SIGNATURE
MORMON CLASSICS

Drawing on a rich literary heritage, Signature Books is pleased to make available a new series of classic Mormon works reprinted with specially commissioned introductions. Each book has left an indelible impression on the LDS church and its members, while also having influenced non-Mormon perceptions of the Saints. The authors, whether believers or skeptics, occupy an important place in the development of LDS culture and identity. The reissue of their works offers readers today an opportunity to better appreciate the origins and growth of a major religious and social movement.

The Articles of Faith

SIGNATURE MORMON CLASSICS

James E. Talmage

The Articles of Faith

A Series of Lectures on the Principal Doctrines of the
Church of Jesus Christ of Latter-day Saints

WRITTEN BY APPOINTMENT AND
PUBLISHED BY THE CHURCH

TO WHICH IS APPENDED

Latter-day Revelation

Selections from the Book of Doctrine and
Covenants Containing Revelations Given through
Joseph Smith the Prophet

COMPILED BY APPOINTMENT AND
PUBLISHED BY THE CHURCH

with a foreword by
James P. Harris

SIGNATURE BOOKS ❧ SALT LAKE CITY ❧ 2003

A NOTE ON THE TEXT

Except for the front matter and foreword, this
Signature Mormon Classics edition of *The Articles of Faith* by
James E. Talmage is an exact reprint of the 1899 first edition, "written by
appointment and published by the church"; the appended *Latter-day
Revelation,* compiled by James E. Talmage, is an exact reprint of the sole
English edition "published by the Church of Jesus Christ of Latter-day
Saints" in 1930; both were published in Salt Lake City.

The Articles of Faith was first printed in the
United States of America in 1899 by the *Deseret News* and
copyrighted by the author; *Latter-day Revelation* was first printed in the
USA in 1930 by the Church of Jesus Christ of Latter-day Saints and
copyrighted by Heber J. Grant, trustee-in-trust for the church.

www.signaturebooks.com

Library of Congress Cataloging-in-Publication Data
Talmage, James Edward, 1862-1933.
The articles of faith : a series of lectures on the principal doctrines of the
Church of Jesus Christ of Latter-day Saints / James E. Talmage ;
with a foreword by James P. Harris.
p. cm. — (Signature Mormon classics)
"Latter-day revelation": p.
First work originally published : Salt Lake City : Deseret News, 1899.
2nd work originally published : Salt Lake City : Church of Jesus Christ of
Latter-day Saints, 1930.
Includes bibliographical references and indexes.
ISBN 1-56085-167-8
1. Church of Jesus Christ of Latter-day Saints—Doctrines.
2. Mormon Church—Doctrines. I. Doctrine and Covenants. Selections.
II. Title. III. Series.
BX8635.T3 2003
230'.9332—dc21   2003045574

TABLE OF CONTENTS

LATTER-DAY REVELATION

*The chapter numbering corresponds to sections of the
Doctrine and Covenants*

FOREWORD

James P. Harris

On Friday, 11 September 1891, future LDS apostle James E. Talmage[1] made the following entry in his journal: "Today I had an interview with the First Presidency of the Church, relative to the Religion Class system. Being the Superintendent of such classes for the Stake, and having found from the labors of the past, that the Bishops of many of the wards feel they have now all they possibly can carry in the way of special organizations, I asked instructions from the authorities as to the proper procedure [to provide support for such classes]. Plans for some change in the system are pending, and another appointment for an interview was set for Monday next."[2] Three days later Talmage met with the First Presidency and there began a course of events that would eventually result in *The Articles of Faith,* a classic in the literature and theology of the Church of Jesus Christ of Latter-day Saints.

Almost eight years passed from Talmage's first mention of the religion class to 4 April 1899, the day *The Articles of Faith* was formally released to an eager public. The chapters of the book had passed through a unique evolution culminating in official endorsement by church president Lorenzo Snow and by his successors in years to come.

Talmage's journals provide a rough outline of his appointment and work on the book. Although not a general authority, he was nevertheless a logical candidate for such an endeavor. When a young man attending Brigham Young Academy in Provo, Utah, he had come to the attention of church president John Taylor, who consented to send him east to be educated at Lehigh and Johns Hopkins universities.[3] In 1888 Talmage was appointed by church president Wilford Woodruff to be the principal of LDS College, the higher end of the Latter-day Saint school system, located in downtown Salt Lake City.[4]

When he met with the First Presidency three years later on 14 September 1891, Talmage recorded:

> Met by appointment with the First Presidency relative to the Religion Class system ... It is the intention of the brethren to cause to be published a class-work on Theology, for use in Church Schools, and in Religion Classes generally. The need for such a work has long been felt among the teachers of the Latter-day Saints. The plan of the work is not fully matured as yet, the probability of issuing a series of two or three books is strong. Several preliminaries have to be arranged before the work is begun; but the First Presidency have expressed to me their intention of appointing me to do the labor. I find myself very busy already, but I have never yet found it necessary to decline any labor appointed to me by the Holy Priesthood; and in the performance of duties so entailed as my day, so my strength has ever been.

Talmage makes no other entry regarding this work for the next year and a half, probably because he was preoccupied as principal of the college. He also taught classes, consulted professionally as a geologist, and fulfilled other church commitments. However, he may well have begun already to prepare outlines and lectures and to index the scriptures and church authorities' statements, as well as to reflect on Mormon theology and how to present it most effectively.[5] On 31 January 1893, he recorded:

> This day in an interview with Presidents [Wilford] Woodruff and [Joseph F.] Smith of the First Presidency, I was appointed to now proceed with a work before given and subsequently withdrawn,[6] I am requested to prepare a work on Theology, suitable as a text-book for our church schools and other organizations. In making the appointment Pres. Woodruff gave me his blessing. Told the brethren that I would accept the appointment as a mission; with no expectation of any pecuniary reward should the work ever be published, hoping that the book would be sold more cheaply if I waived all claim to royalty in the sale. Without the blessing of the Almighty, and the support of the brethren I should shrink from even attempting such a work.

By this time, the treatise had been reduced from a two- or three-volume work to one volume.

Late the next month on 22 February, the First Presidency sent Talmage a letter formally commissioning him:

Dear Brother:

From conversations we have had with you in the past, we know that you in common with many others who are connected with the educational interests of our Church have seen the great need of properly arranged text and reference books in theological and religious subjects, for use in our Church Schools, Sunday Schools, etc.

It is our desire that a book suitable for the purposes named should be placed in the hands of our people as soon as possible. Knowing your experience in this direction we should be pleased to have you prepare such a work. We understand it is your intention not to make any charge for the preparation of this work so that it may be placed on the market at so low a price that it will be within the reach of all; with this suggestion we hastily concur.

Wishing you the fulfillment of every righteous desire in your calling as a teacher of the youth of Israel, we are

Your Brethren:

W. Woodruff

Jos. F. Smith

George Q. Cannon, the other counselor in the First Presidency, was not in the city at the time the letter was signed.

Later that year a formal theological class was organized for LDS University with Talmage as instructor, the class lectures from which would come the substance of Talmage's later book. A leaflet distributed prior to the first class of 29 October 1893 outlined the topic of discussion, as would be the practice for subsequent sessions. Previously it had been decided that the lectures would be based on the format developed in Joseph Smith's thirteen Articles of Faith. The October leaflet stated that: "Theology, as taught by the Latter-day Saints, comprises whole scheme of the Gospel. Many leading principles, but not all, are set forth in the 'Articles of Faith,' accepted by vote of the people, re-adopted October 5, 1890." As the first edition of *The Articles of Faith* explains: "As these Articles of Faith present the leading tenets of the Church in systematic order, they suggest themselves as a convenient outline for our plan of study ... Of the doctrines treated in the authorized standards, the Articles of Faith may be regarded as a fair, though necessarily but an incomplete epitome."[7]

Prior to Talmage, other people had similarly found the Articles of Faith a convenient outline for categorizing church doctrine. In 1882 Elder Franklin D. Richards of the Quorum of the Twelve Apostles and Elder James A. Little compiled *A Compendium of the Doctrines of the Gospel*.[8] In 1887 missionaries from the church's British mission compiled a cut-and-paste collection of scriptures entitled *Ready References* that began with the Articles of Faith and scriptural cross references to support each topic therein.[9]

Talmage kept a notebook entitled "Record of Church University Theology Class" with minutes and newsclippings for each class proceeding. The minutes were kept by a student, Leah Dunford, later the wife of Talmage's colleague in the Quorum of the Twelve Apostles, John A. Widtsoe.[10] Either Talmage or Dunford clipped articles from the *Deseret News* and *Salt Lake Herald* chronicling the progress of each class.[11]

In his journal entry of 29 October 1893, the date of his first lecture, Talmage noted that "the large lecture room in the University building was filled to overflowing: every seat being occupied. Chairs were brought from the College adjoining and every corner taken possession of while the aisles were filled, and the stand crowded, many sitting on the edge of the platform ... So many applicants had to be denied admission that it was decided on the recommendation of Pres[iden]t Angus M. Cannon to adjourn the class at its close to meet next Sunday in the Stake Assembly Hall."

The following week Talmage stated that "[b]etween 500 and 600 persons attended" his class of 5 November. Attendance increased to over 1,200 by 25 February 1894. The purpose of the class may have been to provide Talmage with a kind of focus group to monitor responses to the material presented. The classes initially included review time during which questions were solicited, but this format was abandoned after 11 February due to time constraints.

Talmage wrote in his journal on 6 November 1893: "Today the Presidency of the Church gave instructions that the lectures delivered before the University Theology Class be published in full in serial form, and that the arrangements for republication in book form be left for subsequent consideration. The 'Juvenile Instructor' was selected as the organ of publication." Indeed, from 15 November 1893 to 15 August 1894, the *Juvenile Instructor,* a semi-monthly publication, carried eighteen installments commencing with the introduction to theology, the role of Joseph Smith, and the first Article of Faith through the final lecture given in the series on the Gathering of Israel.

A comparison of the *Juvenile Instructor* and *The Articles of Faith* reveals that Talmage made several changes to the text. However, most of these pertained to grammar and sentence structure. Accompanying the first installment in 1893, the *Instructor's* editor took liberty with a portion of Talmage's text on Joseph Smith. The editor stated:

> Here followed a graphic description of the conditions which led the boy, Joseph, to the Lord for information concerning the true Church; of his first prayer; and the glorious appearance unto him of the Father and the Son; of the persecution that followed his testimony of the vision; of the visits of the angel Moroni; of his receiving the plates of the Book of Mormon from the angel; of his baptism and the bestowal of the Aaronic and the Melchisedek Priesthood upon him; of the organization of the Church of Jesus Christ of Latter-day Saints; and of the Prophet's martyrdom. This, through lack of space, is, with the author's sanction, omitted from the present report. —Ed.

Talmage kept a portion of the removed section in his papers with the note, "omitted from published report," but the brief, two-page draft offers no new details beyond what was included in the book.[12]

Talmage proposed that a "Committee on Criticism" be appointed "to avoid serious error," and the First Presidency responded by appointing Francis M. Lyman of the Quorum of the Twelve Apostles as chair, with Abraham H. Cannon, also of the Quorum of the Twelve, George Reynolds of the First Council of the Seventy, Superintendent of Church Schools Karl G. Maeser, and *Deseret News* associate editor John Nicholson as the remaining committee members.[13] This group reviewed and approved the lectures for publication in the 1893-94 *Juvenile Instructor* and was reappointed on 27 December 1898 with Anthon H. Lund of the Quorum of the Twelve replacing Abraham Cannon who had passed away.[14]

The reason the lecture series ended in 1894 is delineated in Talmage's journal entry of 1 April that year:

> At this the twenty-second session of the Theology Class the attendance was as large as if not indeed larger than that of any previous session. Today marked the last meeting of the class, its discontinuance having been determined upon yesterday or the day before by the First Presidency. The reasons for this action are briefly these:—(1) It is plain that in the event of my accepting any prominent position in the State University it would be manifestly inconsistent for me to occupy so distinguished a place among the Theology Class of our people, the University being a strictly non-sectarian institution. There will be I think opposition enough to the change in the University administration without complicating matters by offering other excuses for

attack. (2) The Presidency are loath to appoint a successor in the instructorship of the Theology Class, as the projected work is still unfinished; and if such an appointment were made, the work would have to be carried in one of two ways,—as the independent treatment of the subject by the new instructor;—and this course they deem objectionable, as it is the design to publish the lectures in book form, and the volume would then be the joint work of two; or the lectures would have to be presented as mine being simply delivered by another; this latter course would remove little if any of the objection now offered to my continuing with the work as in the past. (3) The Presidency have warned me repeatedly of my having too much work on my hands: and they seem determined to relieve me of some.

At the session today, I disposed of as many of the incidental questions as possible, then finished the lecture on the *Gathering*, as per leaflet No. 17: then announced the discontinuance of the class. This announcement caused considerable consternation: and I feel that there has been a true appreciation of the work of the class. A letter from the First Presidency, addressed to myself, advising the discontinuance and citing the reasons therefore, was read by Apostle Abraham H. Cannon, one of the Committee on Theology Class appointed by the First Presidency. He and Elder George Reynolds, another of the Committee made remarks eulogizing the labors of the class. A vote of thanks was heartily rendered the instructor. I feel much regret in seeing the class come to a close,—regret that circumstances render such a course advisable for I believe the class has taken a hold on the minds of the members. I would at least have wished to see the completion of the lectures on the Articles of Faith; but the lectures not yet delivered will be published with those already given. For the need of success that has come to the class I reverentially acknowledge the hand of God. May the seed so planted, yet produce a healthful growth and pleasing fruit.

In 1893 Talmage agreed to be president of the University of Utah, a post he would hold for four years, and he accordingly took a hiatus from working on *The Articles of Faith* until 1898 when he was asked to resume writing. On 27 December of that year, he recorded: "Many requests, personal and official have been made for the continuation of the work. The subjects of the 'articles' not presented before the Church University class were subsequently treated before other classes and theological organizations. Not until this autumn have I been able to resume the work of writing the lectures. For three months past I have been suffering from my baneful affliction of sleeplessness, and my nights, often extending until daybreak have been devoted to writing the matter, which is now practically completed." A few days later he noted, "I was surprised at a suggestion made by the committee a few days ago, and still more so at the approval of the suggestion by the First Presidency that the book be published by the Church. I was not aware that such an honor had ever been paid to one of our writers; and I hardly felt to urge the matter for I don't think the Church is rightly to be made responsible for the slips and errors which will inevitably appear in the book."[15]

Talmage labored on the manuscript with the aid of a student, J. Reuben Clark Jr., who assisted in typing the final draft of the book.[16] The two became good friends, and when Talmage was appointed to officiate as a sealer in the temple, his first act was to marry Clark and his bride, Luacine A. Savage.[17] When Talmage passed away on 27 July 1933,[18] Clark, who had been recently called to the First Presidency, was at his side.

The Articles of Faith was released on 4 April 1899 in time for the church's semi-annual world general conference. Prior to its release, President Lorenzo Snow made the following statement:

> During the early part of April there will be issued by the
> *Deseret News* a Church work, entitled "The Articles of
> Faith," the same being a series of lectures on the principal
> doctrines of the Church of Jesus Christ of Latter-day Saints,
> by Dr. James E. Talmage. The lectures were prepared by
> appointment of the First Presidency, and the book will be
> published by the Church. It is intended for use as a text
> book in the Church schools, Sunday schools, Improve-
> ment associations, quorums of the Priesthood, and other
> Church organizations in which the study of Theology is
> pursued, and also for individual use among the members of
> the Church. The work has been approved by the First Pres-
> idency, and I heartily commend it to members of the
> Church.[19]

As noted, Talmage intended the book to be a gift to the
church with no expectation that he would receive any royalties.
In his journal entry of 17 January 1899, he repeated his intent,
stating: "If I can feel that the Lord has accepted my humble and
imperfect offering I shall count myself richly recompensed." The
matter remained so until 31 May 1901 when Talmage wrote:

> When I submitted [the] manuscript for the "Articles of
> Faith," the book that I had prepared in response to the ap-
> pointment of the First Presidency, I asked no royalty on the
> sales or other pecuniary return; indeed I felt honored in be-
> ing able to do that little for the good of the Church. There
> was some hesitation on the part of the First Presidency in
> accepting the gift, partly owing to a request of mine that
> the book be sold strictly at cost, and partly because of Pres.
> Snow's statement that a proper payment ought to be made.
> The first edition of 10,500 copies has been sold, and copy

for a second issue is now in the hands of the electrotypers
... Several times I have been called into conference with the
publication committee and with the Presidency relative to
the transfer of my copyright to the Church; this the authorities desire, and for the same the Presidency declare a payment ought to be made. The brethren have urged the matter with such kindness that I could not well do otherwise
than express acquiescence. I was asked to name a sum that
would be satisfactory; this I declined to do, saying that I
had offered the work as a gift. Pres. Snow replied that it had
been accepted as a gift, but they desired to make a present
in return. Today Pres. Snow informed me of the decision
reached, and I was handed a check for Fifteen Hundred
Dollars. I made the legal transfer of copyright to the work,
and assigned all claims incident to the first edition.

In the course of writing *The Articles of Faith,* Talmage
encountered several doctrinal uncertainties. On 29 November
1893, he recorded that he was called out of the temple to meet
with the First Presidency on issues related to his theological class
instruction. Among those discussed were the following:

1. The changing of Article 4 of the Articles of Faith from
the old form:
    4. We believe that these ordinances are: First, Faith in
    the Lord Jesus Christ; second, Repentance; third, Bap-
    tism by immersion for the remission of sins; fourth:
    Laying on of Hands for the Gift of the Holy Ghost.
so as to designate faith and repentance in some other way
than as ordinances which they are not. The following form
was adopted
    4. We believe that the first principles and ordinances
    of the Gospel are: (1) Faith in the Lord Jesus Christ;
    (2) Repentance; (3) Baptism by immersion for the re-

mission of sins; (4) Laying on of hands for the Gift of
the Holy Ghost.

2. The proper form and ceremony of baptism whether in
case of rebaptism or in any other occasion, additions to the
revealed formula, such as, "for the remission of your sins"
or "for the renewal of your covenants." The decision was
that any additions to the revealed form, or any other departure therefrom is unauthorized, and to be deprecated. The
authorized form is that given in the Doctrine and Covenants.

3. The authority for rebaptisms: —The authorities were
unanimous in declaring that rebaptism is not recognized as
a regularly constituted principle of the Church; and that
the current practice of requiring rebaptism as a prerequi-
site for admission to the temples, etc. is unauthorized.
Nothing should be put in the way of anyone receiving his
covenants by rebaptism if he feels the necessity of so doing:
and of course, in cases of disfellowship, or excommunication, a repetition of the baptism is required, but the making
of rebaptism a uniform procedure is not proper. It was declared to be at variance with the order of true government
in the Church to require baptism of those who come from
foreign branches to Zion, bringing with them certificates of
membership and of full standing. Pres. Geo. Q. Cannon [of
the First Presidency] expressed the opinion that the practice of repeating baptism came from the example and
teaching of Pres. Brigham Young in the days of first migration to these parts: when the journey meant a long separation from organized branches and wards of the Church:
and consequently an interruption in the observance of regular Church duties. The conditions are changed now: and
the counsel given for special circumstances should not be
made applicable to general procedure under all circumstances. Danger was seen in the practice of repeated bap-

tisms: —such may be made like the confessional of the Catholics: a premium on sinning.

Several minor points were ruled upon, comprising— unpardonable sin: murder and shedding of innocent blood.

In the afternoon a meeting of the Presidency and the Twelve was held at the Temple, at which all the points named above were ratified as set forth. I was told by one of the Apostles on our Committee that I was authorized to proclaim this as doctrine in the Theological Class.

Another theme that occupied Talmage's attention was related to the Holy Ghost. Talmage wrote:

Met with Theological Class Committee and [First] Presidency in lecture work. The subject of "The Holy Ghost" formed the topic. Pres. [George Q.] Cannon in commenting on the ambiguity existing in our printed works concerning the nature or character of the Holy Ghost expressed his opinion that the Holy Ghost was in reality a person, in the image of the other members of the Godhead,—a man in form and figure: and that what we often speak of as the Holy Ghost is in reality but the power or influence of the Spirit. However the Presidency deemed it wise to say as little as possible on this or other disputed subjects.[20]

Talmage mentioned the issue again on 13 January 1899:

One of the questions referred to the First Presidency by the Committee was as to the advisability of reprinting the lecture entitled "The Holy Ghost" which appeared in the "Juvenile Instructor" soon after its delivery in the theology class of the Church University. I remember that considerable discussion attended the reading of the lecture before the former committee prior to its delivery ... The question hung upon the expediency and wisdom of expressing views as definite as those presented in the lecture regarding the personality of the Holy Ghost when marked ambiguity and differences of opinion appeared in the published writings of our Church authorities on the subject. The lecture was approved as it appeared in the "Instructor." I have incorporated it in the prospective book in practically an unaltered form. President [Lorenzo] Snow took the article under advisement today. In conversation Pres. Geo. Q. Cannon supported the view of the distinct personality of the Holy Ghost and stated that he had [here the word "actually" is crossed out] heard the voice of the third member of the Godhead, actually talking to him.

Finally, on 16 January 1899, Talmage recorded that "President [Lorenzo] Snow announced his unqualified approval of the lecture on the 'Holy Ghost'; and directed its insertion."[21]

Not recorded in Talmage's journal is the level of anxiety this issue aroused. When he was subpoenaed in 1905 to testify before the U.S. Senate committee investigating Utah senator Reed Smoot's position as an apostle in the LDS church, Talmage was asked whether a charge of apostasy had been levied against him during the writing of *The Articles of Faith*. He replied, "No charge was actually made, though I was notified I would be so charged. But as one of the church officials had already expressed as holding the views set forth by myself in that work, and he being very much larger game, he was singled out first, and as the proceedings against him ended in a disappointing way, I was never brought to trial."[22] It was never clarified who the "very much larger game" was or what the exact charges were. However, judging from Talmage's remarks on 13 January 1899, the Holy Ghost lecture may have been what elicited the charge of apostasy against him.

On pages 420-21 of the first edition of *The Articles of Faith,* Talmage outlines the concept of progression between the kingdoms of glory in the hereafter, ending with this marvelous observation: "Eternity is progressive; perfection is relative; the essential feature of God's living purpose is its associated power of eternal increase." Talmage may have been influenced in his contemplations by Elder B. H. Roberts who had published a similar sentiment, but the way Talmage articulated it, it was the clearest expression yet of this doctrine and in a form that remains accessible to all members of the church.[23]

A word-by-word comparison of the first edition of *The Articles of Faith* with its 1924 revised edition shows that there were changes in sentence structure and grammar and that questions for review, originally included at the end of the book, were deleted. In addition, Talmage dropped references to the "Lectures of Faith," which he had recommended the church remove from the Doctrine and Covenants when it was revised in 1921, with Talmage as a member of the revision committee. The presentation of the concept of the Kingdom of God was softened in 1924 when "kingdom" was no longer capitalized. Other doctrinal explanations were modified or clarified, one of the most notable being on page 454 of the first edition under the section "Social Order of the Saints," where Talmage speaks of "a plan which seeks without force or violence to establish a natural equality, to take the weapons of despotism from the rich, to aid the lowly and poor ... From the tyranny of wealth, as to every other form of oppression, the truth will make men free." In subsequent editions the phrase "to take the weapons of despotism of the rich" was removed, and "the tyranny of wealth" was modified to "the tyranny of misused wealth." In other instances where rhetoric was perceived to be threatening or overtly political, it was softened.

One major difference between *The Articles of Faith* and works such as *A Compendium of the Doctrines of the Gospel* and *Ready References* was the elimination of scriptural defenses of plural marriage. Talmage's approach to plural marriage was to show how the church today submits to secular authority.[24] In Talmage's papers at Brigham Young University is a 16-page, handwritten document entitled "Items on Polygamy—Omitted from the Published Book" which appears to have been prepared for *The Articles of Faith*. Talmage does not record if the decision to omit the section was his, the committee's, or the First Presidency's.[25]

At times, Talmage's book elaborates themes that earlier church leaders inadequately addressed, in Talmage's view. He challenges Brigham Young's 1859 statement that "[m]ankind are here because they are the offspring of parents who were first brought here from another planet."[26] In an eloquent passage discussing the nature of inquiry into the origin of life, he states:

> The theorist therefore must admit a beginning to earthly life, and such a beginning is explicable only on the assumption of some creative act, or a contribution from outside the earth. If he admit the introduction of life upon the earth from some other and older sphere, he does but extend the limits of his inquiry as to the beginning of vital existence; for to explain the origin of a rose-bush in our own garden by saying that it was transplanted as an offshoot from a rose-tree growing elsewhere, is no answer to the question concerning the origin of roses. Science of necessity assumes a beginning to vital phenomena on this planet, and admits a finite duration of the earth in its current course of progressive change; and in this respect, the earth is a representative of the heavenly bodies in general.[27]

The church leader who had the most impact on Talmage was

Apostle Orson Pratt. Throughout the notes and in the text of *The Articles of Faith,* one sees Pratt's influence. On 9 October 1911, just two months before being called as an apostle, Talmage spoke at a memorial service held during the Pratt family reunion at the Granite Stake Tabernacle. Of Elder Pratt, he said:

> It was not my privilege to have personal acquaintance with Orson Pratt. He was born over half a century before my birth, and he died while I was yet a boy in my teens and but a few years after I came to this continent. I never had the privilege of conversing with him, and saw him only from a distance. And yet I feel that I know him ... At first but a reader of his works I came to be an admirer of his mind, of his personality, of himself. From a critical analysis of what he said, by spoken speech or written word, I have found he was thoroughly imbued with the scientific spirit,—the spirit of search and research, the spirit of investigation and test, the spirit of trial and proof. He knew no dogma nor dictum; he considered proposition, analysis, demonstration.

He went on to praise Pratt's writings both scientific and spiritual.[28]

At the close of an address entitled "The Methods and Motives of Science" given at the Logan temple on 5 February 1898, Talmage said, "The scientific spirit is divine."[29] This view best explains his overall approach to the study of Mormonism in *The Articles of Faith.* Doctrines are categorized, analyzed, and explained, then presented for others to further test and explore. In writing the book, the Spirit was sought through prayer and those in authority were given the opportunity of reviewing the final product. This combination of scholarship and spiritual guidance produced a reliable and authoritative explication of Mormon doctrine and theology.

The disciple-scholar was entrusted with another equally weighty doctrinal assignment a year later when the First Presidency asked him to prepare an edition of the Pearl of Great Price for the church. He worked on the project for two years, removing hymns, deleting items that were duplicated in the Doctrine and Covenants, and adding footnotes. When his compilation was presented to a general conference of the church in 1902, it was accepted as scripture. It would still be nine years before the forty-year-old academic would be called to full-time church service as a member of the Quorum of the Twelve Apostles. In the meantime, he received other church assignments to write a study guide for youth titled *The Great Apostasy* (1909), a pamphlet titled *The Story of Mormonism* (1910) to be used at Temple Square, and a richly illustrated book titled *The House of the Lord* (1911) about LDS temple worship. He was also asked to advise the First Presidency on the topic of evolution in 1909.[30]

Shortly after his call to the Twelve, he wrote *Jesus the Christ,* another classic of Mormon literature commissioned by the First Presidency. He also integrated the *Ready References* into a scripture index for publication in 1916, then was assigned to make corrections, and add chapter headings and footnotes, to the Book of Mormon in 1920.[31] All of this provides some context for understanding his assignment in 1930 to prepare a shortened version of the Doctrine and Covenants.

It was a nondescript little book that appeared on the shelves of Salt Lake City bookstores in late 1930 that bore the title *Latter-day Revelation: Selections from the Book of Doctrine and Covenants of the Church of Jesus Christ of Latter-day Saints.* The volume carried the imprint of the church, yet it disappeared as quickly as it appeared. It did not pretend to be a substitute for the Doctrine and Covenants. The forward stated:

This little book contains selected Sections and parts of Sections from the Doctrine and Covenants, the selections comprising Scriptures of general and enduring value, given as the Word of the Lord through the First Elder and Prophet in the present dispensation, which is verily the "Dispensation of the Fulness of Times."

The complete Doctrine and Covenants is a current publication, accessible to all, so that comparison between that volume and this is a simple undertaking.

A simple undertaking it was. Among those who immediately objected were Mormon fundamentalists accusing the church of changing the scriptures. Of most concern was that the new book omitted verses 1-4 of section 131 pertaining to the "new and everlasting covenant of marriage." Section 132 regarding the eternal marriage covenant and plural marriage was missing altogether. In all, *Latter-day Revelation* retained twenty[32] and parts of twenty-one sections of the Doctrine and Covenants[33] and omitted ninety-five.[34]

In addition, the new version contained theological terminology not generally used by Latter-day Saints. For example, section 27 is titled "Sacramental Emblems and the Future Communion." Section 76 is referred to as "Perdition and Graded Kingdoms of Glory." Section 110 is described as "A Glorious Theophany followed by Visitations of Ancient Prophets." In the title for Section 130, the Godhead is referred to as "The Holy Trinity." There is mention of "the imminence of the Lord's advent," "commandments comprised in the Decalog," and "the Twelve [being called] to ordain evangelical ministers, or Patriarchs."[35]

According to LDS Institute of Religion professor Dale C. LeCheminant, *Latter-day Revelation* became scarce almost immediately after it was released. When historian T. Edgar Lyon inquired about it at Deseret Book, an assistant store manager "took him down to the basement vault where he showed him fifty remaining copies. He then told Lyon that the book had been on display a short time. Some copies had been sold when the fundamentalists got one and immediately charged the Mormon Church with changing the scriptures ... Heber J. Grant then gave orders for the remaining books to be withdrawn and shredded to avoid further conflict with the fundamentalists."[36]

This did not prevent the book from being translated into Dutch, Norwegian, and Spanish. In some countries this would be the only version of the Doctrine and Covenants that would be available for several years.[37]

Because *Latter-day Revelation* offers no information about who the compiler was or how the book came to be, there has been speculation about who it might have been and what the process was. The usual choices for editor have been Elder Talmage or Elder John A. Widtsoe, both of the Quorum of the Twelve Apostles. The speculation regarding Widtsoe came from the doctoral dissertation by Dale C. LeCheminant, who spoke of the appeal the Doctrine and Covenants had for Widtsoe.[38] Nevertheless, two journal entries from Elder Talmage reveal that it was he who compiled the book. The first entry is dated 28 June 1930:

> By prearrangement I sat with the First Presidency during the afternoon, and together we examined in detail the copy I had prepared for the prospective bringing out of a book containing extracts from the Doctrine and Covenants. The purpose of this undertaking is to make the strictly doctrinal parts of the Doctrine and Covenants of easy access and reduce its bulk, furthermore making it suitable for distribution by missionaries and for general use by investiga-

tors. Many of the revelations received by the prophet Joseph related to personal directions in temporal activities incident to the early years of the Church, the immediate importance of which was localized as to time and place. Part of my work in the immediate future will be the carrying of this book of extracts through the press.

For 22 November 1930, he recorded the following:

I had the pleasure of presenting to the First Presidency advance copies of the little book "Latter-day Revelation" which is described on the title pages as "Selections from the book of Doctrine and Covenants." The selections were decided upon by the First Presidency and the Twelve and the matter of arranging, editing, proof reading, etc., has been under my immediate direction, and I must be held personally responsible for the correctness of the type and the matter.[39]

Ironically, Talmage reviewed the book in the *Improvement Era,* and he may also have been responsible for the official 1930 announcement in the *Deseret News* titled "Timely Doctrinal Treatise."[40]

It is interesting to compare *Latter-day Revelation* to what Talmage mentioned were the criteria for deciding what to include in his redaction. The sections and passages retained in full are, in fact, theological, or spiritual rather than temporal, compared to those that were omitted, and most Latter-day Saints would agree that they form the essential core of the revelations.[41] Conversely, many sections of the Doctrine and Covenants contain instructions to specific individuals, calling them on a mission, for instance, or to church callings or assignments. These, along with announcements of meetings, the dedicatory prayer for the Kirtland Temple, general and repetitive calls to repentance, to be patient and prayerful and to preach the gospel, and procedural means for settling disputes and recording ordinances were all deleted.[42]

Other sections were excised because, like polygamy, the church no longer advocated the practice of the tenet. An example is the communal experiment known as the United Order (sections 49, 51, 82, 70, 72, 78, 82, 83, 85, 92, 96, 104, and parts of 42 and 84).[43] Still, there were other cuts that went further than this and cannot be entirely explained by an appeal to changing church practices or the absence of enduring theological content. Examples are the revelation that Satan rules the waters (61), that male children do not need to be circumcised (74), that animals will be resurrected (77), that the Apocrypha should be read (91), and how to differentiate between good and evil spirits (129). These may have been thought to be of minor importance, or perhaps they were considered to be difficult or controversial.[44]

Whatever motivation lay behind such changes, the impression left with the reader is one of scripture and revelation that is fluid and adaptable to new circumstances and of a process rather than a terminable event. Indeed, Talmage writes in the *Articles of Faith* of "the gift of revelation in varying degrees," existing on a continuum with inspiration, and adds that "by neither of these directing processes does the Lord deprive the human subject of agency or individuality; as is proved by the marked peculiarities of style and method characterizing the several books of holy writ." Two pages later he continues even more explicitly: "While the revelations of the past have ever been indispensable as guides to the people, showing forth as they do, the plan and purpose of God's dealings under particular conditions, they may not be universally and directly applicable to the circumstances of succeeding times." In other words, one would expect to see the revelations added upon, modified to fit new situations, and given varying degrees of emphasis.[45]

A lingering question might be why Elder Talmage, rather than the prophet himself, was entrusted with such a responsibility. Upon reflection, he appears to have been uniquely qualified for the task due to his previous experience with preparing scripture for publication as well as his scholarly credentials, his spiritual sensitivity, and his willingness to defer to review by the presidency and Quorum of the Twelve Apostles. Only a few men in the church's history have been asked to modify scripture, but the assignment came repeatedly to him. He proposed minor changes even before he was called as an apostle in 1911; in 1893, for instance, while writing *The Articles of Faith,* he proposed that the wording of the fourth Article of Faith be changed to its current form. His suggestion met with approval by the First Presidency.[46]

In 1902 he revised the Pearl of Great Price, as previously noted.[47] In 1920 he added footnotes to the Book of Mormon. In the processes he made revisions because of the errors he discovered that had crept in over multiple editions. Interestingly, he advised his secretary to tell no one of these changes.[48]

In 1921 Talmage headed a committee of three apostles that added footnotes to the Doctrine and Covenants and removed the Lectures on Faith. The latter had been canonized as part of the 1833 Book of Commandments.

In 1940 BYU student John W. Fitzgerald wrote a master's thesis titled, "A Study of the Doctrine and Covenants." As part of his research, he corresponded with Elder Joseph Fielding Smith of the Quorum of the Twelve, who had also been a member of the 1921 Doctrine and Covenants Committee. When the student asked why the Lectures on Faith had been removed from the Doctrine and Covenants, Elder Smith responded:

> (1) They were not received as revelations by the Prophet Joseph Smith.
> (2) They are only instructions relative to the general subject of faith. They are explanations of this principle but not doctrine.
> (3) They are not complete as to their teachings regarding the Godhead.
> (4) It was thought by Elder James E. Talmage, chairman, and other members of the committee who were responsible for their omission that to avoid confusion and contention on this vital point of belief [the Godhead], it would be better not to have them bound in the same volume as the commandments or revelations which make up the Doctrine and Covenants.[49]

In short, Talmage was intimately involved during his lifetime in preparing new editions of scripture, including modifications in content and wording and what could be called the decanonization process. *Latter-day Revelation* was not in print long enough for the membership to become familiar with it and to be considered for canonization, but it reflected the thinking of the leadership at the time that the Doctrine and Covenants should be simplified and updated. It is often forgotten that, like the Bible, the Doctrine and Covenants itself was the result of a selection process that chose from among many more available texts.

It can only be speculated that other discussions took place in the 1920s and 1930s regarding the content of the Doctrine and Covenants. However, except for Talmage's journal entries, there are no other records available to further explain why a book like

Latter-day Revelation was considered necessary. One scholar suggested that because 1930 was the centennial celebration of the organization of the church, this may have been a way to celebrate the new century.[50]

Latter-day Revelation remains an anomaly because of its association with canonized scripture. The interest shown in the book justifies its reissue, along with the *Articles of Faith,* as a meditation, for its historical value, and to facilitate further discussion about the nature of continuing revelation.

Notes

1. Talmage would become an apostle in December 1911 at the age of fifty.

2. Talmage Journal, 11 Sept. 1891. All journal entries are from the James E. Talmage Journals, Archives and Manuscripts, Harold B. Lee Library, Brigham Young University, Provo, Utah. Talmage produced thirty volumes of diaries from age seventeen (1879) until his death at the age of seventy (1933). The portions pertaining to the first edition of *The Articles of Faith* are contained in the years 1891 to 1899 and are reprinted in James P. Harris, ed., *The Essential James E. Talmage* (Salt Lake City: Signature Books, Salt Lake City, 1997), esp. pp. 44-59; hereafter *Essential James Talmage.*

3. John Talmage, *The Talmage Story* (Salt Lake City: Bookcraft, 1972), 29. See chap. 4; hereafter *Talmage Story.*

4. Ibid., 78-79. See chap. 10.

5. In the Talmage papers at the Lee Library are files containing scriptural references for the Articles of Faith regarding Atonement, Authority, Baptism, Baptism for the Dead, the Bible, Faith, the Fall, Free Agency, God and the Godhead, the Holy Ghost, Idolatry and Atheism, Judgment and the Last Days, Polygamy, Repentance, Sacrament, Satan, and Joseph Smith. The lengths vary from two pages (Idolatry and Atheism) to nineteen pages (Holy Ghost). See James

Edward Talmage Collection, Papers, Division of Archives and Manuscripts, Harold B. Lee Library, Brigham Young University, 22/12-
23/11; hereafter Talmage Papers (including register compiled by
Timothy Wood Slover).

6. It is unclear whether Talmage's term "withdrawn" should be
read literally or if he meant only that until that time he had defaulted
on the First Presidency's assignment.

7. James E. Talmage, *The Articles of Faith: A Series of Lectures on
the Principle Doctrines of the Church of Jesus Christ of Latter-day
Saints* (Salt Lake City: Church of Jesus Christ of Latter-day Saints,
1899), 5. This edition is reproduced in the present publication.

8. Franklin D. Richards and James A. Little, comps., *A Compendium of the Doctrines of the Gospel* (Salt Lake City: by the compilers,
1886), 1-2.

9. *Ready References: A Compilation of Scripture Texts, Arranged
in Subjective Order, with Numerous Annotations from Eminent Writers*
(Salt Lake City: The Deseret News Co., 1887), 7-8. In 1916 Talmage
and Elder Joseph Fielding Smith modified *Ready References* for insertion between the Old and New Testaments in editions of the Bible
printed for the church. See *Essential James Talmage*, xxix, xliin69.

10. John A. Widtsoe, *In a Sunlit Land: The Autobiography of John
A. Widtsoe* (Salt Lake City: Deseret News Press, 1952), 38-39, 53.

11. The Talmage Papers contain the following clippings from
the *Deseret News:* "The Theology Class," 30 Oct. 1893; "Church
University Theology Class," 13, 20, 27 Nov., 4, 11, 18, 26 Dec. 1893,
8 Jan., 5, 12 Feb., 19, 26 Mar., 2 Mar. [Apr.] 1894; from the *Salt Lake
Herald:* "Church University Theology Class," 1 Jan., 19, 26 Feb.
1894; and from an unspecified newspaper: "Church University Theology Class," 15, 22, 29 Jan. 1894.

12. "Smith, Joseph—part of his life story 'omitted from published report' (S109)," n.d., Talmage Papers, 23/11.

13. Talmage Journal, 16 Nov. 1893; *Essential James Talmage*,
48.

14. Talmage Journal, 27 Dec. 1898; *Essential James Talmage*, 54.

15. Talmage Journal, 13 Jan. 1899; *Essential James Talmage,* 55.

16. J. Reuben Clark, "Study of Savior's Ministry Offers Wealth of Faith, Virtue." *Church News,* 23 June 1956, 4, 9.

17. Frank W. Fox, *J. Reuben Clark: The Public Years* (Provo, UT: Brigham Young University Press/Deseret Book Co., 1980), 18; D. Michael Quinn, *J. Reuben Clark: The Church Years* (Provo, UT: Brigham Young University Press, 1983), 9, 286n21; Talmage Journal, 14 Sept. 1898.

18. *Talmage Story,* 237.

19. Talmage Journal, 10 Mar. 1899. A similar announcement appeared in the *Improvement Era,* Apr. 1899, 467.

20. Talmage Journal, 5 Jan. 1894. For a more thorough discussion of issues about the Holy Ghost, see Thomas G. Alexander, *Mormonism in Transition: A History of the Latter-day Saints, 1890-1930* (Urbana: University of Illinois Press, 1986), 281-82; *Essential James Talmage,* xxiii, xxxviinn37-38.

21. A hint as to the controversy may be found in a line from *The Articles of Faith* stating that "the Holy Ghost is capable of manifesting Himself in the true form and figure of God, after which image man is shaped, [a]s indicated by the wonderful interview between the Spirit and Nephi." This could imply that the Holy Ghost exists in some other form, perhaps as something more amorphous. However, Talmage also states that the Holy Ghost "is a Being endowed with the attributes and powers of Deity, and not a mere thing, force, or essence" (165, 164). For more on this, see B. H. Roberts, *The Truth, The Way, The Life: An Elementary Treatise on Theology*, ed. Stan Larson (Salt Lake City: Signature Books, 1994), 478-79n13.

An underlying issue is whether, as Talmage assumes, the "Spirit of the Lord" is the Holy Ghost and not the spirit body of the preexistent Christ as in Ether, chapter 3. In the passage he cites, Nephi seeks an interpretation of his father's vision of the Tree of Life:

> And I said unto him: To know the interpretation thereof—for I spake unto him as a man speaketh; for I beheld that he was in the form of a man; yet nevertheless, I knew that it

> was the Spirit of the Lord; and he spake unto me as a man
> speaketh with another. (I Nephi 11:11)

Talmage's colleagues may have seen in the verse an appearance of
Christ rather than of the Holy Ghost. Still, Talmage wasn't the first
to interpret the verse this way. In his essay, "The Holy Spirit," Orson
Pratt gives a similar reading. See *The Essential Orson Pratt* (Salt Lake
City: Signature Books, 1991), 206-207.

When Talmage added footnotes to the Book of Mormon, he
maintained his interpretation. The singular reference to 1 Nephi
11:11 regarding the "form of a man" referred the reader to John
14:16-17, which reads:

> And I will pray the Father, and he shall give you another
> Comforter, that he may abide with you for ever;
> *Even* the Spirit of truth; whom the world cannot receive,
> because it seeth him not, neither knoweth him: but ye know
> him; for he dwelleth with you, and shall be in you.

The 1981 LDS revised edition of the Book of Mormon, 1 Nephi
11:11, refers the reader to a more general category in the topical
guide called "Spirit Body."

22. *Proceedings before the Committee on Privileges and Elections
of the United States Senate in the Matter of the Protests against the Right
of Hon. Reed Smoot, a Senator from the State of Utah, to Hold His Seat*
(Washington, D.C.: Government Printing Office, 1905), 3:24-25;
Essential James Talmage, xxiv-xxv, xxxviii-xxxixnn45-47.

23. B. H. Roberts, *Outlines in Ecclesiastical History* (Salt Lake
City: Deseret Book Co., Classics in Mormon Literature, 1979),
416-17. The book was originally printed in 1893. Talmage was a
member of the reading committee. See Talmage Journal, 15 Aug.
1892; *Essential James Talmage,* xxxiii, xxxviiin39.

24. *The Articles of Faith,* 435-36, 440. Note the title for Lecture
XXIII: "Submission to Secular Authority." See the twelfth Article of
Faith in the current edition of LDS scripture, The Pearl of Great
Price, 61.

25. "Items on Polygamy Omitted from the Published Book (S.

106)," Talmage Papers, 23/8. Slover or another staff member added "(Published Book: *Jesus the Christ*)" to this description, but the text and style of the manuscript lend themselves more readily to *The Articles of Faith*. The manuscript is printed in its entirety in *Essential James Talmage*, chap. 9.

26. *Journal of Discourses*, 26 vols. (Liverpool, Eng.: Latter-day Saints Book Depot, 1855-86), 7:285. Also see *The Essential Brigham Young* (Salt Lake City: Signature Books, 1992), 126, 95.

27. *The Articles of Faith*, 33-34.

28. Talmage Papers, 22/8. Talmage titled the talk "Orson Pratt," but in his journal entry of 9 October 1911, he referred to it as "Orson Pratt as Scientist and Philosopher." For a further study of the impact of Pratt and his influence on LDS theology, see Gary James Bergera, "The Orson Pratt-Brigham Young Controversies: Conflict within the Quorums, 1853 to 1868," *Dialogue: A Journal of Mormon Thought* 13 (summer 1980): 7-49, hereafter *Dialogue*; and Bergera, ed., "'Let Br. Pratt Do as He Will': Orson Pratt's 29 January 1860 Confessional Discourse—Unrevised," in ibid., 50-58. An extended treatise of the controversy between Brigham Young and Orson Pratt is available in Bergera's *Conflict in the Quorum: Orson Pratt, Brigham Young, Joseph Smith* (Salt Lake City: Signature Books, 2002).

29. James E. Talmage, "The Methods and Motives of Science," *Improvement Era*, Feb. 1900, 250-59; *Essential James Talmage*, chap. 11.

30. *Essential James Talmage*, xxiv-xxvi.

31. Ibid, xxvi, xxix.

32. The following sections were retained in their entirety: 1, 2, 4, 7, 13, 22, 27, 29, 38, 46, 59, 65, 76, 87, 89, 107, 110, 119, 133, and 134. Notice from the reproduction in this volume that the sections retained their original numbering.

33. Parts of the following sections were retained: 18, 19, 20, 42, 43, 45, 50, 56, 58, 63, 64, 68, 84, 88, 93, 98, 101, 121, 124, 130, 131. See H. Michael Marquardt Collection, Marriott Library, University of Utah, Salt Lake City, Utah, 207/10.

34. The following sections were entirely omitted: 3, 5, 6, 8, 9, 10, 11, 12, 14, 15, 16, 17, 21, 23, 24, 25, 26, 28, 30, 31, 32, 33, 34, 35, 36, 37, 39, 40, 41, 44, 47, 48, 49, 51, 52, 53, 54, 55, 57, 60, 61, 62, 66, 67, 69, 70, 71, 72, 73, 74, 75, 77, 78, 79, 80, 81, 82, 83, 85, 86, 90, 91, 92, 94, 95, 96, 97, 99, 100, 102, 103, 104, 105, 106, 108, 109, 111, 112, 113, 114, 115, 116, 117, 118, 120, 122, 123, 125, 126, 127, 128, 129, 132, 135, and 136.

35. *Latter-day Revelation: Selections from the Book of Doctrine and Covenants* (Salt Lake City: Church of Jesus Christ of Latter-day Saints, 1930), 23, 26, 38, 45, 69-70, 134, 146, 156; this edition is reproduced in the present publication; Frederick S. Buchanan, letter, *Dialogue* 24 (spring, 1991), 10. Notice that Talmage uses the term "Holy Trinity" to introduce this verse from the Doctrine and Covenants: "The Father has a body of flesh and bones as tangible as man's; the Son also; but the Holy Ghost has not a body of flesh and bones, but is a personage of spirit" (130:22), while a verse that could be interpreted to be traditionally trinitarian was omitted: "And the Father and I are one. I am in the Father and the Father in me; and inasmuch as ye have received me, ye are in me and I in you" (50:43).

36. Dale Campbell LeCheminant, "John A. Widtsoe: Rational Apologist," Ph.D. diss., University of Utah, 1977, 182-183. This account is also available in the Marquardt Collection, 207/10; I am gratefully indebted to Mr. Marquardt for bringing it to my attention. Because fundamentalist Leroy S. Johnson referred to the book as "Revelations of More Enduring Value," some confusion has been introduced in researching the fundamentalist response. See *L. S. Johnson Sermons,* 6 vols. (Hilldale, Utah: Twin Cities Courier Press, 1983-84), 4:1681, cited by Ken Driggs, letter, *Dialogue,* 23:4, 9.

37. Larry R. Skidmore, reference librarian, Family and Church History Department, The Church of Jesus Christ of Latter-day Saints, to author, 31 Jan. 2003, with summaries of the contents and photocopies of the title pages to three foreign editions: Danish (*Ny Aabenbaring Uddrag af Laerdommens og Pagtens Bog,* 1934), Norwegian (*Ny Apenbaring Utdrag fra Paktens Bok,* 1934), and Spanish (*Revelacion de los Ultimos Dias: Selecciones del Libro de Doctinas y Convenios,* 1933). Interestingly, Talmage's was not the first redac-

tion because an earlier French edition published in Zurich, Switzerland, had only twenty-eight selected sections (*Les Doctrines et Alliances de L'eglise de Jesus-Christ des Saints des Derniers Jours,* 1908).

38. LeCheminant, *op. cit.* See also Buchanan, *op. cit.*

39. Talmage Journal, under dates.

40. *Improvement Era,* 34 (May 1931), 427; *Deseret News,* 24 Nov. 1930, 4.

41. A possible exception would be section 87, the "Prophecy on War," if the test of historical specificity is applied.

42. Some interesting examples of revelations to specific individuals that were deleted are the charge to Emma Smith to prepare a hymnal (26), the requirement that the church provide Joseph Smith with a salary and home (43:11-14; 94), the designation of Ohio as the gathering place (48, 49), the history of the New Zion in Missouri (57, 103, 105, portions of 58 and 101), instructions to Sidney Gilbert not to sell his store (64:26-33; 101:97), and that a group of investors should issue stock to finance a hotel (124:54-122). Talmage defends such omissions in the foreword: "Except as illustrative instances of the Lord's way of directly communicating with His prophets, many of these revelations, once of present and pressing significance, became relatively of reduced importance with the passing of the conditions that had brought them forth" (iv).

43. Additional examples include references to priesthood licenses (20:63-64), a priesthood school (95, 97), searching for treasure (111), a command to build a temple in Far West, Missouri (115), and instructions to found a city in Illinois and to call it Zarahemla (125).

44. A more general description of "discernment of spirits" was retained (50). One can detect careful attention paid to the removal of curses against enemies, including the dusting of feet (sections 24, 60, 75), and of the authorization of violence and retribution (58:53, 98:23-48, 101:10-20, 121:1-20). Other passages that, while historical, contain theological import include Oliver Cowdery's translating with the Rod of Aaron (8), the unauthorized use of a seer stone (28),

the need to retranslate the Bible (45:60-61), a promise that "whatsoever" the elders "speak when moved upon by the Holy Ghost shall be scripture" (68:1-7), the washing of feet (88:127-141), revoking previous commands (56:5-13), and a promise to Joseph Smith that if he lived to be eighty-five years old, he would see the face of the Son of Man (130:14-17).

45. *Articles of Faith,* 308-309, 312, 314. Talmage does note that the words of John the revelator, "having come to him by revelation, were sacred; and to alter such, by omission or addition, would be to modify the words of God. The sin of altering any other part of the revealed word would be equally great." But in the very next sentence, Talmage adds an interesting qualifying statement: "Moreover, in this oft-quoted passage, no intimation is given that the Lord may not add to or take from the word therein revealed; the declaration is that no man shall change the record and escape the penalty" (317).

46. Talmage Journal, 29 November 1893, cited in *Essential James Talmage,* 48-50. Also see xxiii-xxiv, xxxviiin41.

47. *Essential James Talmage,* xxiv.

48. Talmage Papers, 23/13, cited in *Essential James Talmage,* xxix-xliin72. Also see xliinn71, 73.

49. Richard S. Van Wagoner, Steven C. Walker, and Allen D. Roberts. "The 'Lectures on Faith': A Case Study in Decanonization," *Dialogue* 20 (fall 1987), 74-75. See also John W. Fitzgerald, "A Study of the Doctrine and Covenants," M.A. thesis, Brigham Young University, 1940, 343-345, cited in Larry E. Dahl, "The Authorship and History of the Lectures on Faith," eds. Dahl and Charles D. Tate Jr., *The Lectures on Faith in Historical Perspective* (Provo, Utah: Religious Studies Center, Brigham Young University, 1990), 18. For an excellent discussion of canonization, see John W. Welch and David J. Whittaker, *Mormonism's Open Canon: Some Historical Perspectives on Its Religious Limits and Potentials* (Provo, Utah: Foundation for Ancient Research and Mormon Studies, 1987).

50. From a telephone conversation with Stan Larson, Reference Services Archivist, Marriott Library, University of Utah.

The Articles of Faith

The following is an unaltered digital
scan of the first edition of *The Articles of Faith*
published in 1899.

THE

ARTICLES OF FAITH.

A SERIES OF LECTURES ON THE
PRINCIPAL DOCTRINES OF

THE CHURCH OF JESUS CHRIST OF LATTER-DAY SAINTS,

BY

DR. JAMES E. TALMAGE.

WRITTEN BY APPOINTMENT; AND PUBLISHED BY THE CHURCH.

THE DESERET NEWS,
SALT LAKE CITY, UTAH,
1899.

THE ARTICLES OF FAITH

OF THE CHURCH OF JESUS CHRIST OF LATTER-DAY SAINTS.

1 We believe in God, the Eternal Father, and in His Son, Jesus Christ, and in the Holy Ghost.

2 We believe that men will be punished for their own sins, and not for Adam's transgression.

3. We believe that through the atonement of Christ, all mankind may be saved, by obedience to the laws and ordinances of the Gospel.

4. We believe that the first principles and ordinances of the Gospel are:— (1) Faith in the Lord Jesus Christ; (2) Repentance; (3) Baptism by immersion for the remission of sins; (4) Laying on of Hands for the Gift of the Holy Ghost.

5. We believe that a man must be called of God, by prophecy, and by the laying on of hands, by those who are in authority, to preach the Gospel and administer in the ordinances thereof.

6. We believe in the same organization that existed in the Primitive Church, viz: apostles, prophets, pastors, teachers, evangelists, etc.

7. We believe in the gift of tongues, prophecy, revelation, visions, healing, interpretation of tongues, etc.

8. We believe the Bible to be the word of God, as far as it is translated correctly; We also believe the Book of Mormon to be the word of God.

9. We believe all that God has revealed, all that He does now reveal, and we believe that He will yet reveal many great and important things pertaining to the Kingdom of God.

10. We believe in the literal gathering of Israel and in the restoration of the Ten Tribes; That Zion will be built upon this [the American] continent; That Christ will reign personally upon the earth; and, That the earth will be renewed and receive its paradisiacal glory.

11. We claim the privilege of worshiping Almighty God according to the dictates of our conscience, and allow all men the same privilege, let them worship how, where, or what they may.

12. We believe in being subject to kings, presidents, rulers, and magistrates, in obeying, honoring, and sustaining the law.

13. We believe in being honest, true, chaste, benevolent, virtuous, and in doing good to *all men;* indeed, we may say that we follow the admonition of Paul, We believe all things, we hope all things, we have endured many things, and hope to be able to endure all things. If there is anything virtuous, lovely, or of good report or praiseworthy, we seek after these things.—JOSEPH SMITH.

PREFACE.

The lectures herewith presented have been prepared in accordance with the request and appointment of the First Presidency of the Church. The greater number of the addresses were delivered before the Theology Class of the Church University; and, after the close of the class sessions, the lectures were continued before other Church organizations engaged in the study of Theology. To meet the desire expressed by the Church authorities,—that the lectures be published for use in the various educational institutions of the Church,—the matter has been revised, and is now presented in this form.

In anticipation of probable question or criticism regarding the disparity of length of the several lectures, it may be stated that each of the addresses ·occupied two or more class sessions, and that the present arrangement of the matter in separate lectures, is rather one of compilation than of original presentation.

The author's thanks are due and are heartily rendered to the members of the Committee appointed by the First Presidency, whose pains-taking and efficient examination of the manuscript, prior to the delivery of the lectures, has inspired some approach to confidence in the prospective value of the book among members of the Church. The committee here referred to consisted of Elders Francis M. Lyman, Abraham H. Cannon, and Anthon H. Lund, of the Quorum of the Twelve Apostles; Elder George Reynolds, one of the Presidents of the Presiding Quorum of Seventy; Elder John Nicholson, and Dr. Karl G. Maeser.

The lectures are now published by the Church, and with them goes the hope of the author that they may prove of some service to the many students of the scriptures among our people, and to other earnest enquirers into the doctrines and practices of the Church of Jesus Christ of Latter-day Saints. JAMES E. TALMAGE.

Salt Lake City, Utah, April 3, 1899.

CONTENTS.

LECTURE XIX, ARTICLE 10.
Zion.

LECTURE XX, ARTICLE 10.
Christ's Reign on Earth.

LECTURE XXI, ARTICLE 10.
Regeneration and Resurrection.

LECTURE XXII, ARTICLE 11.
Religious Liberty and Toleration.

LECTURE XXIII, ARTICLE 12.
Submission to Secular Authority.

LECTURE XXIV, ARTICLE 13.
Practical Religion.

LECTURES

ON THE

ARTICLES OF FAITH

OF THE CHURCH OF JESUS CHRIST OF
LATTER-DAY SAINTS.

LECTURE I.

INTRODUCTORY.

1. **Importance of Theological Study:**—In the short period
of time that measures the span of mortal existence, it is
not possible for man to explore any considerable portion of
the vast realm of knowledge; it becomes, therefore, the part
of wisdom to select for study the branches that promise to
prove of the greatest worth. All truth is of value—above
price indeed in its place, yet with respect to their possible
application, some truths are of incomparably greater worth
than are others. A knowledge of the principles of trade is
essential to the success of the merchant; an acquaintance
with the laws of navigation is demanded of the mariner;
familiarity with the relation of soil and crops is indispensable to the farmer; an understanding of the profound principles of mathematics is necessary to the engineer and the
astronomer; so too is a practical knowledge of God essential
to the salvation of every human soul that has attained to
powers of judgment and discretion. The value of theological knowledge, therefore, ought not to be under-rated; it

2

is doubtful if its importance can in any way be over-estimated.

2. **What is Theology?**—The word "theology" is of Greek origin; it comes to us from *Theos*, meaning God, and *logos* —a treatise, or discourse, signifying by derivation, therefore, collated knowledge of Divinity, or the science that teaches us of God, implying also the relation existing between the Supreme Being and His creatures. The term is of very ancient usage, and may be traced to pagan sources. Plato and Aristotle speak of theology as the doctrine of Deity and divine things. Concisely defined, theology "is that revealed science which treats of the being and attributes of God, His relations to us, the dispensations of His providence, His will with respect to our actions, and His purposes with respect to our end."[a]

3. It has been held by some as a truth, that theological knowledge is not properly a subject for analytical and otherwise scientific treatment on the part of man; that inasmuch as a true conception of Deity, with which theology has primarily to deal, must necessarily be based upon revelation from the source divine, we can but receive such knowledge as it is graciously given; and that to attempt critical investigation thereof by the fallible powers of human judgment, would be to apply as a measure of the doings of God, the utterly inadequate wisdom of man. Many truths are beyond the scope of unaided human reason, and theological facts have been declared to be above reason; this is true so far as the same remark might be applied to any other kind of truth; for all truth, being eternal, is superior to reason in the sense of being manifest to reason, and not a creation of reason; nevertheless truths are to be estimated and compared by the exercise of reason.

---

[a] See Doc. & Cov. supplement to Lecture I on Faith; Buck's Theological Dictionary p. 582.

4. The Extent of Theology:—Who can survey the boundaries of this science? It deals with Deity—the fountain of knowledge, the source of wisdom; with the proofs of the existence of a Supreme Being, and of other supernatural personalities; with the conditions under which, and the means by which, divine revelation is imparted; with the eternal principles governing the creation of worlds; with the laws of nature in all their varied manifestations. Primarily, theology is the science of God and religion; it seeks to present "the systematic exhibition of revealed truth, the science of Christian faith and life." But in a more general sense, theology has to do with other truths than those which are specifically called spiritual; its domain is co-extensive with that of truth.

5. The industrial pursuits that benefit mankind, the arts that please and refine, the sciences that enlarge and exalt the mind, are but fragments of the great though yet uncompleted volume of truth that has come to earth from a source of eternal and infinite supply. The comprehensive study of theology, therefore, would embrace all known truths. God has constituted Himself as the great teacher;[b] by personal manifestations or through the ministrations of His appointed servants, He instructs His mortal children. To Adam He introduced the art of agriculture,[c] and even taught by example that of tailoring;[d] to Noah and Nephi He gave instructions in ship building;[e] Lehi and Nephi were taught of Him in the arts of navigation;[f] and for their guidance on the water, as in their journeyings on land, He prepared for them the Liahona,[g] a compass operated by a

---

b See Key to Theology, by Parley P. Pratt, chap. i.

c Gen. ii, 8: Pearl of Great Price (1888 ed.), p. 12.

d Gen. iii, 21; Pearl of Great Price, p. 17.

e Gen. vi, 14; I Nephi, xvii 8; xviii, 1-4.

f I Nephi, xviii, 12, 21.

g I Nephi, xvi, 10,16, 26-30; xviii, 12, 21; Alma xxxvii, 38.

force more effective than that of terrestrial magnetism;
furthermore, Moses received divine instructions in architecture.[h]

6. **Theology and Religion**, though closely related, are
by no means identical. A person may be deeply versed in
theological lore, and yet be lacking in religious, and even in
moral traits. Theology may be compared to theory, while
religion represents practice; if theology be precept, then religion is example. Each should be the complement of the
other; theological knowledge should strengthen religious faith
and practice. As accepted by the Latter-day Saints, theology comprehends the whole plan of the gospel. "Theology
is ordered knowledge, representing in the region of the
intellect what religion represents in the heart and life of
man."[i] Knowledge may have to do with the intellect only,
and however sublime its import, it may fail to affect the
hardened heart.

7. **The "Articles of Faith:"**—The beliefs and prescribed
practices of most religious sects are usually set forth in formal creeds. The Latter-day Saints announce no creed as a
complete code of their faith; for while they hold that the
precepts of eternal life are unchangeable, they accept the
principle of continuous revelation as a characteristic feature
of their belief. However, when asked for a concise presentation of the principal religious views of his people, Joseph
Smith, the first prophet of the Church in the present dispensation, announced as a declaration of belief, the "Articles
of Faith of the Church of Jesus Christ of Latter-day Saints."
These include the more essential and characteristic features
of the gospel, as accepted by this Church; but they are not
complete as an exposition of our belief, for by one of the
Articles it is declared, "We believe all that God has revealed,

h Exo. xxv. xxvi. xxvii.
i W. E. Gladstone.

all that He does now reveal, and we believe that He will yet reveal many great and important things pertaining to the Kingdom of God." From the time of their first promulgation, the Articles of Faith have been accepted by the people,[j] and on October 6, 1890, the Latter-day Saints in general conference assembled, re-adopted the Articles as part of their guide in faith and conduct. As these Articles of Faith present the leading tenets of the Church in systematic order, they suggest themselves as a convenient outline for our plan of study.

8. **The Standard Works of the Church** form our written authority in doctrine; but they are by no means our only sources of information and instruction on the theology of the Church. We believe that God is as willing today as He ever has been to reveal His mind and will to man, and that He does so through chosen and appointed channels. We rely therefore on the teachings of the living oracles of God, as of equal validity with the doctrines of the written word, the men in chief authority being acknowledged and accepted by the Church as prophets and revelators, and as being in possession of the power of the holy Priesthood. The written works adopted by the vote of the Church as authoritative guides in faith and doctrine, are four,—the Bible, the Book of Mormon, the Doctrine and Covenants, and the Pearl of Great Price. Other works have been and are being issued by officers and members of the Church, and many such books are unreservedly sanctioned by the people and their ecclesiastical authorities; but the four publications named are the only regularly constituted standard works of the Church. Of the doctrines treated in the authorized standards, the Articles of Faith may be regarded as a fair, though necessarily but an incomplete epitome.

j See Note 1.

JOSEPH SMITH, THE PROPHET.

9.   **Joseph Smith,** whose name is appended to the Articles
of Faith, was the prophet through whom the Lord restored
to earth in these the last days, the gospel, and this in accordance with declarations made in previous dispensations.
The question of the divine authenticity of this man's mission is an all-important one to earnest investigators of
Latter-day Saint doctrines.   If his claims to a God-given
appointment be false, forming, as they do, the foundation
of the Church in the last dispensation, the superstructure
cannot be stable; if, however, his purported ordination under the hands of heavenly personages be a fact, one need
search no further for the cause of the phenomenal strength
and growing power of the restored Church.   The circumstances of the divine dealings with Joseph Smith, the marvelous development of the work instituted by this modern
prophet, the fulfilment through his instrumentality of
many of the grandest predictions of old, and his own prophetic utterances with their literal realization, will yet be
widely acknowledged as proof conclusive of the validity of
his ministry.[k]   The exalted claims maintained for him and
his life's work, the fame that has made his name known for
good or for evil among most of the civilized nations of the
earth, the vitality and growing strength of the religious
and social systems which owe their origin as nineteenth-
century establishments to the ministrations of this man,
give to him an individual importance warranting at least a
passing consideration.

10.   **His Parentage, Youth, etc.:**—Joseph Smith, the third
son and fourth child in a family of ten, was born December
23rd, 1805, at Sharon, Windsor County, Vermont.   He was
the son of Joseph, and Lucy Mack Smith, a worthy couple,

---

[k] See Note 3.

who though in poverty lived happily amid their home scenes of industry and frugality. When the boy, Joseph, was ten years old, the family left Vermont, and settled in the State of New York, first at Palmyra, and later at Manchester, Ontario County. At the place last named, the future prophet spent most of his boyhood days. In common with his brothers and sisters, he had but little schooling; and for the simple rudiments of an education, which by earnest application he was able to gain, he was mostly indebted to his parents, who followed the rule of devoting a portion of their limited leisure to the teaching of the younger members of the household.

11. In their religious inclinations, the family favored the Presbyterian faith, the mother, and three or four of the children having united themselves with that sect; but Joseph, while at one time favorably impressed by the Methodist creed, kept himself free from all sectarian membership, being greatly perplexed over the strife and dissensions manifesting themselves among the churches of the time. He had a right to expect that in the Church of Christ there would be unity and harmony; yet in place of such he saw among the wrangling sects only confusion. While Joseph was in his fifteenth year, the region of his home was visited by a storm of fierce religious excitement, which, beginning with the Methodists soon became general among all the sects; there were revivals and protracted meetings, and the manifestations of sectarian rivalry were many and varied. These conditions added much to the distress of the young searcher after truth.

12. **His Search for Truth and the Result:**—Here is Joseph's own account of his course of action:—

"In the midst of this war of words and tumult of opinions, I often said to myself, what is to be done? who of all these parties are right? or, are they all wrong together? If any one of them be right, which is it, and how shall I know it?

"While I was laboring under the extreme difficulties caused by the contests of these parties of religionists, I was one day reading the Epistle of James, first chapter and fifth verse, which reads, *'If any of you lack wisdom, let him ask of God, that giveth to all men liberally, and upbraideth not, and it shall be given him?'* [l] Never did any passage of scripture come with more power to the heart of man than did this at this time to mine. It seemed to enter with great force into every feeling of my heart. I reflected on it again and again, knowing that if any person needed wisdom from God, I did; for how to act I did not know, and unless I could get more wisdom than I then had, would never know, for the teachers of religion of the different sects understood the same passage so differently as to destroy all confidence in settling the question by an appeal to the Bible. At length I came to the conclusion that I must either remain in darkness and confusion, or else I must do as James directs, that is, ask of God. I at length came to the determination to ask of God, concluding that if He gave wisdom to them that lacked wisdom, and would give liberally and not upbraid, I might venture. So, in accordance with this, my determination to ask of God, I retired to the woods to make the attempt. It was on the morning of a beautiful clear day, early in the spring of 1820. It was the first time in my life that I had made such an attempt, for amidst all my anxieties I had never as yet made the attempt to pray vocally.

"After I had retired into the place where I had previously designed to go, having looked around me and finding myself alone, I kneeled down and began to offer up the desires of my heart to God. I had scarcely done so, when immediately I was seized upon by some power which entirely overcame me, and had such astonishing influence over me as to bind my tongue so that I could not speak. Thick darkness gathered around me, and it seemed to me for a time, as if I were doomed to sudden destruction. But, exerting all my powers to call upon God to deliver me out of the power of

---

l James i, 5.

this enemy which had seized upon me, and at the very moment when I was ready to sink into despair and abandon myself to destruction, not to an imaginary ruin, but to the power of some actual being from the unseen world, who had such a marvelous power as I had never before felt in any being; just at this moment of great alarm, I saw a pillar of light exactly above my head, above the brightness of the sun, which descended gradually until it fell upon me. It no sooner appeared than I found myself delivered from the enemy which held me bound. When the light rested upon me, I saw two personages, whose brightness and glory defy all description, standing above me in the air. One of them spake unto me calling me by name, and said (pointing to the other), *"This is my beloved Son, hear Him."*[m]

13. In answer to his prayer for guidance as to which of the sects was right, he was told to join none of them, for all were wrong, with their creeds which are an abomination in the sight of God, and their professors who are corrupt, in that they draw near with their lips while their hearts are far from the Lord, teaching for doctrine the commandments of men, having a form of godliness while denying the power thereof.

14. Such knowledge as had been communicated in this unprecedented revelation was not to be held captive within the heart of the youth. He hesitated not to impart the glorious truths, first to the members of his family, who received his testimony with reverence, and then to the sectarian ministers, who had labored so diligently to convert him to their several creeds. To his surprise, these professed teachers of Christ treated his statements with the utmost contempt, declaring that the day of revelation from God had long since passed away; and that the manifestation, if indeed he had received any such at all, was surely from Satan. Nevertheless, the ministers exerted them-

---

m Pearl of Great Price, pp. 86-88, (1888 ed.)

selves with a unity of purpose strangely at variance with
their former hostility toward one another, to ridicule the
young man, and to denounce his testimony.   The neighborhood was aroused; persecution, bitter and vindictive, was
waged against him and his family; he was actually fired
upon by a would-be assassin; yet through it all he was preserved from bodily injury; and in spite of increasing opposition, he remained faithfully steadfast to his testimony
of the heavenly visitation.[n]   In this condition of trial, he
continued without further manifestation for three years,
constantly expecting, but never receiving the additional
light and added instructions for which he yearned.   He was
keenly sensitive of his own frailty, and conscious of human
weaknesses.   He pleaded before the Lord, acknowledging
his errors, and craving help.

15. **Angelic Visitations:**—On the night of September
21st, 1823, while praying for forgiveness of sins, and for
guidance as to his future· course, he was blessed with
another heavenly manifestation.   There appeared in his
room a brilliant light, in the midst of which stood a personage clothed in white, and with a countenance of radiant
purity and loveliness.   The celestial visitor announced himself as Moroni, a messenger sent from the presence of God;
and then proceeded to instruct the youth as to some of the
divine purposes, in which Joseph was to take a most important part.   The angel said that through Joseph as the
earthly instrument, the true Church would be again established upon the earth; that his name would be known
among all nations and tongues, honored by the good, reviled
by the wicked; that a record, engraven on plates of gold,
giving a history of the nations that had formerly lived upon
the western continent, and an account of the Savior's ministrations among the people on this land, was hidden in a

[n] See Note 2.

hill near by; that with the plates were two sacred stones, known as Urim and Thummim, by the use of which, men in olden times had become seers, and that through those instruments God would enable Joseph to translate the record engraven on the plates.

16.   The angelic messenger then repeated several prophecies which are recorded in the ancient scriptures; some of the quotations were given with variations from our Bible readings.   Of the words of Malachi the following were quoted: "For behold, the day cometh that shall burn as an oven, and all the proud, yea, and all that do wickedly, shall burn as stubble, for they that come shall burn them, saith the Lord of Hosts, and it shall leave them neither root or branch."[o]   And further:—"Behold, I will reveal unto you the Priesthood by the hand of Elijah the prophet, before the coming of the great and dreadful day of the Lord.   And he shall plant in the hearts of the children the promises made to the fathers, and the hearts of the children shall turn to their fathers; if it were not so, the whole earth would be utterly wasted at his coming."[p]   Among other scriptures, Moroni cited the prophecies of Isaiah relating to the restoration of scattered Israel, and the promised reign of righteousness on earth,[q] saying that the predictions were about to be fulfilled; also the words of Peter to the Jews, concerning the prophet who Moses said would be raised up, explaining that the prophet referred to was Christ, and that the day was near at hand when all who rejected the words of the Savior would be cut off from among the people.[r]

17.   Having delivered his message, the angel departed, the light in the room seeming to condense about his person, and disappearing with him.   But the heavenly visitant re-

o Compare Malachi iv, 1.
p Compare Malachi iv, 5-6.
q See Isaiah xi.
r See Acts iii, 22-23.

turned a second and a third time during the night, each time repeating the instructions, with additional admonitions as to the requirements, and warnings regarding temptations that would assail the youthful seer. On the following day, Moroni appeared to Joseph again, reciting anew the instructions and cautions of the preceding night; and told him to acquaint his father with all he had heard and seen. This the boy did, and the father promptly testified that the communications were from God.

18. Joseph soon repaired to the hill described to him in the vision. He recognized the spot indicated by the angel, and with some labor laid bare a stone box containing the plates and other things spoken of by Moroni. The heavenly messenger again stood beside him; forbade the removal of the contents at that time, saying that four years were to elapse before the plates would be committed to his care; and that it would be his duty to visit the spot at yearly intervals. On the occasion of each of these visits the angel instructed the young man more fully regarding the great work awaiting him.

19. It is not the purpose of the present lecture to review in detail the life and ministry of Joseph Smith;[8] so much attention has been given to the opening scenes of his divinely-appointed mission, in view of the unusual importance associated with the ushering in of the modern or new dispensation of God's providence. The bringing forth of the plates from their resting-place of centuries, their translation by divine power, and the publication of the record as the Book of Mormon, will receive attention on a later occasion; for the present it is sufficient to say that the ancient record has been translated; that the Book of Mormon has been given to the world; and that the volume is accepted as a sacred guide by the Latter-day Saints.

[8] See Note 5.

20. **Later Developments; the Martyrdom:**—In due time, the Church of Jesus Christ of Latter-day Saints was organized; the Priesthood was restored through the ordination of Joseph Smith by those who had held the keys of that authority in former dispensations. From an initial membership of but six persons, the Church grew to include thousands during the life-time of the Prophet Joseph; and the growth has continued with phenomenal rapidity and stability until the present time. One by one the powers and authorities possessed by the Church of old wére restored through the man who was chosen and ordained to be the first elder of the latter-day dispensation. With the spread of the Church, persecution increased, and the effect of evil opposition reached a climax in the cruel martyrdom of the prophet, and his brother Hyrum, then patriarch of the Church, June 27, 1844. The incidents leading up to and culminating in the foul murder of these men at Carthage, Illinois, are matters of common history. Suffice it to say that prophet and patriarch gave the sacred seal of their life's blood to the testimony of the truth, which they had valiantly maintained in the face of intolerant persecution for nearly a quarter of a century.[t]

21. **Authenticity of Joseph Smith's Mission:**—The evidence of divine authority in the work established by Joseph Smith, and of the justification of the claims made by and for the man, may be summarized as follows:

I. Ancient prophecy has been fulfilled in the restoration of the gospel and the re-establishment of the Church upon the earth through his instrumentality.

II. He received by direct ordination and appointment at the hands of those who held the power in former dispensations, the authority to minister in the various ordinances of the gospel.

---

[t] See Note 4.

III.   His possession of the power of true prophecy, and of other spiritual gifts, is shown by the results of his ministry.

IV.   His doctrines are both true and scriptural.

Each of these classes of evidence will receive attention and find ample demonstration in the course of our study of the Articles of Faith; and a detailed consideration will not be attempted at this stage of our investigation; a few illustrations, briefly stated, however, may not be out of place.

22.   I. **The Fulfilment of Prophecy,** wrought through the life work of Joseph Smith is abundantly shown.   John the Revelator, from his prophetic vision of the latter-day dispensation, understood and predicted that the gospel would be again sent from the heavens, and be restored to the earth through the direct ministration of an angel:—"And I saw another angel fly in the midst of heaven, having the everlasting gospel to preach unto them that dwell on the earth, and to every nation, and kindred, and tongue, and people."[u] A partial fulfilment of this prediction is claimed in the manifestation of the angel Moroni to Joseph Smith, as already described, whereby the restoration of the gospel was announced, the speedy realization of other ancient prophecies was promised; and a record, described in part as containing "the fulness of the everlasting gospel," was committed to his care for translation and publication among all nations, kindred, and tongues. The remainder of John's fateful utterance, regarding the authorized call for repentance and the execution of God's judgment preparatory to the awful scenes of the last days, is now in process of rapid and literal fulfilment.

23.   Malachi predicted the coming of Elijah specially commissioned with power to inaugurate the work of co-operation between the fathers and the children, and announced this mission as a necessary preliminary to the advent of "the

_u_ Rev. xiv, 6.

great and dreadful day of the Lord."[v]   The angel Moroni
confirmed the truth and significance of this prediction in an
emphatic reiteration.[w]   Joseph Smith and his associate in
the ministry, Oliver Cowdery, solemnly testify that they
were visited by Elijah the prophet, in the temple at Kirtland, Ohio, on the third day of April, 1836; on which
occasion the heavenly messenger declared that the day
spoken of by Malachi had fully come; "Therefore," continued
he, "the keys of this dispensation are committed into your
hands, and by this ye may know that the great and
dreadful day of the Lord is near, even at the doors."[x]   The
particular nature of the union of the fathers and the children upon which both Malachi and Moroni laid such stress,
has been explained as consisting in the work of vicarious
ordinances, including baptism for the dead who have passed
from earth without a knowledge of the gospel.   In teaching this doctrine, and in complying with its behests, the
Church of Jesus Christ of Latter-day Saints stands today
alone amongst all the sects professing Christianity.

24.   The ancient scriptures are teeming with prophecies
concerning the restoration of Israel in the last days, and
the gathering of the chosen people from among the nations,
and from the lands into which they have been led or driven
as a penalty for their waywardness and sin.[y]   Such prominence and importance are attached to this work of gathering, in the predictions of olden times, that from the days of
Israel's exodus, the last days have been characterized in
sacred writ as a gathering dispensation.   The return of the
tribes after their long and wide dispersion is made a preliminary work to the establishment of the predicted reign

---

v Mal. iv, 5-6.
w See page 11.
x Doc. & Cov., cx, 13-16.
y See lectures on Article 10.

of righteousness with Christ on the throne of the world; and its accomplishment is given as a sure precursor of the millennium. Jerusalem is to be re-established as the City of the Great King on the eastern hemisphere; and Zion, or the New Jerusalem, is to be built on the western continent; the Ten Tribes are to be brought back from their hiding place in the north; and the curse is to be removed from Israel. From the early days of Joseph Smith's ministry, he taught the doctrine of the gathering, as imposing a present duty upon the Church; and this phase of the Latter-day Saint labor is one of its most characteristic features. Joseph Smith and Oliver Cowdery declare that the authority for prosecuting this work was committed to the Church through them by Moses, who held the keys of authority as Israel's leader in former times. Their testimony is thus stated, in the description given of manifestations in the Kirtland Temple, April 3, 1836:—"Moses appeared before us, and committed unto us the keys of the gathering of Israel from the four parts of the earth, and the leading of the ten tribes from the land of the north."[z] As to the earnestness with which this labor has been begun, and the fair progress already made therein, consider the hundreds of thousands belonging to the families of Israel already gathered in the valleys of the Rocky Mountains, about the house of the Lord, now established; and hear the hymn of the chosen seed among the nations, chanted to the accompaniment of effective deeds, "Come, and let us go up to the mountain of the Lord, and to the house of the God of Jacob; and He will teach us of His ways, and we will walk in His paths; for the law shall go forth of Zion, and the word of the Lord from Jerusalem."[a]

25. The bringing forth of the Book of Mormon is held

[z] Doc. & Cov., cx, 11.
[a] Micah iv 1-2.

by the Latter-day Saints to be a direct fulfilment of prophecy.[b]   In predicting the humiliation of Israel, to whom
had been committed the power of the priesthood in early
days, Isaiah gave voice to the word of the Lord in this
wise:—"And thou shalt be brought down, and shalt speak
out of the ground, and thy speech shall be low out of the
dust, and thy voice shall be, as of one that hath a familiar
spirit, out of the ground, and thy speech shall whisper out
of the dust."[c]   The Book of Mormon is verily the voice of
a people brought low, speaking from the dust, from which
indeed the book was literally taken.   The volume professes
to be the history of but a small division of the house of
Israel,—a part of the family of Joseph indeed; who were
led by a miraculous hand to the western continent six
centuries prior to the Christian era.   Of the record of
Joseph, and its coming forth as a parallel testimony to that
of Judah, or the Bible in part, the Lord thus spake through
the prophet Ezekiel:—"Moreover, thou son of man, take
thee one stick, and write upon it, For Judah, and for the
children of Israel his companions: then take another stick,
and write upon it, For Joseph, the stick of Ephraim, and
for all the house of Israel his companions: And join them
one to another into one stick; and they shall become one in
thine hand.   And when the children of thy people shall
speak unto thee, saying, Wilt thou not shew us what thou
meanest by these? Say unto them, Thus saith the Lord
God; Behold, I will take the stick of Joseph, which is in the
hand of Ephraim, and the tribes of Israel his fellows, and
will put them with him, even with the stick of Judah, and
make them one stick, and they shall be one in mine hand."[d]
The succeeding verses declare that the gathering and res-

---

b See lectures on "Book of Mormon," article 8.

c Isa. xxix, 4; see also II Nephi, iii, 19.

d Ezek. xxxvii, 16-19.

3

toration of Israel would immediately follow the united testimony of the records of Judah and Joseph. The two records are before the world, a unit in their testimony of the everlasting gospel, and the work of gathering is in effective progress.

26. It is further evident from the scriptures, that the dispensation of the gospel in the latter days is to be one of restoration, and restitution, a "dispensation of the fulness of times" in very truth. Paul declares it to be the good pleasure of the Lord, "That in the dispensation of the fulness of times he might gather together in one all things in Christ, both which are in heaven, and which are on earth; even in him:"[e] This prediction finds a parallel in an utterance of the prophet Nephi:—"Wherefore all things which have been revealed unto the children of men, shall at that day be revealed."[f] And in accord with this is the teaching of Peter: "Repent ye therefore, and be converted, that your sins may be blotted out, when the times of refreshing shall come from the presence of the Lord; And he shall send Jesus Christ, which before was preached unto you: Whom the heaven must receive until the times of restitution of all things, which God hath spoken by the mouth of all his holy prophets since the world began."[g] Now comes Joseph Smith with the declaration that unto him has been given the authority to open up this, the dispensation of fulness, restitution, and restoration, and that through him the Church has been endowed with all the keys and powers of the priesthood, held and exercised in earlier periods: Unto the Church "is the power of this priesthood given, for the last days, and for the last time, in the which is the dispensation of the fulness of times, which power you hold in

---

e Eph. i, 9-10.
f II Nephi, xxx, 18.
g Acts iii, 19-21.

connection with all those who have received a dispensation at any time from the beginning of creation."[h] The actual possession of these combined and unified powers is sufficiently proved by the comprehensive work of the Church in its present scope of operation.

27. II. **Joseph Smith's Authority** was conferred upon him by direct ministrations of heavenly beings, each of whom had once exercised the same power upon the earth. We have already seen how the angel Moroni, formerly a mortal prophet among the Nephites, transmitted to Joseph the appointment to bring forth the record which he, Moroni, had buried in the earth over fourteen hundred years before. We learn further, that on the 15th of May, 1829, the lesser or Aaronic Priesthood was conferred upon Joseph Smith and Oliver Cowdery by the hand of John the Baptist,[i] who came in his immortalized state with that particular order of priesthood which comprises the keys of the ministrations of angels, the doctrine of repentance and of baptism for remission of sins. This was the same John, who, with the voice of one crying in the wilderness had preached the self-same doctrine, and had administered the same ordinance in Judæa as the immediate forerunner of the Messiah. In delivering his message, John the Baptist stated that he was acting under the direction of Peter, James, and John, apostles of the Lord, in whose hands reposed the keys of the higher or Melchisedek Priesthood, which in time would also be given. This promise was fulfilled a month or so later, when the apostles named manifested themselves to Joseph and Oliver, ordaining them to the apostleship,[j] which comprises all the offices of the higher order of priesthood, and carries authority to minister in all the established ordinances of the gospel.

h Doc. & Cov. cxii, 30-32.

i Doc. & Cov. xiii.

j Doc. & Cov. xxvii. 12.

28. Then, some time after the Church had been duly organized, authority for certain special functions was given, the appointing messenger being in each case the one whose right it was so to officiate by virtue of the commission which he had held in the days of his mortality. Thus, as has been seen, Moses conferred the authority to prosecute the work of gathering; and Elijah, who, not having tasted death, held a peculiar relation to both the living and the dead, delivered the authority of vicarious ministry for the departed. To these appointments by heavenly authority should be added that given by Elias, who appeared to Joseph Smith and Oliver Cowdery, and "committed the dispensation of the gospel of Abraham," saying as was said of the Father of the Faithful and his descendants in olden times, that in them and in their seed should all succeeding generations be blessed.

29. It is evident, then, that the claims made by the Church with respect to its authority, are complete and consistent as to the source of the powers professed, and the channels through which such have been delivered again to earth. Scripture and revelation, both ancient and modern, support as an unalterable law, the principle that no one can delegate to another an authority which the giver does not possess.

30. III. Joseph Smith was himself a true Prophet:— This statement, if fully substantiated, would be of itself sufficient proof of the validity of the claims of this modern prophet, and the test is not difficult of application. In the days of ancient Israel, an effective method of trying the claims of a professed prophet was prescribed:—"When a prophet speaketh in the name of the Lord, if the thing follow not, nor come to pass, that is the thing which the Lord hath not spoken, but the prophet hath spoken it presumptuously; thou shalt not be afraid of him."[k] Conversely, if

k Deut. xviii. 22.

the words of the prophet are made good by fulfilment, there is at least proof presumptive of his genuineness. Of the many predictions uttered by Joseph Smith and already fulfilled or awaiting the set time of their realization, a few citations will suffice for our present purpose.

31. One of the earliest prophecies declared by him, which, while not his independent utterance but that of the angel Moroni, was nevertheless given to the world by Joseph Smith, had special reference to the Book of Mormon, of which the angel said: "The knowledge that this record contains will go to every nation, and kindred, and tongue, and people, under the whole heaven."[l] This declaration was made four years before the work of translation was begun, and fourteen years before the elders of the Church began their missionary labor in foreign lands. Since that time the Book of Mormon has been translated into twelve foreign languages, and is published in ten of these; and the work is still in progress.

32. In August, 1842, while the Church was suffering persecution in Illinois, and when the western part of the continent was but little known, and only as the territory of an alien nation, Joseph Smith prophesied "that the Saints would continue to suffer much affliction, and would be driven to the Rocky Mountains," and that while many then professing allegiance to the Church would apostatize, and others, faithful to their testimony, would meet the martyr's fate, some would live "to assist in making settlements and build cities and see the Saints become a mighty people in the midst of the Rocky Mountains."[m] The literal fulfilment of this prediction, uttered in 1842, and it may be added, foreshadowed by an earlier prophecy in 1831,[n] the one five, the other sixteen years before the migration of the Church

---

l Times and Seasons, Vol. II, No. 13.

m Millennial Star, Vol. XIX, p. 630.

n Doc. and Cov., xlix 24-25.

to the west, is attested by the common history of the settlement and development of this once inhospitable region. Even the skeptic, and the pronounced opponents of the Church, admit the miracle of the establishment of a mighty commonwealth in the valleys of the Rocky Mountains.

33. A most remarkable prediction regarding national affairs was uttered by Joseph Smith, December 25th, 1832; it was soon thereafter promulgated among the members of the Church, and was preached by the elders, but did not appear in print until 1851.° The revelation reads in part as follows:—"Verily thus saith the Lord, concerning the wars that will shortly come to pass, beginning at the rebellion of South Carolina, which will eventually terminate in the death and misery of many souls. The days will come that war will be poured out upon all nations, beginning at that place; For, behold, the Southern States shall be divided against the Northern States, and the Southern States will call on other nations, even the nation of Great Britain;   *   *   * And it shall come to pass, after many days, slaves shall rise up against their masters, who shall be marshalled and disciplined for war." Every student of United States history is acquainted with the facts establishing a complete fulfilment, even to the minutest detail, of this astounding prophecy. In 1861, more than twenty-eight years after the foregoing prediction was recorded, and ten years after its publication in England, the civil war broke out, beginning in South Carolina. The ghastly records of that fratricidal strife sadly support the prediction concerning "the death and misery of many souls." It is well known that slaves deserted the South and were marshalled in the armies of the North, and that the Confederate States solicited aid of Great

o See Pearl of Great Price, British edition of 1851, and Millennial Star, Vol. xlix, p. 396. The prophecy is now a part of the Doctrine and Covenants, see section lxxxvii.

Britain. While no open alliance between the Southern States and England was effected, the British government gave indirect assistance and substantial encouragement to the South, and this in such a way as to produce serious international complications. Vessels were built and equipped at British ports in the interests of the Confederacy; and the results of this violation of the laws of neutrality cost Great Britain the sum of fifteen and a half millions of dollars, which sum was awarded the United States at the Geneva arbitration in settlement of the "Alabama claims." The Confederacy appointed commissioners to Great Britain and France; these appointees were forcibly taken by United States officers from the British steamer on which they had embarked. This act, which the United States government had to admit as overt, threatened for a time to precipitate a war between this nation and Great Britain.

34.   The revelation cited, as given through Joseph Smith, contained other predictions, some of which are yet awaiting fulfilment.[p] The evidence presented is sufficient to prove that Joseph Smith is prominent among men by reason of his instrumentality in fulfilling prophecies uttered by the Lord's representatives in former times, and that his own claim to the rank of prophet is abundantly vindicated. But the endowment of prophecy so richly bestowed upon this Elias of the last days, and so freely yet unerringly exercised by him, is but one of the many spiritual gifts by which he, in common with a host of others who have received the priesthood from him, was distinguished. The scriptures declare that certain signs shall attend the Church of Christ, among them the gifts of tongues, healing, immunity from threatening death, and the power to control evil spirits.[q] The exercise of these powers, resulting in what are ordinarily

p See Doc, and Cov. lxxxvii, 5-7.

q Mark xvi, 16-18; Luke x, 19, etc.; Doc. and Cov. lxxxiv, 65-72.

termed miracles, is by no means an infallible proof of divine authority; for many true prophets have wrought no such wonders, and men have been known to work miracles at the instigation of evil spirits.*r* Nevertheless, the possession of the power implied by the working of miracles is an essential characteristic of the Church; and when such acts are wrought in the accomplishment of holy purposes, they serve as confirmatory evidence of divine authority. Therefore we may expect to find, as find we do, in the ministry of Joseph Smith and in that of the Church in general, the attested record of miracles, comprising manifestations of all the promised gifts of the Spirit. This subject will be further considered on another occasion.*s*

35. IV. The Doctrines Taught by Joseph Smith and by the Church today are true and scriptural. To sustain this statement we must examine the principal teachings of the Church in separate order. The Articles of Faith furnish us a convenient summary of many of the doctrines pertaining to the latter-day work; and these we will proceed to study in the course of the lectures that are to follow.

NOTES.

1. The "Articles of Faith" date from March 1, 1841. They constitute a portion of a letter from the Prophet Joseph Smith to a Mr. Wentworth, of Chicago. The "Articles" were published in the History of Joseph Smith: (See *Millennial Star*, vol. XIX, p. 120; also *Times and Seasons*, vol. III, p. 709.) As stated elsewhere, the Articles have been formally adopted by the Church as an authorized summary of its principal doctrines.

2. Joseph Smith's Early Persecution.—The Prophet wrote as follows concerning the persecution of his boyhood days, which dated from the time of his first mention of his vision of the Father and the Son:—"It has often caused me serious reflection, both then and since, how very strange it was that an obscure boy, a little over fourteen years of age, and one too, who was doomed to the necessity of obtaining a scanty maintenance by his daily labor, should be

---

r Exo. vii, 11, 22: viii, 7, 18; Rev. xiii, 13-15: xvi, 13-14.

s See Lecture on Article 7

thought a character of sufficient importance to attract the attention of the great ones of the most popular sects of the day, so as to create in them a spirit of the hottest persecution and reviling. But strange or not, so it was, and was often cause of great sorrow to myself. However it was, nevertheless, a fact that I had had a vision. I have thought since that I felt much like Paul when he made his defense before King Agrippa, and related the account of the vision he had when he saw a light and heard a voice, but still there were but a few who believed him; some said he was dishonest, others said he was mad, and he was ridiculed and reviled; but all this did not destroy the reality of his vision. He had seen a vision, he knew he had, and all the persecution under heaven could not make it otherwise; * * * * * So it was with me; I had actually seen a light, and in the midst of that light I saw two personages, and they did in reality speak unto me, or one of them did; and though I was hated and persecuted for saying that I had seen a vision, yet it was true; and while they were persecuting me, reviling me, and speaking all manner of evil against me, falsely, for so saying, I was led to say in my heart, Why persecute for telling the truth? I had actually seen a vision, and who am I that I can withstand God?" *Pearl of Great Price:*—Extracts from the History of Joseph Smith: pp. 90-91, (1888 ed.)

3. Tribute to Joseph Smith.—While few people outside the Church have had much to say in commendation of this modern prophet, it is interesting to note that there are some honorable exceptions to the rule. Josiah Quincy, a prominent American, made the acquaintance of Joseph Smith, a short time before the latter's martyrdom; and after the tragic event he wrote: "It is by no means improbable that some future text-book, for the use of generations yet unborn, will contain a question something like this: What historical American of the nineteenth century has exerted the most powerful influence upon the destinies of his countrymen? And it is by no means impossible that the answer to that interrogatory may be thus written: *Joseph Smith, the Mormon Prophet.* And the reply, absurd as it doubtless seems to most men now, may be an obvious commonplace to their descendants. History deals in surprises and paradoxes quite as startling as this. The man who establishes a religion in this age of free debate, who was and is today accepted by hundreds of thousands as a direct emissary from the Most High,—such a rare human being is not to be disposed of by pelting his memory with unsavory epithets. * * * * The most vital questions Americans are asking each other today have to do with this man and what he has left us. * * * * Burning questions they are, which must give a prominent place in the history of the country to that sturdy self-asserter whom I visited at Nauvoo. Joseph Smith, claiming to be an inspired teacher, faced adversity, such as few men have been called to meet, enjoyed a brief season of prosperity, such as few men have ever attained, and, finally, forty-three days after I saw him, went cheerfully to a martyr's death. When he surrendered his person to Governor Ford, in order to prevent the shedding of blood, the Prophet had a presentiment of what was before him. I am going like a lamb to the slaughter,' he is reported to have said, 'but I am as calm as a summer's morning. I have a conscience void of offense, and shall die innocent.' " *Figures of the Past* by Josiah Quincy, p. 376.

4. The Seal of Martyrdom.—"The highest evidence of sincerity that a man can give his fellow-men,—the highest proof that he has spoken the truth in any given case—is that he perseveres in it unto death, and seals his testimony with his blood.   *   *   *   So important did such a testimony become in the estimation of Paul, that he said 'Where a testament is there must also of necessity be the death of the testator.   For a testament is of force after men are dead: otherwise it is of no strength at all while the testator liveth.'   (Heb. ix; 16-17.)   In the light of this principle. and when the importance of the great testimony which he bore to the world is taken into account, it is not to be wondered at that Joseph Smith was called upon to affix the broad seal of martyrdom to his life's work.   Something of incompleteness in his work would likely have been complained of had this been lacking; but now, not so; his character of prophet was rounded out to complete fulness by his falling a martyr under the murderous fire of a mob at Carthage in the State of Illinois."— *Elder B. H. Roberts, in A New Witness for God,* pp. 477-478.

5. **Joseph Smith; Further References.**—For biography, see "*The Life of Joseph Smith, the Prophet,*" by Pres. George Q. Cannon.   See also "*Divine Authority, or the question, Was Joseph Smith Sent of God?*" a pamphlet by Apostle Orson Pratt;   "*Joseph Smith's Prophetic Calling;*"   *Millennial Star,* Vol. XLII; pp 164, 187, 195, 227.   *Letters,* by Elder Orson Spencer to Rev. Wm. Crowell; No. 1; "*A New Witness for God,*" by Elder B. H. Roberts.

LECTURE II.

GOD AND THE GODHEAD.

Article 1:—We believe in God, the Eternal Father, and in His Son, Jesus Christ, and in the Holy Ghost.

1.   **The Existence of God:**—Since faith in God constitutes the foundation of religious belief and practice, and inasmuch as a knowledge of the attributes and character of Deity is essential to an intelligent exercise of faith in Him, this subject claims first place in our study of the doctrines of the Church.

2.   The existence of God is scarcely a question of rational dispute; nor does it call for proof by the feeble demonstrations of man's logic, for the fact is admitted by the human family practically without question, and the consciousness of subjection to a supreme power is an inborn quality of mankind.   The early scriptures are in no sense devoted to a primary demonstration of God's existence, nor to attacks on the sophistries of atheism; from which fact we may infer that the errors of doubt developed in some period later than the first.   The universal assent of mankind to the existence of God is at least a strongly corroborative truth.   There is a filial passion within human nature which flames toward heaven.   Every nation, every tribe, every individual, yearns for some object of reverence.   It is natural for man to worship; his soul is unsatisfied till it finds a deity.   When men through transgression first fell into darkness concerning the true and living God, they established for themselves other deities, and so arose the abominations of idolatry.   And yet, ter-

rible as these practices are, even the most revolting idolatries testify to the existence of a God by declaring man's hereditary passion for worship. Plutarch has wisely remarked of ancient conditions: "If you search the world, you may find cities without walls, without letters, without kings, without money; but no one ever saw a city without a deity, without a temple, or without prayers." This general assent to a belief in the existence of Deity is testimony of a high order; and in this connection the words of Aristotle may be applied:—"What seems true to some wise men is somewhat probable; what seems true to most or all wise men is very probable; what most men, both wise and unwise, assent to, still more resembles truth; but what men generally consent in, has the highest probability, and approaches so near to demonstrated truth, that it may pass for ridiculous arrogance and selfconceitedness, or for intolerable obstinacy and perverseness, to decry it."[a]

3.   The multiplicity of evidence upon which mankind rest their conviction regarding the existence of a Supreme Being, may be classified for convenience of consideration, under the three following heads:

I.   The evidence of history and tradition.
II.   The evidence furnished by the exercise of human reason.
III.   The conclusive evidence of direct revelation from God Himself.

4.   I. History and Tradition:—History as written by man, and tradition as transmitted from generation to generation prior to the date of any written record now extant, give evidence of the actuality of Deity, and of close and personal dealings between God and man in the first epochs of human existence. One of the most ancient records known, the Bible,

a See Notes 1, 2, and 3.

names God as the Creator of all things,[b] and moreover,
declares that He revealed Himself to our first earthly
parents, and to many other holy personages in the early
days of the world.   Adam and Eve heard His voice[c] in the
Garden, and even after their transgression they continued
to call upon God, and to sacrifice to Him.   It is plain, therefore, that they carried with them from the Garden a knowledge of God.   After their expulsion they heard "the voice
of the Lord from the way toward the Garden of Eden,"
though they saw Him not; and He gave unto them commandments, which they obeyed.   Then came to Adam an
angelic messenger, and the Holy Ghost inspired the man
and bare record of the Father and the Son.[d]

5.   Cain and Abel learned of God from the teachings of
their parents, as well as from personal ministrations.   After
the acceptance of Abel's offering, and the rejection of
Cain's, followed by Cain's terrible crime of fratricide, the
Lord talked with Cain, and Cain answered the Lord.[e]   Cain
must, therefore, have taken a personal knowledge of God
from Eden into the land where he went to dwell.[f]   Adam
lived to be nine hundred and thirty years old and many
children were born unto him.   Them he instructed in the
fear of God, and many of them received direct ministrations.   Of Adam's descendants, Seth, Enos, Cainan, Mahalaleel, Jared, Enoch, Methuselah, and Lamech the father of
Noah, each representing a distinct generation, were all living
during Adam's lifetime.   Noah was born but a hundred and
twenty-six years after the time of Adam's death, and moreover lived nearly six hundred years with his father Lamech,
by whom he was doubtless instructed in the traditions con-

---

b Genesis i; see also Pearl of Great Price, Writings of Moses, p. 7, (1888 ed.)

c Genesis iii, 8, and Pearl of Great Price, Writings of Moses, p. 15. (1888 ed.)

d Pearl of Great Price, p. 18, (1888 ed.)

e Genesis iv, 9-16; Pearl of Great Price, p. 21-23, (1888 ed.)

f Genesis iv, 16; Pearl of Great Price, p. 23, (1888 ed.)

cerning God's personal manifestations, which Lamech had learned from the lips of Adam. Through the medium of Noah and his family, a knowledge of God by direct tradition was carried beyond the flood; then Noah held direct communication with God,[g] and lived to instruct ten generations of his descendants. Then followed Abraham, who also enjoyed direct communion with the Creator,[h] and after him Isaac, and Jacob, or Israel, among whose descendants the Lord wrought such wonders through the instrumentality of Moses. Thus, had there been no written records, tradition would have preserved and transmitted a knowledge of God.

6. But even if the accounts of the earliest of man's personal communion with God had become dimmed with time, and therefore weakened in effect, they could but give place to other traditions founded on later manifestations of the Divine personality. Unto Moses the Lord made Himself known, not alone from behind the curtain of fire, and the screen of clouds,[i] but by direct face to face communication, whereby the chosen high-priest, beheld even "the similitude" of his God.[j] This account of direct communion between Moses and God, in part of which the people were permitted to share,[k] as far as their faith and purity permitted, has been preserved by Israel through all the generations of the past. And from Israel the traditions of God's existence have spread throughout the world; so that we find traces of this ancient knowledge even in the most fanciful and perverted mythologies of heathen nations.

7. II. **Human Reason**, operating upon observations of the

---

g Genesis vi, 13, and succeeding chapter.

h Genesis xii, and succeeding chapters.

i Exo. iii, 4; xix, 18; Numb. xii, 5.

j Numb. xii, 8; see also Pearl of Great Price, Visions of Moses, p. 1 (1888 ed.)

k Exo. xix, 9; 11; 17-20.

things of nature, strongly declares the existence of God. The mind already imbued with the historical truths of the Divine existence and its close relationship with man, will find confirmatory evidence in nature on every side; and even to him who rejects the testimony of the past, and assumes to set up his own judgment as superior to the universal belief of ages, the multifarious evidences of design in nature appeal. Every observer must be impressed by the proofs of order and system among created things, and by the absence of superfluities in nature. He notes the regular succession of day and night providing alternate periods of work and rest for man, animals, and vegetables; the sequence of the seasons, each with its longer periods of labor and recuperation, the mutual dependence of animals and plants, the circulation of water from sea to cloud, from cloud to earth again, sustaining the fertility of the soil. As man proceeds to the closer examination of things, he finds that by study and scientific investigation these proofs are multiplied many fold. He may learn something of the laws by which earth and its associated worlds are governed in their orbits; by which satellites are held subordinate to planets, and planets to suns; he may behold the marvels of vegetable and animal anatomy, and the surpassing mechanism of his own body; and with such appeals to his reason increasing at every step, his wonder as to who made all this, gives place to inexpressible admiration for the Creator whose presence and power are thus so forcibly proclaimed; and the observer becomes a worshiper.

8. Everywhere in nature is the evidence of cause and effect; on every side is the demonstration of means adapted to end. But such adaptations, says a thoughtful writer, "indicate contrivance for a given purpose, and contrivance is the evidence of intelligence, and intelligence is the attribute of mind, and the intelligent mind that built the

stupendous universe is God."[l] To admit the existence of a
designer in the evidence of design, to say there must be a
contriver in a world of intelligent contrivance, to believe in
an adapter when man's life is directly dependent upon the
most perfect adaptations conceivable, is but to accept self-
evident truths. These axioms of nature ought to require
no demonstration; the burden of proof as to the non-existence of a God ought to be placed upon him who questions
the solemn truth. "Every house is builded by some man,
but he that built all things is God." So spake the Apostle
of old,[m] and plain as is the truth expressed in these simple
words, there are among men a few, who profess to doubt the
evidence of reason, and who deny the Author of their own
being. Strange is it not, that here and there one, who finds
in the contrivance exhibited by the ant in building her
house, in the architecture of the honey-comb, and in the
myriad instances of orderly instinct among the least of living things, a proof of intelligence from which man may
learn and be wise, will yet question the operation of intelligence in the creation of worlds, and in the constitution of the
universe?[n]

9. Man's inborn consciousness tells him of his own
existence; his ordinary powers of observation prove the
existence of others of his kind, and of uncounted orders of
organized beings; from this he concludes that something
must have existed always, for had there been a time of no
existence, a period of nothingness, existence could never
have begun, for from nothing, nothing can be derived. The
eternal existence of something then, is a fact beyond dispute;
and the only question requiring answer is, what is that
eternal something; that existence which is without begin-

---

[l] Cassell's Bible Dictionary, p 481.
[m] Paul in Heb. iii, 4.
[n] See Note 4.

ning and without end? The skeptic may answer, "Nature; matter has always existed, and the universe is but a manifestation of matter organized by forces operating upon it; however, Nature is not God." But matter is neither vital nor active, nor is force intelligent; yet vitality and ceaseless activity are characteristic of created things, and the effects of intelligence are universally present. True, nature is not God; and to mistake the one for the other is to call the edifice the architect, the fabric the designer, the marble the sculptor, and the thing the power that made it. The system of nature is the manifestation of that order which argues a directing intelligence; and that intelligence is of an eternal character, coeval with existence itself. Nature herself is a declaration of a superior Being, whose will and purpose she portrays in all her varied aspects. Beyond and above nature, stands nature's God.

10. While existence is eternal, and therefore to being there never was a beginning, never will be an end, in a relative sense each stage of organization must have had a beginning, and to every phase of existence as manifested in each of the countless orders and classes of created things, there was a first, as there will be a last; though every ending or consummation in nature is but the beginning of another stage of advancement. Thus, man's ingenuity has invented theories to illustrate, if not to explain, a possible sequence of events by which the earth has been brought from a state of chaos to its present habitable condition; but by those hypotheses, this globe was once a heated ball, on which none of the innumerable forms of life which now tenant it could have existed. The theorist therefore must admit a beginning to earthly life, and such a beginning is explicable only on the assumption of some creative act, or a contribution from outside the earth. If he admit the introduction of life upon the earth from some other and older

4

sphere, he does but extend the limits of his enquiry as to the beginning of vital existence; for to explain the origin of a rose bush in our own garden by saying that it was transplanted as an offshoot from a rose-tree growing elsewhere, is no answer to the question concerning the origin of roses. Science of necessity assumes a beginning to vital phenomena on this planet, and admits a finite duration of the earth in its current course of progressive change; and in this respect, the earth is a representative of the heavenly bodies in general. The eternity of existence then is no more potent as an indication of an eternal Ruler, than is the endless sequence of change, each stage of which has both beginning and end. The origination of created things, the beginning of an organized universe, is utterly inexplicable on any assumption of spontaneous change in matter, or of a fortuitous and accidental operation of its properties.

11. Human reason, so liable to err in dealing with subjects of lesser import even, may not of itself lead its possessor to a full knowledge of God; yet its exercise will aid him in his search, strengthening and confirming his inherited instinct toward his Maker.[o] "The fool hath said in his heart there is no God."[p] In the scriptures, the word fool[q] is used to designate a wicked man, one who has forfeited his wisdom by a long course of wrong doing, bringing darkness over his mind in place of light, and ignorance instead of knowledge. By such a course, the mind becomes depraved and incapable of appreciating the finer arguments in nature. A wilful sinner grows deaf to the voice of reason in holy things, and loses the privilege of communing with his Creator, thus forfeiting the strongest means of attaining a knowledge of God.

---

o See Note 5.
p Psalms xiv, 1.
q Proverbs i, 7; x, 21; xiv, 9.

12. **III. Revelation** gives to man his fullest knowledge of God. We are not left wholly to the exercise of fallible reasoning powers, nor to the testimony of others for a knowledge of our Heavenly Father; we may know Him for ourselves. Instances of God manifesting Himself to His prophets in olden as in later times are so numerous as to render impossible any detailed consideration here; moreover, we will have opportunity of examining many examples in connection with our study of the ninth of the Articles of Faith; for the present, therefore, brief mention must suffice. We have already noted as the foundation of many traditions relating to the existence and personality of God, His revelations of Himself to Adam and other ante-diluvian patriarchs; then to Noah, Abraham, Isaac, Jacob, and Moses. An example but briefly mentioned in the Jewish scriptures is that of Enoch, the father of Methuselah; of him we read that he walked with God.[r] From the "Writings of Moses" we learn that the Lord manifested Himself with special favor to this chosen seer,[s] revealing unto him the course of events until the time of Christ's appointed ministry in the flesh, the plan of salvation through the sacrifice of the Only Begotten, and the scenes that were to follow until the final judgment.

13. Of Moses we read that he received a manifestation from God, who spoke to him from the midst of the burning bush in Mount Horeb, saying "I am the God of thy father, the God of Abraham, the God of Isaac, and the God of Jacob. And Moses hid his face, for he was afraid to look upon God."[t] Unto Moses and assembled Israel God appeared in a cloud, with the terrifying accompaniment of thunders and lightnings, on Sinai; "And the Lord said unto Moses, thus shalt

---

[r] Gen. v, 18-24: see also Jude 14.

[s] Pearl of Great Price, Writings of Moses, p. 28-45, (1888 ed.)

[t] Exodus iii, 6.

thou say unto the children of Israel, ye have seen that I have talked with you from heaven."[u]   Of a later manifestation we are told:—"Then went up Moses, and Aaron, Nadab, and Abihu, and seventy of the elders of Israel: And they saw the God of Israel: and there was under his feet as it were a paved work of a sapphire stone, and as it were the body of heaven in his clearness."[v]

14.   On through the time of Joshua and the judges to the kings and the prophets, the Lord declared His presence and His power. Isaiah saw the Lord enthroned in the midst of a glorious company, and cried out, "Woe is me, for I am undone; because I am a man of unclean lips, and I dwell in the midst of a people of unclean lips, for mine eyes have seen the King, the Lord of hosts."[w]

15.   At a subsequent period, when Christ emerged from the waters of baptism, the voice of the Father was heard declaring "This is my beloved Son, in whom I am well pleased."[x]   And on the occasion of our Lord's transfiguration, the same voice repeated this solemn and glorious acknowledgment.[y]   While Stephen was suffering martyrdom at the hands of his cruel and bigoted countrymen, the heavens were opened, and he "saw the glory of God, and Jesus standing on the right hand of God."[z]

16.   The Book of Mormon is replete with instances of communication between God and His people, mostly through vision and by the ministration of angels, but also through direct manifestation of the Divine presence.   Thus, we read of a colony of people leaving the Tower of Babel and journeying to the western hemisphere, under the leadership

---

u Ex. xx, 18-22.

v Ex. xxiv, 9-10.

w Isa. vi, 1-5.

x Matt. iii, 16-17; Mark i, 11.

y Matt. xvii, 1-5; Luke ix, 35.

z Acts vii, 54-60.

of one who is known in the record as the brother of Jared. In preparing for the voyage across the great deep, the leader prayed that the Lord would touch with His finger, and thereby make luminous, certain stones, that the voyagers might have light in the ships. In answer to this petition, the Lord stretched forth His hand and touched the stones, revealing His finger, which the man was surprised to see resembled the finger of a human being. Then the Lord, pleased with the man's faith, made Himself visible to the brother of Jared, and demonstrated to him that man was formed literally after the image of the Creator.[a] To the Nephites who inhabited the western continent, Christ revealed Himself after His resurrection and ascension. To these sheep of the western fold, He testified of His commission received from the Father; showed the wounds in His hands, feet, and side, and ministered unto the believing multitudes in many ways.[b]

17. In the present dispensation, God has revealed, and does still reveal Himself to His people. We have seen how by faith and sincerity of purpose Joseph Smith, while yet a youth, won for himself a manifestation of God's presence, being privileged to behold both the Father and Christ the Son.[c] His testimony of the existence of God is not dependent upon tradition or logical deduction; he declares to the world that he knows both God and Christ live, for he has beheld their persons, and has heard their voices. In addition to the manifestation cited, Joseph Smith and his fellow servant, Sidney Rigdon, state that on the 16th of February, 1832, they saw the Son of God, and conversed with Him in heavenly vision. In describing this manifestation they say: "And while we meditated upon these things, the

a Book of Mormon, Ether iii.

b Book of Mormon, III Nephi xi-xxviii.

c See page 9.

Lord touched the eyes of our understandings, and they were opened, and the glory of the Lord shone round about; and we beheld the glory of the Son, on the right hand of the Father, and received of His fulness; and saw the holy angels, and they who are sanctified before His throne, worshiping God and the Lamb, who worship Him forever and ever. And now, after the many testimonies which have been given of Him, this is the testimony last of all which we give of Him, that He lives, for we saw Him."[d]

18. Again, on the 3rd of April, 1836, in the temple at Kirtland, Ohio, the Lord manifested Himself to Joseph Smith and Oliver Cowdery, who say of the occasion:—"We saw the Lord standing upon the breastwork of the pulpit before us, and under His feet was a paved work of pure gold in color like amber. His eyes were as a flame of fire, the hair of His head was white like the pure snow, His countenance shone above the brightness of the sun, and His voice was as the sound of the rushing of great waters, even the voice of Jehovah, saying,—I am the first and the last; I am He who liveth; I am He who was slain; I am your advocate with the Father."[e]

19. These are a few of the testimonies establishing the fact of direct revelation from God unto men in ancient and modern times. The privilege of communing with our Maker is restricted to none; true faith, sincerity of purpose, and purity of soul, will win for any one who seeks the boon, the blessing of God's favor, and the light of His presence.

20. **The Godhead: The Trinity:**—Three personages composing the great presiding council of the universe have revealed themselves to man; (1) God the Eternal Father, (2) His Son, Jesus Christ; and (3) the Holy Ghost. That these three are separate individuals, physically distinct from

---

d Doc. and Cov. lxxvi, 11-24.
e Doc. and Cov. cx, 1-4.

each other, is very plainly proved by the accepted records of
the divine dealings with man. On the occasion of the
Savior's baptism before cited, John recognized the sign of
the Holy Ghost; he saw before him in a tabernacle of flesh
the Christ, upon whom he had performed the holy ordinance; and he heard the voice of the Father.[f] The three
personages of the Godhead were present, manifesting themselves each in a different way, and each distinct from the
others. The Savior promised His disciples that the Comforter,[g] which is the Holy Ghost, should be sent unto them
by His Father; here again are the three members of the
Godhead distinctly referred to. Stephen, at the time of his
martyrdom, was blessed with the power of heavenly vision,
and he saw Jesus standing on the right hand of God.[h]
Joseph Smith, while calling upon the Lord in fervent prayer
for wisdom to guide him in his religious professions, saw the
Father and the Son, standing in the midst of light
which shamed the brightness of the sun, one of these declared of the other, "This is my beloved Son, hear Him."[i]
Each of the members of the Trinity is called God,[j] together they constitute the Godhead.

21. **Unity of the Godhead:**—The Godhead is a type of
unity in the attributes, powers, and purposes of its members.
Jesus, while on earth[k] and in manifesting Himself to His
Nephite servants,[l] has repeatedly testified of the unity existing between Himself and the Father, and between them
both and the Holy Ghost. By some this has been construed
to mean that the Father, the Son, and the Holy Ghost are

f Matt. iii, 16-17; Mark i, 9-11; Luke iii, 21-22.

g John xiv, 26; xv, 26.

h Acts vii, 55-56.

i See age 9.

j I Cor. viii, 6; John i, 1-14; Matthew iv, 10; I Tim. iii, 16: I John v, 7: Mosiah
xv, 1, 2.

k John x, 30, 38; xvii, 11, 22.

l III Nephi xi, 27, 36; xxviii, 10; see also Alma xi, 44.

one in substance and in person, that the names in reality
represent the same individual under different aspects. A
single reference to prove the error of this view may suffice:—
Immediately before his betrayal, Christ prayed for His disciples, the Twelve, and other converts, that they should be
preserved in unity,[m] "that they all may be one" as the Father
and the Son are one.   It is absurd to think that Christ
desired His followers to lose their individuality and become
one person, even if a change so directly opposed to the laws
of nature were possible.   Christ desired that all should be
united in heart, and spirit, and purpose; for such is the
unity between His Father and Himself, and between themselves and the Holy Ghost.

22.   This unity is a type of completeness; the mind of
any one member of the Trinity is the mind of the others;
seing as each of them does with the eye of purity and
perfection, they see and understand alike; under similar
conditions and circumstances each would act in the same
way, guided by the same principles of unerring justice and
equity.   The one-ness of the Godhead, to which the scriptures so abundantly testify, implies no mystical union of
substance, or unnatural and therefore impossible blending
of personality; Father, Son, and Holy Ghost are as distinct in their persons and individualities, as are any three
personages in the flesh.   Yet their unity of purpose and
operation is such as to make their edicts one, and their will
the will of God.   To see one is to see all; therefore said
Christ when importuned by Philip to show them the Father,
"Have I been so long time with you, and yet hast thou not
known me, Philip? he that hath seen me hath seen the
Father; and how sayest thou then, Shew us the Father?
Believest thou not that I am in the Father, and the Father
in me? the words that I speak unto you I speak not of

m John xvii, 11-21.

myself: but the Father that dwelleth in me, he doeth the
works.   Believe me that I am in the Father, and the Father
in me.'"[n]

23.   **Personality of Each Member of the Godhead:**—From
the evidence already presented, it is clear that the Father is
a personal Being, possessing a definite form, with bodily
parts, and spiritual passions.   Jesus Christ, who was with
the Father[o] in spirit before coming to dwell in the flesh,
and through whom the worlds were made,[p] lived among men
as a man, with all the physical characteristics of a human
being; after His resurrection He appeared in the same form;[q]
in that form He ascended into heaven;[r] and in that form
He has manifested Himself to the Nephites, and to modern
prophets.   Now we are assured that Christ was in the express image of His Father,[s] after which image man also has
been created.[t]   Therefore we know that both the Father and
the Son are in form and stature perfect men; each of them
possesses a tangible body, infinitely pure and perfect, and attended by transcendent glory, yet a body of flesh and bone.[u]

24.   The Holy Ghost, called also Spirit, and Spirit of the
Lord,[v] Spirit of God,[w] Comforter,[x] and Spirit of Truth,[y] is
not tabernacled in a body of flesh and bone, but is a personage of spirit;[z] yet we know that the Spirit has manifested

----

n John xiv, 9-11.

o John xvii, 5.

p John i, 3; Heb. i, 2; Eph. iii, 9; Col. i, 16.

q John xx, 14-15, 19-20, 26-27; xxi, 1-14; Matt. xxviii, 9; Luke xxiv, 15-31, 36-44.
r Acts i, 9-11.

s Heb. i, 3; Col. i, 15; II Cor. iv, 4.

t Genesis i, 26-27; James iii, 8-9.

u Doc. and. Cov. cxxx, 22.

v I Nephi iv, 6; xi 8; Mos. xiii, 5.   Acts ii, 4; viii. 29; x, 19; Rom viii, 10, 26;
I Thess. v, 19.

w Matt. iii, 16; xii, 28; I Nephi xiii, 1 .

x John xiv, 16.

y John xv, 26; xvi, 13.

z Doc. and Cov. cxxx, 22; also Fifth Lecture on Faith, 2-3

Himself in the form of a man.[a] It is by the ministrations
of the Spirit that the Father and the Son operate in their
dealings with mankind;[b] through Him knowledge is communicated,[c] and by Him the great works of creation are
carried on.[d] The Holy Ghost is the witness of the Father
and the Son,[e] declaring to man their attributes, bearing
record of the other personages of the Godhead.[f]

25. **Some of the Divine Attributes:**—*God is Omnipresent:*
There is no part of creation, however remote, into which He
cannot penetrate; by the power of the Holy Ghost, the
Godhead is in direct communication with all things at all
times. It has been said, therefore, that God is everywhere
present at the same time; but is unreasonable to suppose
that the actual person of any one member of the Godhead
can be in more than one place at one time. The senses of
God are of infinite power, His mind of unlimited capacity;
His eye can penetrate all space, His ear can comprehend every
sound; His powers of transferring Himself from place to
place are not limited; plainly, however, His person cannot
be in more than one place at any one time. Admitting the
personality of God, we are compelled to accept the fact of
His materiality; indeed an "immaterial being," under which
meaningless name some have sought to designate the condition of God, cannot exist, for the very expression is a contradiction in terms. If God possesses a form, that form is
of necessity of definite proportions and therefore of limited
extension in space. It is therefore impossible for Him to
occupy at one time more than one space of such limits; and
it is not surprising therefore to learn from the scriptures

a I Nephi xi, 11

b Neh. ix, 30; Isa. xlii, 1; Acts x, 19; Alma xii, 3; Doc. and Cov. cv, 36; xcvii, 1.

c John xvi, 13; I Nephi x, 19; Doc. and Cov. xxxv, 13: 1, 10.

d Gen. i, 2; Job xxvi, 13; Psalms civ, 30; Doc. and Cov. xxix, 31

e John xv, 26; Acts v, 32; xx, 23; I Cor. ii, 11; xii, 3; III Nephi xi, 32.

f For a fuller treatment of the Holy Ghost, His personality and attributes,
see Lecture viii.

that He moves from place to place. Thus we read in connection with the account of the Tower of Babel "And the Lord came down to see the city and the tower."[g]   Again, God appeared to Abraham, and having declared Himself to be "the Almighty God," He talked with the patriarch, and established a covenant with him; then we read "And He left off talking with him, and God went up from Abraham."[h]

26. *God is Omniscient:*—There is nothing in the physical or spiritual universe which He has not created; every property of matter He has ordained, every law He has framed. He possesses, therefore, a perfect knowledge of all His works. His power cannot be comprehended by man; God's wisdom is infinite. Being Himself eternal and perfect, His knowledge cannot be otherwise than infinite. To comprehend Himself, an infinite Being, He must possess an infinite mind. Through the agency of angels and ministering servants, He is in continuous communication with all parts of creation, and may personally visit as He may will.

27. *God is Omnipotent:*—He is properly called the Almighty. Man can discern proofs of the Divine omnipotence on every side, in the forces that control the elements of earth; that guide the orbs of heaven in their prescribed courses; all are working together for the common good. There can be no limits to the powers of God; whatever His wisdom indicates as fit to be done He can and will do. The means through which He operates may not be of infinite capacity in themselves; but they are directed by an infinite power. A rational conception of His omnipotence is power to do all that He may will to do.

28. *God is kind, benevolent, and loving*, tender, considerate, and long-suffering, bearing patiently with the frailties of His wayward children. He is just, yet merciful in judg-

g Gen. xi, 5.
h Gen. xvii, 1, 22.

ment,[i] showing favor to all alike, and yet combining with these gentler qualities a firmness, almost amounting to fierceness, in avenging wrongs.[j] He is jealous[k] of His own power and the reverence paid to Him by His children; that is to say, He is zealous for the principles of truth and purity, which are nowhere exemplified in a higher degree than in His personal attributes. This Being is the Author of our existence, Him we are permitted to approach as Father. Our faith will increase in Him as we learn of Him.

29. **Idolatry and Atheism:**—From the abundant evidence of the existence of Deity, the idea of which is so generally held by the human family, there would seem to be little ground on which man could rationally assert and maintain a disbelief in God; and in view of the many proofs of the benignant nature of the Divine attributes and disposition, there ought to be little tendency to turn aside after false and unworthy objects of worship. Yet the history of the race shows that theism, which is the doctrine of a belief in and an acceptance of, God as the rightful Ruler, is opposed by many varieties of its opposite,—atheism;[l] and that man is prone to belie his boast as a creature of reason, and to render his worship at idolatrous shrines. Atheism is probably a development of later times, whilst idolatry asserted itself as one of the early sins of the race. Even at the time of Israel's exodus from Egypt, God deemed it proper to command by statute, "Thou shalt have no other gods before me;"[m] yet even while He wrote those words on the stony tablets, His people were bowing before the golden calf which they had fashioned after the pattern of the Egyptian idol.

---

i Deut. iv, 31; II Chron. xxx, 9; Exo. xxxiv, 6; Neh. ix, 17, 31; Psalms cxvi, 5; ciii, 8; lxxxvi, 15; Jer. xxxii, 18; Exo. xx, 6.

j Exo. xx, 5; Deut. vii, 21; x, 17; Psa. vii, 11.

k Exo. xx, 5; xxxiv, 14; Deut. iv, 24; vi, 14, 15; Josh. xxiv, 19, 20.

l See note 6.

m Exo. xx, 3.

30. It has been stated that man possesses an instinct for worship, that he craves and will find some object of adoration. When man fell into the darkness of continued transgression, and forgot the Author of his being, and the God of his fathers, he sought for other deities. Some among men came to regard the sun as the type of the supreme, and before that luminary they prostrated themselves in supplication. Others selected for adoration earthly phenomena; they marvelled over the mystery of fire, and, recognising the beneficent effects of that phenomenon, they worshiped the flame. Some saw, or thought they saw, in water the emblem of the pure and the good, and they rendered their devotions by running streams. Others, awed into reverence by the grandeur of towering mountains, repaired to these natural temples, and worshiped the altar instead of Him in whose honor and by whose power it had been raised. Another class, more strongly imbued with a reverence for the emblematic, sought to create for themselves artificial objects of adoration. They made images and worshiped them; they hewed uncouth figures from tree trunks, and chiseled strange forms in stone, and to these they bowed.[n]

> "Nations, ignorant of God,
> Contrive a wooden one."

31. Idolatrous practices in some of their phases came to be associated with rites of horrible cruelties, as in the custom of sacrificing children to Moloch, and, among the Hindoos, to the Ganges; as also in the wholesale slaughtering of human beings under Druidical tyranny. The gods that human-kind have set up for themselves are heartless, pitiless, cruel.[o]

32. Atheism, as before stated, is the denial of the existence of God; in a milder form it may consist in the mere

[n] See Note 7
[o] See Note 8

ignoring of Deity. But the professed atheist, in common
with his believing fellow-mortals, is subject to man's universal passion for worship; though he refuse to acknowledge
the true and the living God, he consciously or unconsciously
deifies some law, some principle, some passion of the human
soul, or perchance some material creation; and to this he
turns, to seek in contemplation of the unworthy object, a
semblance of the comfort which the believer finds in rich
abundance before the throne of his Father and God. I
doubt the existence of a thorough atheist,—one who with
the sincerity of a settled conviction denies in his heart the
existence of an intelligent Supreme Power. The idea of
God is an essential characteristic of the human soul. The
philosopher recognizes the necessity of such an element in
his theories of being. He may shrink from the open
acknowledgment of a personal Deity, yet he assumes the
existence of a "governing power," of a "great unknown,"
of the "unknowable," the "illimitable," the "unconscious."
Oh, man of learning though not of wisdom; why reject the
privileges extended to you by the omnipotent, omniscient
Being to whom you owe your life, yet whose name you will
not acknowledge? No mortal can approach Him while contemplating His perfections and might with aught but awe
and speechless reverence; regarding Him only as Creator
and God, we are abashed in thought of Him; but He has
given us the right to approach Him as His children,
to call upon Him by the endearing name of Father! And
even the atheist feels, in the more solemn moments of his
life, a yearning of the soul toward a spiritual Parent, as naturally as his human affections turn toward the father who
gave him mortal life. The atheism of to-day is but a
species of idolatry after all.

33. **Sectarian View of the Godhead:**—The consistent,
simple, and authentic doctrine respecting the character and

attributes of God, such as was taught by Christ and the apostles, gave way as revelation ceased, and as the darkness incident to the absence of authority fell upon the world, after the apostles and their priesthood had been driven from the earth; and in its place there appeared numerous theories and dogmas of men, many of which are utterly incomprehensible in their mysticism and inconsistency. In the year 325 A. D., the Council of Nice was convened by the emperor Constantine, who sought through this body to secure a declaration of Christian belief which would be received as authoritative, and be the means of arresting the increasing dissension incident to the general disagreement regarding the nature of the Godhead, and other theological subjects. The Council condemned some of the theories then current; among them that of Arius, which asserted a separate individuality for each member of the Trinity; and promulgated a new code of belief known as the Nicene Creed. A statement of this doctrine, supposedly as announced by Athanasius, is as follows:—"We worship one God in trinity, and trinity in unity; neither confounding the persons, nor dividing the substance. For there is one person of the Father, another of the Son, and another of the Holy Ghost. But the Godhead of the Father, Son, and Holy Ghost, is all one; the glory equal, the majesty co-eternal. Such as the Father is, such is the Son, and such is the Holy Ghost. The Father uncreate, the Son uncreate, and the Holy Ghost uncreate. The Father incomprehensible, the Son incomprehensible, and the Holy Ghost incomprehensible. The Father eternal, the Son eternal, and the Holy Ghost eternal. And yet there are not three eternals, but one eternal. As also there are not three incomprehensibles, nor three uncreated; but one uncreated, and one incomprehensible. So likewise the Father is almighty, the Son almighty, and the Holy Ghost almighty, and yet there are not three Almighties, but one Almighty. So the Father is God, the Son is God, and the Holy Ghost is God, and yet there are not three Gods but one God." It would be difficult to conceive of a greater number of inconsistencies and contradictions, expressed in as few words.

34. The Church of England teaches the present orthodox view of God as follows:—"There is but one living and true God, everlasting, without body, parts, or passions; of infinite power, wisdom, and goodness." The immateriality of God as asserted in these declarations of sectarian faith is entirely at variance with the scriptures, and absolutely contradicted by the revelations of God's person and attributes, as shown by the citations already made.

35. I submit that to deny the materiality of God's person is to deny God; for a thing without parts has no whole, and an immaterial body cannot exist.[p] The Church of Jesus Christ of Latter-day Saints proclaims against the incomprehensible God, devoid of "body, parts, and passions," as a thing impossible of existence, and asserts its belief in and allegiance to the true and living God of scripture and revelation.

NOTES.

1. **Natural to Believe in a God:**—"The great and primary truth 'that there is a God' has obtained among men almost universally, and in all ages; so that the holy scriptures, which speak of God in every page, and which advert to the sentiments of mankind for the period of about four thousand years, always assume this truth as admitted. In the early ages of the world, indeed, there is no positive evidence that speculative theism had any advocates; and if, at a subsequent period, the 'fool said in his heart, There is no God,' the sentiment appears more prominent in his affections than in his judgment; and, withal, had so feeble an influence over the minds of men, that the sacred writers never deemed it necessary to combat the error, either by formal arguments, or by an appeal to miraculous operations. Polytheism, not atheism, was the prevailing sin; and therefore the aim of inspired men was not so much to prove the existence of one God, as the non-existence of others,—to maintain His authority, to enforce His laws, to the exclusion of all rival pretenders."   *   *   *

p See Note 9

"So clear, full, and overpowering is the evidence of God's existence, that it has commanded general belief in all ages and countries,—the only exceptions being a few savage tribes of a most degraded type, among whom the idea of God has faded and disappeared with every vestige of civilization; and a few eccentric would-be philosophers who affect to doubt everything which others believe, and question the truth of their own intuitions, so that the general assent to the being of a God might be added as a testimony of no ·small weight in this argument."—*Cassell's Bible Dictionary; article "God."*

2. Importance of Belief in God:—"The existence of a Supreme Being is, without doubt, the sublimest conception that can enter the human mind, and, even as a scientific question, can have no equal, for it assumes to furnish the cause of causes, the great ultimate fact in philosophy, the last and sublimest generalization of scientific truth. Yet this is the lowest demand it presents for our study; for it lies at the very foundation of morality, virtue, and religion; it supports the social fabric, and gives cohesion to all its parts; it involves the momentous question of man's immortality and responsibility to supreme authority, and is inseparably connected with his brightest hopes and highest enjoyments. It is, indeed, not only a fundamental truth, but the grand central truth of all other truths. All other truths in science, ethics, and religion, radiate from this. It is the source from which they all flow, the center to which they all converge, and the one sublime proposition to which they all bear witness. It has, therefore, no parallel in its solemn grandeur and momentous issues."—*The same.*

3. Belief in God, Natural and Necessary.—Dr. Joseph Le Conte, Professor of Geology and Natural History in the University of California, and a scientist of world-wide renown, has spoken as follows:—"*Theism*, or a belief in God or in gods, or in a supernatural agency of some kind, controlling the phenomena around us, is the fundamental basis and condition of all religion, and is therefore universal, necessary and intuitive. I will not, therefore, attempt to bring forward any proof of that which lies back of all proof, and is already more certain than anything can be made by any process of reasoning. The ground of this belief lies in the very nature of man; it is the very foundation and groundwork of reason. It is this and this only which gives significance to Nature; without it, neither religion nor science, nor indeed human life, would be possible. For, observe what is the characteristic of man in his relation to external Nature. To the brute, the phenomena of Nature are nothing but sensuous phenomena; but man, just in proportion as he uses his human faculties, instinctively ascends from the phenomena to their cause. This is inevitable by a law of our nature, but the process of ascent is different for the cultured and uncultured races. The uncultured man, when a phenomenon occurs, the cause of which is not immediately perceived, passes by one step from the sensuous phenomenon to the first cause; while the cultured, and especially the scientific man, passes from the sensuous phenomena through a chain of secondary causes to the first cause. The region of second causes, and this only, is the domain of science. Science may, in fact, be defined, as the *study of the modes of operation of the first cause.* It is evident, therefore, that the recognition of second causes cannot preclude the idea of the existence of God. * * * Thus, Theism is necessary, intuitive, and therefore universal. We cannot get rid of it if we would. Push it out, as many do, at the front door, and it comes in again, perhaps unrecognized, at the back door. Turn it out in its *nobler forms* as revealed in Scripture, and it comes in again in its *ignoble forms*, it may be as magnetism, electricity, or gravity, or some other sup-

5

posed efficient agent controlling Nature. In some form, noble or ignoble, it will become a guest in the human heart. I therefore repeat, *Theism neither requires nor admits of proof.* But in these latter times, there is a strong tendency for Theism to take the form of *Pantheism,* and thereby religious belief is robbed of all its power over the human heart. It becomes necessary, therefore, for me to attempt to show, not the existence indeed, but the *personality of Deity.*   *   *   *   Among a certain class of cultivated minds, and especially among scientific men, there is a growing sentiment, sometimes openly expressed, sometimes only vaguely felt, that what we call God is only a universal, all-pervading principle animating Nature,—a general principle of evolution—an unconscious, impersonal life-force under which the whole cosmos slowly develops. Now, this form of Theism may possibly satisfy the demands of a purely speculative philosophy, but cannot satisfy the cravings of the human heart.
    *   *   The argument for the personality of Deity is derived from the evidences of intelligent contrivance and design in Nature, or the adjustment of parts for a definite, and an intelligent purpose. It is usually called *·the argument from design.'* The force of this argument is felt at once intuitively by all minds, and its ·effect is irresistible and overwhelming to every plain, honest mind, unplagued by metaphysical subtleties."—*Prof. Joseph Le Conte:* in "Religion and Science," pp. 12-14.

    4. God in Nature:—Sir Isaac Newton, one of the most critical of scientific workers, in writing to his friend Dr. Bentley in 1692, said in reference to the natural universe: "To make such a svstem. with all its motions, required a Cause which understood and compared together the quantities of matter in the several bodies of the sun and planets, and the gravitating powers resulting from them, the several distances of the primary planets from the sun, and of the secondary ones from Saturn, Jupiter, and the earth; and the velocities with which these planets could revolve about those quantities of matter in the central bodies; and to compare and adjust all these things together in so great a variety of bodies argues the Cause to be not blind and fortuitous, but very well skilled in mechanics and geometry."

    5. Natural Indications of God's Existence:—"It may not be, it is not likely, that God can be found with microscope and scalpel, with test-tube or flask, with goniometer or telescope: but with such tools, the student earnestly working, cannot fail to recognize a power beyond his vision, yet a power of which the pulses and the motions are unmistakable. The extent of our solar system once seemed to man more limited than it does at present; and the discovery of the most distant of the planetary family was due to a recognition of an attractive force inexplicable except on the supposition of the existence of another planet. The astronomer, tracing known bodies along their orbital paths, could feel the pull, could see the wire that drew them from a narrower course; he saw not Neptune as he piled calculations sheet on sheet; but the existence of that orb was clearly indicated, and by heeding such indications he sought for it, and it was found. Theory alone could never have revealed it, though theory was incomplete, unsatisfactory without it; but the practical search, instigated by theory, led to the great demonstration. And what is all science but theory compared to the practical influence of prayerful reliance on the assistance of an omnipotent, omniscient power? Disregard not the indications of your science work,—the trembling of the needle that reveals the magnetic influence; the instinct within that speaks of a life and a Life-Giver, far beyond human power of explanation or comprehension. As you sit beneath the canopied vault, pondering in the silence of night over the perturbations, the yearnings which the soul cannot ignore, turn in the direction indicated by those impulses, and with the penetrating, space-annihilating, time-annulling glass of prayer and faith, seek the source of that pervading force."—Jas. E. Talmage in *Baccalaureate Sermon*, June, 1895.

6. Theism; Atheism, etc:—According ·to current usage, *Theism* signifies a belief in God,—the acceptance of one living and eternal Being who has revealed Himself to man. *Deism* implies a professed belief in God, but denies to Deity the power to reveal Himself, and asserts a disbelief in Christianity; the term is used in different senses, prominent among which are:—(1) belief in God as an intelligent and eternal Being, with a denial of all providential care: (2) belief in God, with denial of a future state of the soul: (3) as advocated by Kant, denial of a personal God, while asserting belief in an infinite force, inseparably associated with matter, and operating as the first great cause. *Pantheism* regards matter and mind as one, embracing everything finite and infinite, and calls this universal existence God. In its philosophical aspect, pantheism "has three generic forms with variations: (1) *one-substance pantheism* which ascribes to the universal being the attributes of both mind and matter, thought and extension, as in Spinoza's system; (2) *materialistic pantheism* which ascribes to it only the attributes of matter, as in the system of Strauss: (3) *idealistic pantheism* which ascribes to it only the existence of mind as in Hegel's system." In its doctrinal aspect, pantheism comprises "the worship of nature and humanity founded on the doctrine that the entire phenomenal universe, including man and nature, is the ever-changing manifestation of God." *Polytheism* is the doctrine of a plurality of gods, who are usually regarded as personifications of forces or phenomena of nature. *Monotheism* is the doctrine that there is but one God. *Atheism* signifies disbelief in God, or the denial of God's existence; *dogmatic atheism* denies, while *negative atheism* ignores, the existence of a God. *Infidelity* is sometimes used as synonymous with atheism, though specifically the term signifies a milder form of unbelief, manifesting itself in scepticism on matters religious, a disbelief in the religion of the Bible, and of course a rejection of the doctrines of Christianity. *Agnosticism* holds that God is unknown and unknowable; that His existence can neither be proved nor disproved; it neither affirms nor denies the existence of a personal God; it is the doctrine of "We do not know."—*See Standard Dictionary.*

7. Idolatrous Practices in General:—The soul of man, once abandoned to depravity, is strongly prone to depart from God and his institutions. "Hence," says Burder, "have arisen the altars and demons of heathen antiquity, their extravagant fictions, and abominable orgies. Hence we find among the Babylonians and Arabians, the adoration of the heavenly bodies, the· earliest forms of idolatry; among the Canaanites and Syrians, the worship of Baal, Tammuz, Magog, and Astarte: among the Phœnicians, the immolation of children to Moloch; among the Egyptians, divine honors bestowed on animals, birds, insects, leeks, and onions; among the Persians, religious reverence offered to fire; and among the polished Greeks, the recognition in their system of faith of thirty thousand gods. Hence, moreover, we find at the present time among most Pagan tribes, the deadliest superstitions, the most cruel and bloody rites, and the most shocking licentiousness and vice, practiced under the name of religion."—*History of all Religions*, p. 12.

8. Examples of Atrocious Idolatry.—The worship of Moloch is generally cited as an example of the cruelest and most abhorrent idolatry known to man. Moloch, called also Molech, Malcham, Milcom, Baal-melech, etc., was an Ammonite idol: it is mentioned in scripture in connection with its cruel rites (Lev. xviii, 21; xx, 2-5; see also I Kings xi, 5, 7, 33; II Kings xxiii, 10, 13; Amos v, 26; Zephaniah i, 5; Jeremiah xxxii, 35). Keil and Delitzsch describe the idol as being "represented by a brazen statue which was hollow, and capable of being heated, and formed with a bull's head, and with arms stretched out to receive the children to be sacrificed." While the worship of this idol did not invariably include human sacrifice, it is certain that such hideous rites were characteristic of this abominable shrine. The authors last quoted say "From the time of Ahaz, children were slain at Jerusalem in the valley of Ben-Hinnom, and then sacrificed by being laid in the heated arms and burned. (II Kings xxiii, 10; xvi, 3; xvii, 17; xxi, 6; Jer. xxxii, 35; Ezek. xvi, 20, 21; xx, 31; compare Psalms cvi, 37, 38.) Many authorities state that the sacrifice of children to this hideous monster long ante-dated the time of Ahaz. "The offering of living victims was probably the climax of enormity in connection with this system, and it is said that Tophet, where it was to be witnessed, was so named from the beating of drums to drown the shrieks and groans of those who were burned to death. The same place was called the Valley of Hinnom, and the horrible associations connected with it led to both Tophet and Gehenna ('valley of Hinnom') being adopted as names and symbols of future torment." *For foregoing facts, and others, see "The Pentateuch" by Keil and Delitzsch; and Cassell's Bible Dictionary.*

Scarcely less horrible were the practices of voluntary suicide under the car of the idol Juggernaut, and the drowning of children in the sacred Ganges as found among the Hindoos. According to Burder, ("History of all Religions,") the ponderous and hideous image Juggernaut, was, on festival days, usually placed on a movable tower resting on wheels; and, thus mounted, was drawn through the streets by enthusiastic worshipers. As the car moved along, some of the most zealous of the devotees threw themselves under the wheels and were crushed to death; and such acts were "hailed with the acclamations of the multitude as the most acceptable sacrifices." The same author thus describes the rite of child-sacrifice to the sacred river, as formerly practiced in India:— "People in some parts of India, particularly the inhabitants of Orissa, and of the eastern parts of Bengal, frequently offer their children to the goddess, Gunga. The following reason is assigned for this practice: When a woman has been long married, and has no children, it is common for the man, or his wife, or both of them, to make a vow to the goddess Gunga, that if she will bestow the blessing of children upon them, they will devote the firstborn to her. If, after this vow, they have children, the eldest is nourished till a proper age, which may be three, four, or more years, according to circumstances, when, on a particular day, appointed for bathing in any part of the river, they take the child with them and offer it to the goddess: the child is encouraged to go farther and farther into the water, till it is carried away by the stream, or is pushed off by its inhuman parents."—*History of all Religions,* p. 745-746.

The practices of Druidism among the ancient Britons furnish another example of degradation in religion through the absence of authoritative guidance and the light of revelation. The Druids professed a veneration for the oak, and performed most of their distinctive ceremonies in sacred groves. Human sacrifices were offered as a feature of their system. Of their temples, some, e. g. Stonehenge on Salisbury Plain, Wiltshire, and others in Kent, still remain.

These circular enclosures, which were open to the sky, were called *doom-rings:* near the center of each was an altar (*dolmen*) on which victims were sacrificed. The horrible ceremonies included on special occasions the burning alive of large numbers of human beings, enclosed in immense cages of wicker-work.

9. Immaterialists are Atheists:—"There are two classes of atheists in the world. One class denies the existence of God in the most positive language; the other denies his existence in duration or space. One says 'There is no God;' the other says 'God is not *here* or *there*, any more than he exists *now* and *then*.' The infidel says 'God does not exist anywhere.' The immaterialist says 'He exists *nowhere*.' The infidel says 'There is no such substance as God.' The immaterialist says 'There is such a substance as God, but it is *without parts*.' The atheist says 'There is no such substance as *spirit*.' The immaterialist says 'A spirit, though he lives and acts, occupies no room, and fills no space in the same way and in the same manner as matter, not even so much as does the minutest grain of sand.' The atheist does not seek to hide his infidelity; but the immaterialist, whose declared belief amounts to the same thing as the atheist's, endeavors to hide his infidelity under the shallow covering of a few words. * * * * * The immaterialist is a religious atheist; he only differs from the other class of atheists by clothing an indivisible unextended *nothing* with the powers of a God. One class believes in no God; the other believes that *Nothing* is god and worships it as such."—*Orson Pratt, in pamphlet "Absurdities of Immaterialism,"* p. 11.

10. Atheism, a Fatal Belief:—"During the Reign or Terror, the French were declared to be a nation of atheists, by the National Assembly; but a brief experience convinced them that a nation of atheists could not long exist. Robespierre then 'proclaimed in the convention, that belief in the existence of God was necessary to those principles of virtue and morality upon which the republic was founded; and on the 7th of May, the national representatives, who had so lately prostrated themselves before the Goddess of Reason, voted by acclamation that the French people acknowledged the existence of the Supreme Being, and the immortality of the soul.' "—*Students' France, xxvii, 6;* quoted by Rev. Charles E. Little, in *Historical Lights*, p. 280-281.

LECTURE III.

TRANSGRESSION AND THE FALL.

Article 2:—We believe that men will be punished for their own sins, and not for Adam's transgression.

TRANSGRESSION AND ITS RESULTS.

1. **Man's Free Agency:**—The Church holds and teaches as a strictly scriptural doctrine, that man has inherited among the inalienable rights conferred upon him by his divine Father, absolute freedom to choose the good or the evil in life as he may elect.   This right cannot be guarded with more jealous care than is bestowed upon it by God Himself; for in all His dealings with man, He has left the mortal creature free to choose and to act, with no semblance of compulsion or restraint, beyond the influences of paternal counsel and loving direction.[a] True, He has given commandments, and has established statutes, with promises of blessings for compliance and dire penalties for infraction; but in the choice of these, God's children are untrammeled.   In this respect, man is no less free than are the angels and the Gods, except as he has fettered himself with the bonds of sin, and forfeited his power of will and force of soul.   The individual has as full a measure of liberty to violate the laws of health, the requirements of nature, and the commandments of God in matters both temporal and spiritual, as he has to obey all such; in the one case he brings upon himself the sure penalties that belong to the broken law; as in the other he inherits the specific blessings and the added freedom that attend a law-abiding life.   Obedience to law is the habit of the free man; 'tis the transgressor

a See note 1.

who fears the law, for he brings upon himself deprivation and restraint, not because of the law, which would have protected him in his freedom, but because of his rejection of law.

2. The predominant attribute of justice, recognized as part of the Divine nature, forbids the thought that man should receive promises of reward for righteousness, and threats of punishment for evil deeds, if he possessed no power of independent action. It is no more a part of God's plan to compel men to work righteousness, than it is His purpose to permit evil powers to force His children into sin. In the days of Eden, the first man had placed before him commandment and law,[b] with an explanation of the penalty which would follow a violation of that law. No law could have been given him in righteousness, had he not been free to act for himself. "Nevertheless thou mayest choose for thyself, for it is given unto thee, but remember that I forbid it,"[c] said the Lord God to Adam. Concerning His dealings with the first patriarch of the race, God has declared in this day, "Behold I gave unto him that he should be an agent unto himself."[d]

3. When the brothers Cain and Abel brought their sacrifices before the Lord, the elder one became angry because his offering was rejected; then the Lord reasoned with Cain, and endeavored to teach him that he must expect results of his actions to follow in kind, good or evil as he might elect:—"If thou doest well shalt thou not be accepted? and if thou doest not well, sin lieth at the door."[e]

4. A knowledge of good and evil is essential to the advancement which God has made possible for His children

---

b Genesis ii, 17; Pearl of Great Price, Writings of Moses, pp. 10,12-13 (1888 ed.)

c Pearl of Great Price, p. 13 (1888 ed.)

d Doctrine and Covenants, xxix, 35.

e Genesis iv, 7.

to achieve; this knowledge can be best gained by actual experience, with the contrasts of good and its opposite before the eyes; therefore has man been placed upon the earth subject to the influence of good and wicked powers, with a knowledge of the conditions surrounding him, and the heaven-born right to choose for himself. The words of the prophet, Lehi, are particularly explicit: "Wherefore, the Lord God gave unto man that he should act for himself. Wherefore, man could not act for himself, save it should be that he was enticed by the one or the other. * * * Wherefore, men are free according to the flesh; and all things are given them which are expedient unto man. And they are free to choose liberty and eternal life, through the great mediation of all men, or to choose captivity and death, according to the captivity and power of the devil; for he seeketh that all men might be miserable like unto himself."*f*

5. Alma, another Nephite prophet, in speaking of those who had died, said they had gone "that they might reap their rewards, according to their works, whether they were good or whether they were bad, to reap eternal happiness or eternal misery, according to the spirit which they listed to obey, whether it be a good spirit or a bâd one; For every man receiveth wages of him whom he listeth to obey, and this according to the words of the spirit of prophecy."*g*

6. Samuel, the converted Lamanite, upon whom the spirit of the prophets had fallen, admonished his wayward fellows in this wise: "And now remember, remember my brethren, that whosoever perisheth, perisheth unto himself; and whosoever doeth iniquity, doeth it unto himself; for behold, ye are free; ye are permitted to act for yourselves; for behold, God hath given unto you a knowledge, and he hath

---

f II Nephi ii, 16, and 27; x, 23. See also Alma iii, 23; xii, 31; xxix, 4, 5; xxx, 9; Hel. xiv, 30.

g Alma iii, 26-27

made you free; He hath given unto you that ye might know good from evil, and he hath given unto you that ye might choose life or death."[h]

7. When the plans for creating and peopling the earth were under discussion in heaven, Satan sought to destroy the free agency of man, by obtaining power to force the human family to do his will, promising the Father that by such means he would redeem all mankind, and that not one of them should be lost.[i] This proposition was rejected, while the original purpose of the Father,—to use persuasive influences of wholesome precept and sacrificing example with the inhabitants of the earth, then to leave them free to choose for themselves, was agreed upon, and the Only Begotten Son was chosen as the chief instrument in carrying that purpose into effect.

8. **Man's Responsibility** for his individual acts is as complete as is his agency to elect for himself. The natural result of good deeds is happiness; the consequence of evil is misery; these follow in every man's life by inviolable laws. There is a plan of judgment[j] divinely fore-ordained, by which every man will be called to answer for his deeds; and not for deeds alone but for his words also, and even for the thoughts of his heart. "But I say unto you, that every idle word that men shall speak, they shall give account thereof in the day of judgment."[k] These are the words of the Savior Himself. "And let none of you imagine evil in your hearts against his neighbor, and love no false oath: for all these are things that I hate, saith the Lord."[l] John the Revelator was permitted to learn in vision something of the scenes

---

h Helaman xiv, 30-31.

i Pearl of Great Price: Writings of Moses p. 14; and Book of Abraham p. 63 (1888 ed.)

j Matt. x, 15; xi, 22. II Peter ii, 9; iii, 7. I John iv, 17.

k Matt. xii, 36.

l Zech. viii, 17.

connected with the last judgment; he says: "And] I saw
the dead, small and great, stand before God; and the books
were opened: and another book was opened, which is the
book of life; and the dead were judged out of those things
which were written in the books, according to their works.
And the sea gave up the dead which were in it; and death
and hell delivered up the dead which were in them: and
they were judged every man according to their works."[m]

9. The judgment of God is not always made to follow
immediately the acts of men; good deeds may not be at
once rewarded, evil is rarely peremptorily punished; and
this is according to Divine wisdom; were it appointed otherwise, the test of individual nature, and the trial of human
faith, for which purposes this mortal probation was
primarily ordained, would be greatly lessened; for the
certainty of immediate pleasure or pain would almost
universally determine human acts to secure the one and to
avoid the other. Judgment, therefore, is postponed, that every
one may fully prove his nature, the good man increasing in
righteousness, and the evil doer possessing opportunity of
repentance and reparation before the great and terrible day.
On rare occasions, speedy judgment of a temporal nature
has been executed, the physical results of worldly blessing
for good,[n] and calamity for evil deeds[o] following swiftly
upon the acts. Whether such retribution entirely satisfies
the claims of justice, or a further visitation of judgment is
to take place beyond this world, matters not. Such acts
are exceptional in the Divine administration.

10. It is the prerogative of Jesus Christ[p] to judge the

---

m Rev. xx, 12, 13.

n Job xlii, 10-17.

o Numbers xii, 1-2, 10-15; xv, 32-36; xvi; xxi, 4-6; I Sam. vi, 19; II Sam. vi,
6-7; Acts v, 1-11.

p John v, 22-27; Acts x, 42; xvii, 31; Rom. ii, 16; II Cor. v, 10; II Tim. iv, 1, 8;
Doc. and Cov. cxxxiii, 2.

children of men, and He will do it as His own purposes, which are likewise the purposes of His Father, may be best served.   John the Apostle declares: "For the Father judgeth no man, but hath committed all judgment unto the Son; that all men should honor the Son even as they honor the Father."[q]   And Peter, while expounding the gospel to the devout Gentile, Cornelius, declared concerning Jesus Christ, that "it is He which was ordained of God to be the Judge of quick and dead."[r]   Of the dread fate of the wicked reserved for the judgment day, many prophets have borne record[s] and the presiding Judge of that awful tribunal has given in His own words descriptions[t] so vivid and accurate, as to leave no shadow of doubt that every living soul will be called to acknowledge the record, and to accept the results of his acts.   The Lord's words and those of His prophets are unequivocal, that He is no respecter of persons,[u] and that any species of favor foreign to justice is unknown to Him.   This judgment none but the unrepentant wicked need fear; to the righteous it is a time of triumph.[v]

11.   Sin:—What is the nature of sin?   To this question the Apostle John replies, "Sin is the transgression of the law."[w]   In the original language of the Bible records, many words occur for which our single term sin is used, all however conveying the common idea of opposition to the Divine will.[x]   As God is the embodiment of purity and perfection, such opposition is a rebellion against the principles of ad-

---

q John v, 22.

r Acts x, 42.

s Dan vii, 9; II Thess. i, 7, 8; III Nephi xxvi, 3-5; Doc. and Cov. lxxvi, 31-49; 103-106.

t Matt. xxv, 31-46; Doc. and Cov. i, 9-12.

u Acts x, 34, 35; Rom. ii, 11; Eph. vi, 9; Colos. iii, 25.

v II Tim. iv, 8.

w I John iii, 4.

x See note 2.

vancement, and an acceptance of the practices that lead to degradation. Sin is any condition, whether consisting in omission of things required, or in commission of acts forbidden, which tends to prevent or hinder the development of the human soul. As a righteous course leads to eternal life, so sin tends towards the darkness of the second death. Sin was introduced to the world by the arch-fiend Satan;[y] yet it is by Divine permission that mankind is brought in contact with sin, the contrast between evil and good thus being learned.

12. According to the technical definition of sin, it consists in the violation of law, and in this strict sense sin may be committed inadvertently or in ignorance. It is plain, however, from the scriptural doctrine of human responsibility, and the unerring justice of God, that in his transgressions as in his righteous deeds, man will be judged according to his ability to comprehend law. To him who has never been made acquainted with a higher law, the requirements of that law do not apply in their fulness. For sins committed without knowledge,—that is, for laws violated in ignorance, a propitiation has been provided in the atonement wrought through the sacrifice of the Savior; and sinners of this class do not stand condemned.

13. Nephi, prophesying to the ancient inhabitants of the western continent, taught them this doctrine:—"Where there is no law given there is no punishment; and where there is no punishment, there is no condemnation; and where there is no condemnation, the mercies of the Holy One of Israel have claim upon them, because of the atonement; for they are delivered by the power of him; For the atonement satisfieth the demands of his justice upon all those who have not the law given to them, that they are delivered from that awful monster, death and hell and the

y Pearl of Great Price, Writings of Moses, p. 14 (1888 ed.) Genesis iii.

devil, and the lake of fire and brimstone which is endless torment; and they are restored to that God who gave them breath, which is the Holy One of Israel."[z] And then, in contrast with the lot of those who are thus pardonable, the prophet adds:—"But wo unto him that has the law given; yea, that has all the commandments of God, like unto us, and that transgresseth them, and that wasteth the days of his probation, for awful is his state!"[a] This is in strict agreement with the teachings of Paul to the Romans, "For as many as have sinned without law shall also perish without law; and as many as have sinned in the law shall be judged by the law."[b] And the word of modern scripture is to the same effect, for we are told through recent revelation to the Church, that among those who are to receive the blessings of redemption are "they who died without law."[c] These will include the heathen nations, whose redemption is promised, with the added declaration that "they that knew no law shall have part in the first resurrection."[d]

14. Punishment for Sin:—As rewards for righteous deeds are proportionate to deserving acts, so the punishment prescribed for sin is made adequate to the offense.[e] Punishment is inflicted upon the sinner, for disciplinary and reformatory purposes, and in support of justice. There is nothing of vindictive ss or of desire to cause suffering in the Divine nature; on the contrary, our Father is cognizant of every pang, and permits such to afflict for beneficent purposes only. God's mercy is declared in the retributive pains which He allows, as in the blessings of peace which issue from His hand. It is scarcely profitable to speculate

---

z II Nephi ix, 25-26.

a The same, paragraph 27.

b Rom. ii, 12.

c Doc. and Cov. lxxvi, 72.

d Doc. and Cov. xlv, 54.

e Doc and Cov. lxxvi, 82-85; lxxxii, 21; civ, 9; lxiii, 17; II Nephi i, 13; ix, 27; xxviii, 23.

as to the exact nature of the spiritual suffering imposed as punishment for sin. Comparison with physical pain,[f] such as the tortures of fire, in a sulphurous lake, serve to show that the human mind is incapable of comprehending the depth of these dread penalties. The sufferings entailed by the awful fate of condemnation are more to be feared than are any possible inflictions of purely physical torture; the mind, the spirit, the whole soul is doomed to suffer, and the extent of the torment no man knoweth.

15. Consider the word of the Lord regarding those whose sin is the unpardonable one, whose transgression has carried them beyond the present horizon of possible redemption; those who have sunk so low in their wickedness as to have lost the power and even the desire to attempt reformation.[g] "Sons of Perdition" is the terrible designation by which they are known. These are they who, having learned the power of God, afterward renounce it; those who sin wilfully, in the light of knowledge; those who open their hearts to the Holy Spirit, and then put the Lord to a mockery and a shame by denying it; and those who commit murder, wherein they shed innocent blood [h] these are they of whom the Savior has declared that it would be better for them had they never been born.[i] These are to share the punishment of the devil and his angels—punishment so terrible that the knowledge is withheld from all except those who are consigned to this dread doom, though a momentary glance at the awful picture is permitted to some.[j] These sinners are the only ones over whom the

---

f Doc. and Cov. lxxvi, 36, 44; Jacob vi, 10; Alma xii, 16-17; III Nephi xxvii, 11-12.

g See Doc. and Cov. lxxvi, 26, 32, 43.

h Doc. and Cov. cxxxii, 27.

i John xvii, 12; II Thess, ii 3; Doc. and Cov. lxxvi, 32.

j Doc. and Cov. lxxvi, 45-48.

second death hath power, "Yea, verily, the only ones who shall not be redeemed in the due time of the Lord."[k]

16. **The Duration of Punishment:**—As to the duration of such punishment, we may take assurance that it will be graded according to the sin; and that the popular interpretation of scriptural passages to the effect that every sentence for misdeeds is interminable, is entirely false.[l] Great as is the effect of this life upon the hereafter, and terrible as is the responsibility of opportunities lost for repentance, God holds the power to pardon beyond the grave. And yet the scriptures speak of eternal and endless punishment. Any punishment ordained of God is eternal, for He is eternal.[m] His is a system of endless punishment, for it will always exist as a place or condition prepared for disobedient spirits; yet the infliction of the penalty will have an end in every case of willing repentance and attempted reparation. And repentance is not impossible in the spirit world.[n] Yet, as seen, there are some sins so terrible that their accompanying punishments are not made known to man;[o] these extreme penalties are reserved for the "Sons of Perdition."

17. The false doctrine that the punishment to be visited upon the erring souls is endless, that every sentence for sin is of interminable duration, must be regarded as one of the most pernicious results of unenlightened sectarianism It is but a dogma of unauthorized and erring churches, at once unscriptural, unreasonable, and revolting to one who loves mercy and honors justice. True, the scriptures speak of everlasting burnings, eternal damnation, and the vengeance

---

k Doc. and Cov. lxxvi, 38-39.

l Doc. and Cov. xix, 6-12; lxxvi, 36, 44.

m Doc. and Cov. xix, 10-12.

n I Peter iii, 18-20; iv, 6; Doc. and Cov. lxxvi, 73.

o Doc. and Cov. lxxvi, 44.

of eternal fire,[p] as characteristics of the judgment provided
for the wicked; yet in no instance is there justification for
the inference that the individual sinner will have to suffer
the wrath of offended justice forever and ever. The punishment in any case is sufficiently severe without the added
and supreme horror of unending continuation. Justice
must have her due; but when "the uttermost farthing" is
paid, the prison doors shall open and the captive be free.
But the prison remains, and the law prescribing punishment
for offences will not be repealed.

18. So general were the ill-effects of the commonly-
accepted doctrine, unscriptural and untrue though it was,
regarding the endless torment awaiting every sinner, that
even before the Church had been formally organized in the
present dispensation, God gave a revelation through the
Prophet Joseph Smith, touching this matter, in which we
read:—"And surely every man must repent or suffer; for I,
God, am endless: wherefore I revoke not the judgments
which I shall pass, but woes shall go forth, weeping, wailing and gnashing of teeth, yea to those who are found on
my left hand; nevertheless it is not written that there shall
be no end to this torment, but it is written endless torment.
Again it is written eternal damnation.   *   *   *   for
behold, I am endless, and the punishment which is given
from my hand, is endless punishment, for Endless is my
name; wherefore, eternal punishment is God's punishment.
Endless punishment is God's punishment.[q]"

19. Satan:—We have had occasion to refer frequently to
the author of evil among men. This is Satan,[r] the adversary
or opponent of the Lord, the chief of all evil spirits, called

p Matt. xviii, 8; xxv, 41, 46; II Thess. i, 9; Mark iii, 29; Jude 7.
q Revelation given March, 1830; Doc. and Cov. xix, 4-12.
r Job i, 6-22; ii, 1-7; Zech. iii, 1-2.

also the Devil,[s] Beelzebub,[t] or the Prince of Devils, Perdition[u] and Belial.[v] The figurative appellations Dragon, and Serpent, are applied to Satan, when reference is made to the Fall.[w] We learn from the revealed word[x] that Satan was once an angel of light; he was then known as Lucifer, a Son of the Morning, but his uncontrolled ambition prompted him to aspire to the glory and power of the Father, to secure which, he made the unjust proposition to redeem the human family by compulsion; failing in this purpose, he headed an open rebellion against the Father and the Son, drawing a third of the hosts of heaven into his impious league.[y] These rebellious spirits were expelled from heaven, and have since followed the impulses of their wicked natures by seeking to lead human souls to their own condition of darkness. They are the devil and his angels. The right of free agency, maintained and vindicated by the terrible strife in heaven, prevents the possibility of compulsion being employed in this fiendish work of degradation; but the powers of these malignant spirits to tempt and persuade are used to their utmost limits. Satan tempted Eve to transgress the law of God;[z] it was he who imparted the secret of murder to the fratricide, Cain.[a]

20. Satan exerts a mastery over the spirits that have been corrupted by his practices; he is the foremost of the angels who were thrust down, and the instigator of the ruin of those who fall in this life; he seeks to molest and hinder mankind in good efforts, by tempting to sin; it may be by

---

s Matt. iv, 5, 8, 11: I Peter, v, 8.

t Matt. xii, 24.

u Doc. and Cov. lxxvi, 26.

v II Cor. vi, 15.

w Rev. xii, 9; xx, 2.

x Doc. and Cov. lxxvi, 25-27.

y Doc. & Cov. xxix 36-37; see also Pearl of Great Price, Writings of Moses, p. 14, and Book of Abraham p. 63, (1888 ed.)

z Genesis iii, 4-5, and Pearl of Great Price, p. 14.

a Pearl of Great Price—Writings of Moses, p. 20.

6

imposing sickness,[b] or possibly death. Yet in all these malignant doings, he can go no farther than the transgressions of the victim may enable him, or the wisdom of God may permit him to go, and he may at any time be checked by the superior power. Indeed, even the operations of his utmost malice may be turned to the accomplishment of Divine purposes. The scriptures prove to us that the days of Satan's power are already numbered;[c] his doom has been pronounced, and in the Lord's own time he will be completely overcome. He is to be bound during the millennial reign,[d] and after that thousand years of blessed peace, he will be loosed for a little season; then his defeat will be made complete, and his power over the children of God will be entirely destroyed.

THE FALL.

21. **Our First Parents in Eden:**[e]—The crowning scene of the great drama of creation was the forming of man in the image of his spiritual Father, God.[f] For the reception of the first man, the Creator had specially prepared a choice region of earth, and had embellished it with natural beauties calculated to gladden the heart of its royal possessor. "The Lord God planted a garden eastward in Eden,[g] and there He put the man whom he had formed."[h] Soon after man's advent upon the earth the Lord created for him a companion or help-meet, declaring that it was not good that man should be alone.[i] Thus, male and female, Adam and his wife Eve, were placed in the Garden,

b Luke xiii, 16; Job i.

c John xii, 31; xvi, 11.

d Rev. xx, 1-10.

e Read Genesis, chapters 2 and 3; Pearl of Great Price, Writings of Moses, pp. 11-19, and Book of Abraham, p. 68-70 (1888 ed.)

f Genesis i, 26; Pearl of Great Price, p. 10 (1888 ed.)

g See note 3.

hGenesis ii, 8-9.

i Genesis ii, 18; Pearl of Great Price, p. 13 (1888 ed.)

and were given dominion "over the fish of the sea, and over the fowl of the air, and over every living thing that moveth upon the earth."[j] With this great power were associated certain special commands; the first of which in point of importance was that they "be fruitful and multiply and replenish the earth, and subdue it;" then that they refrain from eating or even touching the fruit of a certain tree, the Tree of Knowledge of Good and Evil, which grew in the midst of the Garden, though of all other fruits they were permitted to freely partake. The words of God concerning this command and its penalty are:—"And I, the Lord God, commanded the man, saying, of every tree in the garden thou mayest freely eat, but of the tree of the knowledge of good and evil; thou shalt not eat of it; nevertheless thou mayest choose for thyself, for it is given unto thee, but remember that I forbid it, for in the day thou eatest thereof thou shalt surely die."[k]

22. **The Temptation** to disobey this command soon came. Satan presented himself before Eve in the Garden, and, speaking by the mouth of the serpent, questioned her about the commands which God had given respecting the Tree of Knowledge of Good and Evil. Eve answered that they were forbidden even to touch the fruit of that tree, under penalty of death. Satan then sought to beguile the woman, contradicting the Lord's statement, and declaring that death would not follow a violation of the Divine injunction; but that, on the other hand, by doing that which the Lord had forbidden, she and her husband would become like unto the gods, knowing good and evil for themselves. The woman was captivated by these representations; and, being eager to possess the advantages pictured by Satan, she disobeyed the command of the Lord, and partook of the fruit

---

j Genesis i, 28.

k Pearl of Great Price, pp. 12-13 (1888 ed.); see also Genesis ii, 16-17.

forbidden. She feared not evil, for she knew it not. Then,
telling Adam what she had done, she urged him to do likewise.

23. Adam found himself in a position that compelled
him to disobey one of the requirements of God. He and
his wife had been commanded to multiply and replenish the
earth. Adam was still immortal; Eve had come under the
penalty of mortality; and in such dissimilar conditions, the
two could not remain together, and therefore could not fulfill the Divine requirement. On the other hand, Adam
would be disobeying another command by yielding to his
wife's request. He deliberately and wisely decided to stand
by the first and greater commandment; and, therefore, with
a full comprehension of the nature of his act, he also partook of the fruit that grew on the Tree of Knowledge. The
fact that Adam acted understandingly in this matter is
affirmed by the scriptures. Paul, in writing to Timothy,
explained that "Adam was not deceived; but the woman,
being deceived, was in the transgression."[l] The prophet,
Lehi, in expounding the scriptures to his sons, declared
"Adam fell that man might be, and men are that they
might have joy."[m]

24. The Tree of Life:—There was another tree of special
virtues in Eden; its fruit insured life to all who ate of it.
While Adam and Eve lived in innocent immortality, this tree
had not been forbidden them; the celestial fruit indeed was
fitting food for their sinless state. Now, that they had
transgressed, however; now that the Divine decree had
issued, fixing death as their lot, it was not proper that the
fruit of the Tree of Life should be longer within their reach.
They were, therefore, expelled from the Garden, and cherubim
with a flaming sword guarded the way, that man might not

l I Timothy ii, 14.
m II Nephi ii, 25.

return in an unforgiven state. By the act of transgression, our first parents acquired a knowledge, which in their condition of pristine innocence they had not possessed,—the experimental knowledge of good and evil. The result of the Fall could have been of none but ill effect had the fallen ones been immediately restored to a condition of immortality, without repentance, without atonement. In the despair that followed their realization of the great change that had come upon them, and in the light of the knowledge gained at such cost as to the virtues of the fruit that grew on the Tree of Life, it would have been but natural for them to seek the seeming advantages of an immediate escape, by partaking of the celestial food. It was in mercy that they were deprived of the means of so doing.

25. The words of the Creator are unmistakable as to the necessity of banishing His first earthly children from Eden:—"And the Lord God said, Behold, the man is become as one of us, to know good and evil: and now, lest he put forth his hand, and take also of the tree of life, and eat, and live forever: Therefore the Lord God sent him forth from the garden of Eden, to till the ground from whence he was taken. So he drove out the man: and he placed at the east of the garden of Eden cherubim, and a flaming sword which turned every way, to keep the way of the tree of life."[n]

26. Alma, the Nephite prophet, comprehended the result that would have followed had Adam and his wife eaten of the Tree of Life; he thus explained the matter:—"Now we see that the man had become as God, knowing good and evil; and lest he should put forth his hand, and take also of the tree of life, and eat and live forever, the Lord God placed Cherubim and the flaming sword, that he should not partake of the fruit; And thus we see, that there was a

[n] Gen. iii, 22-24.

time granted unto man to repent, yea, a probationary time, a time to repent and serve God. For behold, if Adam had put forth his hand immediately, and partook of the tree of life, he would have lived forever, according to the word of God, having no space for repentance; yea, and also the word of God would have been void, and the great plan of salvation would have been frustrated."[o]

27. **The Immediate Result of the Fall** was the substitution of mortality, with all its attendant frailties, for the vigor of the primeval deathless state. Adam felt directly the effects of transgression, in finding a barren and dreary earth, with a sterile soil, instead of the beauty and fruitfulness of Eden. In place of pleasing and useful plants, thorns and thistles sprang up; and he had to labor arduously under the conditions of physical fatigue and suffering, to cultivate the soil that he might obtain necessary food. Upon Eve fell the penalty of bodily infirmity; the pains and sorrows, which since have been regarded as the natural lot of womankind, came upon her, and she was made subject to her husband. Having now lost their sense of former innocence, they became ashamed of their nakedness, and the Lord made for them garments of skins. And upon both the man and the woman was visited the penalty of spiritual death; for in that very day they were banished from Eden, and cast out from the presence of the Lord. The serpent, having served the purposes of Satan, was made a subject of Divine displeasure, being doomed to crawl forever in the dust, and to suffer from the enmity which it was decreed should be placed in the hearts of Eve's children.[p]

28. **Atonement was Provided for:**—God left not His now mortal children without hope. He gave other commandments to Adam, requiring him to offer sacrifices in the name

---

o Alma xlii, 3-5.
p See Note 4.

of the Only Begotten Son, and promising redemption unto him and all his descendants who would comply with the conditions prescribed. The opportunity of winning the victor's reward by overcoming evil was explained to our parents, and they rejoiced. Adam said, "Blessed be the name of God, for because of my transgression my eyes are opened, and in this life I shall have joy, and again in the flesh I shall see God." Eve was glad, declaring, "Were it not for our transgression we never should have had seed, and never should have known good and evil, and the joy of our redemption, and the eternal life which God giveth unto all the obedient."[q]

29. **The Fall came not by Chance:**—It would be unreasonable to suppose that the transgression of Eve and Adam came as a surprise to the Creator. By His infinite fore-knowledge, God knew what would be the result of Satan's temptation to Eve, and what Adam would do under the conditions. And further, it is evident that the Fall was fore-ordained, as a means whereby man could be brought face to face with both good and evil; that of his own agency he might elect the one or the other; and thus be prepared by the experiences of a mortal probation for the exaltation provided in the glorious plan of his creation:—"For this is my work and my glory, to bring to pass the immortality and eternal life of man;"[r] thus spake the Lord unto Moses. It was the purpose of God to place within the reach of the spirits begotten by Him in the heavens, the means of individual effort, and the opportunity of winning, not merely salvation, or exemption from spiritual death, but exaltation, with the powers of eternal progression and increase. Hence, it was necessary that the spiritual offspring of God should leave the mansions of their primeval childhood, and enter the school of mortal experience, meeting,

q Pearl of Great Price p. 19, (1888 ed.)
r Pearl of Great Price, p. 6, (1888 ed.)

conteṇding with, and overcoming evil, according to their several degrees of faith and strength. Adam and Eve could never have been the parents of a mortal posterity, had they not themselves become mortal; mortality, as before stated, was an essential element in the Divine plan respecting the earth and its appointed inhabitants; and as a means of introducing mortality, the Lord placed before the progenitors of the race, a law, knowing full well that transgression would follow.

30.   Eve was fulfilling the foreordained purposes of God by the part she took in the great drama of the Fall; yet she did not partake of the forbidden fruit with that object in view, but with the intent to violate the Divine command, being deceived by the sophistries of the serpent-fiend. Satan also, for that matter, furthered the purposes of the Creator, in tempting Eve; yet his design was to thwart the Lord's plan. We are definitely told that "he knew not the mind of God, wherefore he sought to destroy the world."[s] Yet, his diabolical effort, far from being the initiatory step toward destruction, contributed to the plan of man's eternal exaltation. Adam's part in the great event was essentially different from that of his wife; he was not deceived; on the contrary he deliberately decided to do as Eve desired, that he might carry out the purposes of his Maker with respect to the race of men, whose first patriarch he was ordained to be.

31.   Even the transgressions of man may be turned to the accomplishment of high purposes. As will be shown, the sacrifice of Christ was ordained from before the foundation of the world,[t] yet Judas who betrayed, and the bloodthirsty Jews who crucified the Son of God, are none the less guilty of the awful crime.

---

s Pearl of Great Price, p. 14, (1888 ed.)
t See Lecture iv.

32. It has become a common practice with mankind, to heap reproaches upon the progenitors of the family, and to picture the supposedly blessed state, in which we would be living but for the Fall; whereas our first parents are entitled to our deepest gratitude for their legacy to posterity,—the means of winning glory, exaltation, and eternal lives, on the battlefield of mortality. But for the opportunity thus given, the spirits of God's offspring would have remained forever in a state of innocent childhood; sinless through no effort of their own; negatively saved, not from sin, but from the power of sinning; incapable of winning the honors of victory because prevented from taking part in the battle. As it is, they are heirs to the birthright of Adam's descendants,—mortality, with its immeasurable opportunities, and its God-given freedom of action. From Father Adam we have inherited all the ills to which flesh is heir; but such are necessarily incident to the knowledge of good and evil, by the proper use of which knowledge man may become even as the Gods.[u]

NOTES.

1. **Man's Agency is God-given.**—The following is an extract from a discourse delivered by President Brigham Young July 5, 1855. (See Journal of Discourses of that date, and Millennial Star, vol. xx, p. 43). "What is the foundation of the rights of man? The Lord Almighty has organized man for the express purpose of becoming an independent being like unto Himself, and has given him his individual agency. Man is made in the likeness of his Creator, the great arche-type of the human species, who bestowed upon him the principles of eternity, planting immortality within him, and leaving him at liberty to act in the way that seemeth good unto him;—to choose or refuse for himself, to be a Latter-day Saint or a Wesleyan Methodist, to belong to the Church of England, the oldest daughter of the Mother Church, to the old Mother herself, to her sister the Greek Church, or to be an infidel and belong to no church. When the kingdom of God is fully set up and established on the face of the earth, and takes the pre-eminence over all other nations and kingdoms, it will protect the people in the enjoyment of all their rights, no matter what they believe, what they profess, or what they worship."

---

u See note 5.

2. The Nature of Sin:—The English word "sin" represents a very great variety of terms occurring in the original languages, the literal translations of which bear to one another a very great similarity. Thus, in the Old Testament, the following terms among others occur:—*setim* (referred to in Psalms ci, 3), signifying "to deviate from the way;" *shegagah* (Lev. iv. 2; Num. xv. 27), "to err in the way;" *avon*, "the crooked, or perverted;" *avel*, "to turn aside." In the New Testament we find, *hemartia*, "the missing of a mark;" *parabasis*, "the transgressing of a line;" *parakoe*, "disobedience to a voice;" *paraptoma*, "falling from uprightness;" *agnoema*, "unjustifiable ignorance;" *hettema*, "giving only partial measure;" *anomia*, "non-observance of law;" *plemmeleia*, "a discord." The above illustrations are taken mainly from Müller and French. In all these expressions, the predominant idea is that of departure from the way of God, of separation from His companionship by opposition to the Divine requirements. Sin was introduced into the world from without; it was not a natural product of earth. The seed of disobedience was planted in the mind of Eve by the arch-fiend: that seed took root; and much fruit, of the nature that we, with unguarded words, call calamity, is the result. From these thorns and thistles of mortality, a Savior has been prepared to deliver us.

3. Eden:—In the Hebrew tongue, from which our word "Eden" is taken, this term signifies something particularly delightful,—a place of pleasantness; the place is also called "the garden of the Lord." One particular spot in the land of Eden was prepared by the Lord as a garden; this was situated eastward in Eden. From the garden, the parents of the race were expelled after the Fall, though it is reasonable to suppose that they still dwelt in the land or region of Eden. We read that at a later date, Cain, the first murderer, "went out from the presence of the Lord, and dwelt in the land of Nod, on the east of Eden" (Gen. iv, 16). Though there is no uniform belief among Christian scholars as to the geographical location of Eden, the majority claim that it was in Persia; however, the most radical among the advocates of this view fail to prove any marked resemblance between the region at present, and the place described in the Bible. The Latter-day Saints have more exact knowledge on the matter, a revelation having been given through Joseph Smith, at Spring Hill, Mo., May 19, 1838, in which that place is named by the Lord "Adam-ondi-Ahman, because, said he, it is the place where Adam shall come to visit his people, or the Ancient of Days shall sit, as spoken of by Daniel the prophet"(Doc. and Cov. cxvi). From another revelation we learn (Doc. and Cov. cvii, 52-53) that three years before his death, Adam called together in the valley of Adam-ondi-Ahman those of his sons who had been made High Priests, together with the rest of his righteous posterity, and there bestowed upon them his patriarchal blessings, the event being marked by special manifestations from the Lord (See also Doc. and Cov. cxvii, 8). The Lord has pointed out in this day the exact location of the altar upon which Adam offered sacrifices after his expulsion from the Garden; (See Contributor, Vol. vii, page 314). There is no authentic record of the human race having inhabited the Eastern Hemisphere until after the flood. The Western Continent called now the New World, comprises indeed the oldest inhabited regions of earth. The west, not the east, is the "cradle of nations."

4. The Serpent, as stated, having aided the purposes of Satan, received from the Lord a special curse (See Genesis iii, 13, 15, and the Pearl of Great Price, p. 16). The creature was doomed to a life of degradation. Even from the standpoint of anatomy, the serpent is a degraded type. Though a vertebrate,—a member of the highest sub-kingdom of animals, it is devoid even of external limbs, and its means of locomotion are of no higher order than are those of the worm and the caterpillar. In the scriptures, the serpent is made the symbol of craft, subtlety, cunning, and danger.

5. The Fall Essential:—President John Taylor, after discussing the succession of events leading up to the Fall, says:—"Thus it would appear that if any of the links of this great chain had been broken, it would have interfered with the comprehensive plan of the Almighty pertaining to the salvation and eternal exaltation of those spirits who were His sons, and for whom principally the world was made; that they, through submission to the requirements of the eternal principle and law governing those matters, might possess bodies, and those bodies united with the spirits might become living souls, and being the sons of God, and made in the image of God, they, through the atonement might be exalted, by obedience to the law of the Gospel, to the Godhead."—*Mediation and Atonement*, p. 135.

LECTURE IV.

THE ATONEMENT, AND SALVATION.

Article 3:—We believe that through the atonement of Christ, all mankind may be saved, by obedience to the laws and ordinances of the gospel.

THE ATONEMENT.

1. **The Atonement of Christ** is taught as a leading doctrine by all sects professing Christianity. The expression is so common a one, and the essential point of its signification is so generally admitted, that definitions may appear to be superfluous; nevertheless, there is a peculiar importance attached to the use of the word, atonement, in a theological sense. The doctrine of the atonement comprises proof of the divinity of Christ's earthly ministry; and the vicarious nature of His death, as a fore-ordained and voluntary sacrifice, intended for and efficacious as a propitiation for the sins of mankind, thus becoming the means whereby salvation may be obtained.

2. The New Testament, which is properly regarded as the scripture of Christ's mission among men, is imbued throughout with the doctrine of salvation through the work of atonement wrought by the Savior; and yet the word, atonement, occurs but once in the whole record; and in that single instance, according to the opinion of most biblical authorities, it is confessedly misused. The instance referred to is found in the words of Paul addressed to the saints at Rome:—"But we also joy in God through our Lord Jesus Christ, by whom we have now received the atonement."[a] The marginal rendering gives, instead of atonement, reconciliation, and of this word a related form is used in the

---

[a] Romans v, 11.

preceding verse. A consistent translation, giving a full
agreement between the English and the Greek, would make
the verse quoted, and that immediately preceding it, read
in this way:—"For if, when we were enemies, we were reconciled to God by the death of his Son; much more, being
reconciled, we shall be saved by his life. And not only so,
but we also joy in God through our Lord Jesus Christ, by
whom we have now received the reconciliation."[b] The term,
atonement, occurs repeatedly in the Old Testament, and
with marked frequency in three of the books of the Pentateuch, viz.: Exodus, Leviticus, and Numbers; and the sense
in which it is employed is invariably that of a sacrifice of
propitiation, usually associated with the death of an acceptable victim, whereby reconciliation was to be effected between God and His creatures.

3. The structure of the word in its present form is suggestive of this, the true meaning; it is literally *at-one-ment*,
"denoting reconciliation, or the bringing into agreement of
those who have been estranged."[c] And such is the significance of the saving sacrifice of the Redeemer, whereby He
expiated the transgression of the Fall, through which came
death into the world, and provided ready and efficient means
for man's return to a state of immortality through reconciliation with God.

4. **Nature of the Atonement:**—The atonement wrought
by Jesus Christ is a necessary sequence of the transgression
of Adam; and, as the infinite foreknowledge of God made
clear to Him the one even before Adam was placed on earth,
so the Father's boundless mercy prepared a Savior for mankind before the world was framed. Through the Fall,
Adam and Eve have entailed the conditions of mortality
upon their descendants; therefore all beings born of earthly

---

b Romans v, 10-11.
c Standard Dictionary, under "*propitiation*."

parents are subject to bodily death. The sentence of banishment from the presence of God was in the nature of a
spiritual death; and that penalty, which was visited upon
our first parents in the day of their transgression, has likewise followed as the common heritage of humanity. As
this penalty came into the world through an individual act,
it would be manifestly unjust to cause all to eternally suffer
therefrom, without a chance of deliverance. Therefore was
the promised sacrifice of Jesus Christ ordained as a propitiation for broken law, whereby Justice could be fully satisfied,
and Mercy be left free to exercise her beneficent influence
over the souls of mankind.[d] All the details of the glorious
plan, by which the salvation of the human family is assured,
may not lie within the understanding of man; but surely,
man has learned from his futile attempts to fathom the
primary cause of the phenomena of nature, that his powers
of comprehension are limited; and he will admit, that to
deny the effect because of his inability to elucidate the
cause, would be to forfeit his claims as an observing and
reasoning being.

5. Simple as is the plan of redemption in its general features, it is confessedly a mystery to the finite mind in detail.
President John Taylor has written in this wise:—"In some
mysterious, incomprehensible way, Jesus assumed the responsibility which naturally would have devolved upon
Adam; but which could only be accomplished through the
mediation of Himself; and by taking upon Himself their
sorrows, assuming their responsibilities, and bearing their
transgressions or sins. In a manner to us incomprehensible
and inexplicable, He bore the weight of the sins of the
whole world, not only of Adam, but of his posterity; and
in doing that, opened the kingdom of heaven, not only to all
believers and all who obeyed the law of God, but to more

d See Note 1.

than one half of the human family who die before they come to years of maturity, as well as to the heathen, who, having died without law, will through His mediation be resurrected without law, and be judged without law, and thus participate, according to their capacity, works, and worth, in the blessings of His atonement."[e]

6. But, however incomplete may be our comprehension of the scheme of redemption through Christ's vicarious sacrifice in all its parts, we cannot reject it without becoming infidel; for it stands as the fundamental doctrine of all scripture, the very essence of the spirit of prophecy and revelation, the most prominent of all the declarations of God unto man.

7. **The Atonement a Vicarious Sacrifice:**—It is to many a matter of surpassing wonder, that the voluntary sacrifice of a single being could be made to operate as a means of ransom for the rest of mankind. In this, as in other things, the scriptures are explicable only by the spirit of scriptural interpretation. The sacred writings of ancient times, the words of modern prophets, the traditions of mankind, the rites of sacrifice, and even the sacrileges of heathen idolatries, involve the idea of vicarious atonement. God has never refused to accept an offering made by one who is authorized on behalf of those who are in any way incapable of doing the required service themselves. The scape-goat,[f] and the altar victim[g] of ancient Israel, if offered with repentance and contrition, were accepted by the Lord in mitigation of the sins of the people. It is interesting to note, that while the ceremonies of sacrifice formed so large and so essential a part of the Mosaic requirements, these rites long ante-dated the establishment of Israel as a

[e] Pres. John Taylor, Mediation and Atonement, p. 148-149.

[f] Lev. xvi, 20-22.

[g] Lev. iv.

distinct people; for, as already shown, altar sacrifice was rendered by Adam.[h] The symbolism of the sacrificing of animals as a prototype of the great sacrifice to follow on Calvary, was thus instituted with the beginning of human history.

8. The many kinds of sacrifice prescribed by the Mosaic law are clearly classified under the headings, bloody, and bloodless. Offerings of the first order only, involving the infliction of death, were acceptable in propitiation or atonement for sin, and the victim had to be clean, healthy, and without spot or blemish. And so for the great sacrifice, the effects of which were to be infinite, only an innocent subject could be accepted. It was Christ's right, as the only sinless Being on earth, and as the Only Begotten of the Father, and above all as the One ordained to this mission in the heavens, to be the Redeemer of mankind; and though the exercise of this right involved a sacrifice, the extent of which man cannot comprehend, yet Christ made that sacrifice willingly and voluntarily. To the last He had the means of terminating the tortures of His persecutors, by a simple exercise of His powers as one of the Godhead.[i] In some way, though that way may be inexplicable to us, Christ took upon Himself the sins of mankind. The means may be to our finite minds a mystery, yet the results are our salvation.

9. Something of the Savior's agony as He groaned under this load of guilt, which to Him, as a type of purity, must have been in itself repulsive, He has told us through the prophet's words in this day: "For behold, I, God, have suffered these things for all, that they might not suffer if they would repent; but if they would not repent they must suffer even as I, which suffering caused myself,

h See page 70.
i Matt. xxvi, 53-54; John x, 17, 18.

even God, the greatest of all, to tremble because of pain, and to bleed at every pore, and to suffer both body and spirit; and would that I might not drink the bitter cup, and shrink:—Nevertheless, glory be to the Father, and I partook and finished my preparations unto the children of men."[j] Further instances of the validity of vicarious service are found in the ordinances of baptism for the dead[k] as taught in apostolic and modern times, and in the institution of other temple ceremonies[l] in the present dispensation.

10. **Christ's Sacrifice was Voluntary and Love-inspired:**— We have noted in passing that Christ gave His life willingly and voluntarily for the redemption of mankind. He offered Himself, in the great Council of the Gods, as the subject of the atoning sacrifice made necessary by the fore-seen transgression of the first man; and the free agency shown and exercised in this, the early stage of His saving mission, was retained to the very last of the agonizing fulfilment of the accepted plan. Though He lived on earth a man in every particular that concerns us in our regard for Him as an example of Godliness in humanity, yet it is to be remembered, that though born of a mortal mother, he was begotten by an immortal Sire; and so had combined within His being the capacity to die, and the power to set death at defiance. He gave His life; it was not taken from him. Note the significance of His own declaration:—"Therefore doth my Father love me, because I lay down my life that I may take it up again. No man taketh it from me, but I lay it down of myself. I have power to lay it down, and I have power to take it again."[m] On another occasion Jesus testified of Himself in this way:—"For as the Father hath life in himself, so hath he given to the Son to have life in himself; and

---

[j] Doc. and Cov. xix, 16-19.

[k] I Cor. xv, 29. See Lectures vi and vii.

[l] Doc. and Cov. cxxvii, 4-9; cxxviii.

[m] John x, 17-18.

7

hath given Him authority to execute judgment also, because
he is the Son of man."[n]   And then amid the tragic scenes
of the betrayal, when one who had been a professed follower
and friend gave Him with a traitorous kiss to His persecutors; when Peter, with a rashness prompted by righteous
zeal, drew and used the sword in His defence, the Master
said:—"Thinkest thou that I cannot now pray to my Father,
and he shall presently give me more than twelve legions of
angels?   But how then shall the scriptures be fulfilled, that
thus it must be?"[o]   And on to the bitter end, marked by the
expiring though triumphant cry "It is finished," the incar-
nated God held in subjection within Himself the power to
thwart His murderers, had He so willed.

11.   The motive inspiring and sustaining Him through
all the scenes of His mission, from the time of His primeval
ordination, to the moment of victorious consummation on
the cross, was two-fold; first, the desire to do His Father's
will, in accomplishing the salvation of man; second, His
love for humanity, of whose welfare and destiny He had
assumed charge.   Far from cherishing the least feeling of
vindictiveness against those, who, in defiance of the laws of
God and man, put Him to ignominious death, He entertained for them compassion to the last.   Hear Him in the
hour of supreme agony, praying aloud, "Father, forgive
them, for they know not what they do."[p]   Not less is the
Father's love, as shown by His accepting the Son's offer,
and permitting Him whom He delighted to call His Beloved,
to suffer as only a God could suffer:—"For God so loved
the world, that he gave his only begotten Son, that whosoever believeth in him should not perish, but have everlasting life.   For God sent not his Son into the world to con-

n John v. 26-27.
o Matt. xxvi 53-54.
p Luke xxiii 34.

demn the world, but that the world through him might be saved."[q] And further, we hear the teaching of the apostle, whom the Savior loved so well, "In this was manifested the love of God toward us, because that God sent his only begotten Son into the world that we might live through him."[r]

12. **The Atonement Fore-ordained and Fore-told:**—As already shown, the plan of the Father to open a way for the redemption of mankind, then to leave all men free to exercise their own agency, was adopted by the Council in heaven to the rejection of Lucifer's plan of compulsion. Even at that remote period, Christ was thus ordained as a Mediator for all mankind; in fact, "a covenant was entered into between Him and His Father, in which He agreed to atone for the sins of the world, and He thus, as stated, became a 'Lamb slain from before the foundation of the world.'"[s] The prophets of old, many of whom lived centuries before the time of Christ's coming in the flesh, testified of Him and of the great work He had been ordained to perform. These men of God had been permitted to behold in prophetic vision many of the scenes incident to the Savior's earthly mission; and they solemnly bore record of the manifestations. Indeed, the testimony of Christ is the spirit of prophecy, and without it no person can rightly claim the distinction of being a prophet of God. Adam's despair, on being driven from Eden, was changed to joy, when, through revelation, he learned of the plan of redemption to be wrought by the Son of God in the flesh.[t] Righteous Enoch taught the same truths, which had been declared to him

---

q John iii, 16-17.

r I John iv, 9.

s Pres. John Taylor, in Mediation and Atonement, p. 97.

t See page 71. Pearl of Great Price, p. 19, (1888 ed.)

from the heavens.[u] This testimony was borne by Moses,[v] Job,[w] David,[x] Zechariah,[y] Isaiah,[z] and Micah.[a] The same declaration was made by John the Baptist,[b] the prophet of the Highest, designated by the Savior as more than a prophet; he it was who baptized the Christ, and who witnessed the Father's words associated with the visible sign of the Holy Ghost, concerning the mission of the Son.

13. Should there be any doubt as to the application of such prophecies, we have the conclusive testimony of Christ that they refer to Himself. On that memorable day, immediately following His resurrection, while walking incognito with two of His disciples on the road to Emmaus, He taught them the scriptures that had been written concerning the Son of God; "Beginning at Moses, and all the prophets, he expounded unto them in all the scriptures the things concerning himself."[c] A few hours after this event, the Lord appeared to the Eleven at Jerusalem. He operated upon their minds "that they might understand the scriptures; and said unto them, 'Thus it is written, and thus it behoved Christ to suffer,"[d] in this way testifying that He was fulfilling a previously ordained plan. Peter, one of the Savior's most intimate earthly associates, refers to Him as "a Lamb without blemish and without spot, who verily was foreordained before the foundation of the world."[e] In his epistle to the Romans, Paul characterizes Christ as the one "Whom

---

u Pearl of Great Price, 32-35.
v Deut. xviii, 15, 17-19.
w Job xix, 25-27.
x Psalms ii, 1-12.
y Zech. ix, 9; xii, 10; xiii, 6.
z Isaiah vii, 14; ix, 6-7.
a Micah v, 2.
b Matt. iii, 11.
c Luke xxiv, 27.
d Luke xxiv, 45-46.
e I Peter i, 19-20.

God hath set forth to be a propitiation through faith in his blood, to declare his righteousness for the remission of sins that are past."[f]   These are but a few of the biblical evidences of Christ's appointment and fore-ordination; both Old and New Testament[g] writings abound in proofs of the Messiah's great work.

14.   Book of Mormon prophets are characterized by their full testimonies concerning the Messiah.   Because of his purity of faith, the brother of Jared was permitted to behold the Savior of mankind, twenty-two centuries prior to the meridian of time, and to be shown that man was created after the image of the Lord, at the same time being taught of the Father's purpose that the Son take upon Himself flesh and dwell on earth.[h]   Note the personal declaration of the fore-ordained Redeemer to this prophet:—"Behold, I am he who was prepared from the foundation of the world to redeem my people.   Behold, I am Jesus Christ.   I am the Father and the Son.   In me shall all mankind have light, and that eternally, even they who shall believe on my name; and they shall become my sons and my daughters."[i]

15.   Nephi records the prophecy of his father Lehi concerning the future appearing of the Son in the flesh, His baptism, death and resurrection; this prophetic utterance specifies the exact date of the Savior's birth, viz., six hundred years after the time of Lehi's exodus from Jerusalem.   The mission of John the Baptist is described, and even the place of baptism is designated.[j]   Shortly after the time of Lehi's vision, Nephi was shown by the Spirit the same things, as also many others, some of which he has written, but the greater part

---

[f] Romans iii, 25.

[g] See Rom. xvi, 25-26; Eph. iii, 9-11; Col. i, 24-26; II Tim. 1, 8-10; Titus i, 2-3; Rev. xiii, 8.

[h] Ether iii, 13-14; see also xiii, 10-11.

[i] Ether iii, 14; read also 8-16.

[j] I Nephi x, 3-11.

of which he was forbidden to write, as another, the Apostle
John, had been ordained to set them forth in a book which
should form part of the Bible. But, from his partial account
of his vision, we learn that he saw in Nazareth, Mary the
Virgin, first alone, and shortly afterward with a child in her
arms; the demonstrator of the vision informed him that the
infant was the Lamb of God, the Son of the Eternal Father.
Then Nephi beheld the Son ministering among the children
of men, proclaiming the word, healing the sick, and working many other wondrous miracles; he saw John, the
prophet of the wilderness, going before Him; he beheld the
Savior baptized of John, and the Holy Ghost descending
upon him with the visible sign of the dove. Then he saw
and prophesied that twelve chosen apostles would follow the
Savior in His ministry; that the Son would be taken and
judged of men, and finally be slain. Piercing the future,
even beyond the time of the crucifixion, Nephi beheld the
strife of the world against the apostles of the Lamb, and
the final triumph of God's cause.[k]

16. Jacob, the brother of Nephi, prophesied to his brethren
that Christ would appear in the flesh among the Jews, and
that He would be scourged and crucified of them.[l] King
Benjamin lifted his voice in support of the same testimony,
and preached unto his people the righteous condescension of
God.[m] So also declared Abinadi,[n] Alma,[o] Amulek,[p] and
Samuel the Lamanite prophet.[q] The literal fulfilment of
these prophecies furnishes unquestionable proof of their
truth. The wondrous signs indicative of Christ's birth[r] and

---

k I Nephi xi, 14-35; see also II Nephi ii, 3-21; xxv, 20-27; xxvi, 24.

l II Nephi vi, 8-10; ix, 5-6.

m Mosiah iii, 5-27; iv, 1-8.

n Mosiah xv, 6-9; xvi.

o Alma vii, 9-14.

p Alma xi, 35-44.

q Hela. xiv, 2-8.

r Hela. xiv, 2-5; 21-27.

death were all realized,[s] and after His death and ascension, the Savior manifested Himself among the Nephites, as the Father announced Him to the multitude.[t]

17. The ancient scriptures, then, are plain in declaring that Christ came upon the earth to do a work previously allotted. He lived, suffered and died, in accordance with a plan which was framed in righteousness for the redemption of the children of Adam, even before the world was. Equally important and explicit is the word of modern revelation, through which the Son has declared Himself as Alpha and Omega, the beginning and the end, man's Advocate with the Father, the universal Redeemer.[u] Let us consider a single citation from the many revelations concerning Christ given in the present dispensation:—"Listen to the voice of the Lord your God, even Alpha and Omega, the beginning and the end, whose course is one eternal round, the same today as yesterday and forever. I am Jesus Christ, the Son of God, who was crucified for the sins of the world, even as many as will believe on my name, that they may become the sons of God, even one in me as I am in the Father, as the Father is one in me, that we may be one."[v]

18. **The Extent of the Atonement** is infinite, applying alike to all descendants of Adam. Even the unbeliever, and the heathen, and the child who dies before reaching the years of discretion, are redeemed by the Savior's self-sacrifice from all the consequences of the Fall.[w] It is conclusively proved by the scripture that the resurrection of the body is one of the victories achieved by Christ

---

s III Nephi i, 5-21; viii, 3-25.

t III Nephi xi, 1-17.

u See Doc. and Cov., vi, 21; xiv, 9; xviii, 10-12; xix, 1-2, 24; xxi, 9; xxix. 1; xxxiii; xxxiv, 1-3; xxxv, 1-2; xxxviii, 1-5; xxxix, 1-3; xlv, 3-5; xlvi. 13-14; lxxvi, 1-4, 12-14, 19-24, 68; xciii, 1-6, 12-17, 38.

v Doc. and Cov. xxxv, 1-2.

w See note 2.

through His atoning sacrifice.   He Himself proclaimed the
eternal truth, "I am the resurrection and the life;"[x] and
He among men came first forth from the grave,—"the first
fruits of them that slept."[y]   Now, the scriptures leave no
room for doubt concerning the fact that the resurrection
will be universal.   The Savior announced to his apostles
the beginning of this work of deliverance from the tomb;
hear His words, "Marvel not at this; for the hour is coming,
in the which all that are in their graves shall hear his voice,
and shall come forth; they that have done good unto the
resurrection of life, and they that done evil unto the
resurrection of damnation;"[z] or, as the latter part of the
declaration has been rendered through inspiration in the
present day, "They who have done good, in the resurrection
of the just: and they who have done evil in the resurrection of the unjust."[a]

19.   Paul refers to the doctrine of a universal resurrection
as being so well proved that even his accusers had to admit
the truth, "that there shall be a resurrection of the dead,
both of the just and unjust."[b]   On another occasion he said
"For as in Adam all die, even so in Christ shall all be made
alive."[c]   Furthermore, John the Revelator testifies of his
vision concerning futurity, "And I saw the dead, small and
great stand before God.   *   *   *   And the sea gave up the
dead which were in it, and death and hell delivered up the
dead which were in them."[d]   Thus it is plain that the effect
of the atonement as far as it applies to the victory over
temporal or bodily death, involves the entire race.   It is

---

x John xi, 25.
y I Cor. xv, 20; see Acts xxvi, 23.
z John v, 28-29.
a Doc. and Cov. lxxvi. 17.
b Acts xxiv, 15.
c I Cor. xv, 22.
d Rev. xx, 12-13.

equally clear that the release from Adam's legacy of spiritual death, or banishment from the presence of God, will be similarily universal; so that if any man lose salvation, such loss will be due to himself, and in no way dependent upon the Fall. The doctrine that the gift of redemption through Christ is free to all men, was specifically taught by the apostles of old. Thus Paul says:—"Therefore, as by the offence of one, judgment came upon all men to condemnation; even so by the righteousness of one the free gift came upon all men to the justification of life."[e] And further:—there is "one mediator between God and men, the man Christ Jesus; who gave himself a ransom for all."[f] John spoke of the Redeemer's sacrifice saying:—"And he is the propitiation for our sins; and not for ours only, but also for the sins of the whole world."[g]

20. The same great truths were taught among the Nephites. Benjamin, the righteous king, preached of "the atonement which was prepared from the foundation of the world for all mankind, which ever were ever since the fall of Adam, or who are, or who ever shall be, even unto the end of the world."[h] In revelation of the present day we read of Christ's having come into the world, to suffer and to die, "That through him all might be saved whom the Father had put into his power and made by him."[i]

21. But beside this universal application of the atonement, whereby all men are redeemed from the effects of Adam's transgression, both with respect to the death of the body and the taint of inherited sin, there is a special application of the same great sacrifice, as a means of propitiation for individual sins, through the faith and good

e Rom. v, 18.
f I Tim. ii, 5-6.
g I John ii, 2.
h Mos. iv, 7.
i Doc. and Cov. lxxvi, 42.

works of the sinner. This two-fold effect of the atonement
is implied in the article of our faith now under consideration. The first effect is to secure to all mankind alike,
exemption from the otherwise terrible effects of the Fall,
thus providing a plan of *General Salvation*. The second
effect is to open a way for *Individual Salvation* whereby mankind may secure forgiveness of personal sins. As these sins
are the result of individual acts, it is just that forgiveness
for them should be conditioned on individual compliance
with prescribed requirements,—"obedience to the laws and
ordinances of the gospel."

22. **The General Effect of the Atonement,** so far as it applies to all who have arrived at years of accountability and
judgment, has been made sufficiently clear perhaps from
the scriptures already quoted. Its application to children
may properly receive our further attention. The Church of
Jesus Christ of Latter-day Saints teaches as a doctrine
founded on reason, justice, and scripture, that all children
are innocent in the sight of God, and that, until they reach
an age of personal responsibility, no baptism or other ordinance is requisite or proper in their behalf; that in short,
they are saved through the atonement of Christ. To a
degree, children are born heirs to the good or evil natures of
their parents; the effects of heredity in determining character are readily recognized. Good and evil tendencies,
blessings and curses, are transmitted from generation to
generation. Through this divinely appointed order, the
justice of which is plain in the revealed light of knowledge
concerning the pre-existent state of the spirits of mankind,
the children of Adam are natural heirs to the calamities of
mortality; but through Christ's atonement they are all redeemed from the curses of this fallen state; the debt, which
comes to them as a legacy, is paid for them, and thus are
they left free. Children who die free of sin are entirely

innocent in the eyes of God, even though they be the offspring of transgressors. We read in the Book of Mormon:
"Little children cannot repent; wherefore it is awful wickedness to deny the pure mercies of God unto them, for they
are all alive in him because of his mercy.   *   *   *   For
behold that all little children are alive in Christ, and also
all they that are without the law. For the power of redemption cometh on all that have no law."[j]

23.   The prophet Mormon writing to his son Moroni
expressed in the following manner his conviction of children's
innocence:—"Listen to the words of Christ, your Redeemer,
your Lord and your God.   Behold, I came into the world
not to call the righteous, but sinners to repentance: the whole
need no physician, but they that are sick; wherefore little
children are whole, for they are not capable of committing
sin; wherefore, the curse of Adam is taken from them in me,
that it hath no power over them.   *   *   *   Behold I say
unto you, That this thing shall ye teach, repentance and
baptism unto those who are accountable and capable of
committing sin; yea, teach parents that they must repent
and be baptized, and humble themselves as their little
children, and they shall all be saved with their little
children. And their little children need no repentance,
neither baptism.   Behold, baptism is unto repentance to
the fulfilling the commandments unto the remission of sins.
But little children are alive in Christ even from the foundation of the world."[k]

24.   And in a revelation through the prophet Joseph
Smith in this dispensation, the Lord has said:—"But behold
I say unto you, that little children are redeemed from the
foundation of the world through mine Only Begotten;
wherefore they cannot sin, for power is not given unto

j Moroni viii, 19-22,
k Moroni viii, 8-12.

Satan to tempt little children until they begin to be
come accountable before me."[l]   President John Taylor,
after citing instances of Christ's affection for little children,
and proofs of the innocent condition in which they are
regarded in heaven says:—"Without Adam's transgression,
those children could not have existed; through the atonement they are placed in a state of salvation without any act
of their own.   These would embrace, according to the
opinion of statisticians, more than one half of the human
family, who can attribute their salvation only to the
mediation and atonement of the Savior."[m]

25. **The Special or Individual Effect of the Atonement**
makes it possible for any and every soul to obtain absolution
from the dread effect of personal sins, through the mediation of Christ; but such saving intercession is to be invoked
only through individual effort as manifested through faith,
repentance and continued works of righteousness.   The
laws under which individual salvation is obtainable have
been prescribed by Christ, whose right it is to say how the
blessings of His own sacrifice shall be administered.   All
men are in need of the Savior's mediation, for all are transgressors.   So taught the apostles of old:—"For all have
sinned, and come short of the glory of God."[n]   And again:
—"If we say that we have no sin we deceive ourselves, and
the truth is not in us."[o]   Now, that the blessing of redemption from individual sins, while free for all to attain, is
nevertheless conditioned on individual effort, is as plainly declared as is the truth of unconditional redemption from
the effects of the Fall.   There is a judgment ordained for
all, and all will be judged "according to their works."   The
free agency of man enables him to choose or reject, to fol-

l Doc. and Cov. xxix, 46-47.

m Mediation and Atonement, page 148. See note 3.

n Rom. iii, 23.

o I John i, 8.

low the path of life, or the road that leads to destruction; it is but just that he be held to answer for the exercise of his freedom, and that he meet the results of his acts.

26. Hence the justice of the scriptural doctrine that salvation comes to the individual only through obedience. "He became the author of eternal salvation unto all them that obey him"[p] said Paul of the Christ. And further:— God "will render to every man according to his deeds: To them who, by patient continuance in well doing, seek for glory and honor and immortality, eternal life: But unto them that are contentious, and do not obey the truth, but obey unrighteousness, indignation and wrath, Tribulation and anguish, upon every soul of man that doeth evil, of the Jew first, and also of the Gentile; But glory, honor, and peace, to every man that worketh good, to the Jew first, and also to the Gentile: For there is no respect of persons with God."[q] To these may be added the words of the risen Lord, "He that believeth, and is baptized, shall be saved; and he that believeth not, shall be damned."[r]

27 Consider further the prophecy of King Benjamin proclaimed to the Nephite multitude:—Christ's blood "atoneth for the sins of those who have fallen by the transgression of Adam, who have died, not knowing the will of God concerning them, or who have ignorantly sinned. But wo, wo unto him who knoweth that he rebelleth against God; for salvation cometh to none such, except it be through repentance and faith on the Lord Jesus Christ."[s] But why multiply scriptural citations when the whole tenor of sacred writ supports the doctrine? Without Christ no man can be saved, and the salvation provided at the cost of Christ's sufferings and bodily death is offered upon certain clearly

---

p Heb. v, 9
q Rom. ii, 6-11,
r Mark xvi, 16.
s Mosiah iii, 11-12.

defined conditions only; and these are summarized under "obedience to the laws and ordinances of the gospel."

28. **Salvation and Exaltation:**—Some degree of salvation will come to all who have not forfeited their right to it; exaltation is given to those only, who by active labors have won a claim to God's merciful liberality by which it is bestowed. Of the saved, not all will be exalted to the higher glories; rewards will not be bestowed in violation of justice; punishments will not be meted out to the ignoring of mercy's claims. No one can be admitted to any order of glory; in short, no soul can be saved, until justice has be satisfied for violated law. Our belief in the universal application of the atonement implies no supposition that all mankind will be saved with like endowments of glory and power. In the kingdom of God there are numerous degrees of exaltation, provided for those who are worthy of them; in the house of our Father there are many mansions, into which only those who are prepared are admitted. The old sectarian idea, that in the hereafter there will be but two places for the souls of mankind,—heaven and hell, with the same glory in all parts of the one, and the same terrors throughout the other, is entirely untenable in the light of divine revelation. Through the direct word of the Lord we learn of varied degrees of glory.

29. **Degrees of Glory:**—The revelations of God have defined the following principal kingdoms or degrees of glory, as prepared through Christ for the children of men:

I. *The Celestial Glory:*[t]—There are some who have striven to obey all the Divine commandments, who have accepted the testimony of Christ, and received the Holy Spirit; these are they who have overcome evil by godly works, and who are therefore entitled to the highest glory; these belong to the Church of the First Born, unto whom the Father has

---

t Doc. and Cov. lxxvi, 50-70.

given all things; they are made Kings and Priests of the Most High, after the order of Melchisedek; they possess celestial bodies, "whose glory is that of the sun, even the glory of God, the highest of all, whose glory the sun of the firmament is written of as being typical;" they indeed are admitted to the celestial company, being crowned with the celestial glory, which makes them Gods.

II. *The Terrestrial Glory:*[u]—We read of those who receive glory of a secondary order only, differing from the highest as "the moon differs from the sun in the firmament;" these are they, who, though honorable, were still in darkness, blinded by the craftiness of men, and unable to receive and obey the higher laws of God, they proved "not valiant in the testimony of Jesus," and therefore are not entitled to the fulness of glory.

III. *The Telestial Glory:*—We learn of a still lower kind of glory, differing from the higher orders as the stars differ from the brighter orbs of the firmament; this is given to those who received not the testimony of Christ, but who still did not deny the Holy Spirit; who have led lives exempting them from the heaviest punishment, yet whose redemption will be delayed till the last resurrection. In the telestial world there are innumerable degrees of glory, comparable to the varying lustre of the stars.[v] Yet all who receive of any one of these orders of glory are at last saved, and upon them Satan will finally have no claim. Even the telestial glory, as we are told by those who have been permitted to gaze upon it, "surpasses all understanding; and no man knows it except him to whom God has revealed it."[w] Then there are those who have lost all claim upon the immediate mercy of God; whose deeds have numbered them with Perdition and his angels.[x]

---

u Doc. and Cov. lxxvi, 71-80.
v Doc. and Cov. lxxvi, 81-86.
w Paragraphs 89-90.
x See page 62.

NOTES.

1. **The Atonement Proved by Evidence:**—"It is often asked: 'How is it that through the sacrifice of one who is innocent salvation may be purchased for those under the dominion of death.' We observe in passing that what should most concern man is not so much how it is that such is the case, but is it a fact? * * * * To that question the blood sprinkled upon a thousand Jewish altars, and the smoke that darkened the heavens for ages from burnt offerings answer yes. * * * * Even the mythology of heathen nations retains the idea of an atonement that either has been, or is to be made for mankind. Fantastic, distorted, confused, buried under the rubbish of savage superstition it may be, but it nevertheless exists. So easily traced, so distinct is this feature of heathen mythology, that some writers have endeavored to prove that the gospel plan of redemption was derived from heathen mythology. Whereas the fact is that the gospel was understood and extensively preached in the earliest ages; men retained in their tradition a knowledge of those principles or parts of them, and however much they have been distorted, traces of them may still be found in nearly all the mythologies of the world. The prophets of the Jewish scriptures answer the question in the affirmative. The writers of the New Testament make Christ's atonement the principal theme of their discourses and epistles. The Book of Mormon, speaking as the voice of an entire continent of people whose prophets and righteous men sought and found God, testify to the same great fact. The revelations of God as given through the Prophet Joseph Smith are replete with passages confirming this doctrine."—Roberts' *Outlines of Ecclesiastical History*, Section viii, 6.

2. **Redemption from the Fall Universal and Unconditional:**—"We believe that through the sufferings, death, and atonement of Jesus Christ, all mankind without one exception, are to be completely and fully redeemed, both body and spirit from the endless banishment and curse to which they were consigned by Adam's transgression; and that this universal salvation and redemption of the whole human family from the endless penalty of the original sin, is effected without any conditions, whatever, on their part; that is, they are not required to believe or repent, or be baptized, or do anything else, in order to be redeemed from that penalty; for whether they believe or disbelieve; whether they repent or remain impenitent, whether they are baptized or unbaptized, whether they keep the commandments or break them, whether they are righteous or unrighteous, it will make no difference in relation to their redemption, both soul and body, from the penalty of Adam's transgression. The most righteous man that ever lived on the earth, and the most wicked wretch of the whole human family, were both placed under the same curse without any transgression or agency of their own, and they both alike will be redeemed from that curse, without any agency or conditions on their part."—Apostle Orson Pratt in *"Remarkable Visions."*

3. **Christ the Author of our Salvation:**—President John Taylor speaks of the death of Christ as an expiatory sacrifice, and adds:—"The Savior thus becomes master of the situation,—the debt is paid, the redemption made, the covenant fulfilled, justice satisfied, the will of God done, and all power is now given into the hands of the Son of God,—the power of the resurrection, the

power of the redemption, the power of salvation, the power to enact laws for the carrying out and accomplishment of this design. * * * The plan, the arrangement, the agreement, the covenant was made, entered into and accepted, before the foundation of the world; it was prefigured by sacrifices, and was carried out and consummated on the cross. Hence, being the Mediator between God and man, He becomes by right the Dictator and Director on earth and in heaven for the living and for the dead, for the past, the present, and the future, pertaining to man as associated with this earth or the heavens, in time or eternity, the Captain of our salvation, the Apostle and High Priest of our profession, the Lord and Giver of life."—*Mediation and Atonement*, p. 171.

8

LECTURE V.

FAITH AND REPENTANCE.

Article 4:—We believe that the first principles and ordinances of the Gospel are: (1) Faith in the Lord Jesus Christ; (2) Repentance;   *   *   *

FAITH.

1. **Nature of Faith.**—The predominating sense in which the term faith is used throughout the scriptures, is that of full confidence and trust in the being, purposes and words of God. Such trust, if it be implicit, will remove all doubt concerning things accomplished or promised of God, even though such things be not apparent to or explicable by the ordinary senses of mortality; hence arises the definition of faith given by Paul: "Now faith is the substance [i. e. confidence, or assurance] of things hoped for, the evidence [i. e. the demonstration or proof] of things not seen."[a] It is plain that such a feeling of trust may exist in different persons in varying degrees; indeed, faith may manifest itself, from the incipient feeble state which is little more than mere belief, scarcely free from hesitation and fear, to the strength of abiding confidence which sets doubt and sophistry at defiance.

2. **Belief, Faith, and Knowledge,** while intimately related and oft-times regarded as one, are in reality not identical. The terms faith and belief are sometimes used as synonyms, nevertheless each of them has a specific and definite meaning in our language, although in early English there was virtually no distinction between them, and therefore the words are used interchangably in the ancient scriptures. Belief may consist in a merely intellectual assent, whilst faith im-

a Heb. xi, 1.

plies such confidence and conviction as will impel to action.
Dictionary authority justifies us in drawing a distinction
between the two, according to present usage in English;
and this authority defines belief as a simple assent to the
truth or actuality of anything, excluding however the moral
element of responsibility through such assent, which is embraced by faith.   Belief is in a sense passive,—a mental
agreement or acceptance only; faith is active and positive,—
such a reliance and confidence as will lead to works.   Faith
in Christ comprises belief in Him, combined with trust in
Him.   One cannot have faith without belief; yet he may
believe and still lack faith. Faith is vivified, vitalized, living
belief.

3.   Certainly there is a great difference in degree, even if
no essential distinction in kind be admitted between the
two.   As will be presently demonstrated, faith in the Godhead is requisite to salvation; it is indeed a saving power,
leading its possessor in the paths of godliness; surely a mere
belief in the existence and attributes of Deity is no such
power.   Mark the words of the Apostle James.[b]   In his
general epistle to the Saints, he chided his brethren for
certain empty professions: said he in effect:—You take
pride and satisfaction in declaring your belief in God; you
boast of being distinguished from the idolaters and the
heathen because you accept one God; you do well to so profess, and so believe; but, remember, others do likewise;
even the devils believe; and so firmly that they tremble at
thought of the fate which that belief makes plain to them.—
What, do devils believe in Christ?   Aye, their belief amounts
to certain knowledge, as to who He is, and as to what constitutes His part, past, present, and to come, in the Divine
plan of human existence and salvation.   Call to mind the
case of the man possessed by evil spirits, in the land of the

b See James ii, 19.

Gadarenes; a man so grievously tormented as to be a terror to all who came near him; he could be neither tamed nor bound; people were afraid to approach him; yet when he saw Christ, he ran to Him and worshiped, and the wicked spirit within him begged for mercy at the hands of that Righteous One, calling Him "Jesus, Son of the Most High God."[c]   Again, an unclean spirit in the synagogue at Jerusalem implored Christ not to use His power, crying in fear and agony, "I know thee, who thou art, the Holy One of God."[d]   And then, we are told that Christ was once followed by a multitude made up of people from Idumæa and Jerusalem, from Tyre and Sidon; among them were many who were possessed of evil spirits, and these, when they saw Him, fell down in the attitude of worship, exclaiming: "Thou art the Son of God."[e]   Was there ever mortal believer who confessed more unreservedly a knowledge of God and His Son Jesus Christ than did these same followers of Satan? The evil one knows God and Christ; remembers, perchance, somewhat concerning the position which he once occupied as a Son of the Morning; yet with all such knowledge he is Satan still.   Neither belief nor its superior,—actual knowledge,—is efficient to save; for neither of these is faith. Belief may be a product of the mind, faith is of the heart; belief is founded on reason; faith largely on intuition.

4.   We frequently hear it said that faith is imperfect knowledge; that the first disappears as the second takes its place; that now we walk by faith but some day we will walk by the sure light of knowledge.   In a sense this is true; yet it must be remembered that knowledge may be as dead and unproductive in good works as is faithless belief.   Those confessions of the devils, that Christ was the Son of God,

---

c See Mark v, 1-18; also Matt. viii, 28-34.
d See Mark i, 24.
e Mark iii, 8-11.

were founded on knowledge; yet the great truth which they knew did not change their evil natures. How different was their acknowledgment of the Savior from that of Peter, who, to the Master's question "Whom say ye that I am?" replied in practically the words used by the unclean spirits before cited, "Thou art the Christ, the Son of the living God."[f] Peter's faith had already shown its vital power; it had caused him to forsake much that had been dear, to follow his Lord through persecution and suffering, and to put away worldliness with all its fascinations, for the sacrificing godliness which his faith made so desirable. His knowledge of God as the Father, and of the Son as the Redeemer, was perhaps no greater than that of the unclean spirits; but while to them that knowledge was but an added cause of condemnation, to him it was a means of salvation.

5. The mere possession of knowledge gives no assurance of benefit therefrom. An illustration may perhaps be here indulged. During an epidemic of cholera in a large city, a scientific man proved to his own satisfaction, by chemical and microscopical tests, that the water supply was infected, and that through it contagion was being spread. He proclaimed the great truth throughout the city, and warned all against the use of unboiled water. Many of the people, although incapable of comprehending his methods of investigation, far less of repeating such for themselves, had faith in his warning words, followed his instructions, and escaped the death to which their careless and unbelieving fellows succumbed. Their faith was a saving one. To the man himself, the truth by which so many lives had been spared was a matter of knowledge. He had actually seen, under the microscope, the death-dealing germs in the water; he had tested their virulence; he knew of what he spoke. Nevertheless, in a moment of forgetfulness he drank of the

[f] Matt. xvi, 15-16; see also Mark viii, 29; Luke ix, 20.

unpurified water, and soon thereafter died a victim to the plague. His knowledge did not save him, complete though it was; yet others whose reliance was only that of faith in the truth which he declared, escaped the threatening destruction. Truly he had knowledge; but, was he wise? Knowledge is to wisdom what belief is to faith; one an abstract principle, the other a living application. Not possession merely, but the proper use of knowledge constitutes wisdom. Of belief compared with faith it may be said, as it has been taught of knowledge and wisdom:—

> "Knowledge and wisdom, far from being one,
> Have oft-times no connection. * * *
> Knowledge, a rude unprofitable mass,
> The mere material with which wisdom builds,
> Till smoothed and squared and fitted to its place,
> Does but encumber whom it seems to enrich."

6. **The Foundation of Faith:**—In a theological sense, we understand by faith as already outlined, a living, inspiring confidence in God, and an acceptance of His will as our law, and of His words as our guide, in life. Faith in God is possible only as we come to know, or at least to believe, that He exists, and moreover, that He is a Being of worthy character and attributes. The grounds upon which man founds his belief or knowledge respecting the existence of God, have been examined in a previous lecture;[g] some of the Divine attributes, as made known through God's dealings with mankind have been likewise specified. A restatement of the principal facts relating to the character of the Supreme Being, may be in place here, inasmuch as some knowledge concerning the attributes of Deity is essential to the exercise of faith in Him. Let us adopt the summary of facts as set forth by the prophet, Joseph Smith; he presents, on the testimony of scripture the following statements respecting the character of God.

g Lecture II, page 28.

"(1.) That He was God before the world was created, and the same God that He was after it was created.

"(2.) That He is merciful and gracious, slow to anger, abundant in goodness, and that He was so from everlasting, and will be to everlasting.

"(3.) That He changes not, neither is there variableness with Him; but that He is the same from everlasting to everlasting, being the same yesterday, today, and for ever; and that His course is one eternal round, without variation.

"(4.) That He is a God of truth and cannot lie.

"(5.) That He is no respecter of persons; but in every nation he that fears God and works righteousness is accepted of Him.

"(6.) That He is love."[h]

7. A knowledge of these comprehensive features of the Divine nature will enable one to exercise rational and intelligent faith in God. And upon such knowledge of God's existence, the worthiness of His character, and the perfection of His attributes, is man's faith in Him established. Faith then cannot be exercised in the absence of all knowledge; yet even the benighted heathen show some of the fruits of faith; but they have at least the conviction that arises from man's natural intuition regarding a supreme power, which has been described as a common heritage of humanity. In every human soul, even in that of the savage, there is some basis for faith, however limited and imperfect the darkness of heredity or of wilful sin may have made it. Every child of God is born with the capacity for faith inherent within his own nature; and all yearn in some degree for the strength and aid which only faith can give. We shall yet learn:—

[h] Doc. and Cov. Lectures on Faith, iii, 13-18.

> "That in all ages
> Every human heart is human;
> That in even savage bosoms
> There are longings, yearnings, strivings,
> For the good they comprehend not.
> That the feeble hands and helpless,
> Groping blindly in the darkness,
> Trust God's right hand in that darkness,
> And are lifted up and strengthened."

The heathen's faith may be imperfect and weak, for his ability to recognize the evidence upon which belief in God depends may be small. While the first promptings of faith toward God may be the result of natural intuition,—a faint echo of the songs of praise which were so common during the state of primeval childhood,—the later development will be largely the result of unprejudiced and prayerful investigation and search for truth.

8. From trustworthy evidence, rightly interpreted, true faith will spring; from false evidence, only distorted and misplaced faith can arise.[i] Our conclusions concerning any question under test will be governed largely by the number and credibility of the witnesses, if it so be that we cannot investigate the alleged facts for ourselves; and in either case, by the amount and quality of the evidence obtainable. Now, however improbable a declaration may appear to us, if the truth of it be affirmed by witnesses in whom we have confidence, we are led to admit the statement, at least provisionally as true. If many credible witnesses testify, and moreover, if collateral evidence suggest itself through facts in our possession, we may consider the statement as proved; although we would be unable to affirm the truth of it on the strength of our personal knowledge, until we had seen and heard for ourselves, until in fact each of us had become a competent witness through personal observation. To illustrate: of the citizens of this country but a comparative

[i] See note 1.

few perhaps have visited the seat of government; the masses know nothing by' actual observation of the Capitol, the executive mansion, and other buildings of national interest and importance; very few have personally met the President who resides there. How does any one of the multitudes who have not seen for themselves, know of the city of Washington, of the Capitol and of the President? Solely through the testimony of others. He may have among his acquaintances one or many who have been in the capital of our country and whose statements he accepts as true; assuredly he has heard or read of those who do know for themselves. Then he hears of laws being framed there, and of edicts issuing from the nation's headquarters; his studies in school, his use of maps and books, and many other incidents add to the evidence which soon becomes decisive. His inferences multiply, and develop into a positive conviction. He acquires a faith in the existence of a center of national government, and a regard for the laws which emanate therefrom.

9. Let us take another illustration: Astronomers tell us that the earth is of a kind with certain of the stars; that it is one of a family of planets which revolve about the sun in concentric orbits; and that some of those planets are many times the size of our globe. We may not be skilled in astronomers' methods of observation and calculation, and are therefore unable to test the truth of these statements for ourselves; but we find such a mass of evidence resulting from the united testimony of those in whose skill as scientific workers we have confidence, that the conclusions are accepted by us as fully proved.

10. So too concerning the existence, authority and attributes of God, the testimonies of many holy men in ancient and modern times,—prophets whose credibility is established by the fulfilment of their predictions,—have come to us in

united declaration of the solemn truths, and nature furnishes corroborative testimony on every side. To reject without disproving such evidence is to ignore the most approved methods of investigation and research known to man. The development of faith from evidence is illustrated in the scenes of a certain memorable Pentecost celebration, on which occasion thousands of Jews, imbued with a preconceived prejudice that Jesus was an impostor, heard the apostles' testimonies, and witnessed the attendant signs; three thousand of them were convinced of the truth, and became followers of the Son of God, their prejudice giving place to belief, and their belief developing into faith with its accompanying works.[j] The foundation of faith in God then is a sincere belief in or knowledge of Him, as sustained by evidence and testimony, tested and proved by earnest, prayerful search.

11. **Faith a Principle of Power:**—In its widest sense, faith,—the assurance of things for which we hope, and the evidence of things not discernible through our senses,—is the motive principle that impels men to resolve and to act. Without its exercise, we would make no exertion the results of which are future: without faith that he may gather in the autumn, man would not plant in the spring; neither would he essay to build, did he not have confidence that he would finish the structure and enjoy its use; had the student no faith in the possibility of successfully following his studies, he would not enter upon his courses. Faith thus becomes to us the foundation of hope, from which spring all our aspirations, ambitions and confidences for the future. Remove man's faith in the possibility of any desired success, and you rob him of the incentive to strive. He would not stretch forth his hand to seize did he not believe in the possibility of securing that for which he reaches. This prin-

[j] See Acts ii.

ciple becomes therefore the impelling force by which men struggle for excellence, oftentimes enduring vicissitudes and suffering that they may achieve their purposes. Faith is the secret of ambition, the soul of heroism, the motive power of all effort.

12. The exercise of faith is pleasing unto God, and thereby His interposition may be secured. It was through faith that the Israelites in their exodus from Egypt followed their dauntless leader into the bed of the sea; and through the protecting agencies of God, which that faith drew forth, they were saved, while the Egyptians met destruction in attempting to follow.[k] With full confidence in the instructions and promises of God, Joshua and his intrepid followers laid siege to Jericho; and the walls of that city of sin fell before the faith of the besiegers without the use of battering rams, or other engines of war.[l] By the same power Joshua gained the assistance of the luminaries of heaven, in his work of victory over the Amorites.[m] Paul cites[n] us also to the instances of Gideon,[o] Barak,[p] Samson,[q] Jephthah,[r] David,[s] Samuel,[t] and the prophets, "who through faith, subdued kingdoms, wrought righteousness, obtained promises, stopped the mouths of lions, quenched the violence of fire, escaped the edge of the sword, out of weakness were. made strong." It was by faith that Alma and Amulek were delivered from captivity, while the prison walls which had previously held them were rent and demol-

---

k Exo. xiv, 22-29; Heb. xi, 29.
l Josh. vi, 20; Heb. xi, 30.
m Josh. x, 12.
n Heb. xi, 32-34; Doc. and Cov., Lecture i, 20.
o Judges vi, 11.
p Judges iv, 6,
q Judges xiii, 24.
r Judges xi, 1; xii, 7.
s I Sam. xvi, 1, 13; xvii, 45.
t I Sam. i, 20; xii, 20.

ished." By faith, Nephi and Lehi[v] the sons of Helaman were
protected from their Lamanite foes, even by fire, though they
were not burned; and a still greater work was wrought in
the hearts of their persecutors, for they became enlightened,
and accepted the testimony of truth.   Through the operation of faith even the waves of the sea may be subdued,[w]
trees are subject to the voice of Him who commands by
faith;[x] mountains may be removed by the accomplishment
of righteous purposes,[y] the sick may be healed,[z] evil spirits
may be cast out,[a] and the dead may be raised to life.[b]   All
things are wrought through faith.[c]

13.   But, it may be argued that faith of itself is not a
source of power; that its effect is due to an external interposition of Divine aid, which faith merely secured; and the
skeptic may add that an omniscient God, if truly loving and
kind, would act independently and give without waiting to
be invoked through faith or prayer.   A sufficient answer is
found in the abundant proof furnished by the scriptures,
that the Almighty operates in accordance with law; and that
arbitrary and capricious action is foreign to His nature.
However the laws of heaven may have been formulated, the
application of their beneficent provisions to humanity is
dependent on the faith and obedience of the mortal subjects.
Consider the defeat of Israel by the men of Ai; a law of
righteousness had been violated, and things that were
accursed had been introduced into the camp of God's people;

        u Alma xiv, 26-29; Doc. and Cov., Lecture on Faith, i, 19.

        v Helaman v, 20-52; Doc. and Cov., Lecture on Faith, i, 19.

        w Matt. viii, 23-27; Mark iv, 36-41; Luke viii, 22-25; Matt. xiv, 24-32; Mark
vi, 47-51; John vi, 17-21.

        x Matt. xxi, 17-21.; Mark xi, 12-13, 20-24; Book of Jacob iv, 6.

        y Matt. xvii, 20; Mark xi, 23-24; Ether xii, 30; Jacob iv, 6; Doc. and Cov.,
Lecture on Faith, i, 19.

        z Luke xiii, 11; xiv, 2; xvii, 11; xxii, 50; Matt. viii, 2, 5, 14, 16, etc.

        a Matt. viii, 28; xvii, 18; Mark i, 23.

        b Luke vii, 11-16; John xi, 43-45; I Kings xvii, 17-24.

        c Matt. xvii, 20; Mark ix, 23; Eph. vi, 16; I John v, 4.

this transgression stopped the current of Divine help, and until the people had sanctified themselves, the power was not renewed unto them.[d] Christ was influenced, and to some extent controlled in His miracles among men by the faith or lack of faith of the people. The common benediction, "Thy faith hath made thee whole," with which He announced the healing interposition, is evidence of the fact Then we learn that in His own country He could do no mighty work, being restrained by the unbelief of the people.[e]

14. **A Condition of Living Faith:**—A condition essential to the exercise of a living, growing, sustaining faith in Deity, is the consciousness on man's part that he is at least endeavoring to live in accordance with the laws of God as he has learned them. A knowledge that he is wilfully and wantonly sinning against the truth, will deprive him of sincerity in prayer and faith, and surely estrange him from his Father. He must feel that the trend of his life's course is acceptable to God, that with due allowance for mortal weakness and human frailty, he is in some measure approved of the Lord, or he can never approach the throne of grace with confidence. The consciousness of earnest effort toward godly walk and conduct is a power of itself, strengthening its possessor in sacrifice and under persecution, and sustaining him in all good works. It was this knowledge of assured communion with God that enabled the saints of olden time to endure as they did, though their sufferings were appalling. Of them we read that some "were tortured, not accepting deliverance; that they might obtain a better resurrection: And others had trial of cruel mockings and scourgings, yea, moreover of bonds and imprisonment: They were stoned, they were sawn asunder, were tempted, were slain with the sword: they wandered about in sheepskins and goat-

d Joshua vii-viii.
e Matt. xiii, 58; Mark vi, 5-6.

skins; being destitute, afflicted, tormented; (of whom the world was not worthy:) they wandered in deserts, and in mountains, and in dens and caves of the earth."*f* As in former days so in the present, the saints have been sustained through all their sufferings by the sure knowledge of Divine approval; and the faith of righteous men has ever grown through a consciousness of their good endeavors.

15. **Faith Essential to Salvation:**—Inasmuch as salvation is attainable only through the mediation and atonement of Christ, and since this is made applicable to individual sin only in the cases of those who obey the laws of righteousness, faith in Jesus Christ is indispensable to salvation. But no one can believe in Jesus Christ, and at the same time doubt the existence and authority of either the Father or the Holy Ghost; therefore faith in the entire Godhead is essential to salvation. Paul declares that without faith it is impossible to please God, "for he that cometh to God must believe that He is, and that He is a rewarder of them that diligently seek Him."*g* The scriptures abound in assurances of salvation to those who exercise faith in God, and obey the requirements which that faith makes plain. Christ's words on the matter are conclusive, "He that believeth and is baptized shall be saved, but he that believeth not shall be damned,"*h* and again, "He that believeth on the Son hath everlasting life, and he that believeth not the Son shall not see life, but the wrath of God abideth on him."*i* And similar doctrines did His apostles teach after His death all the days of their ministry.*j* A natural result of implicit

f Heb. xi, 35-38; see also Doc. and Cov. Lectures on Faith vi.

g Heb. xi, 6.

h Mark xvi, 16.

i John iii, 36. See also John iii, 15; iv, 42; v, 24; xi, 25; Gal. ii, 20; I Nephi x, 6, 17; II Nephi xxv, 25; xxvi, 8; Enos i, 8; Mos. iii, 17; III Nephi xxvii, 19; Hel. v, 9; Doc. and Cov. xlv, 8;

j Acts ii, 38; x, 42; xvi, 31; Rom. x, 9; Heb. iii, 19; xi, 6; I Pet. i, 9; I John iii, 23; v, 14.

faith in the Godhead, will be a growing confidence in the scriptures as containing the word of God, and in the words and works of His authorized servants, who speak as the living oracles of heaven.

16. **Faith a Gift of God:**—Though within the reach of all who diligently strive to gain it, faith is nevertheless a Divine gift, and can be obtained only from God.[k] As is fitting for so priceless a pearl, it is given to those only who show by their sincerity that they are worthy of it, and who give promise of abiding by its dictates. Although faith is called the first principle of the gospel of Christ, though it be in fact the foundation of all religion, yet, even faith is preceded by sincerity of disposition, and humility of soul, whereby the word of God may make an impression upon the heart.[l] No compulsion is used in bringing men to a knowledge of God; yet, as fast as we open our hearts to the influences of righteousness, the faith that leads to life eternal will be given us of our Father.

17. **Faith and Works:**—Faith in a passive sense, that is, as mere belief, is inefficient as a means of salvation. This truth was clearly set forth both by Christ and the apostles, and the vigor with which it was declared may be an indication of the early development of a most pernicious doctrine,—that of justification by belief alone. The Savior taught that works were essential to the validity of profession and the efficacy of faith. Mark his words:—"Not every one that sayeth unto me, Lord, Lord, shall enter into the kingdom of heaven; but he that doeth the will of my Father which is in heaven."[m] "He that hath my commandments, and keepeth them, he it is that loveth me: and he that loveth me shall be loved of my Father, and I will love him, and

---

k Matt. xvi, 17; John vi, 44, 65; Eph. ii, 8; I Cor. xii, 9; Rom. xii, 3; Moroni x, 11.
l See Rom. x, 17
m Matt. vii, 21.

will manifest myself to him."[n] The instructions of the Apostle James are particularly explicit:—"What doth it profit, my brethren, though a man say he hath faith, and have not works? can faith save him? If a brother or sister be naked, and destitute of daily food, and one of you say unto them, depart in peace, be ye warmed and filled; notwithstanding ye give them not those things which are needful to the body; what doth it profit? Even so faith, if it hath not works, is dead, being alone. Yea, a man may say, Thou hast faith, and I have works: shew me thy faith without thy works, and I will shew thee my faith by my works."[o] And to this may be added the words of John:—"And hereby we do know that we know him, if we keep his commandments. He that saith, I know him, and keepeth not his commandments, is a liar, and the truth is not in him. But whoso keepeth his word, in him verily is the love of God perfected: hereby know we that we are in him."[p]

18. To these teachings may be added many inspired utterances, from Nephite scriptures[q] and from modern revelation,[r] all affirming the necessity of works, and denying the saving efficacy of mere belief. Yet in spite of the plain word of God, sectarian dogmas have been promulgated to the effect that by faith alone man may achieve salvation, and that a mere profession of belief will open the doors of heaven to the sinner.[s] The scriptures cited and man's inherent sense of justice furnish a sufficient refutation of these pernicious doctrines.

---

[n] John xiv, 21.

[o] James ii, 14-18.

[p] I John ii, 3-5.

[q] See I Nephi xv, 33; II Nephi xxix, 11; Mosiah v, 15; Alma vii, 27; ix, 28; xxxvii, 32-34; xli, 3-5.

[r] Doc. and Cov. throughout.

[s] See Note 2.

REPENTANCE.

19. **Nature of Repentance:**—The term repentance is used in the scriptures with several different meanings, but, as representing the duty required of all who would obtain forgiveness for transgression, it indicates a godly sorrow for sin, producing a reformation of life, and embodies, (1) a conviction of guilt; (2) a desire to escape the hurtful effects of sin; and (3) an earnest determination to forsake sin and to accomplish good. Repentance is a result of contrition of soul, which springs from a deep sense of humility, and this in turn is dependent upon the exercise of an abiding faith in God. Repentance therefore properly ranks as the second principle of the gospel, closely associated with and immediately following faith. As soon as one has come to recognize the existence and authority of God, he feels a respect for Divine laws, and a conviction of his own unworthiness. His wish to please the Father, whom he has so long neglected, will impel him to forsake sin; and this impulse will acquire added strength from the sinner's natural and commendable desire to escape, if possible, the dire results of his own waywardness. With the zeal inspired by fresh conviction, he will crave an opportunity of showing by good works the sincerity of his newly developed faith; and he will regard the remission of his sins as the most desirable of blessings. Then he will learn that this gift of mercy is granted on certain specific conditions only.[t] The first step toward the blessed state of forgiveness consists in the sinner confessing his sins; the second, in his forgiving others who have sinned against him; and the third in his showing his acceptance of Christ's atoning sacrifice by obeying the Divine requirements.

20. (1.) **Confession of Sins** is essential, for without it re-

[t] See Note 3.

9

pentance is incomplete.   The Apostle John tells us, "If we
say that we have no sin we deceive ourselves, and the truth is
not in us.   If we confess our sins, He is faithful and just to
forgive us our sins, and to cleanse us from all unrighteousness."[u]   We read also, "He that covereth his sins shall not
prosper, but whoso confesseth and forsaketh them shall
have mercy."[v]   And unto the Saints in this dispensation the
Lord has said, "Verily I say unto you, I, the Lord, forgive
sins unto those who confess their sins before me and ask
forgiveness, who have not sinned unto death."[w]   And that
this act of confession is included in repentance is shown by
the Lord's words: "By this ye may know if a man repenteth of his sins: Behold he will confess them and forsake them."[x]

21.   (2.)   **The Sinner Must be Willing to Forgive Others,** if
he hopes to obtain forgiveness.   Surely his repentance is but
superficial if his heart be not softened to the degree of
tolerance for the weaknesses of his fellows.   In teaching
His hearers how to pray, the Savior instructed them to
supplicate the Father: "Forgive us our debts as we forgive our debtors."[y]   He led them not to hope for forgiveness if in their hearts they forgave not one another:
"For," said He, "if ye forgive men their trespasses, your
Heavenly Father will also forgive you; but, if ye forgive
not men their trespasses, neither will your Father forgive
your trespasses."[z]   And forgiveness between man and man,
to be acceptable before the Lord, must be unbounded.   In
answering Peter's question, "Lord, how oft shall my brother
sin against me, and I forgive him? till seven times?" the

---

u I John i, 8-9; see also Psalms xxxii, 5; xxxviii, 18; Mosiah xxvi, 29-30.
v Prov. xxviii, 13.
w Doc. and Cov. lxiv, 7.
x Doc. and Cov. lviii, 43.
y Matt. vi, 12; see also Luke xi, 4.
z Matt. vi, 14-15; III Nephi xiii, 14-15.

Master said, "I say not unto thee, until seven times; but until seventy times seven;" clearly intending to teach that man must ever be ready to forgive. On another occasion He taught the disciples, saying, "If thy brother trespass against thee, rebuke him, and if he repent, forgive him. And if he trespass against thee seven times in a day, and seven times in a day turn again to thee saying, I repent, thou shalt forgive him."[a]

22.   Illustrating further the Divine purpose to mete unto men the measure they mete unto their fellows,[b] the Savior put forth to His disciples a parable of a king, to whom one of his subjects owed an enormous sum of money, ten thousand talents; but when the debtor humbled himself and pleaded for mercy, the compassionate heart of the king was moved and he forgave his servant the debt. But the same servant, going out from the presence of the king, met a fellow-servant who was indebted to him in a paltry sum; forgetting the mercy so recently shown unto himself, he seized his fellow-servant and cast him into prison till he would pay the debt. Then the king, hearing of this, sent for the wicked servant, and, denouncing him for his lack of gratitude and consideration, handed him over to the tormentors.[c] The Lord will not listen to petitions nor accept an offering from one who has bitterness in his heart toward others; "First be reconciled to thy brother, and then come and offer thy gift."[d] In His revealed word to the Saints in this day, the Lord has placed particular stress upon this necessary condition: "Wherefore I say unto you that ye ought to forgive one another, for he that forgiveth not his brother his trespasses, standeth condemned before the Lord, for there re-

---

a Luke xvii, 3-4.
b Matt. vii, 2: Mark iv, 24; Luke vi, 38.
c Matt. xviii, 23-35.
d Matt. v, 23-24; III Nephi xii, 23-24.

maineth in him the greater sin;"[e] and to remove all doubt
as to the proper subjects for human forgiveness, it is added:—
"I, the Lord, will forgive whom I will forgive, but of you
it is required to forgive all men."

23.   (3.) **Confidence in Christ's Atoning Sacrifice** constitutes the third essential condition in obtaining remission of
sins.   The name of Christ is the only name under heaven
whereby men may be saved;[f] and we are taught to offer our
petitions to the Father in the name of His Son.   Adam
received this instruction from the mouth of an angel,[g] and
the Savior personally instructed the Nephites to the same
effect.[h]   But no person can truthfully profess faith in
Christ, and refuse to obey His commandments; therefore
obedience is essential to remission of sin; and the repentant
sinner will eagerly seek to learn what is further required of
him.

24.   Repentance, to be worthy of its name, must comprise
something more than a mere self-acknowledgment of error;
it does not consist in lamentations and wordy confessions,
but in the heart-felt recognition of guilt, which carries with
it a horror for sin, and a resolute determination to make
amends for the past and to do better in the future.   If such
a conviction be genuine, it is marked by that godly sorrow,
which, as Paul has said, "worketh repentance to salvation,
not to be repented of; but the sorrow of the world worketh
death."[i]   Apostle Orson Pratt has wisely said:—"It would
be of no use for a sinner to confess his sins to God, unless
he were determined to forsake them; it would be of no
benefit to him to feel sorry that he had done wrong, unless
he intended to do wrong no more; it would be folly for him

---

e Doc. and Cov. lxiv, 9-10.

f Pearl of Great Price p. 32.

g Pearl of Great Price, Writings of Moses, p. 19, (1888 ed.)

h III Nephi xxvii, 5-7.

i II Cor. vii, 10.

to confess before God that he had injured his fellow-man, unless he were determined to do all in his power to make restitution. Repentance, then, is not only a confession of sins, with a sorrowful, contrite heart, but a fixed, settled purpose to refrain from every evil way."

25. **Repentance Essential to Salvation:**—This evidence of sincerity, this beginning of a better life, is required of every candidate for salvation. In the obtaining of Divine mercy, repentance is as indispensable as faith, it must be as extensive as sin. Where can we find an absolutely sinless mortal? Sagely did the Preacher of old declare "There is not a just man upon earth, that doeth good and sinneth not."[j] Who, therefore, has no need of forgiveness? who is exempt from the requirements of repentance? God has promised forgiveness unto those who truly repent before Him, it is unto such that the advantages of individual salvation, through the atonement of Christ, are extended. Isaiah thus admonishes to repentance, with assuring promises of forgiveness: "Seek ye the Lord while he may be found, call ye upon him while he is near. Let the wicked forsake his way, and the unrighteous man his thoughts: and let him return unto the Lord, and he will have mercy upon him; and to our God, for he will abundantly pardon."[k]

26. The burden of inspired teachers in every age has been the call to repentance. To this effect was heard the voice of John crying in the wilderness, "Repent ye, for the kingdom of heaven is at hand."[e] And the Savior followed with "Repent ye and believe the gospel,"[m] for "Except ye repent, ye shall all likewise perish."[n] So too proclaim the

j Eccl. vii, 20; see also Rom. iii, 10; I John i, 8.

k Isa. lv, 6-7; see also II Nephi ix, 24; Alma v, 31-36, 49-56; ix, 12; Doc. and Cov. i, 32-33; xix, 4; xx, 29; xxix, 44; cxxxiii, 16.

l Matt. iii, 2.

m Mark i, 15.

n Luke xiii, 3.

apostles of old, that God "commandeth all men everywhere to repent,"*o* And in the present dispensation has come the word, "We know that all men must repent, and believe on the name of Jesus Christ   *   *   *   or they cannot be saved in the kingdom of God."*p*

27. **Repentance, a Gift from God:**—Repentance is a means of pardon, and is therefore one of God's great gifts to man. It is not to be had for the careless asking; it may not be found upon the highway, it is not of earth, but a treasure of heaven, and is given with care, yet with boundless liberality unto those who have brought forth works that warrant its bestowal.*q* That is to say, all who prepare themselves for repentance will, by the humbling and softening influence of the Holy Spirit, be led to the actual possession of this great gift. When Peter was charged by his fellow-worshipers with a breach of law in that he had associated with Gentiles, he told his hearers of the Divine manifestations he had so recently received; they believed and declared "Then hath God also to the Gentiles granted repentance unto life."*r* Paul also, in writing to the Romans, teaches that repentance comes through the goodness of God.*s*

28. **Repentance not always Possible:**—The gift of repentance is extended to men as they humble themselves before the Lord, it is the testimony of the Spirit in their hearts; if they hearken not unto the monitor it will again leave them, for the Spirit of God strives not ever with man.*t* Repentance becomes more difficult as the sin is more wilful; it is by humility and contrition of the heart that sinners

---

o Acts xvii, 30.

p Doc. and Cov. xx, 29.

q Matt. iii, 7-8; Acts xxvi, 20.

r Acts xi, 18.

s Rom. ii, 4; See also II Tim. ii, 25.
   Gen. vi, 3; Doc. and Cov. i, 33.

may increase their faith in God, and so obtain from Him the priceless gift of repentance. As the time of repentance is procrastinated, the ability to repent grows weaker; neglect of opportunity in holy things brings a forfeit of the chance. In giving commandment to Joseph Smith, in the early days of the present Church, the Lord said, "For I the Lord cannot look upon sin with the least degree of allowance; nevertheless, he that repents and does the commandments of the Lord shall be forgiven, and he that repents not, from him shall be taken even the light which he has received, for my Spirit shall not always strive with man saith the Lord of Hosts."[u]

29. **Repentance Here and Hereafter:**—The Nephite prophet, Alma, described the period of earthly existence as a probationary state, granted unto man for repentance;[v] yet we learn from the scriptures that repentance may be obtained, under certain conditions, beyond the vail of mortality. Between the times of His death and resurrection, Christ "preached unto the spirits in prison, which sometime were disobedient when once the long suffering of God waited in the days of Noah;"[w] these the Son visited, and unto them He preached the gospel, "that they might be judged according to men in the flesh, who received not the testimony of Jesus in the flesh, but afterwards received it."[x]

30. Yet no soul is justified in postponing his efforts to repent because of this assurance of God's long-suffering and mercy. We know not on what terms repentance will be obtainable in the hereafter, but it is unreasonable to suppose that the soul who has wilfully rejected the opportunity of repentance in this life will find it easy to repent there.

---

[u] Doc. and Cov. i, 31-33.
[v] Alma xii, 24; xxxiv, 32; xlii, 4.
[w] I Peter iii, 19-20.
[x] Doc. and Cov. lxxvi, 73-74.

To procrastinate[y] the day of repentance is to deliberately place ourselves in the power of the adversary. As Amulek taught and admonished the multitude of old: "For behold this life is the time for men to prepare to meet God, * * * therefore I beseech of you that ye do not procrastinate the day of your repentance unto the end. * * * Ye cannot say when ye are brought to that awful crisis, that I will repent, that I will return to my God. Nay, ye cannot say this; for that same spirit which doth possess your bodies at the time that ye go out of this life, that same spirit will have power to possess your body in that eternal world. For behold, if ye have procrastinated the day of your repentance, even until death, behold ye have become subjected to the spirit of the devil, and he doth seal you his."[z]

NOTES.

1. **Example of False Faith:**—"When Europeans first began their explorations in the New World, the Indians whom they met were much amazed at the power and explosive properties of gun-powder, and asked many questions respecting the manner in which it was produced. The Europeans, taking advantage of the ignorance of the savages, and seeing an opportunity to increase their wealth by the deception, told the Indians that it was the seed of a plant which grew in the lands they had come from, and doubtless it would thrive in their land also. The Indians, of course, believed this statement, and purchased the supposed seed, giving in exchange for it large quantities of gold. In implicit faith they carefully planted the supposed seed, and anxiously watched for its sprouting and the appearance of the plant; but it never came. They had faith in the statements made to them by the Europeans, but as these statements were false, and therefore the evidence on which the Indians based their belief untrue, their faith was vain."—Orson Pratt.

2. **The Sectarian Dogma of Justification by Faith alone** has exercised an influence for evil since the early days of Christianity. The idea upon which this pernicious doctrine was founded, was at first associated with that of an absolute predestination, by which man was fore-doomed to destruction, or to an utterly undeserved salvation. Thus, Luther taught as follows:—"The excellent, infallible, and sole preparation for grace is the eternal election and predestination of God." "Since the fall of man, free-will is but an idle word." "A man

------

y Alma xxxiv, 33.
z Alma xxxiv, 32-35.

who imagines to arrive at grace by doing all that he is able to do, adds sin to sin, and is doubly guilty." "That man is not justified who performs many works; but he who without works has much faith in Christ." (For these and other doctrines of the so-called "Reformation," see D'Aubigne's *History of the Reformation*, vol. i, pp. 82, 83, 119, 122.) In Miller's *Church History* (vol. iv, p. 514) we read. "The point which the reformer [Luther] had most at heart in all his labors, contests, and dangers, was the justification by faith alone." Melancthon voices the doctrine of Luther in these words: "Man's justification before God proceeds from faith alone. This faith enters man's heart by the grace of God alone;" and further, "As all things which happen, happen necessarily, according to the divine predestination, there is no such thing as liberty in our wills." (D'Aubigne, vol. iii, p. 340). It is true that Luther strongly denounced, and vehemently disclaimed responsibility for, the excesses to which this teaching gave rise, yet he was not less vigorous in proclaiming the doctrine. Note his words:—"I, Doctor Martin Luther, unworthy herald of the gospel of our Lord Jesus Christ, confess this article, that faith alone without works justifies before God; and I declare that it shall stand and remain forever in despite of the emperor of the Romans, the emperor of the Turks, the emperor of the Persians,—in spite of the pope and all the cardinals, with the bishops, priests, monks, and nuns,—in spite of kings, princes, and nobles, and in spite of all the world and of the devils themselves; and that if they endeavor to fight against this truth they will draw the fires of hell upon their heads. This is the true and holy gospel, and the declaration of me, Doctor Luther, according to the teachings of the Holy Ghost." (D'Aubigne, vol. i, p. 70).

Fletcher (*End of Religious Controversy*, p. 90) illustrates the vicious extreme to which this evil doctrine led, by accusing one of its adherents with having said, "Even adultery and murder do not hurt the pleasant children, but rather work for their good. God sees no sin in believers, whatever sin they may commit. * * * * It is a most pernicious error of the schoolmen to distinguish sins according to the fact, and not according to the person. Though I blame those who say, let us sin that grace may abound, yet adultery, incest, and murder, shall upon the whole, make me holier on earth, and merrier in heaven."

A summary of the mediæval controversy regarding the means of grace, including the doctrines of Luther and others, is presented in Roberts' *Outlines of Ecclesiastical History*, part iii, section ii; to which the student is referred. The quotations given above are incorporated therein.

3. Forgiveness not always Immediate:—"On account of the magnitude of sins committed, repentance is not always followed by forgiveness and restoration. For instance, when Peter was preaching to the Jews, who had slain Jesus and taken His blood on themselves and their children, he did not say, repent and be baptized for the remission of sins; but, 'Repent ye therefore, and be converted, that your sins may be blotted out, when the times of refreshing shall come from the presence of the Lord; and [when] He shall send Jesus Christ, which before was preached unto you; whom the heaven must receive until the times of the restitution of all things.' (Acts iii, 19-21.) That is, repent now, and believe in Jesus Christ, that you may be forgiven when He whom you have slain shall come again in the days of the restitution of all things; and prescribe to you the terms on which you may be saved."—Compendium, p. 28.

LECTURE VI.

BAPTISM.

Article 4:—We believe that the first principles and ordinances of the Gospel are:— * * * (3) Baptism by immersion for the remission of sins; * * *

1. **Nature of Baptism:**—Among the Latter-day Saints, water baptism ranks as the third principle, and the first essential ordinance, of the gospel. Baptism is the gateway leading into the fold of Christ, the portal to the Church, the established rite of naturalization in the kingdom of heaven. The candidate for admission into the Church and kingdom, having obtained and professed faith in the Lord Jesus Christ, and having sincerely repented of his sins, is properly required to give evidence of this spiritual sanctification by some outward ordinance, prescribed by authority as the sign or symbol of the new profession. The initiatory ordinance is baptism by water, to be followed by the higher baptism of the Holy Spirit; and, as a result of this act of obedience, remission of sins is granted.

2. How simple are the means thus ordained for admission into the fold; they are within the reach of the poorest and weakest, as also of the rich and powerful! What symbol more expressive of a cleansing from sin could be given, than that of baptism in water? Baptism is made a sign of the covenant entered into between the repentant sinner and his Maker, that thereafter he will seek to observe the Divine commands. Concerning this fact, the Prophet Alma thus admonished and instructed the people of Gideon:—"Yea, I say unto you, come and fear not, and lay aside every sin, which easily doth beset you, which doth bind you down to destruction, yea, come and go forth, and show unto your

God that ye are willing to repent of your sins, and enter into a covenant with him to keep his commandments, and witness it unto him this day, by going into the waters of baptism."[a]

3. The humbled sinner, convicted of his transgression, through the bestowal of God's good gifts of faith and repentance, will hail most joyfully any means of cleansing himself from pollution, now so repulsive in his eyes; all such will cry out as did the stricken Jewish multitude at Pentecost, "What shall we do?" Unto such comes the answering voice of the Spirit, through the medium of scripture, or by the mouths of the Lord's appointed servants, "Repent and be baptized every one of you in the name of Jesus Christ, for the remission of sins."[b] Springing forth as a result of contrition of soul, baptism has been very appropriately called the first fruits of repentance.[d]

4. **The Establishment of Baptism** dates from the time of the earliest history of the race. When the Lord manifested Himself to Adam after the expulsion from the Garden of Eden, He promised the patriarch of the race, "If thou wilt turn unto me and hearken unto my voice, and believe, and repent of all thy transgressions, and be baptized, even in water, in the name of mine Only Begotten Son, who is full of grace and truth, which is Jesus Christ, the only name which shall be given under heaven, whereby salvation shall come unto the children of men, ye shall receive the gift of the Holy Ghost, asking all things in His name, and whatsoever ye shall ask, it shall be given you.　*　*　*
And it came to pass, when the Lord had spoken with Adam, our father, that Adam cried unto the Lord, and he was caught away by the Spirit of the Lord, and was carried

---

a Alma vii, 15.
b Acts ii, 37-38.
d Moroni viii, 25.

down into the water, and was laid under the water, and was brought forth out of the water. And thus he was baptized, and the Spirit of God descended upon him, and thus he was born of the Spirit, and became quickened in the inner man."[b] Enoch preached the doctrine of repentance and baptism, and did baptize the people, and as many as accepted these teachings and submitted to the requirements of the gospel, became sanctified and holy in the sight of God.

5. **The Special Purpose of Baptism** is to afford admission to the Church of Christ with remission of sins. What need of more words to prove the worth of this divinely appointed ordinance? What gift could be offered the human race greater than a ready means of obtaining forgiveness for transgression? Justice forbids the granting of universal and unconditional pardon for sins committed, except through obedience to ordained law; but means simple and effective are provided, whereby the penitent sinner may enter into a covenant with God, sealing that covenant with the sign that commands recognition in heaven, that he will submit himself to the laws of God; thus he places himself within the reach of Mercy, under whose protecting influence he may win eternal life.

6. *Biblical Proofs*, that baptism is designed as a means of securing to man a remission of his sins, are abundant. John the Baptist was the special preacher of this doctrine in the days immediately preceding the Savior's ministry in the flesh; and the voice of this priest of the desert stirred Jerusalem and reverberated through all Judæa, proclaiming remission of sins as the fruits of acceptable baptism.[c]

7. Saul of Tarsus, a zealous persecutor of the followers of Christ, while journeying to Damascus, intent on a further exercise of his ill-directed zeal, received a special manifesta-

---

b Pearl of Great Price, Writings of Moses, pp. 32-34, (1888 ed.)

c Mark i, 4; Luke iii, 3.

tion of the power of God, and was converted with signs and
wonders. He heard and answered the voice of Christ, and
thus became a special witness of his Lord. Yet even this
unusual demonstration of Divine favor was insufficient.
Blinded through the glory that had been manifested unto him,
humbled and earnest, awakening to the terrible fact that
he had been persecuting his Redeemer, he exclaimed in
anguish of soul, "What shall I do, Lord?" He was directed
to go to Damascus, there to learn more of God's will concerning him. Gladly did he receive the Lord's messenger,
devout Ananias, who ministered unto him so that he re-
gained his sight, and then taught him baptism as a means
of obtaining forgiveness.[d]

8. And Saul, known now as Paul, thereafter a preacher
of righteousness, and an apostle of the Lord Jesus Christ,
taught to others the same great saving principle, that by
baptism in water comes regeneration from sin.[e] In forceful
language, and attended with special evidences of Divine
power, Peter declared the same doctrine to the penitent
multitude. Overcome with grief at the recital of what
they had done to the Son of God, they cried out "Men and
brethren, what shall we do?" Promptly came the answer,
with apostolic authority, "Repent, and be baptized every
one of you in the name of Jesus Christ for the remission of
sins."[f]

9. *Book of Mormon prophets* gave the same testimony to
the western fold of Christ. To this effect were the words
of Nephi, the son of Lehi, addressed to his brethren:—"For
the gate by which ye should enter, is repentance, and
baptism by water; and then cometh a remission of your
sins by fire, and by the Holy Ghost."[g] So did Alma teach

d Acts xxii, 1-16.
e Titus iii, 5.
f Acts ii, 36-37; see also I Peter iii, 21.
g II Nephi xxxi, 17.

the people of Gideon, as already quoted.[h] Nephi, the grandson of Helaman, immediately preceding Christ's advent upon earth, went forth amongst his people, baptizing unto repentance, from which followed "a great remission of sins."[i] Nephi ordained assistants in the ministry, "that all such as should come unto them, should be baptized with water, and this as a witness and a testimony before God, and unto the people, that they had repented and received a remission of their sins."[j] Mormon adds his own testimony, as commissioned of Christ, exhorting the people to forsake their sins and be baptized for remission thereof.[k]

10. *Modern Revelation*, concerning baptism and its object, shows that the same importance is ascribed by the Lord to to the ordinance today as in earlier times. That there may be no question as to the application of this doctrine to the Church in the present dispensation, the principle has been re-stated, the law has been re-enacted for our guidance. The elders of the Church are comissioned to preach the remission of sins as obtainable through the means of authorized baptism.[l]

11. **Fit Candidates for Baptism:**—The prime objects of baptism being admission to the Church, with remission of sins, and this coming only through the exercise of faith in God and true repentance before Him, it naturally follows that baptism can in justice be required of those only who are capable of exercising faith and working repentance.[m] In a revelation on Church government given through Joseph the Prophet, April, 1830, the Lord specifically states the

h Alma vii, 14-15.
i III Nephi i, 23.
j III Nephi vii, 24-26.
k III Nephi xxx, 2.
l Doc. and Cov. xix, 31; lv, 2; lxviii, 27; lxxvi, 51, 52; lxxxiv, 27, 74.
m See Note 1.

conditions under which persons may be received into the Church through baptism: these are His words:—"All those who humble themselves before God, and desire to be baptized, and come forth with broken hearts and contrite spirits, and witness before the Church that they have truly repented of all their sins, and are willing to take upon them the name of Jesus Christ, having a determination to serve him to the end, and truly manifest by their works that they have received of the Spirit of Christ unto the remission of their sins, shall be received by baptism into his Church."[n]

12. Such conditions exclude all who have not arrived at the age of discretion and responsibility; and by special commandment the Lord has forbidden the Church to receive any who have not attained to such age.[o] By revelation, the Lord has designated eight years as the age at which children may be properly baptized into the Church, and parents are required to prepare their children for the ordinances of the Church, by teaching them the doctrines of faith, repentance, baptism, and the gift of the Holy Ghost. Failure in this requirement will be accounted by the Lord as a sin resting upon the heads of the parents.[p]

13. **Infant Baptism:**—The Latter-day Saints are opposed to the practice of infant baptism, which indeed they believe to be sacrilege in the eyes of God. No one having faith in the word of God can look upon the child as impure; such an innocent being needs no initiation into the fold, for it has never strayed therefrom; it needs no remission of sins, for it is sinless; and should it die before it has become contaminated by the sins of earth, it will be received again, without baptism, into the presence of its God. Yet there are many professedly Christian teachers who declare that as all chil-

---

n Doc. and Cov. xx, 37.

o Doc. and Cov. xx, 71.

p Doc. and Cov. lxviii, 25-27.

dren are born into a wicked world, they are themselves wicked,
and must be cleansed in the waters of baptism to be made
acceptable to God.   How heinous is such a doctrine!—the
child to whom the Savior pointed as an example of emula-
tion of those even who had received the holy apostleship,[q] the
Lord's selected type of the kingdom of heaven, the favored
spirits whose angels stand forever in the presence of the
Father, faithfully reporting all that may be done unto
their sacred charges"—such souls are to be rejected and cast
into torment because their earthly guardians failed to have
them baptized!   To teach such a doctrine is sin.

14.   **The History of Infant Baptism** is instructive, as throwing light upon the origin of this erratic practice.   It is
certain that the baptism of infants, or pedobaptism (Greek
paidos, child, and *baptismos*, baptism) as it is styled in
theological lore, was not taught by the Savior, nor by His
apostles.   Some point to the incident of Christ blessing
little children, and rebuking those who would forbid the
little ones coming unto Him,[s] as an evidence in favor of
infant baptism; but, as Bishop Jeremy Taylor has tersely
replied:—"From the action of Christ's blessing infants, to
infer they are to be baptized, proves nothing so much as
that there is a want of better argument; for the conclusion
would with more probability be derived thus: Christ blessed
infants, and so dismissed them, but baptized them not;
therefore infants are not to be baptized."

15.   There is no authentic record of infant baptism having been practiced during the first two centuries after
Christ, and the custom probably did not become general till
the fifth century; from the last-named time until the
Reformation, however, it was accepted by most of the pro-

---

q Matt. xviii, 1-6.
r Verse 10.
s Matt. xix, 13; Mark x, 13; Luke xviii, 15.

fessed Christian churches. But even during that dark age, many theological disputants raised their voices against this unholy rite.[t] In the early part of the sixteenth century, a sect rose into prominence in Germany, under the name of Anabaptists (Greek *ana*, again, and *baptizo*, baptize) distinguished for its opposition to the practice of infant baptism, and deriving its name from the requirement made of all its members who had been baptized in infancy that they be baptized again. This denomination, commonly called the Baptists, has become greatly divided by internal disputes; but in general, the Baptists have maintained a unity of belief in opposing the baptism of irresponsible children.

16. Some pedobaptists have attempted to prove an analogy between baptism and circumcision; but for such position there is no scriptural warrant. Circumcision was made the mark of a covenant between God and His chosen servant Abraham,[u] a symbol regarded by the posterity of Abraham as indicative of their freedom from the idolatry of the times, and of God's acceptance of them; and nowhere is circumcision made a means for remission of sins. That rite was applicable to males only; baptism is administered to both sexes. Circumcision was to be performed on the eighth day after birth, even though such should fall on the Sabbath.[w] In the third century a council of bishops was held under the presidency of Cyprian, Bishop of Carthage, at which it was gravely determined, that to postpone baptism until the eighth day after birth was dangerous, and consequently not to be allowed.

17. **Infant Baptism is Forbidden in the Book of Mormon,** from which fact we know that discussion upon this subject must have arisen among the Nephites. Mormon, having

---

t See Note 2.
u Gen. xvii, 1-14.
w John vii, 22-23.
10

received special revelation from the Lord concerning the matter, wrote an epistle thereon to his son Moroni, in which he denounces the practice of infant baptism, and declares that any one who supposeth that little children need baptism is in the gall of bitterness, and in the bonds of iniquity, denying the mercies of Christ, and setting at naught His atonement and the power of His redemption.[x]

18. **Baptism Essential to Salvation:**—Most of the proofs concerning the object of baptism apply with equal force to the proposition that baptism is necessary for salvation; for, inasmuch as remission of sins constitutes a special purpose of baptism, and as no soul can be saved in the kingdom of heaven with unforgiven sins, it is plain that baptism is essential to salvation. Salvation is promised to man on condition of his obedience to the commands of God; and, as the scriptures conclusively prove, baptism is one of the most important of such requirements. Baptism, being commanded of God, must be essential to the purpose for which it is instituted, for our Father deals not with unnecessary forms. Baptism is required of all who have attained to years of accountability; none are exempt.

19. Even Christ, standing as a man without sin in the midst of a sinful world, was baptized, "to fulfill all righteousness,"[y] such being the purpose, as declared by the Savior Himself to the hesitating priest, who, zealous as he was for his great mission, yet demurred when asked to baptize One whom he considered sinless. Centuries before the great event, Nephi, prophesying among the people in the western world, fore-told the baptism of the Savior, and beautifully explained how righteousness would be thereby fulfilled:[z]—"And now if the Lamb of God, he being holy

---

x Moroni viii. Read the entire epistle.

y Matt. iii, 15.

z II Nephi xxxi, 5-8.

should have need to be baptized by water to fulfill all right-eousness, O, then, how much more need have we, being unholy, to be baptized?"

20.   The words of the Savior, spoken while He ministered in the flesh, declare baptism to be essential to salvation. One of the rulers of the Jews, Nicodemus, came to Christ by night and made a profession of confidence in the instruc-tions of the Savior, whom he designated as "a teacher come from God." Seeing his faith, Jesus taught unto him one of the chief laws of heaven, saying, "Except a man be born again, he cannot see the kingdom of God." A question by Nicodemus called forth from the Savior the additional declar-ation, "Verily, verily I say unto thee, except a man be born of water and of the Spirit, he cannot enter into the king-dom of God.[a] It is practically indisputable, that the watery birth here referred to as essential to entrance into the kingdom, is baptism. We learn further concerning Christ's attitude toward baptism, that He required the ordinance of those who professed to become His disciples.[b] When appear-ing to the Eleven in His resurrected state, giving them His farewell blessing and final commission, He commanded them, "Go ye, therefore, and teach all nations, baptizing them in the name of the Father, and of the Son, and of the Holy Ghost;"[c] and, concerning the results of baptism He taught them, that "He that believeth and is baptized shall be saved, but he that believeth not shall be damned."[d]

21.   Plain as seems the spirit of these instructions and promises, there are nevertheless many, who, while profess-ing to teach the doctrine of the Redeemer, evade the mean-ing of His precepts, and declare that because He said "he

a John iii, 1-5.
b John iv, 1-2.
c Matt. xxviii, 19.
d Mark xvi, 16.

that believeth not shall be damned," instead of "he that is
not baptized shall be damned," baptism is after all not
an essential, but a mere convenience or simple propriety,
in the plan of salvation.   It is a mockery of faith to profess
belief in Christ while refusing to abide by His commandments.   To believe the word of God and do it not, is to
increase our culpability; such a course but adds hypocrisy
to other sin.   Surely the full penalty provided for wilful
unbelief will fall to the lot of the professed believer who
refuses to yield obedience to the very principles in which he
boasts of having faith.   And what can be said of the sincerity of one who refuses to obey the Divine commands,
except there be specific penalties provided for disobedience?
Can such a one's repentance be sincere, when he now is submissive only through fear of punishment?   However, in
stating this principle for the government of the Saints in
the present dispensation, the Lord's words are more particular and specific, "And he that believeth and is baptized
shall be saved, and he that believeth not, and is not baptized,
shall be damned."[e]

22.   The same doctrine concerning the necessity of baptism was preached by the disciples of Christ, particularly
those who were immediately associated with Him in the ministry.   John the Baptist testifies that he had been appointed
to baptize with water,[f] and, concerning those who accepted
John's teachings, the Savior declared that they, even though
they were publicans, justified God, while the Pharisees and
lawyers who refused to be baptized, "rejected the counsels
of God against themselves,"[g] thereby, most assuredly forfeiting their claim to salvation.   As already pointed out, Peter,
the chief of the apostles, had but one answer to give to the

---

[e] Doc. and Cov., cxii, 29.
[f] John i, 33.
[g] Luke vii, 30.

eager multitude seeking to know the essentials of salvation, "Repent and be baptized, every one of you."[h]

23. Christ's humble compliance with the will of His Father, by submitting to baptism even though He stood sinless, surely declares to the world in language more forceful than words, that none are exempt from this condition, that baptism indeed is a requisite for salvation. So, no evidence of Divine favor, no bestowal of heavenly gifts, excuses man from obedience to this and other requirements of the gospel. Many illustrations of this fact have been given in connection with the purpose of baptism. Saul of Tarsus, though permitted to hear the voice of His Redeemer, could only enter the Church of Christ through the portals of baptism by water and by the Holy Ghost.[i] Afterward he preached baptism, declaring that by that ordinance may "we put on Christ," becoming the children of God. Cornelius, the centurion, was acknowledged of God through prayers and alms, and an angel came to him, and instructed him to send for Peter, who would tell him what to do. The apostle, having been specially prepared by the Lord for this mission, entered the house of the penitent Gentile, though to do such, was to violate the customs of the Jews; and taught him and his family of Christ Jesus. Even while Peter was speaking, the Holy Ghost fell upon his hearers, so that they testified by the gift of tongues, and greatly magnified God.[j] Yet the bestowal of such great gifts in no degree exempted them from compliance with the law of baptism; and Peter commanded them to be baptized in the name of the Lord.

24. Christ's ministers on the western continent were not less energetic in promulgating the doctrine of baptism.

---

[h] Acts ii, 38; see also I Peter iii, 21
[i] Acts ix, 1-18; xxii, 1-16.
[j] Acts x, 30-48.

Lehi[k] and his son Nephi,[l] each testified of the baptism of the Savior, and of the absolute necessity of baptism by water and by the Holy Ghost on the part of all seekers after salvation. Nephi beautifully compares repentance and baptism by water and the Spirit to the gate leading into the fold of Christ.[m] Alma the first preached baptism as indispensable to salvation, calling upon the people to witness unto the Lord by their observance of this principle, that they covenanted to keep His commandments. The second Alma, son of the former, proclaimed baptism as a means of salvation, and consecrated ministers to baptize.[n]

25. During the last century preceding the birth of Christ, the work of God among the Lamanites was begun, by the preaching of faith, repentance, and baptism; Ammon declared this doctrine to King Lamoni and his people.[o] Helaman preached baptism;[p] and in the time of his ministry, less than half a century before Christ's advent on earth, we read that tens of thousands united themselves with the Church by baptism. So also preached Helaman's sons,[q] and his grandson, Nephi.[r] These baptisms were performed in the name of the Messiah who was to come; but when He came to His western flock, He directed that they should be baptized in the name of the Father, and of the Son, and of the Holy Ghost; and bestowed upon twelve chosen servants the authority to officiate in the ordinance,[s] promising the riches of heaven, unto all who would comply with His law, and unto such only.

---

k I Nephi x, 7-10.
l II Nephi xxxi, 4-14.
m II Nephi xxxi, 17.
n Mos. xviii, 8-17: Alma v, 61, 62: ix, 27.
o Alma xix, 35.
p Alma lxii, 45.
q Hel. v, 14-19.
r III Nephi i, 23.
s III Nephi xi, 22-25: xii, 1-2

26.   Evidence is abundant that the Savior regarded the baptized state as an essential condition of membership in His Church; thus, when instituting the sacrament among the Nephites, He instructed His disciples to administer it unto those only who had been properly baptized.*t* Further, we are informed that those who were baptized as Jesus had directed, were called the Church of Christ.*u* True to the Savior's promise, the Holy Ghost came to those who were baptized by His ordained authority, thus adding to water-baptism the higher baptism of fire and the Holy Ghost;*v* and many of them received wonderful manifestations of the Divine approval, seeing and hearing unspeakable things, not lawful to be written.   The faith of the people showed itself in good works,*w* in prayers and fasting*x* in acknowledgment of which Christ reappeared, this time manifesting Himself to the disciples whom He had called to the ministry; and unto them He reiterated the former promises regarding all who were baptized of Him; and to this He added, that, provided they endured to the end, they should be held guiltless in the day of judgment.*y* On that occasion, He repeated the commandment through obedience to which salvation is promised:—"Repent all ye ends of the earth, and come unto me, and be baptized in my name, that ye may be sanctified by the reception of the Holy Ghost, that ye may stand spotless before me at the last day."*z*

27.   Nearly four centuries later, we hear the same proclamation from the lips of Mormon.*a* And Moroni, his son, the solitary representative of a once mighty people, while

t III Nephi xviii, 5, 11, 28-30.

u III Nephi xxvi, 21.

v III Nephi xxvi, 17-18; xxviii, 18; IV Nephi i, 1.

w III Nephi xxvi, 19-20.

x III Nephi xxvii, 1-2.

y III Nephi xxvii, 16.

z III Nephi xxvii, 20.

a Mormon vii, 8-10.

mourning the destruction of his kindred, leaves what at the time he supposed would be his farewell testimony to the truth of this doctrine;[b] then, being spared contrary to his expectations, he reverts again to the sacred theme, realizing the incalculable worth of the doctrine unto any and all who would read his pages; and in what might be regarded as his last words, he testifies to baptism by water and the Spirit as the means of salvation.[c]

28.   And this great principle, proclaimed of old, remains unaltered today; it is truth and changes not.   The elders of the Church today have been commissioned in almost the same words as were used in authorizing the apostles of old:— "Go ye into all the world, preach the gospel to every creature, acting in the authority which I have given you, baptizing in the name of the Father, and of the Son, and of the Holy Ghost; and he that believeth and is baptized shall be saved, and he that believeth not shall be damned."[d]   And again, hear the word of the Lord through Joseph the Prophet unto the elders of the Church:—"Therefore, as I said unto mine apostles I say unto you again, that every soul who believeth on your words, and is baptized by water for the remission of sins shall receive the Holy Ghost."   But, "verily, verily I say unto you, they who believe not on your words, and are not baptized in water, in my name, for the remission of their sins, that they may receive the Holy Ghost, shall be damned, and shall not come into my Father's kingdom where my Father and I am."[e]   In obedience to these commands, the elders of this Church have continued to proclaim the gospel among the nations, preaching faith, repentance, and baptism by water and the Holy Ghost, as essential to salvation.

b Mormon ix, 22-23

c Moroni vi, 1-4.

d Doc. and Cov. lxviii, 8-9.

e Doc. and Cov. lxxxiv, 64, 74; see also cxii, 28-29.

29.   We have examined the doctrines concerning baptism current among the Jews, the Nephites, and the Church of Jesus Christ in this age, and have found the principles taught to be ever the same.   Indeed, we have gone farther back, even to the earliest history of the human race, and have learned that baptism was announced as a saving principle by which Adam was promised forgiveness and salvation.   No one has reason to hope for salvation except by complying with the law of God, of which baptism is an essential part.

NOTES.

1. **Preparation for Baptism:**—The doctrine that baptism, to be acceptable, must be preceded by efficient preparation, was generally taught and understood in the days of Christ, as also in the so-called apostolic period, and the time immediately following.   But this belief gradually fell away, and baptism came to be regarded as an outward form, the application of which depended little, if at all, on the candidates' appreciation, or conception of its purpose; and, as stated in the text, the Lord deemed it wise to re-announce the doctrine in the present dispensation.   Concerning the former belief a few evidences are here given:

"In the first ages of Christianity, men and women were baptized on a profession of faith in the Lord Jesus Christ."—*Canon Farrar.*

"But as Christ enjoins them (Mark xvi, 15-16) to teach before baptizing, and desires that none but believers shall be admitted to baptism, it would appear that baptism is not properly administered unless when it is preceded by faith." * * * In the apostolic age "no one is found to have been admitted to baptism without a previous profession of faith and repentance."—*Calvin.*

"You are not first baptized, and then begin to receive the faith, and have a desire; but when you are to be baptized, you make known your will to the Teacher, and make a full confession of your faith with your own mouth."— *Arnobius*—a rhetorician who wrote in the latter half of the third century.

"In the primitive church, instruction preceded baptism, agreeable to the order of Jesus Christ—'Go, teach all nations, baptizing them,' etc.—*Saurin,* (a French protestant; 1677—1730.)

"In the first two centuries, no one was baptized, except being instructed in the faith and acquainted with the doctrine of Christ, he was able to profess himself a believer; because of those words, 'He that believeth and is baptized.' " —*Salmasius,* (a French author, 1588—1653.)

2. **Historical Notes on Infant Baptism:**—"The baptism of infants, in the first two centuries after Christ, was altogether unknown. * * * The custom of baptizing infants did not begin before the third age after Christ was

born. In the former ages no trace of it appears; and it was introduced without the command of Christ."—*Curcellaeus.*

"It is certain that Christ did not ordain infant baptism. * * * We cannot prove that the apostles ordained infant baptism. From those places where baptism of a whole family is mentioned (as in Acts xvi, 33; I Cor. i, 16) we can draw no such conclusion, because the inquiry is still to be made, whether there were any children in the families of such an age that they were not capable of any intelligent reception of Christianity; for this is the only point on which the case turns. * * * As baptism was closely united with a conscious entrance on Christian communion, faith and baptism were always connected with one another; and thus it is in the highest degree probable, that baptism was performed only in instances where both could meet together, and that the practice of infant baptism was unknown at this (the apostolic) period. * * * That not till so late a period as (at least certainly not earlier than) Irenæus, a trace of infant baptism appears; and that it first became recognized as an apostolic tradition in the course of the third century, is evidence rather against than for the admission of its apostolic origin."—*Johann Neander,* (a German theologian who flourished in the first half of the present century.)

"Let them therefore come when they are grown up—when they can understand—when they are taught whither they are to come. Let them become Christians when they can know Christ."—*Turtullian,* (one of the Latin "Christian Fathers," he lived from 150 to 220 A. D.) Turtullian's almost violent opposition to the practice of pedobaptism is cited by Neander as "a proof that it was then not usually considered an apostolic ordinance; for in that case he would hardly have ventured to speak so strongly against it."

Martin Luther, writing in the early part of the sixteenth century, declared: "It cannot be proven by the sacred scriptures that infant baptism was instituted by Christ, or begun by the first Christians after the apostles."

"By *tekna* the Apostle understands, not infants, but posterity; in which signification the word occurs in many places of the New Testament; (see among others John viii, 39); whence it appears that the argument which is very commonly taken from this passage for the baptism of infants, is of no force, and good for nothing."—*Limborch,* (a native of Holland, and a theologian of repute; he lived 1633—1712.)

LECTURE VII.

BAPTISM.—Continued.

Article 4:—We believe that the first principles and ordinances of the Gospel are: * * * * (3) Baptism by immersion for the remission of sins; * * * *

MODE OF BAPTISM.

1. **Method of Administering Baptism Important:**—In considering the object and the necessity of baptism, much has been said and implied concerning the importance which the Lord attaches to this initiatory rite; it is natural, that the mode of administering the ordinance should also be specifically prescribed. Many Christian sects have some established rite of initiation, in which water figures as a necessary element; though with some the ceremony consists in nothing more than the placing of the priest's moistened finger on the forehead of the candidate; or in the pouring or sprinkling of water on the face; while others consider immersion of the whole body as requisite. The Latter-day Saints hold that the scriptures are devoid of ambiguity regarding the acceptable mode of baptism; and they boldly declare their belief that immersion of the whole body by a duly authorized servant or representative of the Savior, is the only true form. Their reasons for this belief may be summed up as follows: (1) The derivation and former usage of the word baptism, and its cognates, betoken immersion. (2) The symbolism of the rite is preserved in no other form. (3) Scriptural authority, the revealed word of God through the mouths of ancient and modern prophets, prescribes immersion as the true form of baptism.

2. (1) **The Word "Baptism,"** as is generally admitted by philologists, is derived from the Greek *bapto, baptizo*, mean-

ing literally to dip, or to immerse. As is true in the case
of every living language, words may undergo great changes
of meaning; and some writers declare that the term in
question may be as applicable to pouring or sprinkling
with water as to actual immersion. It becomes interesting, therefore, to enquire as to the current meaning of the
term at or near the time of Christ; for, as the Savior
evidently deemed it unnecessary in the course of His instructions concerning baptism, to modify or in any way to
enlarge upon the meaning of the term, the word "baptize"
evidently conveyed a very definite meaning to those who
received His teachings. From the use made of the original
term by the Latin and Greek authors,[a] it is plain that they
understood an actual immersion in water as the only
true signification. The modern Greeks understand
baptism to mean a burial in water, and therefore, as
they adopt the profession of Christianity, they practice
immersion as the only proper form in baptism.[b] Concerning this kind of argument, it should be remembered
that philological evidence is not of the most decisive order.
Let us pass then to the consideration of other and stronger
reasons.

3. (2.) **The Symbolism of the Baptismal Rite** is preserved
in no form other than immersion. The Savior compared
baptism to a birth, and declared such to be essential to the
life that leads to the kingdom of God.[c] Surely none can
say that a birth is represented by a simple sprinkling of
water on the face or head. Not the least of the distinctions
which have contributed to Christ's pre-eminence as a teacher
of teachers, consists in His precise and forceful use of
language; His comparisons are always telling, His meta-

---

a See Note 1.
b See Note 2.
c John iii, 3-5.

phors ever expressive, His parables convincing; and so inappropriate a comparison as is implied in such a false representation of birth, would be entirely foreign to the Great Teacher's methods.

4. Baptism has also been very expressively compared to a burial, followed by a resurrection; and in this symbol of the bodily death and resurrection of His Son, has God promised to grant remission of sins. In writing to the Romans, Paul says:—"Know ye not, that so many of us as were baptized into Jesus Christ were baptized into his death? Therefore we are buried with him by baptism into death: that like as Christ was raised up from the dead by the glory of the Father, even so we also should walk in newness of life. For if we have been planted together in the likeness of his death, we shall be also in the likeness of his resurrection."[b] And again, the same apostle, writes: "Buried with him in baptism, wherein also ye are risen with him through the faith of the operation of God, who hath raised him from the dead."[c] Among all the varied forms of baptism practiced by man, immersion alone typifies a birth, marking the beginning of a new career; or the sleep of the grave, with subsequent victory over death.

5. (3.) **Scriptural Authority** warrants none other form than immersion. Christ Himself was baptized by immersion. We read that after the ceremony, He "went up straightway out of the water."[d] That the baptism of the Savior was acceptable before His Father is abundantly proved by the manifestations immediately following the ordinance—in the descent of the Holy Ghost, and the declaration, "This is my beloved Son in whom I am well pleased." John, surnamed because of his Divine commission, the Baptist, bap-

---

b Rom. vi, 3-5.
c Col. ii, 12.
d Matt. iii, 16-17; Mark i, 10-11.

tized in the river Jordan;[e] and shortly afterward we hear of him baptizing in Ænon, near to Salim, "because there was much water there;"[f] yet had he been baptizing by sprinkling, a small quantity of water would have sufficed for a multitude.

6. We read of baptism following the somewhat speedy conversion of the Ethiopian eunuch, treasurer to the queen, Candace. To him Philip preached the doctrine of Christ, as they rode together in the Ethiopian's chariot; the eunuch, believing the words of his inspired instructor, desired baptism, and Philip consenting, "he commanded the chariot to stand still, and they both *went down into the water*, both Philip and the eunuch, and he baptized him. And when they were come *up out of the water*, the Spirit of the Lord caught away Philip that the eunuch saw him no more; and he went on his way rejoicing."[g]   Surely the record in this case is explicit, that immersion was the mode practised by Philip.

7. **History, other than Scriptural,** proves that for more than two centuries after Christ, immersion was the only mode of baptism generally practiced by professed Christians; and not indeed till near the close of the thirteenth century did other forms become general.[h]   Distortions of ordinances instituted by authority may be expected, if the outward form of such ordinances be attempted after the authority to minister in them has been taken away; yet such distortions are of gradual growth; deformities resulting from constitutional ailments do not develop in a day; we may with reason, therefore, look for the closest imitation of the true form of baptism, as indeed of any other ordinance instituted by Christ, in the period immediately following His personal

e Mark i, 4, 5.
f John iii, 23.
g Acts viii, 26-39
h See Note 3.

ministry, and that of His apostles. Then, as the darkness
of unbelief deepened, the authority given of Christ having
been taken from the earth with His martyred servants, many
innovations appeared, dignitaries of the various churches
becoming a law unto themselves and to their adherents.
Early in the third century, the Bishop of Carthage decided
that persons of weak health might be acceptably baptized
by sprinkling; and with the license thus given, the true
form of baptism gradually fell into disfavor, and unauthorized practices devised by man took its place.

8. **Baptism Among the Nephites** was performed by immersion only. The wide extent to which baptism was preached
and practised among the people from Lehi to Moroni has
been already shown. When the Savior appeared to His people on this hemisphere, He gave them very explicit instructions as to the method of procedure in administering the
ordinance. These are his words:—"Verily I say unto you,
that whoso repenteth of his sins through your words, and
desireth to be baptized in my name, on this wise shall ye
baptize them: behold, ye shall go down and stand in the
water, and in my name shall ye baptize them. and now
behold, these are the words which ye shall say, calling them
by name, saying, *Having authority given me of Jesus Christ,
I baptize you in the name of the Father, and of the Son,
and of the Holy Ghost: Amen* And then shall ye immerse
them in the water, and come forth again out of the water."[i]

9. **Modern Baptism,** as prescribed by revelation, is after
the same pattern. The first baptisms in the present dispensation were those of Joseph Smith and Oliver Cowdery,
who baptized each other according to the directions of the
heavenly messenger from whom they had received authority
to administer in this holy ordinance, and who was none
other than John the Baptist of a former dispensation, the

i III Nephi xi, 23-27.

forerunner of the Messiah. Joseph Smith thus describes the event:—"Accordingly we went and were baptized; I baptized him [Oliver Cowdery] first, and afterwards he baptized me. * * * Immediately on our coming up out of the water after we had been baptized, we experienced great and glorious blessings."

10. In a revelation concerning Church government, dated April, 1830, the Lord prescribed the exact form of baptism, as He desires the ordinance administered in the present dispensation. He said: "Baptism is to be administered in the following manner unto all those who repent:— The person who is called of God and has authority from Jesus Christ to baptize, shall go down into the water with the person who has presented him or herself for baptism, and shall say, calling him or her by name—*Having been commissioned of Jesus Christ, I baptize you in the name of the Father, and of the Son, and of the Holy Ghost. Amen.* Then shall he immerse him or her in the water, and come forth again out of the water."[j]

11. The Lord would not have prescribed the words of this ceremony did He not desire them used, and therefore elders and priests of the Church of Jesus Christ of Latter-day Saints have no personal authority to change the form given of God, by additions, omissions, or alterations of any kind.

BAPTISM AND "RE-BAPTISM."

12. **A Repetition of the Baptismal Ordinance** on the same individual is allowable under certain specific conditions. Thus, if one, having entered the Church by baptism, withdraws from it, or is excommunicated therefrom, and afterwards repents and desires to regain his standing in the Church, he can do so only through baptism. However,

---

j Doc. and Cov. xx, 72-74.

such is a repetition of the initiatory ordinance as previously administered.   There is no ordinance of "re-baptism" in the Church distinct in nature, form or purpose, from other baptism; and, therefore, in administering baptism to a subject who has been formerly baptized, the form of the ceremony is exactly the same as in first baptisms.   The expressions, "I re-baptize you," in place of "I baptize you," and the additions "for the renewal of your covenants," or "for the remission of your sins," though such have been used by officiating elders and priests of the Church, are not authorized.   The dictates of reason unite with the voice of the presiding authorities of the Church, in discountenancing any erratic departures from the course prescribed by the Lord; changes in ceremonies given by authority, can be effected only by authority, and we must look for direction in these matters to those who hold the keys of power on earth.

13.   A "re-baptism," that is, a repetition of the simple ordinance as at first performed, may be allowed under particular circumstances, which seemingly warrant this extraordinary step.   Thus, in the early days of the Church in Utah, its members having come hither through much tribulation, long and toilsome journeyings, accompanied in many instances by prolonged suspension of Church gatherings and other formal religious observances, it was wisely suggested by President Young that the members of the Church should renew the witness of their allegiance to the cause of God, by each one seeking baptism.   Then, as other companies of immigrants continued to arrive, the same conditions of long travel and rough experience applying in their cases, and further, as many of them hailed from foreign branches of the Church still incompletely organized, through which circumstances the actual standing of the members could not be readily proved, the same rite

11

of a second baptism was allowed to them. However, it was never intended that such a practice should become general; far less that it should be established as a rule of action in the Church. The Latter-day Saints do not profess to be Ana-baptists.

14. **"Re-baptisms" Recorded in Scripture** are very few; and in every instance, the existence of special circumstances justifying the action, are readily seen. Thus, we read of Paul baptizing certain professed disciples at Ephesus, though they had already been baptized after the manner of John's baptism.[k] But in this case, the apostle was evidently, and with good reason, suspicious that the baptism of which these spoke had been performed by unauthorized hands, or at least without the proper preliminary education of the candidates; for when he tested the efficacy of their baptism by asking "Have ye received the Holy Ghost since ye believed?" they answered him, "We have not so much as heard whether there be any Holy Ghost." Then asked he in surprise, "Unto what then were ye baptized?" and they replied, "Unto John's baptism." But Paul knew, as we know, that John preached the baptism of repentance by water, but always declared that such was but a preliminary to the greater baptism by fire, which Christ should bring. Therefore, in view of such unsatisfactory evidence concerning the validity of their baptism, Paul had baptism in the name of the Lord Jesus administered unto these twelve devout Ephesians, after which he laid his hands upon them, and they received the Holy Ghost.

15. The baptism instituted by Christ among the Nephites,[l] was very largely a "rebaptism;" for as we have already seen, the doctrine of baptism had been taught and practiced among the people from the time of Lehi; and

---

k Acts xix, 1-6.
l III Nephi xi, 21-28.

surely, Nephi, the first to whom the Savior gave authority
to baptize after His departure, had been previously baptized, for he and his co-laborers in the ministry had been
most zealous in declaring the necessity of baptism.[m] Yet
in this case also, there had probably arisen much impropriety in the manner, and perhaps in the spirit, of administering the ordinance; for the Savior in giving minute
directions concerning the form of baptism, reproved them
for the spirit of contention and disputation that had
previously existed among them regarding the ordinance.[n]
Therefore, the baptism of these people was made valid by
an authoritative administration, after the manner prescribed
of God.

16. Incidentally, our attention is arrested by the fact that
in these cases of re-baptism among the Nephites, the same
ritual was used as in first baptism, and this by explicit instructions of the Lord, coupled with an impressive warning
against disputation. Why should the priests in this day
seek to alter the form to suit the case of a candidate who
has formerly been baptized?

17. **Repeated Baptisms of the same Person** are not sanctioned in the Church. It is easy to fall into the error of
believing that baptism offers a ready means of gaining forgiveness of sins however oft repeated. Such a belief tends
rather to excuse than to prevent sin, inasmuch as the hurtful effects seem to be so easily averted. Neither the written
law of God, nor the instructions of His living Priesthood,
designate baptism as a means of securing forgiveness by
those who are already within the fold of Christ. Unto
such, forgiveness of all sin, if not unto death, has been
promised on confession, and repentance with full purpose
of heart; of them a repetition of the baptismal rite has not

m III Nephi vii, 23-26, etc.
n III Nephi xi, 27-30.

been required; and, were subjects of this class repeatedly baptized, unto them remission of sins would in no wise come, except they repent most sincerely. The frailties of mortality, and our proneness to sin, lead us continually into error; but if we covenant with the Lord at the waters of baptism, and thereafter seek to observe His law, He is merciful to pardon our little transgressions, through repentance sincere and true; and without such repentance, baptism, however oft repeated, would avail us nothing.

BAPTISM FOR THE DEAD.

18. **Baptism Required of All:**—The universal applicability of the law of baptism has been already dwelt upon. Compliance with the ordinance has been shown to be essential to salvation, and this condition applies to all mankind. Nowhere in scripture is a distinction made in this regard between the living and the dead. The dead are those who have lived in mortality upon earth; the living are mortals who yet will pass through the ordained change which we call death. All are children of the same Father, all to be judged and rewarded or punished by the same unerring justice, with the same interpositions of benignant mercy. Christ's atoning sacrifice was offered, not alone for the few who lived upon the earth while He was in the flesh, nor for those who were to be born in mortality after His death, but for all inhabitants of earth then past, present, and future. He was ordained of the Father to be a judge of both quick and dead;[p] He is Lord alike of living and dead,[q] as men speak of dead and living, though all are to be placed in the same position before Him; there will be but a single class, for all live unto Him.[r]

19. **The Gospel yet Unknown to Many:**—Of the multi-

p Acts x, 42; II Tim. iv, 1; I Peter iv, 5.
q Rom xiv, 9.
r Luke xx, 36, 38.

tudes of human beings who have existed on the earth, but few have heard, and fewer have obeyed, the law of the gospel. In the course of the world's history, there have been long periods of spiritual darkness, when the gospel was not preached upon the earth; when there was no authorized representative of the Lord officiating in the saving ordinances of the kingdom. Such a condition has never existed except as the result of the unbelief and waywardness of the people. When mankind have persistently trodden the pearls of truth into the mire, and have sought to slay and rend the bearers of the jewels, in justice not more than in mercy, these treasures of heaven have been taken away, until a more appreciative posterity could be raised up. It may very properly be asked, What provisions are made in the economy of God for the eventual salvation of those who have thus neglected the requirements of the Word, and for those who have never heard the gospel tidings?

20. According to sectarian dogmas which have prevailed among many so-called Christian sects during the obscurity of the spiritual night, and which are yet zealously promulgated, never-ending punishment or interminable bliss, unchanging in kind or degree, will be the lot of every soul; the award being made according to the condition of the spirit at the time of bodily death; a life of sin being thus entirely nullified by a death-bed repentance; and an honorable career, if unmarked by ceremonies of the established sects, being followed by the tortures of hell without the hope of relief. Such a belief must rank with the dread heresy which proclaims the condemnation of innocent babes who have not been sprinkled by man's assumed authority.

21. It is blasphemous to thus attribute caprice and vindictiveness to the Divine nature. In the justice of God, no soul will be condemned under any law which has not been made known unto him. It is true, eternal punishment has

been decreed as the lot of the wicked; but the true meaning of this terrible expression has been given by the Lord Himself:[s] eternal punishment is God's punishment; endless punishment is God's punishment, for "Endless" and "Eternal" are among His names, and the words are descriptive of His attributes. No soul will be kept in prison or continued in torment beyond the time requisite to work the needed reformation and to vindicate justice, for which ends alone punishment is imposed. And no one will be permitted to enter any kingdom of glory to which he is not entitled through obedience to law.

22. **The Gospel to be Preached to the Dead:**—It is plain, then, that the gospel must be proclaimed in the spirit world; and that such work is provided for, the scriptures abundantly prove. Peter, describing the mission of his Redeemer, thus declares this truth:—"For this cause was the gospel preached also to them that are dead, that they might be judged according to men in the flesh, but live according to God in the spirit."[t] The inauguration of this work among the dead was effected by Christ in the interval between His death and resurrection. While His body lay in the tomb, His spirit was ministering to the spirits of the departed:—"By which also he went and preached unto the spirits in prison; which sometime were disobedient when once the long-suffering of God waited in the days of Noah, while the ark was a preparing, wherein few, that is, eight souls were saved by water."[u]

23. Other scriptures sustain the position, that while in a disembodied state, Christ did not go to the place usually termed Heaven,—the abode of His Father; but was laboring among the dead, who greatly needed His ministry. One of

---

s See page 63; Doc. and Cov. xix, 10-12.

t I Peter iv, 6.

u I Peter iii, 18-20.

the malefactors who suffered crucifixion by His side, through humility, won from the dying Savior the promise, "Today shalt thou be with me in Paradise."[v] Yet, three days afterward, the Lord, then a resurrected Being, declared to the sorrowing Magdalene, "I have not yet ascended to my Father."[w]

24. If it was deemed proper and just that the gospel be carried to the spirits who were disobedient in the days of Noah, is it not reasonable to conclude that like opportunities will be placed within the reach of others who have rejected the word at different times? For the same spirit of neglect and disobedience which characterized the time of Noah, has ever existed.[x] And further, if, in the plan of God, provisions be made for the redemption of the wilfully disobedient, of those who actually spurn the truth, can we believe that the still greater multitudes of spirits who have never heard the gospel, are to be left in punishment eternally? No; God has decreed that even the heathen nations, and those that knew no law, shall be redeemed.[y] The good gifts of the Father are not confined to this sphere of action, but will be distributed in justice throughout eternity. Upon all who reject the word of God in this life will fall the penalties provided for such act; but after the debt has been paid, the prison doors will be opened, and the spirits once confined in suffering, now chastened and clean, will come forth to partake of the glory provided for their class.

25. **Christ's Work among the Dead was Foretold:**—Centuries before Christ came in the flesh, the prophets rejoiced in the knowledge that through Him would salvation be carried to the dead, as well as to the living. Speaking of the punishment to be brought upon the proud and haughty of

v Luke xxiii, 39-43.

w John xx, 17.

x Luke xvii, 26.

y Doc. and Cov. xlv, 54.

the earth, Isaiah declares: "And they shall be gathered together, as prisoners are gathered in the pit, and shall be shut up in the prison, and after many days shall they be visited."[z] The same great prophet thus testifies concerning the work of the coming Redeemer; He is "to open the blind eyes, to bring out the prisoners from the prison, and them that sit in darkness out of the prison house."[a] And David, singing to the music of inspiration concerning the redemption from the grave, exclaims: "Therefore my heart is glad, and my glory rejoiceth: my flesh also shall rest in hope. For thou wilt not leave my soul in hell; neither wilt thou suffer thine Holy One to see corruption. Thou wilt shew me the path of life; in thy presence is fulness of joy; at thy right hand there are pleasures for evermore."[b]

26. **Work of the Living for the Dead:**—The redemption of the dead will be effected in strict accordance with the law of God, which is written in justice, and framed in mercy. It is alike impossible for any spirit, in the flesh or disembodied, to obtain even the promise of eternal glory, except on condition of obedience to the laws and ordinances of the gospel. And, as baptism is essential to the salvation of the living, it is likewise indispensable to the redemption of the dead. This was known by the Saints of old, and hence the doctrine of baptism for the dead was taught among them. In an epistle addressed to the Saints at Corinth, Paul expounded the principles of the resurrection, whereby the bodies of the dead are to be brought forth from the graves. "Christ the first fruits, and afterward they that are Christ's," and as proof that this doctrine of the resurrection was included in the gospel as they had

---

[z] Isa. xxiv, 22.

[a] Isa. xlii, 6-7.

[b] Psa. xvi, 9-11.

received and professed it, the apostle asks: "Else what shall they do which are baptized for the dead, if the dead rise not at all? why are they then baptized for the dead?"[c] These words are unambiguous, and the fact that they are presented without explanation or comment, argues that the principle of baptism for the dead was understood among the people to whom the letter was addressed.

27. The necessity of vicarious work is here shown,—the living laboring in behalf of the dead; the children doing for their progenitors what is beyond the power of the latter to do for themselves. Many and various are the interpretations rendered by erring human wisdom, on this plain statement of Paul's; yet the simple and earnest seeker after truth finds little difficulty in comprehending the meaning. In words which form the closing sentences of the Old Testament, the prophet Malachi predicted the great work to be carried on in behalf of the dead during the latter days: "Behold, I will send you Elijah the prophet before the coming of the great and dreadful day of the Lord: And he shall turn the heart of the fathers to the children, and the heart of the children to their fathers, lest I come and smite the earth with a curse."[d] It is a current belief among many Bible students, that this prophecy had reference to the birth and ministry of John the Baptist,[e] upon whom indeed rested and remained the spirit and power of Elias, as the angel had fortold;[f] but we have no record of Elijah ministering unto John; and moreover the results of the latter's ministry warrant no conclusion that in him did the prophecy find its full realization.

28. We must therefore look to a later date in the world's history for a fulfilment of Malachi's prediction. On the

---

c I Cor. xv 29.

d Mal. iv, 5-6.

e Matt. xi, 14; xvii, 11; Mark ix, 11; Luke i, 17.

f Luke i, 17; Doc. and Cov. xxvii, 7.

21st of September, 1823, Joseph Smith[g] received a visitation of a heavenly being who announced himself as Moroni,
sent from the presence of God.   In the course of his instructions to the chosen youth, this heavenly personage
quoted the prophecy of Malachi, already referred to, but in
language slightly different from, and certainly more expressive than, that appearing in the ordinary translation of
the scriptures; the angel's version is as follows: "For
behold the day cometh that shall burn as an oven, and all
the proud, yea and all that do wickedly, shall burn as
stubble, for they that come shall burn them, saith the Lord
of Hosts, that it shall leave them neither root nor branch.
Behold I will reveal unto you the Priesthood by the hand of
Elijah the prophet, before the coming of the great and
dreadful day of the Lord.   And he shall plant in the hearts
of the children the promises made to the fathers, and the
hearts of the children shall turn to their fathers; if it were
not so the whole earth would be utterly wasted at His
coming."[h]

29.   In a glorious manifestation to Joseph Smith and
Oliver Cowdery, given in the Kirtland Temple, April 3,
1836, there appeared unto them Elijah the prophet, who
was taken to heaven without tasting death; he declared
unto them: "Behold, the time has fully come which was
spoken of by the mouth of Malachi, testifying that he
(Elijah) should be sent before the great and dreadful day of
the Lord come, to turn the hearts of the fathers to the
children and the children to the fathers, lest the whole
earth be smitten with a curse.   Therefore the keys of this
dispensation are committed into your hands, and by this
ye may know that the great and dreadful day of the Lord
is near, even at the doors."[i]

---

g See page 10.
h Compare verses 1, 5, and 6, Mal. iv.
i Doc. and Cov. cx, 13-16.

30. The Fathers and the Children Mutually Dependent:— One of the great principles underlying the doctrine of salvation for the dead is that of the mutual dependence of the fathers and the children. As the Prophet Joseph taught the Saints,[j] but for the establishment of a welding link between the departed fathers and the living children, the earth would be smitten with a curse. The plan of God provides that neither the children nor the fathers can alone be made perfect; and the necessary union is effected through baptism and associated ordinances for the dead. The manner in which the hearts of the children and those of the fathers, are turned toward one another is made plain through these scriptures. As the children learn that without the aid of their progenitors they cannot attain perfection, assuredly will their hearts be opened, their faith will be kindled, and good works will be attempted, for the redemption of their dead; and the departed, learning from the ministers of the gospel laboring among them, that they must depend upon their children as vicarious saviors, will seek to sustain their still mortal representatives with faith and prayer for the perfecting of those labors of love.

31. And love, which is a power in itself, is thus intensified. Aside from the emotions which are stirred within the soul by the presence of the Divine, there are few feelings stronger and purer than the love for kindred. Heaven would not be all we wish were family love unknown there.[k] Affection there will differ from its earthly type, in being deeper, stronger, purer. And thus in the mercy of God, His erring, mortal children, who have taken upon themselves the name of Christ on earth, may become in a limited sphere, each a savior in the house of his fathers, and that too by vicarious labor and sacrifice, rendered in humility,

---

[j] Doc. and Cov. cxxviii, 18; see also this entire section and sec. cxxvii.

[k] See Note 4.

and, as represented in the baptismal ordinance, typical of the death, burial, and resurrection of the Redeemer.

32. **The Labor for the Dead is Two-Fold:**—That performed on earth would be incomplete, but for its supplement and counterpart beyond the vail. Missionary labor is in progress there, whereby the tidings of the gospel are carried to the departed spirits, who thus learn of the work done in their behalf on earth. What glorious possibilities concerning the purposes of God, are thus presented to our view! How the mercy of God is magnified by these evidences of His love! How often do we behold friends and loved ones, whom we count among earth's fairest and best, stricken down by the shafts of death, seemingly in spite of the power of faith and the ministrations of the Priesthood of God! Yet who of us can tell but that the spirits so called away are needed in the labor of redemption beyond, preaching perhaps the gospel to the spirits of their forefathers, while others of the same family are officiating in a similar behalf on earth?

33. As far as the Divine will has been revealed, it requires that the outward ordinances, such as baptism in water, the laying on of hands for the bestowal of the Holy Ghost, and the higher endowments that follow, be attended to on earth, a proper representative in the flesh acting as proxy for the dead. The results of such labors are to be left with God. It is not to be supposed that by these ordinances the departed are in any way compelled to accept the obligation, nor that they are in the least hindered in the exercise of their free agency. They will accept or reject, according to their condition of humility or hostility in respect to things divine; but the work so done for them on earth will be of avail when wholesome argument and reason have shown them their true position.

TEMPLES.

34. Temples or other sacred places are required for the performance of these holy ordinances. Whenever an organization of the priesthood has existed on earth, the Lord has required the preparation of places suited to His use, where the rites of His Church may be performed. It is but proper that such a structure should be the result of the people's best efforts, inasmuch as it is made by them an offering unto the Lord. In every age of the world, the chosen people have been a temple-building people. Shortly after Israel's deliverance from the bondage of Egypt, the Lord called upon the people to construct a sanctuary to His name, the plan of which He minutely explained. Though this was but a tent, it was elaborately furnished and appointed; the choicest possessions of the people being used in its construction.[l] And the Lord accepted this offering of His wandering people, by manifesting His glory therein, and there revealing Himself.[m] When the people had settled in the promised land, the Tabernacle of the congregation was given a more permanent resting place,[n] yet it still was honored for its sacred purpose, until superseded by the Temple of Solomon as the sanctuary of the Lord.

35. This temple, one of the most gorgeous structures ever erected by man for sacred service, was dedicated with imposing ceremonies; but its splendor was of short duration; for, within less than forty years from the time of its completion, its glory declined, and finally it fell a prey to the flames. A partial restoration of the temple was made after the Jews returned from their captivity; and through the friendly influence of Cyrus and Darius, the temple of Zerubbabel

---

l Exo. xxv; xxxv, 22.

m Exo. xl, 34-38.

n Josh. xviii, 1.

was dedicated.[o] That the Lord accepted this effort of His people to maintain a sanctuary to His name, is fully shown by the spirit that actuated its officers, among whom were Zechariah, Haggai, and Malachi. This temple remained standing for nearly five centuries, when, but a few years before the birth of the Savior, a restoration of the edifice was begun by wicked Herod the Great, and the term "Temple of Herod" passed into history.[p] The vail of this temple was rent at the time of the crucifixion, and in the year 70 A. D. the destruction of the building was accomplished by Titus.

36. **Modern Temples:**—From that time until the present dispensation, no other temples have been reared on the eastern continent. It is true, imposing edifices have been erected for the purposes of worship; but a colossal structure does not necessarly constitute a temple. A temple is more than a church-building, a meeting-house, a tabernacle, or a synagogue; it is a place specially prepared by dedication unto the Lord, and marked by His acceptance, for the performing of the ordinances pertaining to the Holy Priesthood. The Latter-day Saints, true to the characteristics of the chosen of God,[r] have been from the first a temple-building people. Only a few months after the organization of the Church in the present dispensation, the Lord made reference to a temple which was to be built.[s] In July, 1831, the Lord designated a spot in Independence, Mo., as the site of a future temple;[t] but the work of construction thereon has not yet been consummated, as is likewise the case with the temple site at Far West, on which the corner-stone was laid July 4, 1838.

o I Kings vi; viii.

p Ezra i, iii, vi.

r Doc. and Cov. cxxiv, 39.

s Doc. and Cov. xxxvi, 8.

t Doc. and Cov. lvii, 3.

37.   There have been already erected and dedicated in the
present dispensation, six temples, in each of which sacred
ordinances have been administered—these comprise the temples at Kirtland, Ohio; Nauvoo, Ill.; St. George, Logan,
Manti, and Salt Lake City, Utah.   The temples at Kirtland
and Nauvoo have been abandoned, as the Saints were driven
westward before the fury of wicked mobs; and the Nauvoo
temple has been demolished.   The Utah temples are still
preserved to the service of God; and the magnitude and
grandeur of the work accomplished within their sacred precincts, tell of the gracious acceptance by the Lord, to whose
name they have been reared, and the continuance of Divine
favor toward them and the people.   In these holy places, the
work of redeeming the dead and endowing the living is in
uninterrupted progress.

NOTES.

1. **Usage of the Term "Baptize" in Ancient Times:**—The following
instances show the ordinary meaning attached to the Greek term from which
our word "baptize" is derived.   In all, the idea of immersion is plainly intended:
—(For these and other examples, see Millennial Star, Vol. XXI, p. 687-8.)

Polybius, a writer of history, who flourished during the second century before
Christ, uses the following expressions:—In describing a naval conflict between
the Carthaginian and Roman fleets off the shores of Sicily he says, "If any were
hard pressed by the enemy they withdrew safely back, on account of their fast
sailing into the open sea: and then turning round and falling on those of their
pursuers who were in advance, they gave them frequent blows and 'baptized'
many of their vessels."—Book I, ch. 51.

The same writer thus refers to the passage of the Roman soldiers through
the river Trebia, "When the passage of the river Trebia came on, which had
risen above its usual current, on account of the rain which had fallen, the
infantry with difficulty, crossed over, being 'baptized' up to the chest."—Book
III, ch. 72.

Describing a catastrophe which befel the Roman ships at Syracuse, Polybius
states: "Some were upset, but the greater number, their prow being thrown
down from a height, were 'baptized' and became full of sea."

Strabo who lived during the time of Christ, used the term "baptized" in the
same sense.   He thus describes an instrument used in fishing:—"And if it fall
into the sea it is not lost: for it is compacted of oak and pine wood: so that even

if the oak is 'baptized' by its weight, the remaining part floats and is easily recovered.''

Strabo refers to the buoyancy of certain saline waters thus:—''These have the taste of salt water, but a different nature, for even persons who cannot swim are not liable to be 'baptized' in them, but float like logs on the surface.''

Referring to a salt spring in Tatta, the same writer says, ''So easily does the water form a crust round everything 'baptized' into it that if persons let down a circlet of rushes they will draw up wreaths of salt.''

Speaking of a species of pitch from the lake Sirbonis, Strabo says:—''It will float on the surface owing to the nature of the water, which, as we said is such as to render swimming unnecessary, and such that one who walks upon it is not 'baptized.' ''

Dio Cassius, speaking of the effects of a severe storm near Rome says, ''The vessels which were in the Tiber, which were lying at anchor near the city, and to the river's mouth, were 'baptized.' ''

The same author thus alludes to the fate of some of Curio's soldiers while fleeting before the forces of Juba:—''Not a few of these fugitives perished, some being knocked down in their attempts to get on board the vessels, and others, even when in the boats, being 'baptized' through their weight.''

Alluding to the fate of the Byzantians who endeavored to escape the siege by taking to the sea, he says, ''Some of those, from the extreme violence of the wind, were 'baptized.' ''

2. Baptism Among the Greeks:—''The native Greeks must understand their own language better than foreigners, and they have always understood the word baptism to signify dipping; and therefore from their first embracing of Christianity to this day they have always baptized, and do yet baptize, by immersion.''—*Robinson.*

3. Early Form of Christian Baptism:—History furnishes ample proof that in the first century after the death of Christ, baptism was administered solely by immersion. Tertullian thus refers to the immersion ceremony common in his day, ''There is no difference whether one is washed in a sea or in a pool, in a river or in a fountain, in a lake or in a channel: nor is there any difference between those whom John dipped in Jordan, and those whom Peter dipped in the Tiber. * * * We are immersed in the water.''

The following are but a few of the instances on record. (See Millennial Star, Vol. XXI, p. 769-770.):

Justin Martyr describes the ceremony as practiced by himself. First describing the preparatory examination of the candidate, he proceeds, ''After that they are led by us to where there is water, and are born again in that kind of new birth by which we ourselves were born again. For upon the name God, the Father and Lord of all, and of Jesus Christ, our Savior, and of the Holy Spirit, the immersion in water is performed, because the Christ hath also said, 'Except a man be born again, he cannot enter into the kingdom of heaven.' ''

Bishop Bennet says concerning the practices of the early Christians:—''They led them into the water and laid them down in the water as a man is laid in a grave; and then they said those words 'I baptize (or wash) thee in the name of the Father, Son, and Holy Ghost;' then they raised them up again, and clean garments were put on them; from whence came the phrases of being baptized into Christ's death, of being buried with Him by baptism into death, of our being risen with Christ, and of our putting on the Lord Jesus Christ, of putting off the old man, and putting on the new."

"That the apostles immersed whom they baptized there is no doubt. * * * And that the ancient church followed their example is very clearly evinced by innumerable testimonies of the fathers."— *Vossius.*

"Burying as it were the person baptized in the water, and raising him out again, without question was anciently the more usual method."—*Archbishop Secker.*

" 'Immersion' was the usual method in which baptism was administered in the early Church. * * * Immersion was undoubtedly a common mode of administering baptism, and was not discontinued when infant baptism prevailed. * * * Sprinkling gradually took the place of immersion without any formal renunciation of the latter."—*Canon Farrar.*

4. The Fathers and the Children:—"The revelation in our day of the doctrine of baptism for the dead may be said to have constituted a new epoch in the history of our race. At the time the Prophet Joseph received that revelation, the belief was general in Christendom that at death the destiny of the soul was fixed irrevocably and for all eternity. If not rewarded with endless happiness, then endless torment was its doom, beyond all possibility of redemption or change. The horrible and monstrous doctrine, so much at variance with every element of Divine justice, was generally believed, that the heathen nations who had died without a knowledge of the true God, and the redemption wrought out by His Son, Jesus Christ, would all be eternally consigned to hell. The belief upon this point is illustrated by the reply of a certain Bishop to the inquiry of the king of the Franks, when the king was about to submit to baptism at the hands of the bishop. The king was a heathen, but had concluded to accept the form of religion then called Christianity. The thought occurred to him that if baptism were necessary for his salvation, what had become of his dear ancestors who had died heathens? This thought framed itself into an inquiry which he addressed to the bishop. The prelate, less politic than many of his sect, bluntly told him they had gone to hell. "Then by Thor, I will go there with them," said the king, and thereupon refused to accept baptism or become a Christian."—Geo. Q. Cannon's *Life of Joseph Smith*, p. 510.

LECTURE VIII.

THE HOLY GHOST.

Article 4:—We believe that the first principles and ordinances of the Gospel are: * * * (4) Laying on of hands for the gift of the Holy Ghost.

1. **The Holy Ghost Promised:**—John the Baptist, proclaiming in the wilderness repentance and baptism by water, foretold a second higher baptism, which he characterized as being of fire and the Holy Ghost; this was to follow his administration,[a] and was to be given by that Mightier One whose shoes the Baptist considered himself unworthy to bear. That the holder of this superior authority was none other than the Christ is proved by John's solemn record:—"Behold the Lamb of God * * * This is he of whom I said, After me cometh a man which is preferred before me * * * And I knew him not, but he that sent me to baptize with water, the same said unto me: Upon whom thou shalt see the Spirit descending and remaining on him, the same is he which baptizeth with the Holy Ghost."[b]

2. In declaring to Nicodemus[c] the necessity of baptism, the Savior did not stop with a reference to the watery birth alone, that being incomplete without the quickening influence of the Spirit; born of water and of the Spirit is the necessary condition of him who is to gain admittance to the kingdom. Many of the scriptural passages quoted in proof of the purpose and necessity of baptism, show baptism by fire and the Holy Ghost to be closely associated with the prescribed ordinance of immersion in water.

a Matt. iii, 2-3, 11; Mark i, 8; Luke iii, 16.
b John i, 29-33.
c John iii, 3-5.

3. Christ's instructions to His apostles comprise repeated promises concerning the coming of the "Comforter," and the "Spirit of Truth,"[d] by which expressive terms the Holy Ghost is designated.   In His last interview with the apostles, at the termination of which He ascended into heaven, the Lord repeated these assurances of a spiritual baptism, which was then soon to take place.[e] The fulfilment of this great prediction was realized at the succeeding Pentecost, when the apostles, having assembled together, were endowed with mighty power from heaven,[f] being filled with the Holy Ghost so that they spake with other tongues as the Spirit gave them utterance.   Among other manifestations of this heavenly gift, may be mentioned the appearance of flames of fire like unto tongues, which rested upon each of them.   The promise so miraculously fulfilled upon themselves was repeated by the apostles to those who sought their instruction.   Peter, addressing the Jews on that same day, declared, on the condition of their acceptable repentance and baptism, "ye shall receive the gift of the Holy Ghost."[g]

4. Book of Mormon evidence is not less conclusive regarding the Holy Spirit's visitation unto those who obey the requirements of water baptism.   Nephi, Lehi's son, bore solemn record of this truth,[h] as made known to him by the voice of God.   And the words of the resurrected Savior to the Nephites come in plainness indisputable, and with authority not to be questioned, proclaiming the baptism of fire and the Holy Ghost unto all those who obey the preliminary requirements.[i]

---

d John xiv, 16-17, 26; xv, 26; xvi, 7, 13.
e Acts i, 5.
f Acts ii, 1-4.
g Acts ii, 38.
h II Nephi xxxi, 8, 12-14, 17.
i III Nephi xi, 36; xii, 2.

5.   Unto the Saints in the dispensation of the fulness of times, the same great promise has been made. "I say unto you again," spake the Lord in addressing certain elders of the Church, "that every soul that believeth on your words, and is baptized by water for the remission of sins shall receive the Holy Ghost."[j]

6.   **Personality and Powers of the Holy Ghost:**—The Holy Ghost is associated with the Father and the Son in the Godhead.   In the light of revelation, we are instructed as to the distinct personality of the Holy Ghost.   He is a Being endowed with the attributes and powers of Deity, and not a mere thing, force, or essence.   The term Holy Ghost and its common synonyms, Spirit of God,[k] Spirit of the Lord, or simply, Spirit,[l] Comforter,[m] and Spirit of Truth,[n] occur in the scriptures with plainly different meanings, referring in some cases to the person of God, the Holy Ghost, and in other instances to the power or authority of this great Being.   The context of such passages will show which of these significations applies.

7.   The Holy Ghost undoubtedly possesses personal powers and affections; these attributes exist in Him in perfection.   Thus, He teaches and guides,[o] testifies of the Father and the Son,[p] reproves for sin,[q] speaks, commands, and commissions,[r] makes intercession for sinners,[s] is grieved,[t]

---

j Doc. and Cov. lxxxiv, 64.

k Matt. iii, 16; xii, 28; I Nephi xiii, 12.

l I Nephi iv, 6; xi, 8; Mos. xiii, 5; Acts ii, 4; viii, 29; x, 19; Rom. viii, 10, 26; I Thess. v, 19.

m John xiv, 16-26; xv, 26.

n John xv, 26; xvi, 13.

o John xiv, 26; xvi, 13.

p John xv, 26.

q John xvi, 8.

r Acts x, 19; xiii, 2; Rev. ii, 7; I Nephi iv, 6; xi, 2-8.

s Rom, viii, 26.

t Eph. iv, 30.

searches and investigates,[u] entices,[v] and knows all things.[w] These are not mere figurative expressions, but plain statements of the attributes and characteristics of this great Personage. That the Holy Ghost is capable of manifesting Himself in the true form and figure of God, after which image man is shaped, is indicated by the wonderful interview between the Spirit and Nephi, in which He revealed Himself to the prophet, questioned him concerning his desires and belief, instructed him in the things of God, speaking face to face with the man. "I spake unto him," says Nephi, "as a man speaketh; for I beheld that he was in the form of a man, yet nevertheless I knew that it was the Spirit of the Lord; and he spake unto me as a man speaketh to another."[x] However, the Holy Ghost does not possess a tangible body of flesh and bones, as do both the Father and the Son, but is a personage of spirit.[y]

8. Much of the confusion existing in our human conceptions concerning the nature of the Holy Ghost, arises from the common failure to segregate our ideas of His person and powers. Plainly, such expressions as being filled with the Holy Ghost,[z] and the Spirit falling upon men, have reference to the powers and influences which emanate from God and which are characteristic of Him; for the Holy Ghost may in this way operate simultaneously upon many persons, even though they be widely separated; whereas the actual person of the Holy Ghost cannot be in more than one place at a time. Yet we read, that through the power of the Spirit, the Father and the Son operate in their creative acts

---

[u] I Cor. ii, 4-10.

[v] Mos. iii, 19.

[w] Alma vii, 13.

[x] I Nephi xi, 11.

[y] Doc. and Cov. cxxx, 22.

[z] Luke i, 15, 67; iv, 1; Acts vi, 3; xiii, 9; Alma xxxvi, 24; Doc. and Cov. cvii, 56.

and in their general dealings with the human family.[a]   The
Holy Ghost may be regarded as the minister of the Godhead,
carrying into effect the decisions of the Supreme Council.

9.   In the execution of these great purposes, the Holy
Ghost directs and controls the numerous forces of Nature,
of which indeed a few, and these perhaps of the minor
order, wonderful as even the least of them seems to man,
have thus far been made known to the human mind.
Gravitation, sound, heat, light, and the still more mysterious, seemingly supernatural power of electricity, are but
the common servants of the Holy Spirit in His operations.
No earnest thinker, no sincere investigator supposes that
he has yet learned of all the forces existing in and operating upon matter; indeed the observed phenomena of nature,
yet wholly inexplicable to him, far outnumber those for
which he has devised even a partial explanation.   There are
powers and forces at the command of God, compared with
which, electricity, the most occult of all the physical
agencies controlled in any degree by man, is as the pack-
horse to the locomotive, the foot messenger to the telegraph,
the raft of logs to the ocean steamer.   Man has scarcely
glanced at the enginery of creation; and yet the few forces
known to him have brought about miracles and wonders,
which but for their actual realization would be beyond
belief.   These mighty agencies, and the mightier ones still
to man unknown, and many perhaps, to the present condition of the human mind unknowable, do not constitute
the Holy Ghost, but the mere means ordained to serve
Divine purposes.

10.   Subtler, mightier, and more far-reaching still than
any or all of the physical forces of nature, are the powers
that operate upon conscious organisms, the means by which

_a_ Gen. i, 2;   Neh. ix, 30; Job xxvi, 13;   Psalms civ, 30.   Isa. xlii, 1;   Acts x, 19;
I Nephi x, 19; Alma xii, 3:   Doc. and Cov. cv, 36;   xcvii, i;

the mind, the heart, the soul of man may be affected. In our ignorance of the true nature of electric energy, we speak of it as a fluid; and so by analogy the forces through which the mind is governed have been called spiritual fluids. The true nature of these higher powers is unknown to us, for the conditions of comparison and analogy, so necessary to our frail human reasoning, are wanting; still the effects are experienced by all. As the conducting medium in an electric current is capable of conveying but a limited current, the maximum strength depending upon the resistance offered by the conductor; and, as separate circuits of different degrees of conductivity may carry currents of widely varying intensity; so human souls are of varied capacity with respect to the diviner powers. But, as the medium is purified, as the obstructions are removed, so the resistance to the energy decreases, and the forces manifest themselves with greater perfection. By analogous processes of purification, may our spirits be made more susceptible to the power of life, which is an emanation from the Spirit of God. Therefore are we taught to pray by word and action for a constantly increasing portion of the Spirit, that is, the power of the Spirit, which is a measure of the favor of God unto us.

11. **The Office of the Holy Ghost** in His ministrations among men is very fully described in scripture. He is a Teacher sent from the Father;[b] and unto those who are entitled to His tuition He will reveal all things necessary for the soul's advancement. Through the influences of the Holy Spirit, the powers of the human mind may be quickened and increased, so that things past may be brought to remembrance. He will serve as a guide in things divine unto all who will obey Him,[c] enlightening every man,[d] in

b John xiv, 26.

c Doc. and Cov, xlv, 57.

d Doc. and Cov. lxxxiv, 45-47.

proportion to his humility and obedience;[e] unfolding the mysteries of God,[f] as the knowledge thus revealed may tend to spiritual growth; conveying knowledge from God to man;[g] sanctifying those who have been cleansed through obedience to the requirements of the gospel;[h] manifesting all things;[i] and bearing witness unto men concerning the existence and infallibility of the Father and the Son.[j]

12.   And not alone does the Holy Ghost bring to mind the past, and explain the things of the present, but His power is manifested likewise in prophecy concerning the future;—"He shall show you things to come," declared the Savior to the apostles in promising the advent of the Comforter.   Adam, the first prophet of earth, under the influence of the Holy Ghost "predicted whatsoever should befall his posterity unto the latest generation."[k]

13.   The power of the Holy Ghost then is the spirit of prophecy and revelation; His office is that of enlightenment of the mind, quickening of the intellect, and sanctification of the soul.

14.   **To Whom is the Holy Ghost given?** Not to all indiscriminately.   The Redeemer declared to the apostles of old, "I will pray to the Father and he shall give you another Comforter, that he may abide with you forever; Even the Spirit of truth; whom the world cannot receive, because it seeth him not, neither knoweth him."[l] Clearly, then, a certain condition of the candidate is requisite before the Holy Ghost can be bestowed, that is to say, before the person can receive a right to the company

---

e Doc. and Cov. cxxxvi, 33.

f I Nephi x, 19.

g Doc. and Cov. cxxi, 43.

h Alma xiii, 12.

i Doc and Cov. xviii, 18.

j John xv, 26; Acts v, 32; xx. 23; I Cor. ii, 11; xii, 3; III Nephi xi, 32.

k Doc. and Cov. cvii, 56.

l John xiv, 16, 17.

and ministrations of the Spirit.   God grants the Holy Ghost unto the obedient; and the bestowal of this gift follows faith, repentance, and baptism by water.

15.   The apostles of old promised the ministration of the Holy Ghost unto those only who had received baptism by water for the remission of sins;[m] John the Baptist gave assurances of the visitation of the Holy Ghost to those only, who were baptized unto repentance.[n] The instance of Paul's rebaptizing the twelve disciples at Ephesus before he conferred upon them the Holy Ghost, on account of a probable lack of propriety or of authority in their first baptism,[o] has already been dwelt upon.   We read of a remarkable manifestation of power among the people of Samaria,[p] to whom Philip went and preached the Lord Jesus; the people with one accord accepted his testimony and sought baptism. Then came unto them Peter and John, through whose ministrations the Holy Ghost came upon the new converts, whereas upon none of them had the Spirit previously fallen, though all had been baptized.

16.   The Holy Ghost dwells not in tabernacles unfit and unworthy.   Paul makes the sublime declaration that the body of man when filled with the power of the Holy Ghost becomes a temple of this Spirit; and the apostle points out the terrible responsibility of defiling a structure sanctified by so holy a presence.[q]   Faith in God leads to repentance of sin, this is followed by baptism in water for the remission of sins, and this in turn by the bestowal of the Holy Ghost, through whose power come sanctification and the specific gifts of God.

17.   **An Exception to the Prescribed Order** is shown in the

m Acts ii, 38.

n Matt, iii, 11: Mark i, 8.

o Acts xix, 1-7.

p Acts viii, 5-8, 12, 14-17.

q I Cor. iii, 6.

case of the devout Gentile, Cornelius, unto whom, together with his family, came the Holy Ghost, with such power that they spake with new tongues to the glorification of God, and this before their baptism.[r]   But sufficient reason for this departure from the usual order is seen in the prejudice that existed among the Jews toward other nations, which, but for the Lord's direct instructions to Peter, would have hindered, if indeed it did not prevent, the apostle from ministering unto the Gentiles; as it was, his act was loudly condemned by his own people; but he answered their criticisms with a recital of the lesson given him of God, and the undeniable evidence of the Divine will as shown in the reception of the Holy Ghost by Cornelius and his family before baptism.

18.   And in another sense the Holy Ghost has frequently operated for good through persons that are unbaptized; indeed, some measure of this power is given to all mankind; for, as seen already, the Holy Spirit is the power of intelligence, of wise direction, of development, of life.   Manifestation of the power of God, as made plain through the operations of the Spirit, are seen in the triumphs of ennobling art, the discoveries of true science, and the events of history; with all of which the carnal mind may believe that God takes no direct concern.   Not a truth has ever been made the property of human kind, except through the power of that great Spirit who exists to do the bidding of the Father and the Son.   And yet the actual companionship of the Holy Ghost, the divinely-bestowed right to His ministrations, the sanctifying baptism with fire, are given as a permanent possession only to the faithful, repentant, baptized candidate for salvation; and with all such this gift will abide, unless forfeited through transgression.

19.   **The Bestowal of the Holy Ghost** is effected through

r Acts x.

the ordinance of an oral blessing, pronounced upon the candidate by the proper authority of the Priesthood, accompanied by the imposition of hands by him or those officiating. That this was the mode followed by the apostles of old is evident from the Jewish scriptures; that it was practised by the early Christian Fathers is proved by history; that it was the acknowledged method among the Nephites is plainly shown by the Book of Mormon records; and for the same practice in the present dispensation authority has come direct from heaven.

20. Among the instances recorded in the New Testament, we may mention the following: Peter and John conferred the Holy Ghost upon Philip's converts at Samaria, as already noted, and the ordinance was performed by prayer and the laying on of hands.[s] Paul operated in the same manner on the Ephesians whom he had caused to be baptized; and "when he had laid his hands upon them, the Holy Ghost came on them, and they spake with tongues and prophesied."[t] Paul also refers to this ordinance in his admonition to Timothy not to neglect the gift so bestowed.[u] The same apostle, in enumerating the cardinal principles and ordinances of the Church of Christ, includes the laying on of hands as following baptism.[v]

21. Alma so invoked the power of the Holy Ghost in behalf of his co-laborers:[w]—"He clapped his hands upon all them who were with him. And behold, as he clapped his hands upon them they were filled with the Holy Spirit." The Savior gave authority to the twelve chosen Nephites,[x]

[s] Acts viii, 14-17. Read the account of Simon, the magician, in the same chapter.

[t] Acts xix, 2-6.

[u] II Tim. i, 6.

[v] Heb. vi, 1-2.

[w] Alma xxxi, 36.

[x] III Nephi xviii, 36, 37.

by touching them one by one; they were thus commissioned
to bestow the Holy Ghost.

22.   In this dispensation, it has been made a duty of the
Priesthood "to confirm those who are baptized into the
Church by the laying on of hands for the baptism of fire
and the Holy Ghost."[y]   The Lord has promised that the
Holy Ghost shall follow these authoritative acts of His
servants.[z]   The ceremony of laying on of hands for the
bestowal of the Holy Ghost is associated with that of confirmation in the Church.   The officiating elder acting in
the name and by the authority of Jesus Christ, says,
"*Receive ye the Holy Ghost;*" and "*I confirm you a member
of the Church of Jesus Christ of Latter-day Saints.*"   Even
these words are not prescribed, but their meaning should be
expressed in the ceremony; and to such may be added other
words of blessing and invocation as the Spirit of the Lord
may dictate to the officiating elder.   This act completes
the outward form of the baptism so indispensable to salvation—the birth of water and of the Spirit.

23.   The authority to so bestow the Holy Ghost belongs
to the higher or Melchisedek Priesthood,[a] whereas water-
baptism may be administered by a priest, officiating in the
ordinances of the lesser or Aaronic order of priesthood.[b]
This order of authority, as made known through revelation,
explains that while Philip had authority to administer the
ordinance of baptism to the converted Samaritans, others
who held the higher priesthood had to be sent to confer
upon them the Holy Ghost.[c]

24.   **Gifts of the Spirit:**—As already pointed out, the
special office of the Holy Ghost is to enlighten and ennoble

y Doc. and Cov. xx, 41, 43.

z Doc. and Cov. xxxv, 6; xxxix, 6, 23; xlix, 11-14.

a Doc. and Cov. xx, 38-43.

b Doc. and Cov, xx, 46, 50.

c See Acts viii, 5-17.

the mind, to purify and sanctify the soul, to incite to good works, and to reveal the things of God. But, beside these general blessings, there are certain specific endowments promised in connection with the gifts of the Holy Ghost. Said the Savior, "These signs shall follow them that believe: In my name shall they cast out devils, they shall speak with new tongues; they shall take up serpents; and if they drink any deadly thing it shall not hurt them: they shall lay hands on the sick and they shall recover."[d]

25.   These gifts of the Spirit are distributed in the wisdom of God for the exaltation of His children. Paul thus discourses concerning them: "Now, concerning spiritual gifts, brethren, I would not have you ignorant.   *   *   * Now there are diversities of gifts, but the same Spirit. * * * * But the manifestation of the Spirit is given to every man to profit withal. For to one is given by the Spirit the word of wisdom; to another the word of knowledge by the same Spirit. To another faith by the same Spirit; to another the gift of healing by the same Spirit. To another the working of miracles; to another prophecy; to another discerning of spirits; to another divers kind of tongues; to another the interpretation of tongues. But all these worketh that one and the selfsame Spirit, dividing to every man severally as he will."[e] No man is without some gift from the Spirit; one person may possess several.

NOTES:

1. **Effect of the Holy Ghost on the Individual:**—"An intelligent being, in the image of God, possesses every organ, attribute, sense, sympathy, affection, of will, wisdom, love, power and gift, which is possessed by God Himself. But these are possessed by man in his rudimental state in a subordinate sense of the word. Or, in other words, these attributes are in embryo, and are to be grad-

---

d Mark xvi, 17-18; Doc. and Cov. lxxxiv, 65-73.

e I Cor. xii, 8; see also Moroni x, 8-18.

ually developed. They resemble a bud, a germ, which gradually develops into bloom, and then, by progress, produces the mature fruit after its own kind. The gift of the Holy Spirit adapts itself to all these organs or attributes. It quickens all the intellectual faculties, increases, enlarges, expands, and purifies all the natural passions and affections, and adapts them by the gift of wisdom, to their lawful use. It inspires, develops, cultivates, and matures all the fine-toned sympathies, joys, tastes, kindred feelings, and affections of our nature. It inspires virtue, kindness, goodness, tenderness, gentleness, and charity. It develops beauty of person, form and features. It tends to health, vigor, animation, and social feeling. It develops and invigorates all the faculties of the physical and intellectual man. It strengthens, invigorates, and gives tone to the nerves. In short, it is, as it were, marrow to the bone, joy to the heart, light to the eyes, music to the ears, and life to the whole being."—Parley P. Pratt; *Key to Theology*, p.p. 96-97, (4th ed.)

2. **The Laying on of Hands:**—From the scriptures cited, it is plain that the usual ceremony of bestowing the gift of the Holy Ghost, consisted in part in the imposition of hands by those in authority. (Acts viii, 17; ix, 17; xix, 2-6; Alma xxxi, 36; III Nephi, xviii, 36-37; Doc. and Cov., xx, 41.) The same outward sign has marked other authoritative acts: for example, ordination to the priesthood; and administration to the sick. It is probable that Paul had reference to Timothy's ordination when he exhorts him thus: "Neglect not the gift that is in thee, which was given thee by prophecy, with the laying on of the hands of the presbytery." (I Tim. iv, 14.) And again, "Stir up the gift of God, which is in thee by the putting on of my hands." (II Tim. i, 6.) The first ordination to the priesthood in latter times was done by the imposition of hands by John the Baptist (Doc. and Cov. xiii.) That Christ in healing the sick sometimes laid His hands upon the afflicted ones is certain (Mark vi, 5); and He left with His apostles a promise that healing should follow the authoritative laying on of hands (Mark xvi, 15, 18.) The same promise has been repeated in this day (Doc and Cov. xlii, 43-44.) Yet, notwithstanding the importance given to this sign of authority, the laying on of hands is but exceptional among the practices of the many sects professing Christianity today.

LECTURE IX.

THE SACRAMENT OF THE LORD'S SUPPER.

In connection with Article 4.

1. **The Sacrament:**—In the course of our study of the principles and ordinances of the Gospel, as specified in the fourth of the Articles of Faith, the subject of the sacrament of the Lord's Supper[a] very properly claims attention, the observance of this ordinance being required of all who have become members of the Church of Christ through compliance with the requirements of faith, repentance, and baptism by water and by the Holy Ghost.

2. **Institution of the Sacrament among the Jews:**—The sacrament of the Lord's Supper dates from the night of the Passover feast[b] immediately preceding the crucifixion of the Savior. On that solemn occasion, Christ and His apostles were assembled in Jerusalem, keeping the feast in an upper room, made ready by His express command.[c] As a Jew, Christ appears to have been ever loyal to the established usages of His people; and it must have been with most extraordinary feelings that He entered upon this commemorative feast, the last of its kind bearing the significance of the type of a future sacrifice, as well as a reminder of God's favor in the past. Knowing well the terrible experiences immediately awaiting Him, He communed with the Twelve at the paschal board in anguish of soul, prophesying concerning His betrayal, which was soon to be accomplished, by the agency of one who there ate with Him. Then He

a See Notes 1 and 2.

b See Note 3.

c Luke xxii, 8-13.

took bread, and blessed it and gave it to His disciples, saying, "Take, eat; this is my body;"[d] "this do in remembrance
of me."[e]   Afterward, taking the cup, He blessed its contents and administered it to them with the words, "Drink
ye all of it; for this is my blood of the new testament,
which is shed for many for the remission of sins."[f] It is
interesting to note that the account of the sacrament and its
purport as given by Paul[g] resembles so closely, as to be
almost identical with, the descriptions recorded by the evangelists.   The designation of the Sacrament as the Lord's
Supper is used by no biblical writer other than Paul.

3. **Institution of the Sacrament Among the Nephites:**—
On the occasion of His visit to the Nephites, which occurred shortly after His resurrection, Christ established
the sacrament among this division of His flock.   He requested the disciples whom He had chosen to bring Him
bread and wine; then, taking the bread He brake it, blessed
it, and gave it to the disciples with the command that they
should eat, and afterward distribute to the people.   The
authority to administer this ordinance He promised to leave
with the people.   "And this shall ye always observe to do,"
said He, "even as I have done.   * * *   And this shall
ye do in remembrance of my body, which I have shewn
unto you.   And it shall be a testimony unto the Father,
that ye do always remember me.   And if ye do always remember me, ye shall have my Spirit to be with you."[h] The
wine was administered in the same order, first to the disciples, then by them to the people.   This also was to be part
of the standing ordinance among the people:—"And ye
shall do it in remembrance of my blood which I have shed

_d_ Matt. xxvi, 26.
_e_ Luke xxii, 19; see also Mark xiv, 22-25.
_f_ Matt. xxvi, 27-28.
_g_ I Cor. xi, 23-25.
_h_ III Nephi xviii, 6, 7.

for you, that ye may witness unto the Father that ye do always remember me." Then followed a reiteration of the great promise, "And if ye do always remember me, ye shall have my Spirit to be with you."[i]

4. Fit Partakers of the Sacrament.—The Divine instructions concerning the sacredness of this ordinance are very explicit; and the consequent need of scrupulous care being exercised lest it be engaged in unworthily, is apparent. In addressing the Corinthian saints, Paul utters solemn warnings against hasty or unworthy action in partaking of the sacrament, and declares that the penalties of sickness, and even death, are visited upon those who violate the sacred requirements.—"For as often as ye eat this bread, and drink this cup, ye do shew the Lord's death till he come. Wherefore whosoever shall eat this bread, and drink this cup of the Lord, unworthily, shall be guilty of the body and blood of the Lord. But let a man examine himself, and so let him eat of that bread, and drink of that cup. For he that eateth and drinketh unworthily, eateth and drinketh damnation to himself, not discerning the Lord's body. For this cause many are weak and sickly among you, and many sleep."[j]

5. When instructing the Nephites, Jesus laid great stress upon the fitness of those who partook of the sacrament; and moreover He placed much responsibility upon the officers of the Church whose duty it was to administer it, that they should permit none whom they knew to be unworthy to take part in the ordinance:—"And now behold, this is the commandment which I give unto you, that ye shall not suffer any one knowingly to partake of my flesh and blood unworthily, when ye shall minister it; for whoso eateth and drinketh my flesh and blood unworthily, eateth and drinketh

i III Nephi xviii, 11.
j I Cor. xi, 26-30.
13

damnation to his soul; therefore, if ye know that a man is unworthy to eat and drink of my flesh and blood, ye shall forbid him."[k]

6.   The direct word of the Lord unto the Saints in this dispensation instructs them to permit no one who has committed trespass to partake of the sacrament until reconciliation has been made; nevertheless the Saints are commanded to exercise abundant charity toward their erring fellows, not casting them out from the assemblies, yet carefully withholding the sacrament from them.[l]   In our system of Church organization, the local ecclesiastical officers are charged with the responsibility of administering the sacrament, and the people are required to keep themselves worthy to partake of the sacred emblems.

7.   There is an entire absence of scriptural sanction for giving the sacrament to any who are not members in full fellowship in the Church of Christ.   Christ administered the ordinance on the eastern continent to His apostles only; and we have record of their giving it to those only who had assumed the name of Christ.   Amongst His western fold, Christ established the law that only the actual members of His Church should partake.   In promising to ordain one among them with power to officiate in the sacrament, the Savior specified that the one so chosen should give it unto the people of His Church, unto all those who believed and were baptized in His name.[m]   Only those indeed who had been so baptized were called the Church of Christ.[n]   Continuing His instructions to the disciples concerning the sacrament, the Savior said: "This shall ye always do to those who repent and are baptized in my name."[o]

---

k III Nephi xviii, 28, 29.
l Doc. and Cov. xlvi, 4.   See also III Nephi xviii, 30.
m III Nephi xviii, 5.
n III Nephi xxvi, 21.
o III Nephi xviii, 11.

8. And the same law is applicable today; it is members of the Church[p] who are admonished to meet together often for the observance of the sacrament; and the Church comprises none who have not been baptized by the authority of the Holy Priesthood.[q]

9. **Purpose of the Sacrament:**—From the scriptural references already made, it is plain that the sacrament is administered to commemorate the atonement of the Lord Jesus, as consummated in His agony and death; it is a testimony before God, that we are mindful of His Son's sacrifice made in our behalf; and that we still profess the name of Christ and are determined to strive to keep His commandments, in the hope that we may ever have His Spirit to be with us. Partaking of the sacrament worthily may be regarded therefore as a means of renewing our covenants before the Lord, of acknowledgment of mutual fellowship among the members, and of solemnly witnessing our claim and profession of membership in the Church of Christ. The sacrament has not been established as a specific means of securing remission of sins; nor for any other special blessing, aside from that of a fresh endowment of the Holy Spirit, which, however, comprises all needful blessings. Were the sacrament ordained for the remission of sins, it would not be forbidden to those who are in greatest need of special forgiveness; yet participation in the ordinance is restricted to those whose consciences are void of serious offense, those, therefore, who are acceptable before the Lord; those indeed who are in as little need of special forgiveness as mortals can be.

10. **The Sacramental Emblems:**—In instituting the sacrament both among the Jews and the Nephites, Christ used

---

p Doc. and Cov. xx, 75.
q Doc. and Cov. xx, 37.

bread and wine as the emblems of His body and blood;[r] and in this, the dispensation of the fulness of times, He has revealed His will that the Saints meet together often to partake of bread and wine in this commemorative ordinance.[s] But the Lord has also shown that other forms of food and drink may be used in place of bread and wine. Very soon after the Church was organized in the present dispensation, the Prophet Joseph was about to purchase some wine for sacramental purposes, when a special messenger from God appeared to him, and delivered the following instructions: "For, behold, I say unto you, that it mattereth not what ye shall eat, or what ye shall drink, when ye partake of the sacrament, if it so be that ye do it with an eye single to my glory; remembering unto the Father my body which was laid down for you, and my blood which was shed for the remission of your sins. Wherefore, a commandment I give unto you, that you shall not purchase wine, neither strong drink, of your enemies: Wherefore you shall partake of none except it is made new among you; yea in this my Father's kingdom which shall be built up upon the earth."[t] Upon this authority, the Latter-day Saints administer water in their sacramental service, in preference to wine, concerning the purity of which they are not assured. However, in the vineyard districts of the Church territory, wine has been generally used.

11. **Manner of Administering the Sacrament:**—It is customary with the Latter-day Saints in all wards or regularly organized branches of the Church, to hold sacramental meetings every Sabbath. The authority of the priest of the Aaronic order of priesthood is requisite in consecrating the emblems; and, as a matter of course, any one holding

r Matt. xxvi, 27-29; III Nephi xviii, 1, 8.

s Doc. and Cov. xx, 75.

t Doc. and Cov. xxvii, 2-4.

the higher order of priesthood has authority to officiate in this ordinance. The bread is first to be broken in small pieces, and placed in suitable receptacles on the sacramental table; and then, according to the Lord's direction, the elder or priest shall administer it, after this manner:—"He shall kneel with the Church and call upon the Father in solemn prayer, saying:—

"O God, the Eternal Father, we ask thee in the name of thy Son Jesus Christ, to bless and sanctify this bread to the souls of all those who partake of it, that they may eat in remembrance of the body of thy Son, and witness unto thee, O God, the Eternal Father, that they are willing to take upon them the name of thy Son, and always remember him, and keep his commandments which he hath given them, that they may always have his Spirit to be with them. Amen."[u]

12. After the bread has been distributed to the congregation, in which labor the teachers and deacons may take part, under the direction of the officiating priest, the wine or water is consecrated in this manner:—

"O God, the Eternal Father, we ask thee, in the name of thy Son Jesus Christ, to bless and sanctify this wine [or water] to the souls of all those who drink of it, that they may do it in remembrance of the blood of thy Son, which was shed for them; that they may witness unto thee, O God, the Eternal Father, that they do always remember him, that they may always have his Spirit to be with them. Amen."[v]

13. The plainness of the Lord's instructions to the Saints regarding this ordinance, leaves no excuse for disputation concerning the ceremony, for assuredly no one who officiates in these holy rites can feel that he is authorized to change the forms by even the alteration of a word. If ever the Lord desires a change in this ordinance, He will doubtless

---

[u] Doc. and Cov. xx, 76, 77.

[v] Doc. and Cov. xx, 78-79.

make it known through His established channels of the priesthood. The records of the Nephites clearly prove that the manner of administering the sacrament as practiced in their day,[w] was the same, even to the exact words of the ceremony, as revealed for the guidance of the Saints in the dispensation of the fulness of times.

NOTES.

1. **The Term "Sacrament"** is commonly used in both a general and a specific sense; according to its derivation, it signifies a sacred thing or holy ceremony, and with this meaning it is applied by different sects to several ceremonies of their churches. Thus, the Protestants speak of two sacraments,—baptism and the Lord's Supper; the Roman and Greek Catholics recognize seven sacraments,—the two named above, and also confirmation, matrimony, the bestowal of church orders, penance, and extreme unction. Some sections of the Greek church are said to exclude confirmation and extreme unction from among the seven sacraments. With even greater latitude, the term is applied to any miraculous or spiritual manifestation; it is so used by Bishop Jeremy Taylor when he says, "God sometime sent a light of fire, and pillar of a cloud * * * and the sacrament of a rainbow, to guide His people through their portion of sorrows." Specifically, however, the word sacrament denotes the Lord's Supper, and in this sense alone does the word occur in Latter-day Saint theology. Eucharist and HolyCommunion are terms employed in certain churches as synonymous with the sacrament of the Lord's supper. From the custom of regarding the ceremony of communion, that is, the partaking of the sacrament, as an evidence of standing in any church, and from the rule which withholds this privilege from those who are judged to be unworthy of fellowship, comes the term *excommunicate*, as applied to deprivation of church fellowship, meaning literally to cast out from communion.

2. **The Lord's Supper:**—As stated, this designation of the sacrament, occurs but once in the Bible. The "Lord's supper" is referred to by Paul in his first epistle to the Corinthians. In all probability this name was used because the rite was first administered at the time of the evening meal. It must be remembered that the *deipnon* or evening supper among the Jews was the principal meal of the day, and really corresponded to our dinner.

3. **The Passover and the Sacrament:**—The feast of the passover was the chief of the annual ceremonials of the Jews, and derived its name from the circumstances of its origin. In setting His hand to deliver Israel from the bondage of Egypt, the Lord wrought many miracles and wonders before Pharoah and his idolatrous house: and, as the last of the ten terrible plagues to which the Egyptians were subjected, the first born of every household was smitten with death during a single night. By previous command, the Israelites had marked

w Moroni iv; v.

the posts and lintels of their doorways with the blood of a lamb slain for the occasion, the blood having been sprinkled by means of a bunch of hyssop. In his passage through the land, the Lord passed over the houses so marked (Exodus xii, 12, 13); while in all the Egyptian homes the stroke of death was felt. Hence arises the name Passover, from *pasach*—to pass by. The flesh of the paschal lamb was eaten amid the haste of departure. To commemorate their deliverance from bondage, the Lord required of the Israelites an annual celebration of this event, the occasion being known as the "Feast of the Passover," also as the "Feast of Unleavened Bread," the latter name arising from the Lord's command that during the specified time of the observance no leaven should be found in the houses of the people (Ex. xii, 15); and the occasion of the feast was to be taken advantage of for instructing the children concerning the merciful dealings of God with their forefathers (Ex. xii, 26,27). But aside from its commemorative purpose, the passover became to the people a type of the sacrifice on Calvary. Paul says, "Christ, our passover, is sacrificed for us" (I Cor. v, 7). As being typical of the future atoning death of Christ, the passover lost part of its significance by the crucifixion, and was superceded by the sacrament. There is perhaps no closer relation between the two ordinances than this. Surely the sacrament was not designed to fully supplant the passover, for the latter was established as a perpetually recurring feast:—"And the day shall be unto you for a memorial; and ye shall keep it a feast to the Lord throughout your generations; ye shall keep it a feast by an ordinance forever." (Ex. xii, 14.)

4. **Errors Concerning the Sacrament,** and its signification, and the manner of administering it, grew rapidly in the professed Christian churches during the early centuries of the Christian era. As soon as the power of the priesthood had departed, much disputation arose in matters of ordinance, and the observance of the sacrament became distorted. Theological teachers strove to foster the idea that there was much mystery attending this naturally simple and most impressive ordinance; that all who were not in full communion with the Church should be excluded, not only from participation in the ordinance, which was justifiable, but from the privilege of witnessing the service, lest they profane the mystic rite by their unhallowed presence. Then arose the heresy of transsubstantiation,—which held that the sacramental emblems by the ceremony of consecration lost their natural character of simple bread and wine, and became in reality flesh and blood,—actually parts of the crucified body of Christ. Argument against such dogmas is useless. Then followed the veneration of the emblems by the people, the bread and wine—regarded as part of Christ's tabernacle, being elevated in the mass for the adoration of the people, and later, the custom of suppressing half of the sacrament was introduced. By the innovation last mentioned, only the bread was administered, the dogmatic assertion being that both the body and the blood were represented in some mystical way in one of the "elements." Certain it is, that Christ required his disciples to both eat and drink in remembrance of Him.

LECTURE X.

AUTHORITY IN THE MINISTRY.

Article 5:—We believe that a man must be called of God, by prophecy and by the laying on of hands by those who are in authority, to preach the Gospel, and administer in the ordinances thereof.

MEN CALLED OF GOD.

1. **Scriptural Examples:**—It is not less agreeable to the dictates of human reason, than it is comformable to the plan of perfect organization which characterizes the Church of Christ, that all who minister in the ordinances of the Gospel should be called and commissioned for their sacred duties by the authority of heaven. The scriptures sustain this view most thoroughly; they present to us an array of men whose Divine callings are specially attested, and whose mighty works declare a power greater than that of man. On the other hand, not an instance is set down in holy writ of anyone taking to himself the authority to officiate in sacred ordinances, and being acknowledged of the Lord in such administration.

2. Consider the case of Noah, who "found grace in the eyes of the Lord"[a] in the midst of a wicked world. Unto him the Lord spake, announcing His displeasure with the wicked inhabitants of earth, and the Divine intention concerning the deluge; and instructed him in the manner of building and stocking the ark. That Noah declared the word of God unto his perverse contemporaries is shown in Peter's declaration of Christ's mission in the spirit world,— that the Savior preached to those who had been disobedient during the period of God's long suffering in the days of

a Gen. vi, 8.

Noah, and who had in consequence endured the privations of the prison house in the interval.[b]   Surely none can question the Divine source of Noah's authority, nor the justice of the retributive punishment following the wilful rejection of his teachings, for his words were the words of God.

3.   So also with Abraham, the father of the faithful; the Lord called him[c] and made covenant with him for all the generations of his posterity.   Isaac[d] was similarly distinguished; likewise Jacob,[e] to whom as he rested upon his pillow of stones in the desert, the Lord appeared.   Unto Moses[f] came the voice of God amidst the fierceness of fire, calling and commissioning the man to go into Egypt, and deliver therefrom the people whose cries had come up with such effect before the throne of heaven.   In this great work Aaron[g] was called to assist his brother; and later, Aaron and his sons[h] were chosen by Divine direction from the midst of the children of Israel to minister in the priest's office.   When Moses[i] saw that his days were numbered, he solicited the Lord to appoint a successor in his holy station; and by special command, Joshua, the son of Nun, was so selected.

4.   Samuel, who became so great a prophet in Israel, commissioned to consecrate, command, and rebuke kings, to direct armies, and to serve as the oracle of God unto the people, was chosen while yet a boy, and called by the voice of the Lord.[j]   And such was the power that followed this call, that all Israel from Dan to Beersheba knew that

---

[b] I Peter iii, 19-20.
[c] Gen. xii-xxv; Pearl of Great Price; Book of Abraham.
[d] Gen. xxvi, 2-5.
[e] Gen. xxviii, 10-15.
[f] Exo. iii. 2-10.
[g] Exo. iv, 14-16, 27.
[h] Exo. xxviii, 1.
[i] Numb. xxvii, 15-23.
[j] I Sam. iii, 4-14.

Samuel was established a prophet of the Lord.[k] Time fails
to permit the mention of many other men of might, who
received their power from God, whose histories portray the
honor with which the Lord regarded his chosen ministers.
Think of the heavenly vision by which Isaiah was called and
directed in the duties of his prophetic office;[l] of Jeremiah,
to whom the word of the Lord came in the days of Josiah;[m]
of the priest Ezekiel, who first received the Divine message
in the land of the Chaldeans,[n] and subsequently on other
occasions; of Hosea,[o] and all the rest of the prophets to
Zechariah[p] and Malachi.[q]

5. The apostles of the Lord were called by His own
voice in the days of His ministry; and surely the Savior's
authority is beyond question, vindicated as it is by the
mighty works of the atonement, wrought through pain and
the anguish of death, and by the authoritative declaration
of the Father at the time of Christ's baptism. Peter, and
Andrew his brother, while casting their nets into the sea,
were called with the instruction,—"Follow me, and I will
make you fishers of men;"[r] and soon after, James and John,
the sons of Zebedee, were similarly called. So with all of
the chosen Twelve who ministered with the Master; and
unto the Eleven who had remained faithful, He appeared
after His resurrection, giving them special commissions for
the work of the kingdom.[s] Christ specifically declares that
He had chosen His apostles, and that He had ordained them
in their exalted stations.[t]

k I Sam. iii, 20.

l Isa. i, 1; ii, 1; vi, 8-9.

m Jer. i, 2-10.

n Ezek. i. 1.

o Hos. i, 1.

p Zech. i, 1.

q Mal. i, 1.

r Matt. iv, 18-20.

s Matt. xviii, 19-20; Mark xvi, 15.

t John vi, 70; xv, 16.

6. In the period immediately following that of Christ's earthly mission, the ministers of the Gospel were all designated and set apart by unquestionable authority. Even Saul of Tarsus, afterward Paul the apostle, who was converted with marvelous signs and wondrous manifestations,[u] had to be formally commissioned for the labor which the Lord desired him to perform; and we are told that the Holy Ghost spake to the prophets and teachers of the Church at Antioch, while they fasted before the Lord, saying, "Separate me Barnabas and Saul for the work whereunto I have called them."[v]

7. **The Ordination of Man to the Ministry,** as sanctioned by scriptural precedent, and established by direct revelation of God's will, is to be effected through the gift of prophecy, and by the imposition of hands by those who are in authority. By prophecy is meant the right to receive, and the power to interpret, manifestations of the Divine will. That the laying on of hands is usual as a part of the ceremony is seen in several of the instances already cited; nevertheless the scriptures record numerous ordinations to the offices of the priesthood, with no specific statement concerning the imposition of hands, or indeed any other details of the ceremony. Such instances do not warrant the conclusion that the laying on of hands was not actually performed; and indeed, in the light of modern revelation it is clear that the imposition of hands was a usual accompaniment of ordination, as it was also a part of the ceremony of confirming blessings,[w] and of bestowing the Holy Ghost.[x]

8. Thus, the priesthood descended from Adam to Noah,

---

[u] Acts ix.

[v] Acts xiii, 1-2.

[w] Gen. xlviii, 14-19. Compare II Kings v, 11; Matt. viii, 15; Mark vi, 5; xvi, 15-18.

[x] See Lecture viii.

under the hands of the fathers;[y] Enos was ordained by the
hand of Adam; and the same was true of Mahalaleel,
Jared, Enoch, and Methuselah. Lamech was ordained
under the hand of Seth; Noah received his authority from
the hand of Methuselah. And so may the priesthood be
traced, bestowed as the spirit of prophecy directed, by the
hand of one upon another, till the time of Moses. Melchisedek, who bestowed this authority upon Abraham,
received his own through the direct lineage of his fathers,
from Noah. Esaias, a contemporary of Abraham, received
his ordination under the hand of God. Through the hand
of Esaias, the authority passed to Gad, thence by the same
means to Jeremy, Elihu, Caleb, and Jethro, the priest of
Midian, under whose hand Moses was ordained.[z] Joshua
the son of Nun was set apart as directed of God, through
the imposition of hands by Moses.[a]

9. In the days of the apostles, circumstances rendered it
expedient to appoint special officers in the Church, to care
for the poor and attend to the distribution of supplies;
these were selected with care, and were set apart through
prayer and laying on of hands.[b] Timothy was so ordained,
as witness the admonitions given him by Paul:—"Neglect
not the gift that is in thee, which was given thee by
prophecy, with the laying on of the hands of the presbytery,"[c] and again, "Stir up the gift of God which is in thee
by the putting on of my hands."[d] The Lord has bound
Himself by solemn covenant to acknowledge the acts of
His authorized servants. Unto whomsoever the elders give
promise after baptism the Holy Ghost will come.[e] What-

y Doc. and Cov. cvii, 40-52.
z Doc. and Cov. lxxxiv, 6-14.
a Numb. xxvii, 18; Deut. xxxiv, 9.
b Acts vi, 1-6.
c I Timothy iv, 14.
d II Tim. i, 6.
e Acts ii, 38; III Nephi xi, 35; xii, 2; Doc. and Cov. lxxxiv, 64.

ever the priesthood shall bind or loose on earth, is to be similarly bound and loosed in heaven;[f] the sick upon whom the elders lay their hands, are to recover;[g] and many other wonders are to follow them that believe.   And so jealous is the Lord of the power to officiate in His name, that at the judgment, all who have aided or persecuted His servants, are to be rewarded or punished as if they had done those things unto Christ Himself.[h]

10. **Unauthorized Ministrations** in priestly functions are not alone invalid, they are indeed grievously sinful.   In His dealings with mankind, God has ever recognized and honored the priesthood established by His direction; and has never countenanced any unauthorized assumption of authority.   A terrible lesson is taught in the case of Korah and his associates, in their rebellion against the authority of the priesthood,—in that they falsely professed the right to minister in the priest's office.   The Lord promptly visited them for their sins, causing the ground to cleave asunder, and to swallow them up with all their belongings.[i]

11. And think of the affliction that fell on Miriam, the sister of Moses, a prophetess among the people.[j] She, with Aaron, railed against Moses, and they said, "Hath the Lord indeed spoken only by Moses? hath He not spoken also by us? and the Lord heard it."[k] He came at once in a cloud, and stood in the door of the tabernacle; denouncing their presumption, and vindicating the authority of His chosen oracle, Moses.   When the cloud passed from the tabernacle, Miriam was seen to be leprous, white as snow; and, according to the law, she was shut out of the camp of

f Matt. xvi, 19; Doc. and Cov. i, 8; cxxviii, 8-11.

g Mark xvi, 15-18,

h Matt. xviii, 4-6; xxv, 31-46, Doc. and Cov. lxxv, 19-22; lxxxiv. 88-90

i Numbers xvi.

j Exo, xv, 21.

k Numbers xii.

Israel.   However, through the earnest entreaties of Moses,
the Lord healed the woman, and she was subsequently
permitted to return to the company.

12.   Consider the fate of Uzza, the Israelite who met
sudden death through the anger of God, because he put
forth his hand to steady the ark of the covenant lest it fall.[l]
This he did in spite of the law that none but the priests
might touch the sacred accompaniments of the ark; we
read that not even the appointed bearers of the vessel were
allowed to touch its holy parts, on pain of death.[m]

13.   Think also of Saul the King of Israel, who had
been called from the farm to be made a monarch favored of
God.   When the Philistines were marshalled against Israel
in Michmash, Saul waited for Samuel,[n] under whose hand
he had received his kingly anointing,[o] and to whom he had
looked in the days of his humility for guidance; he asked
that the prophet come and offer sacrifices to the Lord in
behalf of the people.   But, growing impatient at Samuel's
delay, Saul prepared the burnt offering himself, forgetting
that though he occupied the throne, wore the crown, and
bore the sceptre, these insignia of kingly power gave him
no right to officiate even as a door-keeper in the house of
God; and for this and other instances of his unrighteous
presumption, he was rejected of God and another was
chosen in his place.

14.   A striking instance of Divine jealousy concerning
holy functions is shown in the dreadful experience of
Uzziah, king of Judah.   He was placed upon the throne
when but sixteen years old; and, as long as he sought the
Lord, he was greatly prospered, so that his name became a
terror unto his enemies.   But he allowed pride to grow in

l I Chron. xiii, 10.

m Num. iv, 15.

n I Sam. xiii, 5-14.

o I Sam. x.

his heart, and indulged the delusion that in his kingship he was supreme. He entered the temple and essayed to burn incense on the altar; shocked at his blasphemous action, Azariah, the chief priest of the temple, and fourscore priests with him, forbade the king, saying:—"It appertaineth not unto thee, Uzziah, to burn incense unto the Lord, but to the priests, the sons of Aaron, that are consecrated to burn incense; go out of the sanctuary, for thou hast trespassed." At this rebuke and condemnation from his subjects, though they were priests of the living God, the king became angry; but immediately the dread scourge of leprosy fell upon him; the signs of the horrible disease appeared in his forehead; and, being now physically an unclean creature, his presence tended the more to defile the holy place. So Azariah and his associate priests thrust the king out from the temple, and he, a smitten thing, fled from the house of God never again to enter its sacred precincts. Concerning the rest of his punishment we read, "And Uzziah the king was a leper unto the day of his death, and dwelt in a several house, being a leper; for he was cut off from the house of the Lord."[p]

15. A forcible illustration of the futility of false ceremonies, or of the mere form of sacred ordinances when the authority is absent, is shown in the New Testament record of the seven sons of Sceva. These in common with others had seen, and had marveled at, the miraculous power exhibited by Paul, whom the Lord so blessed in his apostleship that by touching hankerchiefs or aprons sent by him the sick were healed, and even evil spirits were cast out. Sceva's sons, who are reckoned by the sacred chronicler among the exorcists, and the vagabond Jews, sought also to expel an evil spirit: "We adjure you by Jesus whom Paul preacheth" said they; but the evil spirit derided them for their

---
[p] II Chron. xxvi.

lack of authority saying, "Jesus I know, and Paul I know, but who are ye?" Then the afflicted person, in whom the evil spirit dwelt, leaped upon them and overcame them, so that when they escaped from the house they were naked and wounded.*q*

16. **Teachers True and False:**—None but those who are duly authorized to teach can be regarded as true expounders of the word. The remarks of Paul concerning the high priests are alike applicable to every office of the priesthood: "No man taketh this honor to himself, but he that is called of God, as was Aaron."*r* And Aaron, as we have already seen, was called through Moses, unto whom the Lord revealed His will in the matter. This authority to act in the name of the Lord is given to those only who are chosen of God; it is not to be had for the mere asking; it is not to be bought with gold. We read of Simon, the sorcerer, who coveted the power possessed by the apostles; he offered these ministers of Christ money, saying, "Give me also this power that on whomsoever I lay my hands he may receive the Holy Ghost." But Peter answered him with righteous indignation, "Thy money perish with thee, because thou hast thought that the gift of God may be purchased with money; thou has neither part nor lot in this matter, for thy heart is not right in the sight of God."*s*

17. It was known to the apostles of old that men would seek to arrogate unto themselves the right to officiate in things divine, thus becoming servants of Satan. In addressing a conference of the elders at Ephesus, Paul prophesied of these ill events, and warned the shepherds of the flock to look well to their charge.*t* In an epistle to Timothy, the apostle reiterates this prophecy; encouraging

q Acts xix, 13-17.
r Heb. v, 4.
s Acts viii, 18-24.
t Acts xx, 28-30.

to diligence in preaching the word, he declares, "For the time will come when they will not endure sound doctrine, but after their own lusts shall they heap to themselves teachers having itching ears, and they shall turn away their ears from the truth, and shall be turned unto fables."[u] Peter's declarations on the same subject are no less plain. Addressing himself to the Saints of his time, he refers to the false prophets of old, and adds:—"There shall be false teachers among you, who privily shall bring in damnable heresies; even denying the Lord that bought them * * * And many shall follow their pernicious ways, by reason of whom the way of truth shall be evil spoken of."[v]

18. **Divine Authority in the Present Dispensation:**— The Latter-day Saints claim to possess authority to administer in the name of God; and that this right has been conferred in this day under the hands of those who held the same power in former dispensations. That the authority of the holy priesthood was to be taken from the earth as the apostles of old were slain, and that it would of necessity have to be restored from heaven before the Church could be re-established, may be shown by scripture. On the 15th day of May, 1829, while Joseph Smith and Oliver Cowdery were engaged in earnest prayer for instruction concerning baptism for the remission of sins, mention of which they had found in the plates from which they were then engaged in translating the Book of Mormon, a messenger from heaven descended in a cloud of light. He announced himself as John, called of old the Baptist, and said he acted under the direction of Peter, James, and John, who held the keys of the higher priesthood. The messenger laid his hands upon the two young men and ordained them to authority, saying, "Upon you my fellow servants, in the name of Messiah, I

---

u II Tim. iv, 2-4.
v II Pet. ii, 1-3.

confer the priesthood of Aaron, which holds the keys of the ministering of angels, and of the gospel of repentance, and of baptism by immersion for the remission of sins; and this shall never be taken again from the earth, until the sons of Levi do offer again an offering unto the Lord in righteousness."[w]

19. A short time after this event, Peter, James, and John appeared to Joseph and Oliver, and ordained the two to the higher or Melchisedek priesthood, bestowing upon them the keys of the apostleship, which these heavenly messengers had held and exercised in the former gospel dispensation. This order of priesthood holds authority over all the offices in the Church, and includes power to administer in spiritual things;[x] consequently all the authorities and powers necessary to the establishment of the Church were by this visitation restored to earth.

20. No one is authorized to officiate in any of the ordinances of the Church of Jesus Christ of Latter-day Saints unless he has been ordained to that calling by those holding the power; thus, no man receives the priesthood except under the hand of one who holds that priesthood himself; that one must have obtained it from others previously commissioned; and so every holder of the priesthood today can trace his authority to the hands of Joseph the Prophet, who, as already stated, received his ordination under the hands of heavenly messengers clothed with power divine. That men, who are called of God to the authority of the ministry on earth, may have been selected for such appointment even before they took mortal bodies, is evident from the scriptures. This matter may properly claim attention in the present connection; and its consideration leads us to the subjects which follow.

---

w Pearl of Great Price p. 105 (1888 ed.); Doc. and Cov. xiii.
x Doc. and Cov. cvii.

FORE-ORDINATION AND PRE-EXISTENCE.

21. Fore-ordination:—In a wonderful interview with Abraham, the Lord revealed many things ordinarily withheld from mortal eyes. Said the patriarch:—"Now the Lord had shewn unto me, Abraham, the intelligences that were organized before the world was; and among all these there were many of the noble and great ones; and God saw these souls that they were good, and he stood in the midst of them, and he said, These I will make my rulers; for he stood among those that were spirits, and he saw that they were good; and he said unto me, Abraham, thou art one of them, thou wast chosen before thou wast born."[y] This is one of the many scriptural proofs that the spirits of mankind existed prior to their earthly probation:—a condition in which these intelligences lived and exercised their free agency before they assumed bodily tabernacles. Surely then the natures, dispositions, and tendencies of men are known to the Father of their spirits, even before these beings are born in mortality; and He needs not to wait till they develop and prove their capacities on earth before they are appointed to special labors in the fulfilment of Divine purposes.

22. Evidence is abundant that Christ was chosen and ordained to be the Redeemer of the world, even from the beginning. We read of His formost position amongst the sons of God in offering Himself as a sacrifice to carry into effect the will of the Father.[z] He it was, "Who verily was fore-ordained before the foundation of the world."[a]

23. Paul taught the doctrine of Divine selection and pre-appointment thus:—"For whom he did fore-know, he

---

y Pearl of Great Price; Book of Abraham, p. 62, (1888 ed.)

z See page 83.

a I Peter i, 20.

also did predestinate to be conformed to the image of his Son. * * * Moreover, whom he did predestinate, them he also called."[b] And again:—"God hath not cast away his people which he foreknew."[c]

24. Alma, the Nephite prophet, spoke of the priests who had been ordained after the order of the Son, and added:— "And this is the manner after which they were ordained: being called and prepared from the foundation of the world, according to the fore-knowledge of God, on account of their exceeding faith and good works; in the first place being left to choose good or evil; therefore they having chosen good, and exercising exceeding great faith, are called with a holy calling, yea, with that holy calling which was prepared with, and according to, a preparatory redemption for such." [d]

25. Fore-ordination does not Imply Compulsion:—The doctrine of absolute predestination, resulting in a nullification of man's free agency, has been advocated with various modifications by Christian sects. Nevertheless, such teachings are wholly unjustified by both the letter and the spirit of sacred writ. God's fore-knowledge cencerning the natures and capacities of His children enables Him to see the end of their earthly career even from the first:— "Known unto God are all his works from the beginning of the world."[e] Many people have been led to regard this fore-knowledge of God as a sure predestination, whereby souls are assigned to glory or condemnation, even before their birth in the flesh, and independently of any merits or demerits of their own. This heretical doctrine seeks to rob Deity of every trait of mercy, of justice, and of pure love; it makes the Father appear capricious and selfish, directing

b Rom. viii, 29-30.
c Rom. xi, 2.
d Alma xiii, 3; also 10, 11.
e Acts xv, 18.

and creating all things for His own glory alone, caring not for the consequent suffering of the victims of His injustice. How dreadful, how inconsistent is such an idea of God! It leads to the absurd conclusion that the mere knowledge of coming events must act as a determinative influence in bringing about those occurrences. God's knowledge of spiritual and of human nature enables Him to conclude with certainty as to the actions of any of His children under given conditions; yet such knowledge has surely no determining influence upon the creature.

26. Doubtless He knows of some spirits, that they await only the opportunity of choice between good and evil to choose the latter, and to accomplish their own destruction; these are they as spoken of by Jude, "who were before of old ordained to this condemnation;"*f* To avert the fate of such, their free agency would have to be taken away; they can be saved by force alone; and compulsion is forbidden by the laws of heaven, for salvation and for condemnation alike. There are others whose integrity and faithfulness have been demonstrated in their pristine state: the Father knows how unreservedly they may be trusted, and many of them are called even in their mortal youth to special and exalted labors as chosen servants of the Most High.

27. **Pre-existence of Spirits:**—The facts already presented, concerning fore-ordination, furnish proof that the spirits of mankind passed through a stage of existence prior to the earthly probation. This pre-existent period is oft-times spoken of as the stage of "primeval childhood" or "first estate." That these spirits existed as organized intelligences, and exercised their free agency during that primeval stage, is clear from the declaration of the Lord to Abraham: —"And they who keep their first estate shall be added upon, and they who keep not their first estate shall not have glory

---
f Jude 4.

in the same kingdom with those who keep their first estate; and they who keep their second estate shall have glory added upon their heads forever and ever."[g]

28.   No Christian doubts the pre-existence of the Savior, or questions His position as one of the Godhead before He came to earth as Mary's Son.   The common interpretation given to the opening words of John's Gospel sustains the view of Christ's primeval God-ship:—"In the beginning was the Word, and the Word was with God, and the Word was God."   We read further, "And the Word was made flesh and dwelt among us."[h]   The sayings of the Redeemer Himself support this truth.   When His disciples dissented concerning His doctrine of Himself, He said, "What and if ye shall see the Son of man ascend up where he was before?"[i]   On another occasion He spoke in this wise:—"I came forth from the Father, and am come into the world; again, I leave the world and go to the Father."[j]   And His disciples, pleased with this plain declaration confirming the belief which, perchance, they already entertained at heart, rejoined, "Lo, now speakest thou plainly, and speakest no proverb.   *   *   *   by this we believe that thou camest forth from God."[k]   To the wicked Jews who boasted of their descent from Abraham, and sought to hide their sins under the protecting mantle of the great patriarch's name, the Savior declared:—"Verily, verily, I say unto you, Before Abraham was, I am."[l]   In a solemn prayer to His Father, the Son implored, "And now, O Father glorify thou me with thine own self, with the glory which I had with thee before the world was."[m]   Yet Christ was born a

---

g Pearl of Great Price, Book of Abraham, p. 63 (1888 ed.)

h John i, 1, 14.

i John vi, 62.

j John xvi, 28.

k Verses 29-30.

l John viii, 58.

m John xvii, 5.   See also II Nephi ix, 5; xxv, 12; Mos. iii, 5; xiii, 33-34; xv, 1.

child among mortals; and it is fair to infer, that if His earthly birth was the union of a pre-existent immortal spirit with a mortal body, such also is the birth of every member of the human family.

29. But we are not left to mere inference on a basis of analogy only; the scriptures plainly teach that the spirits of mankind are known and numbered unto God before their earthly advent. In his farewell administration to Israel Moses sang, "Remember the days of old. * * * When the Most High divided to the nations their inheritance, when he separated the sons of Adam, he set the bounds of the people according to the number of the children of Israel."[n] From this we learn that the earth was allotted to the nations, according to the number of the children of Israel; it is evident therefore that the number was known prior to the existence of the Israelitish nation in the flesh; this is most easily explained on the assumption of a previous existence in which the spirits of the future nation were known.

30. No chance is possible therefore in the number or extent of the temporal creations of God.[o] The population of the earth is fixed according to the number of spirits appointed to take tabernacles of flesh upon this sphere; when these have all come forth in the order and time decreed of God, then, and not till then, will the end come.

NOTE.

Spiritual Creations:—The pre-existent condition is not characteristic of human souls alone; all things of earth have a spiritual being, of which the temporal structure forms but the counterpart. We read of the creation of "every plant of the field before it was in the earth, and every herb of the field before it grew." (Gen. ii, 5.) This is set forth with greater fulness in another revelation to Moses:—"These are the generations of the heaven and the earth

n Deut. xxxii, 7-8.

o See note, this page.

when they were created, in the day that I, the Lord God, made the heaven and the earth, and every plant of the earth before it was in the earth, and every herb of the field before it grew. For I, the Lord God, created all things of which I have spoken, spiritually, before they were naturally upon the face of the earth. * * * And I, the Lord God, had created all the children of men, and not yet a man to till the ground; for in heaven created I them; and there was not yet flesh upon the earth, neither in the water, neither in the air: but I, the Lord God, spake, and there went up a mist from the earth, and watered the whole face of the ground. And I, the Lord God, formed man from the dust of the ground, and breathed into his nostrils the breath of life; and man became a living soul, the first flesh upon the earth, the first man also; nevertheless, all things were before created, but spiritually were they created and made according to my word."—(Pearl of Great Price, Writings of Moses, p. 11, (1888 ed.)

LECTURE XI.

THE CHURCH AND ITS PLAN OF ORGANIZATION.

Article 6.—We believe in the same organization that existed in the primitive Church, viz: apostles, prophets, pastors, teachers, evangelists, etc.

THE CHURCH IN FORMER AND LATTER DAYS.

1. **The Primitive Church:**—In the dispensation of the Savior's ministry, Christ established His Church upon the earth, appointing therein the officers necessary for the carrying out of the Father's purposes. As shown in the last lecture, every person so appointed was divinely commissioned with authority to officiate in the ordinances of his calling; and, after Christ's ascension, the same organization was continued, those who had received authority ordaining others to the various offices of the priesthood. In this way were given unto the Church, apostles, prophets, evangelists, pastors,[a] high priests,[b] seventies,[c] elders,[d] bishops,[e] priests,[f] teachers,[g] and deacons.[h]

2. Besides these specific offices in the priesthood, there were other callings of a more temporal nature, to which men were also set apart by authority: such for instance was the case of the seven men of honest report, who, in the days of the apostles were chosen and appointed to minister to the poor, thus leaving the Twelve freer to attend to the

---

[a] Eph. iv, 11.
[b] Heb. v, 1-5.
[c] Luke x, 1-11.
[d] Acts xiv, 23; xv, 6; I Peter v, 1.
[e] I Tim. iii, 1; Titus i, 7.
[f] Rev. i, 6.
[g] Acts xiii, 1.
[h] I Tim. iii, 8-12.

particular duties of their office.[i] This special appointment illustrates the nature of the helps and governments[j] set in the Church, to assist in the work under the direction of the regular officers of the priesthood.

3. The ministers so appointed, and the members among whom they labor, constitute the Church of Christ, which has been beautifully compared to a perfect body, the individuals typifying the separate members, each with its special function, all co-operating for the welfare of the whole.[k] Every office so established, every officer so commissioned, is necessary to the development of the Church and to the accomplishment of the work of God. An organization established of God comprises no superfluities; the eye, the ear, the hand, the foot, every organ of the body, is essential to the symmetry and perfection of the physical structure; in the Church no officer can rightly say to another, "I have no need of thee."[l]

4. The existence of these officers, and particularly their operation with accompaniments of Divine assistance and power, may be taken as a distinguishing characteristic of the Church in any age of the world,—a crucial test, whereby the validity or fallacy of any claim to Divine authority may be determined. The gospel of Christ is the everlasting gospel; its principles, laws, and ordinances, and the Church organization founded thereon, must be ever the same. In searching for the true Church, therefore, one must look for an organization comprising the offices established of old; the callings of apostles, prophets, evangelists, high priests, seventies, pastors, bishops, elders, priests, teachers, deacons; not men bearing these names merely, but ministers able to vindicate their claim to position as officers in the Lord's

---

i Acts vi, 1-6.

j I Cor. xii, 28.

k I Cor. xii, 12-27; Rom. xii, 4-5; Eph. iv, 16.

l I Cor. xii, 21.

service, through the evidences of power and authority accompanying their ministry.

5. **Apostasy from the Primitive Church:**—The question may fairly arise in the mind of the earnest investigator, have these authorities and powers, together with their associated gifts of the Spirit, remained with men from the apostolic age to the present; in short, has there been a Church of Christ upon the earth during this long interval? In answer, let these facts be considered: Since the period immediately following the ministrations of the apostles of old, and until the present century, no organization has maintained a claim to direct revelation from God; in fact, the teachings of the professed ministers of the gospel for centuries have been to the effect that such gifts of God have ceased, that the days of miracles have gone, and that the present depends for its guiding code wholly upon the past. A self-suggesting interpretation of history indicates that there has been a great departure from the way of salvation as laid down by the Savior, a universal apostasy from the Church of Christ.[m] Scarcely had the Church been organized by the Savior, whose name it bears, before the powers of darkness arrayed themselves for conflict with the organized body. Even in the days of Christ, persecution was bitterly waged against the disciples; commencing with the Jews, and directed first against the Master Himself and His few immediate associates, this tide of opposition soon enveloped every known follower of the Savior; so that the very name Christian became an epithet of derision.

6. In the first quarter of the fourth century, however, a change in the attitude of paganism toward Christianity was marked by the conversion of Constantine the Great, under whose patronage the Christian profession grew in favor, and became in fact the religion of the state. But what a pro-

[m] See notes 1 and 2.

fession, what a religion was it by this time! Its simplicity
had departed; earnest devotion and self-sacrificing sincerity
were no longer characteristic of the Church's ministers;
these professed followers of the humble Prophet of Nazareth,
these self-styled associates of the meek and lowly Jesus,
these loudly-proclaimed lovers of the Man of Sorrow, lived
amid conditions strangely inconsistent with the life of their
great Exemplar.   Church offices were sought after for the
distinction of honor and wealth accompanying them; ministers of the gospel affected the state of worldly authority;
bishops sought the pomp of princes, archbishops lived as
kings, and popes like emperors.   With these unauthorized
and unscriptural innovations, came many changes in the
ordinances of the so-called church; the rites of baptism
were perverted; the sacrament was altered; public worship
became an exhibition of art; men were canonized; martyrs
were made subjects of adoration; blasphemy grew apace, in
that men without authority essayed to exercise the prerogatives of God in calling others to what still bore the name
of spiritual office.   Ages of darkness came upon the earth;
the power of Satan seemed almost supreme.

7.   For a special consideration of the evidence of a general apostasy from the Church of Christ, the student must
consult authorities on ecclesiastical history.   While the fact
of the apostasy is admitted by but few such writers, the
historical events which they chronicle, suggest the awful
truth.   We may trace from the days of the apostles, down
to near the close of the tenth century, a constantly changing form of Church organization, which, at the later
time named, bore but little semblance to the Church established by the Savior.   This falling away is admitted by some
historians, and as we shall presently see, it was definitely
foretold by authoritative prophecy.

8.   John Wesley, founder of a powerful sect, declared

that the distinctive gifts of the Holy Ghost were no longer with the church, having been taken away on account of the unworthiness of professing Christians, whom he characterized indeed as heathen, with only a dead form of worship.[n] In the Church of England homily regarding the "Perils of Idolatry," we read "that laity and clergy, learned and unlearned, men and women, and children of all ages, sects, and degrees, of whole Christendom, have been at once buried in the most abominable idolatry, and that for the space of eight hundred years or more." Dr. Milner, author of an exhaustive work on church history, admits a pitiable condition of the so-called Church in the tenth century, and finds in that sad state a fulfilment of scriptural predictions.

9. **This Great Apostasy was Foretold:**—The infinite foreknowledge of God made plain to Him even from the beginning this falling away from the truth; and, through inspiration, the prophets of old uttered solemn warnings of the approaching dangers. Surely Isaiah was gazing upon the era of spiritual darkness when he declared, "The earth also is defiled under the inhabitants thereof; because they have transgressed the laws, changed the ordinance, broken the everlasting covenant."[o] And how deeply impressive is the declaration of Jeremiah, "For my people have committed two evils: they have forsaken me, the fountain of living waters, and hewed them out cisterns, broken cisterns that can hold no water."[p]

10. The prophecies of the apostles relative to the false teachers so soon to trouble the flock, already quoted,[q] declare the apostasy then rapidly approaching. Paul warned

---

n. John Wesley's Works, vii, pp. 26-27 . See note 4, following Lecture xii, in connection with Article 7; "Spiritual Gifts."

o Isa. xxiv, 5.

p Jer. ii, 13.

q See pages 192-193.

the Saints of Thessaly that they be not deceived by those who cried that the second coming of Christ was then at hand, "For," said the apostle, "that day shall not come except there come a falling away first, and that man of sin be revealed, the son of perdition; Who opposeth and ex-alteth himself above all that is called God, or that is wor-shiped; so that he as God sitteth in the temple of God, showing himself that he is God."[r] This falling away had begun even in the days of the apostles:— "Even now," says John, "are there many anti-Christs."[s] And Paul, in addressing the Galatians, declared, "There be some that trouble you, and would pervert the gospel of Christ."[t]

11. Not less conclusive are the prophecies contained in the Book of Mormon relating to this great falling away. Nephi, son of Lehi, predicted the oppression of the North American Indians at the hands of the Gentiles, and de-clared that at that time the people will be lifted up in self-pride, having departed from the ordinances of God's house; true, they will build to themselves many churches, but in these they will preach their own wisdom, with envyings, and strife, and malice, denying however the power and miracles of God.[u]

12. Restoration of the Church:—From the facts already stated, it is evident that the Church was literally driven from the earth; in the first ten centuries immediately following the ministry of Christ, the authority of the priesthood was lost from among men, and no worldly power could restore it. But the Lord in His mercy provided for the re-establishment of His Church in the last days, and for the last time; and

---

r II Thess. ii, 3-4.

s I John ii, 18.

t Gal i, 7.

u II Nephi xxvi, 19-22; see also xxvii, 1; xxviii, 3, 6; xxix, 3; I Nephi xiii 5; xxii, 22-23.

prophets of olden time fore-saw this era of renewed enlightenment, and sang in joyous tones of its coming.[v] It has been already shown that this restoration was effected by the Lord through the Prophet Joseph Smith, who, together with Oliver Cowdery, in 1829 received the Aaronic Priesthood under the hands of John the Baptist; and later the Melchisedek Priesthood under the hands of the former-day apostles, Peter, James and John. By the authority thus bestowed, the Church has been again organized, with all its former completeness, and mankind once more rejoices in the priceless privileges of the counsels of God. The Latter-day Saints declare their high claim to the true Church organization, similar in all essentials to the organization effected by Christ among the Jews; this people of the last days profess to have the Priesthood of the Almighty, the power to act in the name of God, which power commands respect both on earth and in heaven. Let us consider the organization of the priesthood as it exists to-day.

PLAN OF GOVERNMENT IN THE RESTORED CHURCH.

13. Orders and Offices in the Priesthood:—The Church of Jesus Christ of Latter-day Saints recognizes two orders of priesthood, the lesser called the Aaronic, the greater known as the Melchisedek order. *The Aaronic Priesthood* is named after Aaron, who was given to Moses as his mouth-piece, to act under his direction in the carrying out of God's purposes respecting Israel.[w] For this reason, it is sometimes called the Lesser Priesthood; but though lesser, it is neither small nor insignificant. While Israel journeyed in the wilderness, Aaron and his sons were called by prophecy and set apart for the duties of the priest's office.[x]

---

v Dan. ii, 44-45; vii, 27; Matt. xxiv, 14; Rev. xiv, 6-8.

w Exo. iv, 14-16.

x Exo. xxviii, 1.

14. At a subsequent period of Israel's history, the Lord chose the tribe of Levi to assist Aaron in the priestly functions, the special duties of the Levites being to keep the instruments and attend to the service of the tabernacle. The Levites, thus chosen of the Lord, were to take the place of the first-born throughout the tribes, whom the Lord had claimed for His service from the time of the last dread plague in Egypt, whereby the first-born in every Egyptian house was slain, while the eldest in every Israelitish house was hallowed and spared.[y] The commission thus given to the Levites is sometimes called the *Levitical Priesthood;*[z] it is to be regarded as an appendage to the priesthood of Aaron, not comprising the highest priestly powers. The Aaronic Priesthood, as restored to the earth in this dispensation, comprises the Levitical order.[a] This priesthood holds the keys of the ministering of angels, and the authority to attend to the outward ordinances, the letter of the gospel;[b] it comprises the offices of deacon, teacher, and priest; with the bishopric holding the keys of presidency.

15 The greater or *Melchizedek Priesthood* is named after the king of Salem, a great High Priest of God;[c] before his day it was known as "the Holy Priesthood, after the order of the Son of God, but out of respect or reverence to the name of the Supreme Being, to avoid the too frequent repetition of His name, they, the Church, in ancient days, called that Priesthood after Melchisedek."[d] This priesthood holds the right of presidency in all the offices of the Church; its special functions lie in the administration of spiritual things; comprising as it does the keys of all spiritual

---

y Numb. iii, 12-13, 39, 44-45, 50-51.

z Heb. vii, 11.

a Doc. and Cov. cvii, 1.

b Doc. and Cov. cvii, 20.

c Gen. xiv, 18; Heb. vii, 1-17.

d Doc. and Cov. cvii, 2-4.

blessings of the Church, the right "to have the heavens opened unto them, to commune with the general assembly and Church of the First Born, and to enjoy the communion and presence of God the Father, and Jesus the Mediator of the new covenant."[e] The special offices of the Melchisedek Priesthood are those of apostle, patriarch or evangelist, high priest, seventy, and elder. Revelation from God has defined the duties associated with each of these callings; and the same high authority has directed the establishment of presiding officers growing out of, or appointed from among those who are ordained to the several offices in these two priesthoods.[f]

16. **Specific Duties in the Priesthood:**—The office of Deacon is the first or lowest in the Aaronic Priesthood. The duties of this calling are generally of a temporal nature, pertaining to the care of the houses of worship and the comfort of the worshipers. In all things, however, the Deacon may be called to assist the Teacher in his labors.[g] Twelve deacons form a quorum;[h] such a body is to be presided over by a president and counselors, selected from among their number.

17. **Teachers** are local officers, whose function it is to mingle with the Saints, exhorting them to their duties, and strengthening the Church by their constant ministry; .they are to see that there is no iniquity in the Church; that the members do not cherish ill-feelings toward one another; but that all observe the law of God respecting Church duties.

---

e Doc. and Cov. cvii, 8, 18-19.

f Doc. aud Cov. cvii, 21.

g Doc. and Cov. xx, 57, cvii, 85.

h **Quorum:**—This term has acquired a special meaning among the Latter-day Saints. It signifies, not alone a majority or such a number of persons of any organized body as is requisite for authoritative action, but the organized body itself. The Church regards a quorum as "a council or an organized body of the priesthood," e. g. *an elders' quorum; the quorum of the Twelve Apostles*, etc. (See Standard Dictionary.)

They may take the lead of meetings when no Priest or higher officer is present. Both Teachers and Deacons may preach the word of God when properly directed so to do; but they have not the power to independently officiate in any spiritual ordinances, such as baptizing, administering the sacrament, or laying on of hands.[i] Twenty-four Teachers constitute a quorum; from among such a body a president and counselors are to be chosen.

18. **The Priests** are appointed to preach, teach, expound the scripture, to baptize, to administer the sacrament, to visit the houses of the members, exhorting them to their duties. When properly directed, the Priest may ordain Deacons, Teachers, and other Priests; and he may be called upon to assist the Elder in his work. A quorum of Priests comprises forty-eight members; such an organization is to be presided over by a Bishop.

19. **Elders** are empowered to officiate in any or all duties connected with lower callings in the priesthood; and in addition, they may ordain other Elders; confirm as members of the Church candidates who have been properly baptized, and confer upon them the Holy Ghost. These officers have authority to bless children in the Church, and to take charge of all meetings, conducting the same as they are led by the Holy Ghost.[j] The Elder may officiate in the stead of the High Priest when the latter is not present. Ninety-six Elders form a quorum; three of these constitute the presidency of the quorum.[k]

20. **Seventies** are traveling ministers, ordained to promulgate the Gospel among the nations of the earth, "unto the Gentiles first, and also unto the Jews." They are to act under the direction of the Apostles in this exalted labor.[l] A

i Doc. and Cov. xx, 53-59, cvii, 86.

j Doc. and Cov. xx, 38-45, 70; cvii, 11-12.

k Doc. and Cov cvii, 89.

l Doc and Cov cvii, 34-35, 97-98.

full quorum comprises seventy members, including seven presidents.

21. **High Priests** are ordained with power to officiate, when properly directed, in all the ordinances and blessings of the Church. They may travel as do the Seventies, carrying the Gospel to the nations; but they are not specially charged with this duty; their specific calling being that of standing presidency. The High Priests of any stake of the Church may be organized into a quorum, and this without limit as to number; over such a quorum, three of the members may be chosen to preside, as president and counselors.[m]

22. **Patriarchs,** or **Evangelists,** are charged with the special duty of blessing the Church; of course they have authority to officiate also in other ordinances. There is one "Patriarch to the Church," with general jurisdiction throughout the whole organization; he holds the keys of the patriarchal office, and unto him the promise is given "that whoever he blesses shall be blessed, and whoever he curses shall be cursed, that whatsoever he shall bind on earth shall be bound in heaven, and whatsoever he shall loose on earth shall be loosed in heaven."[n]

23. Concerning the patriarchial authority, the Lord has said: "The order of this priesthood was confirmed to be handed down from father to son, and rightly belongs to the literal descendants of the chosen seed to whom the promises were made. This order was instituted in the days of Adam, and came down by lineage."[o] But, beside this office of general patriarchial power, there are a number of local Patriarchs appointed in the branches of the Church, all subject to counsel and direction at the hands of the "Patriarch to the Church;" yet possessing the same

---

m Doc. and Cov. cvii, 10; cxxiv. 134-135.

n Doc. and Cov. cxxiv, 92-93.

o Doc. and Cov. cvii, 40-57.

privileges in their district as belong to him throughout the
Church. It is made a duty of the Twelve Apostles to
ordain evangelical ministers, or Patriarchs, in all large
branches of the Church, the selection to be made through
the power of revelation.[p]

24. **Apostles** are called to be special witnesses of the
name of Christ in all the world;[q] they are empowered to
build up and organize the branches of the Church; and
may officiate in any or all of the sacred ordinances. They
are to travel among the Saints, regulating the affairs of the
Church wherever they go, but particularly where there is
no complete local organization. They are authorized to
ordain Patriarchs, and other officers in the priesthood, as
they may be directed by the Spirit of God.[r]

25. **Presidency and Quorum Organizations:**—The revealed
word of God has provided for the establishment of presiding
officers "growing out of, or appointed from among those
who are ordained to the several offices in these two orders of
priesthoods."[s] In accordance with the prevailing principles of
order so characteristic of all His work, the Lord has directed
that the bearers of His priesthood shall be organized into
quorums, the better to aid them in learning the duties of
their stations. Some of these quorums are general in
extent and authority; others are local in their jurisdiction.
All quorums in authority and presiding officers are to be
sustained in their several positions by the vote of the people
over whom they are appointed to preside. Local officers are
thus voted upon by the local organizations, general authorities by the Church in conference assembled. Conferences
of the Church are held at semi-annual intervals, on which
occasions, the names of all the general officers are submitted

p Doc. and Cov. cvii, 39.
q Doc. and Cov. cvii, 23.
r Doc. and Cov. cvii, 39, 58; xx, 38-44.
s Doc. and Cov. cvii, 21.

for the vote of the people.   In like manner the authorities of stakes and wards are sustained by vote at local conferences held for these and other purposes.   The principle of common consent is thus observed in all the organizations of the Church.

26.   **The First Presidency** constitutes the presiding quorum of the Church.   By Divine direction, a president is appointed from among the members of the High Priesthood to preside over the entire Church.   He is known as President of the High Priesthood of the Church, or Presiding High Priest over the High Priesthood of the Church.[t]   He is called "to be a seer, a revelator, a translator, and a prophet, having all the gifts of God which He bestows upon the head of the Church."[u]   His station is compared by the Lord to that of Moses of old, who stood as the mouth-piece of God unto Israel.   In his exalted labors among the Church, this Presiding High Priest is assisted by two others holding the same priesthood, and these three High Priests, when properly appointed and ordained, and upheld by the confidence, faith and prayers of the Church, "form a quorum of the Presidency of the Church."[v]

27.   **The Quorum of the Twelve Apostles:**—Twelve men holding the Apostleship, properly organized, constitute the quorum of the Apostles.   These the Lord has designated as the twelve traveling counselors;[w] they form the traveling presiding High Council, to officiate under the direction of the First Presidency in all parts of the world.   They constitute a quorum, whose unanimous decisions are equally binding in power and authority with those of the First Presidency of the Church.[x]   When the quorum of the First

---

t Doc. and Cov. cvii, 64-68.

u Doc. and Cov. cvii, 91-92.

v Doc and Cov. cvii, 22.

w Doc. and Cov, cvii, 23, 33.

x Doc. and Cov. cvii, 24.

Presidency is disorganized through the death or disability
of the President, the directing authority in government
reverts at once to the quorum of the Twelve Apostles, by
whom the nomination to the Presidency is made.   There
may be, and at present are, Apostles in the Church who are
not members of this quorum of Twelve; but such could
claim no place in the sittings of the quorum.

28.   The Presiding Quorum of Seventy:—The first quorum
of Seventies form a body, whose unanimous decisions are
equally binding with those of the Twelve Apostles.   Many
such quorums of Seventy may be required in the work of
the Church; already there have been effected more than a
hundred of such organizations; each quorum is presided
over by seven presidents.   The seven presidents of the
First Quorum of Seventies, however, preside over all the
other quorums and their presidents.[y]

29.   The Presiding Bishopric, as at present constituted,
comprises the Presiding Bishop of the Church, and two
Counselors.   This quorum holds jurisdiction over the duties
of other Bishops in the Church, and of all organizations
pertaining to the Aaronic Priesthood.   The oldest living
representative among the sons of Aaron is entitled to this
office of presidency, provided he be in all respects worthy and
qualified; he must be designated and ordained by the First
Presidency of the Church.[z]   If such a literal descendant of
Aaron be found and ordained, he may act without counselors, except when he sits in judgment in a trial of one of
the presidents of the High Priesthood, in which case he is
to be assisted by twelve High Priests.[a]   But in the absence
of any lineal descendant of Aaron properly qualified, a High
Priest of the Melchisedek Priesthood may be called and set
apart by the First Presidency of the Church to the office of

y Doc. and Cov. cvii, 25-26; 34, 93-97.
z Doc. and Cov. lxviii. 18-20.
a Doc. and Cov. cvii, 82-83.

Presiding Bishop; he is to be assisted by two other High Priests properly ordained as his counselors.[b]

30. **Local Organizations of the Priesthood:**—Where the Saints are permanently · located, Stakes of Zion are organized, each Stake comprising a number of wards or branches. Over each Stake is placed a *Stake Presidency*, consisting of a president and two counselors, who are High Priests properly chosen and set apart to this office. The Stake Presidency is assisted in judical function by a *Standing High Council*, composed of twelve High Priests chosen and ordained to the office. This Council is presided over by the Stake Presidency, and forms the highest judicial tribunal of the Stake.

31. The presidents of stakes and bishops of wards are properly regarded as pastors to the fold; their duties are doubtless analogous to those of the pastors of former dispensations. The High Priests and the Elders in each Stake are organized into quorums as already described; the former without limitation as to number, the latter forming one or more quorums, each of ninety-six members, as their number may warrant. *Patriarchs* are also set apart to officiate in their holy office among the people of the Stake.

32. **A Ward Bishopric** is established in every fully organized Ward of the Church. This body consists usually of three High Priests set apart as a Bishop and Counselors. If, however, a literal descendant of Aaron be called to the bishopric, it is his privilege to act without counselors, as was stated in the case of the Presiding Bishop. The Bishop has jurisdiction over the quorums of the Lesser Priesthood in his Ward; and also over holders of the Higher Priesthood as members of his Ward; but he has no direct presidency over quorums of the Melchisedek order, as such, which may be embraced within his domain. As a presiding High Priest, he properly presides over his entire Ward. The ward or-

---

b Doc. and Cov. lxviii, 19.

ganization comprises quorums of Priests, Teachers, and Deacons, one or more of each as the numerical extent of the Ward may determine.

33. **Helps in Government:**—Beside these constituted authorities and offices in the priesthood, there are a number of secondary or special organizations established among the people for educational and benevolent purposes. Among these, the following are of such importance as to call for special mention.

(1.) *Primary Associations:*—These provide for the moral instruction and training of young children.

(2.) *Mutual Improvement Associations:*—These comprise separate organizations for the sexes, and are designed for the education and training of the youth, in subjects of general and theological interest. Instruction is provided in theology, literature and history, science and art, the laws of health, and numerous other branches of useful knowledge.

(3.) *Sunday Schools*, comprise graded classes for the study of the scriptures, and for training in theology, in moral and religious duties, and in the discipline of the Church. Sunday schools, while primarily designed for the young are open to all.

(4.) *Church Schools:*—These institutions provide for both secular and religious instruction, and range from the grade of the kindergarten to that of the college.

(5.) *Religion Classes:*—In these is provided a course of graded instruction in theology and religion, which is offered as a supplement and complement to the purely secular teachings of the non-denominational schools.

(6.) *Relief Societies:*—These are composed of women whose self-imposed duties relate to the care of the poor, and the relief of suffering among the afflicted.

34. Most of these auxiliary organizations exist in each ward. Indeed, with the exception of Church Schools, which

usually rank as stake institutions, or even as of wider scope, all of the secondary organizations named are regarded as essential to the complete equipment of any ward. Officers are appointed to preside over the several organizations in each ward; and while such officers are subject in a general way to the local authorities in the priesthood, they look for specific instructions regarding the plan and method of their particular work, to the stake and general authorities of the special organizations. In accordance with the principle of common consent which characterizes the Church in general, the officers of the auxiliary institutions, while they are nominated by, or at least with the consent of the established authorities in the priesthood, are installed and retained in office by the vote of the members in the local or general organization within which they are appointed to labor.

NOTES.

1. **Degeneracy of Worship Incident to the Apostasy:**—That, as the priesthood disappeared from the earth after the apostolic period, the forms of worship were perverted, while many pagan influences and practices crept in, may be reasonably inferred from the records of history. Mosheim, an authority of note in ecclesiastical history, has this to say regarding pagan innovations during the fourth century:—"The Christian bishops introduced, with but slight alterations, into the Christian worship, those rites and institutions by which, formerly, the Greeks and Romans and other nations had manifested their piety and reverence towards their imaginary deities; supposing that the people would more readily embrace Christianity, if they saw that the rites handed down to them from their fathers still existed unchanged among the Christians, and perceived that Christ and the martyrs were worshiped in the same manner as formerly their gods were. There was, of course, little difference in these times, between the public worship of the Christians, and that of the Greeks and Romans. In both alike, there were splendid robes, mitres, tiaras, wax tapers, crosiers, processions, illustrations, images, golden and silver vases, and numberless other things."

Of the form of professedly Christian worship in the fifth century, the same authority says:—"Public worship everywhere assumed a form more calculated for show and for the gratification of the eye. Various ornaments were added to the sacerdotal garments, in order to increase the veneration of the people for the clerical order. * * * In some places it was appointed that the praises of

God should be sung perpetually night and day, the singers succeeding each other without interruption: as if the Supreme Being took pleasure in clamor and noise, and in the flatteries of men. The magnificence of the temples knew no bounds. Splendid images were placed in them; * * * the image of the Virgin Mary holding her infant in her arms occupied the most conspicuous place."

2. **Early Beginning of the Apostasy**:—Orson Pratt, an apostle of the present age, has written as follows concerning the early falling away from the authorized practices of the Church: "The great apostasy of the Christian church commenced in the first century, while there were yet inspired apostles and prophets in their midst: hence Paul, just previous to his martyrdom, enumerates a great number who had 'made shipwreck of their faith.' and 'turned aside into vain jangling,' teaching 'that the resurrection was already past;' giving 'heed to fables and endless genealogies;' 'doubting about questions and strifes of words whereof come envyings, railings, evil surmisings, perverse disputings of men of corrupt minds, and destitute of the truth, supposing that gain is godliness ' This apostasy had become so general that Paul declares to Timothy 'that all they which are in Asia be turned away from me:' and again he says, 'at my first answer, no man stood with me, but all men forsook me;' he further states that 'there are many unruly, and vain talkers, deceivers,' 'teaching things which they ought not, for filthy lucre's sake.' These apostates, no doubt, pretended to be very righteous, 'for,' says the apostle, 'they profess that they know God, but in works they deny him, being abominable and disobedient, and unto every good work reprobate.' "

LECTURE XII.

SPIRITUAL GIFTS.

Article 7. We believe in the gift of tongues, prophecy, revelation, visions, healing, interpretation of tongues, etc.

1. **Spiritual Gifts Characteristic of the Church:**—It has been already affirmed that all men who would officiate with propriety in the ordinances of the Gospel, must be commissioned for their exalted duties by the power and authority of heaven. When so divinely invested, these servants of the Lord will not be lacking in proofs of the Master's favor; for it has ever been characteristic of the dealings of God with His people, to manifest His power by the bestowal of a variety of ennobling graces, which are properly called gifts of the Spirit. These are oft-times exhibited in a manner so diverse from the usual order of things as to be called miraculous and supernatural. In this way did the Lord make Himself known in the early times of scriptural history; and from the days of Adam until the present, prophets of God have generally been endowed with such power. Whenever the priesthood has operated through an organized Church on the earth, the members of the flock have been strengthened in their faith, and otherwise blessed in numerous related ways, by the possession of these graces within the Church. We may safely regard the existence of these spiritual powers as one of the essential characteristics of the true Church; where they are not, the priesthood of God does not operate.

2. Mormon[a] solemnly declares that the days of miracles will not pass from the Church, as long as there shall be a

a Moroni vii, 35-37.

man upon the earth to be saved; "For," says he, "it is by faith that miracles are wrought; and it is by faith that angels appear and minister unto men; wherefore if these things have ceased, wo be unto the children of men, for it is because of unbelief, and all is vain." And Moroni, standing on the threshold of the grave, bears an independent testimony that the gifts and graces of the Spirit will never be done away as long as the world shall stand, except it be through the unbelief of mankind.[b]

3. Hear the words of this prophet addressed to those "who deny the revelations of God and say that they are done away, that there are no revelations nor prophecies, nor gifts, nor healing, nor speaking with tongues, and the interpretation of tongues. Behold I say unto you, he that denieth these things knoweth not the Gospel of Christ; yea he has not read the scriptures; if so, he does not understand them. For do we not read that God is the same yesterday, today, and forever, and in him there is no variableness neither shadow of changing? And now, if ye have imagined up unto yourselves a god who doth vary, and in him there is shadow of changing, then have ye imagined up unto yourselves a god who is not a God of miracles. But behold, I will show unto you a God of miracles, even the God of Abraham, and the God of Isaac, and the God of Jacob; and it is that same God who created the heavens and the earth, and all things that in them are."[c]

4. **Nature of Spiritual Gifts:**—The gifts here spoken of are essentially endowments of power and authority, through which the purposes of God are accomplished, sometimes with accompanying conditions that appear to be supernatural. By such the sick may be healed, malignant influences overcome, spirits of darkness subdued, the Saints, humble

---

[b] Moroni x, 19, 23-27.
[c] Mormon ix, 7-11.

and weak, may proclaim their testimonies and otherwise utter praises unto God in new and strange tongues, and others may interpret these words; the feeble human intellect may be invigorated by the heavenly touch of spiritual vision and blessed dreams, to see and comprehend things ordinarily withheld from mortal senses; direct communication with the fountain of all wisdom may be established, and the revelations of the Divine will may be obtained.

5. These gifts have been promised of the Lord unto those who believe in His name;[d] they are to follow obedience to the requirements of the Gospel. Among believers, they are to serve for encouragement, and as incentives to higher communion with the Spirit.[e] They are not given as signs to gratify carnal curiosity; nor to satisfy a morbid craving for the wonderful. Men have been led to the light through manifestations of the miraculous; but events in the lives of these show that they are either such as would have found a knowledge of the truth in some other way, or they are but superficially affected, and as soon as the novelty of the new sensation has exhausted itself they wander again into the darkness from which they had for the time escaped. Miracles are not primarily intended, surely they are not needed, to prove the power of God; the simpler occurrences, the more ordinary works of creation do that. But unto the heart already softened and purified by the testimony of the truth, to the mind enlightened through the Spirit's power, and conscious of obedient service in the requirements of the gospel, the voice of miracles comes with cheering tidings of a loving Parent's continued favor, with fresh and more abundant evidences of the magnanimity of an all-merciful God.[f]

---

d Mark xvi, 16; Doc. and Cov. lxxxiv, 64-73.

e Matt. xii, 38, 39; xvi, 1-4; Mark viii, 11, 12; Luke xi, 16-30.

f See Note 6.

6.   Yet even to the unbeliever, the testimony of miracles should appeal, at least to the extent of argument favoring an investigation of the power through which these acts are wrought; in such cases miracles are as "a loud voice addressed to those who are hard of hearing." The purpose of spiritual gifts in the Church is explicitly set forth in a revelation from the Lord through Joseph Smith:—"Wherefore, beware lest ye be deceived; and that ye may not be deceived, seek ye earnestly the best gifts, always remembering for what they are given; For verily I say unto you, they are given for the benefit of those who love me and keep all my commandments, and him that seeketh so to do, that all may be benefited that seeketh or that asketh of me, that asketh and not for a sign that he may consume it upon his lusts."[g]

7.   **Miracles** are commonly regarded as supernatural occurrences, taking place in opposition to the laws of nature. Such a conception is plainly erroneous, for the laws of nature are inviolable. However, as human understanding of these laws is at best but imperfect, events strictly in accordance with natural law may appear contrary thereto. The entire constitution of nature is founded on system and order; the laws of nature, however, are graded as are the laws of man. The application of a higher law in any particular case does not destroy the efficacy or validity of an inferior one; the lower law is as fully applicable as before to the cases for which it was framed. For example, society has enacted a law, forbidding, on peril of heavy penalties, any man appropriating the property of another; yet oftentimes officers of the law forcibly seize the possessions of their fellow-men, against whom judgments may have been rendered; and such acts are done to satisfy, not to violate justice. Jehovah commanded "Thou shalt not kill," and

g Doc. and Cov. xlvi, 8, 9.

mankind has re-enacted the law, prescribing penalties for violation thereof. Yet sacred history testifies, that, in certain cases, the Lawgiver, Himself, has directly commanded His servants to vindicate justice by taking human life. The judge who passes the extreme sentence upon a convicted murderer, and the executioner who carries into effect that terrible mandate, act not in opposition of "Thou shalt not kill," but actually in support of this decree.

8. With some of the principles upon which the powers of nature operate, we are in a degree acquainted; and in contemplating them, we are no longer surprised, though deeper reflection may show that even the commonest occurrence is wonderful and strange. But any event beyond the ordinary is pronounced miraculous, supernatural, if not indeed unnatural, and we are more or less awe-stricken by the same.[h] When the prophet Elisha caused the axe to float in the river,[i] he brought to his service, through the exercise of the authority of the priesthood, a power superior to that of gravity. Without doubt, the iron was heavier than the water; yet by the operation of this higher force it was supported, suspended, or otherwise sustained at the surface, as if it were held there by a human hand, or rendered sufficiently buoyant by attached floaters.

9. Wine ordinarily consists of about four-fifths water, the rest being a variety of chemical compounds, the elements of which are abundantly present in the air and soil. The ordinary method,—what we term the natural method— of bringing these elements into proper combination is by planting the grape, then cultivating the vine till the fruit is ready to yield its juice in the press. But by the exercise of a power, not within purely human reach, the Savior, at the marriage in Cana,[j] called those elements together, and

h See note 1.
i II Kings vi, 5-7.
j John ii, 1-11.

brought about a chemical transformation within the water-pots of stone, resulting in the production of pure wine. So, too, when the multitudes were fed, under His priestly touch and authoritative blessing, the bread and fishes increased in substance, as if the seasons of years had been consumed in their growth according to what we consider the natural order. In healing the leprous, the palsied, and the infirm, the disordered bodily parts were brought again into their normal and healthful state; the impurities operating as poisons in the tissues were removed by means more rapid and effectual than those which depend upon the action of drugs and physic.

10. No earnest observer, no reasoning mind, can doubt the existence of intelligences and organisms which the senses of man do not reveal. This world seems but the temporal embodiment of things spiritual. The Creator has told us that He formed all things spiritual before they were made temporal.[k] The flowers that flourish and die on earth are perhaps represented above by imperishable blossoms of transcendent beauty and entertaining fragrance. Man is shaped after the image of Deity; his mind, though darkened by custom and weakened by injurious habit, is still a fallen type of immortal thought and Divine reason; and though the space separating the human and the Divine in thought, desire, and action, be as wide as that between sea and sky, for as the stars are above the earth so are the ways of God above those of man, yet, we cannot doubt a strict analogy between the spiritual and the temporal. When the eyes of Elisha's servant were opened, the man saw the hosts of heavenly warriors covering the mountains about Dothan,—footmen, horsemen, and chariots, armed for fight against the Syrians.[l] When Israel encompassed Jericho,[m] may we

k See note, page 199.
l II Kings vi, 13-18.
m Josh. vi.

not believe that the Captain of the Lord's host[n] and his
heavenly train were there, and that before their angelic
powers, sustained by the faith and obedience of the mortal
army, the walls were leveled?

11. Some of the latest and highest achievements of man
in the utilization of natural forces approach the conditions
of spiritual operations. To count the ticking of a watch a
hundred miles away; to speak in but an ordinary tone and
be heard across the country; to signal from one hemisphere
and be understood on the other, though oceans roll and
roar between; to bring the lightning into our homes and
make it serve as fire and torch;—are not these miracles? The
possibility of such things would not have been received with
credence before their actual accomplishment. The President of the Republic, sitting in his chair of state at the
nation's capital, talks with all parts, even with the ends of
this great country; and if batteries and wire be in order, if
operators and officials be true, he is rightly informed of
every movement of importance anywhere in the land. The
orbs of the universe are as truly connected by a system of
inter-communication, surprisingly perfect in its action and
adaptation. These and the other innumerable miracles of
creation are accomplished in strict accordance with the laws
of nature, which are the laws of God. But we must return
to a further consideration of the specific manifestations of
spiritual gifts within the Church.

12. **An Enumeration of the Gifts of the Spirit** cannot be
made complete by man, so numerous, so extensive are the
blessings of the Father for His children. Yet the more
common of these spiritual manifestations have been specified by inspired scriptural writers, and by the sure word of
revelation. Paul writing to the Corinthian Saints,[o] Moroni

n Josh. v, 13, 14.
o I Cor. xii, 4-11.

16

inditing his last appeal to the Lamanites,[p] and the voice of
the Lord directed to the people of His Church in this dispensation,[q] each names many of the great gifts of the Spirit.
From these scriptures, we learn that every man has received
some gift from God; and in the great diversity of gifts all
do not receive the same. "To some it is given by the Holy
Ghost to know the differences of administration. *   *   *
And again it is given by the Holy Ghost to some to know
the diversities of operations whether it be of God, that the
manifestations of the Spirit may be given to every man to
profit withal. And again, verily I say unto you, to some it
is given by the Spirit of God, the word of wisdom; to
another it is given the word of knowledge, that all may be
taught to be wise, and to have knowledge. And again to
some it is given to have faith to be healed; and to others it
is given to have faith to heal. And again to some it is given
the working of miracles, and to others it is given to
prophesy, and to others the discerning of spirits. And
again, it is given to some to speak with tongues; and to
another it is given the interpretation of tongues; and all
these gifts cometh from God for the benefit of the children
of God."[r]

13. The Gift of Tongues and Interpretation:—The gift
of tongues constituted one of the first miraculous manifestations of the Holy Ghost with the apostles of old. It was
included by the Savior among the special signs appointed to
follow the believer; "In my name," said He, "they shall
speak with new tongues."[s] The early fulfilment of this
promise in the case of the apostles themselves, was realized
on the succeeding Pentecost, when they, having assembled
in one place, were filled with the Holy Ghost and began to

p Moroni x, 7-19.

q Doc. and Cov. xlvi, 8-29.

r Doc. and Cov. xlvi, 11-26; see also I Cor. xii, 4-11.

s Mark xvi, 17.

speak in strange tongues.[t] When the door of the Gospel
was first opened to the Gentiles, the converts rejoiced in the
Holy Ghost which had fallen upon them, and which gave
them utterance in tongues.[u] This gift with others manifested itself among certain disciples at Ephesus,[v] on the
occasion of their receiving the Holy Ghost. In the present
dispensation, this gift, again promised to the Saints, finds
frequent exercise. Its chief employment is in the function
of praise, rather than that of instruction and preaching;
and this is agreeable to Paul's teaching, "For he that
speaketh in an unknown tongue speaketh not unto men
but unto God."[w] An unusual manifestation of the gift
was witnessed on the occasion of the Pentecostal conversion
of the Jews, already referred to, when the apostles speaking
unto the multitude, were understood by all the diversified
company, each listener hearing their teachings in his own
tongue.[x] This special gift was here associated with higher
endowments of power; the occasion was one of instruction,
admonition, and prophecy. The gift of interpretation may
be possessed by the one speaking in tongues, though more
commonly the separate powers are exercised by different
persons.

14. The Gift of Healing was exercised extensively in the
dispensation of the Savior and His apostles; indeed, healing
constituted by far the greater part of the miracles wrought
at that time. By authoritative ministrations, the eyes of
the blind were opened; the dumb were made to speak; the
deaf to hear; the lame leaped for joy; afflicted mortals,
bowed with infirmity, were lifted erect and enjoyed the
vigor of youth; the palsied were made well; lepers were

t Acts ii, 4.
u Acts x, 46.
v Acts xix, 6.
w I Cor. xiv, 2.
x Acts ii, 6-12.

cleansed; impotence was banished; and fevers were as-
suaged. In this, the dispensation of the fulness of times,
this power is possessed by the Church, and its manifestation
is of frequent occurrence among the Saints. Thousands of
blessed recipients can testify to the fulfilment of the Lord's
promise, that if His servants lay hands on the sick, they
shall recover.[y]

15. The usual method of administering to the sick is by
the imposition of hands of those who possess the requisite
authority of the priesthood;—this being agreeable to the
Savior's instructions in former days,[z] and according to
Divine revelation in the present day.[a] This part of the
ordinance is usually preceded by an anointing with oil
previously consecrated. The Latter-day Saints profess to
abide by the counsels of James of old,[b] "Is any sick among
you? Let him call for the elders of the church, and let
them pray over him, anointing him with oil in the name of
the Lord; and the prayer of faith shall save the sick, and
the Lord shall raise him up; and if he have committed sins,
they shall be forgiven him."

16. Though the authority to administer to the sick
belongs to the elders of the Church in general, some possess
this power in an unusual degree, having received it as a
special endowment of the Spirit. Another gift, allied to
this, is the power of exercising faith to be healed;[c] which is
manifested in varying degrees. Not always are the admin-
istrations of the elders followed by immediate healings; the
afflicted may be permitted to suffer in body, perhaps for the
accomplishment of Divine purposes,[d] and in the time ap-

---

y Mark xvi, 18; see also Doc. and Cov. lxxxiv, 68.

z The same: see also James v, 14, 15.

a Doc. and Cov. xlii, 43-44.

b James v, 14, 15.

c Doc. and Cov. xlvi, 19; xlii, 48-51; see also Acts xiv, 9: Matt. viii, 10; ix, 28, 29.

d See instances of Job.

pointed of the Lord, His children pass through bodily death. But let the counsels of God be observed in administering to the afflicted; then if they recover, they live unto the Lord; and the assuring promise is added that those who die under such conditions die unto the Lord.[e]

17. **Visions and Dreams** have constituted a means of communication between God and His children in every dispensation of the priesthood. In general, visions are manifested to the waking senses, whilst dreams are given during sleep. In the vision, however, the senses may be so affected as to render the person practically unconscious, at least oblivious to ordinary occurrences, while he is able to discern the heavenly manifestation. In the earlier dispensations, the Lord very frequently communicated through dreams and visions, often-times revealing to His prophets the events of the future, even to the latest generations. From the multitude of instances recorded, let us select a few. Consider the case of Enoch,[f] unto whom the Lord spake face to face, showing him the course of the human family until and beyond the second coming of the Savior. The brother of Jared,[g] because of his righteousness was so blessed of God, as to be shown all the inhabitants of the earth, both those who had previously existed, and those who were to follow. Unto Moses the will of God was made known with the visual manifestation of fire.[h] Lehi received his instructions to leave Jerusalem[i] through dreams; and on many subsequent occasions the Lord communicated with this patriarch of the western world by visions and by dreams. The Old Testament prophets were generally so favored; e. g., Jacob the

---

e Doc. and Cov. xlii, 44-46.
f Pearl of Great Price; Writings of Moses, p. 28-30.
g Ether iii.
h Exo. iii, 2.
i I Nephi ii, 2-4.

father of all Israel,[j] Job, the patient sufferer,[k] Jeremiah,[l] Ezekiel,[m] Daniel,[n] Habakkuk,[o] Zechariah.[p]

18. The dispensation of Christ and His apostles was marked by similar manifestations. The birth of John the Baptist was foretold to his father while he was officiating in priestly functions.[q] Joseph, betrothed to the Virgin, received through an angel's visit[r] tidings of the Christ yet to be born; and on subsequent occasions he received warnings and instructions in dreams concerning the welfare of the Holy Child.[s] The Magi, returning from their pilgrimage of worship, were warned in dreams of Herod's treacherous designs.[t] Saul of Tarsus was shown in a vision the messenger whom God was about to send to him to minister in the ordinances of the priesthood;[u] and other visions followed.[v] Peter was prepared for the ministry to the Gentiles through a vision;[w] and John was so favored of God in this respect that the book of Revelation is occupied by the record.

19. Most of the visions and dreams recorded in scripture have been given to the chosen people, through the ministering priesthood; but there are exceptional instances of such manifestations unto some, who, at the time, had not entered the fold. Such, for example, was the case with Saul and Cornelius; but in these instances the Divine manifestations were immediately preliminary to conversion. Dreams with

---

j Gen. xlvi, 2.

k Job iv, 12-21.

l Jer. i, 11-16.

m Ezek. i; ii, 9, 10; iii, 22, 23; viii; xxxvii, 1-10, etc.

n Dan. vii; viii.

o Hab. ii, 2, 3.

p Zech. i, 8-11; 18-21; ii, 1, 2; iv; v; vi, 1-8.

q Luke i, 5-22.

r Matt. i, 20.

s Matt. ii, 13, 19, 22.

t Matt. ii, 12.

u Acts ix, 12.

v Acts xvi, 9; xviii, 9, 10; xxii, 17-21.

w Acts x, 10-16; xi, 5-10.

special import were given to Pharaoh,[x] Nebuchadnezzar[y] and others; but it required a higher power than their own to interpret them; and Joseph and Daniel were called to officiate. The dream given to the Midianite soldier, and its interpretation by his fellow,[z] betokening the victory of Gideon, were true manifestations; as also the dream of Pilate's wife,[a] in which she learned of the innocence of the accused Christ.

20. **The Gift of Prophecy** distinguishes its possessor as a prophet,—literally one who speaks for another; specifically, one who speaks for God.[b] It is distinguished by Paul as one of the most desirable of spiritual endowments, and its pre-eminence over the gift of tongues he discusses at length.[c] To prophesy is to receive and declare the word of God, and the statement of His will to the people. The function of prediction, often regarded as the sole essential of prophecy, is but one among many characteristics of this divinely given power. The prophet may have as much concern with the past, as with the present, or the future; he may exercise his gift in teaching through the light of, and by the experience of preceding events, as in fore-telling occurrences. The prophets of God have ever been in special favor with Him, being privileged to learn of His will and designs; indeed the promise is made that the Lord will do nothing except He reveal His secret purposes unto His servants, the prophets.[d] These chosen oracles stand as mediators between God and mortals, pleading for or against the people.[e]

21. No special ordination in the priesthood is essential to

---

x Gen. xli: see other instances in Gen. xl.

y Dan. ii.

z Jud. vii, 13, 14.

a Matt. xxvii, 19.

b See note 2.

c I Cor. xiv, 1-9.

d Amos iii, 7.

e I Kings xviii, 36, 37; Rom. xi, 2, 3; James v, 16-18; Rev. xi, 6.

man's receiving the gift of prophecy; bearers of the Melchizedek order, Adam, Noah, Moses, and a multitude of others were truly prophets, but not more truly so than were many who exercised the Aaronic functions only—as for example most of the Old Testament priests, subsequent to the time of Moses, and John the Baptist.[f] The ministrations of the prophetesses Miriam[g] and Deborah[h] show that this gift may be possessed by women also. In the time of Samuel, the prophets were organized into a special order, to aid their purposes of study and improvement.[i]

22. In the present dispensation, this great gift is enjoyed in a fulness equal to that of any preceding time. The Lord's will concerning present duties is made known to His people through the mouths of prophets; and events of great import are fore-told.[j] The very fact of the present existence and growing condition of the Church is an undeniable testimony of the power and reliability of modern prophecy. The Latter-day Saints constitute a body of witnesses, numbering hundreds of thousands, to the effect of this, one of the great gifts of God.

23. **Revelation** is the means through which the will of God is declared directly and in fulness to man. Under circumstances best suiting the Divine purposes, through the dreams of sleep or in waking visions of the mind, by voices without visional appearance, or by actual manifestations of the Holy Presence before the eye, God makes known His designs, and charges His chosen vessels to bear the sacred messages so imparted. Under the influence of inspiration, or its more potent manifestation—revelation, man's mind is enlightened, and his energies quickened to the accomplish-

---

f Matt. xi, 8-10.

g Exo. xv, 20.

h Jud. iv, 4.

i See note 3.

j Doc. and Cov. i, 4; lxxxvii.

ment of wonders in the work of human progress; touched with
a spark from the heavenly altar, the inspired instrument
cherishes the holy fire within his soul, and imparts it to
others as he may be led to do; he is the channel through
which the will of God is conveyed. The words of him who
speaks by revelation in its highest form, are not his own;
they are the words of God Himself; the mortal mouth-piece
is but the trusted conveyance of these heavenly messages.
With the authoritative, "Thus saith the Lord," the revelator
delivers the burden intrusted to his care.

24. The Lord strictly observes the principles of order and
propriety in giving revelation to His servants. Though it is
the privilege of any person to live so as to merit this gift in
the affairs of his special calling, only those appointed and
ordained to the offices of presidency are to be revelators to
the people at large. Concerning the President of the
Church, who at the time of the revelation here referred to,
was the Prophet Joseph Smith, the Lord has said to
the elders of the Church:—"And this ye shall know
assuredly, that there is none other appointed unto you to
receive commandments and revelations until he be taken, if
he abide in me.   *   *   *   And this shall be a law unto
you, that ye receive not the teachings of any that shall
come before you, as revelations or commandments. And
this I give unto you that you may not be deceived, that you
may know they are not of me."[k]

25. The Testimony of Miracles:—The Savior's promise in
a former day[l] as in the present dispensation[m] is definite, to
the effect that specified gifts of the Spirit are to follow the
believer as signs of Divine favor. The possession and exercise of such gifts may be taken therefore as essential features of the Church of Christ.[n] Nevertheless we are not

k Doc. and Cov. xliii, 3, 5, 6.
l Mark xvi, 17-18.
m Doc. and Cov. lxxxiv, 65-73.
n See notes 4 and 5.

justified in regarding the evidence of miracles as infallible testimony of authority from heaven; on the other hand, the scriptures furnish abundant proof that spiritual powers of the baser sort have wrought miracles, and will continue so to do, to the deceiving of many who lack discernment. If miracles be accepted as infallible evidence of godly power, the magicians of Egypt, through the wonders which they accomplished in opposition to the ordained plan for Israel's deliverance, have as good a claim to our respect as has Moses.[o] John the Revelator saw in vision a wicked power working miracles, and thereby deceiving many; doing great wonders, even bringing fire from heaven.[p] Again, he saw three unclean spirits, whom he knew to be "the spirits of devils working miracles."[q]

26. Consider in connection with this, the prediction made by the Savior:—"There shall arise false Christs, and false prophets, and shall show great signs and wonders, insomuch that, if it were possible, they shall deceive the very elect."[r] The invalidity of miracles as a proof of righteousness is declared in an utterance of Christ Jesus regarding the events of the great judgment:—"Many will say to me in that day, Lord, Lord, have we not prophesied in thy name? and in thy name have cast out devils? and in thy name done many wonderful works? And then will I profess unto them, I never knew you; depart from me, ye that work iniquity."[s] The Jews, to whom these teachings were addressed, knew that wonders could be wrought by evil powers; for they charged Christ with working miracles by the authority of Beelzebub the prince of devils."[t]

27. If the working of miracles were a distinctive char-

---

o Exo. vii-xi.

p Rev. xiii, 11-18.

q Rev. xvi, 13-14.

r Matt. xxiv, 24.

s Matt. vii, 22-23.

t Matt. xii, 22-30; Mark iii, 22; Luke xi, 15.

acteristic of the holy priesthood, we would look for the
testimony of wondrous manifestations in connection with
the work of every prophet and authorized minister of the
Lord; yet we fail to find a record of miracles in the
case of Zechariah, Malachi, and other prophets of old;
while of John the Baptist, whom Christ declared to be
more than a prophet,[u] it was plainly said that he did no
miracle;[v] nevertheless, in rejecting John's doctrine, the unbelievers were ignoring the counsel of God against their
own souls.[w] To be valid as a testimony of truth, miracles
must be wrought in the name of Christ, and to His
honor, in furtherance of the plan of salvation. As stated,
they are not given to satisfy the curious and the lustful,
nor as a means of gaining notoriety for him through whom
they are accomplished. These gifts of the true Spirit are
manifested in support of the message from heaven, and in
corroboration of the words spoken by authority.

28. **Imitations of Spiritual Gifts:**—The proofs already
cited of miraculous achievements by powers other than of
God, and the scriptural predictions concerning such decep-
tive manifestations in the last days, ought to be our warning
against spurious imitations of the gifts of the Holy Spirit.
Satan has shown himself to be an accomplished strategist,
and a skilful imitator; the most deplorable of his victories are due to his simulation of good, whereby the
undiscerning have been led captive. Let us not be deluded
with the thought that any act, the immediate result of
which appears to be benign, is necessarily productive of permanent good. It may serve the dark purposes of man's
arch-enemy to play upon the human sense of goodness,
even to the extent of healing the body, and apparently of
thwarting death.

---

u Matt. xi, 9.

v John x, 41.

w Luke vii, 30.

29.   The restoration of the priesthood to earth in this age of the world, was followed by a phenomenal growth of the vagaries of spiritualism, whereby many have been led to put their trust in Satan's counterfeit of God's eternal power. The development of the healing gift in the Church to-day is imitated in a degree, comparable to that with which the magicians simulated the miracles of Moses, by the varied faith cures and their numerous modifications.   For those to whom miraculous signs are all-sufficient, the imitation will answer as well as would the real; but the soul who regards the miracle in its true nature as but one element of the system of Christ, possessing value as a positive criterion only as it is associated with the numerous other characteristics of the Church, will not be deceived.

30.   **Spiritual Gifts in the Church Today:**—The Latter-day Saints claim to possess within the Church all the sign-gifts promised as the heritage of the believer.   They point to the unimpeached testimonies of thousands who have been blessed with direct and personal manifestations of heavenly power; to the once blind, and dumb, halt, and weak in body, who have been freed from their infirmities through their faith and by the ministrations of the priesthood; to a multitude who have voiced their testimony in tongues with which they were naturally unfamiliar; or who have demonstrated their possession of the gift by a phenomenal mastery of foreign languages, when such was necessary to the discharge of their duties as preachers of the word of God; to many who have enjoyed communion with heavenly beings; to others who have prophesied in words that have found their speedy vindication in literal fulfilment; and to the Church itself, whose growth has been guided by the voice of its Divine Leader, made known through the gift of revelation.[x]

[x] See note 7.

NOTES.

1. A Seeming Miracle:—A few years ago, Herr Werner Siemens, a German scientist of note, visited the pyramid of Gizeh, and, accompanied by a couple of Arab guides, climbed to the top. He observed that the atmospheric conditions were very favorable to electric manifestations. Fastening a large brass button to an empty water-gourd in the hands of one of the Arabs, and then placing his knuckle within a short distance from the button, he drew therefrom a succession of brilliant sparks, accompanied of course by the crackling noises characteristic of electric discharges. The guides viewed this exhibition of supernatural powers with amazement and terror. which reached a climax when their master stretched his staff above his head, and the stick was surmounted by a beautiful St. Elmo's flame. This spectacle was more than the superstitious Bedouins could bear, they trembled before an enchanter who could play with lightning and fire as with a toy, and who carried miniature thunder in his coat pocket; so they fled down the steps with dangerous precipitation, and soon disappeared in the desert. So great was their fright that they forgot to claim their promised fees, which circumstance alone was no insignificent miracle.

2. The Term "Prophet" appears in the English Bible as the translation of a number of Greek terms, the most usual of which is *nabhi*, signifying "to bubble forth like a fountain." Another of the original words is *rheo*, meaning "to flow," and by derivation "to speak forth," "to utter," "to declare." A prophet, then, is one from whom flow forth the words of a higher authority. Aaron is spoken of as a prophet or spokesman to Moses (Exo. vii, 1); but in the usual sense, the prophet is the representative of God. Closely allied with the calling of the prophet is that of the seer; indeed at a time prior to that of Samuel, the common designation of the oracle of God was seer: "for he that is now called a prophet was beforetime called a seer," (I Sam. ix, 9). The seer was permitted to behold the visions of God, the prophet to declare the truths so learned; the two callings were usually united in the same person. Unto the prophet and seer the Lord usually communicated in visions and dreams; but an exception to this order was made in the case of Moses, who was so faithful and so great in all things good, that the Lord discarded the usual means and declared Himself to His servant face to face (Num. xii, 6-8).

3. Prophets Organized:—The prophet's office existed among men in the earliest periods of history. Adam was a prophet (Doc. and Cov. cvii, 53-56); as also were Enoch (Jude xiv: Pearl of Great Price p. 28), Noah (Gen. vi, vii; Pearl of Great Price p. 47; II Peter ii, 5), Abraham (Gen. xx, 7), Moses (Deut. xxxiv, 10), and a multitude of others who ministered at intermediate and subsequent times. Samuel, who was established in the eyes of all Israel as a prophet of the Lord, (I Sam. iii, 19, 20), organized the prophets into a society for common instruction and edification. He established schools for the prophets, theological colleges, where men were trained in things pertaining to holy offices; the students were generally called "sons of the prophets" (I Kings xx, 35: II Kings ii, 3, 5, 7; iv, 1, 38; ix, 1). Such schools were established at Ramah (I Sam. xix, 19, 20), Bethel (II Kings ii, 3), Jericho (II Kings ii, 5), Gilgal (II Kings iv, 38;). The members seem to have lived together as a society (II Kings vi. 1-4). In the present dispensation, a similar organization was effected under the direction of the prophet Joseph Smith; this also received the name of the School of the Prophets.

4. The Decline of Spiritual Gifts in former days is admitted by many authorities on ecclesiastical history and Christian doctrine. As an instance of this kind of testimony to the departure of the spiritual graces from the apostate church, the following words of John Wesley may be applied:—"It does not appear that these extraordinary gifts of the Holy Spirit were common in the church for more than two or three centuries. We seldom hear of them after that fatal period when the emperor Constantine called himself a Christian. and from a vain imagination of promoting the Christian cause thereby, heaped riches and power and honor upon Christians in general. but in particular upon the Christian clergy. From this time they almost totally ceased; very few instances of the kind were found. The cause of this was not as has been supposed because there was no more occasion for them,—because all the world was become Christians. This is a miserable mistake; not a twentieth part of it was then nominally Christian. The real cause of it was the love of many, almost all Christians. so-called, was waxed cold. The Christians had no more of the Spirit of Christ than the other heathens. The Son of Man, when he came to examine His Church, could hardly find faith upon the earth. This was the real cause why the extraordinary gifts of the Holy Ghost were no longer to be found in the Christian Church—because the Christians were turned heathens again, and only had a dead form left."—Wesley's Works vii, 89; 26-27.

5. Sectarian Views Concerning Continuance or Decline of Spiritual Gifts:—"Protestant writers insist that the age of miracles closed with the fourth or fifth century, and that after that the extraordinary gifts of the Holy Ghost must not be looked for. Catholic writers, on the other hand, insist that the power to perform miracles has always continued in the Church; yet those spiritual manifestations which they describe after the fourth and fifth centuries savor of invention on the part of the priests, and childish incredulity on the part of the people; or else, what is claimed to be miraculous falls far short of the power and dignity of those spiritual manifestations which the primitive church was wont to witness. The virtues and prodigies, ascribed to the bones and other relics of the martyrs and saints, are puerile in comparison with the healings by the anointing with oil and the laying on of hands, speaking in tongues, interpretations, prophecies, revelations, casting out devils in the name of Jesus Christ; to say nothing of the gifts of faith, wisdom, knowledge, discernment of spirits, etc.—common in the Church in the days of the apostles (I Cor. xii, 8-10). Nor is there anything in the scriptures or in reason that would lead one to believe that they were to be discontinued. Still this plea is made by modern Christians—explaining the absence of these spiritual powers among them—that the extraordinary gifts of the Holy Ghost were only intended to accompany the proclamation of the gospel during the first few centuries, until the church was able to make its way without them, and they were to be done away. It is sufficient to remark upon this, that it is assumption pure and simple, and stands without warrant either of scripture or right reason: and proves that men had so far changed the religion of Jesus Christ that it became a form of godliness without the power thereof."—Elder B. H. Roberts, *"Outlines of Ecclesiastical History,"* part ii, sec. v, 6-8.

6. Miracles an Aid to Spiritual Growth:—Apostle Orson Pratt, commenting on the utterances of Paul concerning the passing away of certain spiritual gifts (I Cor. xiii), writes in part as follows:—"The church in its militant and imperfect state, compared with its triumphant, immortal and perfect state, is (in the 11th verse) represented by the two very different states of childhood and manhood. "When," says St. Paul, "I was a child, I spake as a child, understood as a child, I thought as a child; but when I became a man I put away childish things." In the various stages of education from childhood to manhood, certain indispensable rules, and diagrams, and scientific instruments are employed for the use and benefit of the pupil, that he may acquire a correct knowledge of the sciences, and be perfected in his studies. When the principles have been once acquired, and the student has been perfected in every branch of education, he can dispense with many of his maps, charts, globes, books, diagrams, etc.; as being, like childish things, no longer necessary; they were useful before his education was perfected, in imparting the desired knowledge, but having fulfilled their purposes, he no longer needs their assistance. * * * * So it is with the Church in relation to spiritual gifts. While in this state of existence it is represented as a child: prophecy, revelations, tongues, and other spiritual gifts, are the instruments of education. The child, or church, can no more be perfected in its education without the aid of these gifts as instruments, than the chemist could in his researches if he were deprived of the necessary apparatus for experiments. As the chemist needs his laboratory for experiments, as long as there remains any undiscovered truths in relation to the elements and compounds of our globe, so does the Church need the great laboratory of spiritual knowledge—namely, revelation and prophecy,—as long as it knows only in part. * * * * As a human being, when a child, speaks as a child, understands as a child, and thinks as a child, so does the Church in this state of existence know only in part; but as the child, when it becomes a man, puts away childish things, so will the Church put away such childish things as 'prophecy in part,' 'knowledge in part,' and 'seeing in part,' when it grows up, through the aid of these things, to a perfect man in Christ Jesus; that which is in part will be done away or merged into the greater fulness of knowledge which there reigns."—"*Divine Authenticity of the Book of Mormon,*" i, 15.

But none of these gifts will be done away as long as the occasion for their exercise continues. That this was the conviction of Apostle Orson Pratt, whose words are quoted above, is evident from the following utterances by the same authority:—"The affliction of devils, the confusion of tongues, deadly poisons and sickness, are all curses which have been introduced into the world by the wickedness of man. The blessings of the gospel are bestowed to counteract these curses. Therefore, as long as these curses exist, the promised signs [Mark xvi, 16-18; Doc. and Cov. lxxxiv, 65-72] are needed to counteract their evil consequences. If Jesus had not intended that the blessings should be as extensive and unlimited in point of time as the curses, He would have intimated something to that effect in His word. But when He makes a universal promise of certain powers, to enable every believer in the gospel throughout the world to overcome certain curses, entailed upon man because of wickedness, it would be the rankest kind of infidelity not to believe the promised blessing necessary, as long as the curses abound among men."

7. **Modern Manifestations:**—The official and incidental publications of the Church abound in instances of miraculous manifestations during the current dispensation. A number of authenticated accounts with many cases are to be found as follows:—Orson Pratt's "Divine Authenticity of the Book of Mormon," chapter v; B. H. Roberts' "A New Witness for God," chapter xviii.

LECTURE XIII.

THE BIBLE.

Article 8.—We believe the Bible to be the word of God, as far as it is translated correctly   *   *   *

1. **Our Acceptance of the Bible:**—The Church of Jesus Christ of Latter-day Saints accepts the Bible as the first and foremost of her standard works, chief among the books which have been proclaimed as her written guides in faith and doctrine. In the respect and sanctity with which the Latter-day Saints regard the Bible, they are of like profession with Christian denominations in general; differing from them only in the additional acknowledgment of certain other scriptures as authentic and holy, which others are in harmony with the Bible, and serve to support and emphasize its facts and doctrines. There is, therefore, no specifically "Mormon" treatment of the Bible to be presented. The historical and other data, upon which is based the current Christian faith as to the genuineness of the biblical record, are accepted as unreservedly by the Latter-day Saints as by the members of any sect; and in literalness of interpretation this Church probably excels.

2. Nevertheless, the Church announces a reservation in the case of erroneous translation, which may occur as a result of human incapacity; and even in this measure of caution we are not alone, for biblical scholars generally admit the presence of errors of the kind, many of them self-apparent. The Latter-day Saints believe the original records to be the word of God unto man, and, as far as these records have been translated correctly, the translations are regarded as equally authentic. The English Bible professes

to be a translation made through the wisdom of man; in its preparation the most scholarly men have been enlisted; yet not a version has been published in which even the unlearned cannot perceive errors. However, an impartial investigator has cause to wonder more at the paucity of errors than that errors are to be found at all.

3. There will be, there can be, no absolutely reliable translation of these or other scriptures, unless it be effected through the gift of translation, as one of the endowments of the Holy Ghost. The translator must have the spirit of the prophet if he would render in another tongue the prophet's words; and human wisdom leads not to that possession. Let the Bible then be read reverently, and with prayerful care, the reader ever seeking the light of the Spirit that he may discern between truth and the mistakes of men.

4. **The Name "Bible:"**—In present usage, the term, *Bible*, designates the collection of sacred writings otherwise known as the Jewish scriptures, containing an account of the dealings of God with the human family; which account is confined wholly, except in the record of ante-diluvian events, to the Eastern hemisphere. The word itself, though singular in form, is the English representative of a Greek plural, *Biblia*, signifying literally *the books*. The use of the word probably dates from the fourth century, at which time we find Chrysostom[a] employing the term to designate the scriptural books then accepted as canonical by the Greek Christians. It is to be noted, that the idea of a collection of books predominates in all early usages of the word *Bible;* the scriptures were, as they are, composed of the special writings of many authors, widely separated in time; and, from the striking harmony and unity prevailing

a See Note 1.

17

throughout these diverse productions, strong evidence of their authenticity may be adduced.

5.   The word *Biblia* was thus endowed with a special meaning in the Greek, signifying *the books*, that is to say the holy books as distinguishing the sacred scriptures from all other writings; and the term soon became current in the Latin, in which tongue it was used from the first in its special sense.   Through Latin usage, perhaps during the thirteenth century, the word came to be regarded as a singular noun, signifying *the book;* this departure from the plural meaning, invariably associated with the term in the Greek original, led up to the popular error of regarding the Bible as having been a unified volume from the first.   Hence we meet with the reputed derivation of the word from the Greek singular noun *Biblos* meaning *the book*, but this is declared by a preponderance of good authority to be founded on a traditional misconception.   It may appear that the derivation of a word is of trifling importance; yet in this case, the original form and first use of the title now current as that of the sacred volume, must be of instructive interest, as throwing some light upon the compilation of the book in its present form.

6.   It is evident that the name *Bible* is not of itself a biblical term; its use as a designation of the Jewish scriptures is wholly external to those scriptures themselves.   In its earliest application, which dates from post-apostolic times, it was made to embrace most if not all the books of the Old and the New Testament.   Prior to the time of Christ, the books of the Old Testament were known by no single collective name, but were designated in groups as (1) the Pentateuch, or five books of the Law; (2) the Prophets; and (3) the Hagiographa, comprising all sacred records not included in the other divisions.   But we may the better consider the parts of the Bible by taking the main divisions

separately. A very natural division of the biblical record is
effected by the earthly work of the Savior; the written productions of pre-Christian times came to be known as the
Old Covenant; those of the days of the Savior and the years
immediately following, as the New Covenant.[b] The term
testament gradually grew in favor until the designations
Old and New Testaments became common.

THE OLD TESTAMENT.

7. **Its Origin and Growth:**—At the time of our Lord's
ministry in the flesh, the Jews were in possession of certain
scriptures which they regarded as canonical or authoritative.   There can be little doubt as to the authenticity of
those works, for they were frequently quoted by both Christ
and the apostles, by whom they were designated as "the
scriptures."[c]   The Savior specifically refers to them under
their accepted terms of classification as "the law of Moses,
the prophets, and the psalms."[d]   The books thus accepted
by the people in the time of Christ are sometimes spoken
of as the Jewish canon of scripture.   The term *canon*,
now generally current, suggests not books that are merely
credible, authentic, or even inspired; but such books as are
recognized as authoritative guides in profession and practice.   The term is instructive in its derivation.   Its Greek
original, *kanon*, signified a straight measuring rod, and hence
it came to mean an authoritative standard of comparison, a
rule, or test, as applied to moral subjects as well as to
material objects.

8. As to the formation of the Jewish canon, or the Old
Testament, we read that Moses wrote the first part of it,
viz. the Law; and that he committed it to the care of the

---

b I Cor. xi, 25; see also Jer. xxxi, 31.

c John v, 39; Acts xvii, 11.

d Luke xxiv, 44.

priests, or Levites, with a command that they preserve it in the ark of the covenant,[e] to be a witness against Israel in their transgressions. Fore-seeing that a king would some day govern Israel, Moses commanded that the monarch should make a copy of the Law for his guidance.[f] Joshua, successor of Moses, as leader and law-giver of Israel, wrote further of the dealings of God with the people, and of the Divine precepts; and this writing he evidently appended to the Law as recorded by Moses.[g] Three centuries and a half after the time of Moses, when the theocracy had been replaced by a monarchy, Samuel, the approved prophet of the Lord, wrote of the change, "in a book, and laid it up before the Lord."[h] And thus we see the law of Moses was augmented by later authoritative records. From the writings of Isaiah, we learn that the people had access to the "Book of the Lord;" for the prophet admonished them to seek it out, and read it.[i] It is evident then, that in the time of Isaiah, the people had a written authority in doctrine and practice.

9. Nearly four centuries later, (640-630 B. C.), while the righteous king Josiah occupied the throne of Judah, as a part of divided Israel, Hilkiah the high priest and father of the prophet Jeremiah, found in the temple "a book of the law of the Lord",[j] which was read before the kings.[k] Then, during the fifth century B. C., in the days of Ezra, the edict of Cyrus permitted the captive people of Judah, a remnant of once united Israel, to return to Jerusalem,[l] there to rebuild the temple of the Lord, according to the

e Deut. xxxi, 9; 24-26.

f Deut. xvii, 18.

g Joshua xxiv, 26.

h I Sam. x, 25.

i Isaiah xxxiv, 16.

j II Chron. xxxiv, 14-15; see also Deut. xxxi, 26.

k II Kings, xxii.

l Ezra i, 1-3.

law[m] of God, then in the hand of Ezra. From this we may infer that the written law was then known; and to Ezra is usually attributed the credit of compiling the books of the Old Testament as far as completed in his day, to which he added his own writings.[n] In this work of compilation he was probably assisted by Nehemiah and the members of the Great Synagogue,—a Jewish college of a hundred and twenty scholars.[o] The book of Nehemiah, which gives a continuation of the historical story as recorded by Ezra, is supposed to have been written by the prophet whose name it bears, in part at least during the life of Ezra. Then, a century later, Malachi, the last of the prophets of note who flourished before the opening of the dispensation of Christ, added his record, completing, and virtually closing the pre-Christian canon, with a prophetic promise of the Messiah, who was to establish a new and an everlasting covenant.[p]

10. Thus, it is evident that the Old Testament grew with the successive writings of authorized and inspired scribes from Moses to Malachi, and that its compilation was a natural and gradual process, each addition being deposited, or, as the sacred record gives it, "laid up before the Lord," in connection with the previous writings. Undoubtedly there were known to the Jews many other books, not included in our present Old Testament; references to such are abundant in the scriptures themselves, which references prove that many of those extra-canonical records were regarded as of great authority. But concerning this, we will enquire further in connection with the Apocrypha. The recognized canonicity of the Old Testament books is at-

---

m See Ezra vii, 12-14.

n The Book of Ezra.

o This historical information is given in certain of the apocryphal works; see II Esdras.

p Mal. iii, iv

tested by the numerous references in the latter to the earlier books, and by the many quotations from the Old Testament occurring in the New. About two hundred and thirty quotations or direct references have been listed; and in addition to these, hundreds of less direct allusions occur.

11. **Language of the Old Testament:**—It is highly probable, almost certain indeed, that nearly all the books of the Old Testament were originally written in Hebrew. Scholars profess to have found evidence that small portions of the books of Ezra, Daniel, and Jeremiah, were written in the Chaldee language; but the prevalence of Hebrew as the language of the original scriptures has given to the Old Testament the common appellation, Hebrew or Jewish canon. Of the Pentateuch, two versions have been recognized,—the Hebrew proper and the Samaritan,*q* the latter of which was preserved in the most ancient of Hebrew characters by the Samaritans, between whom and the Jews there was lasting enmity.

12. **The Septuagint:**—Passing over the Peshito or early Syriac version of the Old Testament, as of minor significance, we recognize as the first important translation of the Hebrew canon, that known as the *Septuagint.*r This was a Greek version of the Old Testament, translated from the Hebrew at the instance of an Egyptian monarch, probably Ptolemy Philadelphus, about 286 B. C. The name *Septuagint* suggests the number seventy, and is said to have been given because the translation was made by a body of seventy-two elders (in round numbers seventy); or, as other traditions say, because the work was accomplished in seventy, or seventy-two days; or, according to yet other stories, because the version received the sanction of the Jewish ecclesiastical council, the Sanhedrin, which comprised

q See Note 2.
r See Note 3.

seventy-two members. Certain it is that the Septuagint, (sometimes indicated by the numerals LXX) was the current version among the Jews in the days of Christ's ministry, and was quoted by the Savior and the apostles in their references to the old canon. It is regarded as the most authentic of the ancient versions, and is accepted at the present time by the Greek Christians and other eastern churches. It is evident then, that from a time nearly three hundred years before Christ, the Old Testament has been current in both Hebrew and Greek; this duplication has been an effective means of protection against alterations.

13. **The Present Compilation** recognizes thirty-nine books in the Old Testament; these were originally combined as twenty-two books, corresponding to the letters in the Hebrew alphabet. The thirty-nine books as at present constituted may be conveniently classified as follows:

(1) The Pentateuch or Books of the Law 5
(2) The Historical Books 12
(3) The Poetical Books 5
(4) The Books of the Prophets 17

14. (1.) **The Books of the Law.** The first five books in the Bible are collectively designated as the *Pentateuch*, (*pente*— five, *teuxos*—volume); and were known among the early Jews as the *Torah*, or the law. Their authorship is traditionally ascribed to Moses,[s] and in consequence the "Five Books of Moses" is another commonly used designation. They give the history, brief though it be, of the human race, from the creation to the flood, from Noah to Israel; then a more particular account of the chosen people through their period of Egyptian bondage; thence during the journey of four decades in the wilderness, to the encampment on the farther side of Jordan.

---

[s] Ezra vi, 8; vii, 6; Neh. viii, 1; John vii, 19.

15. (2.) **The Historical Books**, twelve in number, comprise the following: Joshua, Judges, Ruth, I and II Samuel, I and II Kings, I and II Chronicles, Ezra, Nehemiah, Esther. They tell the story of the Israelites entering the land of promise, and their subsequent career through three distinct periods of their existence as a people:—(1) as a theocratic nation, with a tribal organization, all parts cemented by ties of religion and kinship; (2) as a monarchy, at first a united kingdom, later a nation divided against itself; (3) as a partly conquered people, their independence curtailed by the hand of their victors.

16. (3.) **The Poetical Books** number five,—Job, Psalms, Proverbs, Ecclesiastes, and the Song of Solomon. They are frequently spoken of as the doctrinal or didactic works, and the Greek designation Hagiographa (*hagios*—holy, and *graphe*—a writing) is still applied.[t] These are of widely different ages, and their close association in the Bible is probably due to their common use as guides in devotion amongst the Jewish churches.

17. (4.) **The Books of the Prophets** comprise the five larger works of Isaiah, Jeremiah, the Lamentations of Jeremiah, Ezekiel, and Daniel, commonly known as the works of the *Major Prophets*; and the twelve shorter books of Hosea, Joel, Amos, Obadiah, Jonah, Micah, Nahum, Habakkuk, Zephaniah, Haggai, Zechariah, and Malachi, known to Bible scholars as the books of the *Minor Prophets*. These give the burden of the Lord's word to His people, encouragement, warning and reproof, as suited their condition, before, during, and after their captivity.[u]

---

[t] As stated, the Hagiographa or "sacred writings," are generally understood to include the five poetical works of the Old Testament. By some authorities, the list is extended to include all the books mentioned in the Talmud as hagiographa, viz., Ruth, Chronicles, Ezra and Nehemiah, Esther, Job, Psalms, Proverbs, Ecclesiastes, Song of Solomon, Lamentations, and Daniel.

[u] See note 4.

18. The Apocrypha comprise a number of books of doubtful authenticity, though such have been at times highly esteemed. Thus, they were added to the Septuagint, and for a time were accorded recognition among the Alexandrine Jews. However, they have never been generally admitted, being of uncertain origin. They are not quoted in the New Testament. The designation apocryphal (meaning hidden, or secret) was first applied to the books by Jerome, because, said he, "the church doth read [them] for example of life and instruction of manners, but yet doth it not apply them to establish any doctrine." The Roman church professes to acknowledge them as scripture, action to this end having been taken by the council of Trent (1546); though the doubt of the authenticity of the works seems still to exist even among the Roman Catholic dignitaries. The sixth article in the Liturgy of the Church of England defines the orthodox views of the church as to the meaning and intent of Holy Scripture; and, after specifying the books of the Old Testament which are regarded as canonical, proceeds in this wise:—"And the other books (as Hierome [Jerome] saith) the church doth read for example of life and instruction of manners; but yet doth it not apply them to establish any doctrine; such are these following:—The Third Book of Esdras; The Fourth Book of Esdras; The Book of Tobias; The Book of Judith; The rest of the Book of Esther; The Book of Wisdom; Jesus, the Son of Sirach; Baruch the Prophet; The Song of the Three Children; The Story of Susanna; Of Bel and the Dragon; The Prayer of Manasses; The First Book of Maccabees; The Second Book of Maccabees."

THE NEW TESTAMENT.

19. Its Origin and Authenticity:—Since the latter part of the fourth century of our present era, there has arisen scarcely a single question of importance regarding the authenticity of the books of the New Testament as at present constituted. From that time until the present, the New Testament has been accepted as an unquestioned canon of scriptures by all professed Christians.[v] In the fourth century, there were generally current several lists of the books of the New Testament as we now have them; of these may be mentioned the catalogues of Athanasius, Epiphanius, Jerome, Rufinus, and Augustine of Hippo, and the list announced by the third Council of Carthage. To these may be added four others, which differ from the foregoing in omitting the Revelation of John in three cases, and the same with the Epistle to the Hebrews in one.

20. This superabundance of evidence relating to the constitution of the New Testament canon in the fourth century, is a result of the anti-Christian persecution of that period. At the beginning of the century in question, the oppressive measures of Diocletian, emperor of Rome, were directed not alone against the Christians as individuals and as a sect, but against their sacred writings, which the fanatical and cruel monarch sought to destroy. Some degree of leniency was extended to those persons who yielded up the holy books that had been committed to their care; and not a few embraced this opportunity of saving their lives. When the rigors of persecution were lessened, the churches sought to judge their members who had weakened in their allegiance to the faith, as shown by their surrender of the scriptures, and all such were anathematized as traitors. Inasmuch as many books, that had been thus given up under the pressure of threatening death, were not at that time generally accepted as holy, it became a question of first importance to decide just which books were of such admitted sanctity that their betrayal would make a man a traitor.[w]

---

v See notes 5 and 6.
w See Tregelles' "Historic Evidence of the Origin * * * of the Books of the New Testament" p. 12—

Hence we find Eusebius designating the books of the Messianic and apostolic days as of two classes:—(1) Those of acknowledged canonicity, viz:—the gospels, the epistles of Paul, Acts, I John, I Peter, and probably the Apocalypse. (2) Those of disputed authenticity, viz:—the epistles of James, II Peter, II and III John, and Jude. To these classes he added a third class, including books that were admittedly spurious.[x]

21. As stated, the list published by Athanasius, which dates from near the middle of the fourth century, gives the constitution of the New Testament as we now have it; and at that time, all doubts as to the correctness of the enumeration seem to have been put to rest; and we find the Testament of common acceptance by professing Christians in Rome, Egypt, Africa, Syria, Asia Minor, and Gaul. The testimony of Origen, who flourished in the third century, and that of Tertullian who lived during the second, were tested and pronounced conclusive by the later writers in favor of the canonicity of the gospels and the apostolic writings. Each book was tested on its own merits, and all were declared by common consent to be authoritative and binding on the churches.

22. If there be need to go farther back, we may note the testimony of Irenæus, distinguished in ecclesiastical history as Bishop of Lyons; he lived in the latter half of the second century, and is known as a disciple of Polycarp, who was personally associated with the Revelator, John. His voluminous writings affirm the authenticity of most of the books of the New Testament, and define their authorship as at present admitted. To these testimonies may be added those of the Saints in Gaul, who wrote to their fellow-sufferers in Asia, quoting freely from gospels, epistles, and

---

[x] See Eusebius, Ecclesiastical History, iii, 25.

the Apocalypse;[y] the declarations of Melito, Bishop of Sardis, who journeyed to the east to determine which were the canonical books, particularly of the Old Testament;[z] and the solemn attest of Justin Martyr, who embraced Christianity as a result of his earnest and learned investigations, and who suffered death for his convictions. In addition to individual testimony, we have that of ecclesiastical councils and official bodies, by whom the question of authenticity was tried and decided. In this connection, may be mentioned the Council of Laodicea, 363 A. D.; the Council of Hippo, 393 A. D.; the third and the sixth Councils of Carthage, 397 and 419 A. D.

23.   Since the date last named, no dispute as to the authenticity of the New Testament has claimed much attention; surely the present is too late a date, and the separating distance today is too vast, to warrant the reopening of the question. The New Testament must be accepted for what it claims to be; and though, perhaps, many precious parts have been suppressed or lost, while some corruptions of the sacred texts may have crept in, and errors have been inadvertently introduced through the incapacity of translators, the volume as a whole must be admitted as authentic and credible, and as an essential part of the holy scriptures.[a]

24.   **Classification of the New Testament:**—The New Testament comprises twenty-seven books, conveniently classified as:—

(1.)   Historical............................. 5
(2.)   Didactic.............................. 21
(3.)   Prophetic............................. 1

25.   (1.)   **The Historical Books** include the four Gos-

---

y See Eusebius, book iv.
z Eusebius iv, 26.
a John v, 39.

pels, and the Acts of the Apostles. The authors of these works are spoken of as the evangelists, Matthew, Mark, Luke, and John; to Luke is ascribed the authorship of the Acts.

26. (2.) **The Didactic Books** comprise the epistles; and these we may arrange thus: (*1.*) *The Epistles of Paul*, comprising, (*a*) his doctrinal letters addressed to Romans, Corinthians, Galatians, Ephesians, Philippians, Colossians, Thessalonians, Hebrews; (*b*) his pastoral communications to Timothy, Titus, and Philemon. (*2.*) *The General Epistles* of James, Peter, John, and Jude.

27. (3.) **The Prophetic Works,** consisting of the Revelation of John, commonly known as the Apocalypse.

THE BIBLE AS A WHOLE.

28. **Early Versions of the Bible:**—Many versions of the Old Testament and of the combined Testaments have appeared at different times. The Hebrew text with the Samaritan duplication of the Pentateuch, and the Greek translation, or the Septuagint (LXX), have been already noted. Revisions and modified translations competed for favor with the Septuagint during the early ages of the Christian era, Theodotian, Aquila, and Symmachus, each issuing a new version. One of the first translations into Latin was the *Italic version*, probably prepared in the second century; this was later improved and amended, and then became known as the *Vulgate;* and this is still held to be the authentic version by the church of Rome. This version included both Old and New Testaments.

29. **Many Modern Versions in English,** some fragmentary, others complete, have appeared since the beginning of the thirteenth century. About 1380 A. D., Wycliffe presented an English translation of the New Testament, made from the Vulgate; the Old Testament was afterward

added.   About 1525 A. D., Tyndale's translation of the
New Testament appeared; this was included in Coverdale's
Bible, printed in 1535, which constituted the first version of
the complete Bible.   Matthew's Bible dates from 1537;
Taverner's Bible from 1539, and Cranmer's Great Bible
from the same year.   In 1560, the Geneva Bible appeared;
in 1568 the Bishop's Bible, the first English version having
chapter and verse divisions; and in 1611 the so-called
Authorized English Version, or King James' translation,
this being a new translation of Old and New Testaments
from the Hebrew and Greek, made by forty-seven scholars
at the command of King James I.   This has superseded all
earlier versions, and is the form now in current use among
Protestants.   But even this latest and supposedly best version was found to contain many and serious errors; and in
1885 a revised version was issued, which, however, has not
yet been accorded general acceptance.

30.   Genuineness and Authenticity of the Bible:—However
interesting and instructive these historical and literary data
of the Jewish scriptures may be, the consideration of such
is subordinate to that of the authenticity of the books; for
as we, in common with the rest of the Christian world, have
accepted them as the word of God, it is eminently proper
that we should enquire into the genuineness of the records
upon which our faith is so largely founded.   All evidences
furnished by the Bible itself, such as its language, historical
details, and the coincidences of its contents, unite in supporting its claim to genuineness as the actual works of the
authors to whom the separate parts are ascribed.   In a
multitude of instances, comparisons are easy between the
biblical record and contemporary history not scriptural,
particularly in regard to biography and genealogy, and, in
all such cases, striking agreement has been found.[b] Further

b See note 7.

argument exists in the individuality maintained by each
writer, resulting in a marked diversity of style; while the
wondrous unity pervading the whole declares the operation
of some single guiding influence throughout the ages of the
record's growth; and this can be nothing less than the
power of inspiration which operated upon all alike who
were accepted as instruments in the Divine Hand to prepare
this book of books. Tradition, contemporary history, literary analysis, and above and beyond all these, the test of
prayerful research and truth-seeking investigation, have
ever combined to prove the authenticity of this wondrous
volume, and to point the way, defined within its covers, lead
ing men back to the Eternal Presence.

31. **Book of Mormon Testimony regarding the Bible:**—As
declared in the eighth of the Articles of Faith now under
consideration, the Latter-day Saints accept the Book of
Mormon as a volume of sacred scripture, which, like the
Bible, embodies the word of God. In the next lecture, the
Book of Mormon will receive our special attention; but it
may be profitable to refer here to the collateral evidence
furnished by that work regarding the authenticity of the
Jewish scriptures, and of the general integrity of these latter in their present form. According to the Book of Mormon record, the Prophet Lehi, with his family and some
others, left Jerusalem by the command of God, about 600
B. C., during the first year of King Zedekiah's reign. Before finally forsaking the land of their nativity, the travel-
ers secured certain records, which were engraved on plates
of brass. Among these writings were a history of the Jews
and some of the scriptures then accepted as authentic.

32. Lehi examined the brazen record,—"And he beheld
that they did contain the five books of Moses, which
gave an account of the creation of the world, and also of
Adam and Eve, who were our first parents; and also a

record of the Jews from the beginning, even down to the
commencement of the reign of Zedekiah, king of Judah;
and also the prophecies of the holy prophets, from the
beginning, even down to the commencement of the reign of
Zedekiah; and also many prophecies which have been spoken
by the mouth of Jeremiah."[c] This direct reference to the
Pentateuch and to certain of the Jewish prophets is valuable
external evidence concerning the authenticity of those parts
of the biblical record.

33. In a vision, Nephi, the son of Lehi, learned of the
future of God's plan regarding the human family; and saw
that a book of great worth, containing the word of God,
and the covenants of the Lord with Israel, would go forth
from the Jews to the Gentiles.[d] It is further stated that
Lehi's company, who, as we shall see, were led across the
waters to the western continent, whereon they established
themselves and afterward grew to be a numerous and
powerful people, were accustomed to study the scriptures engraved on the plates of brass; and, moreover, their scribes embodied long quotations there-from in their own growing record.[e] So much for Book of Mormon recognition of the Old
Testament, or at least of such parts of the Jewish canon as
had been completed when Lehi's migrating colony left Jerusalem, during the ministry of the prophet Jeremiah.

34. But further, concerning the New Testament scriptures, this voice from the western world is not silent. In
prophetic vision, many of the Nephite teachers saw and
fore-told the ministry of Christ in the meridian of time, and
recorded predictions concerning the principal events of the
Savior's life and death, with striking fidelity and detail.

---

c I Nephi v, 10-13.

d See I Nephi xiii, 21-23.

e I Nephi xx-xxi; II Nephi vii-viii; xii-xxiv.

This testimony is recorded of Nephi,[f] Benjamin,[g] who was both prophet and king, Abinadi,[h] Samuel the converted Lamanite,[i] and others. In addition to these and many other prophecies regarding the mission of Christ, all of which agree with the New Testament record of their fulfilment, we find in the Book of Mormon an account of the risen Lord's ministrations among the Nephite people, during which He established His Church with them, after the pattern recorded in the New Testament; and, moreover, He gave them many instructions in words almost identical with those of His teachings among the Jews in the east.[j]

NOTES.

1. John Chrysostom, one of the Greek "Christian Fathers," flourished during the latter half of the fourth century; he was patriarch of Constantinople, but was deposed and exiled some time before his death which occurred in 407. His use of the term *biblia* to designate the scriptural canon is among the earliest applications of the sort yet found. He entreated his people to avail themselves of the riches of inspired works in this wise:—"Hear, I exhort, all yet in secular life, and purchase *biblia*, the medicine of the soul." Speaking of the Jewish Christians, he says, "They have the *biblia*, but we have the treasures of the *biblia;* they have the letters, we have the letters and the understanding."

2. The Samaritan Copy of the Pentateuch:—In his valuable course of lectures on Bible subjects, Elder David McKenzie presents the following, with references to the writings of Horne:—"Nine hundred and seventy years before Christ, the nation of Israel was divided into two kingdoms. Both retained the same book of the law. Rivalry prevented either of them from altering or adding to the law. After Israel was carried into Assyria, other nations occupied Samaria. These received the Pentateuch. The language being Hebrew or Phœnician, whereas the Jewish copy was changed into Chaldee, corruption or alteration was thus made impracticable, yet the texts remain almost identical."

3. Versions of the Bible or of Parts Thereof:—*The Septuagint:*—"Various opinions have been put forth to explain its appellation of *Septuagint;* some say that Ptolemy Philadelphus requested of Eleazer the High Priest, a copy of the Hebrew scriptures, and six learned Jews from each tribe (together seventy-

---

f I Nephi x, 4-5; xi-xiii; xiv; II Nephi ix, 5; x, 3; xxv, 26; xxvi, 24.

g Mosiah iii; iv, 3.

h Mosiah xiii-xvi.

i Helaman xiv, 12.

j III Nephi, ix-xxvi; compare for New Testament references with Matthew v-vii, etc.; and for Old Testament mention with Isaiah liv; Malachi iii-iv.

two,) competent to translate it into Greek; these were shut up in the isle of Pharos, and in seventy-two days they completed their task; as they dictated it, Demetrius Phalereus, the king's chief librarian, transcribed it; but this is now considered a fable. Others say that these same interpreters, having been shut up in separate cells, wrote each one a translation; and so extraordinarily did they all coincide together in words as well as sentiment, that evidence was thus afforded of their inspiration by the Holy Spirit; this opinion has also been set aside as too extravagant. It is very possible that seventy-two writers were employed in the translation; but it is more probable that it acquired the name of *Septuagint* from having received the approbation of the Jewish Sanhedrin, which consisted of seventy-two persons. Some affirm it to have been executed at different times; and Horne says it is most probable that this version was made during the joint reigns of Ptolemy Lagus, and his son Philadelphus, about 285 or 286 B. C."

The Vulgate:—"There was a very ancient version of the Bible translated from the Septuagint into Latin, but by whom and when is unknown. It was in general use in the time of Jerome, and was called the *Itala* or *Italie Version.* About the close of the fourth century, Jerome began a new translation into Latin from the Hebrew text, which he gradually completed. It at last gained the approbation of Pope Gregory I, and has been used ever since the seventh century. The present Vulgate, declared authentic by the Council of Trent in the sixteenth century, is the ancient Italic version, revised and improved by the corrections of Jerome and others; and is the only one allowed by the Church of Rome."

The "Authorized Version."—"Certain objections having been made to the *Bishops' Bible* at the Hampton Court conference in A.D. 1603, King James I directed a new translation to be made. Forty-seven persons, eminent for their piety and biblical learning, were chosen to this end; they were divided into six committees, two to sit at Oxford, two at Cambridge, and two at Westminster; and each committee had a certain portion of the scriptures assigned to it. They began their task in A D, 1607, and the whole was completed and in print in A.D. 1611. This is called the *Authorized English Version* and is the one now in use."— From *Analysis of Scripture History*, by Pinnock; pp. 3, 5; (6th ed.)

4. The Prophetical Books of the Old Testament are arranged with little or no regard to their chronological order, the extent of the contained matter placing the larger works first. The chronological arrangement would probably be Jonah, Joel, Amos, Hosea, Isaiah, Micah, Nahum, Zephaniah:—all of these prophesied previous to the captivity; then follow Jeremiah, Habakkuk, Ezekiel, and Daniel, who wrote during the captivity; then Haggai, Zechariah, and Malachi, after the return of the Jews from captivity.

5. Manuscript Copies of the New Testament:—Three manuscripts of New Testament writings now in existence are regarded as authentic. These are known as the *Vatican* (now in Rome), the *Alexandrian* (now in London), and the *Sinaitic*, (now in the St. Petersburg library). The last named or Sinaitic is considered to be the oldest copy of the New Testament in existence. The manuscript was discovered in 1859 among the archives of a monastery on Mount Sinai, hence its name. It was found by Tischendorf, and is now in the imperial library at St. Petersburg.

6. Concerning the Genuineness of Parts of the New Testament:— In answer to objections that have been urged by critics in the matter of genuine-

ness or authenticity of certain books of the New Testament, the following array
of testimony may be considered. The items are presented here as collated by
Elder David McKenzie, and as used by him in his instructive lectures on the
Bible.

(I) *The Four Gospels:*—1. *Matthew.* Papias, Bishop of Hierapolis, was a hearer
of the Apostle John. With respect to St. Matthew's gospel, Eusebius quotes him
as saying:—"Matthew composed the Oracles in the Hebrew tongue, and each
one interpreted them as he could."—(Eusebius, Hist. Eccl. iii, 39.)

2. *Mark.* Of Mark's writing, Papias also says:—"Mark having become the
interpreter of Peter, wrote down accurately everything that he remembered,
without, however, recording in order what was either said or done by Christ. For
neither did he hear the Lord, nor follow Him, but afterward attended Peter, who
adapted his instructions to the needs of his hearers, but had no design of giving
a connected account of the Lord's oracles (or discourses.)"—(Bishop Lightfoot's
translations, in "Contemporary Review," August, 1875.)

3. *Luke.* Internal evidence shows that Luke's Gospel and the Acts of the
Apostles were composed by the same author. St. Paul speaks of Luke as a
physician; and Dr. Hobart, in 1882, published at London, a treatise on "The
Medical Language of St. Luke," and points out the frequent use of medical terms
in Luke's writings, permeating the entire extent of the third Gospel, and the
Acts of the Apostles. Even M. Renan makes a similar admission. He says:—
"One point which is beyond question is that the Acts are by the same author as
the third Gospel, and are a continuation of that Gospel. One need not stop to
prove this proposition, which has never been seriously contested. The prefaces
at the commencement of each work, the dedication of each to Theophilus, the
perfect resemblance of style and of ideas, furnish on this point abundant
demonstrations." "A second proposition is that the author of the Acts is a
disciple of Paul, who accompanied him for a considerable part of his travels."—
(M. Renan, "The Apostles;" see preface.)

4. *John.* Irenæus, Bishop of Lyons, about 177 A. D., a pupil of Polycarp who
was martyred in 155 or 156, relates in a letter to a fellow-pupil his recollections
of what he had heard Polycarp say about his intercourse with John, and with the
rest who had seen the Lord; and about the Lord, and about His miracles, and
about His teaching. All these he would relate altogether in accordance with *the
Scriptures.* (Eusebius, Eccl. Hist, v, 20.) That Irenæus meant by "the Scriptures," Matthew, Mark, Luke and John, is evident from the text. Besides, he
urges "not only that four Gospels alone have been handed down from the beginning, but that in the nature of things there could not be more nor less than
four. There are four regions in the world, and four principal winds, and the
Church therefore, as destined to be conterminous with the world, must be supported by four Gospels as four pillars.—(Contemporary Review, August, 1876,
p. 413.) [The forced analogy assumed by Irenæus between the *four* Gospels and
the *four* winds, etc., is of course without foundation, and its use appears literally
absurd; nevertheless the fact that he noted it furnishes evidence of the acceptance of the four Gospels in his day.—J. E. T.]

(II.) *The Pauline Epistles:*—The following extracts from the testimony of
the Tübingen critics on four of Paul's epistles, are instructive.

De Wette says, in his introduction to the "Books of the New Testament"
(123, a.):—"The letters of Paul bear the marks of his powerful genius. The most
important of them are raised above all contradiction as to their authenticity:
they form the solid kernel of the book of the New Testament."

Baur says, in his "Apostle Paul," (1, 8):—"Not only has no suspicion of the authenticity of these Epistles even arisen, but they bear so incontestably the seal of the originality of Paul, that one cannot comprehend for what reason critics could raise any objection to them."

Weizsæker writes (Apost. Zeitalter, 1866, p. 190):—"The letters to the Galatians and the Corinthians are, without doubt, from the hand of the Apostle; from his hand also came incontestably the Epistle to the Romans."

Holtzmann says("Einleit in's N. T. " p. 224):—"These four epistles are the Pauline Homologoumena, (books universally received) in the modern acceptation of the word. We can realize, with respect to them, the proof of authenticity undertaken by Paley against the free-thinkers of his time."

M. Renan in "*The Gospels*," (pp. 40, 41,) thus expresses himself:—"The epistles of Paul have an unequaled advantage in this history,—that is, their absolute authenticity." Of the Epistles to the Corinthians, the Galatians, and the Romans, Renan speaks as "indisputable and undisputed;" and adds, "The most severe critics, such as Christian Baur, accept them without objection."

7. Archeological Evidence Confirming the Bible:—Prof. A. H. Sayce, M. A., sums up his learned treatise on the testimony of the ancient monuments, thus:—"The critical objections to the truth of the Old Testament, once drawn from the armory of Greek and Latin writers, can never be urged again; they have been met and overthrown once for all. The answers to them have come from papyrus and clay and stone, from the tombs of ancient Egypt, from the mounds of Babylonia, and from the ruined palaces of the Assyrian kings. "

8. Missing Scripture:—Those who oppose the doctrine of continual revelation between God and His Church, on the ground that the Bible is complete as a collection of sacred scriptures, and that alleged revelation not found therein must therefore be spurious, may profitably take note of the many books not included in the Bible, yet mentioned therein, generally in such a way as to leave no doubt that they were once regarded as authentic. Among these extra-biblical scriptures, the following may be named; some of them are in existence today, and are classed with the Apocrypha; but the greater number are unknown. We read of the Book of the Covenant, (Exo, xxiv, 7); Book of the Wars of the Lord, (Numb. xxi, 14); Book of Jasher (Josh. x, 13); Book of the Statutes (I Sam. x, 25); Book of Enoch, (Jude 14); Book of the Acts of Solomon, (I King xi, 41); Book of Nathan the Prophet, and that of Gad the Seer, (I Chron. xxix, 29); Book of Ahijah the Shilonite, and visions of Iddo, the Seer, (II Chron. ix, 29); Book of Shemaiah, (II Chron. xii, 15); Story of the Prophet Iddo (II Chron. xiii, 22); Book of Jehu, (II Chron. xx, 34); the Acts of Uzziah, by Isaiah, the son of Amoz, (II Chron. xxvi, 22); Sayings of the Seers, (II Chron. xxxiii, 19); a missing epistle of Paul to the Corinthians, (I Cor. v, 9); a missing epistle to the Ephesians, (Eph. iii, 3); missing epistle to the Colossians, written from Laodicea, (Col. iv, 16); a missing epistle of Jude, (Jude 3); a declaration of belief mentioned by Luke (i, 1.)

LECTURE XIV.

THE BOOK OF MORMON.

Article 8:—* * * * We also believe the Book of Mormon to be the word of God.

DESCRIPTION AND ORIGIN.

1. **What is the Book of Mormon?**—The claims made for the Book of Mormon affirm it to be a divinely inspired record, made by the prophets of the ancient peoples who inhabited the American continent for centuries before and immediately after the time of Christ; which record has been translated in the present generation through the gift of God and by His special appointment. The authorized and inspired translator of these sacred scriptures, through whose instrumentality they have been given to the world in modern language, is Joseph Smith, whose first acquaintance with the plates was mentioned in the first lecture.[a] As stated, on the 21st of September, 1823, Joseph Smith received, in answer to fervent prayer, a visitation from an angelic personage, who gave his name as Moroni; subsequent revelations showed him to be the last of a long line of prophets whose translated writings constitute the Book of Mormon; by him the ancient records had been closed; by him the graven plates had been deposited in the earth; and through his ministration they were brought into the possession of the modern prophet and seer whose work of translation is now before us.

2. On the occasion of Moroni's first visit to Joseph Smith, the angelic visitor declared the existence of the record, which, he said, was engraved on plates of gold,

a See pages 10, 17.

at that time lying buried in the side of a hill near Joseph's home. The hill, which was known by one division of the ancient peoples as Cumorah, by another as Ramah, is situated near Palmyra in the county of Wayne, State of New York. The precise spot where the plates lay was shown to Joseph in vision; and he had no difficulty in finding it on the day following the visitation referred to. Joseph's statement of Moroni's declaration concerning the plates is as follows:—"He said there was a book deposited, written upon gold plates, giving an account of the former inhabitants of this continent, and the source from which they sprang. He also said that the fulness of the everlasting gospel was contained in it, as delivered by the Savior to the ancient inhabitants. Also, that there were two stones in silver bows, (and these stones, fastened to a breast-plate, constituted what is called the Urim and Thummim), deposited with the plates; and the possession and use of these stones was what constituted Seers in ancient or former times; and that God had prepared them for the purpose of translating the book."[b]

3. Joseph found a large stone at the indicated spot on the hill Cumorah; beneath the stone was a box, also of stone; the lid of this he raised by means of a lever; then he saw within the box the plates, and the breastplate with the Urim and Thummim, as described by the angel. As he was about to remove the contents of the box, Moroni again appeared before him, and forbade him taking the sacred things at that time, saying that four years must pass before they would be committed to his personal care; and that in the meantime, Joseph would be required to visit the place at yearly intervals; this the youthful revelator did, receiving on each occasion additional instruction concerning the record and God's purposes with it. On the 22nd of Septem-

b Pearl of Great Price, p. 94 (1888 ed.)

ber, 1827, Joseph received from the angel Moroni, the plates, and the Urim and Thummim with the breastplate. He was instructed to guard them with strict care, and was promised that if he used his best efforts to protect them, they would be preserved inviolate in his hands; and that on the completion of the labor of translation, Moroni would visit him again, and receive the plates.

4. The reason prompting the angelic caution regarding Joseph's care of the treasures soon appeared; thrice in the course of his brief journey homeward with the sacred relics, he was attacked; but by Divine aid he was enabled to withstand his assailants; and finally reached his home with the plates and other articles unharmed. These attacks were but the beginning of a siege of persecution which was relentlessly waged against him by the powers of evil as long as the plates remained in his custody. News that he had the golden record in his possession soon spread; and numerous attempts, many of them violent, were made to wrest the plates from his hands. But they were preserved; and, slowly, with many hindrances incident to persecution by the wicked, and to the conditions of his own poverty which made it necessary for him to toil and left little leisure for the appointed labor, Joseph proceeded with the translation; and in 1830, the Book of Mormon was first published to the world.

5. **The Title Page of the Book of Mormon:**—Our best answer to the question: What is the Book of Mormon? is found on the title page to the volume. Thereon we read:

"The Book of Mormon: an account written by the hand of Mormon, upon plates taken from the plates of Nephi. Wherefore it is an abridgment of the record of the people of Nephi, and also of the Lamanites; written to the Lamanites who are a remnant of the house of Israel; and also to Jew and Gentile: written by way of commandment, and also by the spirit of prophecy and of revelation. Written and sealed up, and hid up unto the Lord, that they might not be destroyed; to come forth by the gift and power of God unto the interpretation thereof: sealed by the hand of Moroni, and hid up unto the Lord, to come forth in due time by the way of Gentile; the interpretation thereof by the gift of God.

"An abridgment taken from the Book of Ether also; which is a record of the people of Jared; who were scattered at the time the Lord confounded the language of the people when they were building a tower to get to heaven; which is to show unto the remnant of the House of Israel what great things the Lord hath done for their fathers; and that they may know the covenants of the Lord, that they are not cast off forever; and also to the convincing of the Jew and Gentile that Jesus is the Christ, the Eternal God, manifesting Himself unto all nations. And now, if there are faults, they are the mistakes of men: wherefore condemn not the things of God, that ye may be found spotless at the judgment seat of Christ."

This combined title and preface is a translation from the last page of the plates, and was presumably written by Moroni, who, as before stated, sealed and hid up the book in former days.[c]

6. **Main Divisions of the Book:**—From the title page, we learn that in the Book of Mormon we have to deal with the histories of two great nations, who flourished in America as the descendants of small colonies brought hither from the eastern continent by Divine direction. Of these we may conveniently speak as the Nephites and the Jaredites.

7. **The Nephite Nation** was the later, and in point of the fulness of the records, the more important. The progenitors of this nation were led from Jerusalem 600 B. C., by Lehi, a Jewish prophet of the tribe of Manasseh. His immediate family, at the time of their departure from Jerusalem, comprised his wife Sariah, and their sons Laman,

c See note 1.

Lemuel, Sam, and Nephi; at a later stage of the history, daughters are mentioned, but whether any of these were born before the family exodus we are not told. Beside his own family, the colony of Lehi included Zoram, and Ishmael, the latter an Israelite of the tribe of Ephraïm. Ishmael, with his family, joined Lehi in the wilderness; and his descendants were numbered with the nation of whom we are speaking. The company journeyed somewhat east of south, keeping near the borders of the Red Sea; then, changing their course to the eastward, crossed the peninsula of Arabia; and there on the shores of the Arabian Sea, built and provisioned a vessel in which they committed themselves to Divine care upon the waters. Their voyage carried them eastward across the Indian Ocean, then over the south Pacific Ocean to the western coast of South America, whereon they landed (590 B. C.) probably somewhere near the site of the present city of Valparaiso in Chile.

8.   The people established themselves on what to them was the land of promise; many children were born, and in the course of a few generations a numerous posterity held possession of the land. After the death of Lehi, a division occurred, some of the people accepting as their leader, Nephi, who had been duly appointed to the prophetic office; while the rest proclaimed Laman, the eldest of Lehi's sons, as their chief. Henceforth the divided people were known as Nephites and Lamanites respectively. At times they observed toward each other fairly friendly relations; but generally they were opposed, the Lamanites manifesting implacable hatred and hostility toward their Nephite kindred. The Nephites advanced in the arts of civilization, built large cities, and established prosperous commonwealths; yet they often fell into transgression; and the Lord chastened them by making their foes victorious. They

spread northward, occupying the northern part of South America; then, crossing the Isthmus, they extended their domain over the southern, central, and eastern portions of what is now the United States of America. The Lamanites, while increasing in numbers, fell under the curse of darkness; they became dark in skin and benighted in spirit, forgot the God of their fathers, lived a wild nomadic life, and degenerated into the fallen state in which the American Indians,—their lineal descendants,—were found by those who re-discovered the western continent in later times.

9. The final struggles between Nephites and Lamanites were waged in the vicinity of the hill Cumorah, in what is now the state of New York, resulting in the entire destruction of the Nephites, about 400 A. D. The last Nephite representative was Moroni, who, wandering for safety from place to place, daily expecting death from the victorious Lamanites who had decreed the absolute extinction of their white kindred, wrote the concluding parts of the Book of Mormon, hid the record in Cumorah, and soon there-after died. It was this same Moroni, who, as a resurrected being, gave the records into the hands of Joseph Smith in the present dispensation.

10. The Jaredite Nation:—Of the two nations whose histories constitute the Book of Mormon, the first in order of time consisted of the people of Jared, who followed their leader from the Tower of Babel at the time of the confusion of tongues. Their history was written on twenty-four plates of gold, by Ether the last of their prophets, who, fore-seeing the destruction of his people because of their wickedness, hid away the historical plates. They were afterward found, B. C. 123, by an expedition sent out by King Limhi, a Nephite ruler. The record engraved on these plates was subsequently abridged by Moroni, and the condensed account was attached by him to the Book of

Mormon record; it appears in the modern translation under the name of the Book of Ether.

11. The first and chief prophet of the Jaredites is not mentioned by name in the record as we have it; he is known only as the brother of Jared. Of the people, we learn that amid the confusion of Babel, Jared and his brother importuned the Lord that He would spare them and their associates from the impending disruption. Their prayer was heard, and the Lord led them with a considerable company, who, like themselves, were free from the taint of idolatry, away from their homes, promising to conduct them to a land choice above all other lands. Their course of travel is not given with exactness; we learn only that they reached the ocean, and there constructed eight vessels, called barges, in which they set out upon the waters. These vessels were small and dark within; but the Lord made luminous certain stones, which gave light to the imprisoned voyagers. After a passage of three hundred and forty-four days, the colony landed on the western shore of North America, probably at a place south of the Gulf of California, and north of the Isthmus of Panama.

12. Here they became a flourishing nation; but, giving way in time to internal dissensions, they divided into factions, which warred with one another until the people were totally destroyed. This destruction, which occurred near the hill Ramah, afterward known among the Nephites as Cumorah, probably took place at about the time of Lehi's landing in South America,—590 B.C. The last representative of the ill-fated race was Coriantumr, the former king, concerning whom Ether had prophesied that he should survive all his subjects, and live to see another people in possession of the land. This prediction was fulfilled in that the king, whose people had become extinct, came, in the course of his solitary wanderings, to a region occupied by

the people of Mulek, who are to be mentioned here as the third ancient colony of emigrants from the eastern continent.

13. *Mulek*, we are told, was the son of Zedekiah king of Judah, an infant at the time of his brothers' violent deaths and his father's cruel torture at the hands of the king of Babylon.[d] Eleven years after Lehi's departure from Jerusalem, another colony was led from the city, amongst whom was Mulek. His name has been given to the people, probably on account of his recognized rights of leadership by virtue of his lineage. The Book of Mormon record concerning Mulek and his people is scanty; we learn, however, that the colony was brought across the waters, to a landing on the northern part of the continent. The descendants of this colony were discovered by the Nephites under Mosiah; they had grown numerous, but, having had no scriptures for their guidance, had fallen into a condition of spiritual darkness. They joined the Nephites, and their history is merged into that of the greater nation.[e] The Nephites gave to North America the name, Land of Mulek.

THE ANCIENT PLATES AND THE MODERN TRANSLATION.

14. **The Plates of the Book of Mormon** as delivered by the angel Moroni to Joseph Smith, according to the description given by the modern prophet, were of gold, of uniform size, each about seven inches wide by eight inches long; in thickness, a little less than ordinary sheet tin; they were fastened together by three rings running through the plates near one edge; together they formed a book nearly six inches in thickness, but not all has been translated, a part being sealed. Both sides of the plates were engraved with small and beautiful characters, described by those who ex-

---

d See II Kings xxv, 7.

e Omni i, 12-19.

amined them as of curious workmanship, with the appearance of ancient origin.

15. Three classes of plates are mentioned on the title page of the Book of Mormon, viz:—

(1.) *The Plates of Nephi;* which, as will be shown, were of two kinds:—(a) the larger plates; (b) the smaller plates.

(2.) *The Plates of Mormon*, containing an abridgment from the plates of Nephi, with additions made by Mormon and his son Moroni.

(3.) *The Plates of Ether*, containing as we have seen, the history of the Jaredites.

To these may be added another set of plates, as being mentioned in the Book of Mormon, viz:

(4.) *The Brass Plates of Laban*, brought by Lehi's people from Jerusalem, and containing Jewish scriptures and genealogies; many extracts from which appear in the Nephite records. We have now to consider more particularly the plates of Nephi, and Mormon's abridgment thereof.

16. **The Plates of Nephi** are so named from the fact that they were prepared, and their record was begun, by Nephi, the son of Lehi. These plates were of two kinds,*f* which may be distinguished as the "larger plates," and the "smaller plates." Nephi began his labors as a recorder by engraving on plates of gold a historical account of his people, from the time his father left Jerusalem. This account recited the story of their wanderings, their prosperity, and their distress, the reigns of their kings, and the wars and contentions of the people; the record was in the nature of a secular history. These plates were handed from one recorder to another throughout the generations of the Nephite people; so that at the time they were abridged by Mormon, the record covered a period of about a thousand years, dating from 600 B. C., the time of Lehi's

f I Nephi ix; xix, 1-5; II Nephi v, 30; Jacob i, 1-4; Words of Mormon i, 3-7.

exodus from Jerusalem. Although these plates bore the name of their maker, who was also the first of the writers, the separate work of each recorder is known in general by his specific name, so that the record is made up of many distinct books.

17. By command of the Lord, Nephi made other plates, upon which he recorded particularly the ecclesiastical history of his people, citing only such instances of other events as seemed necessary to the proper sequence of the narrative. "I have received a commandment of the Lord," says Nephi, "that I should make these plates for the special purpose that there should be an account engraven of the ministry of my people."[g] The object of this double line of history was unknown to Nephi, it was enough for him that the Lord required the labor; that it was for a wise purpose will be shown.

18. **Mormon's Abridgment:**—In the course of time, the records that had accumulated as the history of the people grew, fell into the hands of Mormon,[h] and he undertook to make an abridgment of these extensive works, upon plates made with his own hands.[i] By such a course, a record was prepared more concise and more nearly uniform in style, language, and treatment, than could possibly be the case with the varied writings of so many authors as had contributed to the great history during the thousand years of its growth. Mormon recognizes and testifies to the inspiration of God by which he was moved to undertake the great labor.[j] In preparing this shorter history, Mormon preserved the same division of the record into books according to the arrangement of the originals; and thus, though the language may be that of Mormon, except in cases of quotations

g I Nephi ix, 3.

h Words of Mormon i, 11; Mormon i, 1-4; iv, 23.

i III Nephi v, 8-11.

j III Nephi v, 14-19.

from the plates of Nephi, which are indeed numerous, we find the Books of Nephi, the Book of Alma, the Book of Helaman, etc., the form of speech known as the first person being generally preserved.

19. When Mormon, in the course of his abridgment, had reached the time of King Benjamin's reign, he was deeply impressed with the record engraved on the smaller plates of Nephi,—the history of God's dealings with the people during the period of about four centuries, extending from the time of Lehi's exodus from Jerusalem down to the time of King Benjamin. This record, comprising so much of prophecy concerning the mission of the Savior, was regarded by Mormon with more than ordinary favor. Of these plates he attempted no transcript, but included the originals with his own abridgment of the larger plates, making of the two one book. The record as compiled by Mormon, contained, therefore, a double account of the descendants of Lehi for the first four hundred years of their history,—the brief secular history condensed from the larger plates, and the full text on the smaller plates. In solemn language, and with an emphasis which subsequent events have shown to be significant, Mormon declares the hidden wisdom of the Divine purpose in this duplication:—"And I do this for a wise purpose; for thus it whispereth me, according to the workings of the Spirit of the Lord which is in me. And now, I do not know all things; but the Lord knoweth all things which are to come; wherefore, he worketh in me to do according to his will."[k]

20. The Lord's Purpose in the matter of preparing and of preserving the smaller plates as testified of by Mormon, and also by Nephi,[l] is rendered plain from certain circumstances in this dispensation attending the translation of the rec-

---

[k] Words of Mormon i, 7.

[l] I Nephi ix, 5.

ords by Joseph Smith.   When the prophet had prepared a translation of the first part of the writings of Mormon, the manuscript was won from his care through the unrighteous solicitations of Martin Harris, to whom he considered himself in a degree indebted for fianancial assistance in the work of publication.   This manuscript, in all 116 pages, was never returned to Joseph, but, through the dark schemes of evil powers, it fell into the hands of enemies, who straightway laid a wicked plan to ridicule the translator, and thwart the purposes of God.   This evil design was that they wait until Joseph had re-translated the missing matter, when the stolen manuscript, which in the meantime had been altered so that the words were made to express the contrary from the true record, would be set forth as a proof that the prophet was unable to translate the same passages twice alike.   But the Lord's wisdom interposed to bring to naught these dark designs.

21.   Having chastened the prophet by depriving him for a season of his gift to translate, as also of the custody of the sacred records, and this for his dereliction in permitting the writings to pass into unappointed hands, the Lord graciously restored His penitent servant to favor, and revealed to him the designs of his enemies;[m] at the same time showing how these evil machinations should be made to fail. Joseph was instructed, therefore, not to attempt a re-translation of that part of Mormon's abridgment, the first translation of which had been stolen; but instead, to translate the record of the same events from the plates of Nephi,—the set of smaller plates which Mormon had incorporated with his own writings.   The translation so made was therefore published as the record of Nephi, and not as the writing of Mormon; and thus no second translation was made of the parts from which the stolen manuscript had been prepared.

---

m Doctrine and Covenants, x.

22. **The Translation of the Book of Mormon** was effected through the power of God manifested in the bestowal of the gift of revelation. The book professes not to be dependent upon the wisdom or learning of man; its translator was not versed in linguistics; his qualifications were of a different and of a far more efficient order. With the plates, Joseph Smith received from the angel other sacred treasures, including a breastplate, to which were attached the Urim and Thummim,[n] called by the Nephites, *Interpreters*; and by the use of these he was enabled to render the ancient records in our modern tongue. The details of the work of translation have not been recorded, beyond the statement that the translator examined the engraved characters by means of the sacred instruments, and then dictated to the scribe the English sentences.

23. Joseph began his work with the plates by patiently copying a number of characters, adding to some of the pages thus prepared, the translations. The prophet's first assistant in the labor, Martin Harris, obtained permission to take away some of these transcripts, with the purpose of submitting them to the examination of men learned in ancient languages. He placed some of the sheets before Professor Charles Anthon, of Columbia College, who, after careful examination, certified that the characters were in general of the ancient Egyptian order, and that the accompanying translations appeared to be correct. Hearing how this ancient record came into Joseph's hands, Professor Anthon requested Mr. Harris to bring the original book for examination, stating that he would undertake the translation of the entire work; then, learning that a part of the book was sealed, he remarked, "I cannot read a sealed book;" and thus unwittingly did this man fulfil the prophecy of Isaiah concerning the coming forth of the volume:—"And the vision of all

---

[n] Doc. and Cov. x, 1; xvii, 1; cxxx, 8, 9; Mos. viii, 13-19; Ether iii, 23-28.
19

is become unto you as the words of a book that is sealed, which men deliver to one that is learned, saying, read this, I pray thee, and he saith, I cannot, for it is sealed."[a] Another linguist, a Dr. Mitchell, of New York, having examined the characters, gave concerning them a testimony in all important respects corresponding to that of Prof. Anthon.

24.   Arrangement of the Book of Mormon:—The Book of Mormon comprises fifteen separate parts, commonly called books, distinguished by the names of their principal authors. Of these, the first six books, viz., I and II Nephi, Jacob, Enos, Jarom, and Omni, are literal translations from corresponding portions of the smaller plates of Nephi. The body of the volume, from the Book of Mosiah to Mormon, chapter vii, inclusive, is the translation of Mormon's abridgment of the larger plates of Nephi. Between the books of Jarom and Mosiah, "The Words of Mormon" occur, connecting the record of Nephi as engraved on the smaller plates, with Mormon's abridgment of the larger plates for the periods following. The Words of Mormon may be regarded as a brief explanation of the preceding portions of the work, and an announcement of the parts then to follow. The last part of the Book of Mormon, from the beginning of Mormon viii, to the end of the volume, is in the language of Moroni, the son of Mormon, who first proceeds to finish the record of his father, and then adds an abridgment of a set of plates which contained an account of the Jaredites; this appears as the Book of Ether.

25.   At the time of Moroni's writing, he stood alone,— the sole surviving representative of his people. The last of the terrible wars between Nephites and Lamanites had resulted in the annihilation of the former as a people; and Moroni supposed that his abridgment of the Book of Ether would be his last literary work; but, finding himself mirac-

a Isaiah xxix, 11

ulously preserved at the conclusion of that undertaking, he added the parts known to us as the Book of Moroni, containing accounts of the ceremonies of ordination, baptism, administration of the sacrament, etc., and a record of certain utterances and writings of his father Mormon.

THE GENUINENESS OF THE BOOK OF MORMON.

26. The earnest student of the Book of Mormon will be most concerned in his consideration of the reliability of the great record; and this subject may be conveniently considered under two headings: 1st, the genuineness and integrity of the Book of Mormon, i. e., the evidence that the book is what it professes to be,—an actual translation of ancient records; 2nd, the authenticity of the original writings, as shown by internal and external evidence.

27. **The Genuineness of the Book** will appear to anyone who undertakes an impartial investigation into the circumstances attending its coming forth. The many so-called theories of its origin, advanced by prejudiced opponents to the work of God, are in general too inconsistent, and in most instances too thoroughly puerile, to merit serious consideration. Such fancies as are set forth in representations of the Book of Mormon as the production of a single author or of men working in collusion, as a work of fiction, or in any manner as a modern composition, are their own refutation.[o] The sacred character of the plates forbade their display as a means of gratifying personal curiosity; nevertheless a number of reputable witnesses examined them, and these men have given to the world their solemn testimony of the fact. In June, 1829, the prophecies respecting the witnesses by whose testimony the word of God as set forth in the Book of Mormon was to be established,[p] saw its

---

o See Note 2.

p II Nephi xi, 3; xxvii, 12-13; Ether v, 3-4; see also Doc. and Cov. v, 11-15; xvii, 1-9.

fulfilment in a manifestation of Divine power, demonstrating the genuineness of the record to three men, whose affirmations accompany all editions of the book.

28. **The Testimony of Three Witnesses:**—Be it known unto all nations, kindreds, tongues, and people unto whom this work shall come, that we, through the grace of God the Father, and our Lord Jesus Christ, have seen the plates which contain this record, which is a record of the people of Nephi, and also of the Lamanites, their brethren, and also of the people of Jared, who came from the tower of which hath been spoken; and we also know that they have been translated by the gift and power of God, for his voice hath declared it unto us,[q] wherefore we know of a surety that the work is true. And we also testify that we have seen the engravings[r] which are upon the plates; and they have been shown unto us by the power of God, and not of man. And we declare with words of soberness, that an angel of God came down from heaven,[s] and he brought and laid before our eyes, that we beheld and saw the plates, and the engravings thereon; and we know that it is by the grace of God the Father, and our Lord Jesus Christ, that we beheld and bear record that these things are true; and it is marvelous in our eyes, nevertheless the voice of the Lord commanded us that we should bear record of it; wherefore, to be obedient unto the commandments of God, we bear testimony of these things. And we know that if we are faithful in Christ, we shall rid our garments of the blood of all men, and be found spotless before the judgment-seat of Christ, and shall dwell with him eternally in the heavens. And the honor be to the Father, and to the Son, and to the Holy Ghost, which is one God. Amen.

OLIVER COWDERY,
DAVID WHITMER,
MARTIN HARRIS.

29. The testimony so declared was never revoked, or even modified by any one of the witnesses whose names are sub-

---

[q] Doc. and Cov. xvii, 6; xx, 8.

[r] II Nephi v, 32; Alma lxiii, 12; Mormon i, 3.

[s] See History of Joseph Smith, June, 1829.

scribed to the foregoing,[t] though all of them withdrew from the Church, and indulged in feelings amounting almost to hatred toward Joseph Smith. To the last of their lives, they maintained the same solemn declaration of the angelic visit, and the testimony that had been implanted in their hearts. Shortly after the witnessing of the plates by the three, other eight persons were permitted to see and handle the ancient records; and in this also was prophecy fulfilled, in that it was of old declared, that beside the three, "God sendeth more witnesses,"[u] whose testimony shall be added to that of the three. It was presumably in July, 1829, that Joseph Smith showed the plates to the eight whose names are attached to the following certificate.

30. **The Testimony of Eight Witnesses:**—Be it known unto all nations, kindreds, tongues, and people unto whom this work shall come, that Joseph Smith, Jun., the translator of this work, has shown unto us the plates of which hath been spoken, which have the appearance of gold; and as many of the leaves as the said Smith has translated, we did handle with our hands; and we also saw the engravings thereon, all of which has the appearance of ancient work, and of curious workmanship. And this we bear record with words of soberness, that the said Smith has shown unto us, for we have seen and hefted, and know of a surety that the said Smith has got the plates of which we have spoken. And we give our names unto the world, to witness unto the world that which we have seen; and we lie not, God bearing witness of it.

CHRISTIAN WHITMER,	HIRAM PAGE,
JACOB WHITMER,	JOSEPH SMITH, SEN.,
PETER WHITMER, JUN.,	HYRUM SMITH,
JOHN WHITMER,	SAMUEL H. SMITH.

31. Three of the eight witnesses died out of the Church, yet not one of the whole number ever was known to deny

---

t See Note 3.
u II Nephi xi, 3.

his testimony concerning the Book of Mormon."   Here
then are proofs of varied kinds regarding the reliability of
this volume.   Learned linguists pronounce the characters
genuine; eleven men of honest report make solemn oath of
the appearance of the plates; and the nature of the book
itself sustains the claim that it is nothing more nor less than
a translation of ancient records.

NOTES.

1. **Book of Mormon Title Page:**—"I wish to mention here that the title
page of the Book of Mormon is a literal translation, taken from the very last
leaf on the left hand side of the collection or book of plates, which contained the
record which has been translated, the language of the whole running the same
as all Hebrew writing in general; and that said title page is not by any means a
modern composition, either of mine or any other man who has lived or does live
in this generation."—*Joseph Smith.*

2. **Theories concerning the Origin of the Book of Mormon: The
Spaulding Story:**—The true account of the origin of the Book of Mormon
was rejected by the public in general, who thus assumed the responsibility of
explaining in some plausible way the source of the record. Many vague theories,
based on the incredible assumption that the book was the work of a single
author, were put forward; of these, the most famous, and, indeed, the only one
that lived long enough in public favor to be discussed, is the so-called "Spaulding Story." Solomon Spaulding, a clergyman of Amity, Pa., wrote a romance, to
which no title other than "Manuscript Story" was prefixed. Twenty years after
the author's death, one Hurlburt, an apostate from the Church of Jesus Christ of
Latter-day Saints, announced a resemblance between the story and the Book of
Mormon, and expressed his conviction that the work presented to the world by
Joseph Smith was nothing but Spaulding's romance revised and amplified. The
manuscript was lost for a time, and, in the absence of proof to the contrary,
stories of the parallelism between the two works multiplied. But, by a fortu-
nate circumstance, in 1884, President James H. Fairchild of Oberlin College,
Ohio, and a literary friend, one Mr. Rice, in examining a heterogeneous collection of old papers that had been purchased by Mr. Rice, found the original story.
The gentlemen made a careful comparison of the manuscript and the Book of
Mormon; and, with the sole desire of subserving the purposes of truth, made
public their results. Pres. Fairchild published an article in the *New York
Observer*, Feb. 5, 1885, in which he said:—"The theory of the origin of the Book
of Mormon in the traditional manuscript of Solomon Spaulding will probably
have to be relinquished. * * * Mr. Rice, myself and others compared it [the
Spaulding manuscript] with the Book of Mormon and could detect no resemblance between the two. * * * Some other explanation of the Book of Mormon
must be found, if any explanation is required."

v See Note 4.

The manuscript was deposited in the library of Oberlin College where it now reposes. Still, the theory of the "Manuscript Found," as Spaulding's story has come to be known, is occasionally pressed into service in the cause of anti-"Mormon" zeal, by some whom we will charitably believe to be ignorant of the facts set forth by Pres. Fairchild. A letter of more recent date, written by that honorable gentleman in reply to an enquiring correspondent, was published in the *Millennial Star*, Liverpool, Nov. 3, 1898, and is as follows:

OBERLIN COLLEGE, OHIO,
October 17, 1895.

J. R. Hindley, Esq.,

DEAR SIR:—We have in our College Library an original manuscript of Solomon Spaulding—unquestionably genuine.

I found it in 1884 in the hands of Hon. L. L. Rice of Honolulu, Hawaiian Islands. He was formerly State Printer at Columbus, O., and before that, publisher of a paper in Painesville, whose preceding publisher had visited Mrs. Spaulding and obtained the manuscript from her. It had lain among his old papers forty years or more, and was brought out by my asking him to look up anti-slavery documents among his papers.

The manuscript has upon it the signatures of several men of Conneaut, O., who had heard Spaulding read it and knew it to be his. No one can see it and question its genuineness. The manuscript has been printed twice at least— once by the Mormons of Salt Lake City, and once by the Josephite Mormons of Iowa. The Utah Mormons obtained the copy of Mr. Rice at Honolulu, and the Josephites got it of me after it came into my possession.

This manuscript is not the original of the Book of Mormon.

Yours very truly,

JAS. H. FAIRCHILD.

Printed copies of the "Manuscript Found" are obtainable, and any enquirer may examine for himself. For further information see "*The Myth of the Manuscript Found*" by Elder George Reynolds, Salt Lake City; Whitney's *History of Utah*, Vol. I, pp. 46-56; Elder George Reynolds' preface to the story as issued by the Deseret News Company, Salt Lake City, 1886; and the story itself.

3. **The Three Witnesses**:—Oliver Cowdery;—Born at Wells, Rutland Co., Vermont, October, 1805; baptized May 15, 1829; died at Richmond, Mo., March 3, 1850.

David Whitmer:—Born near Harrisburg, Pa., January 7, 1805; baptized June, 1829; excommunicated from the Church, April 13, 1838; died at Richmond, Mo., January 25, 1888.

Martin Harris:—Born at East-town, Saratoga Co., New York, May 18, 1783; baptized 1830; removed to Utah, August, 1870, and died at Clarkston, Cache Co., Utah, July 10, 1875.

4. **The Eight Witnesses**:—Christian Whitmer:—Born January 18, 1798; baptized April 11, 1830; died in full fellowship in the Church, Clay County, Missouri, November 27, 1835. He was the eldest son of Peter Whitmer.

Jacob Whitmer:—Second son of Peter Whitmer; born in Pennsylvania, January 27, 1800; baptized April 11, 1830; died April 21, 1856, having previously withdrawn from the Church.

Peter Whitmer, Jr.:—Born September 27, 1809; fifth son of Peter Whitmer; baptized June, 1829; died a faithful member of the Church, at or near Liberty, Clay Co., Missouri, September 22, 1836.

John Whitmer:—Third son of Peter Whitmer; born August 27, 1802; baptized June, 1829; excommunicated from the Church March 10, 1838; died at Far West, Missouri, July 11, 1878.

Hiram Page:—Born in Vermont, 1800; baptized April 11, 1830; withdrew from the Church, 1838; died in Ray Co., Missouri, August 12, 1852.

Joseph Smith, Sen.:—The Prophet Joseph's father; born at Topsfield, Essex Co., Mass., July 12, 1771; baptized April 6, 1830; ordained Patriarch to the Church, December 18, 1833; died in full fellowship in the Church at Nauvoo, Ill., Sept. 14, 1840.

Hyrum Smith:—Second son of Joseph Smith, Sen., born at Tunbridge, Vt. February 9, 1800; baptized June, 1829; appointed one of the First Presidency of the Church November 7, 1837; Patriarch to the Church January 19, 1841; martyred with his brother, the Prophet, at Carthage, Ill., June 27, 1844.

Samuel Harrison Smith:—Born Tunbridge, Vt., March 13, 1808; fourth son of Joseph Smith, Sen., baptized May 15, 1829; died July 30, 1844.

LECTURE XV.

THE BOOK OF MORMON.—(Continued.)

Article 8.— * * * We also believe the Book of Mormon to be the word of God.

AUTHENTICITY OF THE BOOK OF MORMON.

1. **The Divine Authenticity of the Book of Mormon** constitutes our most important consideration of the work. This subject is one of vital interest to every earnest investigator of the ways of God, to every sincere searcher after truth. Claiming to be, as far as the present dispensation is conconcerned, a new scripture; presenting prophecies and revelations not heretofore recognized in modern theology; announcing to the world the message of a departed people; written by way of commandment, and by the spirit of prophecy and revelation; this volume is entitled to the most thorough and impartial examination. Nay, more, not alone does the Book of Mormon merit such consideration, it claims, even demands the same; for surely no one professing the most cursory belief in the power and authority of God can receive with unconcern the announcement of a new commandment, having the seal of Divine authority upon it. The question of the authenticity of the Book of Mormon is therefore one in which the world is interested.

2. The Latter-day Saints base their belief in the authenticity and genuineness of the book on the following proofs:—

I.　The general agreement of the Book of Mormon with the Bible.

II.　The fulfilment of ancient prophecies accomplished by the bringing forth of the Book of Mormon.

III.   The strict agreement and consistency of the Book of Mormon with itself.

IV.   The evident truth of its contained prophecies.

To these may be added certain external, or extra-scriptural evidences, amongst which are:—

V.   The strongly corroborative evidence furnished by modern discoveries in the field of archeological and ethnological science.

I. THE BOOK OF MORMON AND THE BIBLE.

3.   The Nephite and the Jewish Scriptures are found to agree in all matters of tradition, history, doctrine, and prophecy upon which both the separate records treat. These two volumes of scripture were prepared on opposite hemispheres, under conditions and circumstances widely diverse; yet between them there exists a surprising harmony, confirmatory of Divine inspiration in both.   The Book of Mormon contains a number of quotations from the ancient Jewish scriptures, a copy of which, as far as they had been compiled at the time of Lehi's exodus from Jerusalem, was brought to the western continent, as part of the record engraved on the plates of Laban.   In the case of such passages, there is no essential difference between Bible and Book of Mormon versions, except in instances of probable error in translation,—usually apparent through inconsistency or lack of clearness in the biblical reading.   There are, however, numerous minor variations in corresponding parts of the two volumes; and between such, examination usually demonstrates the superior perspicuity of the Nephite scripture.

4.   In a careful comparison of the prophecies of the Bible with corresponding predictions contained in the Book of Mormon, e. g. those relating to the birth, earthly ministry, sacrificial death, and second coming of Christ Jesus; others

referring to the scattering and subsequent gathering of Israel; and such as relate to the establishment of Zion and the re-building of Jerusalem in the last days, each of the records will be seen to be corroborative of the other. True, there are many predictions in one which are not found in the other; but in no instance has a contradiction or an inconsistency between the two been pointed out. Between the doctrinal parts of the two volumes of scripture the same perfect harmony is found to prevail.

5. Of the agreement of the Book of Mormon with the Bible and with other standards of comparison, Apostle Orson Pratt has forcefully and truthfully written:—"If the miracles of the Book of Mormon be compared with the miracles of the Bible, there cannot be found in the former anything that would be more difficult to believe, than what we find in the latter. If we compare the historical, prophetical, and doctrinal parts of the Book of Mormon with the great truths of science and nature, we find no contradictions, no absurdities, nothing unreasonable. The most perfect harmony, therefore, exists between the great truths revealed in the Book of Mormon, and all other known truths, whether religious, historical, or scientific."[a]

II. ANCIENT PROPHECY REGARDING THE BOOK OF MORMON.

6. **Ancient Prophecy** has been literally fulfilled in the coming forth of the Book of Mormon. One of the earliest prophetic utterances directly bearing upon this subject is that of Enoch, the ante-diluvian prophet, unto whom the Lord revealed His purposes for all time. Witnessing in vision the corruption of mankind, after the ascension of the Son of Man, Enoch cried unto his God, "Wilt thou not come again on the earth?" "And the Lord said unto Enoch,

a "*Divine Authenticity of the Book of Mormon*," Orson Pratt's Works, p. 236, (1891, Utah ed.)

As I live, even so will I come in the last days.   *   *   *
And the day shall come that the earth shall rest, but before
that day the heavens shall be darkened, and a veil of darkness shall cover the earth, and the heavens shall shake and
also the earth, and great tribulations shall be among the
children of men; but my people will I preserve, and righteousness will I send down out of heaven, and truth will I
send forth out of the earth, to bear testimony of Mine Only
Begotten.   *   *   *   and righteousness and truth will I
cause to sweep the earth as with a flood to gather out mine
own elect from the four quarters of the earth, unto a place
which I shall prepare."[b] The Latter-day Saints regard
the coming forth of the Book of Mormon, together with the
restoration of the Priesthood by the direct ministration of
heavenly messengers, as a fulfilment of this prophecy, and
of similar predictions contained in the Bible.

7. **Biblical Prophecies and their Fulfilment:**—David, who
sang his psalms over a thousand years before the "Meridian
of Time," declared, "Truth shall spring out of the earth,
and righteousness shall look down from heaven."[c] And so
also declared Isaiah.[d] Ezekiel saw in vision[e] the coming
together of the stick of Judah, and the stick of Joseph,
signifying, as the Latter-day Saints affirm, the Bible and
the Book of Mormon. The passage last referred to reads,
in the words of Ezekiel:—"The word of the Lord came
again unto me, saying, Moreover, thou son of man, take
thee one stick, and write upon it, For Judah, and for the
children of Israel his companions: then take another stick,
and write upon it, For Joseph, the stick of Ephraim, and
for all the house of Israel his companions: And join them

---

b Pearl of Great Price. Writings of Moses, p. 44. (1888 ed.)
c Psalms lxxxv, 11.
d Isa. xlv, 8.
e Ezek. xxxvii, particularly verses 15-20.

one to another into one stick; and they shall become one in thine hand."

8.   When we call to mind the ancient custom in the making of books,—that of writing on long strips of parchment and rolling the same on rods or sticks, the use of the word "stick" as equivalent to "book" in the passage becomes at once apparent.[f] At the time of this utterance, the Israelites had divided into two nations known as the people of Judah, and that of Israel, or Ephraim. There would seem to be little room for doubt that the records of Judah and of Joseph are here referred to.[g] Now, as we have seen, the Nephite nation comprised the descendants of Lehi of the tribe of Manasseh, of Ishmael an Ephraimite, and of Zoram whose tribal relation is not definitely stated. The Nephites were then of the tribes of Joseph; and their record or "stick" is as truly represented by the Book of Mormon as is the "stick" of Judah by the Bible.

9.   That the coming forth of the record of Joseph or Ephraim is to be accomplished through the direct power of God is evident from the Lord's interpretation of the vision of Ezekiel, wherein He says:—"Behold, *I will take* the stick of Joseph   *   *   *   and will put them with him, even with the stick of Judah."[h] And that this union of the two records is to be a characteristic of the latter days is evident from the prediction of an event which is to follow immediately, viz., the gathering of the tribes from the nations among which they had been dispersed.[i] Comparison with other prophecies relating to the gathering will conclusively prove that the great event is to take place in the latter times, preparatory to the second coming of Christ.[j]

f See a corresponding use of the word "roll" in Jeremiah xxxvi, 1, 2; and its synonym "book" in verses 8, 10, 11, and 13.

g Compare with Lehi's prediction made to his son Joseph, II Nephi iii, 12.

h Ezek. xxxvii, 19.

i Verse 21.

j See lecture on "Gathering" in connection with Article 10.

10. Reverting to the writings of Isaiah, we find that prophet voicing the Lord's threatenings against Ariel, or Jerusalem, "the city where David dwelt." Ariel was to be distressed, burdened with heaviness and sorrow; then the prophet refers to some people, other than Judah who occupied Jerusalem, for he makes comparison with the latter, saying "And it shall be unto me *as* Ariel." As to the fate decreed against this other people we read:—"And thou shalt be brought down, and shalt speak out of the ground, and thy speech shall be low out of the dust, and thy voice shall be, as of one that hath a familiar spirit, out of the ground, and thy speech shall whisper out of the dust."[k]

11. Of the fulfilment of these and associated prophecies, a modern apostle has written:—"These predictions of Isaiah could not refer to Ariel, or Jerusalem, because their speech has not been 'out of the ground,' or 'low out of the dust;' but it refers to the remnant of Joseph who were destroyed in America upwards of fourteen hundred years ago. The Book of Mormon describes their downfall, and truly it was great and terrible. At the crucifixion of Christ, 'the multitude of their terrible ones,' as Isaiah predicted, 'became as chaff that passeth away,' and it took place as he further predicts, 'at an instant suddenly.' * * * This remnant of Joseph in their distress and destruction became *as* Ariel. As the Roman army lay siege to Ariel, and brought upon her great distress and sorrow, so did the contending nations of ancient America bring upon each other the most direful scenes of blood and carnage. Therefore, the Lord could, with the greatest propriety, when speaking in reference to this event, declare that, 'It shall be unto me *as* Ariel.'"[l]

12. Isaiah's striking prediction that the nation thus

---

[k] Isaiah xxix, 4—read verses 1-6.

[l] Orson Pratt, *Divine Authenticity of the Book of Mormon*, p.p. 293-294 (Utah ed. 1891). For details of fulfilment of part of the prophecy, see III Nephi viii-ix.

brought down should "speak out of the ground," with
speech "low out of the dust" was literally fulfilled in the
bringing forth of the Book of Mormon, the original of which
was taken out of the ground, and the voice of the record is
as that of one speaking from the dust.   In continuation of
the same prophecy we read:—"And the vision of all is become unto you as the words of a book that is sealed, which
men deliver unto one that is learned, saying, Read this, I
pray thee: and he saith, I cannot; for it is sealed: And
the book is delivered unto him that is not learned, saying,
Read this, I pray thee: and he saith, I am not learned."[m]
The fulfilment of this prediction is claimed in the presentation of the transcript from the plates,—"the words of a
book," not the book itself, to the learned Prof. Anthon,
whose reply almost in the words of the text has been
cited;[n] and in the delivery of the book itself to the un-
lettered lad, Joseph Smith.

III.   CONSISTENCY OF STYLE AND MATTER IN THE BOOK OF MORMON.

13. The Consistency of the Book of Mormon sustains
belief in its Divine origin. The parts bear evidence of having
been written at different times, and under widely varying
conditions.   The style of the component books is in harmony with the times and circumstances of their production.
The portions which were transcribed from the plates bearing
Mormon's abridgment contain numerous interpolations as
comments and explanations of the transcriber; but in the
first six books, which, as already explained, are the verbatim
record of the smaller plates of Nephi, no such interpolations occur.   The book maintains strict consistency through-

---

m Isaiah xxix, 11-12.

n See p. 273-274.

out all its parts; no contradictions, no disagreements have been pointed out.

14. A Marked Diversity of Style characterizes the several parts.° From what has been said regarding the classes of plates which constitute the original records of the Book of Mormon, it is evident that the volume contains the compiled writings of a long line of inspired scribes extending through a thousand years, this time-range being exclusive of the earlier years of Jaredite history. Unity of style is not to be expected under such conditions, and indeed, did such occur, it would be fatal to the claims made for the volume.

IV.   THE BOOK OF MORMON SUSTAINED BY THE FULFIL-
MENT OF ITS CONTAINED PROPHECIES.

15. Book of Mormon Predictions are numerous and important. Amongst the most conclusive proofs of the authenticity of the book is that furnished by the demonstrated truth of its contained prophecies. Prophecy is best proved in the light of its own fulfilment. The predictions contained within the Book of Mormon may be classed as (*a*) Prophecies relating to the time covered by the book itself, the fulfilment of which is recorded therein; and, (*b*) Prophecies relating to times beyond the limits of the history chronicled in the book.

16. *Prophecies of the First Class* named, the fulfilment of which is attested by the Book of Mormon record, are of but minor value as proof of the authenticity of the work; for, had the book been written according to a plot devised by man, both prediction and fulfilment would have been provided for with equal care and ingenuity. Nevertheless, to the studious and conscientious reader, the genuineness of the book will be apparent; and the account of the literal realization of the numerous and varied predictions

---

o See Note 1.

relating to the fate then future of the people whose history
is given in the record, as also of those concerning the details of the birth and death of the Savior, and of His
appearing in a resurrected state, must, by their accuracy
and consistency, appeal with force as evidence of inspiration and authority in the record.

   17. *Prophecies of the Second Class*, relating to a time
which to the writers was far future, are numerous and explicit: many of them have special reference to the last days,
—the dispensation of the fulness of times,—and of these,
some have been already strictly accomplished, others are
now in process of actual realization, while yet others are
awaiting fulfilment under specified conditions which seem
now to be rapidly approaching.   Among the most remarkable of the Book of Mormon predictions incident to the last
dispensation are those that relate to its own coming forth
and the effect of its publication amongst mankind.   Ezekiel's biblical prophecy concerning the coming together of
the "sticks," or records, of Judah and of Ephraim has
received attention; consider a like prediction pronounced as
a blessing by Lehi upon the head of his son Joseph, which
couples the prophecy concerning the book with that of the
seer through whose instrumentality the miracle was to be
accomplished:—"But a seer will I raise up out of the fruit
of thy loins; and unto him will I give power to bring forth
my word unto the seed of thy loins; and not to the bringing
forth my word only, saith the Lord, but to the convincing
them of my word, which shall have already gone forth
among them.   Wherefore, the fruit of thy loins shall write;
and the fruit of the loins of Judah shall write; and that
which shall be written by the fruit of thy loins, and also
that which shall be written by the fruit of the loins of
Judah, shall grow together, unto the confounding of false
doctrines, and laying down of contentions, and establishing
20

peace among the fruit of thy loins, and bringing them to
the knowledge of their fathers in the latter days; and also to
the knowledge of my covenants, saith the Lord. And out
of weakness he shall be made strong, in that day when my
work shall commence among all my people, unto the restor-
ing thee, O house of Israel, saith the Lord."*p* The literal
fulfilment of these utterances in the bringing forth of the
Book of Mormon through Joseph Smith is of itself apparent.

18. Unto Nephi the Lord showed the effect of the new
publication; declaring that in the day of Israel's gathering,
—plainly then the day of the fulness of times, as attested
by the Jewish scriptures,—the words of the Nephites should
be given to the world, and should "hiss forth unto the ends
of the earth, for a standard" unto the house of Israel; and
that then the Gentiles, forgetting even their debt to the
Jews from whom they have received the Bible in which they
profess such faith, would revile and curse that branch of the
covenant people, and would reject the new scripture, exclaiming, "A Bible! a Bible! we have got a Bible, and there
cannot be any more Bible."*q* Is this not the burden of the
frenzied objections raised by the Gentile world against the
Book of Mormon,—that it is of necessity void because new
revelation is not to be expected?

19. Now, in olden times, two witnesses were required to
establish the truth of any allegation; and, says the Lord
concerning the dual records witnessing of Himself:—"Wherefore murmur ye, because that ye shall receive more of my
word? Know ye not that the testimony of two nations is a
witness unto you that I am God, that I remember one nation
like unto another? Wherefore, I speak the same words unto
one nation like unto another. And when the two nations

---

p II Nephi iii, 11-13.
q II Nephi xxix, 3; read the chapter.

shall run together, the testimony of the two nations shall run together also."[r]

20.   Associated with these predictions of the joint testimony of Jewish and Nephite scriptures, is another prophecy, the consummation of which is now eagerly awaited by the faithful.   Other scriptures are promised; note this word of God:—"Wherefore, because that ye have a Bible, ye need not suppose that it contains all my words; neither need ye suppose that I have not caused more to be written: *   *   *   *   *   For behold, I shall speak unto the Jews, and they shall write it; and I shall also speak unto the Nephites, and they shall write it; and I shall also speak unto the other tribes of the house of Israel, which I have led away, and they shall write it; and I shall also speak unto all nations of the earth, and they shall write it.   And it shall come to pass that the Jews shall have the words of the Nephites, and the Nephites shall have the words of the Jews; and the Nephites and the Jews shall have the words of the lost tribes of Israel; and the lost tribes of Israel shall have the words of the Nephites and the Jews."[s]

V.   CORROBORATIVE EVIDENCE FURNISHED BY MODERN DISCOVERIES.

21.   **The Archeology and Ethnology** of the western continent contribute valuable corroborative evidence in support of the Book of Mormon.   These sciences are confessedly unable to explain in any decisive manner the origin of the native American races; nevertheless, investigation in this field has yielded some results that are fairly definite, and with the most important of these the Book of Mormon account is in general accord.   Among the most prominent

---

[r] Verse 8.
[s] Verses 10 and 12.

of the discoveries respecting the aboriginal inhabitants, are
the following:—

I.   That America was inhabited in very ancient times,
probably soon after the building of the Tower of Babel.

II.   That the continent has been successively occupied
by different peoples, at least by two classes, or so-called
"races" at widely separated periods.

III.   That the aboriginal inhabitants came from the east,
probably from Asia, and that the later occupants, or those
of the second period, were closely allied to, if not identical
with, the Israelites.

IV.   That the existing native races of America have
sprung from a common stock.

22.   From the outline already given of the historical part
of the Book of Mormon, it is seen that each of these discoveries is fully attested by that record. Thus it is stated
therein:—

I.   That America was settled by the Jaredites, who
came direct from the scenes of Babel.

II.   That the Jaredites occupied the land for about
eighteen hundred and fifty years, during which time they
spread over a great part of North and South America;
and that at about the time of their extinction (near 590 B.
C.), Lehi and his company came to this continent where
they developed into the segregated nations Nephites and
Lamanites; the former becoming extinct near 385 A. D.,
about a thousand years after Lehi's arrival on these shores;
the latter continuing in a degenerate condition until the
present, being represented by the Indian tribes of today.

III.   That Lehi, Ishmael, and Zoram, the progenitors
of both Nephites and Lamanites, were undoubtedly Israelites, Lehi being of the tribe of Manasseh while Ishmael was
an Ephraimite; and that the colony came direct from Jerusalem, in Asia.

IV.   That the existing Indian tribes are all direct descendants of Lehi and his company, and that therefore they have sprung from men all of whom were of the house of Israel.

Now let us examine some of the evidence bearing on these points presented by individual investigators, most of whom knew nothing of the Book of Mormon, and none of whom accept the book as authentic.[t]

23. I. Concerning the very Ancient Period at which America was Inhabited:—A recognized authority on American antiquities gives the following evidence and inference:—"One of the arts known to the builders of Babel was that of brick making. This art was also known to the people who built the works in the west. The knowledge of copper was known to the people of the plains of Shinar; for Noah must have communicated it, as he lived a hundred and fifty years among them after the flood. Also copper was known to the ante-diluvians. Copper was also known to the authors of the western monuments. Iron was known to the ante-diluvians. It was also known to the ancients of the west. However, it is evident that very little iron was among them, as very few instances of its discovery in their works have occurred; and for this very reason we draw a conclusion that they came to this country soon after the dispersion."[u]

24. Lowry, in his "Reply to official inquiries respecting the Aborigines of America," concludes concerning the peopling of the western continent, "that the first settlement

---

[t] **Acknowledgments:**—Many of the citations which follow, used in connection with the extra-scriptural evidence supporting the Book of Mormon, have been brought together by writers among our people, particularly by Elder George Reynolds; (see his lectures as specified where quoted); also series of articles entitled "American Antiquities," in Millennial Star, Liverpool, vol. xxi; by Moses Thatcher, (See a series of articles on "The Divine Origin of the Book of Mormon," in Contributor, Salt Lake City, vol. II;) and by Elder Edwin F. Parry; (see tract, "A Prophet of Latter-days;" Liverpool, 1898.)

[u] Priest, *American Antiquities.* (1833).

was made shortly after the confusion of tongues at the building of the Tower of Babel."[v]

25. Prof. Waterman of Boston says of the progenitors of the American Indians:—"When and whence did they come? Albert Galatin, one of the profoundest philologists of the age, concluded, that, so far as language afforded any clue, the time of their arrival could not have been long after the dispersion of the human family."[w]

26. Pritchard says of America's ancient inhabitants, that, "the era of their existence as a distinct and isolated race must probably be dated as far back as that time which separated into nations the inhabitants of the old world, and gave to each branch of the human family its primitive language and individuality."[x]

27. A native Mexican author, Ixtilxochitl, "fixes the date of the first peopling of America about the year 2000 B. C.; this closely accords with that given by the Book of Mormon, which positively declares that it occurred at the time of the dispersion, when God in His anger scattered the people upon the face of the whole earth."[y] "Referring to the quotations from Ixtilxochitl, seventeen hundred and sixteen years are said to have elapsed from the creation to the flood. Moses places it sixteen hundred and fifty-six, a difference of only sixty years.[z] They agree exactly as to the number of cubits, fifteen, which the waters prevailed over the highest mountains. Such a coincidence can lead to but one conclusion, the identity of origin of the two accounts."[a]

v Schoolcraft's *Ethnological Researches*, vol. iii, (1853.)

w Extract from lecture by Prof. Waterman, delivered in Bristol, England, 1849; quoted in pamphlet by Edwin F. Parry "*A Prophet of Latter Days*," (Liverpool, 1898.)

x Pritchard, *National History of Man*, (London, 1845.)

y Moses Thatcher, *Contributor*, vol. ii, p. 227, Salt Lake City, 1881.

z See Note 2.

a Moses Thatcher, *Contributor*, vol. ii, p. 228.

28. Prof. Short, quoting from Clavigero, says, "The Chiapanese have been the first peoplers of the New World, if we give credit to their traditions. They say that Votan, the grandson of that respectable old man who built the great ark to save himself and family from the deluge, and one of those who undertook the building of that lofty edifice, which was to reach up to heaven, went by express command of the Lord to people that land. They say also that the first people came from the quarter of the north, and that when they arrived at Soconusco, they separated, some going to inhabit the country of Nicaragua, and others remaining at Chiapas."[a]

29. **II. Concerning the Successive Occupation of America by Different Peoples in Ancient Times:**—It has been declared by eminent students of American archeology, that two distinct classes, by some designated as separate races, of mankind inhabited this continent in early times: Prof. F. W. Putnam[b] is even more definite in his assertion that one of these ancient races spread from the north, the other from the south. This is in agreement with the Book of Mormon record, which describes the occupation of the continent by the Jaredites and the Nephites in turn, the former having established themselves first in North America, the latter in South America. H. C. Walsh, in an article entitled "Copan, a City of the Dead,"[c] gives many interesting details of excavation and other work prosecuted by Gordon under the auspices of the Peabody expedition; and adds, "All this points to successive periods of occupation, of which there are other evidences."[d]

---

a John T. Short, *North Americans of Antiquity*, p. 204. (Harper Bros., New York; 2nd ed. 1888.)　See also *Contributor*, (Salt Lake City; vol. II, p. 259).

b Putnam, "*Prehistoric Remains in the Ohio Valley*," Century Magazine, March, 1890.

c See *Harper's Weekly*, (New York,) October, 1897; article by Henry C. Walsh.

d See note 3

30.   III.   Concerning the Advent of at least One Division of the Ancient Americans from the East, probably from Asia; and their Israelitish Origin:—Comfirmatory evidence of the belief that the aboriginal Americans sprang from the peoples of the eastern hemisphere is found in the similarity of record and tradition on the two continents, regarding the creation, the deluge, and other great events of history. Boturini[f] who is quoted by most writers on American archeology says, "There is no Gentile nation that refers to primitive events with such certainty as the Indians do.   They give us an account of the creation of the world, of the deluge,[g] of the confusion of languages at the Tower of Babel, and of all other periods and ages of the world, and of the long peregrinations which their people had in Asia, representing the specific years by their characters; and in the seven Conejos (rabbits) they tell us of the great eclipse that occurred at the death of Christ, our Lord."

31.   Similar evidence of the common source of eastern and western traditions of great events in primitive times is furnished in the writings of Short, already quoted, and by Baldwin,[h] Clavigero,[i] Kingsborough,[j] Sahagun,[k] Prescott,[l] Schoolcraft,[m] Squiers,[n] Adair,[o] and others.[p]

32.   Prof. Short adds his testimony to the evidence of the

---

f Chevalier Boturini; he spent several years investigating the antiquities of Mexico and Central America, and collected many valuable records, of most of which he was despoiled by the Spanish; he published a work on the subject of his studies in 1746.

g See Note 4.

h Baldwin, "*Ancient America*," (Harper Bros., New York, 1871.)

i Clavigero, quoted by Prof. Short in "*North Americans of Antiquity*."

j Lord Kingsborough, "*Mexican Antiquities*" (1830-37.)

k Bernardo de Sahagun, "*Historia Universal de Nueva Espana*."

l W. H. Prescott, "*Conquest of Mexico*" (see pp. 463-4.)

m Schoolcraft, "*Ethnological Researches*," (1851); see vol. i.

n Squiers, "*Antiquities of the State of New York*," 1851.

o Adair, "*History of the American Indians*," London, 1775.

p See Bancroft's "*Native Races*," etc, vols. iii and v; Donelly's "*Atlantis*," p 391, (1882.)

aboriginal inhabitants of America being of "Old World origin," but admits his inability to determine when or whence they came to this continent.[q] Waterman, before cited, says: "This people could not have been created in Africa, for its inhabitants were widely dissimilar from those of America; nor in Europe, which was without a native people agreeing at all with American races; then to Asia alone could they look for the origin of the Americans."[r]

33. It has been demonstrated that the aboriginal tribes were accustomed to practice under certain conditions the rites of circumcision,[s] baptism, and animal sacrifice.[t] Herrera, a Spanish writer of three centuries ago, states that among the primitive inhabitants of Yucatan baptism was known by a name that meant to be born again.[u] An interesting discovery of an engraved stone presenting a record of the ten commandments has been reported from the Indian mounds of Ohio."[v]

34. But it is not alone in the matter of custom and tradition relating to pre-Christian times that so marked a resemblance is found between the peoples of the old and the new world. Many traditions and some records, telling of the pre-destined Christ and His atoning death, were current among the native races of this continent long prior to the advent of Christian discoverers in recent centuries. Indeed, when the Spaniards first invaded Mexico, their Catholic priests found a native knowledge of Christ and the Godhead, so closely corresponding with the doctrines of ortho-

q John T. Short, *North Americans of Antiquity*, (1888.)

r Extract from lecture by Prof. Waterman, delivered in Bristol, England, 1849; quoted in pamphlet by Edwin F. Parry, "*A Prophet of Latter-days*," Liverpool, 1898.

s Lord Kingsborough.

t Donelly's "*Atlantis*," p. 144.

u Tract "*A Prophet of Latter-days*," by Edwin F. Parry, p. 106.

v See an article by Elder George Reynolds, in "*Contributor*" (Salt Lake City), xvii, pp. 233.

dox Christianity, that they, in their inability to account for
the same, invented the theory that Satan had planted among
the natives of the country, an imitation gospel for the purpose of deluding the people. A rival theory held that
Thomas, the apostle, had visited the western continent, and
had taught the gospel of Christ.[w]

35. Lord Kingsborough, in his comprehensive and
standard work, refers to a manuscript by Las Casas the
Spanish Bishop of Chiapa, which writing is preserved in
the convent of St. Dominic; in this the Bishop states that a
very accurate knowledge of the Godhead was found to exist
among the natives of Yucatan. One of the bishop's emissaries
wrote that "he had met with a principal lord, who informed
him that they believed in God, who resided in heaven, even
the Father, the Son, and the Holy Spirit. The Father was
named Yeona, the Son Bahab, who was born of a virgin, named Chibirias, and that the Holy Spirit was
called Euach. Bahab, the Son, they said, was put to death
by Eupuro, who scourged Him, and put on his head a crown
of thorns, and placed Him with His arms stretched upon a
beam of wood; and that, on the third day, He came to life,
and ascended into heaven, where He is with the Father;
that immediately after, the Euach came as a merchant,
bringing precious merchandise, filling those who would
with gifts and graces, abundant and divine."[x]

36. Rosales affirms a tradition among the Chileans to
the effect that their forefathers were visited by a wonderful
personage, full of grace and power, who wrought many
miracles among them, and taught them of the Creator who
dwelt in heaven in the midst of glorified hosts.[y] Prescott
refers to the symbol of the cross which was found by the

---

w See Pres. John Taylor's *Mediation and Atonement*, p. 201.

x Kingsborough's *Antiquities of Mexico.*

y Rosales, *History of Chile.*   See Prest. Taylor's *Mediation and Atonement*, p.
202.

Catholics who accompanied Cortez, to be common among the natives of Mexico and Central America. In addition to this sign of a belief in Christ, a ceremony akin to that of the Lord's Supper was witnessed with astonishment by the invaders. The Aztec priests were seen to prepare a cake of flour, mixed with blood, which they consecrated and distributed among the people, who as they ate, "showed signs of humiliation and sorrow, declaring it was the flesh of Deity."[z]

37. The Mexicans recognize a Deity in Quetzalcoatl, the traditional account of whose life and death is closely akin to our history of the Christ, so that, says President John Taylor, "we can come to no other conclusion than that Quetzalcoatl and Christ are the same being."[a] Lord Kingsborough speaks of a painting of Quetzalcoatl, "in the attitude of a person crucified, with the impression of nails in his hands and feet, but not actually upon the cross." The same authority further says, "The seventy-third plate of the Borgian MS. is the most remarkable of all, for Quetzalcoatl is not only represented there as crucified upon a cross of Greek form, but his burial and descent into hell are also depicted in a very curious manner." And again:— "The Mexicans believe that Quetzalcoatl took human nature upon him, partaking of all the infirmities of man, and was not exempt from sorrow, pain or death, which he suffered voluntarily to atone for the sins of man."[b]

38. The source of this knowledge of Christ and the God-head, to account for which gave such trouble to the Catholic invaders and caused them to resort to extreme and un-founded theory, is plainly apparent to the student of the Book of Mormon. We learn from that sacred scripture,

---

z Prescott, *Conquest of Mexico*, p. 465.

a *Mediation and Atonement*, p. 201; See Note 5.

b Lord Kingsborough, *Antiquities of Mexico;* see quotations by Pres. John Taylor, *Mediation and Atonement*, p. 202.

that the progenitors of the native American races, for centuries prior to the time of Christ's birth, lived in the light of direct revelation, which, coming to them through their authorized prophets, showed the purposes of God respecting the redemption of mankind; and, moreover, that the risen Redeemer ministered unto them in person, and established His Church among them with all its essential ordinances. The people have fallen into a state of spiritual degeneracy; many of their traditions are sadly distorted, and disfigured by admixture of superstition and human invention; yet the origin of their knowledge is plainly authentic.

39. IV. Concerning the Common Origin of the Native Races on this Continent:—That the many tribes and nations among the Indians and other "native races" of America are of common parentage is very generally admitted; the conclusion is based on the evident close relationship in their languages, traditions, and customs. "Mr. Lewis H. Morgan finds evidence that the American aborigines had a common origin in what he calls 'their system of consanguinity and affinity.' He says, 'The Indian nations from the Atlantic to the Rocky Mountains, and from the Arctic sea to the Gulf of Mexico, with the exception of the Esquimaux, have the same system. It is elaborate and complicated in its general form and details; and, while deviations from uniformity occur in the systems of different stocks, the radical feature, are in the main constant. This identity in the essential characteristics of a system so remarkable tends to show that it must have been transmitted with the blood to each stock from a common original source. It affords the strongest evidence yet obtained of unity in origin of the Indian nations within the regions defined.' "[c]

c Baldwin's "*Ancient America*," p. 56; see citations of conclusions regarding the characteristics of aboriginal Americans by Bradford, in the same work.

40. Baldwin further quotes Bradford's summary of conclusions regarding the origin and characteristics of the ancient Americans, amongst which we read:—"That they were all of the same origin, branches of the same race, and possessed of similar customs and institutions."[d] Adair writes:—"All the various nations of Indians seem to be of one descent;" and, in support of this conclusion he presents abundant evidence of similarity of language, habits, and customs, religious ceremonies; modes of administering justice, etc.[e]

41. **Written Language of the Ancient Americans:**—To these secular, or extra-scriptural, evidences of the authenticity of the Book of Mormon, may be added the agreement of the record with recent discoveries regarding the written language of these ancient peoples. The prophet Nephi states that he made his record on the plates in "the language of the Egyptians,"[f] and we are further told that the brazen plates of Laban were inscribed in the same.[g] Mormon, who abridged the voluminous writings of his predecessors, and prepared the plates from which the modern translation was made, employed also the Egyptian characters. His son Moroni, who completed the record, declares this fact; but, recognizing a difference between the writing of his day and that on the earlier plates, he attributed the change to the natural mutation through time, and speaks of his own record and that of his father, Mormon, as being written in the "reformed Egyptian."[h]

42. Now consider the testimony of Dr. Le Plongeon, announcing his discovery of a sacred alphabet among the Mayas of Central America, which he declares to be practi-

---

d The same.
e Adair's "*History of the American Indians*," London, 1775.
f I Nephi i, 2.
g Mosiah i, 4.
h Mormon ix, 32.

cally identical with the Egyptian alphabet. He states that the structure of the Maya sacred language closely resembles that of the Egyptians; and he boldly proclaims his conviction that the two nations derived their written language from the same source.[i] Another authority says:—"The eye of the antiquarian cannot fail to be both attracted and fixed by evidence of the existence of two great branches of the hieroglyphical language,—both having striking affinities with the Egyptian, and yet distinguished from it by characteristics perfectly American."[j]

43. But the Egyptian is not the only eastern language found to be represented in the relics of American antiquities; the Hebrew occurs in this connection with at least equal significance. That the Hebrew tongue should have been used by Lehi's descendents is most natural, inasmuch as they were of the House of Israel, transferred to the western continent directly from Jerusalem. That the ability to read and write in that language continued with the Nephites until the time of their extinction, is evident from Moroni's statement regarding the language used on the plates of Mormon:—"And now behold, we have written this record according to our knowledge, in the characters which are called among us the reformed Egyptian, being handed down and altered by us according to our manner of speech. And if our plates had been sufficiently large, we should have written in Hebrew; but the Hebrew hath been altered by us also."[k] Many discoveries of engravings and writings in changed Hebrew characters have been reported from various American localities; and a corrupted form of Hebrew has been recognized among the spoken language of some of the native races.

---

i Dr. August Le Plongeon, in *Review* of *Reviews*, July, 1895.

j "*Quarterly Review*," October, 1836; abstracted in "*Millennial Star*," vol. xxi, p. 467.

k Mormon ix, 32-33.

44. The following instances are taken from an instructive array of such, brought together by Elder George Reynolds.[l] Several of the early Spanish writers claim that the natives of some portions of the land were found speaking a corrupt Hebrew. "Las Casas so affirms with regard to the inhabitants of the island of Hayti. Lafitu wrote a history wherein he maintained that the Carribee language was radically Hebrew. Isaac Nasci, a learned Jew of Surinam, says of the language of the people of Guiana, that all their substantives are Hebrew." Spanish historians record the early discovery of Hebrew characters on the western continent. "Malvenda says that the natives of St. Michael had tombstones, which the Spaniards digged up, with several ancient Hebrew inscriptions upon them." Between 1860 and 1865, four stones engraved with Hebrew inscriptions were found in different parts of Ohio. One of these bore an engraved inscription in Hebrew of the Ten Commandments in an abridged form.[m] Parchments have also been found, bearing in Hebrew characters texts from the ancient scriptures.

45. In all such writings, the characters and the language are allied to the most ancient form of Hebrew, and show none of the vowel signs and terminal letters which were introduced into the Hebrew of the eastern continent after the return of the Jews from the Babylonian captivity. This is consistent with the fact that Lehi and his people left Jerusalem shortly before the captivity, and therefore prior to the introduction of the changes in the written language.

46. Another Test:—Let not the reader of the Book of Mormon content himself with such evidences as have been cited concerning the Divine authenticity of this reputed scripture. There is promised a surer and a more effectual

l Reynolds' lecture, "*The Language of the Book of Mormon.*"
m See page 297.

means of ascertaining the truth or falsity of this marvelous volume. Like other scriptures, the Book of Mormon is to be comprehended through the spirit of the scriptures, and this is obtainable only as a gift from God. But this gift, priceless though it be, is promised unto all who would seek for it. Then to all let us commend the counsel of the last writer in the volume, Moroni, the solitary scribe who sealed the book, afterward the angel of the record who brought it forth:—"And when ye shall receive these things, I would exhort you that ye would ask God, the Eternal Father, in the name of Christ, if these things are not true; and if ye shall ask with a sincere heart, with real intent, having faith in Christ, he will manifest the truth of it unto you, by the power of the Holy Ghost; and by the power of the Holy Ghost ye may know the truth of all things."[n]

NOTES:

1. **Diversity of Literary Style in the Book of Mormon:**—"There is a marked difference in the literary style of Nephi and some of the other earlier prophets from that of Mormon and Moroni. Mormon and his son are more direct and take fewer words to express their ideas than did the earlier writers, at least their manner is, to most readers, the more pleasing. Amos, the son of Jacob, has also a style peculiar to himself. There is another noticable fact that when original records or discourses, such as the record of Limhi, the sermons of Alma, Amulek, etc., the epistles of Helaman, and others, are introduced into Mormon's abridgment, words and expressions are used that appear nowhere else in the Book of Mormon. This diversity of style, expression, and wording is a very pleasing incidental testimony to the truth of the claim made for the Book of Mormon,—that it is a compilation of the work of many writers."—From Lectures on the Book of Mormon, by Elder George Reynolds.

2. **Mexican Date of the Deluge:**—In speaking of the time of the Deluge as given by the Mexican author, Ixtilxochitl, Elder George Reynolds says:— "There is a remarkable agreement between this writer's statements and the Book of Genesis. The time from the Fall to the Flood only differs sixty, possibly only five years, if the following statement in the Book of Doctrine and Covenants (cvii, 49) regarding Enoch lengthens the chronology: "And he saw the Lord, and he walked with him, and was before his face continually; and he walked with God 365 years, making him 430 years old when he was translated." The same statement is made in the Pearl of Great Price, page 45, (1888 ed.)—

[n] Moroni x. 4-5.

From lecture on "*External Evidences of the Book of Mormon*," by Elder Geo. Reynolds.

3. Ancient Civilization in America:—"That a civilization once flourished in these regions [Central America and Mexico] much higher than any the Spanish conquerors found upon their arrival, there can be no doubt. By far the most important work that has been done among the remains of the old Maya civilization has been carried on by the Peabody Museum of Harvard College, through a series of expeditions it has sent to the buried city now called Copan, in Spanish Honduras. In a beautiful valley near the borderland of Guatemala, surrounded by steep mountains and watered by a winding river, the hoary city lies wrapped in the sleep of ages. The ruins at Copan, although in a more advanced state of destruction than those of the Maya cities of Yucatan, have a general similarity to the latter in the design of the buildings, and in the sculptures, while the characters in the inscriptions are essentially the same. It would seem, therefore, that Copan was a city of the Mayas; but if so it must have been one of their most ancient settlements, fallen into decay long before the cities of Yucatan reached their prime. The Maya civilization was totally distinct from the Aztec or Mexican; it was an older and also a much higher civilization." Henry C. Walsh, in article "*Copan, a City of the Dead,*" Harpers' Weekly, October 1897.

Baldwin, in his valuable work "Ancient America" incorporates the conclusions announced by Bradford in regard to the ancient occupants of North America, as follows:—

"That they were all of the same origin, branches of the same race, and possessed of similar customs and institutions.

"That they were populous, and occupied a great extent of territory.

"That they had arrived at a considerable degree of civilization, were associated in large communities, and lived in extensive cities.

"That they possessed the use of many of the metals, such as lead, copper, gold, and silver, and probably the art of working in them.

"That they sculptured in stone, and sometimes used that material in the construction of their edifices.

"That they had the knowledge of the arch of receding steps; of the art of pottery, producing urns and utensils formed with taste, and constructed upon the principles of chemical composition; and the art of brick-making.

"That they worked the salt springs, and manufactured salt.

"That they were an agricultural people, living under the influence and protection of regular forms of governments.

"That they possessed a decided system of religion, and a mythology connected with astronomy, which, with its sister science, geometry, was in the hands of the priesthood.

"That they were skilled in the art of fortification.

"That the epoch of their original settlement in the United States is of great antiquity; and that the only indications of their origin to be gathered from the locality of their ruined monuments, point toward Mexico."—Baldwin, *Ancient America*, p. 56.

4. American Traditions Concerning the Deluge:—"Don Francisco Munoz de laVega, the Bishop of that diocese (Chiapas),certifies in the prologue to his 'Diocesan Constitutions,' declaring that an ancient manuscript of the primitive Indians of that province, who had learned the art of writing, was in his

21

record office, who retained the constant tradition that the father and founder of their nation was named Teponahuale, which signifies lord of the hollow piece of wood: and that he was present at the building of the Great Wall, for so they named the Tower of Babel; and beheld with his own eyes the confusion of language; after which event, God, the Creator, commanded him to come to these extensive regions, and to divide them amongst mankind.—Lord Kingsborough, *Mexican Antiquities*, vol. viii, p. 25.

"It is found in the histories of the Toltecs that this age and first world, as they call it, lasted 1716 years: that men were destroyed by tremendous rains and lightnings from the sky, and even all the land, without the exception of anything, and the highest mountains, were covered up and submerged in water fifteen cubits (caxtolmolatli); and here they added other fables of how men came to multiply from the few who escaped from this destruction in a 'toptlipetlocali;' that this word nearly signifies a close chest; and how, after men had multiplied, they erected a very high 'zacuali,'which is today a tower of great height, in order to take refuge in it should the second world (age) be destroyed. Presently their languages were confused, and, not being able to understand each other, they went to different parts of the earth."—The same, vol. ix, p. 321.

"The most important among the American traditions are the Mexican, for they appear to have been definitely fixed by symbolic and mnemonic paintings before any contact with Europeans. According to these documents, the Noah of the Mexican cataclysm was Coxcox, called by certain people Teocipactli or Tezpi. He had saved himself, together with his wife Xochiquetzal, in a bark, or, according to other traditions, on a raft made of cypress-wood, (*Cypressus disticha*). Paintings retracing the deluge of Coxcox have been discovered among the Aztecs, Miztecs, Zapotecs, Tlascaltecs, and Mechoacaneses. The tradition of the latter is still more strikingly in conformity with the story as we have it in Genesis, and in Chaldean sources. It tells how Tezpi embarked in a spacious vessel with his wife, his children, and several animals, and grain, whose preservation was essential to the subsistence of the human race. When the great god Tezcatlipoca decreed that the waters should retire, Tezpi sent a vulture from the bark. The bird, feeding on the carcases with which the earth was laden, did not return. Tezpi sent out other birds, of which the humming bird only came back, with a leafy branch in its beak. Then Tezpi, seeing that the country began to vegetate, left his bark on the mountain of Colhuacan."—Donelly's *Atlantis*, p. 99.

The tradition of a Deluge, "was the received notion under some form or other, of the most civilized people in the Old World, and of the barbarians of the New. The Aztecs combined with this some particular circumstances of a more arbitrary character, resembling the accounts of the east. They believed that two persons survived the Deluge, a man named Coxcox and his wife. Their heads are represented in ancient painting, together with a boat floating on the waters at the foot of a mountain. A dove is also depicted, with a hieroglyphical emblem of language in his mouth; which he is distributing to the children of Coxcox, who were born dumb. The neighboring people of Michoacan, inhabiting the same high plains of the Andes, had a still further tradition, that the boat in which Tegpi, their Noah, escaped, was filled with various kinds of animals and birds. After some time a vulture was sent out from it, but remained feeding on the dead bodies of the giants. which had been left on the earth as the waters subsided. The little humming bird, *huitzitzilin*, was then sent forth, and returned with a twig in his mouth. The coincidence of both these accounts with the Hebrew and Chaldean narratives is obvious."—Prescott; *Conquest of Mexico*, pp. 463-4.

5. Mexican Tradition Concerning the Savior:—"The story of the life of the Mexican divinity, Quetzalcoatl, closely resembles that of the Savior; so closely, indeed, that we can come to no other conclusion than that Quetzalcoatl and Christ are the same being. But the history of the former has been handed down to us through an impure Lamanitish source, which has sadly disfigured and perverted the original incidents and teachings of the Savior's life and ministry. Regarding this god, Humboldt writes, 'How truly surprising is it to find that the Mexicans, who seem to have been unacquainted with the doctrine of the migration of the soul and the Metempsychosis *should have believed in the incarnation of the only Son of the supreme God, Tomacateuctli.* For Mexican mythology, speaking of no other Son of God except Quetzalcoatl, who was born of Chimelman, the virgin of Tula (without man), by His breath alone, by which may be signified His word or will, when it was announced to Chimelman, by the celestial messenger whom He despatched to inform her that she should conceive a son, it must be presumed this was Quetzalcoatl, who was the only son. Other authors might be adduced to show that the Mexicans believe that this Quetzalcoatl was both God and man; that He had, previously to His incarnation, existed from eternity, and that He had been the Creator both of the world and man; and that He had descended to reform the world by endurance, and being King of Tula, was crucified for the sins of mankind, etc., as is plainly declared in the tradition of Yucatan, and mysteriously represented in the Mexican paintings.' "—Pres. John Taylor, *Mediation and Atonement*, p. 201.

6. Discoveries of Hebrew Inscriptions on Stone:—"Between 1860 and 1865, four different stones with Hebrew inscriptions upon them were found in Licking County, Ohio, though not all in the same neighborhood. On one, which some suppose had been worn as an amulet, was a Hebrew inscription, which was translated, 'May the Lord have mercy on him a nephel;' that is, one of untimely birth. Elder Orson Pratt, however, was of the opinion that the final letter was a 't,' and that the legend should read, 'May the Lord have mercy on him a Nephite.'

"Another of the stones bears a Hebrew inscription on each of its four sides. These inscriptions when translated read: 'The King of the Earth; The Law of the Lord; The Word of the Lord; The Holy of Holies.' It would be difficult to conceive that such an inscription would be put upon a stone by persons not acquainted with the law and with the word of the Lord; or who had not some idea regarding temple ordinances, and what the Holy of Holies implies. But a people like the Nephites would in all respects answer the requirements; as they were trained in both the law and the gospel."—Elder Geo. Reynolds, in his lecture, "*The Language of the Book of Mormon.*"

7. Survival of the Hebrew Language among American Tribes:—"It is claimed that such survivals are numerous in the religious songs and ceremonies of many of the tribes. A number of writers who visited or resided among the tribes of the northern continent, assert that the words Yehovah, Yah, Ale, and Hallelujah, could be distinctly heard in these exercises. Laet and Escarbotus assure us that they often heard the South American Indians repeat the sacred word Hallelujah."—Elder George Reynolds: "*The Language of the Book of Mormon.*"

LECTURE XVI.

REVELATION, PAST, PRESENT, AND FUTURE.

Article 9:—We believe all that God has revealed, all that He does now reveal; and we believe that He will yet reveal many great and important things pertaining to the kingdom of God.

1.   **What is Revelation?**—In a theological sense, the term *revelation* signifies the making known of Divine truth by communication from the heavens.   The Greek—*apocalypsis*, which closely corresponds with our word *revelation*, expresses an uncovering, or a disclosure of that which had been wholly or in part hidden,—the drawing aside of a veil.   An Anglicized form of the Greek term,—*Apocalypse*—is sometimes used to designate the particular Revelation given to John upon the Isle of Patmos, the record of which forms the last book of the New Testament as at present compiled.   Divine revelation, as illustrated by numerous examples in scripture, may consist of disclosures or declarations concerning the attributes of Deity, or of an expression of the Divine will regarding the affairs of men.

2.   The word *inspiration* is sometimes invested with a signification almost identical with that of *revelation;* though, by its origin and early usage it possessed a distinctive meaning.   To inspire, is literally to animate with the spirit; a man is inspired when under the influence of a power other than his own.   Divine inspiration may be regarded as a lower or less comprehensive manifestation of the heavenly influence upon man, than is shown in revelation.   The difference therefore is rather one of degree than of kind.   By neither of these directing processes does the Lord deprive

the human subject of agency or individuality;[a] as is proved
by the marked peculiarities of style and method characterizing the several books of holy writ. Yet, in the giving of
revelation, a more direct influence is exercised upon the
human recipient of the God-given message, than is the case
under the weaker, though no less truly Divine, effect of
inspiration.

3. The directness and plainness with which God may
communicate with man, is dependent upon the purity and
general fitness of the person. One may be susceptible to
inspiration in its lower and simpler phases only; another
may be so thoroughly responsive to this power, as to be
capable of receiving direct revelation; and this higher influence again may manifest itself in varying degrees, and
with a greater or lesser shrouding of the Divine personality.
Consider the Lord's words to Aaron and Miriam who had
been guilty of disrespect toward Moses the chosen revelator:
—"And the Lord came down in the pillar of the cloud,
and stood in the door of the tabernacle, and called Aaron
and Miriam: and they both came forth. And he said,
Hear now my words: If there be a prophet among you, I
the Lord will make myself known unto him in a vision, and
will speak unto him in a dream. My servant Moses is not
so, who is faithful in all mine house. With him will I
speak mouth to mouth, even apparently, and not in dark
speeches; and the similitude of the Lord shall he behold."[b]

4. We have seen that among the most conclusive proofs
of the existence of a Supreme Being, is that afforded by
direct revelation from God Himself, and that some knowledge of the attributes and personality of God is essential to
any rational exercise of faith in Him. We can but im-
perfectly respect an authority whose very existence is a

---

a See Notes 1 and 3.

b Numb. xii, 5-8.

matter of uncertainty and conjecture with us; therefore, if we are to implicitly trust and truly love our Creator, we must know something of Him. Though the veil of mortality, with all its thick obscurity, may shut the light of the Divine presence from the sinful heart, that separating curtain may be drawn aside and the heavenly light may shine into the righteous soul. By the listening ear, attuned to the celestial music, the voice of God has been heard, declaring His personality and will; to the eye that is freed from the motes and beams of sin, single in its search after truth, the hand of God has been made visible; within the soul properly purified by devotion and humility, the mind of God has been revealed.

5. **Revelation is God's Means of Communication:**—We have no record of a period of time during which an authorized minister of Christ has dwelt on earth, when the Lord did not make known to that servant the Divine will concerning the people. As has been shown, no man can take upon himself by his own act alone, the honor and dignity of the ministry. To become an authorized minister of the Gospel, "a man must be called of God, by prophecy, and by the laying on of hands, by those who are in authority," and "those in authority" must have been similarly called. When thus commissioned, the chosen one speaks by a power greater than his own, in preaching the gospel and in administering the ordinances thereof; he may verily become a prophet unto the people. The Lord has consistently recognized and honored his servants so appointed. He has magnified their office in proportion to their own worthiness, making them living oracles of the Divine will. This has been true of every dispensation of the work of God.

6. It is a privilege of the Holy Priesthood to commune with the heavens, and to learn the immediate will of the Lord; this communion may be effected through the medium

of dreams and visions, through the visitation of angels, or by the higher endowment of face to face communication with the Lord.[c] The inspired utterances of men who speak by the power of the Holy Ghost are scripture unto the people.[d] In specific terms the promise has been given, that the Lord would recognize the medium of prophecy through which to make His will and purposes known unto man:— "Surely the Lord God will do nothing but He revealeth His secret unto His servants the prophets."[e] Not all men may attain the position of special revelators:—"The secret of the Lord is with them that fear Him, and He will show them His covenant."[f] Such men are oracles of truth, privileged counselors, friends of God.[g]

7. **Revelation in Ancient Times:**—Unto Adam, the patriarch of the race, to whom were committed the keys of the first dispensation, God revealed His will and gave commandments.[h] While living in a state of child-like innocence prior to the Fall, Adam had direct communication with the Lord; then, through transgression the man was driven from Eden; but he took with him some remembrance of his former happy state, including a personal knowledge of the existence and attributes of his Creator. While sweating under the penalty fore-told and fulfilled upon him, tilling the earth in a struggle for bread, he continued to call upon the Lord. As Adam and his wife, Eve, prayed and toiled, "they heard the voice of the Lord from the way towards the garden of Eden, speaking unto them; and they saw Him not, for they were shut out from His presence; and He gave unto them commandments."[i]

---

c See pp. 35-38, and Lecture xii.

d Doc. and Cov, lxviii, 4.

e Amos iii, 7; see also I Nephi xxii, 2.

f Psalms xxv, 14.

g John xv, 14-15,

h Gen. ii, 15-20; Pearl of Great Price, p. 12, (1888 ed.)

i Pearl of Great Price, p. 18; see also Doc. and Cov., Lectures on Faith, ii, 19-25.

8. The patriarchs who succeeded Adam were blessed with the gift of revelation in varying degrees; Enoch, the seventh in the line of descent was particularly endowed. We learn from the Old Testament that Enoch "walked with God," and that, when he had reached the age of 365 years "he was not, for God took him."[j] From the New Testament we learn something more regarding his ministry;[k] and the Pearl of Great Price gives us a fuller account of the Lord's dealings with this chosen Seer.[l] Unto him were made known the plan of redemption, and the prospective history of the race down to the meridian of time, thence to the millennium and the final judgment. Unto Noah, the Lord revealed His intentions regarding the impending deluge; by this prophetic voice the people were warned and urged to repent; disregarding it and rejecting the message, they were destroyed in their iniquity. With Abraham, God's covenant was established; unto him was revealed the course of the creative events.[m] And this covenant was confirmed unto Isaac and Jacob.

9. Through revelation, God commissioned Moses to lead Israel from bondage. From the burning bush on Horeb, the Lord declared to the man thus chosen, "I am the God of thy father, the God of Abraham, the God of Isaac, and the God of Jacob."[m] In all the troublous scenes between Moses and Pharaoh, the Lord continued His communications unto His servant, who appeared amidst the glory of the Divine endowment, a veritable God unto the heathen king.[o] And throughout the wearisome forty years' journeying in the wilderness, the Lord ceased not to honor His chosen

---

j Gen. v, 18-24.
k Jude 14.
l Pearl of Great Price, pp. 28-45, (1888 ed.)
m Gen. xvii, xviii; Pearl of Great Price, pp. 49-70—Book of Abraham.
n Exodus iii, 2-6.
o Exodus iv, 16; vii, 1.

prophet. So may we trace the line of revelators,—men who have stood, each in his time, as the medium between God and the people, receiving instruction from the source Divine, and transmitting it to the masses,—from Moses to Joshua, and on through the Judges to David and Solomon, thence to John, who was the immediate fore-runner of the Messiah.

10. **Christ Himself was a Revelator:**—Notwithstanding His personal authority, God though He had been and was, while the Christ lived as a man among men, He declared His work to be that of One greater than Himself, by whom He had been sent, and from whom He received instructions. Note His words:—"For I have not spoken of myself; but the Father which sent me, he gave me a commandment, what I should say, and what I should speak. And I know that his commandment is life everlasting: whatsoever I speak therefore, even as the Father said unto me, so I speak."*p* Further: "I can of mine own self do nothing: as I hear, I judge: and my judgment is just; because I seek not mine own will, but the will of the Father which hath sent me."*q* And again, "The words that I speak unto you I speak not of myself: but the Father that dwelleth in me, he doeth the works. * * * And as the Father gave me commandment, even so do I."*r*

11. **The Apostles likewise,** left to bear the burden of the Church after the departure of the Master, looked to heaven for guidance, expected and received the word of revelation to direct them in their exalted ministry. Paul writing to the Corinthians said:—"But God hath revealed them [divine truths] unto us by his Spirit: for the Spirit searcheth all things, yea, the deep things of God. For what man knoweth the things of a man, save the spirit of man which

---

p John xii, 49-50.
q John v, 30.
r John xiv, 10, 31

is in him? even so the things of God knoweth no man, but the Spirit of God. Now we have received, not the spirit of the world, but the Spirit which is of God; that we might know the things that are freely given to us of God."[s]

12.   John also, declares that the book which is known specifically as the *Revelation* was not written of his own wisdom, but that it is:—"The Revelation of Jesus Christ, which God gave unto him, to shew unto his servants things which must shortly come to pass; and he sent and signified it by his angel unto his servant John."[t]

13.   **Continual Revelation Necessary:**—The scriptures are conclusive as to the fact, that from Adam to John the Revelator, God directed the affairs of His people by personal communication through chosen servants.   As the written word—the record of revelation previously given,—grew with time, that became a law unto the people; but in no period was that deemed sufficient.   While the revelations of the past have ever been indispensable as guides to the people, showing forth as they do, the plan and purpose of God's dealings under particular conditions, they may not be universally and directly applicable to the circumstances of succeeding times.   Many of the revealed laws are of general application to all men in all ages; e.g.: the commandments "Thou shalt not steal," "Thou shalt not kill," "Thou shalt not bear false witness," and other injunctions regarding the duty of man toward his fellows, most of which are so plainly just as to be approved by the human conscience, even without the direct word of Divine command.   Other laws may be equally general in application, yet they derive their validity as Divine ordinances from the fact that they have been authoritatively instituted as such; as examples of this class, we may consider the requirements concerning the

---

s I Corinthians ii, 10-12.
t Rev. i, 1.

sanctity of the Sabbath; the necessity of baptism as a means of securing forgiveness of sins; the ordinances of confirmation, the sacrament, etc. Revelations of yet another kind are on record, such as have been given to meet the conditions of particular times; these may be regarded as special, or circumstantial revelations; e.g., the instructions to Noah regarding the building of the ark and the warning of the people; the requirement made of Abraham that he leave the land of his nativity and sojourn in a strange country; the command to Moses, and through him to Israel, relative to the exodus from Egypt; the revelations given to Lehi directing the departure of his company from Jerusalem, their journeying in the wilderness, the building of a ship, and their voyage on the great waters to another hemisphere.

14. It is at once unreasonable, and directly contrary to our conception of the unchangeable justice of God, to believe that He will bless the Church in one dispensation with a present living revelation of His will; and in another leave the Church, to which He gives His name, to live as best it may according to the laws of a by-gone age. True, through apostasy, the authority of the priesthood may have been taken from the earth for a season, leaving the people in a condition of darkness, with the windows of heaven shut against them; but at such times, God has recognized no earthly Church as His own, nor any prophet to declare with authority "Thus saith the Lord."

15. In support of the doctrine that revelation specially adapted to existing conditions is characteristic of God's dealings with His people, we have the fact of laws having been ordained and subsequently repealed, when a more advanced stage of the Divine plan had been reached. Thus, the law of Moses[u] was strictly binding upon Israel from the time of the exodus to that of Christ's ministry; but its

u Exo. xxi; Lev. i; Deut. xii.

repeal was declared by the Savior Himself,[v] and a higher law than that "of carnal commandments," which had been given "because of transgression," was instituted in its stead.

16.   From the scriptures cited, and from numerous other assurances of holy writ, it is evident that continual revelation has ever been characteristic of the living Church.   It is equally plain that revelation is essential to the existence of the Church in an organized state on the earth.   If to have authority to preach the gospel, and administer in the ordinances of the same, a man must be called of God, "by prophecy"[w] it is evident that in the absence of direct revelation, the Church would be left without authorized officers, and would, in consequence, become extinct.   The prophets and patriarchs of old, the judges, the priests, and every authorized servant from Adam to Malachi, were called by direct revelation manifested through the special word of prophecy.   This was true also of John the Baptist,[x] of Christ Himself, and of the apostles[y] and lesser officers[z] of the Church, as long as an organization recognized of God remained on the earth. Without the gift of continual revelation there can be no authorized ministry on the earth; and without officers duly commissioned there can be no Church of Christ.

17.   Revelation is essential to the Church, not only for the proper calling and ordination of its ministers, but also that the officers so chosen may be guided in their ministrations:—to teach with authority the doctrines of salvation; to admonish, to encourage, and if necessary to reprove the people; and to declare unto them by prophecy the purposes

v Matt. v, 17-48.

w See Lecture x, page 184.

x Luke i, 13-18.

y John xv; Acts i, 12-26.

z Acts xx, 28; I Tim. iv, 14; Titus i, 5.

and will of God respecting the Church, present and future. The promise of salvation is not limited by time, place, or persons. So taught Peter on Pentecost day, assuring the multitude of their eligibility to blessing:—"For the promise is unto you," said he, "and to your children, and to all that are afar off, even as many as the Lord our God shall call."[a] Salvation with all the gifts of God, was of old for Jew and Greek alike;[b] the same Lord over all, rich unto those that call upon Him, without difference.[c]

18. **Alleged Objections in Scripture:**—The opponents of the doctrine of continual revelation quote, with gross perversion of meaning, certain scriptural passages, to sustain their heresy; among such scriptures are the following. The words of John with which he approaches the conclusion of his book are these:—"For I testify unto every man that heareth the words of the prophecy of this book, If any man shall add unto these things, God shall add unto him the plagues that are written in this book: And if any man shall take away from the words of the book of this prophecy, God shall take away his part out of the book of life, and out of the holy city, and from the things which are written in this book."[d] To apply these sayings to the Bible as it was afterward compiled is wholly unjustified, for surely John did not write with a knowledge that his book would be the concluding section of any such compilation of the scriptures as we now possess in our Bible. John had reference to his own words, which, having come to him by revelation, were sacred; and to alter such, by omission or addition, would be to modify the words of God. The sin of altering any other part of the revealed word would be equally great. Moreover, in this oft-quoted passage, no intimation is given

---

a Acts ii, 39.

b Rom. x, 12; Gal. iii, 28; Col. iii, 11.

c Rom. iii, 22.

d Rev. xxii, 18-19; see also Doc. and Cov. xx, 35.

that the Lord may not add to or take from the word therein revealed; the declaration is that no man shall change the record and escape the penalty.

19.   A similar injunction against altering the message of Divine command was uttered by Moses, over fifteen centuries before the date of John's writing;[e] and with a similarly restricted application.   Another alleged objection to modern revelation is offered in Paul's words to Timothy, regarding the holy scriptures "which are able to make thee wise unto salvation,"[f] and which are "profitable for doctrine, for reproof, for correction, for instruction in righteousness, that the man of God may be perfect, thoroughly furnished unto all good works."[g]   And the remarks of the apostle to the elders at Ephesus are quoted with the same intent; the passage reads: "Ye know   *   *   *   how I kept back nothing that was profitable unto you, but have shewed you, and have taught you publicly, and from house to house.   *   *   *   *   For I have not shunned to declare unto you all the counsel of God."[h]   It is argued that if the scriptures known to Timothy were all sufficient to make him "wise unto salvation," and the man of God "perfect, thoroughly furnished unto all good works," the same scriptures are sufficient for all men to the end of time; and that if the doctrines preached to the Ephesian elders represented "all the counsel of God," no further counsel is to be expected.   In reply, it is perhaps sufficient to say that the objectors to continued revelation who defend their unscriptural position by strained interpretation of such passages, if consistent, would be compelled to reject all revelation given through the apostles after the date of Paul's utterances, including even the Revelation of John.

---

e Deut. iv, 2; xii, 32.
f II Tim. iii, 15.
g II Tim. iii, 16-17.
h Acts xx, 18-27.

20. Equally absurd is the assertion· that Christ's dying exclamation, "It is finished," meant that revelation was at an end; for we find the same Jesus afterward revealing Himself, as the resurrected Lord, to His apostles, promising them further revelation,[i] and assuring them that He would be with them even unto the end.[j] And, moreover, were the words of the Crucified One susceptible of any such intent, the apostles who taught by revelation as long as they lived must be classed as impostors.

21. To justify the anathema with which the opponents of modern revelation seek to persecute those who believe in the continual flow of God's word to His Church, the following prophecy of Zechariah is quoted:—"And it shall come to pass in that day, saith the Lord of hosts, that I will cut off the names of the idols out of the land, and they shall no more be remembered: and also I will cause the prophets and the unclean spirit to pass out of the land. And it shall come to pass, that when any shall yet prophesy, then his father and his mother that begat him shall say unto him, Thou shalt not live; for thou speakest lies in the name of the Lord: and his father and his mother that begat him shall thrust him through when he prophesieth. And it shall come to pass in that day, that the prophets shall be ashamed every one of his vision, when he hath prophesied."[k] The day here spoken of appears to be yet future, for surely the "idols" and the "unclean spirits" still have influence; and, moreover, the fact that the "prophets" here intended are false ones is shown by Zechariah's associating them with idols and unclean spirits.

22. Such attempts to oppose the doctrine of continued revelation as have been made on the authority of the fore-

---

i Luke xxiv, 49.

j Matt. xxviii. 20; see also Mark xvi, 20.

k Zech. xiii, 2-4.

going scriptures are pitiably futile; they carry their own
refutation, and leave untouched the truth, that belief in
modern revelation is wholly reasonable and strictly scriptural.[l]

23. **Modern Revelation:**—In the light of our knowledge
concerning the constancy of revelation as an essential
characteristic of the Church, it is as reasonable to look
for new revelation today as to believe in the existence of
the gift during ancient times. "Where there is no vision
the people perish,"[m] was declared of old; and surely it is
proper to include with vision, revelation also, since the
latter gift is often manifested through dreams and visions.
Nevertheless, in spite of abundant and most explicit testimony of scripture, the so-called Christian sects of the day
are practically a unit in declaring that revelation ceased
with the apostles, or even before their time; that further
communication from the heavens is unnecessary; and that
to expect such is unscriptural. In assuming this position,
the discordant sects of the day are but following the path
that was trodden by unbelievers in earlier times. The
recreant Jews rejected the Savior, because He came to them
with a new revelation. Had they not Moses and the
prophets to guide them? what more could they need? They
openly boasted "We are Moses' disciples," and added "We
know that God spake unto Moses; as for this fellow, we
know not from whence he is."[n]

24. The scriptures, far from predicting a cessation of
revelation in latter times, expressly declare the continuation
of that gift among the people of the Lord. John foresaw
the restoration of the gospel in the last days, through
angelic ministration:—"And I saw another angel fly in the

---

l See Note 2.
m Prov. xxix, 18.
n John ix, 28-29.

midst of heaven, having the everlasting gospel to preach unto them that dwell on the earth, and to every nation, and kindred, and tongue, and people."[p]   He knew further that the voice of God would be heard in the last days, calling His people from Babylon to a place of safety:—"And I heard another voice from heaven, saying, Come out of her, my people, that ye be not partakers of her sins, and that ye receive not of her plagues."[q]

25.   The Book of Mormon is not less explicit in declaring that direct revelation shall abide as a blessing upon the Church in the latter days.   Note the prediction given through Ether the Jaredite; the context shows that the time spoken of is that of the last dispensation:—"And in that day, they [the Gentiles] shall exercise faith in me, saith the Lord, even as the brother of Jared did, that they may become sanctified in me, then will I manifest unto them the things which the brother of Jared saw, even to the unfolding unto them all my revelations, saith Jesus Christ, the Son of God, the Father of the heavens and of the earth, and all things that in them are.   *   *   *   *   But he that believeth these things which I have spoken, him will I visit with the manifestations of my Spirit, and he shall know and bear record."[r]

26.   Lehi, instructing his sons, quoted a prophecy of Joseph the son of Jacob, which is not recorded in the compilation of books known as the Bible; it has special reference to the work of Joseph the modern prophet:—"Yea, Joseph truly said, Thus saith the Lord unto me: A choice seer will I raise up out of the fruit of thy loins; and he shall be esteemed highly among the fruit of thy loins. And unto him will I give commandment, that he shall do a

---

p Rev. xiv, 6.
q Rev. xviii, 4.
r Ether iv, 7, 11.
22

work for the fruit of thy loins, his brethren, which shall be of great worth unto them, even to the bringing of them to the knowledge of the covenants which I have made with thy fathers."[s]

27. Nephi, the son of Lehi, spoke by prophecy of the last days, in which the Gentiles should receive a testimony of Christ with many signs and wondrous manifestations:— "He manifesteth himself unto all those who believe in him, by the power of the Holy Ghost; yea, unto every nation, kindred, tongue, and people, working mighty miracles, signs, and wonders, among the children of men, according to their faith. But behold, I prophecy unto you concerning the last days; concerning the days when the Lord God shall bring these things forth unto the children of men."[t]

28. The same prophet, apostrophising with warning words the unbelievers of the last days, predicted the coming forth of additional scriptures:—"And it shall come to pass, that the Lord God shall bring forth unto you the words of a book, and they shall be the words of them which have slumbered. And behold the book shall be sealed: and in the book shall be a revelation from God, from the beginning of the world to the ending thereof."[u]

29. The Savior, addressing the Nephites, repeated the prediction of Malachi concerning the revelation to be given through Elijah, before the day of the Lord's second coming:—"Behold, I will send you Elijah the prophet before the coming of the great and dreadful day of the Lord; and he shall turn the heart of the fathers to the children, and the heart of the children to their fathers, lest I come and smite the earth with a curse."[v]

s II Nephi iii, 7.
t II Nephi xxvi, 13-14.
u II Nephi xxvii, 6-7.
v III Nephi xxv, 5-6; see also Mal. iv, 5, 6: pp. 11, 153-154 this book; and for the fulfilment, Doc. and Cov. cx, 13.

30.   By revelation in the present day, the Lord has confirmed and fulfilled His early promises, and has specifically rebuked those who would close His mouth, and estrange Him from His people.   His voice is heard today, "proving to the world that the Holy Scriptures are true, and that God does inspire men and call them to His holy work in this age and generation, as well as in generations of old, thereby showing that He is the same God, yesterday, today, and forever."[w]

31.   **Revelation Yet Future:**—In view of the demonstrated facts that revelation between God and man has ever been and is a characteristic of the Church of Christ, it is reasonable to await with confident expectation the coming of other messages from heaven, even until the end of man's probation on earth.   The Church is, and will continue to be, as truly founded on the rock of revelation, as it was in the day of Christ's prophetic blessing upon Peter, who by this gift of God was able to testify of his Lord's divinity.[x]   Current revelation is equally plain with that of former days, in predicting the yet future manifestations of God through this appointed channel.[y]   The canon of scripture is still open; many lines, many precepts, are yet to be added; revelation, surpassing in importance and glorious fulness any that has been recorded, will yet be given to the Church, and be declared to the world.

32.   What shadow of justification or pretense of consistency can man claim for denying the power and purposes of God to reveal Himself and His will in these days as He assuredly did, in former times?   In every department of human knowledge and activity, in everything for which man

---

w Doc. and Cov. xx, 11-12. See also i, 11; xi, 25; xx, 26-28; xxxv, 8; xlii, 61; l, 35; lix, 4; lxx, 3; and the entire volume, as evidence of the continuation of revelation in the Church today.

x Matt. xvi, 16-19; Mark viii, 27-30; Luke ix, 18-20: John vi, 69.

y Doc. and Cov xx, 35; xxxv, 8; and the Doc. & Cov. references last cited.

arrogates to himself glory, he prides himself in the possibilities of enlargement and growth: yet in the Divine science of theology, he holds that progress is impossible, and advancement forbidden. Against such heresy and blasphemous denial of the Divine prerogatives and power, God has proclaimed His edict in words of terrible import:—"Wo be unto him that shall say We have received the word of God, and we need no more of the word of God for we have enough."[z] "Deny not the spirit of revelation, nor the spirit of prophecy, for wo unto him that denieth these things."[a]

NOTES.

1. **Freedom Under Inspiration:**—Faussett has this to say of man's agency under the influence of inspiration:—"Inspiration does not divest the writers of their several individualities of style, just as the inspired teachers in the early Church were not passive machines in prophesying (I Cor. xiv, 32). "Where the Spirit of the Lord is, there is liberty (II Cor. iii, 17,) Their will became one with God's will; His Spirit acted on their spirit, so that their individuality had full play in the sphere of His inspiration. As to religious truths, the collective Scriptures have unity of authorship; as to other matters their authorship is palpably as manifold as the writers. The variety is human, the unity Divine. If the four evangelists were mere machines, narrating the same events in the same order and words, they would cease to be independent witnesses. Their very discrepancies (only *seeming* ones) disprove collusion. * * * The slight variations in the decalogue between Exo. xx and its repetition Deut. v, and in Ps. xviii, compared with II Sam. xxii; in Ps. xiv compared with Ps. liii, and in New Testament quotations of Old Testament, (sometimes from the Septuagint, which varies from the Hebrew, sometimes from neither in every word,) all prove the spirit-produced independence of the sacred writers, who, under Divine guidance and sanction, presented on different occasions the same substantial truths under different aspects, the one complementing the other."—*Bible Cyclopedia*, p. 308.

2. **The Doctrine of no Further Revelation, New and False:**—"The history of the people of God, from the earliest ages, shows that *continued revelation* was the only way by which they could possibly learn all their duties, or God's will concerning them. They never once thought that the revelations given to previous generations were sufficient to guide them into every duty. A doctrine which rejects new revelation is a new doctrine, invented by the devil and his agents during the second century after Christ; it is a doctrine in direct

z II Nephi, xxviii, 29; see also 30; and xxix, 6-12.

a Doc. and Cov. xi, 25.

opposition to the one believed in and enjoyed by the saints in all ages. Now, to subvert and do away a doctrine four thousand years old, and introduce a new one in its stead can only be done by divine authority. * * * * * As the doctrine, then, of continued revelation is one that was always believed by the saints, it ought not to be required of any man to prove the necessity of the continuation of such a doctrine. If it were a new doctrine, never before introduced into the world, it would become necessary to establish its divine origin; but inasmuch as it is only the continuation of an old doctrine, established thousands of years ago, and which has never ceased to be believed and enjoyed by the saints, it would be the greatest presumption to call it in question at this late period; and hence it would seem almost superfluous to undertake to prove the necessity of its continuance. Instead of being required to do this, all people have the right to call upon the new-revelation deniers of the last seventeen centuries to bring forward their strong reasonings and testimonies for breaking in upon the long-established order of heaven, and introducing a new doctrine so entirely different from the old. If they wish their new doctrine to be believed, let them demonstrate it to be of divine origin, or else all people will be justified in rejecting it, and clinging to the old."—Orson Pratt, "*Divine Authenticity of the Book of Mormon,*"I (2) 15,16.

3. Inspiration a Sure Guide:—"Inspiration has been defined to be the 'actuating energy of the Holy Spirit, in whatever degree or manner it may have been exercised, guided by which the human agents chosen by God have officially proclaimed his will by word of mouth or have committed to writing the several portions of the Bible.' By *plenary inspiration* we mean that this energy was so fully and perfectly exercised, as to make the teaching of the sacred writers to be in the most literal sense of the words, God's teaching, as proceeding from him, truly expressing his mind, and bearing with it the sanction of his authority. By *verbal inspiration* we mean that this energy was not exhausted in suggesting to the writers the matter of Scripture, and then leaving them to themselves to convey, in their own manner and after an exclusively human sort, what had been supernaturally suggested; but that they were assisted and guided in the conveyance of the truth received. * * * When the doctrine of plenary and verbal inspiration is thus disentangled from the misapprehensions which have been entertained of it, it presents in no point of view any just ground of objection. It is consistent with all the conclusions relative to the Word which modern scholarship has succeeded in establishing; for the dreams of the 'higher criticism' are little more than the vagaries of arbitrary caprice; and it is much to be regretted that they have been honored with a deference wholly undeserved, and have been rashly placed side by side with the valuable and precious results of genuine criticism. These results, in many respects, point decisively in the direction of plenary inspiration, when the doctrine itself is rightly understood, as supplying the only consistent and logical ground on which the authority of the canonical writings can be safely based."—Cassell's *Bible Dictionary,* pp. 559, 561.

LECTURE XVII.

THE DISPERSION OF ISRAEL.

Article 10.—We believe in the literal gathering of Israel and in the restoration of the Ten Tribes, etc.

1. Israel:—The term *Israel*, in its original sense, expressed the thought of one who had succeeded in his supplication before the Lord; "soldier of God," "one who contends with God," "a prince of God," are among the common English renderings. The name first appears in sacred writ as a title conferred by the Lord upon Jacob, when the latter prevailed in his determination to secure a blessing from his heavenly visitor in the wilderness, receiving the promise "Thy name shall be called no more Jacob, but Israel, for, as a prince hast thou power with God and with men, and hast prevailed."[a] We read further:—"And God appeared unto Jacob again, when he came out of Padan-aram, and blessed him. And God said unto him, Thy name is Jacob; thy name shall not be called any more Jacob, but Israel shall be thy name: and he called his name Israel."[b]

2.   But the combined name and title thus bestowed under conditions of such solemn dignity, soon acquired a wider application, and came in course of time to represent the entire posterity of Abraham, through Isaac and Jacob,[c] with each of whom the Lord had covenanted, that through his descendants should all nations of the earth be blessed.[d]   The

---

a Gen. xxxii, 28.

b Gen. xxxv, 9-10.

c I Sam. xxv, 1; Isa. xlviii, 1; Rom. ix, 4; xi, 1.

d Gen. xii, 1-3; xvii, 1-8; xxvi, 3-4; xxviii, 13-15.

name of the individual patriarch thus grew into the designation of the nation, including the twelve tribes; who delighted in the title Israelites, or children of Israel. By such names they were collectively known during the dark days of their Egyptian bondage;[e] throughout the four decades of the exodus, and the journey to the land of promise;[f] so on through the period of their existence as a powerful people under the government of the judges; and as a united nation during the hundred and twenty years comprised in the successive reigns of Saul, David, and Solomon.[g]

3. At the death of Solomon, probably about 975 B.C., the kingdom was divided; the tribe of Judah and part of the tribe of Benjamin accepted Rehoboam, the son and successor of Solomon, as their king; while the rest of the people, usually spoken of as the ten tribes, revolted against Rehoboam, thus breaking their allegiance with the house of David; they chose Jeroboam as their king. The ten tribes under Jeroboam retained the title *Kingdom of Israel*, though the kingdom was likewise known by the name of Ephraim,[h] from its most prominent tribe; while Rehoboam and his subjects were known as the *Kingdom of Judah*. For about two hundred and fifty years the two kingdoms maintained a separate existence; after which (721 B. C.), the independent status of the kingdom of Israel was destroyed, and the people were brought into captivity by the Assyrians under Shalmanezer. The kingdom of Judah was recognized for over a century longer, after which it was brought to an end by Nebuchadnezzar, who inaugurated the Babylonian captivity. For about seventy years, the people remained in subjection; which fact was in accordance with the prophecy

---

[e] Exo. i, 1, 7; ix, 6-7: xii, 3, etc.

[f] Exo. xii, 35, 40; xiii, 19; xv, 1; xxxv, 20, 30; Lev. i, 2; Numb. xx, 1, 19, 24, etc.

[g] See references in great number throughout the books of Judges, I and II Samuel, and I and II Kings.

[h] Isa. xi, 13; xvii, 3; Ezek. xxxvii, 16-22; Hos. iv, 17.

of Jeremiah;[i] then the Lord softened the hearts of the ruling kings, and the work of emancipation was begun by Cyrus the Persian. The Hebrew people were permitted to return to Judea, and, to rebuild the temple at Jerusalem.

4. The people, then commonly known as Hebrews, or Jews,[j] retained as the name of their nation the designation Israel, though they comprised fewer than two complete tribes out of the twelve. The name, Israel, thus held with commendable pride by the remnant of a once mighty people, was used in a figurative manner to designate the chosen and accepted ones, who constituted the Church of Christ;[k] and in that sense it is still employed. The people of Israel, as first we meet them in history, were a united people. That we may comprehend the true import of the gathering, to which reference is made in the tenth of the Articles of Faith, it is necessary that we first consider the dispersions and scattering to which the people have been subjected. The scriptures abound in predictions concerning such dispersions; holy scripture and history in general unite in testimony of the fulfilment of these prophecies.

5. The Dispersion of Israel Foretold:—It has been said, that "If a complete history of the house of Israel were written, it would be the history of histories, the key of the world's history for the past twenty centuries."[l] Justification for this sweeping statement is found in the fact that the Israelites have been so completely dispersed among the nations as to give to this scattered people a place of importance as a factor in the rise and development of almost every large division of the human family. This work of dispersion was brought about by many stages, and extended through millenniums. It was foreseen by the early

i Jer. xxv, 11-12; xxix, 10.

j See Notes 1 and 2.

k Rom. ix, 6; Gal. vi, 16.

l Compendium, p. 85, (1884 ed.)

prophets among the chosen people; and the spiritual leaders of every generation prior to and immediately following the Messianic era predicted the scattering of the people, as an ordained result of their increasing wickedness; or referred to the fulfilment of former prophecies regarding the dispersion, then already accomplished, and foretold a further and more complete disruption of the nation.

6.   **Biblical Prophecies:**—In the course of Israels' troubled journey from Egypt, where they had dwelt as in a "house of bondage," to Canaan, the land of their promised inheritance, the Lord gave them many laws, and established ordinances for their government in temporal and spiritual affairs.   He arrayed for their contemplation blessings beyond the power of the un-aided mind of man to conceive, predicating these upon their obedience to the laws of righteousness, and their allegiance to Himself as God and King.   In contrast with this picture of blessed prosperity, the Lord described with terrible distinctness, and soul-harrowing detail, a state of abject misfortune and blighting suffering, into which they would surely fall if they departed from the path of rectitude and adopted the sinful practices of the heathen peoples with whom they would have dealings. The darkest parts of this dread picture were those that depicted the prospective breaking up of the nation, and the scattering of the people among those who knew not God.   These extreme calamities, however, were to befall Israel only after less severe chastisements had proved ineffective.[m]

7.   When the journey following the exodus was nearing its close, as the Israelites were preparing to cross the Jordan and to take possession of the land of promise; when Moses, patriarch, law-giver, and prophet, was about to ascend Nebo, from which he was to look over the goodly land and

[m] Read the fateful predictions in Leviticus xxvi, 14-33.

then die there; he repeated the story of contrasted blessings and cursings which formed the condition of God's covenant with the people. "The Lord shall cause thee to be smitten before thine enemies"[n] was declared unto them; and again:—"The Lord shall bring thee, and thy king which thou shalt set over thee, unto a nation which neither thou nor thy fathers have known; and there shalt thou serve other Gods, wood and stone. And thou shalt become an astonishment, a proverb, and a by-word, among all nations whither the Lord shall lead thee."[o] And yet further:—"The Lord shall bring a nation against thee from far, from the end of the earth, as swift as the eagle flieth; a nation whose tongue thou shalt not understand; a nation of fierce countenance, which shall not regard the person of the old, nor shew favor to the young:[p] * * * * And the Lord shall scatter thee among all people, from the one end of the earth even unto the other; and there thou shalt serve other gods, which neither thou nor thy fathers have known, even wood and stone."[q]

8. As the sacred record progresses, the fact is made plain that Israel had chosen the evil alternative, forfeiting the blessings and reaping the curses. When the son of sinful Jeroboam lay sick almost unto death, the troubled king sent his wife in disguise to Ahijah the blind prophet of Israel, to enquire concerning the fate of the child. The prophet, seeing beyond the physical blindness of his old age, predicted the child's death and the overthrow of the house of Jeroboam; and declared further:—"For the Lord shall smite Israel, as a reed is shaken in the water, and he shall root up Israel out of this good land, which he gave to their fathers,

----

n Deut. xxviii, 25.
o Verses 36-37.
p Verses 49, 50.
q Verse 64.

and shall scatter them beyond the river, because they have made their groves, provoking the Lord to anger."[r]

9.   Through Isaiah the Lord justifies His judgment upon the people, likening them to an unprofitable vineyard,[s] which, in spite of protecting hedge and fullest care, had yielded but wild grapes, and which was fit only for spoliation; "therefore" He continues, "my people have gone into captivity."[t]   And yet other tribulations were to follow, against which the people were warned lest they alienate themselves entirely from the God of their fathers:—"And what will ye do in the day of visitation, and in the desolation which shall come from far? to whom will ye flee for help?"[u]   The prophet directs the attention of his erring people to the fact that their tribulations are from the Lord:—"Who gave Jacob for a spoil and Israel to the robbers? did not the Lord, he against whom we have sinned? for they would not walk in his ways, neither were they obedient unto his law. Therefore he has poured upon them the fury of his anger, and the strength of battle."[v]

10.   After the captivity of Ephraim, or the kingdom of Israel, specifically so called, the people of Judah needed yet other admonishings and threatenings.   Through Jeremiah the fate of their brethren was brought to their remembrance;[w] then, as a result of their continued and increasing wickedness, the Lord said:—"And I will cast you out of my sight, as I have cast out all your brethren, even the whole seed of Ephraim."[x]   Their land was to be despoiled; all the cities of Judah were to be consigned to desolation,[y] and

---

[r] I Kings xiv, 15.
[s] Isa. v, 1-7.
[t] Verse 13.
[u] Isa. x, 3.
[v] Isa. xlii, 24-25.
[w] Jer. vii, 12.
[x] Verse 15.
[y] Jer. ix, 11; x, 22.

the people were to be scattered among the kingdoms of the earth.[z]   Other prophets[a] revealed the Lord's words of anger and dire warning; and the Divine decree is recorded:—"I will sift the house of Israel among all nations, like as corn is sifted in a sieve,"[b] and again "I will sow them among the people, and they shall remember me in far countries."[c]

11. **Book of Mormon Predictions:**—The record made by that division of the house of Israel which took its departure from Jerusalem and made its way to the western hemisphere about 600 B. C., contains many references to the dispersions that had already taken place, and to the continuation of the scattering which was to the writers of the Book of Mormon yet future.   In the course of the journey to the coast, the prophet Lehi, while encamped with his family and other followers in the valley of Lemuel on the borders of the Red Sea, declared what he had learned by revelation of the future "dwindling of the Jews in unbelief," of their crucifying the Messiah, and of their scattering "upon all the face of the earth."[d]   He compared Israel to an olive tree,[e] the branches of which were to be broken off and distributed; and he recognized the exodus of his colony, and their journeying afar as an incident in the general plan of dispersion.[f]   Nephi, the son of Lehi, also beheld in vision the scattering of the covenant people of God, and on this point added his testimony to that of his prophet-father.[g]   He saw also that the seed of his brethren, subsequently known as the Lamanites, were to be chastened

z Jer. xxxiv, 17.

a Ezek. xx, 23; xxii, 15; xxxiv, 6; xxxvi, 19; Amos vii, 17; ix, 9; Micah iii, 12.

b Amos ix, 9.

c Zech. x, 9.

d I Nephi x, 11-12.

e Verse 12; xv, 12, 13; see also Jacob v, and vi.

f I Nephi x, 13.

g I Nephi xiv, 14.

for their unbelief, and that they were destined to become subject to the Gentiles, and to be scattered before them.[h] Down the prophetic vista of years, he saw also the bringing forth of sacred records, other than those then known, "unto the convincing of the Gentiles, and the remnant of the seed of my brethren,[i] and also the Jews who were scattered upon all the face of the earth."[j]

12. After their arrival on the promised land, the colony led by Lehi received further information regarding the dispersion of Israel. The prophet Zenos,[k] quoted by Nephi, had predicted the unbelief of the house of Israel, in consequence of which these covenant ones of God were to "wander in the flesh, and perish, and become a hiss and a by-word, and be hated among all nations."[l] The brothers of Nephi, skeptical in regard to these teachings, asked whether the things of which he spake was to come to pass in a spiritual sense, or more literally; and were informed that "the house of Israel, sooner or later, will be scattered upon all the face of the earth, and also among all nations;" and further, in reference to dispersions then already accomplished, that "the more part of all the tribes have been led away; and they are scattered to and fro upon the isles of the sea;"[m] and then, by way of prediction concerning further division and separation, Nephi adds that the Gentiles shall be given power over the people of Israel, "and by them shall our seed be scattered."[n] Though an ocean rolled between the country of their nativity and the land to which they had been miraculously led, the children of Lehi learned through revelation by the mouth of Jacob,

---

[h] I Nephi xiii, 11-14.

[i] The division of Lehi's posterity, known at a later date as Lamanites.

[j] I Nephi xiii, 39.

[k] See Note 3.

[l] I Nephi xix, 12-14.

[m] I Nephi xxii, 1-4.

[n] I Nephi xxii, 7.

Nephi's brother, of the captivity of the Jews whom they had left at Jerusalem.[o] By Nephi they were further told of troubles then impending over the city of their birth,[p] and of a further dispersion of their kindred, the Jews.[q]

13. The Lamanites, a division of Lehi's colony, were also to be disrupted and scattered, as witness the words of Samuel, a prophet of that benighted people.[r] Nephi, the third prophet of that name, grandson of Helaman, emphasizes the dispersion of his people by declaring that their "dwellings shall become desolate."[s] Jesus Himself, after His resurrection, while ministering to the division of His flock on the western hemisphere, refers solemnly to the remnant of the chosen seed who are to be "scattered forth upon the face of the earth because of their unbelief."[t]

14. From these references it is plain that the followers of Lehi, including his own family, and Zoram,[u] together with Ishmael and his family,[v] from whom sprang the mighty peoples the Nephites, who suffered extermination because of their unfaithfulness, and the Lamanites, who, now known as the American Indians, have continued in troubled existence until the present day, were informed by revelation of the dispersion of their former compatriots in the land of Palestine, and of their own certain doom as a result of their disobedience to the laws of God. We have said that the transfer of Lehi and his followers from the eastern to the western hemisphere was itself a part of the general dispersion. It should be remembered that another colony of Jews came to the western hemisphere, the start dating about

o II Nephi vi, 8.
p II Nephi xxv, 14-15.
q Verse 15.
r Helaman xv, 12.
s III Nephi x, 7.
t III Nephi xvi, 4.
u I Nephi iv, 20-26; 30-37,
v I Nephi vii, 2-6; 19; 22; xvi, 7.

eleven years after the time of Lehi's departure. This second company was led by Mulek, a son of Zedekiah the last king of Judah; they left Jerusalem immediately after the capture of the city by Nebuchadnezzar, about 588 B. C.[w]

15. **The Fulfilment of these Prophecies:**—The sacred scriptures, as well as other writings for which the claim of direct inspiration is not asserted, record the literal fulfilment of prophecy in the desolation of the house of Israel. The dividing of the united nation into the separate kingdoms of Judah and Israel led to the downfall of both. As the people grew in their disregard for the laws of their fathers, their enemies were permitted to triumph over them. After many minor losses in war, the kingdom of Israel met an overwhelming defeat at the hands of the Assyrians, in or about the year 721 B. C. We read that Shalmanezer IV, king of Assyria, besieged Samaria, the third and last capital of the kingdom,[x] and that after three years the city was taken by Sargon, Shalmanezer's successor. The people of Israel were carried captive into Assyria, and distributed among the cities of the Medes.[y] Thus was the dread prediction of Ahijah to the wife of Jeroboam fulfilled. Israel was "scattered beyond the river,"[z] probably the Euphrates, and from the time of this event the ten tribes are entirely lost to history.

16. The sad fate of the kingdom of Israel had some effect in partially awakening among the people of Judah a sense of their own impending doom. Hezekiah reigned as king for nine and twenty years, and proved himself a bright exception to a line of wicked rulers who had preceded him.

---

[w] Omni i, 14-19; Mos. xxv, 2-4; Alma xxii, 30-32; Hel. vi, 10; viii, 21; p. 268.

[x] Shechem was the first capital of the kingdom of Israel (I Kings xii, 25); later, Tirzah became the capital: it was famous for its beauty, (I Kings xiv, 17; xv, 33; xvi, 8, 17, 23; Song of Sol. vi, 4); and lastly Samaria, (I Kings xvi, 24.)

[y] II Kings xvii, 5-6; xviii, 9-11.

[z] I Kings xiv, 15.

Of him we are told that "he did that which was right in the sight of the Lord."[a] During his reign, the Assyrians under Sennacherib invaded the land; but the Lord's favor was in part restored to the people, and Hezekiah roused them to a reliance upon their God, bidding them take courage and fear not the Assyrian king nor his hosts, "for" said this righteous prince, "there be more with us than with him; With him is an arm of flesh, but with us is the Lord our God, to help us and to fight our battles."[b] The Assyrian army was miraculously destroyed.[c] But Hezekiah died, and Manasseh ruled in his stead; this king did evil in the sight of the Lord,[d] and the wickedness of the people continued for half a century or more, broken only by the good works of one righteous king, Josiah.[e]

17. While Zedekiah occupied the throne, Nebuchadnezzar, king of Babylon, laid siege to Jerusalem,[f] took the city about 488 B. C., and led the people captive into Babylon, thus virtually putting an end to the kingdom of Judah. The people were scattered among the cities of Asia; and groaned under the vicissitudes of the Babylonian captivity for nearly seventy years,[g] after which they were given permission by Cyrus the Persian, who had subdued the Babylonians, to return to Jerusalem. Multitudes of the exiled Hebrews availed themselves of this opportunity, though many remained in the land of their captivity; and while those who did return earnestly sought to re-establish themselves on a scale of their former power, they were never again truly an independent people. They were assailed by Syria and Egypt, and later became tributary to Rome, in

a II Kings xviii, 1-3; II Chron. xxix, 1-11.

b II Chron. xxxii, 7-8.

c II Chron. xxxii, 21-22.

d II Chron. xxxiii, 1-10; II Kings xxi, 1-9.

e II Kings xxii, 1; II Chron. xxxiv, 1.

f II Kings xxv, 1-3; II Chron. xxvi, 17.

g See pp. 327-328.

which condition they were during the personal ministry of Christ among them.

18.   Jeremiah's prophecy still lacked a complete fulfilment, but time proved that not a word was to fail. "Judah shall be carried away captive, all of it; it shall be wholly carried away captive;"[h] this was the prediction. A rebellious disturbance among the Jews gave a semblance of excuse for a terrible chastisement to be visited upon them by their Roman masters, which culminated in the destruction of Jerusalem A. D. 71.   The city fell after a six months' siege before the Roman arms led by Titus, son of the emperor Vespasian.   Josephus, the famous historian, to whom we owe most of our knowledge as to the details of the struggle, was himself a resident in Galilee and was carried to Rome among the captives.   From his record we learn that more than a million Jews lost their lives through the famine incident to the siege; many more were sold into slavery, and uncounted numbers were forced into exile.   The city was utterly destroyed, and the site upon which the temple had stood was plowed up by the Romans in their search for treasure.   Thus literally were the words of Christ fulfilled, "There shall not be left here one stone upon another that shall not be thrown down."[i]

19.   Since the destruction of Jerusalem and the final disruption of the organized people, the Jews have been wanderers upon the face of the earth, outcasts among the nations, a people without a country, a nation without a home.   The prophecy uttered by Amos of old has had its literal fulfilment: truly have Israel been sifted among all nations "like as corn is sifted in a sieve;"[j] let it be remembered, however, that, coupled with this dread prediction

---

h Jer. xiii, 19.
i Matt. xxiv, 1-2; see also Luke xix, 44.
j Amos ix, 9.
    23

was the promise "Yet shall not the least grain fall upon the earth."

20.   **The Lost Tribes:**—As already stated, in the division of the Israelites after the death of Solomon, ten tribes, really ten and a half, established themselves as an independent kingdom.   This, the kingdom of Israel, was terminated as far as history is concerned, by the Assyrian captivity, 721 B. C.   The people were led into Assyria; and later disappeared so completely that they have been called the Lost Tribes.   They seem to have departed from Assyria, and while we lack definite information as to their final destination, and present location, there is abundant evidence that their journey was toward the north.[k]   The Lord's word through Jeremiah promises that the people shall be brought back "from the land of the north,"[l] and a similar declaration has been made through Divine revelation during the present dispensation.[m]

21.   In the writings of Esdras or Ezra, which however are not included among the canonical books of the Bible, but are known as apocryphal, we find references to the north-bound migration of the ten tribes, which they undertook in accordance with a plan to escape the heathen by going to "a further country where never man dwelt, that they might there keep their statutes which they never kept in their own land."[n]   The same writer informs us further that they journeyed a year and a half into the north country; but he gives us evidence that many remained in the land of their captivity.

22.   The resurrected Christ, while ministering among the Nephites on this hemisphere, specifically mentioned "the other tribes of the house of Israel, whom the Father hath

k Jer. iii, 12.
l Jer. xvi, 15; xxiii, 8; xxxi, 8.
m Doc. and Cov. cxxxiii, 26-27.
n II Esdras xiii.   See Note 4.

led away out of the land;"[o] and again He referred to them as "other sheep which are not of this land, neither of the land of Jerusalem; neither in any parts of that land around about, whither I have been to minister."[p] Christ announced a commandment of the Father that He should reveal Himself to them. The present location of the Lost Tribes has not been accurately revealed.

NOTES.

1. **Hebrews:**—Shem is called "the father of all the children of Eber" as Ham is called father of Canaan. The Hebrews and Canaanites were often brought into contact, and exhibited the respective characteristics of the Shemites and the Hamites. The term "Hebrews" thus is derived from "Eber." (Gen. x, 21; comp. Numb. xxiv, 24.)"—*Bible Cyclopedia*, by Fausset.

The writer of the article "Hebrew" in Cassell's Bible Dictionary questions the evidence on which the derivation of "Hebrew" from "Eber" or "Heber" is asserted and says: "All that can be confidently affirmed is that the term is employed of Abraham, and of the descendants of Jacob in general. The interest attaching to the word, coupled with its obscure origin, suffices to account for the many speculations in regard to it. It may be added that some scholars have found the name 'Hebrews,' a little changed, on the monuments of Egypt. If this interpretation is verified, it will be of value, as showing that when the Egyptians called Joseph a Hebrew, they employed the designation which was accepted among them."

2. **Jews:**—The term properly signifies "a man of Judah, or a descendant of Judah, but the word came to be applied to all those who were otherwise designated 'Hebrews.' It does not appear to have come into use until long after the revolt of Jeroboam and the ten tribes, and so long as the kingdom stood, it was naturally employed of the citizens of the kingdom of Judah (II Kings xvi, 6; xxv, 25); but it rarely occurs in this sense. After the exile it took the extension of meaning which it has to the present day. It was adopted by the remnants of all the tribes, and was the one name by which the descendants of Jacob were known throughout the ancient world; certainly it was far more common than 'Hebrew.' It occurs in the books of Ezra, Nehemiah, Esther, Daniel, etc., is found in the Apocrypha; and is common in Josephus, and in the New Testament."—*Cassell's Bible Dictionary*.

"Under the theocracy they were known as Hebrews, under the monarchy as Israelites, and during foreign domination as Jews. The modern representatives

---

o III Nephi xv, 15.

p III Nephi xvi. 1.

of this stock call themselves Hebrews in race and language, and Israelites in religion, but Jews in both senses."—*Standard Dictionary.*

3. Zenos:—"A Hebrew prophet, often quoted by the Nephite servants of God. All we are told of his personal history is that he was slain because he testified boldly of what God revealed to him. That he was a man greatly blessed of the Lord with the spirit of prophecy is shown by that wonderful and almost incomparable parable of the Vineyard, given at length by Jacob, (Jacob chap. v). His prophecies are also quoted by Nephi (I Nephi xix, 10, 12, 16), Alma (Alma xxxiii, 3, 13, 15), Amulek, Alma (xxxiv, 7), Samuel the Lamanite, (Helaman xv, 11), and Mormon (III Nephi x, 16).—*Dictionary of the Book of Mormon,* by Elder George Reynolds.

4. The Journeyings of the Lost Tribes:—Esdras, whose books, as stated in the text, are classed among the apocrypha, describes a vision, in the course of which the Ten Tribes are noticed in this way:—"Those are the tribes which were carried away captives out of their own land in the time of Oseas [Hosea] the king, whom Shalmanezer, the king of the Assyrians, took captive, and crossed them beyond the river; so were they brought into another land. But they took counsel to themselves, that they would leave the multitude of the heathen, and go forth unto a further country where never man dwelt, that they there might keep their statutes, which they never kept in their own land. And they entered in at the narrow passage of the River Euphrates. For the Most High then showed them signs, and stayed the springs of the flood till they were passed over. For through the country there was a great journey, even of a year and a half, and the same region is called Arsareth (or Ararah). Then dwelt they there until the latter time, and when they come forth again, the Most High shall hold still the springs of the river again, that they may go through."—II Esdras, xiii.

Concerning the journeyings of the Ten Tribes toward the north, Elder George Reynolds in his little work *"Are We of Israel,"* says:—"They determined to go to a country 'where never man dwelt,' that they might be free from all contaminating influences. That country could only be found ·in the north. Southern Africa was already the seat of a comparatively ancient civilization; Egypt flourished in northern Africa; and southern Europe was rapidly filling with the future rulers of the world. They had therefore no choice but to turn their faces northward. The first portion of their journey was not however north; according to the account of Esdras, they appear to have at first moved in the direction of their old home; and it is possible that they originally started with the intention of returning thereto; or probably, in order to deceive the Assyrians they started as if to return to Canaan, and when they crossed the Euphrates and were out of danger from the hosts of Medes and Persians, then they turned their journeying feet toward the polar star. Esdras states that they entered in at the narrow passage of the river Euphrates, the Lord staying the springs of the flood until they were passed over. The point on the river Euphrates at which they crossed would necessarily be in its upper portion, as lower down would be too far south for their purpose. The upper course of the Euphrates lies among lofty mountains near the village of Pastash; it plunges through a gorge formed by precipices more than a thousand feet in height, and so narrow that it is bridged at the top: it shortly afterward enters the plain of Mesopotamia. How accurately this portion of the river answers to the discription of Esdras of the 'Narrows' where the Israelites crossed."

LECTURE XVIII.

THE GATHERING OF ISRAEL.

Article 10:—We believe in the literal gathering of Israel, and in the restoration of the Ten Tribes, etc.

1. The Gathering Predicted:—Terrible as was the chastisement decreed on Israel for their waywardness and sin, amounting, as it did, to their dissolution as a nation, and to a virtual expulsion from the sight of the Lord's favor; fearful as has been their denunciation by Him who delighted to call them His people; through all their sufferings and deprivations, while wandering as outcasts among alien nations who have never ceased to treat them with contumely and insult, when their very name has been made a hiss and a byword in the earth;—they have ever been sustained by the sure word of Divine promise, that a day of glorious deliverance and blessed restoration awaits them. Associated with the curses under which they writhed and groaned, were assurances of blessings. From the heart of the people, as from the soul of their mighty king in the day of his deserved affliction, has poured forth a song of tearful rejoicing:—"Thou wilt not leave my soul in hell."[a] The sufferings of Israel have been but necessary chastening by a grieved yet loving Father, who planned by these effective means to purify His sin-stained children. To them He has freely told His purpose in thus afflicting them, and in His punishments they have seen His love, "For whom the Lord loveth he chasteneth,"[b] and "Blessed is the man whom thou chasteneth, O Lord."[c]

---

a Psa. xvi, 10; Acts ii, 27.

b Heb. xii, 6.

c Psa. xciv, 12; see also Prov. iii, 12; James i, 12; Rev. iii, 19.

2.   Though smitten of men, a large part of them gone from a knowledge of the world, Israel are not lost unto their Father; He knows whither they have been led or driven; toward them His heart still yearns with paternal love; and surely will He bring them forth, in due time and by appointed means, into a condition of favor and power, befitting His chosen and covenant people.   In spite of their sin, and the tribulations which they would assuredly bring upon themselves, the Lord said:—"And yet for all that, when they be in the land of their enemies, I will not cast them away, neither will I abhor them, to destroy them utterly, and to break my covenant with them: for I am the Lord their God."[d]   As complete as was the scattering, so will be the gathering of Israel.

3.   **Bible Prophecies concerning the Gathering:**—We have examined a few of the biblical predictions concerning the dispersion of Israel; in all cases the blessing of eventual restoration was associated with the curse.   Among the early prophecies, we hear the Lord declaring that it shall come to pass that when thou, Israel, "shalt return unto the Lord thy God, and shalt obey his voice according to all that I command thee this day, thou and thy children, with all thine heart, and with all thy soul; that then the Lord thy God will turn thy captivity, and have compassion upon thee, and will return and gather thee from all the nations, whither the Lord thy God hath scattered thee.   If any of thine be driven out unto the utmost parts of heaven, from thence will the Lord thy God gather thee, and from thence will he fetch thee: and the Lord thy God will bring thee into the land which thy fathers possessed, and thou shalt possess it; and he will do thee good, and multiply thee above thy fathers."[e]

d Levit.xxvi. 44; see also Deut. iv. 27-31.
e Deut. xxx, 2-5.

4. Nehemiah pleads in fasting and prayer that the Lord would remember His promise of restoration if the people would turn unto righteousness.[f] Isaiah speaks with no uncertain words of the assured return and re-union of scattered Israel, saying:—"And it shall come to pass in that day, that the Lord shall set his hand again the second time to recover the remnant of his people, which shall be left * * * * And he shall set up an ensign for the nations, and shall assemble the outcasts of Israel, and gather together the dispersed of Judah from the four corners of the earth."[g]

5. The restoration is to be complete; there shall be a united people, no longer two kingdoms, each at enmity with the other; for, "The envy also of Ephraim shall depart, and the adversaries of Judah shall be cut off: Ephraim shall not envy Judah, and Judah shall not vex Ephraim."[h] With the words of a fond Father, the Lord thus speaks of His treatment of Israel and brightens their desolation with promises:—"For a small moment have I forsaken thee; but with great mercies will I gather thee. In a little wrath I hid my face from thee for a moment; but with everlasting kindness will I have mercy on thee, saith the Lord thy Redeemer."[i]

6. After giving a terrible recital of the people's sins and the penalties to follow, Jeremiah thus voices the will and purpose of God, concerning the subsequent deliverance:— "Therefore, behold, the days come, saith the Lord, that it shall no more be said, the Lord liveth, that brought up the children of Israel out of the land of Egypt; but, the Lord liveth, that brought up the children of Israel from the land of the north, and from all the lands whither he had driven

f Neh. i, 9.

g Isaiah xi, 11-12.

h Verse 13; see also Ezek. xxxvii, 21.

i Isa. liv, 7-8.

them: and I will bring them again into their land that I gave unto their fathers. Behold, I will send for many fishers, saith the Lord, and they shall fish them; and after will I send for many hunters, and they shall hunt them from every mountain, and from every hill, and out of the holes of the rocks."[j] And again:—"Behold, I will bring them from the north country, and gather them from the coasts of the earth. * * * Hear the word of the Lord, O ye nations, and declare it in the isles afar off, and say, He that scattered Israel will gather him, and keep him, as a shepherd doth his flock. For the Lord hath redeemed Jacob, and ransomed him from the hand of him that was stronger than he. Therefore they shall come and sing in the height of Zion, and shall flow together to the goodness of the Lord."[k]

7. "Backsliding Israel," "treacherous Judah," are the terms of reproof with which the Lord addressed His recreant children, then He commanded the prophet saying: "Go and proclaim these words toward the north, and say, Return thou backsliding Israel, saith the Lord; and I will not cause mine anger to fall upon you: for I am merciful, saith the Lord, and I will not keep anger for ever. Only acknowledge thine iniquity, that thou hast transgressed against the Lord thy God, and hast scattered thy ways to the strangers under every green tree, and ye have not obeyed my voice, saith the Lord. Turn, O backsliding children, saith the Lord; for I am married unto you: and I will take you one of a city, and two of a family, and I will bring you to Zion: And I will give you pastors according to mine heart, which shall feed you with knowledge and understanding. And it shall come to pass, when ye be multiplied and increased in the land, in those days, saith the Lord, they shall say no more, The ark of the covenant of the Lord:

---

j Jer xvi, 12-16.
k Jer. xxxi, 7-8, 10-12.

neither shall it come to mind; neither shall they remember it; neither shall they visit it; neither shall that be done any more. At that time they shall call Jerusalem the throne of the Lord; and all the nations shall be gathered unto it, to the name of the Lord, to Jerusalem; neither shall they walk any more after the imagination of their evil heart. In those days the house of Judah shall walk with the house of Israel, and they shall come together out of the land of the north to the land that I have given for an inheritance unto your fathers."[l]

8. To Ezekiel, the Lord also declared the plan of Israel's restoration:—"Thus saith the Lord God; behold, I will take the children of Israel from among the heathen, whither they be gone, and will gather them on every side, and bring them into their own land: And I will make them one nation in the land upon the mountains of Israel: and one king shall be king to them all: and they shall be no more two nations, neither shall they be divided into two kingdoms any more at all."[m]

9. That the re-establishment is to be a permanent one is evident from the revelation given through Amos, wherein we read that the Lord said:—"And I will bring again the captivity of my people of Israel, and they shall build the waste cities, and inhabit them; and they shall plant vineyards, and drink the wine thereof; they shall also make gardens, and eat the fruit of them. And I will plant them upon their land, and they shall no more be pulled up out of their land which I have given them, saith the Lord thy God."[n]

10. As a fitting close to our selection of biblical prophecies, let the words of Jesus of Nazareth be read, spoken

---

l Jer. iii, 12-18. See also xxiii, 8; xxv, 34; **xxx**, 3; xxxii, 37.

m Ezek. xxxvii, 21-22; see also xi, 17; xx, 34-42; xxviii, 25; xxxiv, 11, 31.

n Amos ix, 14-15.

while He lived among men: "And he shall send his angels with a great sound of a trumpet, and they shall gather together his elect from the four winds, from one end of heaven to the other."[o]

11. Book of Mormon Prophecies:—The gathering of Israel claimed the attention of many prophets whose teachings are recorded in the Book of Mormon, and not a little direct revelation concerning the subject is preserved within the pages of that volume. We have noted Lehi's discourse in the valley of Lemuel, in the course of which that patriarch-prophet compared the house of Israel to an olive tree, the branches of which were to be broken off and scattered; now may we add his prediction regarding the subsequent grafting-in of the branches; he taught, that, "after the house of Israel shall be scattered, they should be gathered together again; or, in fine, after the Gentiles had received the fulness of the Gospel, the natural branches of the olive tree, or the remnants of the house of Israel, should be grafted in, or come to a knowledge of the true Messiah, their Lord and their Redeemer."[p]

12. Nephi, quoting the words of the prophet Zenos,[q] emphasizes the declaration that when purified by suffering, Israel shall come again into the favor of the Lord, and then shall they be gathered from the four quarters of the earth, and the isles of the sea shall be remembered.[r] Jacob, the brother of Nephi, testified to the truth of the prophecies of Zenos, and indicated the time of the gathering as a characteristic sign of the last days. Consider his words:—"And in the day that he shall set his hand again the second time to recover his people, is the day, yea, even the last time, that the servants of the Lord shall go forth in his power, to

---

o Matt. xxiv, 31.

p I Nephi x, 14; see also Jacob v.

q See Note 3, p 340.

r I Nephi xix, 16; see also I Nephi xxii, 11, 12, 25; II Nephi vi, 8-11.

nourish and prune his vineyard; and after that the end soon cometh."[s]

13. Among the most comprehensive predictions regarding the restoration of the Jews is the following utterance of Nephi:—"Wherefore, the Jews shall be scattered among all nations; yea, and also Babylon shall be destroyed; wherefore, the Jews shall be scattered by other nations; and after they have been scattered, and the Lord God hath scourged them by other nations, for the space of many generations, yea, even down from generation to generation, until they shall be persuaded to believe in Christ, the Son of God, and the atonement, which is infinite for all mankind; and when that day shall come, that they shall believe in Christ, and worship the Father in his name, with pure hearts and clean hands, and look not forward any more for another Messiah, then, at that time, the day will come that it must needs to be expedient that they should believe these things, and the Lord will set his hand again the second time to restore his people from their lost and fallen state. Wherefore, he will proceed to do a marvelous work and a wonder among the children of men."[t]

14. Nephi, commenting on the words of Isaiah regarding the sufferings and subsequent triumph of the people of Israel, states the condition upon which their gathering is predicated, and says of God:—"That he has spoken unto the Jews, by the mouth of his holy prophets, even from the beginning down, from generation to generation, until the time comes that they shall be restored to the true church and fold of God; when they shall be gathered home to the lands of their inheritance, and shall be established in all their lands of promise."[u]

---

[s] Jacob vi, 2.

[t] II Nephi xxv, 15-17.

[u] II Nephi ix, 2; see also I Nephi xv, 19; xix, 13-16; II Nephi xxv, 16, 17, 20; III Nephi v, 21-26; xxi, 26-29; xxix, 1-8; Mormon v, 14.

15. It is evident from this and many other passages, that the time of the Jews' return is to be determined by their acceptance of Christ as their Lord. When that time comes, they are to be gathered to the land of their fathers; and in the work of gathering, the Gentiles are destined to take a great and honorable part, as witness the further words of Nephi:—"But behold, thus saith the Lord God: When the day cometh that they shall believe in me, that I am Christ, then have I covenanted with their fathers that they shall be restored in the flesh, upon the earth, unto the lands of their inheritance. And it shall come to pass that they shall be gathered in from their long dispersion, from the isles of the sea, and from the four parts of the earth; and the nations of the Gentiles shall be great in the eyes of me, saith God, in carrying them forth to the land of their inheritance. Yea, the kings of the Gentiles shall be nursing fathers unto them, and their queens shall become nursing mothers; wherefore, the promises of the Lord are great unto the Gentiles, for he hath spoken it, and who can dispute."[v]

16. The assistance which the Gentiles are to give in the preparation of the Jews, and of the remnant of the house of Israel established on the western continent, is affirmed by several Book of Mormon prophets; and, moreover, the blessings which the Gentiles may thus bring upon themselves are described in detail.[w] A single quotation must suffice for our present purpose; and this the declaration of the risen Lord, during His brief ministration among the Nephites:—"But if they [the Gentiles] will repent, and hearken unto my words, and harden not their hearts, I will establish my church among them, and they shall come in unto the covenant, and be numbered among this the remnant of Jacob, unto whom I have given this land for

v II Nephi x, 7-9; xxx, 7; See also Isaiah xlix, 23; III Nephi v, 26; xx, 29.
w III Nephi xxi, 21-27; Ether xiii, 8-10.

their inheritance, and they shall assist my people, the remnant of Jacob, and also, as many of the house of Israel
as shall come, that they may build a city, which shall be
called the New Jerusalem; and then shall they assist my
people that they may be gathered in, who are scattered upon
all the face of the land, in unto the New Jerusalem. And
then shall the power of heaven come down among them; and
I also will be in the midst; and then shall the work of the
Father commence at that day, even when this gospel shall be
preached among the remnant of this people. Verily I say
unto you, at that day shall the work of the Father commence among all the dispersed of my people; yea, even the
tribes which have been lost, which the Father hath led away
out of Jerusalem. Yea, the work shall commence among
all the dispersed of my people, with the Father, to prepare
the way whereby they may come unto me, that they may
call on the Father in my name; yea, and then shall the
work commence, with the Father, among all nations, in
preparing the way whereby his people may be gathered
home to the land of their inheritance."[x]

17. **Modern Revelation Concerning the Gathering:**—We
have found abundant proof of the severely literal fulfilment
of prophecies relating to Israel's dispersion. The predictions relative to the gathering have been but partly fulfilled;
for, while the work of concentration has been well begun,
and is now in active progress, the consummation of the
labor is yet future. It is reasonable, then, to look for revelation and prophecy concerning the subject, in modern
scripture as well as in the inspired writings of former times.
Speaking to the elders of the Church in this dispensation,
the Lord declares His purpose to gather His people "even as
a hen gathereth her chickens under her wings,"[y] and adds

---

[x] III Nephi xxi, 22-28.

[y] Revelation given 1830, Doc. and Cov. xxix, 2; see also x, 65;xliii, 24.

"and ye are called to bring to pass the gathering of mine elect, for mine elect hear my voice, and harden not their hearts; wherefore the decree hath gone forth from the Father, that they shall be gathered in unto one place upon the face of this land, to prepare their hearts and be prepared in all things against the day when tribulation and desolation are sent forth upon the wicked."[z]

18.   Hear further, the word of the Lord unto the people of His Church in the present day, not only predicting the gathering of the Saints to Zion, but announcing that the hour for the gathering has come:—"Wherefore, prepare ye, prepare ye, O my people; sanctify yourselves; gather ye together, O ye people of my church.   *   *   *   Yea, verily I say unto you again, the time has come when the voice of the Lord is unto you, go ye out of Babylon, gather ye out from among the nations, from the four winds, from one end of heaven to the other."[a]

19. Extent and Purpose of the Gathering:—Some of the prophecies already cited have special reference to the restoration of the Ten Tribes; others relate to the return of the people of Judah to the land of their inheritance; yet others refer to the re-establishment of Israel in general, without mention of tribal or other divisions; while many passages in the revelations of the present dispensation deal with the gathering of the Saints who have numbered themselves with the Church of Christ as re-established.   It is evident that the plan of gathering comprises:—

1.   Return of the Jews to Jerusalem.

2.   Restoration of the Ten Tribes.

3.   Assembling in the land of Zion of the people of Israel from the nations of the earth.

---

z Doc. and Cov. xxix, 7-8; see also xxxi, 8; xxxiii, 6; xxxviii, 31; cxxxiii, 7; xlv, 25; lxxvii, 14; lxxxiv, 2.

a Doc. and Cov. cxxxiii, 4, 7.

20. The sequence of these subdivisions as here presented, is that of convenience only, and has no significance
as to the order in which the work is to be done. The division last named constitutes the present great work of the
Church, though the labor of assisting in the restoration of
the Lost Tribes is included. We are informed by revelation,
given in the Kirtland Temple, that the appointment to and
the authority for this work were solemnly committed to the
Church. And through whom should such authority be expected to come? Surely through him who had received it
by Divine commission in a former dispensation of united
Israel. Moses, who was the chief representative of Israel's
God when the Lord set His hand the first time to lead His
people to the land of their appointed inheritance, has come
in person and has committed to the latter-day Church the
authority to minister in the work now that the Lord has
"set his hand the second time" to recover His people.

21. Joseph Smith and Oliver Cowdery, each of whom
had been duly ordained to the apostleship, testify of the
manifestations made to them, in these words:—"The
heavens were again opened unto us, and Moses appeared
before us, and committed unto us the keys of the gathering
of Israel from the four parts of the earth, and the leading
of the ten tribes from the land of the north."[b] The importance of the work thus required of the Church was
emphasized by a later revelation, in which the Lord gave
this command:—"Send forth the elders of my church unto
the nations which are afar off; unto the islands of the sea;
send forth unto foreign lands; call upon all nations; firstly
upon the Gentiles, and then upon the Jews. And behold,
and lo, this shall be their cry, and the voice of the Lord
unto all people: Go ye forth unto the land of Zion. * * *
Let them therefore, who are among the Gentiles flee

---

[b] Doc. and Cov. cx. 11.

unto Zion. And let them who be of Judah flee unto
Jerusalem, unto the mountain of the Lord's house. Go ye
out from among the nations, even from Babylon, from the
midst of wickedness, which is spirtual Babylon."[c]

22. The last sentence of the foregoing quotation expresses the purpose for which this work of gathering the
Saints from the nations of the earth has been ordained. The
Lord would have His people separate themselves from the
sins of the world, and depart from spiritual Babylon, that
they may learn the ways of God and serve Him the
more fully. John the Revelator, while in exile on Patmos,
saw in vision the fate of the sinful world. An angel came
down from heaven, "and he cried mightily with a strong
voice, saying, Babylon the great is fallen, is fallen, and is
become the habitation of devils, and the hold of every foul
spirit, and a cage of every unclean and hateful bird. * * *
And I heard another voice from heaven, saying, Come out
of her, my people, that ye be not partakers of her sins, and
that ye receive not of her plagues. For her sins have reached
unto heaven, and God hath remembered her iniquities."[d]

23. The faith of the Saints teaches that in the day of the
Lord's righteous fury, safety will be found in Zion. The
importance which the Latter-day Saints associate with the
work of gathering, and the fidelity with which they seek to
discharge the duty enjoined upon them by Divine authority in the matter of warning the world of the impending
dangers, as described in the Revelator's vision, are sufficiently
demonstrated by the great extent of the missionary labor as
at present prosecuted by this people.[e]

24. **Israel a Chosen People:**—It is evident that the Lord
has conferred the choicest of blessings upon His people

c Doc. and Cov. cxxxiii, 8-9, 12-14.

d Rev. xviii, 2, 4-5.

e See Note 1.

Israel.[f] With Abraham, the patriarch of the nation, God entered into a covenant and said:—"I will make of thee a great nation, and I will bless thee and make thy name great; and thou shalt be a blessing; and I will bless them that bless thee, and curse him that curseth thee, and in thee shall all families of the earth be blessed."[g] This was to be an everlasting covenant.[h] It was confirmed upon Isaac,[i] and in turn upon Jacob who was called Israel.[j] The promises regarding the multitudinous posterity, among whom were to be counted many of royal rank, have been literally fulfilled. No less certain is the realization of the second part of the prediction, that in and through Abraham's descendants should all nations of the earth be blessed. For, by a world-wide dispersion, the children of Israel have been mingled with the nations; and the blood of the chosen seed has been sprinkled among the peoples.[k] And now, in this the day of gathering, when the Lord is again bringing His people together to honor and bless them above all that the world can give, every nation with the blood of Israel in the veins of its members will partake of the blessings.

25. But there is another and more striking proof of blessings flowing to all nations through the house of Israel. Was not the Redeemer born in the flesh through the lineage of Abraham? Surely the blessings of that Divine birth are extended, not only to the nations and families of the earth collectively, but to every individual in mortality.

26. **Restoration of the Ten Tribes:**—From the scriptural passages already considered, it is plain, that while many of those belonging to the Ten Tribes were dispersed among the nations, a sufficient number to justify the retention of the original name were led away as a body, and are now in ex-

---

[f] See Note 2.
[g] Gen. xii, 1-2; see also Gal. iii, 14, 16.
[h] Gen. xvii, 6-8.
[i] Gen. xxvi, 3-4.
[j] Gen. xxxv, 11-12.
[k] See Note 3.

24

istence in some place where the Lord has hidden them.
To them Christ went to minister after His visit to the
Nephites, as before stated.[l] Their return constitutes a very
important part of the gathering, characteristic of the dispensation of the fulness of times.

27. To the scriptures already quoted as relating to their
return, the following should be added: As a feature of the
work of God in the day of restoration we are told:—"And
they who are in the north countries shall come in remembrance before the Lord, and their prophets shall hear his
voice, and shall no longer stay themselves, and they shall
smite the rocks, and the ice shall flow down at their presence. And an highway shall be cast up in the midst of the
great deep. Their enemies shall become a prey unto them.
And in the barren deserts there shall come forth pools of
living water; and the parched ground shall no longer be
a thirsty land. And they shall bring forth their rich
treasures unto the children of Ephraim my servants.
And the boundaries of the everlasting hills shall tremble at
their presence. And there shall they fall down, and be
crowned with glory, even in Zion, by the hands of the
servants of the Lord, even the children of Ephraim; and
they shall be filled with songs of everlasting joy. Behold
this is the blessing of the everlasting God upon the tribes
of Israel, and the richer blessing upon the head of Ephraim
and his fellows."[m]

28. From the express and repeated declaration, that in
their exodus from the north, the Ten Tribes are to be led to
Zion, there to receive honor at the hands of some of the
children of Ephraim, who necessarily are to have previously gathered there, it is plain that Zion is to be first
established. The establishment of Zion will receive attention in the next lecture.

l pp. 338-339.
m Doc. and Cov. cxxxiii, 26-34.

NOTES.

1. Gathering Now in Progress:—The Latter-day Saints "are building up stakes of Zion in the Rocky Mountain valleys, and in this way are fulfilling predictions of the ancient prophets. Isaiah hath it written, "And it shall come to pass in the last days, that the mountain of the Lord's house shall be established in the top of the mountains, and shall be exalted above the hills; and all nations shall flow unto it. And many people shall go and say, Come ye, and let us go up to the mountain of the Lord, to the house of the God of Jacob; and he will teach us of his ways, and we will walk in his paths; for out of Zion shall go forth the law, and the word of the Lord from Jerusalem." (Isaiah ii, 2-3.) It is remarkable how minutely the Latter-day Saints are fulfilling the terms of this prophecy: 1. They are building the temples of God in the tops of the mountains, so that the house of the Lord is truly where Isaiah saw it would be. 2. The Saints engaged in this work are people gathered from nearly all the nations under heaven, so that all nations are flowing unto the house of the Lord in the top of the mountains. 3. The people who receive the gospel in foreign lands joyfully say to their relatives and friends: Come ye, and let us go up to the house of the Lord, and he will teach us of his ways and we will walk in his paths."—*Roberts' Outlines of Ecclesiastical History*, p. 409.

2. Israel a Chosen People:—"The promise to Abram that he should become a great nation, has been fulfilled in his chosen seed occupying the land of Palestine, as such, for fifteen hundred years. It will again be fulfilled when they become a nation on that land forever. The history of the eastern hemisphere for the two thousand years which intervened between the calling of Abraham and the destruction of Jerusalem by the Romans, witnesses that every nation that fought against Israel, or in any way oppressed them passed away. Time will show the same general result from the destruction of Jerusalem to the millennium. The Prophet Isaiah, speaking of the time when the Lord should favor Israel, said, "All they that were incensed against thee shall be ashamed and confounded; they shall be as nothing; and they that strive with thee shall perish." (xli, 11.) "I will feed them that oppress thee with their own flesh; and they shall be drunken with their own blood." (xlix, 27.) "I have taken out of thine hand the cup of trembling, even the dregs of the cup of my fury; thou shalt no more drink of it again: but I will put it into the hand of them that afflict thee; which have said to thy soul, Bow down, that we may go over."—*A Compendium of the Doctrines of the Gospel*, by Elders Franklin D. Richards and James A. Little, pp. 246-247.

3. Israel Among the Nations:—"When we reflect that it is thirty-two centuries since the enemies of Israel began to oppress them in the land of Canaan, that about one-third of the time they were a people in that land they were more or less in bondage to their enemies; that seven hundred years before the coming of Christ the ten tribes were scattered throughout western Asia; that we have no record that any have as yet returned to the land of their inheritance; that nearly six hundred years before Christ, the Babylonish captivity took place, and that, according to the Book of Esther, only a small part of the Jews ever returned, but were scattered through the 127 provinces of the Persian empire; that Asia was the hive from which swarmed the nomadic tribes who over-ran Europe; that at the destruction of Jerusalem by the Romans the Jews were scattered over the known world; we may well ask the question, Does not Israel today constitute a large proportion of the human family?"—*Compendium*, by Elders F. D. Richards and Jas. A. Little, p. 90.

LECTURE XIX.

ZION.

Article 10.—We believe   *   *   *   That Zion will be built upon this [the American] continent, etc.

1.   Two Gathering Places:—Some of the passages quoted in connection with the dispersion and the subsequent re-union of Israel, make reference to Jerusalem which is to be re-established, and Zion which is to be built.   True, the latter name is in many cases used as a synonym of the first, owing to the fact that a certain hill within the Jerusalem of old was known specifically as Zion, or Mount Zion; and the name of a part, is often used figuratively to designate the whole; but in other passages, the separate and distinctive meaning of the terms is clear.   The prophet Micah, who ministered during the seventh century before the birth of Christ, "full of power by the spirit of the Lord, and of judgment, and of might,"[a] predicted the destruction of Jerusalem and its associated Zion, the former to "become heaps," and the latter to be "plowed as a field;"[b] and then announced a new condition which is to exist in the last days, when another "mountain of the house of the Lord" is to be established, and this is to be called Zion.[c]   The two places are mentioned separately in the prophecy:—"For the law shall go forth of Zion, and the word of the Lord from Jerusalem."[d]

2.   Joel adds this testimony regarding the two places from which the Lord shall rule over His people:—"The

---

a Micah iii, 8,

b Micah iii, 12; see also page 337 of this book.

c Micah iv, 1.

d Micah iv, 2; Isaiah ii, 2-3.

Lord also shall roar out of Zion, and utter his voice from Jerusalem."[e] Zephaniah breaks forth into song, with the triumph of Israel as his theme, and addresses the daughters of both cities:—"Sing, O daughter of Zion; shout, O Israel; be glad and rejoice with all the heart, O daughter of Jerusalem."[f] Then, the prophet predicts separately of each place:—"In that day it shall be said to Jerusalem, Fear thou not: and to Zion, Let not thine hands be slack."[g] Furthermore, Zechariah records the revealed will in this way:— "And the Lord shall yet comfort Zion, and shall yet choose Jerusalem."[h]

3. When the people of the house of Jacob are prepared to receive the Redeemer as their rightful king, when the scattered sheep of Israel have been sufficiently humbled through suffering and sorrow to know and to follow their Shepherd, then, indeed, will He come to reign among them. Then a literal kingdom will be established, wide as the world, with the King of Kings on the throne; and the two capitals of this mighty empire will be, Jerusalem on the eastern hemisphere, and Zion on the western. Isaiah speaks of the glory of Christ's kingdom in the latter days, and ascribes separately to Zion and to Jerusalem the blessings of triumph:[i]—"O Zion, that bringest good tidings, get thee up into the high mountain; O Jerusalem, that bringest good tidings, lift up thy voice with strength; lift it up, be not afraid; say unto the cities of Judah, behold your God."[j]

4. **The Name "Zion"** is used in several distinct senses. By derivation, the word *Zion*, or as written by the Greeks, *Sion*, probably meant *bright*, or *sunny;* but this common-

---

e Joel iii, 16.
f Zeph. iii, 14.
g Verse 16.
h Zech. i, 17; see also ii, 7-12.
i Isa. iv, 3-4.
j Isa. xl. 9.

place signification is lost in the deeper and more affecting meaning which the word as a name and title came to acquire. As stated, a particular hill within the site of the city of Jerusalem was called Zion. When David gained his victory over the Jebusites, he captured and occupied the "stronghold of Zion," and named it the city of David.[k] "Zion" then was the name of a place; and it has been applied as follows:

1. To the hill itself, or Mount Zion, and, by extension of meaning, to Jerusalem.

2. To the location of the "mountain of the house of the Lord," which Micah predicts shall be established in the last days, distinct from Jerusalem. To these we may add another application of the name as made known through modern revelation, viz.

3. To the city of Holiness, founded by Enoch, the seventh patriarch in descent from Adam, and called by him Zion.[l]

4. Yet another use of the term is to be noted, viz. a metaphorical one, by which the Church of God is called Zion, comprising, according to the Lord's own definition, the pure in heart.[m]

5. **Jerusalem:**—As a fitting introduction to our study regarding the new Zion, yet to be built, as we shall presently see, on the western hemisphere, let us briefly consider the history and destiny of Jerusalem,[n] the Zion of the eastern continent. The word Jerusalem is generally believed to mean by derivation the *foundation* or *city of peace.* We meet it for the first time as Salem, the abode of Melchisedek, high-priest and king, to whom Abram paid tithes, in the nineteenth century before Christ.[o] We find a direct statement concerning the identity of Salem and Jerusalem

---

k II Sam. v, 6-7; see also I Kings ii, 10, and viii, 1.

l "Wrtings of Moses." Pearl of Great Price, pp. 37, 38. (1888 ed.)

m Doc. and Cov. xcvii, 21.

n See Note 1.

o Gen. xiv, 18-20.

by Josephus.[p] As noted, the city was wrested from the Jebusites by David;[q] this was about 1048 B. C. During the reigns of David and Solomon, the city as the capital of the kingdom of undivided Israel acquired great fame for its riches, beauty, and strength, its chief attraction being the marvelous temple of Solomon which adorned Mount Moriah.[r] After the division of the kingdom, Jerusalem remained the capital of the smaller kingdom of Judah.

6. Among its many and varied vicissitudes incident to the fortunes of war,[s] may be mentioned:—the destruction of the city and the enslaving of the inhabitants by Nebuchadnezzar 585 B. C.;[t] its re-establishment at the close of the Babylonian captivity,[u] (about 515 B. C.); and its final overthrow at the disruption of the Jewish nation by the Romans 70-71 A. D. In importance, and in the love of the Jews, the city was the very heart of Judea: and in the estimation of Christians, it has ever been invested with the fullest sanctity. It occupied an important place in the earthly mission of the Redeemer, and was the scene of His death, resurrection, and ascension. The Savior's high regard for the chief city of His people is beyond question. He forbade that any should swear by it, "for it is the city of the great King;"[v] and because of its sins, He lamented over it as a father for a wayward child.[w]

7. But, great as is Jerusalem's past, a yet greater future awaits her. Again will the city become a royal seat, her throne that of the King of Kings, with permanency of glory assured.

---

[p] Ant. of the Jews I, chapter x.

[q] II Sam. v, 6-7.

[r] I Kin. v-viii; II Chron. ii-vii.

[s] I Kings xiv, 25; II Kings xiv, 13-14: xxv: II Chron. xii, 2-5; xxxvi, 14-21; Jer. xxxix, 5-8.

[t] Jer. lii, 12-15.

[u] Ezra. i-iii; Neh. ii.

[v] Matt. v, 35; see also Psa. xlviii, 2; lxxxvii. 3.

[w] Matt. xxiii, 37; Luke xiii, 34.

8. The Latter-day Zion; New Jerusalem:—The biblical statements concerning the Zion of the last days as separate
from the ancient or the re-established Jerusalem of the east,
are silent regarding the geographical location of this second
and modern capital of Christ's kingdom. We learn something, however, from the Bible as to the physical characteristics of the region wherein Zion is to be built. Thus, Micah,
after predicting the desolation of the hill, Mount Zion, and
of Jerusalem in general, describes in contrast the new Zion,
wherein the house of the Lord is to be built in the last days.
These are his words:—"But in the last days it shall come to
pass, that the mountain of the house of the Lord shall be
established in the top of the mountains, and it shall be
exalted above the hills; and people shall flow unto it. And
many nations shall come, and say, Come, and let us go up
to the mountain of the Lord, and to the house of the God
of Jacob; and he will teach us of his ways, and we will
walk in his paths; for the law shall go forth of Zion, and
the word of the Lord from Jerusalem."[x]

9. The prophecy of Isaiah is not less explicit regarding
the mountainous character of the country of modern Zion;[y]
and, furthermore, this writer assures us that the righteous
man only shall be able to dwell amid the fiery splendor of
this new abode; and of him the prophet says:—"He shall
dwell on high: his place of defence shall be the munitions
of rocks;" and adds the statement that the land shall be
very far off.[z] In another passage, he mentions a gathering
place "beyond the rivers of Ethiopia," and, "on the mountains" where the Lord is to "set up an ensign" to the world.[a]

10. The teachings of the Book of Mormon, and the
truths made known through revelation in the present dis-

---

x Micah iv, 1-2.
y Isa. ii, 2-3.
z Isa. xxxiii, 15-17.
a Isa. xviii. 1-3.

pensation, regarding the Zion of the last days, while agreeing with the biblical record as to the general description of
the situation, and the glories of the city, are more explicit
in regard to the location. In these scriptures, the names
Zion and New Jerusalem are used synonymously, the latter
designation being given in honor of the Jerusalem of the
east. John the Revelator saw in vision a New Jerusalem as
characteristic of the latter times.[b] Ether, writing 600 B.C.
as a prophet among the Jaredites,—a people who had inhabited parts of North America for centuries before Lehi and
his followers came to this hemisphere,[c] foretold the establishment of the New Jerusalem on this continent, and emphasized the distinction between that city and the Jerusalem of
old.

11. The Nephite prophet, Moroni, in the synopsis of the
writings of Ether, says of the latter, that he saw concerning
the land of North America, "That it was the place of the
New Jerusalem, which should come down out of heaven,
and the Holy Sanctuary of the Lord." And adds: "Behold, Ether saw the days of Christ, and he spake concerning a new Jerusalem, upon this land; And he spake also
concerning the house of Israel, and the Jerusalem from
whence Lehi should come; after it should be destroyed, it
should be built up again a holy city unto the Lord, wherefore it could not be a New Jerusalem, for it had been in a
time of old, but it should be built up again, and become a
holy city of the Lord; and it should be built unto the house
of Israel: And that a New Jerusalem should be built up
upon this land, unto the remnant of the seed of Joseph, for
which things there has been a type: For as Joseph brought
his father down into the land of Egypt, even so he died
there; wherefore the Lord brought a remnant of the seed of

---

b Rev. xxi, 2.
c See page 266.

Joseph out of the land of Jerusalem, that he might be merciful unto the seed of Joseph, that they should perish not, even as he was merciful unto the father of Joseph, that he should perish not; Wherefore the remnant of the house of Joseph shall be built upon this land; and it shall be a land of their inheritance; and they shall build up a holy city unto the Lord, like unto the Jerusalem of old; and they shall no more be confounded, until the end come, when the earth shall pass away."[d]

12. Jesus Christ visited the Nephites in North America soon after His resurrection, and in the course of His teachings said—"And behold, this people will I establish in this land, unto the fulfilling of the covenant which I made with your father Jacob; and it shall be a New Jerusalem. And the powers of heaven shall be in the midst of this people; yea, even I will be in the midst of you."[e] Our Savior predicted further, as set forth in a previous lecture,[f] that the Gentiles, if they would repent of their sins, and not harden their hearts, should be included in the covenant, and be permitted to assist in the building of a city to be called the New Jerusalem.[g]

13. Ether the Jaredite, and John the Revelator, separated by more than six centuries of time and prophesying on opposite hemispheres, each saw the New Jerusalem come down from heaven, "prepared" says the Jewish apostle "as a bride adorned for her husband."[h] We have already spoken of the Zion of Enoch,[i] a city once situated on the North American continent, whose inhabitants were so righteous that they too were called Zion, "because they were of one

---

d Book of Mormon, Ether xiii, 3-8.
e III Nephi xx, 22.
f See pp. 348-349.
g III Nephi xxi, 22-24.
h Rev. xxi, 2.
i Page 358.

heart and one mind."[j] They, with their patriarch leader, were translated from the earth, or, as we read, "it came to pass that Zion was not, for God received it up into His own bosom, and from thence went forth the saying "Zion is fled."[k] But before this event, the Lord had revealed unto Enoch the Divine purpose in regard to humanity, even unto the last of time. Great events are to mark the latter days; the elect are to be gathered from the four quarters of the earth to a place prepared for them; the tabernacle of the Lord is to be established there, and the place "shall be called Zion, a New Jerusalem." Then Enoch and his people are to return to earth and meet the gathered elect in the holy place.

14. We have seen that the names Zion and New Jerusalem are used interchangably; and, furthermore, that righteous people as well as sanctified places are called Zion; for, by the Lord's special word, Zion to Him means "the pure in heart."[l] The Church in this day teaches that the New Jerusalem seen by St. John, and by the prophet Ether, as descending from the heavens in glory, is the return of exalted Enoch and his righteous people; and that the people or Zion of Enoch, and the modern Zion, or the gathered elect on the western continent, will become one people.

15. The Book of Mormon is explicit in foretelling the establishment of Zion on the western continent; but the precise location was not revealed until after the restoration of the priesthood in the present dispensation. In 1831, the Lord commanded the elders of His Church in this wise:— "Go ye forth into the western countries, call upon the inhabitants to repent, and inasmuch as they do repent, build up churches unto me; and with one heart and with one mind,

j Pearl of Great Price,—Writings of Moses, p. 37 (1888 ed.)

k Pearl of Great Price, p, 45; Doc. and Cov. xxxviii, 4; xlv, 11-12; lxxxiv, 99-100

l Doc. and Cov. xcvii, 21; Pearl of Great Price, p. 37, (1888 ed.); also Doc. and Cov. lxxxiv, 100.

gather up your riches that ye may purchase an inheritance which shall hereafter be appointed unto you; and it shall be called the New Jerusalem, a land of peace, a city of refuge, a place of safety for the saints of the Most High God; and the glory of the Lord shall be there, and the terror of the Lord shall also be there, insomuch that the wicked will not come unto it, and it shall be called Zion."[m]

16. Later revelations called the elders of the Church to assemble in western Missouri,[n] and designated that place as the land appointed and consecrated for the gathering of the Saints.[o] "Wherefore this is the land of promise, and the place for the city of Zion."[p] The town of Independence was named as "the center place," and the site for the temple was designated, the Saints being counseled to purchase land there, "that they may obtain it for an everlasting inheritance."[q] On August 3rd, 1831, the temple site thus named was solemnly dedicated by the prophet, Joseph Smith, and his associates in the priesthood.[r] The region round about was also dedicated, that it might be a gathering place for the people of God.

17. Such, then, is the belief of the Latter-day Saints; such are the teachings of the Church. But the plan of building up Zion has not yet been consummated. The Saints were not permitted to enter into immediate possession of the land, which was promised them as an everlasting inheritance. Even as years elapsed between the time of the Lord's promise to Israel of old that Canaan should be their inheritance, and the time of their entering into possession thereof,—years devoted to the people's toilsome and sorrowful preparation for the fulfilment,—so in these latter-days, the Divine purpose is held in abeyance, while the people are

m Doc. and Cov. xlv, 64-67; read further, verses 68-71.
n Doc. and Cov. lii, 2-3; see Note 2.
o Doc. and Cov. lvii, 1-2.
p Verse 2.
q Verses 4-5.
r See Note 3.

being sanctified for the great gift, and for the greater responsibilities associated with it. In the mean-time, the honest in heart are gathering to the valleys of the Rocky Mountains; and here, in the tops of the mountains, exalted above the hills, temples have been erected, and all nations are flowing unto this region. But Zion will yet be established on the chosen site; she "shall not be moved out of her place," and the pure in heart shall surely return, "with songs of everlasting joy to build up the waste places of Zion."[s]

18. But gathered Israel cannot be confined to the "center place," nor to the region immediately adjacent; other places have been and will be appointed, and these are called Stakes of Zion.[t] Many stakes have been established in the regions inhabited by the Latter-day Saints, and these are to be permanent possessions; and thence will go those who are appointed from among the worthy to receive possession of their inheritances. Zion is to be chastened, but only for a little season,[u] then will come the time of her redemption.

19. That time will be appointed of God, yet it is to be determined according to the faithfulness of the people. Their wickedness causeth the Lord to tarry; for, saith He:—"Therefore, in consequence of the transgression of my people, it is expedient in me that mine elders should wait for a little season for the redemption of Zion."[v] And again,—"Zion shall be redeemed in mine own due time."[w] But the Lord's time in giving blessings unto His people is dependent upon them. As long ago as 1834 came the word of the Lord unto the Church:—"Behold, I say unto you, were it not for the transgressions of my people   *   *   * they might have been redeemed even now."[x]

s Doc. and Cov. ci, 17-18; see also ci, 43, 74, 75; ciii, 1, 11, 13, 15; cv, 1, 2, 9 13, 16, 34; cix, 47; cxxxvi, 18.
t Doc. and Cov. ci, 21; see page 215.
u Doc. and Cov. c, 13.
v Doc. and Cov. cv, 9; also cxxxvi, 31.
w Doc. and Cov. cxxxvi, 18.
x Doc. and Cov. cv, 1-2.

NOTES.

1. Jerusalem:—"The city has, in different ages, borne a variety of names, and
. even in the Bible it has several designations. Salem, mentioned in Gen. xiv, 18,
was perhaps its name in the time of Melchisedek, and it is certainly so called in
Psa. lxxvi, 2. Isaiah (xxix, 1, 7) calls it Ariel. Jebus, or Jebusi, the city of the
Jebusites, was its name in the days of Joshua and the Judges (Josh. xv, 8; xviii,
16, 28; Judges xix, 10, 11), and this name continued in use till David's time (I
Chron. xi, 4, 5). Some have thought that Jerusalem is itself a corruption of
Jebus-Salem, but it is a theory unsupported by facts. Jerusalem is also termed
'the city of David,' 'the city of Judah,' 'the holy city,' 'the city of God.'
(II Kings xiv, 20; II Chron. xxv, 28; Neh. xi, 18; Psa. lxxxvii, 3.) To this day it
is called el-Kuds, or 'the holy,' in most countries of the East. No city in the
world has received more honorable appellations: our Savior himself called it
'the city of the great King.' "—*Bible Dictionary* Cassell & Co , p 600

2. The Founding of Zion in Missouri:—" * * A company of Saints
known as the Colesville Branch—from their having lived at Colesville, Broome
County , New York, had arrived in Missouri, and having received instructions to
purchase the lands in the regions around about Zion, they secured a tract of
land in a fertile prairie some ten or twelve miles west of Independence, in Kaw
township, not far from the present location of Kansas City. On the 2nd of
August [1831],—the day preceding the dedication of the temple site,—in the settlement of the Colesville Saints, the first log was laid for a house as the foundation
of Zion. The log was carried by twelve men, in honor of the Twelve Tribes of
Israel; and Elder Sidney Rigdon consecrated and dedicated the land of Zion for
the gathering of the Saints."—*Outlines of Ecclesiastical History* by Elder B. H.
Roberts, p. 352.

3. Temple Site, Independence, Jackson County, Missouri:—"Taking the road running west from the Court House for a scant half mile, you come
to the summit of a crowning hill, the slope of which to the south and west is
quite abrupt, but very gradual toward the north and east. * * * * This is the
temple site. It was upon this spot on the third day of August, 1831, that Joseph
Smith, Sidney Rigdon, Edward Partridge, W. W. Phelps, Oliver Cowdery, Martin Harris, and Joseph Coe, and another person whose name I cannot learn, for
there were eight in all,—men in whom the Lord was well pleased, assembled to
dedicate this place as the temple site in Zion. The eighty-seventh psalm was
read. Joseph [the prophet] then dedicated the spot, where is to be built a temple
on which the glory of God shall rest. Yea, the great God hath so decreed it
saying: "Verily this generation shall not pass away, until an house shall be
built unto the Lord, and a cloud shall rest upon it, which cloud shall be even the
glory of the Lord, which shall fill the house. * * * * And the sons of Moses,
and also the sons of Aaron, shall offer an acceptable offering and sacrifice in the
house of the Lord, which house shall be built unto the Lord in this generation,
upon the consecrated spot as I have appointed.—(Doc. and Cov. sec. lxxxiv, 5,
31.)"—Elder B. H. Roberts, *Missouri Persecutions.*

LECTURE XX.

CHRIST'S REIGN ON EARTH.

Article 10:—We believe * * * That Christ will reign personally upon the earth, etc.

1.   Christ's First and Second Advents:—The facts of Christ's birth in the flesh, of His thirty and three years of life among mortals, of His ministry, sufferings, and death, are universally accepted as attested history.   Not alone do the records which the Christian world regards as sacred and inspired bear testimony concerning these facts, but the history written by man, and, in contrast, called profane, is generally in harmony with the biblical account.   Even those who reject the doctrine of Christ's divinity, even they who refuse to accept Him as their Redeemer, admit the historical facts of His marvelous life, and acknowledge the incalculable effect of His precepts and example upon the human family.

2.   Nearly nineteen centuries ago, Christ was born to earth, amid humble surroundings,—in obscurity, indeed, to all except the faithful few who had been watching for the expected advent.   His coming had been heralded through the previous centuries, even from the dawn of human existence; every prophet of God had borne record of the great events which were to characterize the "Meridian of Time;" every important incident connected with His birth, life, death, triumphal resurrection, and ultimate glory as King, Lord, and God, had been predicted; and even the details of the circumstances were given with exactness.   Judah and Israel had been told to prepare for the coming of the

Annointed One;[a] yet, behold, when He came to His own
they received Him not. Persecuted and despised, He trod
the thorny path of duty, "a man of sorrows and acquainted
with grief;" and, finally condemned by His people, who
clamored to an alien power for authority to execute their
own diabolical sentence upon their Lord, He went to the
death prescribed for malefactors.

3. To human judgment, it surely seemed that the Divine
mision of Christ had been nullified, that His work had
failed, and that the powers of darkness had become triumphant. Blind, deaf, and hard of heart, were those who refused
to see, hear, and comprehend the purport of the Savior's
mission. Similarly benighted are they who reject the
prophetic evidence of His second coming, and who fail to
read the signs of the times, which declare the event, at once
so terrible and glorious, to be near at hand. Both before
and after His death, Christ prophesied of His appointed re-
appearance upon the earth; and His faithful followers are
today waiting and watching for the signs of the great fulfilment. The heavens are flaming with those signals, and
the burden of inspired teaching is again heard,—Repent,
repent, for the kingdom of heaven is at hand.

4. **Christ's Second Coming Predicted; and Signs Described:
Bible Prophecies:**—The prophets of the Old Testament,
and those of Book of Mormon record who lived and wrote
before the era of Christ, had little to say regarding the
second coming of the Lord, little indeed in comparison with
their numerous and explicit predictions concerning His first
advent.   As they looked into the sky of futurity, and with
prophetic power read the story of the heavenly orbs, their
vision was dazzled with the brilliancy of the Meridian Sun,
and they saw little of the glorious luminary beyond, whose
proportions and radiance were veiled by the mists of dis

a See Note 1.

tance. A few of them saw and so testified, as the following
passages show: The Psalmist sang:—"Our God shall come,
and shall not keep silence; a fire shall devour before him,
and it shall be very tempestuous round about him."[b]   These
devouring and tempestuous conditions did not attend the
coming of Bethlehem's Babe.

5.   Isaiah cries:—"Say to them that are of a fearful heart,
Be strong, fear not; behold your God will come with
vengeance, even God with a recompence; he will come and
save you."[c]   Aside from the evident fact that these conditions did not attend the first coming of Christ, the context of the prophet's words shows that he applied them to
the last days, the time of restitution, the day of the "ransomed of the Lord," and of the triumph of Zion.[d]   Again
Isaiah speaks:—"Behold, the Lord God will come with
strong hand, and his arm shall rule for him: behold, his
reward is with him, and his work before him."[e]

6.   The prophet Enoch, who lived twenty centuries before the first of those whose words are given above, spoke
with vigor on the subject.   His teachings do not appear
under his own name in the Bible, though Jude, a New
Testament writer cites them.[f]   From the Writings of Moses
in the Pearl of Great Price, we learn concerning the revelation given to Enoch:—"And the Lord said unto Enoch, As
I live, even so will I come in the last days of wickedness and
vengeance, to fulfil the oath which I made unto you concerning the children of Noah."[g]

7.   Jesus taught the disciples that His mission in the flesh
was to be of short duration, and that He would come again

---

b Psalms l, 3.
c Isa. xxxv, 4.
d Verses 5-10.
e Isa. xl, 10.
f Jude 14-15,
g Pearl of Great Price, p. 44,(1888 ed.)
25

to earth, for we find them enquiring in this wise, "Tell us
when shall these things be? And what shall be the sign of
thy coming, and of the end of the world?"[h] In reply, our
Lord detailed many of the signs of the latter times, the last
and greatest of which He thus stated:—"And this gospel of
the kingdom shall be preached in all the world for a witness
unto all nations; and then shall the end come."[i] With great
clearness, Jesus spoke of the worldliness in which the children of men had continued to indulge, even on the eve of the
Deluge, and on the day of the fiery destruction which befel
the Cities of the Plains, and added "Even thus shall it be
in the day when the Son of man is revealed."[j]

8. Another of our Lord's predictions concerning His
second coming is as follows; His citation of the signs by
which the approach of the event may be known is so impressive that we should read the description in its entirety:—
"And they [the disciples] asked him, saying, Master, but
when shall these things be? and what sign will there be
when these things shall come to pass? And he said, Take
heed that ye be not deceived: for many shall come in my
name, saying, I am Christ; and the time draweth near: go
ye not therefore after them. But when ye shall hear of
wars and commotions, be not terrified: for these things
must first come to pass; but the end is not by and by.
Then said he unto them, Nation shall rise against
nation, and kingdom against kingdom: and great earthquakes shall be in divers places, and famines, and pestilences; and fearful sights and great signs shall there be
from heaven. But before all these, they shall lay their
hands on you, and persecute you, delivering you up to the
synagogues, and into prisons, being brought before kings

---

h Matt. xxiv, 3.
i Verse 14.
j Luke xvii, 26-30.

and rulers for my name's sake. And it shall turn to you
for a testimony. Settle it therefore in your hearts, not to
meditate before what ye shall answer: For I will give you
a mouth and wisdom, which all your adversaries shall not
be able to gainsay nor resist. And ye shall be betrayed
both by parents, and brethren, and kinsfolks, and friends;
and some of you shall they cause to be put to death. And
ye shall be hated of all men for my name's sake. * * *
And there shall be signs in the sun, and in the moon, and
in the stars; and upon the earth distress of nations, with
perplexity; the sea and the waves roaring; men's hearts
failing them for fear, and for looking after those things
which are coming on the earth: for the powers of heaven
shall be shaken. And then shall they see the Son of man
coming in a cloud with power and great glory. And when
these things begin to come to pass, then look up, and lift
up your heads; for your redemption draweth nigh."[k]

9. Again, by way of warning, the Lord said:—"Whosoever therefore shall be ashamed of me and of my words, in
this adulterous and sinful generation, of him also shall the
Son of man be ashamed, when he cometh in the glory of his
Father with the holy angels."[l]

10. At the time of the Ascension, as the apostles stood
gazing into the firmament, where a cloud had hidden their
resurrected Lord from sight, they became aware of the
presence of two heavenly visitors, who said:—"Ye men of
Galilee, why stand ye gazing up into heaven? this same
Jesus, which is taken up from you into heaven, shall so
come in like manner as ye have seen him go into heaven."[m]
Paul instructed the churches in the doctrines of Christ's

---

k Luke xxi, 7-28; see also Mark xiii, 14-26: Rev. vi, 12-17.
l Mark viii, 38.
m Acts i, 11.

second advent, and described the glory of His coming.[n] So also did others of the apostles.[o]

11. **Among Book of Mormon Prophecies** concerning our present subject, we find the teachings of Christ Himself at the time of His ministrations to the Nephites in His resurrected state. To the multitude He explained many matters, "even from the beginning until the time that He should come in His glory."[p] In promising the three disciples the desire of their hearts, which was that they might be spared in the flesh to continue the work of the ministry, the Lord said to them:—"Ye shall live to behold all the doings of the Father, unto the children of men, even until all things shall be fulfilled, according to the will of the Father, when I shall come in my glory, with the powers of heaven.[q]

12. **The Word of Modern Revelation** is no less sure regarding the appointed advent of the Redeemer. To servants, specially commissioned, instructions were given to this effect:—"Wherefore, be faithful, praying always, having your lamps trimmed and burning, and oil with you,[r] that you may be ready at the coming of the Bridegroom. For behold, verily, verily, I say unto you that I come quickly."[s] And again, this instruction is given:—"Cry repentance unto a crooked and perverse generation, preparing the way of the Lord for his second coming; for behold, verily, verily, I say unto you, the time is soon at hand that I shall come in a cloud with power and great glory."[t]

13. In a revelation to the people of the Church, March 7, 1831, the Lord speaks of the signs of His coming, and counsels diligence. Consider His words:—"Ye look and

n I Thess. iv, 16; II Thess. i, 7-8; Heb. ix, 28.

o I Peter iv, 13; I John ii, 28; iii, 2.

p III Nephi xxvi, 3; see also xxv, 5.

q III Nephi xxviii, 7; see also 8.

r An allusion to the parable of the Ten Virgins, see Matt. xxv, 1-13.

s Doc. and Cov. xxxiii, 17.

t Doc. and Cov, xxxiv, 6-7.

behold the fig-trees, and ye see them with your eyes, and ye say when they begin to shoot forth, and their leaves are yet tender, that summer is now nigh at hand; even so it shall be in that day when they shall see all these things, then shall they know that the hour is nigh. And it shall come to pass that he that feareth me shall be looking forth for the great day of the Lord to come, even for the signs of the coming of the Son of man; and they shall see signs and wonders, for they shall be shown forth in the heavens above, and in the earth beneath; and they shall behold blood and fire, and vapors of smoke; and before the day of the Lord shall come, the sun shall be darkened, and the moon be turned into blood, and stars fall from heaven; and the remnant shall be gathered unto this place, and then they shall look for me, and behold I will come; and they shall see me in the clouds of heaven, clothed with power and great glory, with all the holy angels; and he that watches not for me shall be cut off."[u]

14. The distinctive characteristic of the revelations as given in the present dispensation, regarding the second coming of our Lord, is the emphatic and oft-repeated declaration that the event is near at hand.[v] The call is "Prepare ye, prepare ye, for that which is to come, for the Lord is nigh." Instead of the cry of one man in the wilderness of Judea, the voice of thousands is heard authoritatively warning the nations, and inviting them to repent and flee to Zion for safety. The fig tree is rapidly putting forth its leaves; the signs in heaven and earth are increasing; surely the great and dreadful day of the Lord is near.

15. **The Precise Time of Christ's Coming** has not been made known to man. By learning to comprehend the signs of the times, by watching the development of the work

---

u Doc. and Cov. xlv, 37-44; see also paragraphs 74-75.

v See the numerous references in connection with Doc. and Cov. i, 12.

of God among the nations, and by noting the rapid fulfilment of significant prophecies, we may perceive the
progressive evidence of the approaching event, "But the
hour and the day no man knoweth, neither the angels in
heaven, nor shall they know until he comes."[w] His coming will be a surprise to those who have rejected His warnings, and who have failed to watch. "Like a thief in the
night"[x] will be the coming of the day of the Lord unto the
wicked. "Watch therefore, for ye know neither the day nor
the hour wherein the Son of man cometh."[y]

16. **Christ's Reign: The Kingdom:**—We have seen, that,
according to the words of holy prophets ancient and modern,
Christ is to come, in a literal sense, and so manifest Himself
in person in the last days. He is to dwell among His Saints.
"Yea, even I will be in the midst of you,"[z] He declared to
the people on this continent, whom He promised to establish
in the land of the New Jerusalem; and similar assurances
were given through the prophets of the east.[a] In this
prospective ministration among His gathered Saints, Christ
is to be at once their God and their King. His government
is to be that of a perfect theocracy; the laws of righteousness will be the code, and control will be administered under one authority, undisputed because indisputable.

17. The scriptures abound with declarations that the
Lord will yet reign among His people. To this effect sang
Moses before the hosts of Israel after their miraculous passage through the Red Sea,—"The Lord shall reign for ever
and ever;"[b] and the psalmist echoes the refrain, "The Lord
is King for ever and ever."[c] Jeremiah calls Him "an ever-

---

w Doc. and Cov. xlix, 7.

x II Peter iii, 10; I Thess. v, 2, etc.

y Matt. xxv. 13; see also xxiv, 42, 44; Mark xiii, 33, 35; Luke xii, 40.

z III Nephi xx, 22; see also xxi, 25.

a Ezek. xxxvii, 26-27; Zech. ii, 10, 11; viii, 3; II Cor. vi. 16.

b Exo. xv, 18.

c Psa. x, 16; see also xxix, 10; cxlv, 13; cxlvi, 10.

lasting king," before whose wrath the earth will tremble, and the nations yield;[d] and Nebuchadnezzar, humbled through tribulation, rejoiced in honoring the King of Heaven, "whose dominion is an everlasting dominion, and his kingdom is from generation to generation."[e]

18. Even chosen Israel were not always willing to accept God as their king. Remember how they protested that Samuel, the anointed prophet and judge, was old,—a poor excuse for their claim, as the old man ministered with vigor among them for thirty-five years beyond that time,—and how they cried for a king to rule them, that they might be like other nations.[f] Note the pathetic words with which the Lord replied to Samuel's prayer regarding this demand of the people, and the sorrow with which He granted them their wish:—"Hearken unto the voice of the people in all that they say unto thee; for they have not rejected thee, but they have rejected me that I should not reign over them."[g] But the Lord will not be ever rejected by His people; at the time appointed He will come with power and great glory, and will assume His rightful place of authority as King of earth.

19. Daniel interpreted the dream of Nebuchadnezzar, and spoke of the many kingdoms and divisions of kingdoms which were to be established, then added:—"And in the days of these kings shall the God of heaven set up a kingdom, which shall never be destroyed: and the kingdom shall not be left to other people, but it shall break in pieces and consume all these kingdoms, and it shall stand forever."[h] Touching the extent of the great kingdom to be established the same prophet declared:—"And the kingdom and domin-

d Jer. x, 10.

e Dan. iv, 34-37.

f I Sam. viii, 5.

g Verse 7; see also x, 19; Hosea xiii, 10-11.

h Dan. ii, 44.

ion, and the greatness of the kingdom under the whole heaven, shall be given to the people of the saints of the Most High, whose kingdom is an everlasting kingdom, and all dominions shall serve and obey him."[i]

20. Speaking of the restoration of Judah and Israel in the last days, Micah prophecies:—"And the Lord shall reign over them in mount Zion from henceforth, even for ever."[j] In the annunciation to the Virgin, the angel said of the unborn Christ:—"He shall reign over the house of Jacob forever, and of his kingdom there shall be no end."[k] In the visions of Patmos, the Apostle John saw the glorious consummation, and a universal recognition of the eternal King:—"And the seventh angel sounded; and there were great voices in heaven, saying, The kingdoms of this world are become the kingdoms of our Lord, and of his Christ; and he shall reign for ever and ever."[l] Modern revelation is rich in evidence of an approaching reign of righteousness, with Christ as King; witness the following:—"And also the Lord shall have power over his saints, and shall reign in their midst."[m] "For in my own due time will I come upon the earth in judgment, and my people shall be redeemed and shall reign with me on earth."[n]

21. **Kingdom and Church:**—In the Gospel according to Matthew, the phrase "kingdom of heaven" is of frequent occurrence; while in the books of the other evangelists, and throughout the epistles, the expression is "kingdom of God," "kingdom of Christ," or simply "kingdom." It is evident that these expressions may be used interchangably

------

i Dan vii, 27.
j Micah iv, 7; see also Isa. xxiv, 23.
k Luke i, 33.
l Rev. xi, 15.
m Doc. and Cov i, 36.
n Doc. and Cov. xliii, 29; see also lxxxiv, 119.

without violence to the true meaning. However, the term kingdom is used in more senses than one, and a careful study of the context in each instance may be necessary to a proper comprehension of the writer's intent. The most common usages are two:—1. An expression synonymous with "the Church," having reference to the followers of Christ without distinction as to their temporal or spiritual organizations. 2. The designation of the literal kingdom over which Christ is to reign on earth in the last days.

22. When we contemplate the Kingdom in the latter and more general sense, the Church must be regarded as a part thereof; an essential indeed, for it is the germ from which the Kingdom is to be developed, and the very heart of the perfected organization. The Church has existed and now continues in an organized form, without the Kingdom as a visibly established power with temporal authority in the world; but the Kingdom cannot be maintained without the Church.

23. In modern revelation, the expressions "kingdom of God" and "kingdom of heaven" are sometimes used with distinctive meanings,—the former phrase signifying the Church, and the latter the literal kingdom which is to over-shadow and comprise all existing national divisions. In this sense, the Kingdom of God has been set up already in these the last days; its beginning, in and for the present dispensation, was the establishment of the Church on its latter-day and permanent foundation. This is consistent with our conception of the Church as the vital organ of the Kingdom in general. The powers and authority committed to the Church, are then the keys of the Kingdom. Such meaning is made clear in the following revelation to the Church:—"The keys of the kingdom of God are committed unto man on the earth, and from thence shall the gospel roll forth unto the ends of the earth, as the stone

which is cut out of the mountain without hands[o] shall roll
forth, until it has filled the whole earth   *   *   *   Call
upon the Lord, that his kingdom may go forth upon the
earth, that the inhabitants thereof may receive it, and be
prepared for the days to come, in the which the Son of man
shall come down in heaven, clothed in the brightness of his
glory, to meet the kingdom of God which is set up on the
earth; wherefore may the kingdom of God go forth, that
the kingdom of heaven may come, that thou O God mayest
be glorified in heaven so on earth, that thy enemies may
be subdued; for thine is the honor, power and glory for
ever and ever."[p]

24.   At the time of His glorious advent, Christ will be
accompanied by the hosts of righteous ones who have already
passed from earth; and the Saints who are still alive on
earth are to be quickened and caught up to meet Him, and
to descend with Him as partakers of His glory.[q] With Him
too will come Enoch and his band of the pure in heart;[r] and
a union will be effected with the Kingdom of God, or that
part of the Kingdom of Heaven previously established as the
Church of Christ on earth; and the Kingdom on earth will
be one with that in heaven. Then will be realized a complete fulfilment of the Lord's own prayer, given as a pattern
to all who pray:—"Thy kingdom come, thy will be done in
earth, as it is in heaven."[s]

25. The disputed question "Is the Kingdom already set
up on earth or are we to wait for its establishment until the
time of the future advent of Christ, the King?" may properly receive answer either affirmative or negative, according

---

[o] Allusion to Daniel's interpretation of the dream of Nebuchadnezzar: see
Dan. ii, 34, 44.

[p] Doc. and Cov. lxv, 2, 5-6

[q] Doc. and Cov. lxxxviii, 91-98.

[r] See pp. 358, 362-363.

[s] Matt. vi, 10; Luke xi, 2.

to the sense in which the term kingdom is understood. The Kingdom of God as identical with the Church of Christ has assuredly been established; its history is that of the Church in these the last days; its officers are divinely commissioned, their power is that of the holy priesthood. They claim an authority which is spiritual, but also temporal in dealing with the members of the organization,—Church or Kingdom as you may choose to call it,—but they make no attempt, nor do they assert the right, to modify, assail, or in any way interfere with, existing governments; far less to subdue nations or to set up rival systems of control. The Kingdom of Heaven, including the Church, and comprising all nations, will be set up with power and great glory when the triumphant King comes with His heavenly retinue to personally rule and reign on the earth which He has redeemed at the sacrifice of His own life.

26. As seen, the Kingdom of Heaven will comprise more than the Church. The honorable and honest among men will be accorded protection and the privileges of citizenship under the perfect system of government which Christ will administer; and this will be their happy lot whether they are actually members of the Church or not. Law-breakers and men of impure heart will meet the judgment of destruction according to their sin; but those who live according to the truth as they have been able to receive and comprehend it, will enjoy the fullest liberty under the benign influences of a perfect administration. The special privileges and blessings associated with the Church, the right to hold and exercise the priesthood with its boundless possibilities and eternal powers, will be, as now they are, for those only who enter into the covenant and become part of the Church of the Redeemer.

27. **The Millennium:**—In connection with scriptural mention of Christ's reign on earth, a duration of a thousand

years is frequently specified.   While we cannot regard this
as indicating a time limit to the Kingdom's existence, or a
measure of the Savior's administration of power, we are
justified in the belief that the thousand years immediately
following the establishment of the Kingdom are to be
specially characterized, so as to be different from both preceding and succeeding time.   The gathering of Israel and
the establishment of an earthly Zion are to be effected, preparatory to His coming.   His advent will be marked by a
destruction of the wicked, and by the inauguration of an
era of peace.   The Revelator saw the souls of the martyrs,
and of other righteous men, in power, living and reigning
with Christ a thousand years.[t]   At the beginning of this
period Satan is to be bound, "that he should deceive the
nations no more until the thousand years should be fulfilled."[u]
Certain of the dead are not to live again, until the thousand
years are passed;[v] while the righteous "shall be priests of
God and of Christ, and shall reign with him a thousand
years."[w]   Among the most ancient of revelations regarding
the Millennium, is that given to Enoch:—"And it came to
pass that Enoch saw the day of the coming of the Son of
Man, in the last days, to dwell on the earth in righteousness
for the space of a thousand years."[x]

   28.   It is evident then, that in speaking of the Millennium,
we have to consider a definite period, with important events
marking its beginning and its close, and conditions of unusual blessedness extending throughout.   It will be a sabbat-
ical era,[y]—a thousand years of peace.   Enmity between man
and beast shall cease; the fierceness and venom of the brute

---

t Rev. xx, 4; see also 6.

u Rev. xx, 2-3.

v Verse 5.

w Verse 6.

x Pearl of Great Price, p. 45, (1888 ed.)

y See Note 2.

creation shall be done away,[z] and love shall rule.[a] A new condition of affairs will prevail, as was declared in the word of the Lord to Isaiah:—"For behold, I create new heavens and a new earth; and the former shall not be remembered, nor come into mind."[b]

29. Concerning the state of peace, prosperity, and duration of human life, characteristic of that period, we read:— "There shall be no more thence an infant of days, nor an old man that hath not filled his days: for the child shall die an hundred years old; but the sinner being an hundred years old shall be accursed. And they shall build houses, and inhabit them; and they shall plant vineyards, and eat the fruit of them. They shall not build, and another inhabit; they shall not plant, and another eat: for as the days of a tree are the days of my people, and mine elect shall long enjoy the work of their hands. They shall not labor in vain, nor bring forth for trouble; for they are the seed of the blessed of the Lord, and their offspring with them. And it shall come to pass, that before they call, I will answer: and while they are yet speaking, I will hear. The wolf and the lamb shall feed together, and the lion shall eat straw like the bullock: and dust shall be the serpent's meat. They shall not hurt nor destroy in all my holy mountain, saith the Lord."[c]

30. The Lord's voice is heard today declaring the same prophetic truths, as is shown in the revelations touching the Millennium given in the present dispensation of the Church.[d] In 1831, the Lord addressed the elders of His Church, and said:—"For the great Millennium, of which I have spoken by the mouth of my servants, shall come; for

---

z Isa. xi, 6-9; lxv, 25.

a See Notes 3 and 4.

b Isa. lxv, 17.

c Verses 20-25.

d Doc. and Cov. lxiii, 49-51.

Satan shall be bound, and when he is loosed again, he shall only reign for a little season, and then cometh the end of the earth."[e] On another occasion these words were spoken:— "For I will reveal myself from heaven with power and great glory, with all the hosts thereof, and dwell in righteousness with men on earth a thousand years, and the wicked shall not stand. * * * * And again, verily, verily, I say unto you, that when the thousand years are ended, and men again begin to deny their God, then will I spare the earth but for a little season, and the end shall come."[f]

31. The Millennium then is to precede the events usually indicated by the scriptural phrase, "the end of the world." During that period, all conditions will be propitious for righteousness; Satan's power will be suspended; and men, relieved to some extent from temptation, will be zealous in the service of their reigning Lord. Nevertheless, sin will not be wholly abolished, nor will death be banished; though children will live to reach maturity in the flesh, and then may be changed to a condition of immortality in the "twinkling of an eye."[g] Both mortal and immortal beings will tenant the earth, and communion with the heavenly powers will be common. The Latter-day Saints believe that during that millennial era, they will be privileged to continue the vicarious work for the dead, which constitutes so important and and so characteristic a feature of their duty,[h] and that the facilities for direct communication with the heavens will enable them to carry on their labor of love without hindrance. When the thousand years are passed, Satan will again assert his power, and those who are not then numbered among the pure in heart will yield to his in-

---

e Doc. and Cov. xliii, 30-31.

f Doc. and Cov. xxix, 11, 22-23.

g Doc. and Cov. lxiii, 50-51.

h See pp. 148-159.

fluence.   But the liberty thus recovered by "the prince of
the power of the air"[i] will be of short duration; his final
doom will speedily follow, and with him will go to the punishment that is everlasting, all who are his.   Then the earth
will pass to its celestial condition, and become a fit abode for
the glorified sons and daughters of our God.

NOTES.

1. "The Anointed One:"—"Christ, the official name of the Redeemer of
mankind, as Jesus, or in the Hebrew, *Joshua*, 'Savior,' was His natural name.
Christ means 'anointed,' from *chrio*, 'to anoint.' Under the Old Testament dispensation, high priests, kings, and prophets were appointed to their office by the
pouring of the sacred oil upon their heads. The rite was performed by the recognized officer of Jehovah, and was an outward testimony that their appointment
proceeded direct from God himself, as the source of all authority, and as being
under the ancient covenant, in a peculiar way the governor of his people. The oil
used in the consecration of priests, and the anointing of the tabernacle and
sacred vessels, was a special preparation of myrrh, cinnamon, calamus, and
cassia, (Exo. xxx, 23-25), which the Jews were forbidden to apply to the body, or
to copy under pain of death. It was no doubt intended to typify the gifts and
graces of the Holy Spirit."—Cassell's *Bible Dictionary*, p. 257.

2. The Seventh Thousand Years:—"As each *seventh* year was Israel's
year of remission, so of the world's seven thousands, the seventh shall be its
sabbatism." *Fausset's Bible Cyclopedia*, p. 685. "There remaineth therefore a
rest to the people of God;" or, as given by marginal reference, instead of "rest,"
the "keeping of a sabbath."—Heb. iv, 9.

3. Millennial Peace:—"The wolf also shall dwell with the lamb, and the
leopard shall lie down with the kid: and the calf and the young lion and the
fatling together; and a little child shall lead them. And the cow and the bear
shall feed; their young ones shall lie down together: and the lion shall eat straw
like the ox. And the sucking child shall play on the hole of the asp, and the
weaned child shall put his hand on the cockatrice' den. They shall not hurt nor
destroy in all my holy mountain: for the earth shall be full of the knowledge of
the Lord, as the waters cover the sea."—Isa. xi, 6-9; see also lxv, 25.

4. The Earth, before, during, and after the Millennium:—"There
are three conditions of the earth spoken of in the inspired writings,—the
present, in which everything pertaining to it must go through a change which
we call death; the millennial condition, in which it will be sanctified for the resi-
dence of purer intelligences, some mortal and some immortal; and the celestial
condition, spoken of in the twenty-first and twenty-second chapters of Revelation, which will be one of immortality and eternal life."—*Compendium*, by
Elders F. D. Richards and James A. Little, p. 202.

---

i Eph. ii, 2.

LECTURE XXI.

REGENERATION AND RESURRECTION.

Article 10.—We believe * * * * That the earth will be renewed and receive its paradisiacal glory.

RENEWAL OF THE EARTH.

1. **The Earth Under the Curse:**—The blessed conditions, under which the earth shall exist and man shall live during the millennial era, are almost beyond human powers of comprehension, so different are they from all to which history testifies and which experience confirms. A reign of righteousness throughout the earth has never yet been known to the fallen race of man. So marked has been the universal curse, so great the power of the tempter; so bitter the selfish and ungodly strife betwixt man and man, and between nation and nation; so general has been the enmity of the animal creation, among its own members, and toward the being, who, though in a degraded state, yet holds the Divine commission to the authority of dominion; so prolific has been the soil in bringing forth thorns, briers, and noxious weeds, that the description of Eden is to us as the story of another world, an orb of a higher order of existence, wholly unlike this dreary sphere. Yet, we learn that Eden was truly a feature of our planet, and that the earth is destined to become a celestialized body,—fit for the abode of the most exalted intelligences. The millennium, with all its splendor, is but a more advanced stage of preparation, by which the earth and its inhabitants will approach the foreordained perfection.

2. **Regeneration of the Earth:**—The term regeneration, (translated from the Greek, *palingenesia*, and signifying a new birth, or more literally, one who is born again) occurs twice[a] in the New Testament; while other expressions of equivalent meaning are used in many places. However, the terms are usually applied to the renewal of the soul of man through the spiritual birth, by which salvation is made obtainable; though our Lord's use of the term, in the promise of future glory which He confirmed upon the apostles, has probable reference to the rejuvenation of the earth, its inhabitants and their institutions, in connection with the millennial era —"I say unto you, That ye which have followed me, in the regeneration when the Son of man shall sit in the throne of his glory, ye also shall sit upon twelve thrones, judging the twelve tribes of Israel."[b]

3. A time of restitution is foretold. Consider the words of Peter, spoken to the people who had come together in Solomon's porch, marveling over the miraculous healing of the lame beggar at the gate Beautiful:—"Repent ye therefore, and be converted, that your sins may be blotted out, when the times of refreshing shall come from the presence of the Lord; and he shall send Jesus Christ, which before was preached unto you: whom the heavens must receive until the times of restitution of all things, which God hath spoken by the mouth of all his holy prophets since the world began."[c]

4. That the change to a state more nearly approaching perfection is to affect both nature and man is evident from the teachings of Paul, as recorded in his letter to the Romans:—"Because the creature itself also shall be delivered from the bondage of corruption into the glorious

---

a Matt. xix, 28; Titus iii, 5.
b Matt. xix, 28
c Acts iii, 19.
26

liberty of the children of God. For we know that the whole
creation groaneth and travaileth in pain together until now.
And not only they, but ourselves also, which have the first-
fruits of the Spirit, even we ourselves groan within ourselves,
waiting for the adoption, to wit, the redemption of our
body."*d*

5. This work of regeneration has already begun. As a
necessary preliminary, whereby the curse that would otherwise afflict the earth, might be averted, Elijah the
prophet was to visit the earth, bringing with him the
keys and authority of a great work; concerning which event
while yet future, the Lord said:—"Behold, I will send you
Elijah the prophet before the coming of the great and
dreadful day of the Lord: And he shall turn the heart of
the fathers to the children, and the heart of the children to
their fathers, lest I come and smite the earth with a curse."*e*

6. The Latter-day Saints solemnly declare that this
prophecy has had a literal fulfilment, in that on the third
day of April, A. D. 1836, Elijah visited the Prophet Joseph
Smith and Oliver Cowdery, in the newly dedicated temple at
Kirtland, Ohio, announced his mission as that spoken of by
the mouth of Malachi, declared that the day for the fulfilment
of the prediction had come, and committed the keys of this
work of the last dispensation to the Church, that the labor
of restoration might be carried on; and moreover, as a sign
"that the great and dreadful day of the Lord is near, even
at the doors."*f* Throughout the Millennium, this process
of regeneration will be continued. Society shall be purified;
nations shall exist in peace; wars shall cease; the ferocity of
beasts shall be subdued; the earth, escaping in a great

d Rom. viii, 21-23.
e Mal. iv, 5-6; see also III Nephi xxv.
f Doc. and Cov. cx, 14-16; p. 154, this book.

measure the curse of the Fall, shall yield bounteously to the husbandman; and the planet shall be redeemed.

7. The final stages of this regeneration of nature will not be reached until the Millennium has run its blessed course. Describing the events to take place after the completion of the thousand years, John the Revelator says:— "And I saw a new heaven and a new earth: for the first heaven and the first earth were passed away; and there was no more sea. * * * * And I heard a great voice out of heaven saying, Behold, the tabernacle of God is with men, and he will dwell with them, and they shall be his people, and God himself shall be with them, and be their God. And God shall wipe away all tears from their eyes; and there shall be no more death, neither sorrow, nor crying, neither shall there be any more pain: for the former things are passed away."[g] A similar prediction was made by Ether the Jaredite, six hundred years before Christ was born:—"And there shall be a new heaven, and a new earth; and they shall be like unto the old, save the old have passed away, and all things have become new."[h] This event is to follow the scenes of the Millennium, as the context makes plain.

8. In the year 1830 of our present era, the Lord said:— "When the thousand years are ended, and men again begin to deny their God, then will I spare the earth but for a little season; and the end shall come, and the heaven and the earth shall be consumed and pass away, and there shall be a new heaven and a new earth, for all old things shall pass away, and all things shall become new, even the heaven and the earth, and all the fulness thereof, both men and beasts, the fowls of the air and the fishes of the sea; and

---

g Rev. xxi. 1. 3-4.
h Book of Mormon. Ether xiii, 9.

not one hair, neither mote, shall be lost, for it is the work-manship of mine hand."[i]

9.   According to the scriptures, the earth has to undergo a change analogous to death, and to be regenerated in a manner comparable to a resurrection. References to the elements melting with heat, and to the earth being con-sumed and passing away, such as occur in many scriptures already cited, are suggestive of death; and the new earth, really the renewed or regenerated planet, which is to result, may be compared with a resurrected organism. The change has been likened unto a transfiguration.[j] Every created thing has been made for a purpose; and everything that fills the measure of its creation is to be advanced in the scale of progression, be it an atom or a world, an animalcule, or man—the direct and literal offspring of Deity. In speaking of the degrees of glory provided for His creations, and of the laws of regeneration and sancti-fication, the Lord, in a revelation dated 1832, speaks plainly of the approaching death and subsequent quicken-ing of the earth. These are His words:—"And again, verily, I say unto you, the earth abideth the law of a celestial kingdom, for it filleth the measure of its creation, and transgresseth not the law. Wherefore it shall be sanctified; yea, notwithstanding it shall die, it shall be quickened again, and shall abide the power by which it is quickened, and the righteous shall inherit it."[k]

10.   During the Millennium, the earth, while preparing for the final change, will be tenanted by both mortal and immortal beings; but after the regeneration is complete, death will no longer be known among its inhabitants. Then, the Redeemer of earth "shall deliver up the kingdom, and

i Doc. and Cov. xxix, 22-25.

j Doc. and Cov. lxiii, 20-21.

k Doc. and Cov. lxxxviii, 25-26.

present it unto the Father spotless, saying, I have overcome."[l]
Before victory is thus achieved and triumph won, the enemies of righteousness must be subdued; the last foe to be
vanquished is death. Thus saith Paul the Apostle:—"Then
cometh the end, when he shall have delivered up the kingdom to God, even the Father; when he shall have put down
all rule, and all authority and power. For he must reign,
till he hath put all enemies under his feet. The last enemy
that shall be destroyed is death. For he hath put all things
under his feet. But when he saith, All things are put under
him, it is manifest that he is excepted, which did put all
things under him. And when all things shall be subdued
unto him, then shall the Son also himself be subject unto
him that put all things under him, that God may be all in
all."[m]

11. The following partial description of the earth in its
immortalized condition has been given by the Prophet
Joseph Smith in this dispensation:—"This earth, in its
sanctified and immortal state, will be made like unto crystal,
and will be a Urim and Thummim[n] to the inhabitants who
dwell thereon, whereby all things pertaining to an inferior
kingdom, or all kingdoms of a lower order, will be manifest
to those who dwell on it; and this earth will be Christ's."[o]

12. **Absence of Evidence from Science:**—Attempts have
been made to demonstrate an agreement between the teachings of science concerning the destiny of the earth, and the
scriptural predictions regarding the ordained regeneration
of our planet, by which it is to be made fit for the abode of
immortal souls. Without considering the details of the alleged evidence of mutual support between science and the
revealed word in this matter, it may suffice to say, that the

  l Doc. and Cov. lxxvi, 107.
  m I Cor. xv, 24-26.
  n See page 273.
  o Doc. and Cov. cxxx, 9.

so-called evidence is unsatisfactory, and that science is practically silent on the subject.   The geologist views the earth
as a body in process of continual change; its surface a
heterogeneous mass of fragmental material; he reads, in the
record inscribed on its stony pages, the story of past development through many successive stages of progress, each
making the globe more fit for habitation by man; he witnesses the work of constructive and destructive agencies now
in operation, land masses yielding to the lowering action of
air and water, and by their destruction furnishing material
for other formations now in process of construction;—the
general effect of all such being to level the surface by de-
grading the hills and exalting the valleys.   On the other
hand, he observes volcanic agencies operating to increase the
inequality of level by violent eruption and crustal elevation.
He confesses inability, from his observations of the present,
and his deductions concerning the past of the earth, to pre-
dict even a probable future.   So futile have been his efforts
to ascertain the origin or determine the destiny of the globe,
that he has generally abandoned the attempt.   The epoch-
making declaration of an acknowledged leader in the science
has now become proverbial:—Geology furnishes "no traces
of a beginning, no prospect of an end."[p]

13.   The astronomer, studying the varied conditions of
other worlds, may seek by analogy to learn of the probable
fate of our own.   Gazing into space with greatly augmented
vision, he sees, within the system to which the earth belongs,
spheres exhibiting a great range of development,—some in
their fiery stage, seemingly unfit for the abode of beings
constituted as are we; others in a state more nearly resembling that of the earth; and yet others seemingly old and
lifeless.   Of the mighty systems beyond the comparatively
small company under control of our own sun, he knows

[p] James Hutton.

nothing but the existence of these central orbs. But, nowhere has he discovered a celestialized world. Think you that mortal eye could discern such even if it were within the limits of vision as determined by distance alone?

14. The poet has written:—

> "Nor think though men were not,
> That heaven would want spectators,
> God want praise!
> Millions of spiritual beings
> Walk the earth,
> Unseen both when we wake,
> And when we sleep."

If this thought be founded on truth, and the Christian soul will hardly doubt it, we may as readily believe in the existence of other worlds than those of structure so gross as to be capable of reflecting light to our dull eyes. I repeat, that in regard to the revealed word concerning the regeneration of earth, and the acquirement of a celestial glory by our planet, science has nothing to offer, either by way of support or contradiction. Let us not because of this, disparage science, or decry the labors of its votaries. No one realizes more fully than does the truly scientific man how much we do not know.

RESURRECTION OF THE BODY.

15. The Resurrection from the Dead:—Closely associated with, and analogous to, the ordained rejuvenation of earth, whereby our planet is to pass from its present dreary and broken state to a condition of glorified perfection, is the resurrection of the bodies of all beings who have had an existence upon its surface. The Church of Jesus Christ of Latter-day Saints teaches the doctrine of a literal resurrection; an actual re-union of departed spirits and the tabernacles with which they were clothed during mortal probation; and a transition from mortality to immortality in the

case of some who will be in the flesh at the time of the great change, and who, because of individual righteousness, are to be spared the sleep of the grave. But in such teachings, the Church is not essentially different from most Christian sects, except perhaps in the literalness of the bodily resurrection as taught by it, and in the belief concerning the nature of the resurrected state. The Bible is replete with evidence regarding the quickening of the dead. Human knowledge of the resurrection rests wholly upon revelation. Pagan peoples have therefore no conception of an actual coming forth of the dead unto life.[q]

16. In accepting the doctrine of a resurrection, we are to be guided by faith; which, however, is supported by abundant revelation, given in a manner unequivocal and sure. Science, the result of human research, fails to afford us any indication of such an event in the history of living things, and men have sought in vain for an analogy in external nature. True, comparisons have been made, metaphors have been employed, and similes pressed into service, to show in nature some counterpart or semblance of the immortalizing change, to which the Christian soul looks forward with unwavering confidence; but all such figures of speech are defective in the application, and untrue in their professed analogies.

17. The return of spring after the death-like sleep of winter; the passing of the crawling caterpillar into the corpse-like chrysalis, and the subsequent emergence of the winged butterfly; the coming forth of a living bird from the tomb-like recess of the egg; these and other natural processes of development have been used as illustrative of the resurrection. Each of them is defective, for in no instance of such awakening has there been an actual death. If the tree die, it will not resume its leafage with the return

q See Note 1.

of the sun; if the pupa within the chrysalis, or the life-germ within the egg be killed, no butterfly or bird will emerge. When we indulge such figurative illustrations without most thorough caution, we are apt to conceive the thought that the body pre-destined to resurrection is not truly dead; and that therefore the quickening which is to follow, is not what the revealed word declares it to be. Observation proves that the separation of the spirit from the body leaves the latter an inanimate mass, no longer able to resist the processes of physical and chemical dissolution. The body, deserted by its immortal tenant, is literally dead; it will be resolved into its natural components, and its sub· stance will enter again upon the round of universal circulation of matter. Yet the resurrection from the dead is assured; the faith of those who trust in the word of revealed truth will be vindicated,[r] and the Divine decree will be carried into full effect.

18. **Predictions concerning the Resurrection:** — The prophets in the past dispensations of the world's history have fore-seen and fore-told the final conquest of death. Some of them testified specifically of Christ's victory over the tomb; others have dwelt upon the resurrection in a general way. Job, the man of patience under tribulation, sang joyously even in his agony:—"For I know that my Redeemer liveth, and that he shall stand at the latter day upon the earth: and though after my skin worms destroy this body, yet in my flesh shall I see God."[s] Enoch, to whom the Lord revealed His plan for the redemption of mankind, fore-saw the resurrection of Christ, the coming forth of the righteous dead with Him, and the eventual resurrection of all men.[t]

———
 r See Note 2.
 s Job. xix, 25-26; see also Isa. xxvi, 19; Ezek. xxxvii, 11-14; Hos. xiii, 14.
 t Pearl of Great Price, pp. 43, (1888 ed.)

19. Nephi testified to his brethren that the Redeemer's death was a fore-ordained necessity, provided in order that resurrection from the dead might be given to man. These are his words:—"For as death hath passed upon all men, to fulfil the merciful plan of the great Creator there must needs be a power of resurrection, and the resurrection must needs come unto man by reason of the fall; and the fall came by reason of transgression; and because man became fallen they were cut off from the presence of the Lord; * * * * And this death of which I have spoken, which is the spiritual death, shall deliver up its dead; which spiritual death is hell; wherefore, death and hell must deliver up their dead, and hell must deliver up its captive spirits, and the grave must deliver up its captive bodies, and the bodies and the spirits of men will be restored one to the other; and it is by the power of the resurrection of the Holy One of Israel. O how great the plan of our God! For on the other hand, the paradise of God must deliver up the spirits of the righteous, and the grave deliver up the body of the righteous; and the spirit and the body is restored to itself again, and all men become incorruptible, and immortal, and they are living souls, having a perfect knowledge like unto us in the flesh; save it be that our knowledge shall be perfect."[u]

20. Samuel, the Lamanite prophet, predicted the Savior's birth, ministry, death, and resurrection, and explained the resulting resurrection of mankind:—"For behold, he surely must die, that salvation may come; yea, it behoveth him, and becometh expedient that he dieth, to bring to pass the resurrection of the dead, that thereby men may be brought into the presence of the Lord; Yea, behold this death bringeth to pass the resurrection, and redeemeth all mankind from the first death—that spiritual death; for all mankind, by

[u] II Nephi ix, 6, 12-13.

the fall of Adam, being cut off from the presence of the
Lord, are considered as dead, both as to things temporal and
to things spiritual. But, behold, the resurrection of Christ
redeemeth mankind, yea, even all mankind, and bringeth
them back into the presence of the Lord."[v]

21. The New Testament furnishes abundant evidence
that the doctrine of the resurrection was very generally
understood during the time of Christ's earthly mission, and
in the succeeding apostolic era.[w] The Master Himself proclaimed these teachings. In reply to the hypercritical Sadducees,[x] He said:—"But as touching the resurrection of the
dead, have ye not read that which was spoken unto you by
God, saying, I am the God of Abraham, and the God of
Isaac, and the God of Jacob? God is not the God of the
dead, but of the living."[y] To the Jews who sought His
life because of His deeds and doctrine He spoke in this
way:—"Verily, verily, I say unto you, He that heareth my
word, and believeth on him that sent me, hath everlasting
life, and shall not come into condemnation; but is passed
from death unto life. Verily, verily, I say unto you, The
hour is coming, and now is, when the dead shall hear the
voice of the Son of God: and they that hear shall live."[z]

22. That Christ fully comprehended the purpose of His
approaching martyrdom, and the resurrection which was to
follow, is abundantly proved by His own utterances while
yet in the flesh. To Nicodemus He said:—"And as Moses
lifted up the serpent in the wilderness, even so must the
Son of man be lifted up: That whosoever believeth in him
should not perish, but have eternal life."[a] And to Martha,

---

v Helaman xiv, 15-17; see also Mosiah xv, 20-24, and Alma xl, 2, 16.

w Matt. xiv, 1-2; John xi, 24.

x See Note 3.

y Matt. xxii. 31-32; see also Luke xiv, 14.

z John v, 24-25; see also verse 21, and xi, 23-25.

a John iii, 14-15.

who was bewailing the death of her brother Lazarus, he declared: "I am the resurrection, and the life: he that believeth in me, though he were dead, yet shall he live."[b]   Of His own resurrection He prophesied freely; specifying the time during which His body would be entombed.[c]

23.   **Two General Resurrections** are mentioned in the scriptures: these my be specified as first and final, or as the resurrection of the just and the resurrection of the unjust. The first was inaugurated by the resurrection of Jesus Christ; immediately following which, many of the departed Saints came forth from their graves; a continuation of this, the resurrection of the just, has been in operation,[d] and will be brought to pass in a general way in connection with the coming of Christ in His glory, and will be incident therefore to the beginning of the Millennium.   The final resurrection will be deferred until the end of the thousand years of peace, and will be in connection with the last judgment.

24.   **The First Resurrection;—Christ's Resurrection, and that immediately following:**—The facts of Christ's resurrection from the dead are attested by such an array of scriptural proofs that no doubt of the reality finds place in the mind of any believer in the inspired records.   To the women who came early to the sepulchre, the angel, who had rolled the stone from the door of the tomb, spoke saying:—"He is not here, for he is risen, as he said."[e]   Afterward the resurrected Lord showed Himself to many[f] during the forty days interval between His resurrection and ascension.[g]   Sub-

---

b John xi, 25.

c Matt. xii, 40; xvi, 21; xvii, 23; xx, 19.

d Note the fact that Moroni, the last of the Nephite prophets, who died in the first quarter of the fifth century A. D., appeared as a resurrected being to Joseph Smith in 1823 (see pp. 10-12).

e Matt. xxviii, 6.

f Matt. xxviii, 9, 16; Mark xvi, 14; Luke xxiv, 13-31, 34; John xx, 14-17, 19, 26; xxi, 1-4; I Cor. xv, 5-8.

g Luke xxiv, 49-51; Acts i, 1-11.

sequent to the ascension He manifested Himself to the Nephites on the western hemisphere, as already noted in another connection.[h] The apostles, as we shall see, ceased not to testify of the genuineness of their Lord's resurrection, nor did they fail to proclaim the resurrections of the future.

25.   Christ, "the first fruits of them that slept"[i] was the first among men to come forth from the grave in an immortalized body; but, we read that soon after His resurrection, many of the Saints were brought from their tombs:—"And the graves were opened; and many bodies of the saints which slept arose, and came out of the graves after his resurrection, and went into the holy city, and appeared unto many."[j]

26.   Alma the Nephite prophet, whose writings antedate by nearly a century the birth of Christ, clearly understood that there would be no resurrection prior to that of the Redeemer, for he said:—"Behold I say unto you, that there is no resurrection; or, I would say, in other words, that this mortal does not put on immortality; this corruption does not put on incorruption, until after the coming of Christ."[k] And furthermore, he foresaw a general resurrection in connection with Christ's coming forth from the dead, as the context of the fore-going quotation clearly proves.[l] Inspired men among the Nephites spoke of the death and resurrection of Christ[m] even during the time of His actual ministry in the flesh; and their teachings were speedily confirmed by the appearance of the risen Lord among them,[n] as had been foretold by their earlier prophets.[o]

---

[h] See page 37.
[i] I Cor. xv, 20, 23; see also Acts xxvi, 23; Col. i, 18; Rev. i, 5.
[j] Matt. xxvii, 52-53.
[k] Alma xl, 2.
[l] Paragraph 16.
[m] III Nephi vi. 20.
[n] III Nephi xi.
[o] I Nephi xii, 6; II Nephi xxvi, 1, 9; Alma xvi, 20; III Nephi xi, 12.

27.   In the latter-days, the Lord has again manifested Himself, declaring the facts of His death and resurrection:— "For behold, the Lord your Redeemer suffered death in the flesh; wherefore he suffered the pain of all men, that all men might repent and come unto him.   And he hath risen again from the dead, that he might bring all men unto him on conditions of repentance."[p]

28.   **Resurrection at the time of Christ's Second Coming:**— —Immediately after the departure of Christ from the earth, the apostles, upon whom then devolved the direct responsibility of the Church, were found preaching the doctrine of a future and universal resurrection.   This teaching appears to have formed a very prominent feature of their instructions; for it was made a special cause of complaint by the Sadducees, who assailed the apostles, even within the sacred confines of the temple, the accusers "being grieved that they [the apostles] taught the people, and preached through Jesus the resurrection from the dead."[q]   Paul gave offence by the zeal with which he preached the resurrection which was to come; as witness his contention with certain philosophers of the Epicureans and of the Stoics; in the course of which some said:—"What will this babbler say? other some, He seemeth to be a setter forth of strange gods: because he preached unto them Jesus, and the resurrection."[r]   The discussion was continued at Areopagus, or Mars' Hill, where Paul preached the gospel of the true and living God, including the tenets of the resurrection.   "And when they heard of the resurrection of the dead, some mocked: and others said, We will hear thee again of this matter."[s]   He declared the same truth to Felix, the governor

---

p Doc. and Cov. xviii, 11-12.
q Acts iv, 2; see also Matt. xxii, 23, 31-32, and Acts xxiii, 8.
r Acts xvii, 18.
s Verse 32.

of Judea;[t] and when brought in bonds before Agrippa, the king, he asked, as if dealing with one of the principal accusations against him, "Why should it be thought a thing incredible with you, that God should raise the dead?"[u]

29. The resurrection appears to have been a favorite theme with Paul; in his epistles to the Saints, he gives it a prominent place.[v] From him, also, we learn that an order of precedence will be observed in the resurrection:—"But now is Christ risen from the dead, and become the firstfruits of them that slept. For since by man came death, by man came also the resurrection of the dead. For as in Adam all die, even so in Christ shall all be made alive. But every man in his own order: Christ the first-fruits; afterward they that are Christ's at his coming."[w]

30. It is expressly declared that many graves will yield up their dead at the time of Christ's advent in glory, and the just who have slept, together with many who have not died, will be caught up to meet the Lord. Paul thus wrote to the Saints in Thessaly:—"Even so them also which sleep in Jesus will God bring with him. * * * For the Lord himself shall descend from heaven with a shout, with the voice of the archangel, and with the trump of God: and the dead in Christ shall rise first. Then we which are alive and remain shall be caught up together with them in the clouds to meet the Lord in the air."[x]

31. To the three Nephite disciples, who had asked the blessing of John the beloved apostle, Christ said:—"And ye shall never endure the pains of death; but when I shall come in my glory, ye shall be changed in the twinkling of an eye from mortality to immortality."[y]

---

t Acts xxiv, 15.
u Acts xxvi, 8.
v Rom. vi, 5; viii, 11; I Cor. xv: II Cor. iv, 14; Phil. iii, 21; Col. iii, 4; I Thess. iv, 14: Heb. vi, 2.
w I Cor. xv, 20-23; the entire chapter should be studied.
x I Thess. iv, 14-17.
y III Nephi xxviii, 8.

32. Through the medium of latter-day revelation, the Lord has said:—"Behold I will come, and they shall see me in the clouds of heaven, clothed with power and great glory, with all the holy angels; and he that watches not for me shall be cut off. But before the arm of the Lord shall fall, an angel shall sound his trump, and the Saints that have slept, shall come forth to meet me in the cloud."[z] Of the many signs and wonders which shall attend the Lord's glorious coming we have this partial description:—"And the face of the Lord shall be unveiled: and the saints that are upon the earth, who are alive, shall be quickened, and be caught up to meet him. And they who have slept in their graves shall come forth; for their graves shall be opened, and they also shall be caught up to meet him in the midst of the pillar of heaven. They are Christ's, the first-fruits; they who shall descend with him first, and they who are on the earth and in their graves, who are first caught up to meet him."[a]

33. Such are some of the glories to attend the first resurrection; in which only the righteous are to have part. But, the company of the righteous will include all who have faithfully lived according to the laws of God as made known to them; children who have died in their innocence; and even the just among the heathen nations who have lived in comparative darkness while groping for light, and who have died in ignorance.[b] This doctrine is made plain by modern revelation:—"And then shall the heathen nations be redeemed, and they that knew no law shall have part in the first resurrection."[c] The Millennium then is to be inaugurated by a glorious deliverance of the just from

---

z Doc. and Cov. xlv, 44-45.

a Doc. and Cov. lxxxviii, 95-98.

b See Note 4.

c Doc. and Cov. xlv, 54; see also Ezek. xxxvi, 23-24; xxxvii, 28; xxxix, 7, 21, 23.

the power of death; and of this company of the redeemed
it is written:—"Blessed and holy is he that hath part in the
first resurrection; on such the second death hath no
power, but they shall be priests of God and of Christ, and
shall reign with him a thousand years."[d]

34.   **The Final Resurrection:**—"But the rest of the dead
lived not again until the thousand years were finished,"[e]
So said the Revelator after having described the glorious
blessings of the just, who are given part in the first resurrection.   The unworthy will be called to the judgment of
condemnation, when the regenerated world is ready to be
presented to the Father.[f]

35.   The contrast between those whose part in the first
resurrection is assured, and those whose doom it is to wait
until the time of final judgment, is a strong one, and in no
case do the scriptures lighten it.   We are told that it is
proper for us to weep over bereavement by death, "and
more especially for those that have not hope of a glorious
resurrection."[g]   In the present day, the voice of the Mighty
One is heard in solemn warning:—"Hearken ye, for, behold,
the great day of the Lord is nigh at hand.   For the day cometh
that the Lord shall utter his voice out of heaven; the heavens
shall shake, and the earth shall tremble, and the trump of
God shall sound both long and loud, and shall say to the
sleeping nations, Ye saints arise and live; ye sinners stay
and sleep until I shall call again."[h]

36.   The vision of the final scene is thus described by
John:—"And I saw the dead, small and great, stand before
God; and the books were opened; and another book was
opened, which is the book of life; and the dead were judged

---

d Rev. xx, 6.
e Rev. xx, 5.
f See Note 5.
g Doc. and Cov. xlii, 45.
h Doc. and Cov. xliii, 17-18
27

out of those things which were written in the books, according to their works. And the sea gave up the dead which were in it; and death and hell delivered up the dead which were in them: and they were judged every man according to their works."[i] This stage marks the completion of the work of resurrection. As the scriptures conclusively prove, the resurrection will be universal; while it is true that the dead will be brought forth in order, each as he is prepared for the first or the final stage, yet everyone who has tabernacled in the flesh will again assume his body and with such be judged.

37. The Book of Mormon is explicit in the description of the literal and universal resurrection:—"Now, there is a death which is called a temporal death; and the death of Christ shall loose the bands of this temporal death, that all shall be raised from this temporal death; The spirit and the body shall be re-united again in its perfect form; both limb and joint shall be restored to its proper frame, even as we now are at this time, and we shall be brought to stand before God, knowing even as we know now, and have a bright recollection of all our guilt. Now this restoration shall come to all, both old and young, both bond and free, both male and female, both the wicked and the righteous; and even there shall not so much as a hair of their heads be lost; but all things shall be restored to its perfect frame, as it is now, or in the body, and shall be brought and be arraigned before the bar of Christ the Son, and God the Father, and the Holy Spirit, which is one eternal God, to be judged according to their works, whether they be good or whether they be evil. Now, behold, I have spoken unto you, concerning the death of the mortal body, and also cencerning the resurrection of the mortal body. I say unto you

---

i Rev. xx, 12-13.

that this mortal body is raised to an immortal body; that is from death; even from the first death unto life."[j]

38. Consider also the following:—"The death of Christ bringeth to pass the resurrection, which bringeth to pass a redemption from an endless sleep, from which sleep all men shall be awoke by the power of God when the trump shall sound; and they shall come forth, both small and great, and all shall stand before his bar, being redeemed and loosed from this eternal band of death, which death is a temporal death; And then cometh the judgment of the Holy One upon them, and then cometh the time that he that is filthy shall be filthy still; and he that is righteous, shall be righteous still; he that is happy shall be happy still; and he that is unhappy, shall be unhappy still."[k]

39. So far has the word of revealed truth extended our knowledge regarding the destiny of the children of God. Beyond the regeneration of the earth, and the final judgment of the just and the wicked, we know little except that a plan of eternal progression has been provided.

NOTES:

1. **Pagan Ignorance Concerning the Resurrection:**—In connection with the statement that human knowledge of the resurrection is based on revelation, the following is of interest:—"Whatever heathen philosophers may have *guessed* as to the immortality of the soul, even admitting that this was really the result of their own speculations, and not at all due to the relics of tradition, it is certain that they never reached so far as the doctrine of a bodily resurrection. Pliny, when enumerating the things which it was not even in the power of God to do, specified these two—the endowment of mortals with an eternal existence, and the recalling of the departed from the grave. (ii, c, vii). A similar opinion is enunciated by Æschylus in the 'Eumenides' (647, 648). The utmost to which they attained in their ethical speculations was a conception of the possible continuance of life, in some new forms and conditions, beyond the grave; but this was all. A resurrection in the scripture sense of the word they never imagined."—Cassell's *Bible Dictionary.* p. 936.

---

[j] Alma xi, 42-45.
[k] Mormon ix, 13-14.

2. General Belief in a Resurrection:—"This great event of the future, like the doctrine of the resurrection of Christ, is so entirely a cardinal truth, that there never has been a time in which it has not been an article of the Christian creed, the only difference between the ancient creeds and our own, being that the latter has the phrase 'resurrection of the body' whereas the former invariably uses the form 'resurrection of the flesh.' The reason for the ancient mode of expression is stated by Jerome to be, that since there are spiritual bodies, some might readily accept a resurrection of the body in that sense, who would deny the actual resurrection of the flesh."—Cassell's *Bible Dictionary*, p.935.

3. The Sadducees, when mentioned in the New Testament, are usually represented as being in opposition to the Pharisees, the two classes constituting the most influential of the sects existing among the Jews at the time of Christ, The two differed on many fundamental matters of belief and practice, including pre-existence of spirits; the reality of spiritual punishment and future retribution for sin; the necessity of self-denial in individual life; the immortality of the soul; and the resurrection from the dead; in all of which the Pharisees stood for the affirmative, while the Sadducees denied. Josephus says:—"The doctrine of the Sadducees is that the soul and body perish together; the law is all that they are concerned to observe." (Ant. xviii, 1, 4.) The sect consisted mainly of members of the aristocracy. Special mention of the Sadducees here is suggested by their determined opposition to the doctrine of the resurrection, which they sought to assail by arrogant assumption or to belittle by ridicule. Cassell's *Bible Dictionary* gives place to the following:—"The Sadducees are never mentioned in John's Gospel. The only occasion on which they are spoken of in the Gospels of Mark and Luke is that referred to also by St. Matthew, on which they attempted to ridicule the doctrine of the resurrection, by asking our Lord's opinion as to whose wife a woman would be in the future world, who had been married to several in this world. (Matt. xxii, 23-32; Mark xii, 18-27; Luke xx, 27-38.) Their question proceeded on the assumption that the levirate law, as promulgated by Moses (Deut. xxv, 5-6) implied that the Jewish lawgiver had no resurrection of the dead in view. Our Lord's answer explained the difficulty, affirmed the resurrection of the dead, and asserted the existence of angels, which the Sadducees also denied; (Matt. xxii, 30; Mark xii, 25; Luke xx, 35, 36; compare with Acts, xxiii, 8.) He also quoted the divine announcement,—"I am the God of Abraham, the God of Isaac, and the God of Jacob," (Exod. iii, 6, 15, 16), and founded thereon by inference, an argument not only for immortality, but also for the resurrection. The words quoted must have been regarded by our Lord as implying that the patriarchs, as parties to the covenant, were still in a state of conscious relation to God."

4. Heathen in the First Resurrection:—The statement that the heathen dead will have place in the first resurrection is sustained by the word of scripture, and by a consideration of the principles of true justice according to which humanity is to be judged. Man will be accounted blameless or guilty, according to his deeds as interpreted in the light of the law under which he is required to live. It is inconsistent with our conception of a just God, to believe Him capable of inflicting condemnation upon any one for non-compliance with a requirement of which the person had no knowledge. Nevertheless, the laws of the Church will not be suspended even in the case of those who have sinned in darkness and ignorance: but it is reasonable to believe that the plan of redemption will afford such benighted ones an opportunity of learning the laws of

God; and surely, as fast as they so learn, will obedience be required on pain of the penalty. Note the following passages in addition to the citations in the text.

"And if there was no law given if men sinned, what could justice do, or mercy either; for they would have no claim upon the creature?"—Alma xlii, 21.

"Wherefore he has given a law; and where there is no law given, there is no punishment; and where there is no punishment, there is no condemnation; and where there is no condemnation, the mercies of the Holy One of Israel have claim upon them, because of the atonement; for they are delivered by the power of him."—II Nephi ix, 25.

"And moreover, I say unto you, that the time shall come, when the knowledge of a Savior shall spread throughout every nation, kindred, tongue, and people. And behold, when that time cometh, none shall be found blameless before God, except it be little children, only through repentance and faith on the name of the Lord God Omnipotent. '—Mos. iii, 20-21. See also Helaman xv, 14-15.

5. **The Intermediate State of the Soul; Paradise:**—The condition of the spirits of men between death and the resurrection is a subject of great interest, and one concerning which much dispute has arisen. The scriptures prove, that at the time of man's final judgment, he will stand before the bar of God, clothed in his resurrected body, and this, irrespective of his condition of purity or guilt. While awaiting the time of their coming forth, disembodied spirits exist in an intermediate state, of happiness and rest or of suffering and suspense according to their works in mortality, The prophet Alma said:—"Now concerning the state of the soul between death and the resurrection. Behold, it has been made known unto me, by an angel, that the spirits of all men, as soon as they are departed from this mortal body; yea, the spirits of all men, whether they be good or evil, are taken home to that God who gave them life. And then shall it come to pass that the spirits of those who are righteous are received into a state of happiness, which is called paradise; a state of rest; a state of peace, where they shall rest from all their troubles and from all care, and sorrow, &c. And then shall it come to pass, that the spirits of the wicked, yea, who are evil; for behold, they have no part nor portion of the Spirit of the Lord; for behold, they chose evil works rather than good; therefore the spirit of the devil did enter into them, and take possession of their house; and these shall be cast out into outer darkness; there shall be weeping, and wailing, and gnashing of teeth; and this because of their own iniquity; being led captive by the will of the devil. Now this is the state of the souls of the wicked; yea, in darkness, and a state of awful, fearful looking, for the fiery indignation of the wrath of God upon them; thus they remain in this state, as well as the righteous in paradise until the time of their resurrection."—Alma xl, 11-14.

Reference to paradise, as a place prepared for righteous spirits while awaiting the resurrection, is made also by the first Nephi (II Nephi ix, 13), by a later prophet of the same name (IV Nephi 14), and by Moroni (Moroni x, 34). New Testament mention supports the same. (Luke xxiii, 43; II Cor. xii, 4; Rev. ii, 7.) Paradise, then, is not the place of final glory; for such the thief who died with Christ was assuredly not prepared, yet we cannot doubt the fulfilment of our Lord's promise that the penitent malefactor should be with Him in paradise that day; and, moreover, the declaration of the risen Savior to Mary Magdalene, three days later, that He had not at that time ascended to His Father, is proof of His having spent the intermediate time in paradise.

The word "paradise," by its derivation through the Greek from the Persian, signifies a pleasure ground.

LECTURE XXII.

RELIGIOUS LIBERTY AND TOLERATION.

Article 11.—We claim the privilege of worshiping Almighty God according to the dictates of our conscience, and allow all men the same privilege, let let them worship how, where, or what they may.

1. **Man's Right to Freedom in Worship:**—In this article of their faith, the Latter-day Saints declare unqualified allegiance to the principles of religious liberty and religious toleration. Freedom to worship Almighty God as the conscience may dictate, they claim as one of the inherent and inalienable rights of humanity. The inspired framers of our charter of national independence proclaimed to the world, as a self-evident truth, that the common birthright of humanity gives to every man a claim to life, liberty, and the pursuit of happiness. Happiness is foreign, liberty but a name, and life a disappointment, to him who is denied the freedom to worship as he may desire. No person possessing a regard for Deity and a sense of duty toward that power Divine, can be happy if he be restricted in the performance of the highest duty of his existence. Could one be happy, though he were housed in a palace, surrounded with all material comforts and provided with every facility for intellectual enjoyment, if he were cut off from communion with the being whom he loved the most? To the man who has learned to know his Divine Father, freedom of worship is preferable even to life.

2. **What is Worship?**—The derivation of the term suggests an answer. It comes to us as the lineal descendant of a pair of Anglo-Saxon words, (*weorth*, meaning worthy, and *scipe*,—the old form of *ship*, signifying

condition or state), and conveys the thought of *worthy-ship*. The worship of which one is capable, depends upon his comprehension of the worthiness characterizing the object of his reverence. Man's capacity for worship is a measure of his comprehension of God. The fuller the acquaintance, the closer the communion between the worshiper and his Deity, the more thorough and sincere will be his homage. When we say of one, in figurative speech, that he is a worshiper of the good, the beautiful, the true, we affirm that he possesses a deeper and a more complete conception of worth in the object of his adoration, than has another whose conscience does not lead him to reverence those ennobling qualities.

3.   Man, then, will worship God according to his conception of the Divine attributes and powers; and this conception will approach the correct one in proportion to the spiritual light that has come to him.   True worship cannot exist where there is no reverence or love for the object. This reverence may be ill-founded; the adoration may be a species of idolatry; the object may be in fact unworthy; yet of the devotee it must be said that he worships if his conscience clothe the idol with the attribute of worthy-ship. We have spoken of "true worship;" the expression is a pleonasm.   Worship, as has been affirmed, is the heart-felt adoration that is rendered as a result of a sincere conception of worthiness on the part of the object; any manifestation of reverence prompted by a conviction inferior to this is but a counterfeit of worship; call such "false worship" if you choose; but let it be remembered that worship is necessarily true; the word requires no adjective to extend its meaning, nor to attest its genuineness.   Worship is not a matter of form, any more than is prayer.   It consists not in posture nor in gesture, in ritual nor in creed.   Worship most profound may be rendered with none of the arti-

ficial accessories of ritualistic service; for altar, the stone
in the desert may serve; the peaks of the everlasting hills
are temple spires; the vault of heaven is of all the grandest
cathedral dome.

4.   Man is at heart an inferior pattern of that which he
worships.   The savage, who knows no triumph greater than
that of bloody victory over his enemy, who regards prowess
and physical strength as the most desirable qualities of his
race, and who looks upon revenge and vindictiveness as the
sweetest gratifications of life, will assuredly ascribe such
attributes to his deity; and will offer his profoundest reverence in sacrifices of blood.   All the revolting practices of
idolatry are traceable to perverted and fiendish conceptions
of human excellence, and these are reflected in the hideous
creations of man-made, devil-inspired, deities.   On the
other hand, the man whose enlightened soul has received
the impress of love, pure and undefiled, will ascribe to his
God the attributes of gentleness and affection, and will say
in his heart "God is love."   He alone who has acquired a
proper understanding of the glory and responsiblity of
parenthood, can intelligently use the Son's title of invocation, "Our Father."   Knowledge, therefore, is essential to
worship; man cannot adequately serve God in ignorance;
and the greater his knowledge of the Divine personality, the
fuller, truer, will be his adoration; he may learn to know
the Father, and the Son who was sent; and such knowledge is man's guarantee to eternal life.

5.   Worship is the voluntary homage of the soul.   Under
compulsion, or for the hypocritical purposes of effect,
one may insincerely perform all the outward ceremonies
of an established style of adoration; he may voice
words of prescribed prayers; his lips may profess a creed;
yet his effort is but a mockery of worship, and its indul-
gence a sin.   Our Father desires no reluctant homage nor

unwilling praise.   Formalism in worship is acceptable only
so far as it is accompanied by an intelligent devoutness; and
it is of use only as an aid to the spiritual devotion which
leads to communion with Deity.   The spoken prayer is but
empty sound if it be anything less than an index to the
volume of the soul's righteous desire.   Communications
addressed to the throne of Grace must bear the stamp of
sincerity if they are to reach their high destination.   The
most acceptable form of worship is that which rests on an
unreserved compliance with the laws of God as the worshiper has learned their intent.

   6. Religious Intolerance:—The Church holds, that the
right to worship according to the dictates of conscience has
been conferred upon man by an authority higher than any
of earth; and that, in consequence, no worldly power can
justly interfere with its exercise.   The Latter-day Saints
accept as inspired the constitutional provision, by which
religious liberty within our own nation is professedly
guarded, that no law shall ever be made "respecting an
establishment of religion, or prohibiting the free exercise
thereof;"[a] and they confidently believe, that with the spread
of enlightenment throughout the world, a similar guarantee
will be acquired by every nation.   Intolerance has been the
greatest hindrance to true progress in every period of
time; yet under the sable cloak of perverted zeal for
religion, nations while boasting of their civilization, and
professed ministers of the gospel of Christ, have stained
the pages of the world's history with the record of such
unholy deeds of persecution as to make the heavens weep.
In this respect, so-called Christianity ought to bow its head
in shame before the record of even pagan toleration.
Rome, while arrogantly, though none the less actually,
posing as the mistress of the world, granted to her van-

---

a Constitution of the United States, first amendment.

quished subjects the rights of free worship, requiring of them only that they refrain from molesting others or one another in the exercise of such freedom.

7. But, as soon as the gospel of Christ was established upon the earth, its devout adherents immediately, and its more pretentious though less sincere devotees of a later day, came to regard themselves of such sanctity and excellence, that all who believed and professed not as did they, were wholly unworthy of consideration. Nay, even long prior to the advent of the Teacher of Love, Israel, knowing the covenant of Divine favor under which they had flourished, counted themselves sure of an exalted station, and looked upon all who were not of the chosen seed as unworthy. Christ, in His ministry among the Jews, saw with compassionate sorrow the spiritual and intellectual bondage of the times, and declared unto them the saving word, saying, "the truth shall make you free." At this, those self-righteous children of the covenant became angry, and boastfully answered, "We be Abraham's seed, and were never in bondage to any man; how sayest thou, Ye shall be made free?" Then the Master reproved them for their bigotry, "I know that ye are Abraham's seed, but ye seek to kill me, because my word has no place in you."[c]

8. There is little cause for wonder in the fact that the early Christians, zealous for the new faith unto which they had been baptized, and newly converted from idolatrous practices and pagan superstitions, should consider themselves superior to the rest of humanity still sitting in darkness and ignorance. Even John, now known as the Apostle of Love, but surnamed by the Christ, both he and his brother James, Boanerges, or Sons of Thunder,[d] was intolerant and resentful toward those who followed not his path;

---

c John viii, 32-45; see also Matt. iii, 9.
d Mark iii, 17.

and more than once he had to be rebuked by his Master. Note this incident:—"And John answered him, saying, Master, we saw one casting out devils in thy name, and he followeth not us; and we forbade him because he followeth not us. But Jesus said, Forbid him not: for there is no man which shall do a miracle in my name, that can lightly speak evil of me. For he that is not against us is on our part. For whosoever shall give you a cup of water to drink in my name, because ye belong to Christ, verily I say unto you, he shall not lose his reward."[e]   And again, while traveling with their Lord through Samaria, the apostles James and John were incensed at the Samaritans' neglect shown toward the Master; and they craved permission to call fire from heaven to consume the unbelievers, but their revengeful desire was promptly rebuked by the Lord, who said, "Ye know not what manner of spirit ye are of. For the Son of man is not come to destroy men's lives, but to save them."[f]

9. **Intolerance is Unscriptural:**—The teachings of our Lord breathe the spirit of forbearance and love even to enemies. He tolerated, though he could not approve, the practices of the heathen in their idolatry, the Samaritans with their mongrel and un-orthodox customs of worship, the luxury-loving Sadducees, and the law-bound Pharisees. Hatred was not countenanced even toward foes. His instructions were:—"Love your enemies, bless them that curse you, do good to them that hate you, and pray for them which despitefully use you, and persecute you; that ye may be the children of your Father which is in heaven: for he maketh his sun to rise on the evil and on the good, and sendeth rain on the just and on the unjust."[g]   The Twelve were commanded to salute with their blessing every

---

e Mark xi, 38-41; see also Luke ix, 49-50, and compare Numb. xi, 27-29

f Luke ix, 51-56; see also John iii, 17, and xii, 47.

g Matt. v, 44-45,

house at which they applied for hospitality. True, if the
people rejected them and their message, retribution was to
follow; but this visitation of cursing was to be reserved as
a Divine prerogative for the judgment day. In His Parable
of the Tares, Christ taught the same lesson of forbearance;
the hasty servants wanted to pluck out the weeds straightway, but they were forbidden lest they root up the wheat
also; and were assured of the harvest when a separation
would be effected.[h]

10. In spite of the prevailing spirit of toleration and
love which pervades the teachings of the Savior and His
apostles, attempts have been made to draw from the scriptures justification for intolerance and persecution.[i] Paul's
stinging words, addressed to the Galatians, have been given
a meaning wholly foreign to the spirit which prompted
them. Warning the Saints of false teachers, he said:—"As
we said before, so say I now again, If any man preach any
other gospel unto you than that ye have received, let him
be accursed."[j] With such an utterance, self-styled ministers of Christ, who, if the whole truth were considered are
perhaps preaching doctrines foreign to the apostolic precepts, seek to justify their sectarian hatred and unchristian
cruelty; forgetting that vengeance and recompense belong
to the Lord.[k]

11. The intent of John's words of counsel to the Elect
Lady has been perverted, and his teachings have been made
a cover of refuge for persecutors and bigots. Warning
her of the ministers of Antichrist who were industriously
disseminating their heresies, the Apostle wrote:—"If there
come any unto you, and bring not this doctrine, receive him
not into your house, neither bid him God-speed: for he

h Matt. xiii, 24-30.
i See Note 1.
j Gal. i, 9; also 8.
k Deut. xxxii, 35; Psa. xciv, 1; Rom, xii, 19; Heb. x, 30.

that biddeth him God-speed is partaker of his evil deeds."[l]
By no rightful interpretation can these words be made to
sanction intolerance, persecution, and hatred.

12.   The apostle's true meaning has been set forth with
clearness and force by a renowned Christian writer of the
present day, who, after deploring the "narrow intolerance
of an ignorant dogmatism," says:—"The Apostle of Love
would have belied all that is best in his own teaching if he
had consciously given an absolution, nay, an incentive, to
furious intolerance.   * * *   Meanwhile, this incidental
expression of St. John's brief letter will not lend itself to
these gross perversions.   What St. John really says and
really means, is something wholly different.   False teachers were rife, who, professing to be Christians, robbed the
nature of Christ of all which gave its efficacy to the atonement, and its significance to the incarnation.   These teachers, like other Christian missionaries, traveled from city to
city; and, in the absence of public inns, were received into
the houses of Christian converts.   The Christian lady to
whom St. John writes is warned, that if she offers her hospitality to these dangerous emissaries, who were subverting
the central truth of Christianity, she is expressing a public
sanction of them; and by doing this, and offering them
her best wishes, she is taking a direct share in the harm they
do.   This is common sense, nor is there anything uncharit-
able in it.   No one is bound to help forward the dissemina-
tion of teaching what he regards as erroneous respecting
the most essential doctrines of his own faith.   Still less
would it have been right to do this in the days when Christian communities were so small and weak.   But, to interpret
this as it has in all ages been practically interpreted,—to
pervert it into a sort of command to exaggerate the minor
ariations between religious opinions, and to persecute those

---
[l] II John, 10-11.

whose views differ from our own,—to make our own opinions
the conclusive test of heresy, and to say with Cornelius-a-
Lapide, that this verse reprobates 'all conversations, all intercourse, all dealings with heretics'—is to interpret scripture
by the glare of partisanship and spiritual self-satisfaction,
not to read it under the light of holy love.'"[m]

13. **Toleration is not Acceptance:**—The human frailty
of running to extremes in thought and action finds few more
glaring examples than are presented in man's dealings with
his fellows on matters religious. On the one hand, he is
prone to regard the faith of others as not merely inferior to
his own, but as utterly unworthy of his respect; or, on the
other, he brings himself to believe that all sects are equally
justified in their professions and practices, and that therefore there is no distinctively true order of religion. It is in
no-wise inconsistent for Latter-day Saints to boldly proclaim the conviction, that their own Church is the accepted
one, the only one entitled to the designation "Church of
Jesus Christ," and the sole earthly repository of the eternal
priesthood in the present age; and yet to willingly accord
kind treatment and a recognition of sincerity of purpose to
every soul or sect honestly professing Christ, or merely
showing a respect for truth, and manifesting a sincere
desire to walk according to the light received. My allegiance to the Church of my choice is based on a conviction of
the validity and genuineness of its high claim to distinction, as the one and only Church possessing a God-given
charter of authority; nevertheless, I count other sects as
sincere until they demonstrate that they are otherwise, and
am prepared to defend them in their rights.

14. Joseph Smith, the first prophet of the last dispensation, while reproving certain of his brethren for intolerance
toward the cherished beliefs of other sects, taught that even

---

m Canon Farrar, *The Early Days of Christianity* pp. 587, 588.

idolaters ought to be protected in their worship; that, while it would be the strict duty of any Christian to direct his efforts toward enlightening such benighted minds, he would not be justified in forcibly depriving the heathen of their rights of adoration.   In the pure eyes of God, idolatry is one of the most heinous of sins: yet He is tolerant of those who, knowing Him not, yield to their inherited instinct for worship by rendering homage even to stocks and stones. Deadly as is the sin of idolatrous worship on the part of him to whom light has come, it may represent in the savage the sincerest reverence of which he is capable.   And, as set forth in a preceding lecture,[n] the voice of the Eternal One has declared that the heathen who have known no law shall have part in the first resurrection.

   15.   What justification can man find for intolerance toward his fellow, when God, who is grieved over every sin, manifests so marked a forbearance?   The free agency of the human soul is sacred to Deity.

> "Know this, that every soul is free,
> To choose his life. and what he'll be;
> For this eternal truth is given,
> That God will force no man to heaven.
> He'll call, persuade, direct aright,
> Bless him with wisdom, love, and light,
> In nameless ways be good and kind,
> But never force the human mind."

   16.   Man is strictly answerable for his Acts:—The unbounded liberality and true tolerance with which the Church of Jesus Christ of Latter-day Saints regards other religious denominations, and the teachings of the Church respecting the assurance of final redemption for all men except the few who have fallen so far as to have committed the unpardonable sin, thereby becoming Sons of Perdition, may suggest the erroneous conclusion, that we believe that

n See page 61.

all so redeemed shall be admitted to equal powers, privileges, and glories in the Heaven of our God. Far from this, the Church proclaims the doctrine of many and varied degrees of glory, which the redeemed will inherit in strict accordance with their merits.[o] We believe in no general plan of universal forgiveness or reward, by which sinners of high and low degree shall be exempted from the effects of their deeds, while the righteous are ushered into heaven as a dwelling place in common, all glorified in the same measure. As stated, the heathen whose sins are those of ignorance, are to come forth with the just in the first resurrection; but this does not imply that those children of the lower races are to inherit the glory provided for the able, the valiant, and the true, in the cause of God on earth.

17.   Our condition in the world to come will be strictly a result of the life we lead in this probation, as, by the light of revealed truth regarding the pre-existent state,[p] we perceive our present condition to be determined by the fidelity with which we kept our first estate. The scriptures repeatedly declare that man will reap the natural harvest of his works in life, be such good or evil; in the effective language with which the Father encourages and warns his frail children, every one will be rewarded or punished according to his works.[q] In eternity, man will enjoy or loath the "fruit of his doing."

18.   Degrees of Glory:—That the privileges and glories of heaven are graded to suit the various capacities of the blessed, is indicated in Christ's teachings. To His apostles He said:—"In my Father's house are many mansions: if it were not so, I would have told you. I go to prepare a place for you. And if I go and prepare a place for you, I will

---

o See pp. 94-95.

p See pp. 195-198.

q Job. xxxiv, 11; Psal. lxii, 12; Jer. xvii, 10; xxxii, 19; Matt. xvi, 17; Rom. ii, 6-12; xiv, 12; I Cor. iii, 8; II Cor. v, 10; Rev. ii, 23; xx, 12; xxii, 12.

come again, and receive you unto myself; that where I am, there ye may be also."[r]

19. This utterance is supplemented by that of Paul, who speaks of the graded glories of the resurrection as follows:— "There are also celestial bodies, and bodies terrestrial: but the glory of the celestial is one, and the glory of the terrestrial is another. There is one glory of the sun, and another glory of the moon, and another glory of the stars; for one star differeth from another star in glory. So also is the resurrection of the dead."[s]

20. A fuller knowledge of this subject has been imparted in the present dispensation. From a revelation given in 1832[t] we learn the following:—Three great kingdoms or degrees of glory are established for the future habitation of the human race; these are known as the Celestial, the Terrestrial, and the Telestial. Far below the last and least of these, is the state of eternal punishment prepared for the Sons of Perdition.

21. **The Celestial Glory** is provided for those who merit the highest honors of heaven. In the revelation referred to, we read of them:—"They are they who received the testimony of Jesus, and believed on his name and were baptized after the manner of his burial, being buried in the water in his name, and this according to the commandment which he has given, that by keeping the commandments they might be washed and cleansed from all their sins, and receive the Holy Spirit by the laying on of the hands of him who is ordained and sealed unto this power, and who overcome by faith, and are sealed by the Holy Spirit of promise, which the Father sheds forth upon all those who are just and true. They are they who are the Church of the First-born. They

---

[r] John xiv, 1-3.
[s] I Cor. xv, 40-42.
[t] Doc. and Cov. lxxvi.

28

are they into whose hands the Father has given all things,—
They are they who are Priests and Kings, who have
received of his fulness, and of his glory, and are Priests of
the Most High, after the order of Melchisedek, which was
after the order of Enoch, which was after the order of the
Only Begotten Son; wherefore, as it is written, they are
Gods, even the sons of God;—wherefore all things are theirs,
whether life or death, or things present, or things to come,
all are theirs, and they are Christ's, and Christ is God's.
* * * These shall dwell in the presence of God and his
Christ for ever and ever. These are they whom he shall
bring with him, when he shall come in the clouds of heaven,
to reign on the earth over his people. These are they who
shall have part in the first resurrection. These are they
who shall come forth in the resurrection of the just. * * *
These are they who are just men made perfect through
Jesus, the mediator of the new covenant, who wrought out
this perfect atonement through the shedding of his own
blood. These are they whose bodies are celestial, whose
glory is that of the sun, even the glory of God, the highest
of all, whose glory the sun of the firmament is written of as
being typical."[u]

22.   **The Terrestrial Glory:**—This, the next lower degree,
will be received by many whose works do not merit the highest reward. We read of them:—"These are they who are of
the terrestrial, whose glory differs from that of the Church
of the First-born, who have received the fulness of the
Father, even as that of the moon differs from the sun in the
firmament. Behold, these are they who died without law, and
also they who are the spirits of men kept in prison, whom
the Son visited, and preached the Gospel unto them, that
they might be judged according to men in the flesh, who
received not the testimony of Jesus in the flesh, but after-

_u_ Paragraphs 51-70.

wards received it. These are they who are honorable men
of the earth, who were blinded by the craftiness of men.
These are they who receive of his glory, but not of his
fulness. These are they who receive of the presence of the
Son, but not of the fulness of the Father; wherefore they
are bodies terrestrial, and not bodies celestial, and differ in
glory as the moon differs from the sun. These are they
who are not valiant in the testimony of Jesus; wherefore
they obtain not the crown over the kingdom of our God."[v]

23. **The Telestial Glory:**—The revelation continues:—
"And again, we saw the glory of the telestial,[w] which glory
is that of the lesser, even as the glory of the stars differs
from that of the glory of the moon in the firmament.
These are they who received not the gospel of Christ, neither
the testimony of Jesus. These are they who deny not the
Holy Spirit. These are they who are thrust down to hell.
These are they who shall not be redeemed from the devil,
until the last resurrection, until the Lord, even Christ the
Lamb shall have finished his work."[x] We learn further
that the inhabitants of this kingdom are to be graded
among themselves, comprising as they do the unenlightened among the varied opposing sects and divisions of
men, and sinners of many types, whose offences are not
those of utter perdition;—"For as one star differs from
another star in glory, even so differs one from another in
glory in the telestial world; for these are they who are of
Paul, and of Apollos, and of Cephas. These are they who
say they are some of one and some of another—some of
Christ, and some of John, and some of Moses, and some of
Elias, and some of Esaias, and some of Isaiah, and some of
Enoch; but received not the gospel, neither the testimony

v Paragraphs 71-79.
w See Note 2.
x Paragraphs 81-86.

of Jesus, neither the prophets, neither the everlasting covenant."[y]   Evidently a considerable part of the human family
will fail of all glory beyond that of the telestial kingdom,
for we are told,—"But behold, and lo, we saw the glory and
the inhabitants of the telestial world, that they were as
innumerable as the stars in the firmament of heaven, or as
the sand upon the sea shore."[z]   They are thus not wholly
rejected; their every merit will be respected.   "For they
shall be judged according to their works, and every man
shall receive according to his own works, his own dominion
in the mansions which are prepared; and they shall be
servants of the Most High, but where God and Christ dwell,
they cannot come, worlds without end."[a]

24.   **The Kingdoms with Respect to One Another:**—The
three kingdoms of widely differing glories are themselves
organized on an orderly plan of gradation.   We have seen
that the telestial kingdom comprises a multitude of subdivisions; this also is the case, we are told, with the
celestial;[b] and, by analogy, we conclude that a similar condition prevails in the terrestrial.   Thus the innumerable
degrees of merit amongst mankind are provided for in an
infinity of graded glories.   The Celestial kingdom is
supremely honored by the personal ministrations of the
Father and the Son.[c]   The Terrestrial kingdom will be
administered through the higher, without a fulness of
glory.   The Telestial is governed through the ministrations
of the Terrestrial, by "angels who are appointed to minister
for them."[d]

25.   It is reasonable to believe, in the absence of direct

---

y Doc. and Cov. lxxvi, 98-101.

z Par. 109.

a Par. 111-112.'

b Doc. and Cov. cxxxi, 1; see also II Cor. xii, 1-4.

c Doc. and Cov. lxxvi, 68.

d Par. 86, 88.

revelation by which alone absolute knowledge of the matter could be acquired, that, in accordance with God's plan of eternal progression, advancement from grade to grade within any kingdom, and from kingdom to kingdom, will be provided for. But if the recipients of a lower glory be enabled to advance, surely the intelligences of higher rank will not be stopped in their progress; and thus we may conclude, that degrees and grades will ever characterize the kingdoms of our God. Eternity is progressive; perfection is relative; the essential feature of God's living purpose is its associated power of eternal increase.

26. **The Sons of Perdition:**—We learn of another class of souls whose sins are such as to place them beyond the present possibility of redemption. These are called Sons of Perdition; children of the fallen angel, once a Son of the Morning, now Lucifer, or Perdition.[e] These are they who have violated truth in the full blaze of the light of knowledge; who, having received the testimony of Christ, and having been endowed by the Holy Spirit, then deny the same and defy the power of God, crucifying the Lord afresh, and putting Him to an open shame. This, the unpardonable sin, can be committed by those only who have received the knowledge and the sacred conviction of the truth, against which they then rebel. Their sin is comparable to the treason of Lucifer, by which he sought to usurp the power and glory of his God. Concerning them and their dreadful fate, the Almighty has said;—"I say that it had been better for them never to have been born; for they are vessels of wrath, doomed to suffer the wrath of God, with the devil and his angels in eternity; concerning whom I have said, there is no forgiveness in this world nor in the world to come. * * * They shall go away into everlasting punishment, which is endless punishment, which is

e Doc. and Cov. lxxvi, 25-27.

eternal punishment, to reign with the devil and his angels in eternity, where their worm dieth not, and the fire is not quenched, which is their torment; And the end thereof, neither the place thereof, nor their torment, no man knows; neither was it revealed, neither is, neither will be revealed unto man, except to them who are made partakers thereof: Nevertheless I, the Lord, show it by vision unto many, but straightway shut it up again; wherefore the end, the width, the height, the depth, and the misery thereof, they understand not, neither any man except them who are ordained unto this condemnation."[f]

27.   Surely the doctrines of the Church are explicit in defining the relationship between the mortal probation and the future state, and in teaching the individual accountability, and the free agency of man.   The Church affirms that in view of the terrible responsibility under which every man rests, as the unrestrained director of his own course, he must be and is free to choose in all things, from the life that leads to the celestial home, to the career that is but the introduction to the miseries of perdition.   Freedom to worship, or to refuse to worship at all, is a God-given right.

NOTES.

1. **Intolerance Among Christians Today:**—"It must be said,—though I say it with the deepest sorrow—that the cold exclusiveness of the Pharisee, the bitter ignorance of the self-styled theologian, the usurped infallibility of the half-educated religionist, have been ever the curse of Christianity.   They have imposed 'the senses of men upon the words of God, the special senses of men on the general words of God;' and have tried to enforce them on all men's consciences with all kinds of burnings and anathemas under equal threats of death and damnation.   And thus they incurred the terrible responsibility of presenting

[f] Doc. and Cov. lxxvi, 31-48; see also Heb. vi, 4-:6 Alma xxxix, 6.   For other references see page 62.

religion to mankind in a false and repellant guise. Is theological hatred still to be a proverb for the world's just contempt? Is such hatred—hatred in its bitterest and most ruthless form—to be regarded as the legitimate and normal outcome of the religion of love? Is the spirit of peace never to be brought to bear on religious opinions? Are such questions always to excite the most intense animosities, and the most terrible divisions? * * * Is the world to be forever confirmed in its opinion that theological partisans are less truthful, less candid, less high-minded, less honorable even than the partisans of political and social causes, who make no profession as to the duty of love? Are the so-called 'religious' champions to be forever as they now are, the most unscrupu-lously bitter, the most conspicuously unfair? Alas! they might be so with far less danger to the cause of religion if they would forego the luxury of 'quoting scripture for their purpose.' "—Canon Farrar, "*The Early Days of Christianity*," pp. 584-585.

2. **"Telestial:"**—The adjective "telestial" has not become current in the language; its use is at present confined to the theology of the Church of Jesus Christ of Latter-day Saints. It is applied as a distinguishing term to the lowest of the three kingdoms of glory provided for the redeemed. The only English word approaching it in form, is the adjective "telestic," which is defined thus:— "tending toward the end or final accomplishment; tending to accomplish a purpose."

LECTURE XXIII.

SUBMISSION TO SECULAR AUTHORITY.

Article 12.—We believe in being subject to kings, presidents, rulers, and magistrates, in obeying, honoring, and sustaining the law.

1. **Introductory:**—It is but reasonable to expect of a people professing the Gospel of Christ, and claiming membership in the one accepted and divinely authorized Church, that they manifest in practice the virtues which their precepts inculcate. True, we may look in vain for perfection among those even who make the fullest and most justifiable claims to orthodoxy; but we have a right to expect in their creed, ample requirements concerning the most approved course of action; and in their lives, sincere and earnest effort toward the practical realization of their professions. Religion, to be of service and at all worthy of acceptance, must be of wholesome influence in the individual lives and the temporal affairs of its adherents. Among other virtues, the Church in its teachings should impress the duty of a law-abiding course; and the people should show forth the effect of such precepts in their excellence as citizens of the nation, and as individuals in the community of which they are part.

2. The Church of Jesus Christ of Latter-day Saints makes emphatic declaration of its belief and precepts regarding the duty of its members toward the laws of the land; and sustains its position by the authority of specific revelation in ancient as in present times. Moreover, the people are confident, that when the true story of their rise and progress as an established body of religious worshipers

is written, the loyalty of the Church and the patriotic devotion of its members will be vindicated and extolled by the world in general, as now are these virtues recognized by the few unprejudiced investigators who have studied with honest purpose the history of this remarkable organization.

3. **Obedience to Authority Enjoined by Scripture:**—During the patriarchal period, when the head of the family possessed virtually the power of judge and king over his household, the authority of the ruler and the rights of the family were respected. Consider the instance of Hagar, the "plural" wife of Abram, and the handmaid of Sarai. Jealousy and ill-feeling had arisen between Hagar and her mistress, the senior wife of the patriarch. Abram listened to the complaint of Sarai, and, recognizing her authority over Hagar, who, though his wife, was still the servant of Sarai, said:—"Behold thy maid is in thy hand; do to her as it pleaseth thee." Then, as the mistress dealt harshly with her servant, Hagar fled into the wilderness; there she was visited by an angel of the Lord, who addressed her thus:—"Hagar, Sarai's maid, whence camest thou, and whither wilt thou go? And she said, I flee from the face of my mistress Sarai. And the angel of the Lord said unto her, Return to thy mistress, and submit thyself under her hands."[a] Observe that the heavenly messenger recognized the authority of the mistress over the bond-woman, even though the latter had been given the rank of wifehood in the family.

4. The ready submission of Isaac to the will of his father, even to the extent of offering his life[b] on the altar of bloody sacrifice, is evidence of the sancity with which the authority of the family ruler was regarded. It may

---

a Gen. xvi, 1-9.
b Gen. xxii, 1-10.

appear, as indeed it has been claimed, that the requirement which the Lord made of Abraham as a test of faith, in the matter of giving his son's life as a sacrifice, was a violation of existing laws, and therefore opposed to stable government. The claim is poorly placed in view of the fact, that the patriarchal head was possessed of absolute authority over the members of his household, the power extending even to judgment of life or death.[c]

5. In the days of the exodus, when Israel were ruled by a theocracy, the Lord gave divers laws and commandments for the government of His chosen people; among them we read:—"Thou shalt not revile the gods, nor curse the ruler of thy people."[d] Judges were appointed by Divine direction to exercise authority amongst Israel. Moses, in reiterating the Lord's commands, charged the people to this effect:— "Judges and officers shalt thou make thee in all thy gates, which the Lord thy God giveth thee, throughout thy tribes; and they shall judge the people with just judgment."[e]

6. When the people wearied of God's direct control, and clamored for a king, the Lord yielded to their desire, and gave the new ruler authority by a holy anointing.[f] David, even though he had been anointed to succeed Saul on the throne, recognized the sanctity of the king's person, and bitterly reproached himself, because on one occasion he had mutilated the robe of the monarch. True, Saul was at that time seeking David's life, and the latter sought only a means of showing that he had no intent to kill his royal enemy; yet we are told:—"That David's heart smote him, because he had cut off Saul's skirt. And he said unto his men, The Lord forbid that I should do this thing unto my

---

c Gen. xxxviii, 24.

d Exo. xxii, 28; The word "gods" in this passage, is rendered by some translators "judges;" (see marginal reference, Bible.)

e Deut. xvi, 18: see also i, 16; I Chron. xxiii, 4; xxvi, 29.

f I Sam. viii, 6-7, 22; ix, 15-16; x, 1.

master, the Lord's anointed, to stretch forth mine hand against him, seeing he is the anointed of the Lord."[g]

7. Note, further, the following scriptural adjurations as recorded in the Old Testament:—"My son, fear thou the Lord, and the king."[h] "I counsel thee to keep the king's commandment, and that in regard of the oath of God."[i] "Curse not the king, no not in thy thought."[j]

8. **Examples Set by Christ and His Apostles:**—Our Savior's work on earth was marked throughout by His acknowledgment of the existing powers of the land, even though the authority had been won by cruel conquest, and was exercised unjustly. When the tax-collector called for the dues demanded by an alien king, Christ, while privately protesting against the injustice of the claim, directed that it be paid, and even invoked a miraculous circumstance whereby the money could be provided. Of Peter he asked:— "What thinkest thou, Simon? of whom do the kings of the earth take custom or tribute? of their own children, or of strangers? Peter saith unto him, of strangers. Jesus saith unto him, Then are the children free. Notwithstanding, lest we should offend them, go thou to the sea, and cast an hook, and take up the fish that first cometh up; and when thou hast opened his mouth, thou shall find a piece of money: that take, and give unto them for me and thee."[k]

9. At the instigation of certain wicked Pharisees, a treacherous plot was laid to make Christ appear as an offender against the ruling powers. They sought to catch Him by the hypocritical question,—"What thinkest thou? Is it lawful to give tribute unto Cæsar or not?" His answer

---

g I Sam. xxiv, 5-6, 10; see also xxvi, 9-12, 16.

h Prov. xxiv, 21.

i Eccles. viii. 2.

j Eccles. x, 20.

k Matt. xvii. 24-27.

was an unequivocal endorsement of submission to the laws. To his questioners he replied:—"Shew me the tribute money. And they brought unto him a penny. And he saith unto them, whose is this image and superscription? They say unto him, Cæsar's. Then saith he unto them, Render therefore unto Cæsar the things which are Cæsar's; and unto God the things that are God's."[l]

10. Throughout the solemnly tragic circumstances of His trial and condemnation, Christ maintained a submissive demeanor even toward the chief priests and council who were plotting his death. These officers, however unworthy of their priestly power, were nevertheless in authority, and had a certain measure of jurisdiction in secular as in ecclesiastical affairs. When He stood before Caiaphas, laden with insult and accused by false witnesses, He maintained a dignified silence. To the high priest's question,—"Answereth thou nothing? What is it these witness against thee?" He deigned no reply. Then the high priest added:—"I adjure thee by the living God, that thou tell us whether thou be the Christ, the Son of God."[m] To this solemn adjuration, spoken with official authority, the Savior gave an immediate answer; thus recognizing the office of the high priest, however unworthy the man.

11. A similar respect for the high priest's office was shown by Paul while a prisoner before the tribunal. His remarks displeased the high priest, who gave immediate command to those who stood near Paul to smite him on the mouth.[n] This angered the apostle, and he cried out:—"God shall smite thee, thou whited wall: for sittest thou to judge me after the law, and commandest me to be smitten contrary to the law? And they that stood by said, Revilest

---

l Matt. xxii, 15-21; see also Mark xii, 13-17; Luke xx, 20-25.

m Matt. xxvi, 57-64; Mark xiv, 55-62.

n See Note 1.

thou God's high priest?   Then said Paul, I wist not, brethren, that he was the high priest: for it is written, Thou
shalt not speak evil of the ruler of thy people."[o]

12. **Teachings of the Apostles:**—Paul, writing to Titus
who had been left in charge of the Church among the
Cretans, warns him of the weaknesses of his flock, and
urges him to teach them to be orderly and law-abiding:—
"Put them in mind to be subject to principalities and
powers, to obey magistrates, to be ready to every good
work."[p] In another place, Paul is emphatic in declaring the
duty of the Saints toward the civil power, such authority
being ordained of God. He points out the necessity of
secular government, and the need of officers in authority,
whose power will be feared by evil-doers only. He designates
the civil authorities as ministers of God; and justifies taxa-
tion by the state, with an admonition that the Saints fail
not in their dues.

13. These are his words addressed to the Church at
Rome:—"Let every soul be subject unto the higher powers.
For there is no power but of God: the powers that be are
ordained of God. Whosoever therefore resisteth the power,
resisteth the ordinance of God: and they that resist shall
receive to themselves damnation. For rulers are not a terror
to good works, but to the evil. Wilt thou then not be afraid
of the power? do that which is good, and thou shalt have
praise of the same: For he is the minister of God to thee
for good. But if thou do that which is evil, be afraid; for
he beareth not the sword in vain: for he is the minister of
God, a revenger to execute wrath upon him that doeth evil.
Wherefore ye must needs be subject, not only for wrath,
but also for conscience sake. For, for this cause pay ye
tribute also: for they are God's ministers, attending contin-

o Acts xxiii, 1-5.
p Titus iii. 1.

ually upon this very thing. Render therefore to all their dues: tribute to whom tribute is due; custom to whom custom; fear to whom fear; honor to whom honor."[q]

14. In a letter to Timothy, Paul teaches that in the prayers of the Saints, kings and all in authority should be remembered, adding that such remembrance is pleasing in the sight of God:—"I exhort therefore, that, first of all, supplications, prayers, intercessions, and giving of thanks, be made for all men; For kings, and for all that are in authority; that we may lead a quiet and peaceable life in all godliness and honesty. For this is good and acceptable in the sight of God our Savior."[r]

15. The duty of willing submission to authority is elaborated in the epistles to the Ephesians and the Colossians; and illustrations are applied to the relations of social and domestic life. Wives are taught to be submissive to their husbands,—"For the husband is the head of the wife, even as Christ is the head of the church;" but this duty within the family is reciprocal, and therefore husbands are instructed as to the manner in which authority ought to be exercised. Children are to obey their parents; yet the parents are cautioned against provoking or otherwise offending their little ones. Servants are told to render willing and earnest service to their masters, recognizing in all things the superior authority; and masters are instructed in their duty toward their servants, being counseled to abandon threatening and other harsh treatment, remembering that they also will have to answer to a Master greater than themselves.[s]

16. Peter is not less emphatic in teaching the sanctity with which the civil power should be regarded;[t] he admon-

[q] Rom. xiii. 1-7.
[r] I Tim. ii, 1-3.
[s] Eph. v, 22-23; vi, 1-9; Col. iii, 18-22; iv, 1.
[t] See Note 2.

ishes the Saints in this wise:—"Submit yourselves to every
ordinance of man for the Lord's sake: whether it be to the
king, as supreme; or unto governors, as unto them that are
sent by him for the punishment of evil doers, and for the
praise of them that do well. For so is the will of God,
that with well doing ye may put to silence the ignorance of
foolish men: as free, and not using your liberty for a cloak
of maliciousness, but as the servants of God. Honor all
men. Love the brotherhood. Fear God. Honor the king."[u]

17. These general rules, relating to submission to authority, he applies, as did Paul similarly, to the conditions of
domestic life. Servants are to be obedient, even though
their masters be harsh and severe:—"For this is thank-
worthy, if a man for conscience toward God endure grief,
suffering wrongfully. For what glory is it, if, when ye be
buffeted for your faults, ye take it patiently? but if,
when you do well, and suffer for it, ye take it patiently,
this is acceptable with God."[v] Wives also, even though
their husbands be not of their faith, are not to vaunt
themselves and defy authority, but to be submissive, and to
rely upon gentler and more effective means of influencing
those whose name they bear.[w] He gives assurance of the
judgment which shall overtake evil doers, and specifies as
fit subjects for condemnation, "chiefly them that walk after
the flesh in the lust of uncleanness, and despise government. Presumptuous are they, self-willed, they are not
afraid to speak evil of dignities."[x]

18. Doubtless there existed excellent reason for these
explicit and repeated counsels against the spirit of revolt,
with which the apostles of old sought to lead and strengthen
the Church. The Saints rejoiced in their testimony of the

---

u I Peter ii, 13-17.

v Verses 19-20.

w I Peter iii, 1-7.

x II Peter ii, 10.

truth that had found place in their hearts,—the truth that was to make them free,—and it would have been but natural for them to regard all others as inferior to themselves, and to rebel against all authority of man in favor of their allegiance to a higher power.   There was constant danger that their zeal would lead them to acts of indiscretion, and thus furnish excuse, if not reason, for the assaults of persecutors, who would have denounced them as law-breakers and workers of sedition.   Even half-hearted submission to the civil powers would have been unwise at least, in view of the disfavor with which the new sect had come to be regarded by their pagan contemporaries.   The voice of their inspired leaders was heard, therefore, in timely counsel for humility and submission.   But there were then, as ever have there been, weightier reasons than such as rest on motives of policy, requiring submission to the established powers.   Such is no less the law of God than of man.   Governments are essential to human existence; they are recognized, given indeed, of the Lord; and His people are in duty bound to sustain them.

19. **Book of Mormon Teachings** concerning the duty of the people as subjects of the law of the land are abundant throughout the volume. However, as the civil and the ecclesiastical powers were usually vested together, the king or chief judge being also the high priest, there are comparatively few admonitions of allegiance to the civil authority as distinct from that of the priesthood. From the time of Nephi, son of Lehi, to that of the death of Mosiah,—a period of nearly five hundred years, the Nephites were ruled by a succession of kings; during the remaining time of their recorded history,—more than five hundred years, the people were subject to judges of their own choosing. Under each of these varieties of government, the secular laws were rigidly enforced, the power of the state being supplemented and strengthened by that of the Church. The sanctity

with which the laws were regarded is illustrated in the judgment pronounced by Alma upon Nehor, a murderer, and an advocate of sedition and priestcraft:—"Thou art condemned to die," said the judge, "according to the law which has been given us by Mosiah, our last king; and they have been acknowledged by this people; therefore, this people must abide by the law."[y]

20. **Modern Revelation** requires of the Saints in the present dispensation a strict allegiance to the civil laws. In a communication dated August 1, 1831, the Lord said to the Church:—"Let no man break the laws of the land, for he that keepeth the laws of God hath no need to break the laws of the land: Wherefore, be subject to the powers that be, until He reigns whose right it is to reign, and subdues all enemies under his feet."[z] At a later date, August 6, 1833, the voice of the Lord was heard again on this matter, saying:—"And now, verily I say unto you concerning the laws of the land, it is my will that my people should observe to do all things whatsoever I command them; and that law of the land which is constitutional, supporting that principle of freedom in maintaining rights and privileges, belongs to all mankind, and is justifiable before me; Therefore, I, the Lord, justify you, and your brethren of my church, in befriending that law which is the constitutional law of the land."[a]

21. A question has many times been asked of the Church and of its individual members, to this effect:—In the case of a conflict between the requirements made by the revealed word of God, and those imposed by the secular law, which of these authorities would the members of the Church be bound to obey? In answer, the words of Christ may be

---

y Alma i, 14.
z Doc. and Cov. lviii, 21-22.
a Doc. and Cov. xcviii, 4-6.
  29

applied:—it is the duty of the people to render "unto Cæsar the things that are Cæsar's, and unto God the things that are God's." At the present time, the Kingdom of Heaven as an earthly power, with a reigning King exercising direct and personal authority in temporal matters, has not been established upon the earth; the branches of the Church as such, and the members composing the same, are subjects of the several governments within whose separate realms the Church organizations exist. In this day of comparative enlightenment and freedom, there is small cause for expecting any direct interference with the rights of private worship and individual devotion; in all civilized nations the people are accorded the right to pray, and this right is assured by what may be properly called a common law of human-kind. No earnest soul is cut off from communion with his God; and with such an open channel of communication, relief from burdensome laws and redress for grievances may be sought from the Power that holds control of nations.

22. Pending the over-ruling by Providence in favor of religious liberty, it is the duty of the Saints to submit themselves to the laws of their country. Nevertheless, they should use every proper method, as citizens or subjects of their several governments, to secure the boon of freedom in religious duties, for themselves and for all men. It is not required of them to suffer without protest imposition by lawless persecutors, or through the operation of unjust laws; but their protests should be offered in peaceful and proper order. The Saints have practically demonstrated their acceptance of the doctrine that it is better to suffer evil than to do wrong by purely human opposition to unjust authority. And if by thus submitting themselves to the laws of the land, in the event of such laws being unjust and subversive of human freedom, the Saints be prevented

from doing the work appointed them of God, they will not be held accountable for the failure to act under the higher law.   The word of the Lord has been given explicitly defining the position and duty of the people in such a contingency:—"Verily, verily, I say unto you, that when I give a commandment to any of the sons of men, to do a work unto my name, and those sons of men go with all their might, and with all they have, to perform that work, and cease not their diligence, and their enemies come upon them, and hinder them from performing that work; behold, it behoveth me to require that work no more at the hands of those sons of men, but to accept of their offerings; And the iniquity and transgression of my holy laws and commandments, I will visit upon the heads of those who hindered my work, unto the third and fourth generation, so long as they repent not and hate me, saith the Lord God."[b]

23. An Illustration of such suspension of Divine law is found in the action of the Church regarding the matter of plural or polygamous marriage. The practice referred to was established as a result of direct revelation,[c] and many of those who followed the same felt that they were divinely commanded so to do.   For ten years after polygamy had been introduced into Utah as a Church observance, no law was enacted in opposition to the practice. Beginning with 1862, however, federal statutes were framed declaring the practice unlawful and providing penalties therefor. The Church claimed that these enactments were unconstitutional, and therefore void, inasmuch as they violated the provision in the national constitution which denies the government power to make laws respecting any establishment of religion, or prohibiting the free exercise thereof.[d]   Many

---

[b] Doc. and Cov. cxxiv, 49-50; see Note 3.

[c] Doc. and Cov. cxxxii.

[d] Article I, of the Amendments to the Constitution of the United States.

appeals were taken to the national court of final resort, and at last a decision was rendered sustaining the anti-polygamy laws as constitutional and therefore binding. The Church, through its chief officer, thereupon discontinued the practice of plural marriage, and announced its action to the world; solemnly placing the responsibility for the change upon the nation by whose laws the renunciation had been forced. This action has been approved and confirmed by the official vote of the Church in conference assembled.[e]

24. **Teachings of the Church today:**—Perhaps no more proper summary could be presented of the teachings of the Church of Jesus Christ of Latter-day Saints regarding its relation to the civil power, and the respect due to the laws of the land, than the official declaration of belief which was issued by the Prophet Joseph Smith, and which has been incorporated in the Doctrine and Covenants,—one of the standard works of the Church, adopted by vote of the Church as one of the accepted guides in faith, doctrine, and practice.[f] It reads as follows:—

"OF GOVERNMENTS AND LAWS IN GENERAL.

"1.   We believe that governments were instituted of God for the benefit of man, and that he holds men accountable for their acts in relation to them, either in making laws or administering them, for the good and safety of society.

"2.   We believe that no government can exist in peace, except such laws are framed and held inviolate as will secure to each individual the free exercise of conscience, the right and control of property, and the protection of life.

"3.   We believe that all governments necessarily require civil officers and magistrates to enforce the laws of the same, and that such as will administer the law in equity and justice, should be sought for and upheld by the voice of the people (if a republic,) or the will of the sovereign.

e See Note 4.

f Doc. and Cov. cxxxiv.

"4. We believe that religion is instituted of God, and
that men are amenable to him, and to him only, for the
exercise of it, unless their religious opinions prompt them
to infringe upon the rights and liberties of others; but we
do not believe that human law has a right to interfere in
prescribing rules of worship to bind the consciences of men,
nor dictate forms for public or private devotion; that the
civil magistrate should restrain crime, but never control
conscience; should punish guilt, but never suppress the
freedom of the soul.

"5. We believe that all men are bound to sustain and
uphold the respective governments in which they reside,
while protected in their inherent and inalienable rights by
the laws of such governments; and that sedition and rebellion are unbecoming every citizen thus protected, and should
be punished accordingly; and that all governments have a
right to enact such laws as in their own judgment are best
calculated to secure the public interest, at the same time,
however, holding sacred the freedom of conscience.

"6. We believe that every man should be honored in his
station: rulers and magistrates as such, being placed for
the protection of the innocent, and the punishment of
the guilty; and that to the laws, all men owe respect and
deference, as without them peace and harmony would be
supplanted by anarchy and terror; human laws being instituted for the express purpose of regulating our interests as
individuals and nations, between man and man, and divine
laws given of heaven, prescribing rules on spiritual concerns, for faith and worship, both to be answered by man to
his Maker.

"7. We believe that rulers, states, and governments, have
a right, and are bound to enact laws for the protection of
all citizens in the free exercise of their religious belief; but
we do not believe that they have a right in justice, to deprive
citizens of this privilege, or proscribe them in their opinions, so long as a regard and reverence are shown to the
laws, and such religious opinions do not justify sedition nor
conspiracy.

"8. We believe that the commission of crime should be
punished according to the nature of the offence; that murder, treason, robbery, theft, and the breach of the general

peace, in all respects, should be punished according to their criminality, and their tendency to evil among men, by the laws of that government in which the offence is committed; and for the public peace and tranquility, all men should step forward and use their ability in bringing offenders against good laws to punishment.

"9. We do not believe it just to mingle religious influence with civil government, whereby one religious society is fostered, and another proscribed in its spiritual privileges, and the individual rights of its members as citizens, denied.

"10. We believe that all religious societies have a right to deal with their members for disorderly conduct according to the rules and regulations of such societies, provided that such dealing be for fellowship and good standing; but we do not believe that any religious society has authority to try men on the right of property or life, to take from them this world's goods, or to put them in jeopardy of either life or limb, neither to inflict any physical punishment upon them; they can only excommunicate them from their society, and withdraw from them their fellowship.

"11. We believe that men should appeal to the civil law for redress of all wrongs and grievances, where personal abuse is inflicted, or the right of property or character infringed, where such laws exist as will protect the same; but we believe that all men are justified in defending themselves, their friends, and property, and the government, from the unlawful assaults and encroachments of all persons, in times of exigency, where immediate appeal cannot be made to the laws, and relief afforded.

"12. We believe it just to preach the gospel to the nations of the earth, and warn the righteous to save themselves from the corruption of the world; but we do not believe it right to interfere with bond servants, neither preach the gospel to, nor baptize them, contrary to the will and wish of their masters, nor to meddle with or influence them in the least, to cause them to be dissatisfied with their situations in this life, thereby jeopardizing the lives of men; such interference we believe to be unlawful and unjust, and dangerous to the peace of every government allowing human beings to be held in servitude."

NOTES.

1. **Insults to Paul and to Christ**:—See Acts xxiii, 1-5. "Scarcely had the apostle uttered the first sentence of his defense, when, with disgraceful illegality, Ananias ordered the officers of the court to smite him on the mouth. Stung by an insult so flagrant, an outrage so undeserved, the naturally choleric temperament of Paul flamed into that sudden sense of anger which ought to be controlled, but which can hardly be wanting in a truly noble character. No character can be perfect which does not cherish in itself a deeply-seated, though perfectly generous and forbearing, indignation against intolerable wrong. Smarting from the blow, 'God shall smite thee,' he exclaimed, 'thou white-washed wall! What! Dost thou sit there judging me according to the Law, and in violation of law biddest me to be smitten?' The language has been censured as unbecoming in its violence, and has been unfavorably compared with the meekness of Christ before the tribunal of his enemies. [See John xviii, 19-23.] 'Where,' asks St. Jerome, 'is that patience of the Savior, who—as a lamb led to the slaughter opens not his mouth—so gently asks the smiter, 'If I have spoken evil, bear witness to the evil; but if well, why smitest thou me?' We are not detracting from the apostle, but declaring the glory of God, who, suffering in the flesh, reigns above the wrong and frailty of the flesh.' Yet we need not remind the reader that not once or twice only did Christ give the rein to righteous anger, and blight hypocrisy and insolence with a flash of holy wrath. The bystanders seem to have been startled by the boldness of St. Paul's rebuke, for they said to him, 'Dost thou revile the high priest of God?' The apostle's anger had expended itself in that one outburst, and he instantly apologised with exquisite urbanity and self-control. 'I did not know,' he said, 'brethren, that he is the high priest;' adding that, had he known this, he would not have addressed to him the opprobrious name of 'whited wall,' because he reverenced and acted upon the rule of scripture, 'Thou shalt not speak ill of a ruler of thy people.'"—Farrar, *The Life and Work of St. Paul*, p. 539-540.

2. **Peter's Teachings Regarding Submission to Law**:—A special "duty of Christians in those days was due respect in all things lawful, to the civil government. * * * Occasions there are—and none knew this better than an apostle who had himself set an example of splendid disobedience to unwarranted commands [Acts iii, 19, 31; v, 28-32; 40-42]—when 'we must obey God rather than men.' But those occasions are exceptional to the common rule of life. Normally, and as a whole, human law is on the side of divine order, and, by whomsoever administered, has a just claim to obedience and respect. It was a lesson so deeply needed by the Christians of the day that it is taught as emphatically by St. John [John xix, 11], and by St. Peter, as by St. Paul himself. It was more than ever needed at a time when dangerous revolts were gathering to a head in Judea: when the hearts of Jews throughout the world were burning with a fierce flame of hatred against the abominations of a tyrannous idolatry; when Christians were being charged with 'turning the world upside-down;' [Acts xvii, 6]; when some poor Christian slave, led to martyrdom or put to the torture, might easily relieve the tension of his soul by bursting into apocalyptic denunciations of sudden doom against the crimes of the mystic Babylon; when the heathen, in their impatient contempt, might wilfully interpret a prophecy of the final conflagration as though it were a revolutionary and incendiary threat; and when Christians at Rome were, on this very account, already suffering the agonies

ot the Neronian persecution. Submission, therefore, was at this time a primary duty of all who wished to win over the heathen, and to save the Church from being overwhelmed in some outburst of indignation which would be justified even to reasonable and tolerant pagans as a political necessity. * * * 'Submit, therefore,' the apostle says, 'to every human ordinance, for the Lord's sake, whether to the emperor as supreme [the name "king" was freely used of the emperor in the provinces], or to governors, as missioned by him for punishment of malefactors and praise to well-doers; for this is the will of God, that by your well-doing ye should gag the stolid ignorance of foolish persons: as free, yet not using your freedom for a cloak of baseness, but as slaves of God. Honor all men' as a principle; and as your habitual practice, 'love the brotherhood. Fear God. Honor the King.'" [See I Peter ii, 13-17.]—Farrar, *Early Days of Christianity*, pp. 89-90.

3. The Law of God, and the Law of Man:—The teaching of the Church of Jesus Christ of Latter-day Saints respecting the duty of its members in obeying the laws of the land wherein they live, is more comprehensive and definite than is that of many other Christian sects. In January, 1899, an association of the free Evangelical churches of England officially published "a common statement of faith in the form of a new catechism." Touching the relation between church and state, the following formal questions and prescribed answers occur:—

"36. Q.—What is a free church? A.—A church which acknowledges none but Jesus Christ as Head, and, therefore, exercises its right to interpret and administer His laws without restraint or control by the state.

"37. Q.—What is the duty of the church to the state? A.—To observe all the laws of the state unless contrary to the teachings of Christ," etc.

According to the report of the committee in charge of the work of publication, the catechism "represents, directly or indirectly, the beliefs of not less, and probably many more, than sixty millions of avowed Christians in all parts of the world."

4. Discontinuance of Plural Marriage:—The official act terminating the practice of plural marriage among the Latter-day Saints was the adoption by the Church, in conference assembled, of a manifesto proclaimed by the President of the Church. The language of the document illustrates the law-abiding character of the people and the Church, as is shown by the following clause:—"Inasmuch as laws have been enacted by Congress forbidding plural marriages, which laws have been pronounced constitutional by the court of last resort, I [President Wilford Woodruff] hereby declare my intention to submit to those laws, and to use my influence with the members of the Church over which I preside to have them do likewise." In the course of a sermon immediately following the proclaiming of the manifesto, Prest. Woodruff said regarding the action taken: —"I have done my duty, and the nation of which we form a part must be responsible for that which has been done in relation to that principle," (i. e. plural marriage).

LECTURE XXIV.

PRACTICAL RELIGION.

Article 13:—We believe in being honest, true, chaste, benevolent, virtuous, and in doing good to all men; indeed, we may say that we follow the admonition of Paul,—We believe all things, we hope all things, we have endured many things, and hope to be able to endure all things. If there is anything virtuous, lovely, or of good report or praiseworthy, we seek after these things.

1. Religion of Daily Life:—In this article of their faith, the Latter-day Saints declare their acceptance of a practical religion; a religion that shall consist, not alone of professions in spiritual matters, and belief as to the conditions of the hereafter; of the doctrine of original sin and the actuality of a future heaven and hell; but also, and more particularly, of present and every-day duties, in which respect for self, love for fellow-men, and devotion to God, are the guiding principles. Religion without morality, professions of godliness without charity, church-membership without an adequate responsibility as to individual conduct in daily life, are but as sounding brass and tinkling cymbals;—noise without music, the words without the spirit of prayer. "Pure religion and undefiled before God and the Father is this, To visit the fatherless and widows in their affliction, and to keep himself unspotted from the world."[a] Honesty of purpose, integrity of soul, individual purity, absolute freedom of conscience, willingness to do good to all men even enemies, pure benevolence,—these are some of the fruits by which the religion of Christ may be known, far exceeding in importance and value the promulgation of dogmas, and the enunciation of theories. Yet a knowledge of things more than temporal, doctrines of spir-

---

a James i, 27.

itual matters, founded on revelation and not resting on the sands of man's frail hypotheses, are likewise characteristic of the true Church.

2. **The Comprehensiveness of Our Faith** must appeal to every earnest investigator of the principles taught by the Church, and still more to the unprejudiced observer of the results as manifested in the course of life character-istic of the Latter-day Saints. Within the pale of the Church, there is a place for all truth,—for everything that is praiseworthy, virtuous, lovely, or of good report. The liberality with which the Church regards other religious denominations; the earnestness of its teach-ing that God is no respecter of persons, but that He will judge all men according to their deeds; the breadth and depth of its precepts concerning the state of immortality, and the gradations of eternal glory awaiting the honest in heart of all nations, kindred, and churches, civilized and heathen, enlightened and benighted; have been set forth in preceding lectures. We have seen further, that the belief of this people carries them forward, even beyond the bounds of all knowledge thus far revealed, and teaches them to look with unwavering confidence for other revelation, truths yet to be added, glories grander than have yet been made known, eternities of powers, dominions, and progress, beyond the mind of man to conceive or the soul to contain. We believe in a God who is Himself progressive, whose majesty is intelligence; whose perfection con-sists in eternal advancement; the perpetual work of whose creation stands "finished, yet renewed forever;"[b] —a Being who has attained His exalted state by a path which now His children are permitted to follow; whose glory it is their heritage to share. In spite of the opposition of all other sects, in the face of direct charges of

[b] Bryant.

blasphemy, the Church proclaims the eternal truth, "*As man is, God once was; as God is, man may become.*" With such a future, well may man open his heart to the stream of revelation, past, present, and to come; and truthfully should we be able to say of every enlightened child of God, that he "Beareth all things, believeth all things, hopeth all things, endureth all things."[c] As incidental to the declaration of belief embodied in this article of faith, many topics relating to the organization, precepts, and practice of the Church, suggest themselves. Of these the following may claim our present attention.

3. **Benevolence:**—Benevolence is founded on love for fellow-men; it embraces, though it far exceeds charity, in the modern sense in which the latter word is used. By the Divine Teacher it was placed as second only to love for God. On one occasion, certain Pharisees came to Christ, tempting Him with questions on doctrine, in the hope that they could entangle Him, and so make Him an offender against the Jewish law. Their spokesman was a lawyer; note his question and the Savior's answer:—"Master, which is the great commandment in the law? Jesus said unto him, Thou shalt love the Lord thy God with all thy heart, and with all thy soul, and with all thy mind. This is the first and great commandment. And the second is like unto it, Thou shalt love thy neighbor as thyself. On these two commandments hang all the law and the prophets."[d] The two commandments, here spoken of as first and second, are so closely related as to be virtually one, and that one:—"Thou shalt love." He who abideth one of the two will abide both. And without love for our fellows, it is impossible to please God. Hence wrote John,—the Apostle of Love,—"Beloved, let us love one another: for love is of God; and every one that

c I Cor. xiii, 7.

d Matt. xxii, 36-40; see also Luke x, 25-27.

loveth is born of God, and knoweth God.   He that loveth not knoweth not God, for God is love.   *   *   *   If a man say, I love God, and hateth his brother, he is a liar; for he that loveth not his brother whom he hath seen, how can he love God whom he hath not seen?   And this commandment have we from him, That he who loveth God love his brother also."[e]

4.   But perhaps the grandest and most sublime of the apostolic utterances concerning the love that saves, is found in the epistle of Paul to the Saints at Corinth.[f]   In our current English translation of the Bible, the virtue which the apostle declares superior to all the miraculous gifts of the Spirit, and which is to continue after all the rest have passed away, is designated as *charity;* but the original word meant *love;* and surely Paul had in mind something grander than mere alms-giving, as is evident from his expression:—"And though I bestow all my goods to feed the poor,   *   *   *   and have not charity, it profiteth me nothing."[g]   Though a man speak with the tongue of angels; though he possess the power of prophecy—the greatest of the ordinary gifts; though he be versed in knowledge and understand all mysteries; though his faith enable him to move mountains; and though he give his all, including even his life,—yet without love is he nothing.   Charity, or alms-giving, even though it be performed with the sincerest of motives, devoid of all desire for praise or hope of return, is but a feeble manifestation of the love that is to make one's neighbor as dear to him as himself; the love that suffers long; that envies not others; that vaunts not itself; that knows no pride; that subdues selfishness; that rejoices in the truth.   When "that which is perfect" is come, the gifts which have been bestowed in part only will be superseded.

---

e I John iv, 7-8, 20-21.

f I Cor. xiii; see also Alma xxxiv, 28-29; Mosiah iv, 16-24.

g Verse 3.

"Perfection will then swallow up imperfection; the healing power will then be done away, for no sickness will be there; tongues and interpretations will then cease, for one pure language alone will be spoken; the casting out of devils and power against deadly poisons will not then be needed, for in heaven circumstances will render them unnecessary. But charity, which is the pure love of God, never faileth; it will sit enthroned in the midst of the glorified throng, clothed in all the glory and splendor of its native heaven."[h] If man would win eternal life, he cannot afford to neglect the duty of love to his fellow, for "Love is the fulfilling of the law."[i]

5. **Benevolence Manifested by the Church:**—The Church of the present day can point to a stupendous labor of benevolence already accomplished and still in progress. One of the most glorious monuments of its work is seen in the missionary labor which has ever been a characteristic feature of its existence. Actuated by no other motives than pure love for humanity and a desire to fulfil the commands of God respecting such, the Church sends out every year hundreds of missionaries to proclaim the gospel of eternal life to the world, without money or price. Multitudes of these devoted servants have suffered contumely and insult at the hands of those whom they seek to benefit; and not a few have given their lives with the seal of the martyr upon their testimony and work. The charity that manifests itself in material giving is not neglected in the Church; indeed this form of benevolence is impressed as a sacred duty upon every Latter-day Saint. While each one is urged to impart of his substance to the needy in his individual capacity, a system of orderly giving has been developed within the

h Orson Pratt, *Divine Authenticity of the Book of Mormon*, i, 15-16.
i Rom. xiii, 10; see also Gal. v, 14; I Peter iv, 8.

Church; and of this some features are worthy of special consideration.

6. **Free-will Offerings:**—It has ever been characteristic of the Church and people of God, that they take upon themselves the care of the poor, if any such exist among them. To subserve this purpose, as also to foster a spirit of liberality, kindness, and benevolence, voluntary gifts and free-will offerings have been asked of those who profess to be living according to the law of God. In the Church today, a systematic plan of giving for the poor is in operation. Thus, in almost every ward or branch, an organization among the women, known as the Relief Society,[j] is in existence. Its purpose is in part to gather from the society and from the members of the Church in general, contributions of .money and other property, particularly the commodities of life; and to distribute such to the deserving and needy, under the direction of the local officers in the priesthood. But the Relief Society operates also on a plan of systematic visitation to the houses of the afflicted, extending aid in nursing, administering comfort in bereavement, and seeking in every possible way to relieve distress. The good work of this organization has won the admiration of many who profess no connection with the Church; its methods have been followed by other benevolent associations, and the Society has been accorded a national status in the United States.

7. **The Fast Offerings** represent a still more general system of donation. The Church teaches the efficacy of continual prayer and of periodical fasting, as a means of acquiring the humility that is meet for Divine approval; and a monthly fast-day has been appointed for observance throughout the Church. For many years, the first Thursday in each month was so observed; but, with the object of secur-

---

j.See page 216.

ing a more general attendance at the fast-service, a benefi-
cial change has been introduced, and at present the first
Sunday of the month is so devoted. The Saints are asked
to manifest their sincerity in fasting, by making an offering
on that day for the benefit of the poor; and, by common
consent, the giving of at least an equivalent of the meals
omitted by the fasting of the family is expected. These
offerings may be made in money, food, or other usable com-
modity; they are received by the bishopric or its representatives, and by the same authority are distributed to the
worthy poor of the ward or branch. In these and in numerous other ways, do the Latter-day Saints contribute of
their substance to the needy, realizing that the poor among
them may be the Lord's poor; and that, irrespective of
worthiness on the part of the recipient, want and distress
must be alleviated. The people believe that the harmony
of their prayers will become a discord if the cry of the poor
accompany their supplications to the throne of Grace.

8. **Tithing:**—The Church recognizes today the doctrine of
tithe-paying, similar in its general provision to that taught
and practiced of old. Before considering the present
authorized practice in this matter, it may be instructive to
study the ancient practice of tithe-paying. Strictly speaking, a tithe is a tenth, and such a proportion of individual
possessions appears to have been formerly regarded as the
Lord's due. The institution of tithing ante-dates even the
Mosaic dispensation, for we find both Abraham and Jacob
paying tithes. Abraham, returning from a victorious battle,
met Melchisedek king of Salem and "priest of the most
high God;" and, recognizing his priestly authority, "gave him
tithes of all."[k] Jacob made a voluntary vow with the Lord to
render a tenth of all that should come into his possession.[l]

---

k Gen. xiv, 18-20; see also Heb. vii, 1-3, 5, and Alma xiii, 13-16.

l Gen. xxviii, 22.

9.   The Mosaic statutes are explicit in requiring tithes:—
"And all the tithe of the land, whether of the seed of the
land, or of the fruit of the tree, is the Lord's; it is holy
unto the Lord.   *   *   *   And concerning the tithe of the
herd, even of whatsoever passeth under the rod, the tenth
shall be holy unto the Lord."[m]   The tenth was to be paid
as it came, without search for good or bad; under some conditions, however, a man could redeem the tithe by paying its
value in some other way, but in such a case he had to add a
fifth of the tithe.   The tenth of all the property in Israel was
to be paid to the Levites, as an inheritance given in acknowledgment of their service in the labor of the tabernacle; and
they in turn were to pay tithing on what they received, and
this tithe of the tithe was to go to the priests.[n]   A second
tithe was demanded of Israel to be used for the appointed
festivals.[o]   It is evident, that while no specific penalty for
neglect of the law of tithing is recorded, the proper observance of the requirement was regarded as a sacred duty.   In
the course of the reformation by Hezekiah, the people
manifested their repentance by an immediate payment of
tithes;[p] and so liberally did they give, that a great surplus
accumulated; observing which, Hezekiah enquired as to the
source of such plenty:—"And Azariah the chief priest of
the house of Zadok answered him, and said, since the people
began to bring the offerings into the house of the Lord, we
have had enough to eat, and have left plenty: for the Lord
hath blessed his people; and that which is left is this great
store."   Nehemiah took care to regulate the tithe-paying of
the people;[r] and both Amos[s] and Malachi[t] chided the people

m Lev. xxvii, 30-34.
n Numb. xviii, 21-28.
o Deut. xii, 5-17; xiv, 22-23.
p II Chron. xxxi, 5-6.
r Neh. x, 37; xii, 44.
s Amos iv, 4.
t Mal. iii, 10.

for their neglect of this duty. Through the prophet last
named, the Lord charged the people with having robbed
Him; but promised them blessings beyond their capacity to
receive if they would return to their allegiance to Him:
"Will a man rob God? Yet ye have robbed me. But ye
say, Wherein have we robbed thee? In tithes and offerings.
Ye are cursed with a curse: for ye have robbed me, even
this whole nation. Bring ye all the tithes into the storehouse, that there may be meat in mine house, and prove
me now herewith, saith the Lord of hosts, if I will not open
you the windows of heaven, and pour you out a blessing, that
there shall not be room enough to receive it."[u]   In visiting
the Nephites after His resurrection, the Savior told them of
these sayings of Malachi, repeating the words of the Jewish
prophet.[v] The Pharisees, at the time of Christ's ministry,
were particularly scrupulous in the matter of tithe paying,—
even to the neglect of the "weightier matters of the law,"—
and for this inconsistency they were severely rebuked by the
Master.[w]

10. In the present dispensation, the law of tithing has
been given a place of great importance; and particular blessings have been promised for its faithful observance.   This
day has been called by the Lord, "a day of sacrifice, and a
day for the tithing of my people; for he that is tithed shall
not be burned."[x] In a revelation, given through the Prophet
Joseph Smith, July 8, 1838, the Lord has explicitly set
forth His requirement of the people in this matter.[y]

11. **Consecration and Stewardship:**—The law of tithing,
as accepted and professedly observed by the Church today,
is after all but a lesser law, given by the Lord in consequence

---

u Mal. iii, 8-10; see also III Nephi xxiv, 7-12.

v III Nephi xxiv, 7-10.

w Matt. xxiii, 23; Luke xi, 42.

x Doc. and Cov. lxiv, 23-24; see also lxxxv, 3.

y Doc. and Cov. cxix.

of the human weaknesses, selfishness, covetousness, and
greed, which prevented the Saints from accepting the higher
principles, according to which the Father would have His
children live.   Specific requirements regarding the payment of tithes were made through revelation in 1838; but
seven years prior to that time, the voice of the Lord had
been heard on the subject of consecration,[z] or the dedication of all one's property, together with his time, talents,
and natural endowments, to the service of God, to be used
as occasion may require.   This again is not new; to the
present dispensation the law of consecration is given as a
re-enactment; it was recognized and observed with profit
in olden times.[a]   But even in the apostolic period, the doctrine of consecration of property and common ownership
was old; thirty-four centuries before that time, the same
principle had been practiced by the patriarch Enoch and
his people, and with such success that "the Lord came and
dwelt with His people;   *   *   *   And the Lord called His
people Zion, because they were of one heart and one mind,
and dwelt in righteousness; and there was no poor among
them."[b]   In each of the instances cited,—that of the people
of Enoch, and that of the Saints in the early part of the
Christian era, we learn of the unity of purpose and consequent power acquired by the people who lived in this social
order; they were "of one heart and one mind."   Through
the spiritual strength so attained, the apostles were able to
perform many mighty works;[c] and of Enoch and his followers we read that the Lord took them unto Himself.[d]

12.   The people of whom the Book of Mormon gives us
record also attained to the blessed state of equality, and

z Doc. and Cov. xlii, 71.

a Acts iv, 32, 34-35; see also ii, 44-46.

b Pearl of Great Price, Writings of Moses, p. 37, (1888 ed.)

c Acts ii, 43.

d See pp. 362-363.

with corresponding results. The disciples, whom Christ had personally commissioned, taught with power, and, "they had all things common among them, every man dealing justly, one with another."[e] Further, we read of a general conversion by which the people came to a condition of ideal peace; "there were no contentions or disputations among them * * * And they had all things common among them, therefore they were not rich and poor, bond and free, but they were all made free, and partakers of the heavenly gift."[f] They were so blessed, that of them the prophet said:—"Surely there could not be a happier people among all the people who had been created by the hand of God."[g] But after nearly two centuries of this happy condition, the people gave way to pride; some of them yielded to a passion for costly apparel; then they refused to longer have their goods in common; and straightway many classes came into existence; dissenting sects were established; and then began a rapid course of disruption, which led to the extinction of the Nephite nation.[h]

13. **Stewardship in the Church today:**—A system of unity in temporal matters has been revealed to the Church in this day; such is currently known as the Order of Enoch,[i] or the United Order,[j] and is founded on the law of consecration. As already stated, in the early days of the modern Church the people demonstrated their inability to abide this law in its fulness, and, in consequence, the lesser law of tithing was given; but the Saints confidently await the day in which they will devote, not merely a tithe of their sub-

---

e III Nephi xxvi, 19.
f IV Nephi i, 2-3.
g Verse 16.
h Verse 24, etc.
i Doc. and Cov lxxviii.
j Doc. and Cov. civ, 48.

stance, but all that they have, and all that they are, to the
service of their God; a day in which no man will speak of
mine and thine, but all things shall be theirs and the
Lord's.

14. In this expectation, they indulge no vague dream of
communism, encouraging individual irresponsibility, and
giving the idler an excuse for hoping to live at the expense
of the thrifty; but rather, a calm trust that in the promised social order which God can approve, every man will be
a steward in the full enjoyment of liberty to do as he will
with the talents committed to his care; but with the sure
knowlege that an account of his stewardship will be required at his hands.   As far as the plan of this prospective
organization has been revealed, it provides that a person
entering the order shall consecrate to the Lord all that he
has, be it little or much, giving to the Church a deed of
his property sealed with a covenant that cannot be broken.[k]
The person thus having given his all, is to be made a steward over a part of the property of the Church, according
to his ability to use it.   The varying grades of occupation
will still exist; there will be laborers, whose qualifications
fit them best for common toil; and managers who have
proved their ability to lead and direct; some who can serve
the cause of God best with the pen, others with the plow;
there will be engineers and mechanics, artisans and artists,
farmers and scholars, teachers, professors, and authors;—
every one laboring as far as practicable in the sphere of his
choice, but each required to work, and to work where and
how he can be of the greatest service.   His stewardship is
to be assured him by written deed, and as long as he is
faithful to his charge, no man can take it from him.[l]   Of
the proceeds of his labors, every man will use as he may

k Doc. and Cov., xlii, 30.
l Doc. and Cov., li, 4-5.

require for the support of himself and his family; the surplus is to be rendered to the Church for public and general works, and for the assistance of those who are worthily deficient.[m] As further illustrative of the uses to which the surplus is to be devoted, we read:—"All children have claim upon their parents for their maintenance until they are of age. And after that they have claim upon the Church, or in other words, upon the Lord's storehouse, if their parents have not wherewith to give them inheritances. And the storehouse shall be kept by the consecrations of the Church, and widows and orphans shall be provided for, as also the poor.[n] Any faithful steward, requiring additional capital for the improvement of his work, has a claim for such upon the custodians of the general fund, they in turn being held accountable for their management, which constitutes their stewardship.[o] Equal rights are to be secured to all. The Lord said:—"And you are to be equal, or, in other words, you are to have equal claims on the properties, for the benefit of managing the concerns of your stewardships, every man according to his wants, and his needs, inasmuch as his wants are just; and all this for the benefit of the Church of the living God, that every man may improve upon his talent, that every man may gain other talents, yea, even an hundred fold, to be cast into the Lord's storehouse, to become the common property of the whole church."[p]

15. Freedom of agency is to be secured to every individual; if he be unfaithful he will be dealt with according to the prescribed rules of church discipline. A corresponding power of self-government will be exercised by the several stakes or other branches of the Church, each having inde-

m Doc. and Cov. xlii, 32-35.

n Doc. and Cov. lxxxiii, 4-6.

o Doc. and Cov. civ, 70-77.

p Doc. and. Cov. lxxxii, 17-18.

pendent jurisdiction over its own store-houses and its affairs of administration,[q] all being subject to the general authorities of the Church. Only the idler would suffer in such an order as is here outlined; he shall surely meet the results of his negligence. Against him the edict of the Almighty has gone forth. We read in the revelations:—"Thou shalt not be idle; for he that is idle shall not eat the bread nor wear the garments of the laborer."[r] "The idler shall not have place in the church except he repents and mends his ways."[s] "And the inhabitants of Zion, also, shall remember their labors, inasmuch as they are appointed to labor in all faithfulness; for the idler shall be had in remembrance before the Lord."[t]

16. **Social Order of the Saints:**—In view of the prevailing conditions of social unrest, of the loud protest against existing systems, whereby the distribution of wealth is becoming more and more unequal,—the rich growing richer from the increasing poverty of the poor, the hand of oppression resting more and more heavily upon the masses, the consequent dissatisfaction with governments, and the half-smothered fires of anarchy discernible in almost every nation,—may we not take comfort in the God-given promise of a better plan?—a plan which seeks without force or violence to establish a natural equality, to take the weapons of despotism from the rich, to aid the lowly and the poor,[u] and to give every man an opportunity to live and to labor in the sphere to which he is adapted. From the tyranny of wealth, as from every other form of oppression, the truth will make men free. To be partakers of such freedom, mankind must

---

q Doc. and Cov. li, 10-13, 18.
r Doc. and Cov. xlii, 42; see also lx, 13; lxxv, 3.
s Doc. and Cov. lxxv, 29.
t Doc. and Cov. lxviii, 30; see also lxxxviii, 124.
u Doc. and Cov. xlii, 39.

subdue selfishness, which is one of the most potent enemies of godliness.

17. The Church teaches the necessity of proper social organization, in harmony with the laws of the land; the sanctity of the institution and covenant of marriage as essential to the stability of society; the fulfilment of the Divine law with respect to the perpetuation of the human family; and the importance of strictest personal purity.

18. **Marriage:**—The teachings of the scriptures concerning the necessity of marriage are numerous and explicit. "The Lord God said, It is not good that the man should be alone;"[v] this comprehensive declaration was made concerning Adam, immediately after his location in Eden; Eve was given unto him, and the man recognized the necessity of a continued association of the sexes in marriage, and said:— "Therefore shall a man leave his father and his mother, and shall cleave unto his wife; and they shall be one flesh."[w] Neither of the sexes is complete in itself as a counterpart of God. Of the creation of human kind we read:— "So God created man in his own image, in the image of God created he him; male and female created he them."[x] The purpose of this dual creation is set forth in the next verse of the sacred narrative:—"And God blessed them; and God said unto them, Be fruitful and multiply and replenish the earth."[y] Such a command would have been meaningless and void if addressed to either of the sexes alone; for only by the union of both is the propagation of the species possible. And without the power of perpetuating his kind, how insignificant would appear the glory and majesty of man! How little can be accom-

---

v Gen. ii, 18.

w Verse 24.

x Gen. i, 27; see also v, 2.

y Verse 28; see also ix, 1, 7; Lev. xxvi, 9.

plished by the individual within the limited range of a single mortal existence!

19. Grand as may seem the achievements of a man who is truly great, the culmination of his glorious heritage lies in the possibility of his leaving offspring from his own being to continue, perchance, the triumphs of their sire. And if such be true of mortals with respect to the things of earth, how transcendently greater is the power of eternal increase, as viewed in the light of revealed truth concerning the un-ending progression of the future state! Truly the apostle was wise when he said, "Neither is the man without the woman, neither the woman without the man, in the Lord."[z]

20. The Latter-day Saints accept the doctrine that marriage is honorable,[a] and apply it as a requirement to all who are not prevented by physical or other disability from assuming the sacred responsibilities of the wedded state. They consider, as part of the birthright of every worthy man, the privilege and duty to stand as the head of a household, the father of a posterity, which by the blessing of God shall never become extinct; and equally strong is the right of every worthy woman to be a wife and a mother in the family of mankind.   In spite of the simplicity, reasonableness, and naturalness of these teachings, false teachers have arisen among men, declaring the pernicious doctrine that the married state is but a carnal necessity, inherited by man as an incident of his degraded nature; and that celibacy is a mark of a higher state, more acceptable in the pure sight of God.   Concerning such the Lord has spoken in this day:—"Whoso forbiddeth to marry is not ordained of God, for marriage is ordained of God unto man   *   *   *   that the earth might answer the end of its creation; and that it

z I Cor. xi, 11.
a Heb. xiii. 4.

might be filled with the measure of man, according to his creation before the world was made."[b]

21. **Celestial Marriage:**—Marriage, as regarded by the Latter-day Saints, is ordained of God and designed to be an eternal relationship of the sexes. With this people it is not merely a temporal contract to be of effect on earth during the mortal existence of the parties, but a solemn agreement which is to extend beyond the grave. In the complete ceremony of marriage, as prescribed by the Church, the man and the woman are placed under covenant of mutual fidelity, not "until death do you part," but "for time and for all eternity." A contract as far reaching as this, extending not only throughout time, but into the domain of the hereafter, requires for its validation an authority superior to that of earth; and such an authority is found in the holy priesthood, which, given of God, is eternal. Any power less than this, while perchance of effect in this life, will surely be void as to the state of the human soul beyond the grave. As the Lord has said:—"All covenants, contracts, bonds, obligations, oaths, vows, performances, connections, associations, or expectations, that are not made, and entered into, and sealed, by the Holy Spirit of promise, of him who is anointed, both as well for time and for all eternity, and that too most holy, by revelation, and commandment, through the medium of mine anointed, whom I have appointed on the earth to hold this power, * * * * are of no efficacy, virtue, or force, in and after the resurrection from the dead; for all contracts that are not made unto this end, have an end when men are dead."[c] And, as touching the application of the principle of earthly authority for things of earth, and eternal authority for things beyond the grave, to the sacred contract of marriage, the

b Doc. and Cov. xlix, 15-17.

c Doc. and Cov. cxxxii, 7.

revelation continues:—"Therefore, if a man marry him a wife in the world, and he marry her not by me, nor by my word, and he covenant with her so long as he is in the world, and she with him, their covenant and marriage are not of force when they are dead, and when they are out of the world; therefore they are not bound by any law when they are out of the world; Therefore, when they are out of the world, they neither marry, nor are given in marriage; but are appointed angels in heaven, which angels are ministering servants, to minister for those who are worthy of a far more, and an exceeding, and an eternal weight of glory; For these angels did not abide my law, therefore they cannot be enlarged, but remain separately and singly, without exaltation in their saved condition, to all eternity, and from henceforth are not Gods, but are angels of God, for ever and ever."[d]

22.   This system of holy matrimony, involving covenants as to time and eternity, is known distinctively as Celestial Marriage,—the order of marriage that exists in the celestial worlds.   The sacred ordinance of celestial marriage is permitted to those members of the Church only who are adjudged worthy of participation in the special blessings of the House of the Lord; for this ordinance, together with others of eternal validity, is to be performed in the temples which are reared and dedicated for such holy service.[e] Children, who are born of parents thus married, are natural heirs to the priesthood; "children of the covenant" they are called; they require no ceremony of adoption or sealing to insure them place in the posterity of promise.   But the Church sanctions marriages for earthly time only, and bestows upon such the seal of the priesthood, among those who are

---

d Doc. and Cov. cxxxii, 15-17.
e Doc. and Cov. cxxiv, 30-40.

not admitted to the temples of the Lord, or who voluntarily prefer the lesser and temporal order of matrimony.

23. Unlawful Associations of the Sexes have been designated by the Lord as among the most heinous of sins; and the Church today regards individual purity in the sexual relation as an indispensable condition of membership. The teachings of the Nephite prophet, Alma, concerning the enormity of offences against virtue and chastity, are accepted by the Latter-day Saints without modification; and such are to the effect:—"That these things are an abomination in the sight of the Lord; yea, most abominable above all sins, save it be the shedding of innocent blood, or denying the Holy Ghost."*f* The command:—"Thou shalt not commit adultery,"—once written by the finger of God amid the thunders and lightnings of Sinai, has been renewed as a specific injunction in these the last days; and the penalty of excommunication has been prescribed for the offender.*g* Moreover, the Lord regards any approach to sexual sin as inconsistent with the professions of those who have received the Holy Spirit, for he has declared that "he that looketh on a woman to lust after her, or if any shall commit adultery in their hearts, they shall not have the Spirit, but shall deny the faith."*h*

24. Sanctity of the Body:— The Church counsels its members that each regard his body as "the temple of God;"*i* and that he maintain its purity and sanctity as such. He is taught that the Spirit of the Lord dwells not in unclean tabernacles; and that, therefore, he is required to live according to the laws of health, which constitute part of the law of God. For the special guidance of His Saints,

---

f Alma xxxix, 5.

g Doc. and Cov. xlii, 24, 80-83; lxiii, 16-17.

h Doc. and Cov. lxiii, 16: see also xlii, 23.

i I Cor. iii, 16.

the Lord has revealed a "Word of Wisdom"[j] unto the
people; in accordance with which they are counseled to eat
wholesome food only; to abstain from strong drink, hot
drinks, and all kinds of stimulants and narcotics; to eat
flesh but sparingly, and to maintain in all respects a healthful state of the physical organism. And, on condition of
their compliance with these behests, the Saints have been
promised, that all "Who remember to keep and do these
sayings, walking in obedience to the commandments, shall
receive health in their navel, and marrow in their bones,
and shall find wisdom and great treasures of knowledge,
even hidden treasures; and shall run and not be weary, and
shall walk and not faint; And I, the Lord, give unto them
a promise, that the destroying angel shall pass by them, as
the children of Israel."[k]

NOTES.

1. **Love, the Fulfiling of the Law:**—"Peter says, 'Above all things have
fervent love [charity] among yourselves.' [I Peter iv, 8]. *Above all things.* And
John goes farther, 'God is love.' [I John iv, 8]. And you remember the profound
remark which Paul makes elsewhere, 'Love is the fulfiling of the law.' [Rom.
xiii, 10; Gal. v, 14.] Did you ever think what he meant by that? In those days
men were working their passage to heaven by keeping the ten commandments,
and the hundred and ten other commandments which they had manufactured out
of them. Christ said, I will show you a more simple way. If you do one thing,
you will do these hundred and ten things without ever thinking about them. If
you love, you will unconsciously fulfil the whole law. * * * * Take any of the
commandments, 'Thou shalt have no other gods before me.' If a man love God
you will not require to tell him that. Love is the fulfiling of that law. 'Take not
his name in vain.' Would he ever dream of taking his name in vain if he loved
him? 'Remember the Sabbath day to keep it holy.' Would he not be too glad
to have one day in seven to dedicate more exclusively to the object of his affection? Love would fulfil all these laws regarding God. And so if he loved man,
you would never think of telling him to honor his father and mother. He could
never do anything else. It would be preposterous to tell him not to kill. You
could only insult him if you suggested that he should not steal,—how could he
steal from those he loved? It would be superfluous to beg him not to bear false

---

[j] Doc. and Cov. lxxxix; read the revelation entire.

[k] Doc. and Cov. lxxxix, 18-21.

witness against his neighbor. If he loved him it would be the last thing he would do. And you would never dream of urging him not to covet what his neighbors had. He would rather they possessed it than himself. In this way 'Love is the fulfiling of the law.' "—Drummond—*The Greatest Thing in the World.*

2. **Charity and Love:**—"According to the etymology and original usage, *beneficence* is the doing well, *benevolence* the wishing or willing well to others; but *benevolence* has come to include *beneficence* and to displace it. * * * *Charity* which originally meant the love for God and man (as in I Cor. xiii) is now almost universally applied to some form of *alms-giving* and is much more limited in meaning than *benevolence.*"—*Standard Dictionary.*

Charity means "properly, love, and hence acts of kindness. The word never occurs in the Old Testament; in the New Testament it is always, with one exception, synonymous with love, and in every case the love of man toward his fellow man, and to that which is good (see especially I Cor. xiii.) The 'feasts of charity' in Jude 12, are commonly understood to be the *agapæ*, or 'love-feasts,' which were prevalent in the early church, and which consisted in a simple fraternal meeting for worship, and an equally simple social repast."—*Bible Dictionary*, Cassell.

"Charity is only a little bit of love; one of the innumerable avenues of love, and there may even be, and there is, a great deal of charity without love. It is a very easy thing to toss a copper to a beggar on the street; it is generally an easier thing than not to do it. * * * We purchase relief from the sympathetic feelings roused by the spectacle of misery, at the copper's cost, It is too cheap— too cheap for us, and often too dear for the beggar. If we really loved him, we would either do more for him or less."—Drummond:—*The Greatest Theory in the World.*

APPENDIX.

Note:—In view of the expressed wish of the Church authorities by whose direction this work is published,—that the Lectures on the "Articles of Faith," be used as a text-book and work of reference in the various theological organizations of the Church, a series of questions and suggestive exercises, for the work of class review, is herewith presented.

LECTURE I.

INTRODUCTORY.

1. What is Theology? (State, 1, derivation of the word; 2, extent of the science.)

2. Compare Theology and Religion.

3. Define the "Articles of Faith." (Give:—1, circumstance of their origin, see note, p. 24; 2, their re-adoption by the Church; 3, their necessary incompleteness as an expression of our belief.)

4. Name the standard works of the Church.

5. State the principal incidents connected with the parentage, birth, and youth of the Prophet Joseph Smith.

6. Give the circumstances of Joseph Smith's prayerful search for truth.

7. Describe his first vision.

8. What prominent feature of modern sectarian teaching, regarding the personality of the Father and His Son, Jesus Christ, was disproved by this vision?

9. How was Joseph's statement of his vision received by sectarian teachers of that time?

10. Describe the visitations of Moroni to Joseph Smith. (Give:—1, dates; 2, most important messages delivered by the angel.)

11. Describe the re-establishment of the Church through the ministry of Joseph Smith in the present dispensation.

12. Relate the circumstances of the martyrdom of Joseph and his brother Hyrum.—(Doc. and Cov. cxxxv.)

13. Show the importance of the Divine authenticity of Joseph Smith's calling, in respect to the claims made for the Church of Jesus Christ of Latter-day Saints.

14. Summarize the evidence of Divine authority in the work accomplished by Joseph Smith.

15. Give instances of the fulfilment of ancient prophecy in his work.

16. Show the Divine source of Joseph Smith's authority in the priesthood.

17. Show the validity of the claim made, that he was a true prophet. (Give:—1, the Lord's test of a true prophet; 2, give instances of important prophecies uttered by Joseph Smith and already fulfilled.)

LECTURE II, ARTICLE 1.

GOD AND THE GODHEAD.

1. Show that the exercise of faith in God is dependent upon a knowledge of His existence.

2. State what you know of the general belief of mankind as to the existence of God.

3. Summarize the evidence on which our belief in the existence of God is founded.

4. Give evidence drawn from human history and tradition.

5. Show how the exercise of reason affords evidence of the same.

6. Give the evidence of revelation. (1, Instances recorded in the Bible; 2, Book of Mormon instances; 3, examples from modern revelation.)

7. Show that the Godhead is a Trinity.

8. What do you understand by the scriptural declarations concerning the unity of the Godhead?

9. Give evidence of the personality of each member of the Godhead (with scriptural references).

10. Summarize the most important of the Divine attributes as attested by scripture.

11. Define:—1, Idolatry; 2, Atheism; 3, Theism, with its varied modifications.

12. Show that atheism is of comparatively modern development.

13. Show that a belief in God is natural and necessary amongst human-kind. (See pp. 49, 53.)

14. In what way does the idolatry of heathen nations support a belief in the existence of God?

15. Show the close relationship between atheism and immaterialism.

LECTURE III, ARTICLE 2.

TRANSGRESSION.

1. Give the principal scriptural proofs of man's free agency (quote evidence from each of the standard works of the Church.)

2. Show that man's accountability for his acts is just, in view of his rights of free agency.

3. What is sin? (1, Compare wilful sins with those committed in ignorance; 2, give scriptural evidence of the Lord's plan of dealing in the two cases.)

4. Show that punishment for sin is ordained of God.

5. Give a statement of scriptural teachings regarding the duration of punishment in the hereafter. (State the Lord's definition of endless and eternal punishment.)

6. Give scriptural proofs of the personality of Satan. (1, His former position in heaven; 2, his title before his fall; 3, his expulsion from heaven; 4, his present opposition to the purposes of God; 5, his predicted fate.)

THE FALL.

7. Describe the condition of our first parents in Eden.

8. What important commands were given them by the Lord?

9. Give the scriptural statements concerning Satan tempting Eve.

10. Show that Adam understood the nature of his act in partaking of the forbidden fruit.

11. What is known of the Tree of Life in the Garden of Eden?

31

12. Show that the expulsion of our first parents from Eden was a necessity after their transgression.

13. What were the immediate results of the Fall?

14. Give scriptural proof that the Fall was necessary and fore-ordained.

15. Show that mortality is a blessed heritage to mankind.

16. State the doctrine of the Atonement as declared to Adam after the Fall.

17. Describe the joy of Adam and Eve when they learned of the effect of the Fall and the Atonement provided.

LECTURE IV, ARTICLE 3.

THE ATONEMENT AND SALVATION.

1. Define "atonement" in its scriptural usage. (Compare its meaning with that of "reconciliation," as the latter term occurs in the New Testament.)

2. State what you know of the nature of the Atonement.

3. Show that the Atonement is a necessary sequence of the Fall.

4. What is meant by a vicarious sacrifice? (Give scriptural instances of such as recorded in the Old Testament.)

5. Show that Christ's sacrifice was, 1, vicarious; 2, voluntary on His part; 3, love-inspired.

6. Give scriptural proofs (from each of the standard works) that the Atonement was fore-ordained, and foretold.

7. Show:—1, the general, and 2, the individual effect, of the Atonement amongst mankind.

8. Define:—1, "salvation;" 2, "exaltation."

9. Name the "Degrees of Glory" in their order, as revealed of God.

10. Give a summary of the scriptural descriptions of:— 1, the Celestial kingdom or glory; 2, the Terrestrial; 3, the Telestial.

LECTURE V, ARTICLE 4.

FAITH.

1. State the nature of faith.

2. Define the terms "faith," "belief" and "knowledge," in their relation to one another.

3. Give scriptural instances of belief in Christ, which had no saving power.

4. What do you regard as the essential foundation of faith in God?

5. Give Joseph Smith's summary of facts respecting the character and attributes of God.

6. Show how misplaced faith may result from false evidence.

7. What is meant by the statement that faith is a principle of power? (Give scriptural instances).

8. Prove that faith is essential to salvation.

9. Show from the scriptures that faith is a gift from God.

10. Show that faith, to be effective must be accompanied by good works.

REPENTANCE.

11. What is meant by true repentance?

12. State the conditions under which forgiveness of sins is promised.

13. Prove that repentance is essential to salvation.

14. Show that repentance is a gift from God.

15. How may this gift be lost or forfeited?

16. What evidence have we that repentance is possible in the hereafter?

17. Give a summary of the teachings of Amulek regarding the danger of procrastination in the matter of repentance.

LECTURES VI AND VII, ARTICLE 4.

BAPTISM.

1. State what you know of the earliest revelation from God regarding baptism.

2. What is the special purpose of baptism? (Give proofs, 1, from the Bible; 2, from the Book of Mormon; 3, from modern revelation.)

3. Who are fit subjects for Baptism?

4. Show that infant baptism is unscriptural. (1, That it is unsustained by the Bible; 2, that it is forbidden in the Book of Mormon, and by modern revelation.)

5. Give a brief account of the history of infant baptism.

6. Define:—"Pedobaptists;" "Anabaptists."(Give derivation of the terms and their present meanings.)

7. Prove by scriptural evidence that baptism is essential to salvation; (1, from the Bible; 2, from the Book of Mormon; 3, from the Doctrine and Covenants.)

8. Why was Christ's baptism a necessity?

9. Give a summary of the reasons upon which the Latter-day Saints base their belief that immersion is the only true mode of baptism.

10. Show what evidence is furnished by the derivation of the word "baptize," and its early usage.

11. Show how the symbolism of the baptismal rite is best preserved by immersion.

12. Give scriptural and other historical evidence that immersion is the only form sanctioned by the Lord.

13. Give the revealed formula for baptism; (1, among the Nephites; 2, in the present dispensation).

14. Under what conditions may baptism be repeated on the same person?

15. Give instances of "re-baptism" mentioned in scripture, and allowed in the present dispensation, showing the special or exceptional nature of such repetitions of the ordinance.

16. Show the impropriety of repeated baptisms of the same person.

17. Demonstrate the necessity of baptism for the dead.

18. What evidence have we that the gospel is preached to the dead?

19. Cite scriptural predictions of Christ's ministry amongst the dead.

20. Prove that the vicarious work of the living for the dead in the last dispensation was foretold.

21. Show that the authority for this labor has been already given to the Church.

22. Explain the two-fold nature of this vicarious labor for the dead.

23. What is a temple?

24. Give a brief account of ancient temples accepted by the Lord.

25. Describe the work of temple-building already accomplished by the Church in the present dispensation.

LECTURE VIII, ARTICLE 4.

THE HOLY GHOST.

1. Cite biblical promises concerning the advent of the Holy Ghost.

2. Give other scriptural proof, (1, from the Book of Mormon; 2, from the record of modern revelation), that the Holy Ghost is to minister unto all who have been properly baptized.

3. Give the principal names and titles by which the Holy Ghost is described in scripture.

4. What is the special office of the Holy Ghost as a member of the Godhead?

5. Give scriptural proofs of the Holy Ghost's personality.

6. Describe the office of the Holy Ghost in His ministrations among men.

7. To whom is the Holy Ghost promised?

8. Give instances of the Holy Ghost's ministrations unto sincere believers who had not been baptized; explain such exceptional instances.

9. Describe the ordinance of conferring the Holy Ghost in the case of those who have been baptized.

10. Show that the authoritative laying-on of hands was a feature of the ordinance in former days; (1, among the Jews; 2, among the Nephites.)

11. To which order of priesthood does the authority to confer the Holy Ghost belong? (Give scriptural proofs.)

12. Show that the imposition of hands by those in authority is characteristic of other ordinances in the Church.

13. What is meant by "Gifts of the Spirit?"

LECTURE IX, IN CONNECTION WITH ARTICLE 4.

THE SACRAMENT OF THE LORD'S SUPPER.

1. Define the term "sacrament" in its general and specific uses.

2. Describe the institution of the Sacrament by the Savior, (1, among the Jews; 2, among the Nephites.)

3. Who are fit partakers of the Sacrament?

4. Cite scriptural caution, 1, against partaking of the Sacrament unworthily; 2, against knowingly administering it to the unfit.

5. What is the purpose of the Sacrament?

6. What did Christ administer as the emblems of His body and blood?

7. What justification has the Church for using water instead of wine under certain conditions?

8. Give the prescribed prayers of consecration; 1, for the bread; 2, for the wine or water.

9. What grade of authority in the priesthood is requisite in consecrating the sacramental emblems?

10. What relationship exists between the Sacrament and the Jewish Passover?

Lecture X, Article 5.

AUTHORITY IN THE MINISTRY.

1. Give scriptural examples of men who were called of God by special revelation or by personal ministration: 1, before the "Meridian of Time;" 2, in the days of Christ; 3, in the apostolic period; 4, in the "Dispensation of the Fulness of Times."

2. In what manner is the priesthood conferred?

3. Name the principal holders of the priesthood from Adam to Moses.

4. Cite instances of God's disapproval of unauthorized ministrations. (Give the circumstances in the following cases; 1, Korah and his associates; 2, Miriam and Aaron; 3, Uzza; 4, Saul; 5, Uzziah; 6, sons of Sceva.)

5. Give scriptural predictions concerning false teachers who would arise.

6. Prove the existence of the priesthood in the Church today.

7. Give an account of the restoration of 1, the Aaronic, and, 2, the Melchisedek priesthood, in the present dispensation.

FORE-ORDINATION AND PRE-EXISTENCE.

8. How was the fact of fore-ordination made known to Abraham?

9. Give scriptural proofs of Christ's fore-ordination as the Redeemer of mankind.

10. Cite other scriptures supporting the doctrine of fore-ordination. (1, New Testament; 2, Book of Mormon.)

11. Show that fore-ordination does not infringe upon free agency.

12. Give scriptural proofs of the pre-existence of spirits.

LECTURE XI, ARTICLE 6.

CHURCH ORGANIZATION.

1. What is the Church? (Sustain your definition by scriptural records.)

2. What is meant by the Primitive Church?

3. What evidence have you that a general apostasy from the Primitive Church occurred?

4. Show by the scriptures that this apostasy was foretold. (Give evidence, 1, from the Old Testament; 2, from the New Testament; 3, from the Book of Mormon.)

5. Show that the restoration of the Church to earth was foretold.

6. Define "priesthood."

7. Name the principal orders of priesthood as revealed.

8. What relationship exists between the Aaronic and the Levitical priesthood?

9. Name the special offices in the Aaronic priesthood in order, with a statement of the specific duties and authority of each.

10. Name the special offices in the Melchisedek priesthood, in order, describing the authority and duties of each.

11. Describe the constitution and authority of each of the following presiding "quorums" in the priesthood:—1, The First Presidency; 2, The Quorum of the Twelve Apostles; 3, The Presiding Quorum of Seventy; 4, The Presiding Bishopric.

12. Define "branch," "ward," and "stake," as used to designate divisions of the Church.

13. Explain the constitution, authority and special duties of:—1, Stake Presidency; 2, Standing High Council; 3, Ward Bishopric.

14.   What ordination in the priesthood is requisite in the case of members of the presiding organizations last named?

15.   Define "quorum" in its special sense as used by the Latter-day Saints.

16.   What is a Patriarch? (1. Define in this connection the term "evangelist;" 2, show in what respect succession to the presiding patriarchal office differs from that in other offices and callings in the priesthood.)

17.   Name the auxiliary organizations which operate as "helps in government" within the Church.

18.   Give the special duties of each of these.   (Named on p. 216.)

19.   Show how the principle of common consent is observed in appointments to office within the Church.

LECTURE XII, ARTICLE 7.

SPIRITUAL GIFTS.

1.   Show that the existence of spiritual gifts has ever been characteristic of the priesthood.

2.   Give scriptural proof that such gifts will always be found in the Church.

3.   What is a miracle?

4.   Why are miracles called by some, supernatural occurrences?

5.   For what purpose are spiritual gifts manifested in the Church?

6.   Show that miraculous manifestations are not an infallible indication of the operation of the priesthood.

7.   Name the spiritual gifts specifically mentioned in the scriptures.

8.   Describe the usual manifestation characterizing each of the following gifts, with scriptural illustrations of each:—1, The gift of tongues and interpretation; 2, of healing, and the gift of faith to be healed; 3, of visions; 4, of dreams; 5, of prophecy; 6, of revelation.

9.   Cite scriptural promises that certain sign-gifts of the Spirit shall follow the believer.

10.   Give instances of miracles wrought by evil powers.

11.   Cite the predictions of John the Revelator regarding

such imitations of the gifts of the Spirit, which are to characterize the work of God in the last days.

12. What did Christ say about signs and wonders that would be wrought by wicked men?

13. What evidence have you of the existence of spiritual gifts in the Church today?

LECTURE XIII, ARTICLE 8.

THE BIBLE.

1. What position does the Bible occupy among the standard works of the Church?

2. What reservation does the Church make in accepting the modern versions of the Bible as the unchanged word of God?

3. Define "Bible;"—1.(Give the derivation of the word; and, 2, its modern usage.)

4. Show that the division into Old and New Testaments is natural, and self-suggestive.

5. Explain the term "canon of scripture" as applied to the Bible.

6. Explain, with scriptural references, the growth of the Old Testament from the time of Moses to that of Malachi.

7. State what you know of the language in which the books of the Old Testament were originally written.

8. What is the Septuagint? (1, Give the meaning of the term; 2, describe the origin of the book.)

9. Classify the books of the Old Testament as at present compiled.

10. What classification of Old Testament writings was recognized in the days of the Savior's ministry?

11. What is the Pentateuch? (1, Define the term; 2, enumerate the books comprised; 3, state what you know of their authorship; 4, give an account of the copies or versions possessed by the Jews and the Samaritans anciently.)

12 Name the Historical books in order.

13. Name the Poetical books. (In this connection, define the term "Hagiographa.")

14. Name the Prophetical books. (1, In their order as

at present compiled; 2, in the probable order of their production).

18.   What is meant by the Apocrypha?

19.   What is the New Testament?

20.   Give the principal historical evidence of investigation regarding the authenticity of the New Testament
books.

21.   Name and classify the books of the New Testament.

22.   What is the Vulgate?

23.   Specify the principal modern versions of the Bible.

24.   Give evidence supporting belief in the genuineness
and authenticity of the Bible.

25.   State the principal items of evidence from the Book
of Mormon, corroborating the authenticity of the Bible.

26.   Give the important conclusions of biblical scholars
regarding the genuineness of the New Testament or of parts
thereof.

27.   Give the principal biblical references to scriptures
not contained in the Bible.

LECTURE XIV, ARTICLE 8.

THE BOOK OF MORMON.

1.   What is the Book of Mormon?

2.   How was the ancient record brought to modern
notice?

3.   What do we learn from the title-page of the Book of
Mormon as to the nations or peoples whose history is dealt
with in the volume?

4.   Which was the earliest of the nations, mentioned in
the Book of Mormon, which established itself on the American continent?

5.   Give an account of the journey of Lehi and his
colony from Jerusalem to America. (State: 1, the Divine
instructions directing Lehi to leave; 2, time of this occurrence; 3, the course of their overland journey; 4, journey
across the ocean; 5, place of landing in America.)

6.   Describe the origin of Nephites and Lamanites
respectively.

7.   Who were the Jaredites? (1, Why so named; 2, time

and manner of their migration to this continent; 3, brief statement of their history.)

8. How came the record of the Jaredites to be incorporated with the Nephite writings?

9. What is known of Mulek and his people?

10. Name the classes of plates referred to in the Book of Mormon; (1, on the title page; 2, elsewhere in the volume).

11. State what is known of the plates of Nephi; (1, their origin; 2, the "larger" as distinguished from the "smaller" plates; 3, method by which the record grew.)

12. What is Mormon's abridgment of the plates of Nephi?

13. Which of the plates of Nephi did Mormon include with his own abridgment?

14. What great purpose of the Lord was subserved by this duplication of part of the ancient record?

15. Describe the circumstances resulting in the plates coming into the custody of Joseph Smith: (1, his first information regarding their existence; 2, his first view of the plates; 3, his four years of probation; 4, his possession of the plates.)

16. What other sacred articles were buried with the plates?

17. What is meant by the Urim and Thummim?

18. What purpose did these instruments serve in the work of translation?

19. Give an outline of the circumstances attending the translation and publication of the Book of Mormon: (1, difficulties attending the work; 2, date of first publication).

20. What is the testimony of the learned regarding the characters of parts of the original record?

21. Summarize the evidence of the genuineness of the Book of Mormon: (Show the distinction between genuineness and authenticity).

22. Who were the three witnesses to the genuineness of the book? Give an outline of their testimony.

23. Name the eight witnesses. To what did they testify?

24. What is the so-called "Spaulding Story" of the origin of the Book of Mormon? Show its absurdity.

25. Explain the arrangement of the several parts of the Book of Mormon.

LECTURE XV, ARTICLE 8.

AUTHENTICITY OF THE BOOK OF MORMON.

1. Summarize the proofs of the authenticity of the Book of Mormon.

2. Show that the Book of Mormon and the Bible corroborate each other in matters on which they treat in common.

3. Demonstrate the fulfilment of ancient prophecy in the coming forth of the Book of Mormon; (1, of prophecies contained in the Pearl of Great Price; 2, of Old Testament prophecies, specifically those of Isaiah and Ezekiel).

4. State what you know of the consistency of the Book of Mormon in style and matter.

5. Give examples of Book of Mormon prophecies, the fulfilment of which is recorded therein.

6. Give examples of Book of Mormon prophecies, the fulfilment of which has taken place since the closing of the record.

7. State what you know of Book of Mormon prophecy yet awaiting fulfilment.

8. Summarize the general results of modern investigation and research with which the Book of Mormon is in striking accord.

9. Give evidence that America was inhabited at a very ancient period; (1, cite the conclusions of investigators; and 2, compare with the Book of Mormon account.)

10. Give the principal evidence of the successive occupation of the American continent by different peoples in ancient times; confirm by the Book of Mormon account.

11. Give the principal conclusions of investigators concerning the Asiatic origin of the first colonies who came to America.

12. Summarize the evidence indicating their Israelitish origin.

13. State in a general way the traditions of America's native people concerning:—1, The Deluge; 2, the Divinity of Christ, and His crucifixion.

14. Show the resemblance of certain religious cere-

monies as practised by the Jews, and by some of the native American peoples.

15. What evidence is there, external to the Book of Mormon, indicating the common origin of all the American "races?"

16. Confirm the foregoing conclusions (11 to 15) by the Book of Mormon record.

17. What is known of the written languages current among the Nephites? In what language were the plates of Nephi and those of Mormon inscribed?

18. What external evidence is there of the Egyptian language having been known among the American peoples?

19. Give evidence of the survival of the Hebrew language among the native tribes.

20. What test of the authenticity of the Book of Mormon is given by the last of the writers?

Lecture XVI, Article 9.

REVELATION, PAST, PRESENT, AND FUTURE.

1. What is revelation? Compare with inspiration.

2. Show that revelation is God's chosen method of communication through the priesthood.

3. What is known of God's revelations to:—1, Adam; 2, Enoch; 3, Noah; 4, Abraham; 5, Isaac; 6, Jacob; 7, Moses?

4. Give examples of Divine revelation through other Old Testament prophets.

5. Show that Christ was a revelator, while He dwelt among men.

6. Give scriptural evidence of revelation having been given through the apostles of old.

7. Show that the doctrine of continual revelation is reasonable.

8. Show that it is scriptural.

9. Show that continual revelation has ever been characteristic of the operations of the priesthood.

10. Cite the principal objections to this doctrine, professedly founded on scripture. Show their unscriptural foundation.

11. Give specific scriptures predicting that revelation is

to characterize the Church in the last dispensation: (1, from the Bible; 2, from the Book of Mormon).

12. Give instances of modern revelation. Cite promises of the Lord in this dispensation assuring the continuation of revelation in the Church.

13. Show the reasonableness of expecting yet further revelation.

14. Show that the doctrine of no further revelation is comparatively modern, and unscriptural.

15. Show that inspiration does not deprive man of his freedom or individuality.

LECTURE XVII, ARTICLE 10.

THE DISPERSION OF ISRAEL.

1. Explain the term "Israel." (1, Derivation of the word; 2, bestowal of the title on Jacob; 3, its use as the name of Jacob's posterity; 4, as a name of one of the kingdoms after the division of the nation; 5, as a title of the chosen people of God in a collective sense.)

2. Give a general outline of the Israelites' history from the time of Jacob receiving the name Israel, to the time of the first king.

3. Outline the history of Israel as a united nation under the kings.

4. State the circumstances attending the division of the nation.

5. Outline the history of the kingdom of Judah after the division.

6. The same of the kingdom of Israel. By what other name is this division of the people sometimes known?

7. Define the terms "Hebrew" and "Jew."

8. Show that the dispersion of Israel was foretold by their prophets from very early times.

9. On what conditions was this dispersion predicated?

10. Cite Book of Mormon predictions concerning the dispersion. State specifically the prophecies of Zenos. Who was he?

11. Give historical evidences of the fulfilment of these prophecies of dispersion in the case of the kingdom of Judah. What part did Nebuchadnezzar take in the work of

dispersion? At what time? Give an account of the Babylonian captivity. How did Titus contribute to the work of dispersion?

12. Give historical evidence of the fulfilment of prophecy relating to the dispersion of the kingdom of Israel. How did Shalmanezer and Sargon contribute to the dispersion? At what time? Show the literal fulfilment of Ahijah's prophecy to the wife of Jeroboam.

13. Explain the term, "Lost Tribes."

14. What is known of the journeyings of the Lost Tribes?

LECTURE XVIII, ARTICLE 10.

THE GATHERING OF ISRAEL.

1. Cite Bible promises of the gathering associated with predictions of the dispersion; specifically those by, 1, Moses; 2, Nehemiah; 3, Isaiah; 4, Jeremiah; 5, Ezekiel; 6, Amos.

2. Give Book of Mormon prophecies regarding the gathering, especially those uttered 1, by Lehi; 2, by Nephi, his son; 3, by Christ in the course of His ministrations among the Nephites.

3. Cite instances of modern revelation concerning the gathering.

4. What does the plan of the gathering of Israel in the last days comprise?

5. Show that the authority for prosecuting the work of gathering has been given to the Church in this dispensation.

6. What is the purpose of the gathering?

7. Give an account of the work as now in progress.

8. In what respect are the people of Israel a chosen people?

9. Show how the fulfilment of the promise made to Abraham, that through his descendants all nations of the earth should be blessed, has been brought about through the dispersion of Israel.

10. Give another evidence of the fulfilment of that prediction, based on the lineage of Christ.

11.   Give scriptural prophecies relating to the restoration of the Ten Tribes.

12.   Show that the establishment of Zion is to precede the restoration of the Ten Tribes.

LECTURE XIX, ARTICLE 10.

ZION.

1.   Show from the scriptures that two gathering places are to be established in the last dispensation.

2.   Define "Zion." (1, Meaning of the term; 2, its varied applications.)

3.   Give an outline of the history of Jerusalem from the time of its first mention in scripture to that of its overthrow by the Romans.

4.   Cite scriptural promises relating to the future glory of Jerusalem.

5.   Explain the application of the term "New Jerusalem."

6.   Show from Book of Mormon and modern scripture that the Zion of the western continent and the New Jerusalem are identical.

7.   Cite the prophecy of Christ to the Nephites that a New Jerusalem shall be established on the western continent.

8.   Give the prediction of Ether the Jaredite relating to the establishment of the New Jerusalem.

9.   What is meant by the Zion of Enoch? (1, Give outline of the history of the ancient people so designated; 2, cite promises of the return of Enoch and his people.)

10.   What is known through modern revelation as to the location of Zion or the New Jerusalem?

11.   What is meant by Stakes of Zion?

12.   What conditions will determine the time of the redemption of Zion in the present dispensation?

LECTURE XX, ARTICLE 10.

CHRIST'S REIGN ON EARTH.

1.   Compare the conditions attending Christ's first advent, with those predicted for His second coming.

2. Cite scriptural prophecies regarding the second coming of Christ, with attendant signs; (1, Biblical; 2, Book of Mormon; 3, modern.)

3. What evidence have you to prove that the predicted second coming of Christ is near at hand?

4. What is known as to the time of His coming?

5. Show by scripture that Christ is to reign as King on earth.

6. Demonstrate the relation between the Kingdom of God and the Church of Christ.

7. Show the distinctive sense in which the Kingdom of God and the Kingdom of Heaven are spoken of in modern revelation.

8. What will be the position of honest and honorable men who are not members of the Church when the Kingdom of Heaven is established?

9. What is the Millennium?

10. Give scriptural authority for your belief as to the conditions that are to characterize the Millennium.

11. What will be the condition of Satan during and after the Millennium?

LECTURE XXI, ARTICLE 10.

REGENERATION AND RESURRECTION.

1. Explain the statement, that the earth is under a curse.

2. What is meant by the predicted regeneration of the earth?

3. When will this change be completed?

4. What is known as to the future condition of the earth in its regenerated state?

5. What is the attitude of science regarding the earth's regeneration?

6. What is meant by the resurrection of the body?

7. What are the teachings of the Church regarding the literalness of the resurrection?

8. Upon what does our belief in the doctrine of the resurrection depend?

9. Give scriptural evidence supporting belief in the resurrection: (1, Old Testament; 2, New Testament: 3, Book of Mormon; 4, modern.)

10. Specify the general resurrections spoken of in the scriptures.

11. How was the first resurrection inaugurated?

12. Give an account of the resurrection of the just immediately following the resurrection of Christ.

13. Cite Book of Mormon prophecy regarding the resurrection of Christ and that of the righteous immediately following.

14. Give a summary of the teachings by the apostles of old, regarding the resurrection at the time of Christ's second coming.

15. Cite modern revelation on the same subject.

16. Compare the scriptural descriptions of the first resurrection, or the resurrection of the just, with those of the second, or the resurrection of the unjust.

17. Show that the resurrection is to be universal, applying both to righteous and wicked.

18. What will be the lot of the heathen in the resurrection? (Support your answer by scripture).

19. What is known of the intermediate state of the soul, between death and the resurrection?

20. Define "Paradise." Show that Paradise is not the place of final glory.

LECTURE XXII, ARTICLE 11.

RELIGIOUS LIBERTY AND TOLERATION.

1. What is worship?

2. Show that man's ability to worship rightly is a measure of his conception of God's attributes and powers.

3. Show that worship, to be valid, must be voluntary.

4. Demonstrate man's right to freedom in worship.

5. Explain the intolerance in matters of worship, characterizing early and modern times.

6. Show that intolerance is unscriptural.

7. Demonstrate that tolerance is not necessarily acceptance.

8. Show that man, being free to choose for himself, is justly held accountable for his acts.

9. Explain Christ's expression, "In my Father's house are many mansions."

10. What kingdoms or degrees of glory are specified in the revealed word?

11. Who are to inherit the Celestial glory?

12. For whom is the Terrestrial glory provided?

13. Who will be consigned to the Telestial kingdom?

14. What is known of the gradation of glory within each of the kingdoms specified?

15. Who are the Sons of Perdition? What is known of their fate?

LECTURE XXIII, ARTICLE 12.

SUBMISSION TO THE LAW OF THE LAND.

1. What are the teachings of the Church regarding the duties of its members with respect to the secular law?

2. Cite instances recorded in the Old Testament of Divine approval and admonition regarding the secular laws.

3. Give examples from the life of the Savior.

4. What were the teachings of the apostles of old regarding the observance of the law of the land by the members of the Church?

5. Cite the word of the Lord as given through modern revelation regarding the attitude of members of the Church toward the governments under which they live.

6. What has the Lord said as to His judgment concerning those who are effectually prevented by their enemies from a strict compliance with His requirements?

7. Give a modern instance of an abandonment by the Church, under pressure of secular law, of a Divine requirement?

8. Show that secular authority is recognized of God as necessary to the government of mankind, and that the officers of the law are therefore to be obeyed.

9. Summarize the declarations of belief regarding the duty of the Church toward the law of the land, as formulated by Joseph Smith, and as adopted by the Church.

LECTURE XXIV, ARTICLE 13.

PRACTICAL RELIGION.

1. Give James' definition of pure religion.

2. Show that religion is not theological formula, but practical application of recognized principles of right.

32

3. What is the teaching of the Church regarding man's relationship to God?

4. Show that benevolence is enjoined by scripture. (Give, 1, instances from the teachings of the Savior; 2, those of His apostles; 3, those of modern requirement.)

5. Specify the means of donation for benevolent purposes, provided by the Church today.

6. Outline the modern Church plan of 1, Free-will offerings; 2, fast offerings as a modification of the foregoing.

7. Explain the advantages of fast-day observance, and fast-offerings, among members of the Church.

8. What is tithing?

9. Cite biblical authority for the observance of the law of tithing in ancient times.

10. State the requirements made by revelation for the tithing of the people today.

11. What is meant by consecration and stewardship?

12. Give scriptural instances of God's people having lived in the United Order. (Cite, 1, from Pearl of Great Price; 2, from Bible; 3, from Book of Mormon.)

13. Explain the United Order, or the Order of Enoch, as provided for the Church through modern revelation.

14. Show that individual freedom is provided for in the plan of the United Order.

15. Cite scriptural instances of the Lord's denunciation of the idler.

16. What is the teaching of the Church regarding the propriety and necessity of marriage?

17. What has the Lord said through revelation of those who forbid marriage?

18. What is Celestial Marriage?

19. Show that the authority of the priesthood is necessary in the making of contracts that are to be of effect after the death of the parties.

20. What does the Church teach regarding the enormity of the sin of unlawful association of the sexes? Cite the declaration of Alma in this connection.

21. State the provisions of the revelation known as the Word of Wisdom.

INDEX.

purpose of, 350; two places appointed, 356; in progress now, 355; predicted, 341.

General resurrections, two, 396.

General salvation, 90.

Genuineness and authenticity of Bible, 254; of parts of New Testament, 258; of Book of Mormon, 275.

Ghost, Holy; see "Holy Ghost."

Gift of God,—faith a, 111; repentance a, 118.

Gift of healing, 227; of prophecy, 231; of revelation, 232; of tongues and interpretation, 226; of visions and dreams, 229.

Gifts of the Spirit, see "Spiritual gifts."

Gifts, spiritual, imitation of, 235.

Glory, Degrees of, 94, 416,420; Celestial, 94, 417; Terrestrial, 95, 418; Telestial, 95, 419, 423.

God and the Godhead, 27.

God, attributes of, 42, 103; belief in, natural, 48; and necessary, 49; importance of belief in, 49; existence of, 27; evidence from history and tradition, 28; evidence from reason, 30; evidence from revelation, 35; in nature, 50; natural indications of, 50; personality of, 41.

Godhead, personality of each member of, 41; a Trinity, 38; unity of, 39; sectarian view of, 46.

Gospel to be preached to the dead, 150.

Government, Church, helps in, 216.

Governments, secular, obedience to, 424.

Greeks, baptism among, 160.

Hagiographa, 248.

Hands, imposition of, in ordinances, 174, 187.

Healing, gift of, 227.

Heathen, in first resurrection, 404.

Hebrew language, survival of among American aborigines, 302, 307.

Hebrews, 339.

Helps in church government, 216.

High Council, The Standing, 215; The Traveling, (quorum of the Twelve Apostles) 213.

High Priesthood, President of the, 213.

High Priests, office of, and quorum organization, 211; Presiding, 213.

Historical books, of Old Testament, 248; of New Testament, 252.

History and tradition, supporting evidence of God's existence, 28.

Holy Ghost, bestowal of, 170; effect of, on the individual, 173; exceptional visitations, 169; gifts of, see "Spiritual Gifts;" office of 167; personality and powers of, 164; promised, 163; scriptural titles of, 41-42; to whom given, 168.

Holy Spirit, see "Holy Ghost."

Idolatry and atheism, 44; idolatry, examples of atrocious, 51; practices in general, 51.

Imitations of spiritual gifts, 235.

Immaterialism and atheism, 53.

Immersion, the proper mode of baptism, 139.

Importance of belief in God, 49.

Imposition of hands, in ordinances, 174, 187.

Improvement Associations, Mutual, 216.

Indians, American, (Lamanites), 300.

Individual salvation, 90, 92.

Infant Baptism, see "Baptism."

Inspiration and revelation, 308, 324.

Intermediate state of the soul (Paradise), 405.

Interpretation of tongues, gift of, 226.

Intolerance, in religion, 409, 414, 422.

Innocence of children, 90-92.

Israel, 326; a chosen people, 352, 355; dispersion of, 326-328, 329, 332, 355; gathering of, 341; gathering of, now in progress, 351, 355; kingdom of, 327.

Jaredite nation, 266.

Jerusalem, history of, 358, 359, 366.

Jerusalem, The New, (Zion), 360.

Jews, 339.

John the Baptist, conferred the Aaronic priesthood, 19, 193.

Joseph Smith, authenticity of his mission, 13; authority received by, 19; parentage, youth, etc., 6; his first vision, 9; visited by Moroni, 10; persecution of, 24; a true prophet, 20; tribute to, 25; martyrdom of, 13, 25; references to life of, 26.

Journeyings of the Ten Tribes, 340.

Latter-day Revelation

The following is an unaltered
digital scan of *Latter-day Revelation*
published in 1930.

LATTER-DAY REVELATION

Selections from the

BOOK OF
DOCTRINE and COVENANTS

OF

THE CHURCH OF JESUS CHRIST
OF LATTER-DAY SAINTS

———

Containing Revelations Given Through
JOSEPH SMITH THE PROPHET

———

Published by
The Church of Jesus Christ of
Latter-day Saints
Salt Lake City, Utah, U. S. A.
1930

FOREWORD

THE CHURCH OF JESUS CHRIST OF LATTER-DAY SAINTS was organized as an institution among men on the sixth day of April, 1830. Through a period of more than six years prior to that date, Joseph Smith, the Prophet, had received at intervals many Divine revelations and commandments.

Of these the first and of all most glorious was the visitation in which, in answer to the young man's prayer for guidance as to which of the numerous and opposing sects of the day he should join, the Eternal Father, and His Son, Jesus Christ, personally manifested Themselves, and the Father, pointing to the Christ, thus affirmed and commanded: THIS IS MY BELOVED SON. HEAR HIM!

This took place in the early spring of 1820. In September, 1823, and at later times, Joseph Smith received visitations from Moroni, an angel of light, who revealed the resting place of the ancient record from which the *Book of Mormon* was afterward translated.

Many revelations followed in preparation for the reestablishment of the Church of Jesus Christ on earth, and later for the direction of the Church so organized. As early as the summer of 1830, the Prophet, acting under Divine commandment, was engaged in compiling the revelations received up to that time, with a view to their publication in book form. On November 1, 1831, at a conference of the Elders of the Church held at Hiram, Ohio, definite action relating to the publication of the revelations was taken, and the compilation was called the *Book of Commandments*. The

Lord's acceptance of the undertaking was made manifest by the giving of the revelation herein appearing as Section 1, which is currently known as the *Preface*. As successive revelations were added the title was changed to *Doctrine and Covenants*.

Many of the revelations given prior to the organization of the Church and during its early years related to immediate duties and callings of individuals; others dealt especially with conditions in the Church at particular times. A distinguishing feature of these communications from the Lord appears in their timeliness; they were granted to meet circumstances calling for Divine direction of specific nature. Except as illustrative instances of the Lord's way of directly communicating with His prophets, many of these revelations, once of present and pressing significance, became relatively of reduced importance with the passing of the conditions that had brought them forth.

This little book contains selected Sections and parts of Sections from the *Doctrine and Covenants*, the selections comprising Scriptures of general and enduring value, given as the Word of the Lord through the First Elder and Prophet in the present dispensation, which is verily the "Dispensation of the Fulness of Times."

The complete *Doctrine and Covenants* is a current publication, accessible to all, so that comparison between that volume and this is a simple undertaking. Every omission from the full text is indicated in these pages—by asterisks where parts of Sections are left out and by the absence of some Sections in their entirety.

CONTENTS

CONTENTS

Latter-day Revelation

Selections from the

BOOK OF

DOCTRINE AND COVENANTS

THE VOICE OF THE LORD TO ALL PEOPLE

SECTION 1.—*Revelation given through Joseph Smith the Prophet, during a special conference of Elders of the Church of Jesus Christ of Latter-day Saints, held at Hiram, Ohio, November 1, 1831. Many revelations had been received from the Lord prior to this time; and the compilation of these for publication in book form was one of the principal subjects passed upon at the conference. This Section constitutes the Lord's Preface to the doctrines, covenants, and commandments given in this dispensation. —— Proclamation of warning and commandment to the Church and to the inhabitants of the earth at large—Authority of the Priesthood in this dispensation attested—Second advent of the Lord Jesus Christ foretold—Authenticity of the Book of Mormon affirmed.*

HEARKEN, O ye people of my church, saith the voice of him who dwells on high and whose eyes are upon all men; yea, verily I say: Hearken ye people from afar; and ye that are upon the islands of the sea listen together!

For verily the voice of the Lord is unto all men and there is none to escape; and there is no eye that shall not see, neither ear that shall not hear,

neither heart that shall not be penetrated.   And
the rebellious shall be pierced with much sorrow;
for their iniquities shall be spoken upon the house-
tops, and their secret acts shall be revealed.   And
the voice of warning shall be unto all people, by
the mouths of my disciples whom I have chosen
in these last days.   And they shall go forth and
none shall stay them, for I the Lord have commanded them.

Behold, this is mine authority, and the authority of my servants, and my preface unto the book
of my commandments, which I have given them to
publish unto you, O inhabitants of the earth.
Wherefore, fear and tremble, O ye people, for
what I the Lord have decreed in them shall be
fulfilled.

And verily I say unto you, that they who go
forth, bearing these tidings unto the inhabitants
of the earth, to them is power given to seal both
on earth and in heaven the unbelieving and rebellious; yea, verily, to seal them up unto the day
when the wrath of God shall be poured out upon
the wicked without measure—unto the day when
the Lord shall come to recompense unto every
man according to his work, and measure to every
man according to the measure which he has meas-
ured to his fellow man.

Wherefore the voice of the Lord is unto the
ends of the earth, that all that will hear may
hear: Prepare ye, prepare ye for that which is
to come, for the Lord is nigh; and the anger of

the Lord is kindled, and his sword is bathed in heaven, and it shall fall upon the inhabitants of the earth.   And the arm of the Lord shall be revealed; and the day cometh that they who will not hear the voice of the Lord, neither the voice of his servants, neither give heed to the words of the prophets and apostles, shall be cut off from among the people.

For they have strayed from mine ordinances, and have broken mine everlasting covenant.   They seek not the Lord to establish his righteousness, but every man walketh in his own way, and after the image of his own god, whose image is in the likeness of the world, and whose substance is that of an idol, which waxeth old and shall perish in Babylon, even Babylon the great, which shall fall.

Wherefore, I, the Lord, knowing the calamity which should come upon the inhabitants of the earth, called upon my servant Joseph Smith, Jun., and spake unto him from heaven, and gave him commandments; and also gave commandments to others, that they should proclaim these things unto the world; and all this that it might be fulfilled, which was written by the prophets: The weak things of the world shall come forth and break down the mighty and strong ones, that man should not counsel his fellow man, neither trust in the arm of flesh; but that every man might speak in the name of God the Lord, even the Savior of the world—that faith also might increase in the earth; that mine everlasting covenant might be established; that the fulness of my gospel might be proclaimed by the weak and the simple unto the ends of the world, and before kings and rulers.

Behold, I am God and have spoken it; these commandments are of me, and were given unto my servants in their weakness, after the manner of their language, that they might come to understanding; and inasmuch as they erred it might be made known; and inasmuch as they sought wisdom they might be instructed; and inasmuch as they sinned they might be chastened, that they might repent; and inasmuch as they were humble they might be made strong, and blessed from on high, and receive knowledge from time to time.

And after having received the record of the Nephites, yea, even my servant Joseph Smith, Jun., might have power to translate through the mercy of God, by the power of God, the *Book of Mormon*. And also those to whom these commandments were given might have power to lay the foundation of this church, and to bring it forth out of obscurity and out of darkness, the only true and living church upon the face of the whole earth, with which I, the Lord, am well pleased, speaking unto the church collectively and not individually—

For I, the Lord, cannot look upon sin with the least degree of allowance. Nevertheless, he that repents and does the commandments of the Lord shall be forgiven; and he that repents not, from him shall be taken even the light which he has received; for my Spirit shall not always strive with man, saith the Lord of Hosts.

And again, verily I say unto you, O inhabitants of the earth: I, the Lord, am willing to make these things known unto all flesh; for I am no respecter of persons, and will that all men shall know that the day speedily cometh——the hour is not yet, but is nigh at hand——when peace shall be taken from the earth, and the devil shall have power over his own dominion. And also the Lord shall have power over his saints, and shall reign in their midst, and shall come down in judgment upon Idumea, or the world.

Search these commandments, for they are true and faithful, and the prophecies and promises which are in them shall all be fulfilled. What I the Lord have spoken I have spoken, and I excuse not myself; and though the heavens and the earth pass away my word shall not pass away, but shall all be fulfilled, whether by mine own voice or by the voice of my servants, it is the same. For behold, and lo, the Lord is God, and the Spirit beareth record, and the record is true, and the truth abideth forever and ever. Amen.

PREDICTED ADVENT OF ELIJAH THE PROPHET

SECTION 2——*Words spoken by Moroni, the Angel, to Joseph Smith the Prophet, while in his father's house at Manchester, New York, on the evening of Septem-*

*ber 21, 1823. Moroni was the last of a long line of
historians who had made the record that is now before
the world as the Book of Mormon. Compare Malachi
4:5, 6.*

BEHOLD, I will reveal unto you the Priesthood
by the hand of Elijah the prophet, before the coming of the great and dreadful day of the Lord. And
he shall plant in the hearts of the children the
promises made to the fathers, and the hearts of
the children shall turn to their fathers. If it were
not so the whole earth would be utterly wasted at
his coming.

QUALIFICATIONS FOR THE MINISTRY

SECTION 4—*Revelation given through Joseph Smith
the Prophet, to his father, Joseph Smith, Sen., at Harmony, Pennsylvania, February, 1829.*

NOW BEHOLD, a marvelous work is about to
come forth among the children of men. Therefore, O ye that embark in the service of God, see
that ye serve him with all your heart, might,
mind and strength, that ye may stand blameless
before God at the last day. Therefore, if ye have
desires to serve God ye are called to the work; for
behold the field is white already to harvest; and lo,
he that thrusteth in his sickle with his might, the
same layeth up in store that he perisheth not, but
bringeth salvation to his soul. And faith, hope,
charity and love, with an eye single to the glory
of God, qualify him for the work. Remember
faith, virtue, knowledge, temperance, patience,

brotherly kindness, godliness, charity, humility, diligence. Ask, and ye shall receive; knock, and it shall be opened unto you. Amen.

DESIRE OF JOHN THE APOSTLE GRANTED

SECTION 7—*Revelation given to Joseph Smith the Prophet and Oliver Cowdery at Harmony, Pennsylvania, April, 1829, when they inquired through the Urim and Thummim as to whether John, the beloved disciple, tarried in the flesh or had died.*

AND THE LORD SAID UNTO ME: John, my beloved, what desirest thou?   For if you shall ask what you will it shall be granted unto you.   And I said unto him: Lord, give unto me power over death, that I may live and bring souls unto thee. And the Lord said unto me: Verily, verily, I say unto thee, because thou desirest this thou shalt tarry until I come in my glory, and shalt prophesy before nations, kindreds, tongues and people.

And for this cause the Lord said unto Peter: If I will that he tarry till I come, what is that to thee?   For he desired of me that he might bring souls unto me, but thou desiredst that thou mightest speedily come unto me in my kingdom.   I say unto thee, Peter, this was a good desire; but my beloved has desired that he might do more, or a greater work yet among men than what he has before done.   Yea, he has undertaken a greater work; therefore I will make him as flaming fire and a ministering angel; he shall minister for those who shall be heirs of salvation who dwell on the earth.

And I will make thee to minister for him and for thy brother James; and unto you three I will give this power and the keys of this ministry until I come. Verily I say unto you, ye shall both have according to your desires, for ye both joy in that which ye have desired.

RESTORATION OF THE AARONIC PRIESTHOOD

SECTION 13—*Ordination of Joseph Smith and Oliver Cowdery to the Aaronic Priesthood, at Harmony, Pennsylvania, May 15, 1829, under the hands of an Angel, who announced himself as John, the same that is called John the Baptist in the New Testament. The angelic visitant averred that he was acting under the direction of Peter, James and John, the ancient Apostles, who held the keys of the higher Priesthood, which was called the Priesthood of Melchizedek. The promise was given to Joseph and Oliver that in due time the Priesthood of Melchizedek would be conferred upon them.*

UPON YOU, my fellow servants, in the name of Messiah I confer the Priesthood of Aaron, which holds the keys of the ministering of angels, and of the gospel of repentance, and of baptism by immersion for the remission of sins. And this shall never be taken again from the earth, until the sons of Levi do offer again an offering unto the Lord in righteousness.

CALLING OF THE TWELVE DIRECTED

SECTION 18—*Revelation to Joseph Smith the Prophet, Oliver Cowdery and David Whitmer, given at Fayette, New York, June, 1829: Making known the calling of Twelve Apostles in these last days; and also containing instructions relative to building up the Church of Christ according to the fulness of the Gospel. When the Aaronic Priesthood was conferred, the bestowal of the Melchizedek Priesthood was promised. In response to fervent supplication for greater knowledge on the matter the Lord gave this revelation. —— Value of souls emphasized—The great joy attending conversion of souls to the Gospel of Christ—Calling of twelve men to assist in the ministry foreshadowed—The Twelve, here called disciples, were later named Apostles.*

* * *

REMEMBER, the worth of souls is great in the sight of God. For, behold, the Lord your Redeemer suffered death in the flesh; wherefore he suffered the pain of all men, that all men might repent and come unto him. And he hath risen again from the dead, that he might bring all men unto him, on conditions of repentance. And how great is his joy in the soul that repenteth!

Wherefore, you are called to cry repentance unto this people. And if it so be that you should labor all your days in crying repentance unto this people, and bring, save it be one soul unto me, how great shall be your joy with him in the kingdom of my Father! And now, if your joy will be great with one soul that you have brought unto me into the kingdom of my Father, how great will be your joy if you should bring many souls unto me!

Behold, you have my gospel before you, and my rock, and my salvation. Ask the Father in my name, in faith believing that you shall receive, and you shall have the Holy Ghost, which manifesteth all things which are expedient unto the children of men. And if you have not faith, hope, and charity, you can do nothing. Contend against no church, save it be the church of the devil. Take upon you the name of Christ, and speak the truth in soberness. And as many as repent and are baptized in my name, which is Jesus Christ, and endure to the end, the same shall be saved.

Behold, Jesus Christ is the name which is given of the Father, and there is none other name given whereby man can be saved. Wherefore, all men must take upon them the name which is given of the Father, for in that name shall they be called at the last day; wherefore, if they know not the name by which they are called they cannot have place in the kingdom of my Father.

And now, behold, there are others who are called to declare my gospel, both unto Gentile and unto Jew—yea, even twelve; and the Twelve shall be my disciples, and they shall take upon them my name; and the Twelve are they who shall desire to take upon them my name with full purpose of heart. And if they desire to take upon them my name with full purpose of heart they are called to go into all the world to preach my gospel unto every creature.   And they are they who are ordained of me to baptize in my name, according to that which is written; and you have that which is written before you; wherefore, you must perform it according to the words which are written.

And now I speak unto you, the Twelve: Behold, my grace is sufficient for you; you must walk uprightly before me and sin not.   And, behold, you are they who are ordained of me to ordain priests and teachers; to declare my gospel, according to the power of the Holy Ghost which is in you, and according to the callings and gifts of God unto men.   And I, Jesus Christ, your Lord and your God, have spoken it.   These words are not of men nor of man, but of me; wherefore, you shall testify they are of me and not of man. For it is my voice which speaketh them unto you; for they are given by my Spirit unto you, and by my power you can read them one to another; and save it were by my power you could not have them.   Wherefore, you can testify that you have heard my voice, and know my words.

And now, behold, I give unto you, Oliver Cowdery, and also unto David Whitmer, that you shall search out the Twelve, who shall have the desires of which I have spoken.   And by their desires and their works you shall know them. And when you have found them you shall show these things unto them.   And you shall fall down and worship the Father in my name.   And you must preach unto the world, saying: You must repent and be baptized, in the name of Jesus Christ. For all men must repent and be baptized, and not only men, but women, and children who have arrived at the years of accountability.

And now, after that you have received this, you must keep my commandments in all things; and by your hands I will work a marvelous work among the children of men, unto the convincing of many of their sins, that they may come unto repentance, and that they may come unto the kingdom of my Father. Wherefore, the blessings which I give unto you are above all things. And after that you have received this, if you keep not my commandments you cannot be saved in the kingdom of my Father. Behold, I, Jesus Christ, your Lord and your God, and your Redeemer, by the power of my Spirit have spoken it. Amen.

CHRIST VICTORIOUS AND OMNIPOTENT

SECTION 19—*A Commandment of God, and not of man, revealed through Joseph Smith the Prophet, to Martin Harris, at Manchester, New York, March, 1830, by him who is Eternal. —— Christ affirms his omnipotence—Declares that punishment and suffering are inevitable consequences of unrepented sins—Explains the signification of endless torment and eternal damnation—Reaffirms the actuality of his own suffering in the flesh.*

I AM ALPHA AND OMEGA, Christ the Lord; yea, even I am he, the beginning and the end, the Redeemer of the world. I, having accomplished

and finished the will of him whose I am, even the
Father, concerning me—having done this that I
might subdue all things unto myself—retaining
all power, even to the destroying of Satan and his
works at the end of the world, and the last great
day of judgment, which I shall pass upon the inhabitants thereof, judging every man according
to his works and the deeds which he hath done—
and surely every man must repent or suffer, for I,
God, am endless—wherefore, I revoke not the
judgments which I shall pass, but woes shall go
forth, weeping, wailing and gnashing of teeth,
yea, to those who are found on my left hand.

Nevertheless, it is not written that there shall
be no end to this torment, but it is written *endless
torment.* Again, it is written *eternal damnation;*
wherefore it is more express than other scriptures,
that it might work upon the hearts of the children of men, altogether for my name's glory.
Wherefore, I will explain unto you this mystery,
for it is meet unto you to know even as mine
apostles. I speak unto you that are chosen in this
thing, even as one, that you may enter into my
rest.

For, behold, the mystery of godliness, how great
is it! For, behold, I am *endless,* and the punishment which is given from my hand is *endless punishment,* for *Endless* is my name. Wherefore—
eternal punishment is God's punishment. Endless punishment is God's punishment.

Wherefore, I command you to repent, and keep

the commandments which you have received by the hand of my servant Joseph Smith, Jun., in my name; and it is by my almighty power that you have received them.　Therefore I command you to repent—repent, lest I smite you by the rod of my mouth, and by my wrath, and by my anger, and your sufferings be sore—how sore you know not, how exquisite you know not, yea, how hard to bear you know not.

For behold, I, God, have suffered these things for all, that they might not suffer if they would repent.　But if they would not repent they must suffer even as I; which suffering caused myself, even God, the greatest of all, to tremble because of pain, and to bleed at every pore, and to suffer both body and spirit—and would that I might not drink the bitter cup, and shrink—nevertheless, glory be to the Father, and I partook and finished my preparations unto the children of men.

*　　*　　*

FUNDAMENTAL PRINCIPLES AND ORDINANCES

SECTION 20—*Revelation on Church Organization and Government, given through Joseph Smith the Prophet, April, 1830.　Preceding his record of this revelation the Prophet wrote: "We obtained of him [Jesus Christ] the following, by the spirit of prophecy and revelation; which not only gave us much information, but also pointed out to us the precise day upon which, according to his will and commandment, we should proceed to organize his Church once more upon the earth." ——— The Lord again attests the genuineness of the Book of*

Mormon—He gives commandment respecting baptism—Defines the functions of the several offices in the Priesthood—Specifies the duties of members—Prescribes the mode of baptism, and of administering the sacrament—Directs the keeping of records of Church membership.

THE RISE OF THE CHURCH of Christ in these last days, being one thousand eight hundred and thirty years since the coming of our Lord and Savior Jesus Christ in the flesh, it being regularly organized and established agreeable to the laws of our country, by the will and commandments of God, in the fourth month, and on the sixth day of the month which is called April— which commandments were given to Joseph Smith, Jun., who was called of God and ordained an apostle of Jesus Christ, to be the first elder of this church; and to Oliver Cowdery, who was also called of God, an apostle of Jesus Christ, to be the second elder of this church, and ordained under his hand; and this according to the grace of our Lord and Savior Jesus Christ, to whom be all glory both now and forever.   Amen.

After it was truly manifested unto this first elder that he had received a remission of his sins, he was entangled again in the vanities of the world; but after repenting, and humbling himself sincerely through faith, God ministered unto him by an holy angel, whose countenance was as lightning, and whose garments were pure and white above all other whiteness.   And gave unto him commandments which inspired him; and gave him power from on high, by the means which were before prepared, to translate the *Book of Mormon,* which contains a record of a fallen people, and the fulness of the gospel of Jesus Christ to the Gentiles and to the Jews also.

Which was given by inspiration, and is confirmed to others by the ministering of angels, and is declared unto the world by them—proving to the world that the holy scriptures are true, and that God does inspire men and call them to his holy work in this age and generation, as well as in generations of old; thereby showing that he is the same God yesterday, today, and forever.   Amen.

Therefore, having so great witnesses by them shall the world be judged, even as many as shall hereafter come to a knowledge of this work.   And those who receive it in faith, and work righteousness, shall receive a crown of eternal life; but those who harden their hearts in unbelief and reject it, it shall turn to their own condemnation.   For the Lord God has spoken it; and we, the elders of the church, have heard and bear witness to the words of the glorious Majesty on high, to whom be glory forever and ever.   Amen.

By these things we know that there is a God in heaven, who is infinite and eternal, from everlasting to everlasting the same unchangeable God, the framer of heaven and earth and all things which are in them; and that he created man, male and female, after his own image and in his own likeness created he them, and gave unto them commandments that they should love and serve him, the only living and true God, and that he should be the only being whom they should worship. But by the transgression of these holy laws man became sensual and devilish, and became fallen man.

Wherefore, the Almighty God gave his Only Begotten Son, as it is written in those scriptures which have been given of him. He suffered temptations but gave no heed unto them. He was crucified, died, and rose again the third day, and ascended into heaven, to sit down on the right hand of the Father, to reign with almighty power according to the will of the Father—That as many as would believe and be baptized in his holy name, and endure in faith to the end, should be saved—Not only those who believed after he came in the meridian of time, in the flesh, but all those from the beginning, even as many as were before he came, who believed in the words of the holy prophets, who spake as they were inspired by the gift of the Holy Ghost, who truly testified of him in all things, should have eternal life, as well as those who should come after, who should believe in the gifts and callings of God by the Holy Ghost, which beareth record of the Father and of the Son. Which Father, Son, and Holy Ghost are one God, infinite and eternal, without end.   Amen.

And we know that all men must repent and believe on the name of Jesus Christ, and worship

2

the Father in his name, and endure in faith on his name to the end, or they cannot be saved in the kingdom of God. And we know that justification through the grace of our Lord and Savior Jesus Christ is just and true; and we know also that sanctification through the grace of our Lord and Savior Jesus Christ is just and true—to all those who love and serve God with all their mights, minds, and strength.

But there is a possibility that man may fall from grace and depart from the living God; therefore let the church take heed and pray always, lest they fall into temptation; yea, and even let those who are sanctified take heed also. And we know that these things are true and according to the revelations of John, neither adding to, nor diminishing from the prophecy of his book, the holy scriptures, or the revelations of God which shall come hereafter by the gift and power of the Holy Ghost, the voice of God, or the ministering of angels. And the Lord God has spoken it; and honor, power and glory be rendered to his holy name, both now and ever. Amen.

And again, by way of commandment to the church concerning the manner of baptism: All those who humble themselves before God, and desire to be baptized, and come forth with broken hearts and contrite spirits, and witness before the church that they have truly repented of all their sins, and are willing to take upon them the name of Jesus Christ, having a determination to serve him to the end, and truly manifest by their works that they have received of the Spirit of Christ unto the remission of their sins, shall be received by baptism into his church.

The duty of the elders, priests, teachers, deacons, and members of the church of Christ: An apostle is an elder, and it is his calling to baptize; and to ordain other elders, priests, teachers, and deacons; and to administer bread and wine—the emblems of the flesh and blood of Christ; and to confirm those who are baptized into the church, by the laying on of hands for the baptism of fire and the Holy Ghost, according to the scriptures; and to teach, expound, exhort, baptize, and watch over the church; and to confirm the church by the laying on of the hands, and the giving of the Holy Ghost; and to take the lead of all meetings.   The elders are to conduct the meetings as they are led by the Holy Ghost, according to the commandments and revelations of God.

The priest's duty is to preach, teach, expound, exhort, and baptize, and administer the sacrament, and visit the house of each member, and exhort them to pray vocally and in secret and attend to all family duties.   And he may also ordain other priests, teachers, and deacons.   And he is to take the lead of meetings when there is no elder present; but when there is an elder present, he is only to preach, teach, expound, exhort, and baptize, and visit the house of each member, exhorting them to pray vocally and in secret and attend to all family duties.   In all these duties the priest is to assist the elder if occasion requires.

The teacher's duty is to watch over the church always, and be with and strengthen them, and see that there is no iniquity in the church, neither hardness with each other, neither lying, backbiting, nor evil speaking; and see that the church meet together often, and also see that all the members do their duty.   And he is to take the lead of meetings in the absence of the elder or priest, and is to be assisted always, in all his duties in the church, by the deacons, if occasion requires.   But neither teachers nor deacons have authority to baptize, administer the sacrament, or lay on hands; they are, however, to warn, expound, exhort, and teach, and invite all to come unto Christ.

Every elder, priest, teacher, or deacon is to be ordained according to the gifts and callings of God unto him; and he is to be ordained by the power of the Holy Ghost, which is in the one who ordains him.   The several elders composing this church of Christ are to meet in conference once in three months, or from time to time as said conferences shall direct or appoint; and said conferences are to do whatever church business is necessary to be done at the time.

*   *   *

No person is to be ordained to any office in this church, where there is a regularly organized branch of the same, without the vote of that church; but the presiding elders, traveling bishops, high councilors, high priests, and elders, may have the privilege of ordaining, where there is no branch of the church that a vote may be called.   Every president of the high priesthood (or presiding elder), bishop, high councilor, and high priest, is to be ordained by the direction of a high council or general conference.

The duty of the members after they are received by baptism: The elders or priests are to have a sufficient time to expound all things concerning the church of Christ to their understanding, previous to their partaking of the sacrament and being confirmed by the laying on of the hands of the elders, so that all things may be done in order. And the members shall manifest before the church, and also before the elders, by a godly walk and conversation, that they are worthy of it, that there may be works and faith agreeable to the holy scriptures—walking in holiness before the Lord.

Every member of the church of Christ having children is to bring them unto the elders before the church, who are to lay their hands upon them in the name of Jesus Christ, and bless them in his name.   No one can be received into the church of Christ unless he has arrived unto the years of accountability before God, and is capable of repentance.

Baptism is to be administered in the following manner unto all those who repent—the person who is called of God and has authority from

Jesus Christ to baptize, shall go down into the water with the person who has presented himself or herself for baptism, and shall say, calling him or her by name: *Having been commissioned of Jesus Christ, I baptize you in the name of the Father, and of the Son, and of the Holy Ghost. Amen.* Then shall he immerse him or her in the water, and come forth again out of the water.

It is expedient that the church meet together often to partake of bread and wine in the remembrance of the Lord Jesus. And the elder or priest shall administer it; and after this manner shall he administer it——he shall kneel with the church and call upon the Father in solemn prayer, saying: *O God, the Eternal Father, we ask thee in the name of thy Son, Jesus Christ, to bless and sanctify this bread to the souls of all those who partake of it, that they may eat in remembrance of the body of thy Son, and witness unto thee, O God, the Eternal Father, that they are willing to take upon them the name of thy Son, and always remember him and keep his commandments which he has given them; that they may always have his Spirit to be with them. Amen.*

The manner of administering the wine——he shall take the cup also, and say: *O God, the Eternal Father, we ask thee in the name of thy Son, Jesus Christ, to bless and sanctify this wine to the souls of all those who drink of it, that they may do it in remembrance of the blood of thy Son, which was shed for them; that they may witness unto thee, O*

*God, the Eternal Father, that they do always re-
member him, that they may have his spirit to be
with them.   Amen.*

* * *

A NEW AND EVERLASTING COVENANT

SECTION 22—*Revelation given through Joseph Smith
the Prophet, to the Church of Jesus Christ of Latter-day
Saints, at Manchester, New York, April, 1830, in consequence of some who had previously been baptized into
other churches desiring to unite with the Church without rebaptism. —— Indispensability of baptism in the
way prescribed and through the authority given by the
Lord.*

BEHOLD, I say unto you that all old covenants have I caused to be done away in this thing;
and this is a new and an everlasting covenant, even
that which was from the beginning.   Wherefore,
although a man should be baptized an hundred
times it availeth him nothing, for you cannot enter in at the strait gate by the law of Moses, neither by your dead works.   For it is because of your
dead works that I have caused this last covenant
and this church to be built up unto me, even as in
days of old.   Wherefore, enter ye in at the gate,
as I have commanded, and seek not to counsel your
God.   Amen.

SACRAMENTAL EMBLEMS AND THE FUTURE COMMUNION

SECTION 27—*Revelation given to Joseph Smith the
Prophet, at Harmony, Pennsylvania, August, 1830. In*

preparation for a religious service at which the sacrament of bread and wine was to be administered, Joseph set out to procure wine for the occasion. He was met by a heavenly messenger, and received this revelation. Water is commonly used instead of wine in the sacramental services of the Church. —— Warning against the use of wine of unassured purity in the sacrament— Many ancient prophets named, with whom, as with latter-day prophets, the Lord promises to partake— Prior ordinations to the Apostleship affirmed—Encouraging admonition given.

LISTEN to the voice of Jesus Christ, your Lord, your God, and your Redeemer, whose word is quick and powerful. For, behold, I say unto you, that it mattereth not what ye shall eat or what ye shall drink when ye partake of the sacrament, if it so be that ye do it with an eye single to my glory—remembering unto the Father my body which was laid down for you, and my blood which was shed for the remission of your sins. Wherefore, a commandment I give unto you, that you shall not purchase wine neither strong drink of your enemies. Wherefore, you shall partake of none except it is made new among you, yea, in this my Father's kingdom which shall be built up on the earth.

Behold, this is wisdom in me; wherefore, marvel not, for the hour cometh that I will drink of the fruit of the vine with you on the earth, and with Moroni, whom I have sent unto you to reveal the *Book of Mormon*, containing the fulness of my everlasting gospel, to whom I have committed the keys of the record of the stick of Ephraim—

And also with Elias, to whom I have committed the keys of bringing to pass the restoration of all things spoken by the mouth of all the holy prophets since the world began, concerning the last days—And also John the son of Zacharias, which Zacharias he (Elias) visited and gave promise that he should have a son, and his name should be John, and he should be filled with the spirit of Elias—Which John I have sent unto you, my servants, Joseph Smith, Jun., and Oliver Cowdery, to ordain you unto the first priesthood which you have received, that you might be called and ordained even as Aaron—

And also Elijah, unto whom I have committed the keys of the power of turning the hearts of the fathers to the children, and the hearts of the children to the fathers, that the whole earth may not be smitten with a curse—And also with Joseph and Jacob, and Isaac, and Abraham, your fathers, by whom the promises remain—And also with Michael, or Adam, the father of all, the prince of all, the ancient of days—

And also with Peter, and James, and John, whom I have sent unto you, by whom I have ordained you and confirmed you to be apostles, and especial witnesses of my name, and bear the keys of your ministry and of the same things which I revealed unto them—Unto whom I have committed the keys of my kingdom, and a dispensation of the gospel for the last times, and for the fulness of times, in the which I will gather together in one all things, both which are in heaven, and which are on earth—And also with all those whom my Father hath given me out of the world.

Wherefore, lift up your hearts and rejoice, and gird up your loins, and take upon you my whole armor, that ye may be able to withstand the evil day, having done all, that ye may be able to stand. Stand, therefore, having your loins girt about with truth, having on the breastplate of righteousness, and your feet shod with the preparation of the gospel of peace, which I have sent mine angels to commit unto you, taking the shield of faith wherewith ye shall be able to quench all the fiery darts of the wicked. And take the helmet of salvation, and the sword of my Spirit, which I will pour out upon you, and my word which I reveal unto you, and be agreed as touching all things whatsoever ye ask of me, and be faithful until I come, and ye shall be caught up, that where I am ye shall be also. Amen.

TRIBULATIONS AND JUDGMENT

SECTION 29—*Revelation given through Joseph Smith the Prophet, in the presence of six Elders, at Fayette, New York, September, 1830. —— Gathering of the elect—Imminence of the Lord's advent—Calamities incident to sinful state of the world—The Millennium and scenes of judgment to follow—Distinction between spiritual and temporal creations—Purpose of the mortal probation—The agency of man—Assured redemption of children who die in infancy.*

LISTEN to the voice of Jesus Christ, your Redeemer, the Great I AM, whose arm of mercy hath atoned for your sins, who will gather his people even as a hen gathereth her chickens under her wings, even as many as will hearken to my voice and humble themselves before me, and call upon me in mighty prayer. Behold, verily, verily, I say unto you, that at this time your sins are forgiven you, therefore ye receive these things; but remember to sin no more, lest perils shall come upon you.

Verily I say unto you that ye are chosen out of the world to declare my gospel with the sound of rejoicing, as with the voice of a trump. Lift up your hearts and be glad, for I am in your midst, and am your advocate with the Father; and it is his good will to give you the kingdom. And, as it is written—Whatsoever ye shall ask in faith, being united in prayer according to my command, ye shall receive. And ye are called to bring to pass the gathering of mine elect; for mine elect hear my voice and harden not their hearts. Wherefore, the decree hath gone forth from the Father that they shall be gathered in unto one place upon the face of this land, to prepare their hearts and be prepared in all things against the day when tribulation and desolation are sent forth upon the wicked.

For the hour is nigh and the day soon at hand when the earth is ripe; and all the proud and they that do wickedly shall be as stubble; and I will burn them up, saith the Lord of Hosts, that wickedness shall not be upon the earth. For the hour is nigh, and that which was spoken by mine apostles must be fulfilled; for as they spoke so shall it come to pass; for I will reveal myself from heaven with power and great glory, with all the hosts thereof, and dwell in righteousness with men on earth a thousand years, and the wicked shall not stand.

And again, verily, verily, I say unto you, and it hath gone forth in a firm decree, by the will of the Father, that mine apostles, the Twelve which were with me in my ministry at Jerusalem, shall stand at my right hand at the day of my coming in a pillar of fire, being clothed with robes of righteousness, with crowns upon their heads, in glory even as I am, to judge the whole house of Israel, even as many as have loved me and kept my commandments and none else. For a trump shall sound both long and loud, even as upon Mount Sinai, and all the earth shall quake, and they shall come forth, yea, even the dead which died in me, to receive a crown of righteousness, and to be clothed upon, even as I am, to be with me, that we may be one.

But, behold, I say unto you that before this great day shall come the sun shall be darkened, and the moon shall be turned into blood, and the stars shall fall from heaven, and there shall be greater signs in heaven above and in the earth beneath. And there shall be weeping and wailing among the hosts of men. And there shall be a great hailstorm sent forth to destroy the crops of the earth. And it shall come to pass, because of the wickedness of the world, that I will take vengeance upon the wicked, for they will not repent; for the cup of mine indignation is full; for behold, my blood shall not cleanse them if they hear me not.

Wherefore, I, the Lord God, will send forth flies upon the face of the earth, which shall take hold of the inhabitants thereof, and shall eat their flesh, and shall cause maggots to come in upon them; and their tongues shall be stayed that they shall not utter against me; and their flesh shall fall from off their bones, and their eyes from their sockets. And it shall come to pass that the beasts of the forest and the fowls of the air shall devour them up. And the great and abominable church, which is the whore of all the earth, shall be cast down by devouring fire, according as it is spoken by the mouth of Ezekiel the prophet, who spoke of these things, which have not come to pass but surely must, as I live, for abominations shall not reign.

And again, verily, verily, I say unto you that when the thousand years are ended, and men again begin to deny their God, then will I spare the earth but for a little season and the end shall come, and the heaven and the earth shall be consumed and pass away, and there shall be a new heaven and a new earth. For all old things shall pass away, and all things shall become new, even the heaven and the earth, and all the fulness thereof, both men and beasts, the fowls of the air, and the fishes of the sea; and not one hair, neither mote, shall be lost, for it is the workmanship of mine hand.

But, behold, verily I say unto you, before the earth shall pass away, Michael, mine archangel, shall sound his trump, and then shall all the dead awake, for their graves shall be opened, and they shall come forth, yea, even all. And the righteous shall be gathered on my right hand unto eternal life; and the wicked on my left hand will I be ashamed to own before the Father; wherefore I will say unto them: Depart from me, ye cursed, into everlasting fire, prepared for the devil and his angels. And now, behold, I say unto you, never at any time have I declared from mine own mouth that they should return, for where I am they cannot come, for they have no power.

But remember that all my judgments are not given unto men; and as the words have gone forth out of my mouth even so shall they be fulfilled, that the first shall be last, and that the last shall be first in all things whatsoever I have created by the word of my power, which is the power of my Spirit. For by the power of my Spirit created I them; yea, all things both spiritual and temporal—first spiritual, secondly temporal, which is the beginning of my work; and again, first temporal, and secondly spiritual, which is the last of my work—speaking unto you that you may naturally understand; but unto myself my works have no end, neither beginning; but it is given unto you that ye may understand, because ye have asked it of me and are agreed.

Wherefore, verily I say unto you that all things unto me are spiritual, and not at any time have I given unto you a law which was temporal; neither any man, nor the children of men; neither Adam, your father, whom I created. Behold, I gave unto him that he should be an agent unto himself; and I gave unto him commandment, but no temporal commandment gave I unto him, for my commandments are spiritual; they are not natural nor temporal, neither carnal nor sensual.

And it came to pass that Adam, being tempted of the devil—for, behold, the devil was before Adam, for he rebelled against me, saying, Give me thine honor, which is my power; and also a third part of the hosts of heaven turned he away from me because of their agency. And they were thrust down, and thus came the devil and his angels; and, behold, there is a place prepared for them from the beginning, which place is hell.

And it must needs be that the devil should tempt the children of men, or they could not be agents unto themselves; for if they never should have bitter they could not know the sweet. Wherefore, it came to pass that the devil tempted Adam, and he partook of the forbidden fruit and transgressed the commandment, wherein he became subject to the will of the devil, because he yielded unto temptation. Wherefore, I, the Lord God, caused that he should be cast out from the Garden

of Eden, from my presence, because of his transgression, wherein he became spiritually dead,
which is the first death, even that same death which
is the last death, which is spiritual, which shall be
pronounced upon the wicked when I shall say:
Depart, ye cursed.

But, behold, I say unto you that I, the Lord
God, gave unto Adam and unto his seed, that they
should not die as to the temporal death until I,
the Lord God, should send forth angels to declare
unto them repentance and redemption, through
faith on the name of mine Only Begotten Son.
And thus did I, the Lord God, appoint unto man
the days of his probation—that by his natural
death he might be raised in immortality unto eternal life, even as many as would believe; and they
that believe not unto eternal damnation; for they
cannot be redeemed from their spiritual fall, because they repent not; for they love darkness rather
than light, and their deeds are evil, and they receive their wages of whom they list to obey.

But, behold, I say unto you, that little children
are redeemed from the foundation of the world
through mine Only Begotten. Wherefore, they
cannot sin, for power is not given unto Satan to
tempt little children until they begin to become accountable before me. For it is given unto them
even as I will, according to mine own pleasure,
that great things may be required at the hand of
their fathers. And, again, I say unto you, that
whoso having knowledge have I not commanded

to repent?   And he that hath no understanding, it remaineth in me to do according as it is written. And now I declare no more unto you at this time. Amen.

―――――――

DILIGENCE ENJOINED

SECTION 38—*Revelation given through Joseph Smith the Prophet, at Fayette, New York, January 2, 1831, at a conference of the Church. —— Jesus Christ proclaims himself as the Creator—Future of the wicked and the righteous—Definite promise of endowment with power from on high—Riches of eternity extolled—Diligent service required.*

THUS SAITH THE LORD your God, even Jesus Christ, the Great I AM, Alpha and Omega, the beginning and the end, the same which looked upon the wide expanse of eternity, and all the seraphic hosts of heaven, before the world was made; the same which knoweth all things, for all things are present before mine eyes.   I am the same which spake, and the world was made, and all things came by me.

I am the same which have taken the Zion of Enoch into mine own bosom; and verily, I say, even as many as have believed in my name, for I am Christ, and in mine own name, by the virtue of the blood which I have spilt, have I pleaded before the Father for them.

But behold, the residue of the wicked have I kept in chains of darkness until the judgment of the

3

great day, which shall come at the end of the earth. And even so will I cause the wicked to be kept, that will not hear my voice but harden their hearts, and wo, wo, wo, is their doom.

But behold, verily, verily, I say unto you that mine eyes are upon you. I am in your midst and ye cannot see me; but the day soon cometh that ye shall see me, and know that I am; for the veil of darkness shall soon be rent, and he that is not purified shall not abide the day. Wherefore, gird up your loins and be prepared. Behold, the kingdom is yours, and the enemy shall not overcome.

Verily I say unto you, ye are clean, but not all; and there is none else with whom I am well pleased; for all flesh is corrupted before me; and the powers of darkness prevail upon the earth, among the children of men, in the presence of all the hosts of heaven—which causeth silence to reign, and all eternity is pained, and the angels are waiting the great command to reap down the earth, to gather the tares that they may be burned; and, behold, the enemy is combined.

And now I show unto you a mystery, a thing which is had in secret chambers, to bring to pass even your destruction in process of time, and ye knew it not. But now I tell it unto you, and ye are blessed, not because of your iniquity, neither your hearts of unbelief; for verily some of you are guilty before me, but I will be merciful unto your weakness. Therefore, be ye strong from henceforth; fear not, for the kingdom is yours.

And for your salvation I give unto you a commandment, for I have heard your prayers, and the poor have complained before me, and the rich have I made, and all flesh is mine, and I am no respecter of persons. And I have made the earth rich, and behold it is my footstool, wherefore, again I will stand upon it. And I hold forth and deign to give unto you greater riches, even a land of promise, a land flowing with milk and honey, upon which there shall be no curse when the Lord cometh; and I will give it unto you for the land of your inheritance, if you seek it with all your hearts.

And this shall be my covenant with you, ye shall have it for the land of your inheritance, and for the inheritance of your children forever while the earth shall stand, and ye shall possess it again in eternity, no more to pass away. But, verily I say unto you that in time ye shall have no king nor ruler, for I will be your king and watch over you. Wherefore, hear my voice and follow me, and you shall be a free people, and ye shall have no laws but my laws when I come, for I am your lawgiver, and what can stay my hand?

But, verily I say unto you, teach one another according to the office wherewith I have appointed you; and let every man esteem his brother as himself, and practise virtue and holiness before me. And again I say unto you, let every man esteem his brother as himself. For what man among you having twelve sons, and is no respecter of them, and they serve him obediently, and he saith unto the one: Be thou clothed in robes and sit thou here; and to the other: Be thou clothed in rags and sit thou there—and looketh upon his sons and saith, I am just? Behold, this I have given unto you as a parable, and it is even as I am. I say unto you, be one; and if ye are not one ye are not mine.

And again, I say unto you that the enemy in the secret chambers seeketh your lives. Ye hear of wars in far countries, and you say that there will soon be great wars in far countries, but ye know not the hearts of men in your own land. I tell you these things because of your prayers; wherefore, treasure up wisdom in your bosoms, lest the wickedness of men reveal these things unto you by their wickedness, in a manner which shall speak in your ears with a voice louder than that which shall shake the earth; but if ye are prepared ye shall not fear.

And that ye might escape the power of the enemy, and be gathered unto me a righteous people, without spot and blameless, wherefore, for this cause I gave unto you the commandment that ye should go to the Ohio; and there I will give unto you my law; and there you shall be endowed with power from on high. And from thence, whosoever I will shall go forth among all nations, and it shall be told them what they shall do; for I have a great work laid up in store, for Israel shall be saved, and I will lead them whithersoever I will, and no power shall stay my hand.

And now, I give unto the church in these parts a commandment, that certain men among them shall be appointed, and they shall be appointed by the voice of the church. And they shall look to the poor and the needy, and administer to their relief that they shall not suffer; and send them forth to the place which I have commanded them, and this shall be their work, to govern the affairs of the property of this church. And they that have farms that cannot be sold, let them be left or rented as seemeth them good. See that all things are preserved; and when men are endowed with power from on high and sent forth, all these things shall be gathered unto the bosom of the church.

And if ye seek the riches which it is the will of the Father to give unto you, ye shall be the richest of all people, for ye shall have the riches of eternity; and it must needs be that the riches of the earth are mine to give; but beware of pride, lest ye become as the Nephites of old. And again, I say unto you, I give unto you a commandment, that every man, both elder, priest, teacher, and also member, go to with his might, with the labor of his hands, to prepare and accomplish the things which I have commanded. And let your preaching be the warning voice, every man to his neighbor, in mildness and in meekness. And go ye out from among the wicked. Save yourselves. Be ye clean that bear the vessels of the Lord. Even so. Amen.

LAW AND ORDER IN THE CHURCH

SECTION 42—*Revelation given through Joseph Smith the Prophet, at Kirtland, Ohio, February 9, 1831, in the presence of twelve Elders, and in fulfilment of the Lord's promise previously made. The Prophet specifies this revelation as embracing the law of the Church. —— Elders commanded to go forth two by two—Several commandments comprised in the Decalog reiterated—The idler denounced—Administration to the afflicted by the laying on of hands of the Elders—Comforting assurance concerning those who die in the Lord—Sexual sin proclaimed against—Church members who commit crimes to be handed over to the law of the land—Fundamental principles of Church discipline.*

HEARKEN, O ye elders of my church, who have assembled yourselves together in my name, even Jesus Christ the Son of the living God, the Savior of the world; inasmuch as ye believe on my name and keep my commandments. Again I say unto you: Hearken and hear and obey the law which I shall give unto you. For verily I say, as ye have assembled yourselves together according to the commandment wherewith I commanded you, and are agreed as touching this one thing, and have asked the Father in my name, even so ye shall receive.

Behold, verily I say unto you, I give unto you this first commandment, that ye shall go forth in my name, every one of you, excepting my servants Joseph Smith, Jun., and Sidney Rigdon. And I give unto them a commandment that they shall go forth for a little season, and it shall be given by the power of the Spirit when they shall return.   And ye shall go forth in the power of my Spirit. preaching my gospel, two by two, in my name, lifting up your voices as with the sound of a trump, declaring my word like unto angels of God.   And ye shall go forth baptizing with water, saying: Repent ye, repent ye, for the kingdom of heaven is at hand.

And from this place ye shall go forth into the regions westward; and inasmuch as ye shall find them that will receive you ye shall build up my church in every region, until the time shall come when it shall be revealed unto you from on high, when the city of the New Jerusalem shall be prepared, that ye may be gathered in one, that ye may be my people and I will be your God.

*   *   *

Again, I say unto you, that it shall not be given to any one to go forth to preach my gospel, or to build up my church, except he be ordained by some one who has authority, and it is known to the church that he has authority and has been regularly ordained by the heads of the church.   And again, the elders, priests and teachers of this church shall teach the principles of my gospel, which are in the *Bible* and the *Book of Mormon,* in the which is the fulness of the gospel.

And they shall observe the covenants and church

articles to do them, and these shall be their teachings, as they shall be directed by the Spirit. And the Spirit shall be given unto you by the prayer of faith; and if ye receive not the Spirit ye shall not teach. And all this ye shall observe to do as I have commanded concerning your teaching, until the fulness of my scriptures is given. And as ye shall lift up your voices by the Comforter, ye shall speak and prophesy as seemeth me good; for, behold, the Comforter knoweth all things, and beareth record of the Father and of the Son.

And now, behold, I speak unto the church: Thou shalt not kill; and he that kills shall not have forgiveness in this world nor in the world to come. And again, I say, thou shalt not kill; but he that killeth shall die. Thou shalt not steal; and he that stealeth and will not repent shall be cast out. Thou shalt not lie; he that lieth and will not repent shall be cast out.

Thou shalt love thy wife with all thy heart, and shalt cleave unto her and none else. And he that looketh upon a woman to lust after her shall deny the faith, and shall not have the Spirit; and if he repents not he shall be cast out. Thou shalt not commit adultery, and he that committeth adultery, and repenteth not, shall be cast out. But he that has committed adultery and repents with all his heart, and forsaketh it, and doeth it no more, thou shalt forgive; but if he doeth it again, he shall not be forgiven, but shall be cast out. Thou shalt not speak evil of thy neighbor, nor do him any harm. Thou knowest my laws concerning these things are given in my scriptures; he that sinneth and repenteth not shall be cast out. If thou lovest me thou shalt serve me and keep all my commandments.

*   *   *

And again, thou shalt not be proud in thy heart; let all thy garments be plain, and their beauty the beauty of the work of thine own hands; and let all things be done in cleanliness before me. Thou shalt not be idle; for he that is idle shall not eat the bread nor wear the garments of the laborer.

And whosoever among you are sick, and have not faith to be healed, but believe, shall be nourished with all tenderness, with herbs and mild food, and that not by the hand of an enemy. And the elders of the church, two or more, shall be called, and shall pray for and lay their hands upon them in my name; and if they die they shall die unto me, and if they live they shall live unto me. Thou shalt live together in love, insomuch that thou shalt weep for the loss of them that die, and more especially for those that have not hope of a glorious resurrection. And it shall come to pass that those that die in me shall not taste of death, for it shall be sweet unto them; and they that die not in me, wo unto them, for their death is bitter.

And again, it shall come to pass that he that hath faith in me to be healed, and is not appointed unto death, shall be healed. He who hath faith to see shall see. He who hath faith to hear shall hear. The lame who hath faith to leap shall leap. And they who have not faith to do these things, but believe in me, have power to become my sons; and inasmuch as they break not my laws thou shalt bear their infirmities.

* * *

Thou shalt ask, and my scriptures shall be given as I have appointed, and they shall be preserved in safety; and it is expedient that thou shouldst hold thy peace concerning them, and not teach them until ye have received them in full. And I give unto you a commandment that then ye shall teach them unto all men; for they shall be taught unto all nations, kindreds, tongues and people. Thou shalt take the things which thou hast received, which have been given unto thee in my scriptures for a law, to be my law to govern my church; and he that doeth according to these things shall be saved, and he that doeth them not shall be damned if he so continue.

If thou shalt ask, thou shalt receive revelation upon revelation, knowledge upon knowledge, that thou mayest know the mysteries and peaceable things—that which bringeth joy, that which bringeth life eternal. Thou shalt ask, and it shall be revealed unto you in mine own due time where the New Jerusalem shall be built. And behold, it shall come to pass that my servants shall be sent forth to the east and to the west, to the north and to the south. And even now, let him that goeth to the east teach them that shall be converted to flee to the west, and this in consequence of that which is coming on the earth, and of secret combinations. Behold, thou shalt observe all these things, and great shall be thy reward; for unto you it is given to know the mysteries of the kingdom, but unto the world it is not given to know them.

Ye shall observe the laws which ye have received and be faithful. And ye shall hereafter receive church covenants, such as shall be sufficient to establish you, both here and in the New Jerusalem. Therefore, he that lacketh wisdom, let him ask of me, and I will give him liberally and upbraid him not. Lift up your hearts and rejoice, for unto you the kingdom, or in other words, the keys of the church, have been given. Even so. Amen.

* * *

Behold, verily I say unto you, that whatever persons among you, having put away their companions for the cause of fornication, or in other words, if they shall testify before you in all lowliness of heart that this is the case, ye shall not cast them out from among you. But if ye shall find that any persons have left their companions for the sake of adultery, and they themselves are the offenders, and their companions are living, they shall be cast out from among you. And again, I say unto you, that ye shall be watchful and careful, with all inquiry, that ye receive none such among you if they are married; and if they are not married, they shall repent of all their sins or ye shall not receive them.

And again, every person who belongeth to this church of Christ, shall observe to keep all the commandments and covenants of the church. And it shall come to pass, that if any persons among you shall kill they shall be delivered up and dealt with according to the laws of the land; for remember that he hath no forgiveness; and it shall be proved according to the laws of the land.

* * *

And if a man or woman shall rob, he or she shall be delivered up unto the law of the land. And if he or she shall steal, he or she shall be delivered up unto the law of the land. And if he or she shall lie, he or she shall be delivered up unto the law of the land. And if he or she do any manner of iniquity, he or she shall be delivered up unto the law, even that of God.

And if thy brother or sister offend thee, thou shalt take him or her between him or her and thee alone; and if he or she confess thou shalt be reconciled. And if he or she confess not thou shalt deliver him or her up unto the church, not to the members, but to the elders. And it shall be done in a meeting, and that not before the world. And if thy brother or sister offend many, he or she

shall be chastened before many.   And if any one
offend openly, he or she shall be rebuked openly,
that he or she may be ashamed.   And if he or she
confess not, he or she shall be delivered up unto
the law of God.   If any shall offend in secret, he
or she shall be rebuked in secret, that he or she
may have opportunity to confess in secret to him
or her whom he or she has offended, and to God,
that the church may not speak reproachfully of
him or her.   And thus shall ye conduct in all
things.

IN PREPARATION FOR THE LORD'S COMING

SECTION 43—*Revelation given through Joseph Smith
the Prophet, at Kirtland, Ohio, in February, 1831.   At
this time some members of the Church were disturbed
by people making false claims as revelators. —— Revelations to the Church given only through the one appointed to receive such—Elders warned against spurious
claims and false teachings—Elders sent forth to teach
according to the spirit of revelation—Assurances of the
Lord's future advent—Calamities to precede his coming—Warning, proclamation, and commandment.*

O HEARKEN, ye elders of my church, and give
ear to the words which I shall speak unto you.
For behold, verily, verily, I say unto you, that ye
have received a commandment for a law unto my
church, through him whom I have appointed unto you to receive commandments and revelations
from my hand.   And this ye shall know assuredly
—that there is none other appointed unto you to

receive commandments and revelations until he be taken, if he abide in me. But verily, verily, I say unto you, that none else shall be appointed unto this gift except it be through him; for if it be taken from him he shall not have power except to appoint another in his stead.

And this shall be a law unto you, that ye receive not the teachings of any that shall come before you as revelations or commandments; and this I give unto you that you may not be deceived, that you may know they are not of me. For verily I say unto you, that he that is ordained of me shall come in at the gate and be ordained as I have told you before, to teach those revelations which you have received and shall receive through him whom I have appointed.

And now, behold, I give unto you a commandment, that when ye are assembled together ye shall instruct and edify each other, that ye may know how to act and direct my church, how to act upon the points of my law and commandments, which I have given. And thus ye shall become instructed in the law of my church, and be sanctified by that which ye have received, and ye shall bind yourselves to act in all holiness before me. That inasmuch as ye do this, glory shall be added to the kingdom which ye have received. Inasmuch as ye do it not, it shall be taken, even that which ye have received.

* * *

Again I say, hearken ye elders of my church, whom I have appointed: Ye are not sent forth to be taught, but to teach the children of men the things which I have put into your hands by the power of my Spirit; and ye are to be taught from on high. Sanctify yourselves and ye shall be endowed with power, that ye may give even as I have spoken.

Hearken ye, for, behold, the great day of the Lord is nigh at hand. For the day cometh that the Lord shall utter his voice out of heaven; the heavens shall shake and the earth shall tremble, and the trump of God shall sound both long and loud, and shall say to the sleeping nations: Ye saints arise and live; ye sinners stay and sleep until I shall call again.

Wherefore gird up your loins lest ye be found among the wicked. Lift up your voices and spare not. Call upon the nations to repent, both old and young, both bond and free, saying: Prepare yourselves for the great day of the Lord; for if I, who am a man, do lift up my voice and call upon you to repent, and ye hate me, what will ye say when the day cometh when the thunders shall utter their voices from the ends of the earth, speaking to the ears of all that live, saying—Repent, and prepare for the great day of the Lord? Yea, and again, when the lightnings shall streak forth from the east unto the west, and shall utter forth their voices unto all that live, and make the ears of all tingle that hear, saying these words—Repent ye, for the great day of the Lord is come?

And again, the Lord shall utter his voice out of heaven, saying: Hearken, O ye nations of the earth, and hear the words of that God who made you. O, ye nations of the earth, how often would I have gathered you together as a hen gathereth her chickens under her wings, but ye would not! How oft have I called upon you by the mouth of my servants, and by the ministering of angels, and by mine own voice, and by the voice of thunderings, and by the voice of lightnings, and by the voice of tempests, and by the voice of earthquakes, and great hailstorms, and by the voice of famines and pestilences of every kind, and by the great sound of a trump, and by the voice of judgment, and by the voice of mercy all the day long, and by the voice of glory and honor and the riches of eternal life, and would have saved you with an everlasting salvation, but ye would not!

Behold the day has come, when the cup of the wrath of mine indignation is full. Behold, verily I say unto you, that these are the words of the Lord your God. Wherefore, labor ye, labor ye in my vineyard for the last time—for the last time call upon the inhabitants of the earth. For in mine own due time will I come upon the earth in judgment, and my people shall be redeemed and shall reign with me on earth.

For the great Millennium, of which I have spoken by the mouth of my servants, shall come.

For Satan shall be bound, and when he is loosed again he shall only reign for a little season, and then cometh the end of the earth.   And he that liveth in righteousness shall be changed in the twinkling of an eye, and the earth shall pass away so as by fire.   And the wicked shall go away into unquenchable fire, and their end no man knoweth on earth, nor ever shall know, until they come before me in judgment. Hearken ye to these words. Behold, I am Jesus Christ, the Savior of the world. Treasure these things up in your hearts, and let the solemnities of eternity rest upon your minds. Be sober.   Keep all my commandments.   Even so. Amen.

AS THE LORD SPAKE SO HE SPEAKS

SECTION 45—*Revelation given through Joseph Smith the Prophet, to the Church, at Kirtland, Ohio, March 7, 1831. Prefacing his record of this revelation, the Prophet states that at this age of the Church many false reports and foolish stories were published and circulated, to prevent people from investigating the work or embracing the faith. ——— Jesus Christ the Advocate with the Father—Blessed state of Enoch and his people— Prediction to the disciples in former days cited—Times of the Gentiles signalized by the light of the Gospel— A desolating sickness named among the many tribulations—Gathering of the people—Eventual triumph of Zion.*

HEARKEN, O ye people of my church, to whom the kingdom has been given; hearken ye and give

4

ear to him who laid the foundation of the earth, who made the heavens and all the hosts thereof, and by whom all things were made which live, and move, and have a being. And again I say, hearken unto my voice, lest death shall overtake you; in an hour when ye think not the summer shall be past, and the harvest ended, and your souls not saved.

Listen to him who is the advocate with the Father, who is pleading your cause before him, saying: Father, behold the sufferings and death of him who did no sin, in whom thou wast well pleased; behold the blood of thy Son which was shed, the blood of him whom thou gavest that thyself might be glorified; wherefore, Father, spare these my brethren that believe on my name, that they may come unto me and have everlasting life.

Hearken, O ye people of my church, and ye elders listen together, and hear my voice while it is called *today,* and harden not your hearts. For verily I say unto you that I am Alpha and Omega, the beginning and the end, the light and the life of the world—a light that shineth in darkness and the darkness comprehendeth it not. I came unto mine own, and mine own received me not; but unto as many as received me gave I power to do many miracles, and to become the sons of God; and even unto them that believed on my name gave I power to obtain eternal life.

And even so I have sent mine everlasting covenant into the world, to be a light to the world, and to be a standard for my people, and for the Gentiles to seek to it, and to be a messenger before my face to prepare the way before me. Wherefore, come ye unto it, and with him that cometh I will reason as with men in days of old, and I will show unto you my strong reasoning.

Wherefore, hearken ye together and let me show unto you even my wisdom—the wisdom of him whom ye say is the God of Enoch, and his brethren, who were separated from the earth, and were received unto myself—a city reserved until a day of righteousness shall come—a day which was sought for by all holy men, and they found it not because of wickedness and abominations; and confessed they were strangers and pilgrims on the earth; but obtained a promise that they should find it and see it in their flesh.

Wherefore, hearken and I will reason with you, and I will speak unto you and prophesy, as unto men in days of old. And I will show it plainly as I showed it unto my disciples as I stood before them in the flesh, and spake unto them, saying:

"As ye have asked of me concerning the signs of my coming, in the day when I shall come in my glory in the clouds of heaven, to fulfil the promises that I have made unto your fathers—for as ye have looked upon the long absence of your spirits from your bodies to be a bondage, I will show unto you how the day of redemption shall come, and also the restoration of the scattered Israel.

"And now ye behold this temple which is in Jerusalem, which ye call the house of God, and your enemies say that this house shall never fall. But, verily I say unto you, that desolation shall come upon this generation as a thief in the night, and this people shall be destroyed and scattered among all nations. And this temple which ye now see shall be thrown down that there shall not be left one stone upon another. And it shall come to pass, that this generation of Jews shall not pass away until every desolation which I have told you concerning them shall come to pass.

"Ye say that ye know that the end of the world cometh; ye say also that ye know that the heavens and the earth shall pass away. And in this ye say truly, for so it is; but these things which I have told you shall not pass away until all shall be fulfilled. And this I have told you concerning Jerusalem; and when that day shall come, shall a remnant be scattered among all nations; but they shall be gathered again; but they shall remain until the times of the Gentiles be fulfilled. And in that day shall be heard of wars and rumors of wars, and the whole earth shall be in commotion, and men's hearts shall fail them, and they shall say that Christ delayeth his coming until the end of the earth. And the love of men shall wax cold, and iniquity shall abound.

"And when the times of the Gentiles is come in, a light shall break forth among them that sit in darkness, and it shall be the fulness of my gospel; but they receive it not; for they perceive not the light, and they turn their hearts from me because of the precepts of men.   And in that generation shall the times of the Gentiles be fulfilled.

"And there shall be men standing in that generation that shall not pass until they shall see an overflowing scourge; for a desolating sickness shall cover the land.   But my disciples shall stand in holy places, and shall not be moved; but among the wicked, men shall lift up their voices and curse God and die.   And there shall be earthquakes also in divers places, and many desolations; yet men will harden their hearts against me, and they will take up the sword one against another and they will kill one another."

And now, when I, the Lord, had spoken these words unto my disciples, they were troubled. And I said unto them: "Be not troubled, for, when all these things shall come to pass, ye may know that the promises which have been made unto you shall be fulfilled.   And when the light shall begin to break forth it shall be with them like unto a parable which I will show you: Ye look and behold the fig-trees, and ye see them with your eyes, and ye say when they begin to shoot forth and their leaves are yet tender that summer is now nigh at hand.   Even so it shall be in that day when they shall see all these things, then shall they know that the hour is nigh.

"And it shall come to pass that he that feareth me shall be looking forth for the great day of the Lord to come, even for the signs of the coming of the Son of Man. And they shall see signs and wonders, for they shall be shown forth in the heavens above, and in the earth beneath; and they shall behold blood, and fire, and vapors of smoke. And before the day of the Lord shall come, the sun shall be darkened, and the moon be turned into blood, and the stars fall from heaven. And the remnant shall be gathered unto this place; and then they shall look for me, and, behold, I will come; and they shall see me in the clouds of heaven, clothed with power and great glory, with all the holy angels; and he that watches not for me shall be cut off.

"But before the arm of the Lord shall fall, an angel shall sound his trump, and the saints that have slept shall come forth to meet me in the cloud. Wherefore, if ye have slept in peace blessed are you; for as you now behold me and know that I am, even so shall ye come unto me and your souls shall live, and your redemption shall be perfected; and the saints shall come forth from the four quarters of the earth. Then shall the arm of the Lord fall upon the nations. And then shall the Lord set his foot upon this mount, and it shall cleave in twain, and the earth shall tremble, and reel to and fro, and the heavens also shall shake.

"And the Lord shall utter his voice, and all the ends of the earth shall hear it; and the nations of the earth shall mourn, and they that have laughed shall see their folly. And calamity shall cover the mocker, and the scorner shall be consumed; and they that have watched for iniquity shall be hewn down and cast into the fire. And then shall the Jews look upon me and say: What are these wounds in thine hands and in thy feet? Then shall they know that I am the Lord; for I will say unto them: These wounds are the wounds with which I was wounded in the house of my friends. I am he who was lifted up. I am Jesus that was crucified. I am the Son of God. And then shall they weep because of their iniquities; then shall they lament because they persecuted their king.

"And then shall the heathen nations be redeemed, and they that knew no law shall have part in the first resurrection; and it shall be tolerable for them. And Satan shall be bound, that he shall have no place in the hearts of the children of men. And at that day, when I shall come in my glory, shall the parable be fulfilled which I spake concerning the ten virgins. For they that are wise and have received the truth, and have taken the Holy Spirit for their guide, and have not been deceived—verily I say unto you, they shall not be hewn down and cast into the fire, but shall abide the day. And the earth shall be given unto them for an inheritance; and they shall multiply and wax strong, and their children shall grow up without sin unto salvation. For the Lord shall be in their midst, and his glory shall be upon them, and he will be their king and their lawgiver."

* * *

For verily I say unto you, that great things await you: Ye hear of wars in foreign lands; but, behold, I say unto you, they are nigh, even at your doors, and not many years hence ye shall hear of wars in your own lands. Wherefore I, the Lord, have said: Gather ye out from the eastern lands, assemble ye yourselves together ye elders of my church; go ye forth into the western countries, call upon the inhabitants to repent, and inasmuch as they do repent, build up churches unto me.

And with one heart and with one mind, gather up your riches that ye may purchase an inheritance which shall hereafter be appointed unto you. And it shall be called the New Jerusalem, a land of peace, a city of refuge, a place of safety for the saints of the Most High God; and the glory of the Lord shall be there, and the terror of the Lord also shall be there, insomuch that the wicked will not come unto it, and it shall be called Zion. And it shall come to pass among the wicked, that every man that will not take his sword against his neighbor must needs flee unto Zion for safety. And there shall be gathered unto it out of every nation under heaven; and it shall be the only people that shall not be at war one with another. And it shall be said among the wicked: Let us not go up to battle against Zion, for the inhabitants of Zion are terrible; wherefore we cannot stand.

And it shall come to pass that the righteous shall be gathered out from among all nations, and shall come to Zion, singing with songs of everlasting joy. And now I say unto you, keep these things from going abroad unto the world until it is expedient in me, that ye may accomplish this work in the eyes of the people, and in the eyes of your enemies, that they may not know your works until ye have accomplished the thing which I have commanded you; that when they shall know it they may consider these things. For when the Lord shall appear he shall be terrible unto them, that fear may seize upon them, and they shall stand afar off and tremble. And all nations shall be afraid because of the terror of the Lord, and the power of his might. Even so. Amen.

GIFTS OF THE SPIRIT

SECTION 46—*Revelation given through Joseph Smith the Prophet, to the Church, at Kirtland, Ohio, March 8, 1831. A custom of admitting to the sacramental meetings and other assemblies of the Church only members and earnest investigators had become somewhat general. —— Meetings of the Church to be conducted as the Holy Spirit shall guide—Neither members nor earnest seekers after the truth to be excluded from sacramental services—Gifts of the Holy Spirit enumerated—Power of discernment promised.*

HEARKEN, O ye people of my church; for verily I say unto you that these things were spoken unto you for your profit and learning. But notwithstanding those things which are written, it always has been given to the elders of my church from the beginning, and ever shall be, to conduct all meetings as they are directed and guided by the Holy Spirit.

Nevertheless ye are commanded never to cast any one out from your public meetings, which are held before the world. Ye are also commanded not to cast any one who belongeth to the church out of your sacrament meetings; nevertheless, if any have trespassed, let him not partake until he makes reconciliation. And again I say unto you, ye shall not cast any out of your sacrament meetings who are earnestly seeking the kingdom—I speak this concerning those who are not of the church. And again I say unto you, concerning your confirmation meetings, that if there be any that are not of the church, that are earnestly seeking after the kingdom, ye shall not cast them out.

But ye are commanded in all things to ask of God, who giveth liberally; and that which the Spirit testifies unto you even so I would that ye should do in all holiness of heart, walking uprightly before me, considering the end of your salvation, doing all things with prayer and thanksgiving, that ye may not be seduced by evil spirits, or doctrines of devils, or the commandments of men; for some are of men, and others of devils.

Wherefore, beware lest ye are deceived; and that ye may not be deceived seek ye earnestly the best gifts, always remembering for what they are given; for verily I say unto you, they are given for the benefit of those who love me and keep all my commandments, and him that seeketh so to do; that all may be benefited that seek or that ask of me, that ask and not for a sign that they may consume it upon their lusts.

And again, verily I say unto you, I would that ye should always remember, and always retain in your minds what those gifts are, that are given unto the church. For all have not every gift given unto them; for there are many gifts, and to every man is given a gift by the Spirit of God. To some is given one, and to some is given another, that all may be profited thereby. To some it is given by the Holy Ghost to know that Jesus Christ is the Son of God, and that he was crucified for the sins of the world. To others it is given to believe on their words, that they also might have eternal life if they continue faithful.

And again, to some it is given by the Holy Ghost to know the differences of administration, as it will be pleasing unto the same Lord, according as the Lord will, suiting his mercies according to the conditions of the children of men. And again, it is given by the Holy Ghost to some to know the diversities of operations, whether they be of God, that the manifestations of the Spirit may be given to every man to profit withal. And again, verily I say unto you, to some is given, by the Spirit of God, the word of wisdom. To another is given the word of knowledge, that all may be taught to be wise and to have knowledge.

And again, to some it is given to have faith to be healed; and to others it is given to have faith to heal. And again, to some is given the working of miracles; and to others it is given to prophesy; and to others the discerning of spirits. And again, it is given to some to speak with tongues; and to another is given the interpretation of tongues. And all these gifts come from God, for the benefit of the children of God.

And unto the bishop of the church, and unto such as God shall appoint and ordain to watch over the church and to be elders unto the church, are to have it given unto them to discern all those gifts lest there shall be any among you professing and yet be not of God. And it shall come to pass that he that asketh in Spirit shall receive in Spirit; that unto some it may be given to have all those gifts, that there may be a head, in order that every member may be profited thereby.

He that asketh in the Spirit asketh according to the will of God; wherefore it is done even as he asketh. And again, I say unto you, all things must be done in the name of Christ, whatsoever you do in the Spirit; and ye must give thanks unto

God in the Spirit for whatsoever blessing ye are blessed with. And ye must practise virtue and holiness before me continually. Even so. Amen.

DISCERNMENT OF SPIRITS

SECTION 50—*Revelation given through Joseph Smith the Prophet, at Kirtland, Ohio, May, 1831. The Prophet states that some of the Elders present did not understand the manifestations of different spirits abroad in the earth, and that this revelation was given in response to his special inquiry on the matter. So-called spiritual phenomena were not uncommon among the members, some of whom claimed to be receiving visions and revelations. —— False spirits deceiving the world— Means by which they may be detected.*

HEARKEN, O ye elders of my church, and give ear to the voice of the living God; and attend to the words of wisdom which shall be given unto you, according as ye have asked and are agreed as touching the church, and the spirits which have gone abroad in the earth. Behold, verily I say unto you, that there are many spirits which are false spirits, which have gone forth in the earth, deceiving the world. And also Satan hath sought to deceive you, that he might overthrow you.

Behold, I, the Lord, have looked upon you, and have seen abominations in the church that profess my name. But blessed are they who are faithful and endure, whether in life or in death, for they shall inherit eternal life. But wo unto them that are deceivers and hypocrites, for, thus saith the Lord, I will bring them to judgment.

Behold, verily I say unto you, there are hypocrites among you, who have deceived some, which has given the adversary power; but behold such shall be reclaimed, but the hypocrites shall be detected and shall be cut off, either in life or in death, even as I will; and wo unto them who are cut off from my church, for the same are overcome of the world. Wherefore, let every man beware lest he do that which is not in truth and righteousness before me.

And now come, saith the Lord, by the Spirit, unto the elders of his church, and let us reason together, that ye may understand; let us reason even as a man reasoneth one with another face to face. Now, when a man reasoneth he is understood of man, because he reasoneth as a man; even so will I, the Lord, reason with you that you may understand.

Wherefore, I, the Lord, ask you this question: Unto what were ye ordained? To preach my gospel by the Spirit, even the Comforter which was sent forth to teach the truth. And then received ye spirits which ye could not understand, and received them to be of God; and in this are ye justified? Behold ye shall answer this question yourselves; nevertheless, I will be merciful unto you; he that is weak among you hereafter shall be made strong.

Verily I say unto you, he that is ordained of me and sent forth to preach the word of truth by the Comforter, in the Spirit of truth, doth he preach it by the Spirit of truth or some other way? And if it be by some other way it is not of God. And again, he that receiveth the word of truth, doth he receive it by the Spirit of truth or some other way? If it be some other way it is not of God.

Therefore, why is it that ye cannot understand and know that he that receiveth the word by the Spirit of truth receiveth it as it is preached by the Spirit of truth? Wherefore, he that preacheth and he that receiveth understand one another, and both are edified and rejoice together. And that which doth not edify is not of God, and is darkness. That which is of God is light; and he that receiveth light, and continueth in God, receiveth more light; and that light groweth brighter and brighter until the perfect day.

And again, verily I say unto you, and I say it that you may know the truth, that you may chase darkness from among you: He that is ordained of God and sent forth, the same is appointed to be the greatest, notwithstanding he is the least and the servant of all. Wherefore, he is possessor of all things; for all things are subject unto him, both in heaven and on the earth, the life and the light, the Spirit and the power, sent forth by the will of the Father through Jesus Christ, his Son. But no man is possessor of all things except he be purified and cleansed from all sin. And if ye are purified and cleansed from all sin, ye shall ask whatsoever you will in the name of Jesus and it shall be done. But know this, it shall be given you what you shall ask; and as ye are appointed to the head, the spirits shall be subject unto you.

Wherefore, it shall come to pass, that if you behold a spirit manifested that you cannot understand, and you receive not that spirit, ye shall ask of the Father in the name of Jesus; and if he give not unto you that spirit, then you may know that it is not of God. And it shall be given unto you, power over that spirit; and you shall proclaim against that spirit with a loud voice that it is not of God—not with railing accusation, that ye be not overcome, neither with boasting nor rejoicing, lest you be seized therewith.

He that receiveth of God, let him account it of God; and let him rejoice that he is accounted of God worthy to receive. And by giving heed and doing these things which ye have received, and which ye shall hereafter receive—and the kingdom is given you of the Father, and power to overcome all things which are not ordained of him—and behold, verily I say unto you, blessed are you who are now hearing these words of mine from the mouth of my servant, for your sins are forgiven you.

*   *   *

WOES AND BLESSINGS

SECTION 56—*Revelation given through Joseph Smith the Prophet, at Kirtland, Ohio, June, 1831. One of the elders who had been appointed to travel in the ministry was not ready to start on his mission at the appointed time, and the Lord answered the Prophet's inquiry on the matter by this utterance.*

HEARKEN, O ye people who profess my name, saith the Lord your God; for behold, mine anger is kindled against the rebellious, and they shall know mine arm and mine indignation in the day of visitation and of wrath upon the nations. And he that will not take up his cross and follow me, and keep my commandments, the same shall not be saved. Behold, I, the Lord, command; and he that will not obey shall be cut off in mine own due time, after I have commanded and the commandment is broken. Wherefore I, the Lord, command and revoke, as it seemeth me good; and all this to be answered upon the heads of the rebellious, saith the Lord.

*   *   *

Behold, thus saith the Lord unto my people— you have many things to do and to repent of; for behold, your sins have come up unto me, and are not pardoned, because you seek to counsel in your own ways. And your hearts are not satisfied. And ye obey not the truth, but have pleasure in unrighteousness. Wo unto you rich men, that will not give your substance to the poor, for your riches will canker your souls; and this shall be your lamentation in the day of visitation, and of judgment, and of indignation: The harvest is past, the summer is ended, and my soul is not saved! Wo unto you poor men, whose hearts are not broken, whose spirits are not contrite, and whose bellies are not satisfied, and whose hands are not stayed from laying hold upon other men's goods, whose eyes are full of greediness, and who will not labor with your own hands!

But blessed are the poor who are pure in heart, whose hearts are broken and whose spirits are contrite, for they shall see the kingdom of God coming in power and great glory unto their deliverance; for the fatness of the earth shall be theirs. For behold, the Lord shall come, and his recompense shall be with him, and he shall reward every man, and the poor shall rejoice, and their generations shall inherit the earth from generation to generation, forever and ever. And now I make an end of speaking unto you. Even so. Amen.

COMMANDMENT AND OBEDIENCE

SECTION 58—*Revelation given through Joseph Smith the Prophet, in Zion, Jackson County, Missouri, August 1, 1831. On the first Sabbath after the arrival of the Prophet and party in Jackson County, Missouri, a religious service was held and members were received by baptism. Many were eager to learn the will of the Lord concerning them in the new place of gathering. —— Great things to follow, with glory after much tribulation—People instructed to observe the laws of the land, and to regard the commandments given through revelation as the laws of the Church—Servants not to be compelled in all things but to be diligent and active.*

HEARKEN, O ye elders of my church, and give ear to my word, and learn of me what I will concerning you, and also concerning this land unto which I have sent you. For verily I say unto you, blessed is he that keepeth my commandments, whether in life or in death; and he that is faithful in tribulation, the reward of the same is greater in the kingdom of heaven.

Ye cannot behold with your natural eyes, for the present time, the design of your God concerning those things which shall come hereafter, and the glory which shall follow after much tribulation. For after much tribulation come the blessings. Wherefore the day cometh that ye shall be crowned with much glory; the hour is not yet but is nigh at hand. Remember this, which I tell you before that you may lay it to heart, and receive that which is to follow.

Behold, verily I say unto you, for this cause I have sent you—that you might be obedient, and that your hearts might be prepared to bear testimony of the things which are to come; and also that you might be honored in laying the foundation, and in bearing record of the land upon which the Zion of God shall stand. And also that a feast of fat things might be prepared for the poor; yea, a feast of fat things, of wine on the lees well refined, that the earth may know that the mouths of the prophets shall not fail; yea, a supper of the house of the Lord, well prepared, unto which all nations shall be invited. First, the rich and the learned, the wise and the noble; and after that cometh the day of my power; then shall the poor, the lame, and the blind, and the deaf, come in unto the marriage of the Lamb, and partake of the supper of the Lord, prepared for the great day to come. Behold, I, the Lord, have spoken it.

* * *

Let no man think he is ruler; but let God rule him that judgeth, according to the counsel of his own will, or, in other words, him that counseleth or sitteth upon the judgment seat. Let no man break the laws of the land, for he that keepeth the laws of God hath no need to break the laws of the land. Wherefore, be subject to the powers that be, until he reigns whose right it is to reign, and subdues all enemies under his feet. Behold, the laws which ye have received from my hand are the laws of the church, and in this light ye shall hold them forth. Behold, here is wisdom.

* * *

For behold, it is not meet that I should command in all things; for he that is compelled in all things, the same is a slothful and not a wise servant; wherefore he receiveth no reward. Verily I say, men should be anxiously engaged in a good cause, and do many things of their own free will, and bring to pass much righteousness; for the power is in them, wherein they are agents unto themselves. And inasmuch as men do good they shall in nowise lose their reward. But he that doeth not anything until he is commanded, and receiveth a commandment with doubtful heart, and keepeth it with slothfulness, the same is damned.

Who am I that made man, saith the Lord, that will hold him guiltless that obeys not my commandments? Who am I, saith the Lord, that have promised and have not fulfilled? I command and men obey not; I revoke and they receive not the blessing. Then they say in their hearts: This is not the work of the Lord, for his promises are not fulfilled. But wo unto such, for their reward lurketh beneath, and not from above.

* * *

COMMENDATION AND FURTHER PROMISE

SECTION 59—*Revelation given through Joseph Smith the Prophet, in Zion, Jackson County, Missouri, August 7, 1831. Preceding his record of this revelation the Prophet writes descriptively of the land of Zion wherein the people were then assembled. The land was consecrated, as the Lord had directed, and the site for a future Temple was dedicated. The Lord makes these commandments especially applicable to the Saints in Zion. —— The people commended for their obedience—Cer-*

tain of the commandments given in the Decalog re-
iterated—Sanctity of the Sabbath emphasized—Not
confessing the hand of God in all things a grievous
offense.

BEHOLD, blessed, saith the Lord, are they who
have come up unto this land with an eye single
to my glory, according to my commandments. For
those that live shall inherit the earth, and those
that die shall rest from all their labors, and their
works shall follow them; and they shall receive a
crown in the mansions of my Father, which I have
prepared for them.   Yea, blessed are they whose
feet stand upon the land of Zion, who have obeyed
my gospel; for they shall receive for their reward
the good things of the earth, and it shall bring
forth in its strength.   And they shall also be
crowned with blessings from above, yea, and with
commandments not a few, and with revelations in
their time—they that are faithful and diligent before me.

Wherefore, I give unto them a commandment,
saying thus: Thou shalt love the Lord thy God
with all thy heart, with all thy might, mind,
and strength; and in the name of Jesus Christ
thou shalt serve him.   Thou shalt love thy neighbor as thyself.   Thou shalt not steal; neither
commit adultery, nor kill, nor do anything like
unto it.   Thou shalt thank the Lord thy God
in all things.   Thou shalt offer a sacrifice unto
the Lord thy God in righteousness, even that of a
broken heart and a contrite spirit.

And that thou mayest more fully keep thyself unspotted from the world, thou shalt go to the house of prayer and offer up thy sacraments upon my holy day; for verily this is a day appointed unto you to rest from your labors and to pay thy devotions unto the Most High.   Nevertheless thy vows shall be offered up in righteousness on all days and at all times; but remember that on this, the *Lord's Day*, thou shalt offer thine oblations and thy sacraments unto the Most High, confessing thy sins unto thy brethren, and before the Lord.   And on this day thou shalt do none other thing, only let thy food be prepared with singleness of heart that thy fasting may be perfect, or, in other words, that thy joy may be full.   Verily, this is fasting and prayer, or in other words, rejoicing and prayer.

And inasmuch as ye do these things with thanksgiving, with cheerful hearts and countenances, not with much laughter, for this is sin, but with a glad heart and a cheerful countenance, verily I say, that inasmuch as ye do this, the fulness of the earth is yours, the beasts of the field and the fowls of the air, and that which climbeth upon the trees and walketh upon the earth.   Yea, and the herb, and the good things which come of the earth, whether for food or for raiment, or for houses, or for barns, or for orchards, or for gardens, or for vineyards; yea, all things which come of the earth, in the season thereof, are made for the benefit and the use of man, both to please the eye and to gladden the heart; yea, for food and for raiment, for taste and for smell, to strengthen the body and to enliven the soul.

And it pleaseth God that he hath given all these things unto man; for unto this end were they made to be used, with judgment, not to excess, neither by extortion. And in nothing doth man offend God, or against none is his wrath kindled, save those who confess not his hand in all things, and obey not his commandments. Behold, this is according to the law and the prophets; wherefore, trouble me no more concerning this matter. But learn that he who doeth the works of righteousness shall receive his reward, even peace in this world, and eternal life in the world to come. I, the Lord, have spoken it, and the Spirit beareth record. Amen.

CALAMITIES TO BEFALL THE WICKED

SECTION 63—*Revelation given through Joseph Smith the Prophet, at Kirtland, Ohio, August, 1831. Prefacing his record of this revelation the Prophet wrote: "In these infant days of the Church, there was a great anxiety to obtain the word of the Lord upon every subject that in any way concerned our salvation; and as the land of Zion was now the most important temporal object in view, I inquired of the Lord for further information upon the gathering of the Saints, and the purchase of the land, and other matters." —— Solemn warning to the wicked—Divine manifestations, and signs wrought by evil powers—Sin of adultery espe-*

*cially condemned—Lands in Zion to be secured by pur-
chase and not by seizure—Blessed are they who die in
the Lord—Condition of those who shall die during the
Millennium—Those who use the name of the Lord without authority declared to be under condemnation.*

HEARKEN, O ye people, and open your hearts
and give ear from afar; and listen, you that call
yourselves the people of the Lord, and hear the
word of the Lord and his will concerning you.
Yea, verily, I say, hear the word of him whose
anger is kindled against the wicked and rebellious
—who willeth to take even them whom he will
take, and preserveth in life them whom he will
preserve; who buildeth up at his own will and
pleasure; and destroyeth when he pleases, and is
able to cast the soul down to hell.   Behold, I, the
Lord, utter my voice and it shall be obeyed.

Wherefore, verily I say, let the wicked take heed
and let the rebellious fear and tremble, and let the
unbelieving hold their lips, for the day of wrath
shall come upon them as a whirlwind, and all
flesh shall know that I am God.   And he that
seeketh signs shall see signs, but not unto salvation.   Verily, I say unto you, there are those
among you who seek signs, and there have been
such even from the beginning; but, behold, faith
cometh not by signs, but signs follow those that
believe.   Yea, signs come by faith, not by the will
of men, nor as they please, but by the will of God.
Yea, signs come by faith unto mighty works,
for without faith no man pleaseth God; and with

whom God is angry he is not well pleased; wherefore, unto such he showeth no signs, only in
wrath unto their condemnation.   Wherefore, I,
the Lord, am not pleased with those among you
who have sought after signs and wonders for
faith, and not for the good of men unto my
glory.

Nevertheless, I give commandments, and many
have turned away from my commandments and
have not kept them.   There were among you
adulterers and adulteresses; some of whom have
turned away from you, and others remain with
you that hereafter shall be revealed.   Let such beware and repent speedily, lest judgment shall come
upon them as a snare, and their folly shall be made
manifest, and their works shall follow them in
the eyes of the people.

And verily I say unto you, as I have said before, he that looketh on a woman to lust after her,
or if any shall commit adultery in their hearts, they
shall not have the Spirit, but shall deny the faith
and shall fear.   Wherefore, I, the Lord, have said
that the fearful, and the unbelieving, and all liars,
and whosoever loveth and maketh a lie, and the
whoremonger, and the sorcerer, shall have their
part in that lake which burneth with fire and brimstone, which is the second death.   Verily I say,
that they shall not have part in the first resurrection.

And now behold, I, the Lord, say unto you

that ye are not justified, because these things are among you.   Nevertheless, he that endureth in faith and doeth my will, the same shall overcome, and shall receive an inheritance upon the earth when the day of transfiguration shall come; when the earth shall be transfigured, even according to the pattern which was shown unto mine apostles upon the mount; of which account the fulness ye have not yet received.

And now, verily I say unto you, that as I said that I would make known my will unto you, behold I will make it known unto you, not by the way of commandment, for there are many who observe not to keep my commandments.   But unto him that keepeth my commandments I will give the mysteries of my kingdom, and the same shall be in him a well of living water, springing up unto everlasting life.

And now, behold, this is the will of the Lord your God concerning his saints, that they should assemble themselves together unto the land of Zion, not in haste, lest there should be confusion, which bringeth pestilence.   Behold, the land of Zion—I, the Lord, hold it in mine own hands! Nevertheless, I, the Lord, render unto Caesar the things which are Caesar's. Wherefore, I, the Lord, will that you should purchase the lands, that you may have advantage of the world, that you may have claim on the world, that they may not be stirred up unto anger.   For Satan putteth it into their hearts to anger against you, and to the shedding of blood.

Wherefore, the land of Zion shall not be obtained but by purchase or by blood, otherwise there is none inheritance for you. And if by purchase, behold you are blessed. And if by blood, as you are forbidden to shed blood, lo, your enemies are upon you, and ye shall be scourged from city to city, and from synagog to synagog, and but few shall stand to receive an inheritance.

I, the Lord, am angry with the wicked; I am holding my Spirit from the inhabitants of the earth. I have sworn in my wrath, and decreed wars upon the face of the earth, and the wicked shall slay the wicked and fear shall come upon every man. And the saints also shall hardly escape; nevertheless, I, the Lord, am with them, and will come down in heaven from the presence of my Father and consume the wicked with unquenchable fire. And behold, this is not yet, but by and by.

Wherefore, seeing that I, the Lord, have decreed all these things upon the face of the earth, I will that my saints should be assembled upon the land of Zion; and that every man should take righteousness in his hands and faithfulness upon his loins, and lift a warning voice unto the inhabitants of the earth; and declare both by word and by flight that desolation shall come upon the wicked.

*　　*　　*

Yea, and blessed are the dead that die in the Lord, from henceforth.   When the Lord shall come, and old things shall pass away and all things become new, they shall rise from the dead and shall not die after, and shall receive an inheritance before the Lord in the holy city.   And he that liveth when the Lord shall come, and hath kept the faith, blessed is he; nevertheless, it is appointed to him to die at the age of man. Wherefore, children shall grow up until they become old; old men shall die; but they shall not sleep in the dust, but they shall be changed in the twinkling of an eye.   Wherefore, for this cause preached the apostles unto the world the resurrection of the dead.

These things are the things that ye must look for; and, speaking after the manner of the Lord, they are now nigh at hand and in a time to come, even in the day of the coming of the Son of Man. And until that hour there will be foolish virgins among the wise; and at that hour cometh an entire separation of the righteous and the wicked; and in that day will I send mine angels to pluck out the wicked and cast them into unquenchable fire.

*   *   *

For this is a day of warning, and not a day of many words.   For I, the Lord, am not to be mocked in the last days. Behold, I am from above, and my power lieth beneath.   I am over all, and in all, and through all, and search all things, and the day cometh that all things shall be subject unto me.

Behold, I am Alpha and Omega, even Jesus Christ. Wherefore, let all men beware how they take my name in their lips; for behold, verily I say, that many there be who are under this condemnation, who use the name of the Lord, and use it in vain, having not authority. Wherefore, let the church repent of their sins, and I, the Lord, will own them; otherwise they shall be cut off. Remember that that which cometh from above is sacred, and must be spoken with care, and by constraint of the Spirit; and in this there is no condemnation, and ye receive the Spirit through prayer; wherefore, without this there remaineth condemnation.

* * *

FORGIVENESS AND SACRIFICE REQUIRED

SECTION 64—*Revelation given through Joseph Smith the Prophet, to the Elders of the Church, at Kirtland, Ohio, September 11, 1831. A company of brethren who had been commanded to journey to Zion were busily engaged in making preparations to leave. —— Forgiveness for the repentant sinner—Forgive one another, and all men—The intervening time, until the coming of the Son of Man, called today—This a time of sacrifice and for the tithing of the people.*

* * *

MY DISCIPLES, in days of old, sought occasion against one another and forgave not one another in their hearts; and for this evil they were afflicted and sorely chastened.   Wherefore, I say unto you, that ye ought to forgive one another; for he that forgiveth not his brother his trespasses standeth condemned before the Lord; for there remaineth in him the greater sin.   I, the Lord, will forgive whom I will forgive, but of you it is required to forgive all men.   And ye ought to say in your hearts—let God judge between me and thee, and reward thee according to thy deeds.

And him that repenteth not of his sins, and confesseth them not, ye shall bring before the church, and do with him as the scripture saith unto you, either by commandment or by revelation.   And this ye shall do that God may be glorified—not because ye forgive not, having not compassion, but that ye may be justified in the eyes of the law, that ye may not offend him who is your lawgiver—verily I say, for this cause ye shall do these things.

*   *   *

Behold, now it is called *today,* until the coming of the Son of Man, and verily it is a day of sacrifice, and a day for the tithing of my people; for he that is tithed shall not be burned at his coming.   For after today cometh the burning— this is speaking after the manner of the Lord—for verily I say, tomorrow all the proud and they that do wickedly shall be as stubble; and I will burn them up, for I am the Lord of Hosts; and I will not spare any that remain in Babylon. Wherefore, if ye believe me, ye will labor while it is called *today*.

* * *

KINGDOM OF GOD AND KINGDOM OF HEAVEN

SECTION 65—*Revelation given through Joseph Smith the Prophet, at Hiram, Ohio, October, 1831. The Prophet designates this revelation as a prayer. —— Commitment of the keys of the kingdom of God unto man—Supplication that the kingdom of God, already on earth, may go forth that the kingdom of Heaven may come.*

HEARKEN, and lo, a voice as of one sent down from on high, who is mighty and powerful, whose going forth is unto the ends of the earth, yea, whose voice is unto men—Prepare ye the way of the Lord, make his paths straight.

The keys of the kingdom of God are committed unto man on the earth, and from thence shall the gospel roll forth unto the ends of the earth, as the stone which is cut out of the mountain without hands shall roll forth, until it has filled the whole earth. Yea, a voice crying—Prepare ye the way of the Lord, prepare ye the supper of the Lamb, make ready for the Bridegroom. Pray unto the Lord, call upon his holy name, make known his wonderful works among the people.

Call upon the Lord, that his kingdom may go

forth upon the earth, that the inhabitants thereof may receive it, and be prepared for the days to come, in the which the Son of Man shall come down in heaven, clothed in the brightness of his glory, to meet the kingdom of God which is set up on the earth.

Wherefore, may the kingdom of God go forth, that the kingdom of heaven may come, that thou, O God, mayest be glorified in heaven so on earth, that thine enemies may be subdued; for thine is the honor, power and glory, forever and ever. Amen.

TO ELDERS AND PARENTS ESPECIALLY

SECTION 68—*Revelation given through Joseph Smith the Prophet, at Hiram, Ohio, November, 1831, in response to supplication that the mind of the Lord be made known regarding the immediate duties of certain Elders. —— Duties of parents respecting their children, particularly as to the teaching of the principles of the Gospel—Observance of the Sabbath as a holy day—Idleness and greed for worldly things condemned.*

* * *

GO YE into all the world, preach the gospel to every creature, acting in the authority which I have given you, baptizing in the name of the Father, and of the Son, and of the Holy Ghost. And he that believeth and is baptized shall be saved, and he that believeth not shall be damned. And he that believeth shall be blest with signs following,

6

even as it is written.   And unto you it shall be
given to know the signs of the times, and the signs
of the coming of the Son of Man.   And of as
many as the Father shall bear record, to you shall
be given power to seal them up unto eternal life.
Amen.

*   *   *

And again, inasmuch as parents have children
in Zion, or in any of her stakes which are organized, that teach them not to understand the doctrine of repentance, faith in Christ the Son of the
living God, and of baptism and the gift of the
Holy Ghost by the laying on of the hands, when
eight years old, the sin be upon the heads of the
parents. For this shall be a law unto the inhabitants of Zion, or in any of her stakes which are
organized.   And their children shall be baptized
for the remission of their sins when eight years
old, and receive the laying on of the hands.   And
they shall also teach their children to pray, and to
walk uprightly before the Lord.

And the inhabitants of Zion shall also observe
the Sabbath day to keep it holy.   And the inhabitants of Zion also shall remember their labors,
inasmuch as they are appointed to labor, in all
faithfulness; for the idler shall be had in remembrance before the Lord.   Now, I, the Lord, am not
well pleased with the inhabitants of Zion, for
there are idlers among them; and their children
are also growing up in wickedness; they also seek

not earnestly the riches of eternity, but their eyes are full of greediness. These things ought not to be, and must be done away from among them; wherefore, let my servant Oliver Cowdery carry these sayings unto the land of Zion.

And a commandment I give unto them—that he that observeth not his prayers before the Lord in the season thereof, let him be had in remembrance before the judge of my people. These sayings are true and faithful; wherefore, transgress them not, neither take therefrom. Behold, I am Alpha and Omega, and I come quickly. Amen.

PERDITION AND GRADED KINGDOMS OF GLORY

SECTION 76—*A vision, given to Joseph Smith, the Prophet, and Sidney Rigdon, at Hiram, Ohio, February 16, 1832. Prefacing his record of this vision the Prophet wrote: "From sundry revelations which had been received, it was apparent that many important points touching the salvation of man had been taken from the Bible, or lost before it was compiled. It appeared self-evident from what truths were left, that if God rewarded every one according to the deeds done in the body, the term Heaven, as intended for the Saints' eternal home, must include more kingdoms than one." While he and Sidney Rigdon were engaged in studious and prayerful consideration of this matter, the glorious vision here recorded was given them. —— Revelation of truth, wisdom, and even mysteries promised unto those who are worthy—The eventual resurrection of both just and unjust—The two Elders bear solemn personal testimony that Jesus Christ lives—The expulsion of Lucifer, and his evil activities as Satan on the earth—*

Awful fate of those who become sons of Perdition—
Distinctive glories of the Celestial, the Terrestrial, and
the Telestial states—Qualifications of souls that shall be
assigned to each—Glorious consummation of the Sav-
ior's work.

HEAR, O YE HEAVENS, and give ear, O Earth, and rejoice ye inhabitants thereof, for the Lord is God, and beside him there is no Savior. Great is his wisdom, marvelous are his ways, and the extent of his doings none can find out. His purposes fail not, neither are there any who can stay his hand. From eternity to eternity he is the same, and his years never fail.

For thus saith the Lord: I, the Lord, am merciful and gracious unto those who fear me, and delight to honor those who serve me in righteousness and in truth unto the end. Great shall be their reward and eternal shall be their glory. And to them will I reveal all mysteries; yea, all the hidden mysteries of my kingdom from days of old, and for ages to come, will I make known unto them— the good pleasure of my will concerning all things pertaining to my kingdom.

Yea, even the wonders of eternity shall they know, and things to come will I show them, even the things of many generations. And their wisdom shall be great, and their understanding reach to heaven; and before them the wisdom of the wise shall perish, and the understanding of the prudent shall come to naught. For by my Spirit will I enlighten them, and by my power will I

make known unto them the secrets of my will—
yea, even those things which eye has not seen, nor
ear heard, nor yet entered into the heart of man.

We, Joseph Smith, Jun., and Sidney Rigdon,
being in the Spirit on the sixteenth day of February, in the year of our Lord one thousand eight
hundred and thirty-two—by the power of the
Spirit our eyes were opened and our understandings were enlightened, so as to see and understand
the things of God—even those things which were
from the beginning before the world was, which
were ordained of the Father, through his Only Begotten Son, who was in the bosom of the Father,
even from the beginning; of whom we bear record; and the record which we bear is the fulness of
the gospel of Jesus Christ, who is the Son, whom
we saw and with whom we conversed in the heavenly vision.

For while we were doing the work of translation, which the Lord had appointed unto us, we
came to the twenty-ninth verse of the fifth chapter
of John, which was given unto us as follows:
Speaking of the resurrection of the dead, concerning
those who shall hear the voice of the Son of Man,
and shall come forth—they who have done good
in the resurrection of the just, and they who have
done evil in the resurrection of the unjust—now
this caused us to marvel, for it was given unto us
of the Spirit.

And while we meditated upon these things, the

Lord touched the eyes of our understandings and they were opened, and the glory of the Lord shone round about. And we beheld the glory of the Son, on the right hand of the Father, and received of his fulness, and saw the holy angels, and them who are sanctified before his throne, worshiping God, and the Lamb, who worship him forever and ever.

And now, after the many testimonies which have been given of him, this is the testimony, last of all, which we give of him: That he lives! For we saw him, even on the right hand of God; and we heard the voice bearing record that he is the Only Begotten of the Father—that by him, and through him, and of him, the worlds are and were created, and the inhabitants thereof are begotten sons and daughters unto God.

And this we saw also, and bear record, that an angel of God who was in authority in the presence of God, who rebelled against the Only Begotten Son whom the Father loved and who was in the bosom of the Father, was thrust down from the presence of God and the Son, and was called Perdition, for the heavens wept over him—he was Lucifer, a son of the morning. And we beheld, and lo, he is fallen! is fallen, even a son of the morning!

And while we were yet in the Spirit, the Lord commanded us that we should write the vision; for we beheld Satan, that old serpent, even the devil, who rebelled against God, and sought to take the kingdom of our God and his Christ—wherefore, he maketh war with the saints of God, and encompasseth them round about. And we saw a vision of the sufferings of those with whom he made war and overcame, for thus came the voice of the Lord unto us:

Thus saith the Lord concerning all those who know my power, and have been made partakers thereof, and suffered themselves through the power of the devil to be overcome, and to deny the truth and defy my power—they are they who are the sons of Perdition, of whom I say that it had been better for them never to have been born; for they are vessels of wrath, doomed to suffer the wrath of God, with the devil and his angels in eternity; concerning whom I have said there is no forgiveness in this world nor in the world to come—having denied the Holy Spirit after having received it, and having denied the Only Begotten Son of the Father, having crucified him unto themselves and put him to an open shame.

These are they who shall go away into the lake of fire and brimstone, with the devil and his angels —and the only ones on whom the second death shall have any power; yea, verily, the only ones who shall not be redeemed in the due time of the Lord, after the sufferings of his wrath. For all the rest shall be brought forth by the resurrection of the dead, through the triumph and the glory of the Lamb, who was slain, who was in the bosom of the Father before the worlds were made.

And this is the gospel, the glad tidings, which the voice out of the heavens bore record unto us: That he came into the world, even Jesus, to be crucified for the world, and to bear the sins of the world, and to sanctify the world, and to cleanse it from all unrighteousness; that through him all might be saved whom the Father had put into his power and made by him; who glorifies the Father, and saves all the works of his hands, except those sons of Perdition who deny the Son after the Father has revealed him.

Wherefore, he saves all except them—they shall go away into everlasting punishment, which is endless punishment, which is eternal punishment, to reign with the devil and his angels in eternity, where their worm dieth not, and the fire is not quenched, which is their torment. And the end thereof, neither the place thereof, nor their torment, no man knows; neither was it revealed, neither is, neither will be revealed unto man, except to them who are made partakers thereof. Nevertheless, I, the Lord, show it by vision unto many, but straightway shut it up again; wherefore, the end, the width, the height, the depth, and the misery thereof, they understand not, neither any man except those who are ordained unto this condemnation. And we heard the voice, saying: Write the vision, for lo, this is the end of the vision of the sufferings of the ungodly.

And again we bear record—for we saw and heard, and this is the testimony of the gospel of Christ concerning them who shall come forth in the resurrection of the just: They are they who received the testimony of Jesus, and believed on his name and were baptized after the manner of his burial, being buried in the water in his name, and this according to the commandment which he has given, that by keeping the commandments they might be washed and cleansed from all their sins, and receive the Holy Spirit by the laying on of the hands of him who is ordained and sealed unto this power; and who overcome by faith, and are sealed by the Holy Spirit of promise, which the Father sheds forth upon all those who are just and true.

They are they who are the church of the Firstborn. They are they into whose hands the Father has given all things; they are they who are priests and kings, who have received of his fulness, and of his glory, and are priests of the Most High, after the order of Melchizedek, which was after the order of Enoch, which was after the order of the Only Begotten Son. Wherefore, as it is written, they are gods, even the sons of God. Wherefore, all things are theirs, whether life or death, or things present, or things to come, all are theirs and they are Christ's, and Christ is God's. And they shall overcome all things.

Wherefore, let no man glory in man, but rather let him glory in God, who shall subdue all enemies under his feet. These shall dwell in the presence of God and his Christ forever and ever. These are they whom he shall bring with him, when he shall come in the clouds of heaven to reign on the earth over his people. These are they who shall have part in the first resurrection. These are they who shall come forth in the resurrection of the just. These are they who are come unto Mount Zion, and unto the city of the living God, the heavenly place, the holiest of all. These are they who have come to an innumerable company of angels, to the general assembly and church of Enoch, and of the Firstborn.

These are they whose names are written in heaven, where God and Christ are the judge of all. These are they who are just men made perfect through Jesus the mediator of the new covenant, who wrought out this perfect atonement through the shedding of his own blood. These are they whose bodies are *celestial*, whose glory is that of the sun, even the glory of God, the highest of all, whose glory the sun of the firmament is written of as being typical.

And again, we saw the *terrestrial* world; and behold and lo, these are they who are of the terrestrial, whose glory differs from that of the church of the Firstborn who have received the fulness of the Father, even as that of the moon differs from the sun in the firmament. Behold, these are they who died without law; and also they who are the spirits of men kept in prison, whom the Son visited, and preached the gospel unto them, that they

might be judged according to men in the flesh—
who received not the testimony of Jesus in the
flesh, but afterwards received it.

These are they who are honorable men of the
earth, who were blinded by the craftiness of men.
These are they who receive of his glory, but not
of his fulness. These are they who receive of the
presence of the Son, but not of the fulness of the
Father. Wherefore, they are bodies *terrestrial*,
and not bodies *celestial*, and differ in glory as the
moon differs from the sun. These are they who
are not valiant in the testimony of Jesus; wherefore, they obtain not the crown over the kingdom
of our God. And now this is the end of the vision
which we saw of the terrestrial, that the Lord commanded us to write while we were yet in the Spirit.

And again, we saw the glory of the *telestial*,
which glory is that of the lesser, even as the glory
of the stars differs from that of the glory of the
moon in the firmament. These are they who received not the gospel of Christ, neither the testimony of Jesus. These are they who deny not the
Holy Spirit. These are they who are thrust down
to hell. These are they who shall not be redeemed
from the devil until the last resurrection, until the
Lord, even Christ the Lamb, shall have finished
his work. These are they who receive not of his
fulness in the eternal world, but of the Holy Spirit
through the ministration of the terrestrial; and the
terrestrial through the ministration of the celestial. And also the telestial receive it of the ad-

ministering of angels who are appointed to minister for them, or who are appointed to be ministering spirits for them; for they shall be heirs of salvation. ·

And thus we saw, in the heavenly vision, the glory of the *telestial*, which surpasses all understanding; and no man knows it except him to whom God has revealed it. And thus we saw the glory of the *terrestrial* which excels in all things the glory of the telestial, even in glory, and in power, and in might, and in dominion. And thus we saw the glory of the *celestial*, which excels in all things—where God, even the Father, reigns upon his throne forever and ever—before whose throne all things bow in humble reverence, and give him glory forever and ever. They who dwell in his presence are the church of the Firstborn; and they see as they are seen, and know as they are known, having received of his fulness and of his grace; and he makes them equal in power, and in might, and in dominion.

And the glory of the *celestial* is one, even as the glory of the sun is one. And the glory of the *terrestrial* is one, even as the glory of the moon is one. And the glory of the *telestial* is one, even as the glory of the stars is one; for as one star differs from another star in glory even so differs one from another in glory in the telestial world; for these are they who are of Paul, and of Apollos, and of Cephas. These are they who say they are some of one and some of another—some of Christ and some of John, and some of Moses, and some of Elias, and some of Esaias, and some of Isaiah, and some of Enoch—but received not the gospel, neither the testimony of Jesus, neither the prophets, neither the everlasting covenant.

Last of all, these all are they who will not be gathered with the saints, to be caught up unto the church of the Firstborn, and received into the cloud. These are they who are liars, and sorcerers, and adulterers, and whoremongers, and whosoever loves and makes a lie. These are they who suffer the wrath of God on earth. These are they who suffer the vengeance of eternal fire. These are they who are cast down to hell and suffer the wrath of Almighty God, until the fulness of times, when Christ shall have subdued all enemies under his feet, and shall have perfected his work; when he shall deliver up the kingdom, and present it unto the Father, spotless, saying: I have overcome and have trodden the winepress alone, even the winepress of the fierceness of the wrath of Almighty God. Then shall he be crowned with the crown of his glory, to sit on the throne of his power to reign forever and ever.

But behold, and lo, we saw the glory and the inhabitants of the telestial world, that they were as innumerable as the stars in the firmament of heaven, or as the sand upon the seashore; and heard the voice of the Lord, saying: These all shall bow the knee, and every tongue shall confess to him who sits upon the throne forever and ever; for they shall be judged according to their works, and every man shall receive according to his own works, his own dominion, in the mansions which are prepared. And they shall be servants of the Most High; but where God and Christ dwell they cannot come, worlds without end.

This is the end of the vision which we saw, which we were commanded to write while we were yet in the Spirit. But great and marvelous are the works of the Lord, and the mysteries of his kingdom which he showed unto us, which surpass all understanding in glory, and in might, and in dominion—which he commanded us we should not write while we were yet in the Spirit, and are not lawful for man to utter. Neither is man capable to make them known, for they are only to be seen and understood by the power of the Holy Spirit, which God bestows on those who love him, and purify themselves before him; to whom he grants this privilege of seeing and knowing for themselves, that through the power and manifestation of the Spirit, while in the flesh, they may be able to bear his presence in the world of glory. And to God and the Lamb be glory, and honor, and dominion forever and ever. Amen.

ON PRIESTHOOD

SECTION 84—*Revelation given through Joseph Smith the Prophet, at Kirtland, Ohio, September 22 and 23, 1832. During the month of September, Elders had be-*

gun to return from their missions in the eastern States, and to make reports of their labors. It was while they were together in this season of joy that the following communication was received. The Prophet designates it a Revelation on Priesthood. —— A Temple to be built in the land of Zion during this generation—The line of the Holy Priesthood from Moses back to Adam—Relation between the Holy Priesthood and the Lesser Priesthood—Bearers of these two Priesthoods called the sons of Moses and of Aaron respectively—Blessings and privileges of those who attain to these Priesthoods—The bondage of sin—The new and everlasting covenant—Gifts of the spirit specified—The Lord calls his servants, friends—Missionary service imperative—Plagues impending because of wickedness.

A REVELATION OF JESUS CHRIST unto his servant Joseph Smith, Jun., and six elders, as they united their hearts and lifted their voices on high. Yea, the word of the Lord concerning his church, established in the last days for the restoration of his people, as he has spoken by the mouth of his prophets, and for the gathering of his saints to stand upon Mount Zion, which shall be the city of New Jerusalem. Which city shall be built, beginning at the temple lot, which is appointed by the finger of the Lord, in the western boundaries of the State of Missouri, and dedicated by the hand of Joseph Smith, Jun., and others with whom the Lord was well pleased.

Verily this is the word of the Lord, that the city New Jerusalem shall be built by the gathering of the saints, beginning at this place, even the place of the temple, which temple shall be reared in this generation. For verily this generation shall not all pass away until an house shall be built unto the Lord, and a cloud shall rest upon it, which cloud shall be even the glory of the Lord, which shall fill the house.

And the sons of Moses, according to the Holy Priesthood which he received under the hand of his father-in-law, Jethro; and Jethro received it under the hand of Caleb; and Caleb received it under the hand of Elihu; and Elihu under the hand of Jeremy; and Jeremy under the hand of Gad; and Gad under the hand of Esaias; and Esaias received it under the hand of God. Esaias also lived in the days of Abraham, and was blessed of him; which Abraham received the priesthood from Melchizedek, who received it through the lineage of his fathers, even till Noah; and from Noah till Enoch, through the lineage of their fathers; and from Enoch to Abel, who was slain by the conspiracy of his brother, who received the priesthood by the commandments of God, by the hand of his father Adam, who was the first man. Which priesthood continueth in the church of God in all generations, and is without beginning of days or end of years.

And the Lord confirmed a priesthood also upon Aaron and his seed, throughout all their generations, which priesthood also continueth and abideth forever with the priesthood which is after the holiest order of God. And this greater priesthood administereth the gospel and holdeth the key of the mysteries of the kingdom, even the key of the knowledge of God. Therefore, in the ordinances thereof, the power of godliness is manifest. And without the ordinances thereof, and the authority of the priesthood, the power of godliness is not manifest unto men in the flesh. For without this no man can see the face of God, even the Father, and live.

Now this Moses plainly taught to the children of Israel in the wilderness, and sought diligently to sanctify his people that they might behold the face of God; but they hardened their hearts and could not endure his presence; therefore, the Lord in his wrath, for his anger was kindled against them, swore that they should not enter into his rest while in the wilderness, which rest is the fulness of his glory. Therefore, he took Moses out of their midst, and the Holy Priesthood also.

And the lesser priesthood continued, which priesthood holdeth the key of the ministering of angels and the preparatory gospel. Which gospel is the gospel of repentance and of baptism, and the remission of sins, and the law of carnal commandments, which the Lord in his wrath caused to continue with the house of Aaron among the children of Israel until John, whom God raised up, being filled with the Holy Ghost from his mother's womb. For he was baptized while he was yet in his childhood, and was ordained by the angel of God at the time he was eight days old

7

unto this power, to overthrow the kingdom of the Jews, and to make straight the way of the Lord before the face of his people, to prepare them for the coming of the Lord, in whose hand is given all power.

And again, the offices of elder and bishop are necessary appendages belonging unto the high priesthood. And again, the offices of teacher and deacon are necessary appendages belonging to the lesser priesthood, which priesthood was confirmed upon Aaron and his sons. Therefore, as I said concerning the sons of Moses—for the sons of Moses and also the sons of Aaron shall offer an acceptable offering and sacrifice in the house of the Lord, which house shall be built unto the Lord in this generation, upon the consecrated spot as I have appointed—and the sons of Moses and of Aaron shall be filled with the glory of the Lord, upon Mount Zion in the Lord's house, whose sons are ye; and also many whom I have called and sent forth to build up my church.

For whoso is faithful unto the obtaining these two priesthoods of which I have spoken, and the magnifying their calling, are sanctified by the Spirit unto the renewing of their bodies. They become the sons of Moses and of Aaron and the seed of Abraham, and the church and kingdom, and the elect of God. And also all they who receive this priesthood receive me, saith the Lord; for he that receiveth my servants receiveth me; and he that receiveth me receiveth my Father; and he that receiveth my Father receiveth my Father's kingdom; therefore all that my Father hath shall be given unto him.

And this is according to the oath and covenant which belongeth to the priesthood. Therefore, all those who receive the priesthood receive this oath and covenant of my Father, which he cannot break, neither can it be moved. But whoso breaketh this covenant after he hath received it, and altogether turneth therefrom, shall not have forgiveness of sins in this world nor in the world to come. And wo unto all those who come not unto this priesthood which ye have received, which I now confirm upon you who are present this day, by mine own voice out of the heavens; and even I have given the heavenly hosts and mine angels charge concerning you.

And I now give unto you a commandment to beware concerning yourselves, to give diligent heed to the words of eternal life. For you shall live by every word that proceedeth forth from the mouth of God. For the word of the Lord is truth, and whatsoever is truth is light, and whatsoever is light is Spirit, even the Spirit of Jesus Christ. And the Spirit giveth light to every man that cometh into the world; and the Spirit enlighteneth every man through the world, that hearkeneth to the voice of the Spirit. And every one that hearkeneth to the voice of the Spirit cometh unto God, even the Father. And the Father teacheth him of the covenant which he has renewed and confirmed upon you, which is confirmed upon you for your sakes, and not for your sakes only, but for the sake of the whole world.

And the whole world lieth in sin, and groaneth under darkness and under the bondage of sin. And by this you may know they are under the bondage of sin, because they come not unto me. For whoso cometh not unto me is under the bondage of sin. And whoso receiveth not my voice is not acquainted with my voice, and is not of me. And by this you may know the righteous from the wicked, and that the whole world groaneth under sin and darkness even now.

And your minds in times past have been darkened because of unbelief, and because you have treated lightly the things you have received—which vanity and unbelief have brought the whole church under condemnation. And this condemnation resteth upon the children of Zion, even all. And they shall remain under this condemnation until they repent and remember the new covenant, even the *Book of Mormon* and the former commandments which I have given them, not only to say, but to do according to that which I have written —that they may bring forth fruit meet for their Father's kingdom; otherwise there remaineth a scourge and judgment to be poured out upon the children of Zion. For shall the children of the kingdom pollute my holy land?   Verily, I say unto you, Nay.

Verily, verily, I say unto you who now hear my words, which are my voice, blessed are ye inasmuch as you receive these things; for I will forgive you of your sins with this commandment—that you remain steadfast in your minds in solemnity and the spirit of prayer, in bearing testimony to all the world of those things which are communicated unto you.   Therefore, go ye into all the world; and unto whatsoever place ye cannot go ye shall send, that the testimony may go from you into all the world unto every creature.

And as I said unto mine apostles even so I say unto you, for you are mine apostles, even God's high priests; ye are they whom my Father hath given me; ye are my friends; therefore, as I said unto mine apostles I say unto you again, that every soul who believeth on your words, and is baptized by water for the remission of sins, shall receive the Holy Ghost.

And these signs shall follow them that believe: In my name they shall do many wonderful works; in my name they shall cast out devils; in my name they shall heal the sick; in my name they shall open the eyes of the blind, and unstop the ears of the deaf; and the tongue of the dumb shall speak. And if any man shall administer poison unto them it shall not hurt them; and the poison of a serpent shall not have power to harm them.   But a commandment I give unto them, that they shall not boast themselves of these things, neither speak them before the world; for these things are given unto you for your profit and for salvation.

Verily, verily, I say unto you, they who believe not on your words, and are not baptized in water in my name, for the remission of their sins, that they may receive the Holy Ghost, shall be damned, and shall not come into my Father's kingdom where my Father and I am. And this revelation unto you, and commandment, is in force from this very hour upon all the world, and the gospel is unto all who have not received it. But, verily I say unto all those to whom the kingdom has been given—from you it must be preached unto them, that they shall repent of their former evil works; for they are to be upbraided for their evil hearts of unbelief, and your brethren in Zion for their rebellion against you at the time I sent you.

And again I say unto you, my friends, for from henceforth I shall call you friends, it is expedient that I give unto you this commandment, that ye become even as my friends in days when I was with them, traveling to preach the gospel in my power; for I suffered them not to have purse or scrip, neither two coats. Behold, I send you out to prove the world, and the laborer is worthy of his hire. And any man that shall go and preach this gospel of the kingdom, and fail not to continue faithful in all things, shall not be weary in mind, neither darkened, neither in body, limb, nor joint; and a hair of his head shall not fall to the ground unnoticed. And they shall not go hungry, neither athirst.

Therefore, take ye no thought for the morrow, for what ye shall eat, or what ye shall drink, or wherewithal ye shall be clothed. For, consider the lilies of the field, how they grow, they toil not, neither do they spin; and the kingdoms of the world, in all their glory, are not arrayed like one of these. For your Father, who is in heaven, knoweth that you have need of all these things. Therefore, let the morrow take thought for the things of itself.

Neither take ye thought beforehand what ye shall say; but treasure up in your minds continually the words of life, and it shall be given you in the very hour that portion that shall be meted unto every man. Therefore, let no man among you, for this commandment is unto all the faithful who are called of God in the church unto the ministry, from this hour take purse or scrip, that goeth forth to proclaim this gospel of the kingdom. Behold, I send you out to reprove the world of all their unrighteous deeds, and to teach them of a judgment which is to come.

And whoso receiveth you, there I will be also, for I will go before your face. I will be on your right hand and on your left, and my Spirit shall be in your hearts, and mine angels round about you, to bear you up. Whoso receiveth you receiveth me; and the same will feed you, and clothe you, and give you money. And he who feeds you, or clothes you, or gives you money, shall in nowise lose his reward. And he that doeth not these things is not my disciple; by this you may know my disciples.

He that receiveth you not, go away from him alone by yourselves, and cleanse your feet even with water, pure water, whether in heat or in cold, and bear testimony of it unto your Father which is in heaven, and return not again unto that man. And in whatsoever village or city ye enter, do likewise. Nevertheless, search diligently and spare not; and wo unto that house, or that village or city that rejecteth you, or your words, or your testimony concerning me.

Wo, I say again, unto that house, or that village or city that rejecteth you, or your words, or your testimony of me. For I, the Almighty, have laid my hands upon the nations, to scourge them for their wickedness. And plagues shall go forth, and they shall not be taken from the earth until I have completed my work, which shall be cut short in righteousness—until all shall know me, who remain, even from the least unto the greatest, and shall be filled with the knowledge of the Lord, and shall see eye to eye, and shall lift up their voice, and with the voice together sing this new song, saying:

The Lord hath brought again Zion;
The Lord hath redeemed his people, Israel,
According to the election of grace,
Which was brought to pass by the faith
And covenant of their fathers.
The Lord hath redeemed his people;
And Satan is bound and time is no longer.
The Lord hath gathered all things in one.
The Lord hath brought down Zion from above.
The Lord hath brought up Zion from beneath.
The earth hath travailed and brought forth her
    strength;
And truth is established in her bowels;
And the heavens have smiled upon her;
And she is clothed with the glory of her God;
For he stands in the midst of his people.
Glory, and honor, and power, and might
Be ascribed to our God; for he is full of mercy,
Justice, grace and truth and peace,
Forever and ever, Amen.

*   *   *

And if any man among you be strong in the Spirit, let him take with him him that is weak, that he may be edified in all meekness, that he may become strong also. Therefore, take with you those who are ordained unto the lesser priesthood, and send them before you to make appointments, and to prepare the way, and to fill appointments that you yourselves are not able to fill. Behold, this is the way that mine apostles, in ancient days, built up my church unto me. Therefore, let every man stand in his own office, and labor in his own calling; and let not the head say unto the feet it hath no need of the feet; for without the feet how shall the body be able to stand? Also the body hath need of every member, that all may be edified together, that the system may be kept perfect. And behold, the high priests should travel, and also the elders, and also the lesser priests, but the deacons and teachers should be appointed to watch over the church, to be standing ministers unto the church.

* * *

PROPHECY ON WAR

SECTION 87—*Revelation and Prophecy on War, given through Joseph Smith the Prophet, December 25, 1832.* —— *This portentous prediction was very widely promulgated among members of the Church and preached by the Elders from the time of its utterance. Manuscript copies were carried by the missionaries and publicly read wherever they traveled in the United States and abroad. In July, 1851, the prophecy appeared in print in the "Millennial Star" and in the first edition of the "Pearl of Great Price," both published at Liverpool, England, by the British Mission of the Church. In 1861 the Civil War between North and South broke out, on the initiative of South Carolina, more than twenty-eight years after the revelation was first proclaimed and ten years after its publication in print. The World War has carried to progressive realization the prediction that "war shall be poured out upon all nations." The complete fulfilment of the Lord's pronouncement is yet to come.*

VERILY, THUS SAITH THE LORD concerning the wars that will shortly come to pass, beginning at the rebellion of South Carolina, which will eventually terminate in the death and misery of many souls: And the time will come that war will be poured out upon all nations, beginning at this place.

For behold, the Southern States shall be divided against the Northern States, and the Southern States will call on other nations, even the nation of Great Britain, as it is called, and they shall also call upon other nations, in order to defend themselves against other nations; and then war shall be poured out upon all nations.

And it shall come to pass, after many days, slaves shall rise up against their masters, who shall be marshaled and disciplined for war.   And it shall come to pass also that the remnants who are left of the land will marshal themselves, and shall become exceedingly angry, and shall vex the Gentiles with a sore vexation.

And thus, with the sword and by bloodshed the inhabitants of the earth shall mourn; and with famine, and plague, and earthquake, and the thunder of heaven, and the fierce and vivid lightning also, shall the inhabitants of the earth be made to feel the wrath, and indignation, and chastening hand of an Almighty God, until the consumption decreed hath made a full end of all nations: That the cry of the saints, and of the blood of the saints, shall cease to come up into the ears of the Lord of Sabaoth, from the earth, to be avenged of their enemies. Wherefore, stand ye in holy places, and be not moved, until the day of the Lord come; for behold, it cometh quickly, saith the Lord. Amen.

THE OLIVE LEAF

SECTION 88—*Revelation given through Joseph Smith the Prophet, at Kirtland, Ohio, December 27, 1832. Designated by the Prophet, the Olive Leaf. —— Ministrations of the Comforter—The light of truth is the light of Christ—The spirit and the body constitute the soul—Search for the truth through study and prayer enjoined—Testimony of the Elders to be followed by that of calamity—Scenes incident to the Lord's coming —The angels sounding their trumpets in turn as appointed.*

VERILY, THUS SAITH THE LORD unto you who have assembled yourselves together to receive his will concerning you: Behold, this is pleasing unto your Lord, and the angels rejoice over you; the alms of your prayers have come up into the ears of the Lord of Sabaoth, and are recorded in the book of the names of the sanctified, even them of the celestial world. Wherefore, I now send upon you another Comforter, even upon you my friends, that it may abide in your hearts, even the Holy Spirit of promise; which other Comforter is the same that I promised unto my disciples, as is recorded in the testimony of John.

This Comforter is the promise which I give unto you of eternal life, even the glory of the celestial kingdom; which glory is that of the church of the Firstborn, even of God, the holiest of all, through Jesus Christ his Son—he that ascended up on high, as also he descended below all things, in that he comprehended all things, that he might be in all and through all things, the light of truth; which truth shineth.

This is the light of Christ.   As also he is in the sun, and the light of the sun, and the power thereof by which it was made.   As also he is in the moon, and is the light of the moon, and the power thereof by which it was made; as also the light of the stars, and the power thereof by which they were made; and the earth also, and the power thereof, even the earth upon which you stand. And the light which shineth, which giveth you light, is through him who enlighteneth your eyes, which is the same light that quickeneth your understandings —which light proceedeth forth from the presence of God to fill the immensity of space—the light which is in all things, which giveth life to all things, which is the law by which all things are governed, even the power of God who sitteth upon his throne, who is in the bosom of eternity, who is in the midst of all things.

Now, verily I say unto you, that through the redemption which is made for you is brought to pass the resurrection from the dead. *And the spirit and the body are the soul of man. And the resurrection from the dead is the redemption of the soul.* And the redemption of the soul is through him that quickeneth all things, in whose bosom it is decreed that the poor and the meek of the earth shall inherit it.

Therefore, it must needs be sanctified from all unrighteousness, that it may be prepared for the *celestial* glory; for after it hath filled the measure of its creation it shall be crowned with glory, even with the presence of God the Father; that bodies who are of the *celestial kingdom* may possess it forever and ever; for, for this intent was it made and created, and for this intent are they sanctified.

And they who are not sanctified through the law which I have given unto you, even the law of Christ, must inherit another kingdom, even that of a *terrestrial kingdom,* or that of a *telestial kingdom.* For he who is not able to abide the law of a celestial kingdom cannot abide a celestial glory. And he who cannot abide the law of a terrestrial kingdom cannot abide a terrestrial glory. And he who cannot abide the law of a telestial kingdom cannot abide a telestial glory; therefore he is not meet for a kingdom of glory. Therefore he must abide a kingdom which is not a kingdom of glory.

And again, verily I say unto you, the earth abideth the law of a celestial kingdom, for it filleth the measure of its creation, and transgresseth not the law; wherefore, it shall be sanctified; yea, notwithstanding it shall die, it shall be quickened again, and shall abide the power by which it is quickened, and the righteous shall inherit it. For notwithstanding they die, they also shall rise again, a spiritual body. They who are of a celestial spirit shall receive the same body which was a natural body; even ye shall receive your bodies, and your glory shall be that glory by which your bodies are quickened. Ye who are quickened by a portion of the celestial glory shall then receive of the same, even a fulness. And they who are quickened by a portion of the terrestrial glory shall then receive of the same, even a fulness. And also they who are quickened by a portion of the telestial glory shall then receive of the same, even a fulness.

And they who remain shall also be quickened; nevertheless, they shall return again to their own place, to enjoy that which they are willing to receive, because they were not willing to enjoy that which they might have received. For what doth it profit a man if a gift is bestowed upon him, and he receive not the gift? Behold, he rejoices not in that which is given unto him, neither rejoices in him who is the giver of the gift.

And again, verily I say unto you, that which is governed by law is also preserved by law and perfected and sanctified by the same. That which breaketh a law, and abideth not by law, but seeketh to become a law unto itself, and willeth to abide in sin, and altogether abideth in sin, cannot be sanctified by law, neither by mercy, justice, nor judgment.   Therefore, they must remain filthy still.

All kingdoms have a law given.   And there are many kingdoms; for there is no space in the which there is no kingdom; and there is no kingdom in which there is no space, either a greater or a lesser kingdom.   And unto every kingdom is given a law; and unto every law there are certain bounds also and conditions.   All beings who abide not in those conditions are not justified.

For intelligence cleaveth unto intelligence; wisdom receiveth wisdom; truth embraceth truth; virtue loveth virtue; light cleaveth unto light; mercy hath compassion on mercy and claimeth her own; justice continueth its course and claimeth its own; judgment goeth before the face of him who sitteth upon the throne and governeth and executeth all things.   He comprehendeth all things, and all things are before him, and all things are round about him; and he is above all things, and in all things, and is through all things, and is round about all things, and all things are by him, and of him, even God, forever and ever.

And again, verily I say unto you, he hath given a law unto all things, by which they move in their times and their seasons; and their courses are fixed, even the courses of the heavens and the earth, which comprehend the earth and all the planets.   And they give light to each other in their times and in their seasons, in their minutes, in their hours, in their days, in their weeks, in their months, in their years—all these are one year with God, but not with man.   The earth rolls upon her wings, and the sun giveth his light by day, and the moon giveth her light by night, and the stars also give their light, as they roll upon their wings in their glory, in the midst of the power of God.

Unto what shall I liken these kingdoms, that ye may understand?   Behold, all these are kingdoms, and any man who hath seen any or the least of these hath seen God moving in his majesty and power.   I say unto you, he hath seen him; nevertheless, he who came unto his own was not comprehended.   The light shineth in darkness, and the darkness comprehendeth it not; nevertheless, the day shall come when you shall comprehend even God, being quickened in him and by him.   Then shall ye know that ye have seen me, that I am, and that I am the true light that is in you, and that you are in me; otherwise ye could not abound.

Behold, I will liken these kingdoms unto a man having a field, and he sent forth his servants into the field to dig in the field.   And he said unto the first: Go ye and labor in the field, and in the first hour I will come unto you, and ye shall behold the joy of my countenance.   And he said unto the second: Go ye also into the field, and in the second hour I will visit you with the joy of my countenance—and also unto the third, saying: I will visit you; and unto the fourth, and so on unto the twelfth.   And the lord of the field went unto the

8

first in the first hour, and tarried with him all that hour, and he was made glad with the light of the countenance of his lord.

And then he withdrew from the first that he might visit the second also, and the third, and the fourth, and so on unto the twelfth. And thus they all received the light of the countenance of their lord, every man in his hour, and in his time, and in his season—beginning at the first, and so on unto the last, and from the last unto the first, and from the first unto the last; every man in his own order, until his hour was finished, even according as his lord had commanded him, that his lord might be glorified in him, and he in his lord, that they all might be glorified.

Therefore, unto this parable I will liken all these kingdoms, and the inhabitants thereof—every kingdom in its hour, and in its time, and in its season, even according to the decree which God hath made. And again, verily I say unto you, my friends, I leave these sayings with you to ponder in your hearts, with this commandment which I give unto you, that ye shall call upon me while I am near. Draw near unto me and I will draw near unto you; seek me diligently and ye shall find me; ask, and ye shall receive; knock, and it shall be opened unto you. Whatsoever ye ask the Father in my name it shall be given unto you, that is expedient for you; and if ye ask anything that is not expedient for you, it shall turn unto your condemnation.

Behold, that which you hear is as the voice of one crying in the wilderness—in the wilderness, because you cannot see him—my voice, because my voice is Spirit; my Spirit is truth; truth abideth and hath no end; and if it be in you it shall abound. And if your eye be single to my glory, your whole bodies shall be filled with light, and there shall be no darkness in you; and that body which is filled with light comprehendeth all things. Therefore, sanctify yourselves that your minds become single to God, and the days will come that you shall see him; for he will unveil his face unto you, and it shall be in his own time, and in his own way, and according to his own will.

Remember the great and last promise which I have made unto you; cast away your idle thoughts and your excess of laughter far from you. Tarry ye, tarry ye in this place, and call a solemn assembly, even of those who are the first laborers in this last kingdom. And let those whom they have warned in their traveling call on the Lord, and ponder the warning in their hearts which they have received, for a little season. Behold, and lo, I will take care of your flocks, and will raise up elders and send unto them. Behold, I will hasten my work in its time.

And I give unto you, who are the first laborers in this last kingdom, a commandment that you assemble yourselves together, and organize yourselves, and prepare yourselves, and sanctify yourselves; yea, purify your hearts, and cleanse your hands and your feet before me, that I may make you clean—that I may testify unto your Father, and your God, and my God, that you are clean from the blood of this wicked generation; that I may fulfil this promise, this great and last promise, which I have made unto you, when I will. Also, I give unto you a commandment that ye shall continue in prayer and fasting from this time forth.

And I give unto you a commandment that you shall teach one another the doctrine of the kingdom. Teach ye diligently and my grace shall attend you, that you may be instructed more perfectly in theory, in principle, in doctrine, in the law of the gospel, in all things that pertain unto the kingdom of God, that are expedient for you to understand; of things both in heaven and in the earth, and under the earth; things which have been, things which are, things which must shortly come to pass; things which are at home, things which are abroad; the wars and the perplexities of the nations, and the judgments which are on the land; and a knowledge also of countries and of kingdoms—that ye may be prepared in all things when I shall send you again to magnify the calling whereunto I have called you, and the mission with which I have commissioned you.

Behold, I sent you out to testify and warn the people, and it becometh every man who hath been warned to warn his neighbor. Therefore, they are left without excuse, and their sins are upon their own heads. He that seeketh me early shall find

me, and shall not be forsaken.   Therefore, tarry
ye, and labor diligently, that you may be perfected
in your ministry to go forth among the Gentiles
for the last time, as many as the mouth of the Lord
shall name, to bind up the law and seal up the testimony, and to prepare the saints for the hour of
judgment which is to come—that their souls may
escape the wrath of God, the desolation of abomination which awaits the wicked, both in this
world and in the world to come.   Verily, I say
unto you, let those who are not the first elders
continue in the vineyard until the mouth of the
Lord shall call them, for their time is not yet
come; their garments are not clean from the blood
of this generation.

Abide ye in the liberty wherewith ye are made
free; entangle not yourselves in sin, but let your
hands be clean, until the Lord comes.   For not
many days hence and the earth shall tremble and
reel to and fro as a drunken man; and the sun
shall hide his face, and shall refuse to give light;
and the moon shall be bathed in blood; and the
stars shall become exceedingly angry, and shall
cast themselves down as a fig that falleth from off
a fig-tree.   And after your testimony cometh wrath
and indignation upon the people.

For after your testimony cometh the testimony
of earthquakes, that shall cause groanings in the
midst of her, and men shall fall upon the ground
and shall not be able to stand.   And also cometh
the testimony of the voice of thunderings, and the

voice of lightnings, and the voice of tempests, and the voice of the waves of the sea heaving themselves beyond their bounds. And all things shall be in commotion; and surely, men's hearts shall fail them, for fear shall come upon all people.

And angels shall fly through the midst of heaven, crying with a loud voice, sounding the trump of God, saying: Prepare ye, prepare ye, O inhabitants of the earth; for the judgment of our God is come. Behold, and lo, the Bridegroom cometh; go ye out to meet him. And immediately there shall appear a great sign in heaven, and all people shall see it together.

And another angel shall sound his trump, saying: That great church, the mother of abominations, that made all nations drink of the wine of the wrath of her fornication, that persecuteth the saints of God, that shed their blood—she who sitteth upon many waters, and upon the islands of the sea—behold, she is the tares of the earth; she is bound in bundles; her bands are made strong, no man can loose them; therefore, she is ready to be burned. And he shall sound his trump both long and loud, and all nations shall hear it.

And there shall be silence in heaven for the space of half an hour; and immediately after shall the curtain of heaven be unfolded, as a scroll is unfolded after it is rolled up, and the face of the Lord shall be unveiled. And the saints that are upon the earth, who are alive, shall be quickened and be caught up to meet him.   And they who have slept in their graves shall come forth, for their graves shall be opened; and they also shall be caught up to meet him in the midst of the pillar of heaven.   They are Christ's, the firstfruits, they who shall descend with him first, and they who are on the earth and in their graves, who are first caught up to meet him; and all this by the voice of the sounding of the trump of the angel of God.

And after this another angel shall sound, which is the second trump; and then cometh the redemption of those who are Christ's at his coming; who have received their part in that prison which is prepared for them, that they might receive the gospel, and be judged according to men in the flesh.   And again, another trump shall sound, which is the third trump; and then come the spirits of men who are to be judged, and are found under condemnation.   And these are the rest of the dead; and they live not again until the thousand years are ended, neither again, until the end of the earth.

And another trump shall sound, which is the fourth trump, saying: There are found among those who are to remain until that great and last day, even the end, who shall remain filthy still.   And another trump shall sound, which is the fifth trump, which is the fifth angel who committeth the everlasting gospel—flying through the midst of heaven, unto all nations, kindreds, tongues, and people: And this shall be the sound of his trump, saying to all people, both in heaven and in earth, and that are under the earth—for every ear shall hear it, and every knee shall bow, and every tongue shall confess, while they hear the sound of the trump, saying: Fear God, and give glory to him who sitteth upon the throne, forever and ever; for the hour of his judgment is come.

And again, another angel shall sound his trump, which is the sixth angel, saying: She is fallen who made all nations drink of the wine of the wrath of her fornication; she is fallen, is fallen! And again, another angel shall sound his trump, which is the seventh angel, saying: It is finished; it is finished! The Lamb of God hath overcome and trodden the wine-press alone, even the wine-press of the fierceness of the wrath of Almighty God. And then shall the angels be crowned with the glory of his might, and the saints shall be filled with his glory, and receive their inheritance and be made equal with him.

And then shall the first angel again sound his trump in the ears of all living, and reveal the secret acts of men, and the mighty works of God in the first thousand years. And then shall the second angel sound his trump, and reveal the secret acts of men, and the thoughts and intents of their hearts, and the mighty works of God in the second thousand years. And so on, until the seventh angel shall sound his trump; and he shall stand forth upon the land and upon the sea, and swear in the name of him who sitteth upon the throne, that there shall be time no longer; and Satan shall be bound, that old serpent, who is called the devil, and shall not be loosed for the space of a thousand years.

And then he shall be loosed for a little season, that he may gather together his armies. And Michael, the seventh angel, even the archangel, shall gather together his armies, even the hosts of heaven. And the devil shall gather together his armies; even the hosts of hell, and shall come up to battle against Michael and his armies. And then cometh the battle of the great God; and the devil and his armies shall be cast away into their own place, that they shall not have power over the saints any more at all. For Michael shall fight their battles, and shall overcome him who seeketh the throne of him who sitteth upon the throne, even the Lamb. This is the glory of God, and the sanctified; and they shall not any more see death.

Therefore, verily I say unto you, my friends, call your solemn assembly, as I have commanded you. And as all have not faith, seek ye diligently and teach one another words of wisdom; yea, seek ye out of the best books words of wisdom; seek learning, even by study and also by faith. Organize yourselves; prepare every needful thing; and establish a house, even a house of prayer, a house of fasting, a house of faith, a house of learning, a house of glory, a house of order, a house of God; that your incomings may be in the name of the Lord; that your outgoings may be in the name of the Lord; that all your salutations may be in the name of the Lord, with uplifted hands unto the Most High.

Therefore, cease from all your light speeches, from all laughter, from all your lustful desires, from all your pride and light-mindedness, and from all your wicked doings. Appoint among yourselves a teacher, and let not all be spokesmen at once; but let one speak at a time and let all listen unto his sayings, that when all have spoken that all may be edified of all, and that every man may have an equal privilege.

See that ye love one another; cease to be covetous; learn to impart one to another as the gospel requires. Cease to be idle; cease to be unclean; cease to find fault one with another; cease to sleep longer than is needful; retire to thy bed early, that ye may not be weary; arise early, that your bodies and your minds may be invigorated. And above all things, clothe yourselves with the bond of charity, as with a mantle, which is the bond of perfectness and peace. Pray always, that ye may not faint, until I come. Behold, and lo, I will come quickly, and receive you unto myself. Amen.

* * *

THE WORD OF WISDOM

SECTION 89—*Revelation given through Joseph Smith the Prophet, at Kirtland, Ohio, February 27, 1833, known as the Word of Wisdom. —— Abstinence from wine, strong drink, tobacco and hot drinks enjoined—*

*Moderation in the eating of meat—Wholesome foods—
Promises to those who live according to these precepts.*

A WORD OF WISDOM, for the benefit of the
council of high priests, assembled in Kirtland, and
the church, and also the saints in Zion—to be sent
greeting; not by commandment or constraint, but
by revelation and the word of wisdom, showing
forth the order and will of God in the temporal
salvation of all saints in the last days—Given for
a principle with promise, adapted to the capacity
of the weak and the weakest of all saints, who are
or can be called saints.   Behold, verily, thus saith
the Lord unto you: In consequence of evils and
designs which do and will exist in the hearts of
conspiring men in the last days, I have warned you,
and forewarn you, by giving unto you this word
of wisdom by revelation.

That inasmuch as any man drinketh wine or
strong drink among you, behold it is not good,
neither meet in the sight of your Father, only in
assembling yourselves together to offer up your
sacraments before him.   And, behold, this should
be wine, yea, pure wine of the grape of the vine,
of your own make.   And, again, strong drinks are
not for the belly, but for the washing of your
bodies.   And again, tobacco is not for the body,
neither for the belly, and is not good for man, but
is an herb for bruises and all sick cattle, to be used
with judgment and skill.   And again, hot drinks
are not for the body or belly.

And again, verily I say unto you, all wholesome herbs God hath ordained for the constitution, nature, and use of man—every herb in the season thereof, and every fruit in the season thereof, all these to be used with prudence and thanksgiving. Yea, flesh also of beasts and of the fowls of the air, I, the Lord, have ordained for the use of man with thanksgiving; nevertheless they are to be used sparingly; and it is pleasing unto me that they should not be used, only in times of winter, or of cold, or famine.

All grain is ordained for the use of man and of beasts, to be the staff of life, not only for man but for the beasts of the field, and the fowls of heaven, and all wild animals that run or creep on the earth; and these hath God made for the use of man only in times of famine and excess of hunger. All grain is good for the food of man; as also the fruit of the vine; that which yieldeth fruit, whether in the ground or above the ground—nevertheless, wheat for man, and corn for the ox, and oats for the horse, and rye for the fowls and for swine, and for all beasts of the field, and barley for all useful animals, and for mild drinks, as also other grain.

And all saints who remember to keep and do these sayings, walking in obedience to the commandments, shall receive health in their navel and marrow to their bones; and shall find wisdom and great treasures of knowledge, even hidden treasures; and shall run and not be weary, and shall walk and not faint. And I, the Lord, give unto them a promise, that the destroying angel shall pass by them, as the children of Israel, and not slay them.   Amen.

THE GLORY OF GOD IS INTELLIGENCE

SECTION 93—*Revelation given through Joseph Smith the Prophet, at Kirtland, Ohio, May 6, 1833. —— The Lord defines the relation between himself and the Father—The record of John, the Apostle and Revelator —Jesus Christ the Firstborn—Man was in the beginning with God—The elements are eternal—The glory of God is intelligence—Man innocent in the beginning.*

VERILY, THUS SAITH THE LORD: It shall come to pass that every soul who forsaketh his sins and cometh unto me, and calleth on my name, and obeyeth my voice, and keepeth my commandments, shall see my face and know that I am; and that I am the true light that lighteth every man that cometh into the world; and that I am in the Father; and the Father in me, and the Father and I are one—the Father because he gave me of his fulness, and the Son because I was in the world and made flesh my tabernacle, and dwelt among the sons of men.   I was in the world and received of my Father, and the works of him were plainly manifest.

And John saw and bore record of the fulness of my glory, and the fulness of John's record is hereafter to be revealed.   And he bore record, saying: I saw his glory, that he was in the beginning, before the world was; therefore, in the beginning the Word was, for he was the Word, even the messenger of salvation—the light and the Redeemer of the world; the Spirit of truth, who came into the world, because the world was made by him, and in him was the life of men and the light of men. The worlds were made by him; men were made by him; all things were made by him, and through him, and of him.

And I, John, bear record that I beheld his glory, as the glory of the Only Begotten of the Father, full of grace and truth, even the Spirit of truth, which came and dwelt in the flesh, and dwelt among us. And I, John, saw that he received not of the fulness at the first, but received grace for grace; and he received not of the fulness at first, but continued from grace to grace, until he received a fulness; and thus he was called the Son of God, because he received not of the fulness at the first. And I, John, bear record, and lo, the heavens were opened, and the Holy Ghost descended upon him in the form of a dove, and sat upon him, and there came a voice out of heaven saying: This is my beloved Son. And I, John, bear record that he received a fulness of the glory of the Father; and he received all power, both in heaven and on earth, and the glory of the Father was with him, for he dwelt in him.

And it shall come to pass, that if you are faithful you shall receive the fulness of the record of

John. I give unto you these sayings that you may understand and know how to worship, and know what you worship, that you may come unto the Father in my name, and in due time receive of his fulness. For if you keep my commandments you shall receive of his fulness, and be glorified in me as I am in the Father; therefore, I say unto you, you shall receive grace for grace. And now, verily I say unto you, I was in the beginning with the Father, and am the Firstborn; and all those who are begotten through me are partakers of the glory of the same, and are the church of the Firstborn.

Ye were also in the beginning with the Father; that which is Spirit, even the Spirit of truth; and truth is knowledge of things as they are, and as they were, and as they are to come; and whatsoever is more or less than this is the spirit of that wickèd one who was a liar from the beginning. The Spirit of truth is of God. I am the Spirit of truth, and John bore record of me, saying: He received a fulness of truth, yea, even of all truth. And no man receiveth a fulness unless he keepeth his commandments. He that keepeth his commandments receiveth truth and light, until he is glorified in truth and knoweth all things.

Man was also in the beginning with God. Intelligence, or the light of truth, was not created or made, neither indeed can be. All truth is independent in that sphere in which God has placed it, to act for itself, as all intelligence also; otherwise there is no existence. Behold, here is the agency of man, and here is the condemnation of man; because that which was from the beginning is plainly manifest unto them, and they receive not the light. And every man whose spirit receiveth not the light is under condemnation.

For man is spirit. The elements are eternal, and spirit and element, inseparably connected, receive a fulness of joy; and when separated, man cannot receive a fulness of joy. The elements are the tabernacle of God; yea, man is the tabernacle of God, even temples; and whatsoever temple is defiled, God shall destroy that temple. The glory of God is intelligence, or, in other words, light and truth. Light and truth forsake that evil one.

Every spirit of man was innocent in the beginning; and God having redeemed man from the fall, men became again, in their infant state, innocent before God. And that wicked one cometh and taketh away light and truth, through disobedience, from the children of men, and because of the tradition of their fathers. But I have commanded you to bring up your children in light and truth.

*   *   *

DIVINE AND SECULAR LAW

SECTION 98—*Revelation given through Joseph Smith the Prophet, at Kirtland, Ohio, August 6, 1833. —— Patience in persecution enjoined—Good to come out of affliction—The constitutional law of the land to be supported by the Saints—Good men to be supported for secular office.*

VERILY I SAY UNTO YOU my friends, fear not, let your hearts be comforted; yea, rejoice evermore, and in everything give thanks; waiting patiently on the Lord, for your prayers have entered into the ears of the Lord of Sabaoth, and are recorded with this seal and testament—the Lord hath sworn and decreed that they shall be granted. Therefore, he giveth this promise unto you, with an immutable covenant that they shall be fulfilled; and all things wherewith you have been afflicted shall work together for your good, and to my name's glory, saith the Lord.

And now, verily I say unto you concerning the laws of the land, it is my will that my people should observe to do all things whatsoever I command them.   And that law of the land which is constitutional, supporting that principle of freedom in maintaining rights and privileges, belongs to all mankind, and is justifiable before me. Therefore, I, the Lord, justify you, and your brethren of my church, in befriending that law which is the constitutional law of the land; and as pertaining to law of man, whatsoever is more or less than this cometh of evil.

I, the Lord God, make you free, therefore ye are free indeed; and the law also maketh you free. Nevertheless, when the wicked rule the people mourn.   Wherefore, honest men and wise men should be sought for diligently, and good men and wise men ye should observe to uphold; otherwise whatsoever is less than these cometh of evil. And I give unto you a commandment, that ye shall forsake all evil and cleave unto all good, that ye shall live by every word which proceedeth forth out of the mouth of God. For he will give unto the faithful line upon line, precept upon precept; and I will try you and prove you herewith.

And whoso layeth down his life in my cause, for my name's sake, shall find it again, even life eternal. Therefore, be not afraid of your enemies, for I have decreed in my heart, saith the Lord, that I will prove you in all things, whether you will abide in my covenant, even unto death, that you may be found worthy. For if ye will not abide in my covenant ye are not worthy of me.

Therefore, renounce war and proclaim peace, and seek diligently to turn the hearts of the children to their fathers, and the hearts of the fathers to the children; and again, the hearts of the Jews unto the prophets, and the prophets unto the Jews; lest I come and smite the whole earth with a curse, and all flesh be consumed before me. Let not your hearts be troubled; for in my Father's house are many mansions, and I have prepared a place for you; and where my Father and I am, there ye shall be also.

* * *

ENCOURAGEMENT AND ASSURANCE

SECTION 101—*Revelation given to Joseph Smith the Prophet, at Kirtland, Ohio, December 16, 1833. At this time the Saints who had gathered in Missouri were suffering great persecution. Mobs had driven them from their homes in Jackson County, and some of the Saints had tried to establish themselves in Van Buren County, but persecution followed them. The main body of the Church was at that time in Clay County, Missouri. Threats of death against individuals of the Church were many. The people had lost household furniture, clothing, livestock and other personal property, and many of their crops had been destroyed. —— Gathering of the Saints to be continued—Blessed state incident to the millennial era of peace—Those who have been oppressed by their enemies to importune for redress—Creation of the Constitution of the United States directed by the Lord.*

* * *

BEHOLD, IT IS MY WILL, that all they who call on my name, and worship me according to mine everlasting gospel, should gather together, and stand in holy places, and prepare for the revelation which is to come, when the veil of the covering of my temple, in my tabernacle, which hideth the earth, shall be taken off, and all flesh shall see me together.   And every corruptible thing, both of man, or of the beasts of the field, or of the fowls of the heavens, or of the fish of the sea, that dwells upon all the face of the earth, shall be consumed; and also that of element shall melt with fervent heat; and all things shall become new, that my knowledge and glory may dwell upon all the earth.

And in that day the enmity of man, and the enmity of beasts, yea, the enmity of all flesh, shall cease from before my face. And in that day whatsoever any man shall ask, it shall be given unto him. And in that day Satan shall not have power to tempt any man. And there shall be no sorrow because there is no death. In that day an infant shall not die until he is old; and his life shall be as the age of a tree; and when he dies he shall not sleep, that is to say in the earth, but shall be changed in the twinkling of an eye, and shall be caught up, and his rest shall be glorious.

Yea, verily I say unto you, in that day when the Lord shall come, he shall reveal all things—things which have passed, and hidden things which no man knew, things of the earth, by which it was made, and the purpose and the end thereof; things most precious, things that are above, and things that are beneath, things that are in the earth, and upon the earth, and in heaven.

And all they who suffer persecution for my name, and endure in faith, though they are called to lay down their lives for my sake yet shall they partake of all this glory. Wherefore, fear not even unto death; for in this world your joy is not full, but in me your joy is full. Therefore, care not for the body, neither the life of the body; but care for the soul, and for the life of the soul. And seek the face of the Lord always, that in patience ye may possess your souls, and ye shall have eternal life.

When men are called unto mine everlasting gospel, and covenant with an everlasting covenant, they are accounted as the salt of the earth and the savor of men; they are called to be the savor of men; therefore, if that salt of the earth lose its savor, behold, it is thenceforth good for nothing only to be cast out and trodden under the feet of men.

* * *

And again I say unto you, those who have been scattered by their enemies, it is my will that they should continue to importune for redress, and redemption, by the hands of those who are placed as rulers and are in authority over you—according to the laws and constitution of the people, which I have suffered to be established, and should be maintained for the rights and protection of all flesh, according to just and holy principles: That every man may act in doctrine and principle pertaining to futurity according to the moral agency which I have given unto him, that every man may be accountable for his own sins in the day of judgment.

Therefore, it is not right that any man should be in bondage one to another. And for this purpose have I established the Constitution of this land, by the hands of wise men whom I raised up unto this very purpose, and redeemed the land by the shedding of blood.

* * *

ORDERS AND OFFICES OF PRIESTHOOD

SECTION 107—*Revelation on Priesthood, given through Joseph Smith the Prophet, at Kirtland, Ohio, dated March 28, 1835. On the date named the Twelve met in council, confessing their individual weaknesses and shortcomings, expressing repentance, and seeking the further guidance of the Lord. They were about to separate on missions to districts assigned. —— Distinction between the Aaronic and the Melchizedek Priesthoods—High authority of the Presidency of the High Priesthood—The Bishopric as the Presidency of the Aaronic Priesthood—The Twelve to ordain evangelical ministers, or Patriarchs—The order of Church tribunals —No one in the Church exempt from accountability.*

THERE ARE, in the church, two Priesthoods, namely, the Melchizedek and Aaronic, including the Levitical Priesthood. Why the first is called the Melchizedek Priesthood is because Melchizedek was such a great high priest. Before his day it was called *the Holy Priesthood, after the Order of the Son of God.* But out of respect or reverence to the name of the Supreme Being, to avoid the too frequent repetition of his name, they, the church, in ancient days, called that priesthood after Melchizedek, or the Melchizedek Priesthood.

All other authorities or offices in the church are appendages to this priesthood. But there are two divisions or grand heads—one is the Melchizedek Priesthood, and the other is the Aaronic or Levitical Priesthood. The office of an elder comes under the priesthood of Melchizedek.

The Melchizedek Priesthood holds the right of

presidency, and has power and authority over all the offices in the church in all ages of the world, to administer in spiritual things. The Presidency of the High Priesthood, after the order of Melchizedek, have a right to officiate in all the offices in the church.

High priests after the order of the Melchizedek Priesthood have a right to officiate in their own standing, under the direction of the presidency, in administering spiritual things, and also in the office of an elder, priest of the Levitical order, teacher, deacon, and member. An elder has a right to officiate in his stead when the high priest is not present. The high priest and elder are to administer in spiritual things, agreeable to the covenants and commandments of the church; and they have a right to officiate in all these offices of the church when there are no higher authorities present.

The second priesthood is called the Priesthood of Aaron, because it was conferred upon Aaron and his seed, throughout all their generations. Why it is called the lesser priesthood is because it is an appendage to the greater, or the Melchizedek Priesthood, and has power in administering outward ordinances. The bishopric is the presidency of this priesthood, and holds the keys or authority of the same. No man has a legal right to this office, to hold the keys of this priesthood, except he be a literal descendant of Aaron. But as a high priest of the Melchizedek Priesthood has authority to officiate in all the lesser offices, he may officiate in the office of bishop when no literal descendant of Aaron can be found, provided he is called and set apart and ordained unto this power by the hands of the Presidency of the Melchizedek Priesthood.

The power and authority of the higher, or Melchizedek Priesthood, is to hold the keys of all the spiritual blessings of the church——to have the privilege of receiving the mysteries of the kingdom of heaven, to have the heavens opened unto them, to commune with the general assembly and church of the Firstborn, and to enjoy the communion and presence of God the Father, and Jesus the mediator of the new covenant.

The power and authority of the lesser, or Aaronic Priesthood, is to hold the keys of the ministering of angels, and to administer in outward ordinances, the letter of the gospel, the baptism of repentance for the remission of sins, agreeable to the covenants and commandments.

Of necessity there are presidents, or presiding officers growing out of, or appointed of or from among those who are ordained to the several offices in these two priesthoods. Of the Melchizedek Priesthood, three Presiding High Priests, chosen by the body, appointed and ordained to that office, and upheld by the confidence, faith, and prayer of the church, form a quorum of the *Presidency of the Church*. The twelve traveling councilors are called to be the *Twelve Apostles*, or special wit-

nesses of the name of Christ in all the world—
thus differing from other officers in the church in
the duties of their calling.   And they form a quorum, equal in authority and power to the three
presidents previously mentioned.

The *Seventy* are also called to preach the gospel, and to be especial witnesses unto the Gentiles
and in all the world—thus differing from other
officers in the church in the duties of their calling.
And they form a quorum, equal in authority to
that of the Twelve special witnesses or Apostles
just named.

And every decision made by either of these quorums must be by the unanimous voice of the
same; that is, every member in each quorum must
be agreed to its decisions, in order to make their
decisions of the same power or validity one with
the other—a majority may form a quorum when
circumstances render it impossible to be otherwise
—unless this is the case, their decisions are not entitled to the same blessings which the decisions
of a quorum of three presidents were anciently,
who were ordained after the order of Melchizedek,
and were righteous and holy men.

The decisions of these quorums, or either of
them, are to be made in all righteousness, in holiness, and lowliness of heart, meekness and long-
suffering, and in faith, and virtue, and knowledge,
temperance, patience, godliness, brotherly kindness
and charity.   Because the promise is, if these

things abound in them they shall not be unfruitful in the knowledge of the Lord. And in case that any decision of these quorums is made in unrighteousness, it may be brought before a general assembly of the several quorums, which constitute the spiritual authorities of the church; otherwise there can be no appeal from their decision.

The Twelve are a Traveling Presiding High Council, to officiate in the name of the Lord, under the direction of the Presidency of the Church, agreeable to the institution of heaven; to build up the church, and regulate all the affairs of the same in all nations, first unto the Gentiles and secondly unto the Jews. The Seventy are to act in the name of the Lord, under the direction of the Twelve or the traveling high council, in building up the church and regulating all the affairs of the same in all nations, first unto the Gentiles and then to the Jews—the Twelve being sent out, holding the keys, to open the door by the proclamation of the gospel of Jesus Christ, and first unto the Gentiles and then unto the Jews.

The standing high councils, at the stakes of Zion, form a quorum equal in authority in the affairs of the church, in all their decisions, to the quorum of the presidency, or to the traveling high council. The high council in Zion form a quorum equal in authority in the affairs of the church, in all their decisions, to the councils of the Twelve at the stakes of Zion.

It is the duty of the traveling high council to call upon the Seventy, when they need assistance, to fill the several calls for preaching and administering the gospel, instead of any others.

It is the duty of the Twelve, in all large branches of the church, to ordain evangelical ministers, as they shall be designated unto them by revelation. The order of this priesthood was confirmed to be handed down from father to son, and rightly belongs to the literal descendants of the chosen seed, to whom the promises were made. This order was instituted in the days of Adam, and came down by lineage in the following manner:

From Adam to Seth, who was ordained by Adam at the age of sixty-nine years, and was blessed by him three years previous to his (Adam's) death, and received the promise of God by his father, that his posterity should be the chosen of the Lord, and that they should be preserved unto the end of the earth; because he (Seth) was a perfect man, and his likeness was the express likeness of his father, insomuch that he seemed to be like unto his father in all things, and could be distinguished from him only by his age.

Enos was ordained at the age of one hundred and thirty-four years and four months, by the hand of Adam. God called upon Cainan in the wilderness in the fortieth year of his age; and he met Adam in journeying to the place Shedolamak.

He was eighty-seven years old when he received his ordination. Mahalaleel was four hundred and ninety-six years and seven days old when he was ordained by the hand of Adam, who also blessed him. Jared was two hundred years old when he was ordained under the hand of Adam, who also blessed him.

Enoch was twenty-five years old when he was ordained under the hand of Adam; and he was sixty-five and Adam blessed him. And he saw the Lord, and he walked with him, and was before his face continually; and he walked with God three hundred and sixty-five years, making him four hundred and thirty years old when he was translated. Methuselah was one hundred years old when he was ordained under the hand of Adam. Lamech was thirty-two years old when he was ordained under the hand of Seth. Noah was ten years old when he was ordained under the hand of Methuselah.

Three years previous to the death of Adam, he called Seth, Enos, Cainan, Mahalaleel, Jared, Enoch, and Methuselah, who were all high priests, with the residue of his posterity who were righteous, into the valley of Adam-ondi-Ahman, and there bestowed upon them his last blessing. And the Lord appeared unto them, and they rose up and blessed Adam, and called him Michael, the prince, the archangel. And the Lord administered comfort unto Adam, and said unto him: I have set thee to be at the head; a multitude of nations shall come of thee, and thou art a prince over them forever.   And Adam stood up in the midst of the congregation; and, notwithstanding he was bowed down with age, being full of the Holy Ghost, predicted whatsoever should befall his posterity unto the latest generation.   These things were all written in the book of Enoch, and are to be testified of in due time.

It is the duty of the Twelve, also, to ordain and set in order all the other officers of the church, agreeable to the revelation which says: To the church of Christ in the land of Zion, in addition to the church laws respecting church business, verily, I say unto you, saith the Lord of Hosts, there must needs be presiding elders to preside over those who are of the office of an elder; and also priests to preside over those who are of the office of a priest; and also teachers to preside over those who are of the office of a teacher, in like manner, and also the deacons—wherefore, from deacon to teacher, and from teacher to priest, and from priest to elder, severally as they are appointed, according to the covenants and commandments of the church.

Then comes the High Priesthood, which is the greatest of all.   Wherefore, it must needs be that one be appointed of the High Priesthood to preside over the priesthood, and he shall be called President of the High Priesthood of the Church; or, in other words, the Presiding High Priest over the High Priesthood of the Church.   From the same comes the administering of ordinances and blessings upon the church, by the laying on of the hands. Wherefore, the office of a bishop is not equal unto it; for the office of a bishop is in administering all temporal things.

Nevertheless, a bishop must be chosen from the High Priesthood, unless he is a literal descendant of Aaron; for unless he is a literal descendant of Aaron he cannot hold the keys of that priesthood. Nevertheless, a high priest, that is, after the order of Melchizedek, may be set apart unto the ministering of temporal things, having a knowledge of them by the Spirit of truth; and also to be a judge in Israel, to do the business of the church, to sit in judgment upon transgressors upon testimony as it shall be laid before him according to the laws, by the assistance of his counselors, whom he has chosen or will choose among the elders of the church.

This is the duty of a bishop who is not a literal descendant of Aaron, but has been ordained to the High Priesthood after the order of Melchizedek. Thus shall he be a judge, even a common judge among the inhabitants of Zion, or in a stake of Zion, or in any branch of the church where he shall be set apart unto this ministry, until the borders of Zion are enlarged and it becomes necessary to have other bishops or judges in Zion or elsewhere.

And inasmuch as there are other bishops appointed they shall act in the same office.   But a literal descendant of Aaron has a legal right to the presidency of this priesthood, to the keys of this ministry, to act in the office of bishop independently, without counselors, except in a case where a President of the High Priesthood, after the order of Melchizedek, is tried, to sit as a judge in Israel. And the decision of either of these councils, agreeable to the commandment which says: Again, verily, I say unto you, the most important business of the church, and the most difficult cases of the church, inasmuch as there is not satisfaction upon the decision of the bishop or judges, it shall be handed over and carried up unto the council of the church, before the Presidency of the High Priesthood.

And the Presidency of the council of the High Priesthood shall have power to call other high priests, even twelve, to assist as counselors; and thus the Presidency of the High Priesthood and its counselors shall have power to decide upon testimony according to the laws of the church.   And after this decision it shall be had in remembrance no more before the Lord; for this is the highest council of the church of God, and a final decision upon controversies in spiritual matters.   There is not any person belonging to the church who is exempt from this council of the church.

And inasmuch as a President of the High Priesthood shall transgress, he shall be had in remembrance before the common council of the church, who shall be assisted by twelve counselors of the High Priesthood; and their decision upon his head shall be an end of controversy concerning him. Thus, none shall be exempted from the justice and the laws of God, that all things may be done in order and in solemnity before him, according to truth and righteousness.

And again, verily I say unto you, the duty of a president over the office of a deacon is to preside over twelve deacons, to sit in council with them, and to teach them their duty, edifying one another, as it is given according to the covenants. And also the duty of the president over the office of the teachers is to preside over twenty-four of the teachers, and to sit in council with them, teaching them the duties of their office, as given in the covenants. Also the duty of the president over the Priesthood of Aaron is to preside over forty-eight priests, and sit in council with them, to teach them the duties of their office, as is given in the covenants—this president is to be a bishop, for this is one of the duties of this priesthood.

Again, the duty of the president over the office of elders is to preside over ninety-six elders, and to sit in council with them, and to teach them according to the covenants. This presidency is a distinct one from that of the seventy, and is designed for those who do not travel into all the world.

And again, the duty of the President of the office of the High Priesthood is to preside over the whole church, and to be like unto Moses—behold, here is wisdom; yea, to be a seer, a revelator, a translator, and a prophet, having all the gifts of God which he bestows upon the head of the church.

And it is according to the vision showing the order of the Seventy, that they should have seven presidents to preside over them, chosen out of the number of the seventy; and the seventh president of these presidents is to preside over the six. And these seven presidents are to choose other seventy besides the first seventy to whom they belong, and are to preside over them; and also other seventy, until seven times seventy, if the labor in the vineyard of necessity requires it. And these seventy are to be traveling ministers, unto the Gentiles first and also unto the Jews. Whereas other officers of the church, who belong not unto the Twelve, neither to the Seventy, are not under the responsibility to travel among all nations, but are to travel as their circumstances shall allow, notwithstanding they may hold as high and responsible offices in the church.

Wherefore, now let every man learn his duty, and to act in the office in which he is appointed, in all diligence. He that is slothful shall not be counted worthy to stand, and he that learns not his duty and shows himself not approved shall not be counted worthy to stand. Even so. Amen.

———————

10

A GLORIOUS THEOPHANY FOLLOWED BY
VISITATIONS OF ANCIENT PROPHETS

SECTION 110—*Visions manifested to Joseph Smith the Prophet, and Oliver Cowdery, in the Temple at Kirtland, Ohio, April 3, 1836. The occasion was that of a Sabbath-day meeting. The Prophet prefaces his record of the manifestations with these words: "In the afternoon, I assisted the other presidents in distributing the Lord's Supper to the Church, receiving it from the Twelve, whose privilege it was to officiate at the sacred desk this day. After having performed this service to my brethren, I retired to the pulpit, the veils being dropped, and bowed myself, with Oliver Cowdery, in solemn and silent prayer. After rising from prayer, the following vision was opened to both of us." —— Personal manifestation of the Lord Jesus Christ—His acceptance of the Temple—Visitation by Moses and his commitment of the keys of the gathering—Visitation by Elias and his conferment of authority—Visitation by Elijah in direct fulfilment of Malachi's prediction. (See Mal. 4:5, 6.)*

THE VEIL WAS TAKEN from our minds, and the eyes of our understanding were opened. We saw the Lord standing upon the breastwork of the pulpit, before us; and under his feet was a paved work of pure gold, in color like amber. His eyes were as a flame of fire; the hair of his head was white like the pure snow; his countenance shone above the brightness of the sun; and his voice was as the sound of the rushing of great waters, even the voice of Jehovah, saying:

I am the first and the last; I am he who liveth, I am he who was slain; I am your advocate with the Father. Behold, your sins are forgiven you; you are clean before me; therefore, lift up your heads and rejoice. Let the hearts of your brethren rejoice, and let the hearts of all my people rejoice, who have, with their might, built this house to my name. For behold, I have accepted this house, and my name shall be here; and I will manifest myself to my people in mercy in this house. Yea, I will appear unto my servants, and speak unto them with mine own voice, if my people will keep my commandments, and do not pollute this holy house. Yea the hearts of thousands and tens of thousands shall greatly rejoice in consequence of the blessings which shall be poured out, and the endowment with which my servants have been endowed in this house. And the fame of this house shall spread to foreign lands; and this is the beginning of the blessing which shall be poured out upon the heads of my people. Even so. Amen.

After this vision closed, the heavens were again opened unto us; and Moses appeared before us, and committed unto us the keys of the gathering of Israel from the four parts of the earth, and the leading of the ten tribes from the land of the north.

After this, Elias appeared, and committed the dispensation of the gospel of Abraham, saying that in us and our seed all generations after us should be blessed.

After this vision had closed, another great and

glorious vision burst upon us; for Elijah the prophet, who was taken to heaven without tasting death, stood before us, and said: Behold, the time has fully come, which was spoken of by the mouth of Malachi—testifying that he [Elijah] should be sent, before the great and dreadful day of the Lord come—to turn the hearts of the fathers to the children, and the children to the fathers, lest the whole earth be smitten with a curse—therefore, the keys of this dispensation are committed into your hands; and by this ye may know that the great and dreadful day of the Lord is near, even at the doors.

THE LAW OF THE TITHE

SECTION 119—*Revelation given through Joseph Smith the Prophet, at Far West, Missouri, July 8, 1838, in answer to the supplication: "O Lord, show unto thy servants how much thou requirest of the properties of thy people for a tithing."*

VERILY, THUS SAITH THE LORD, I require all their surplus property to be put into the hands of the bishop of my church in Zion, for the building of mine house, and for the laying of the foundation of Zion and for the priesthood, and for the debts of the Presidency of my Church. And this shall be the beginning of the tithing of my people. And after that, those who have thus been tithed shall pay one-tenth of all their interest annually; and this shall be a standing law unto them forever, for my holy priesthood, saith the Lord.

Verily I say unto you, it shall come to pass that all those who gather unto the land of Zion shall be tithed of their surplus properties, and shall observe this law, or they shall not be found worthy to abide among you.   And I say unto you, if my people observe not this law, to keep it holy, and by this law sanctify the land of Zion unto me, that my statutes and my judgments may be kept thereon, that it may be most holy, behold, verily I say unto you, it shall not be a land of Zion unto you.   And this shall be an ensample unto all the stakes of Zion.   Even so.   Amen.

MANY CALLED BUT FEW CHOSEN

Section 121—*Prayer and Prophecies, written by Joseph Smith the Prophet, while a prisoner in the jail at Liberty, Missouri, dated March 20, 1839.   The Prophet with several companions had been months in prison.   Their petitions and appeals directed to the executive officers and the judiciary had failed to bring them relief.* —— *Men though called may not be chosen —The rights of the Priesthood inseparably connected with the powers of heaven—Unrighteous exercise of the powers of the Priesthood leads to apostasy—Powers of the Priesthood to be exercised in justice and mercy.*

* * *

How LONG can rolling waters remain impure? What power shall stay the heavens? As well might man stretch forth his puny arm to stop the Missouri River in its decreed course, or to turn it up stream, as to hinder the Almighty from pouring down knowledge from heaven upon the heads of the Latter-day Saints.

Behold, there are many called, but few are chosen. And why are they not chosen? Because their hearts are set so much upon the things of this world, and aspire to the honors of men, that they do not learn this one lesson: That the rights of the priesthood are inseparably connected with the powers of heaven, and that the powers of heaven cannot be controlled nor handled only upon the principles of righteousness.

That they may be conferred upon us, it is true; but when we undertake to cover our sins, or to gratify our pride, our vain ambition, or to exercise control or dominion or compulsion upon the souls of the children of men, in any degree of unrighteousness, behold, the heavens withdraw themselves; the Spirit of the Lord is grieved; and when it is withdrawn, Amen to the priesthood or the authority of that man! Behold, ere he is aware, he is left unto himself, to kick against the pricks, to persecute the saints, and to fight against God.

We have learned by sad experience that it is the nature and disposition of almost all men, as soon as they get a little authority, as they suppose, they will immediately begin to exercise unrighteous dominion. Hence many are called, but few are chosen.

No power or influence can or ought to be maintained by virtue of the priesthood, only by persuasion, by long-suffering, by gentleness and meekness, and by love unfeigned; by kindness, and pure knowledge, which shall greatly enlarge the soul without hypocrisy, and without guile: Reproving betimes with sharpness, when moved upon by the Holy Ghost; and then showing forth afterwards an increase of love toward him whom thou hast reproved, lest he esteem thee to be his enemy—that he may know that thy faithfulness is stronger than the cords of death.

Let thy bowels also be full of charity towards all men, and to the household of faith, and let virtue garnish thy thoughts unceasingly; then shall thy confidence wax strong in the presence of God; and the doctrine of the priesthood shall distil upon thy soul as the dews from heaven. The Holy Ghost shall be thy constant companion, and thy scepter an unchanging scepter of righteousness and truth; and thy dominion shall be an everlasting dominion, and without compulsory means it shall flow unto thee forever and ever.

COMMANDMENT TO BUILD A HOUSE OF THE LORD

Section 124—*Revelation given to Joseph Smith the Prophet, at Nauvoo, Illinois, January 19, 1841. Because of increasing persecutions and illegal procedures against them by public officers, the Saints had been compelled to leave Missouri. The exterminating order issued by Lilburn W. Boggs, Governor of Missouri, dated October 27, 1838, had left them no alternative. In 1841, when this revelation was given, the city of Nauvoo, occupying the site of the former village of Commerce, Illinois, had been built up by the Saints, and here the headquarters of the Church had been established. —— No baptismal font upon the earth for the administration of baptisms for the dead—Reason for the command to Moses to build a tabernacle in the wilderness—Promise of revelations concerning sacred things thus far hidden —Men who prevent the Saints from carrying out the commandments of God to be held accountable—Delay in building a Temple in Jackson county, Missouri, tolerated.*

* * *

FOR THERE IS NOT A PLACE found on earth that he may come to and restore again that which was lost unto you, or which he hath taken away, even the fulness of the priesthood. For a baptismal font there is not upon the earth, that they, my saints, may be baptized for those who are dead— for this ordinance belongeth to my house, and cannot be acceptable to me, only in the days of your poverty, wherein ye are not able to build a house unto me. But I command you, all ye my saints, to build a house unto me; and I grant unto you a sufficient time to build a house unto me; and during this time your baptisms shall be acceptable unto me.

But behold, at the end of this appointment your baptisms for your dead shall not be acceptable unto me; and if you do not these things at the end of the appointment ye shall be rejected as a church, with your dead, saith the Lord your God.   For verily I say unto you, that after you have had sufficient time to build a house to me, wherein the ordinance of baptizing for the dead belongeth, and for which the same was instituted from before the foundation of the world, your baptisms for your dead cannot be acceptable unto me.   For therein are the keys of the holy priesthood ordained, that you may receive honor and glory.   And after this time, your baptisms for the dead, by those who are scattered abroad, are not acceptable unto me, saith the Lord.   For it is ordained that in Zion, and in her stakes, and in Jerusalem, those places which I have appointed for refuge, shall be the places for your baptisms for your dead.

And again, verily I say unto you, how shall your washings be acceptable unto me, except ye perform them in a house which you have built to my name? For, for this cause I commanded Moses that he should build a tabernacle, that they should bear it with them in the wilderness, and to build a house in the land of promise, that those ordinances might be revealed which had been hid from before the world was.

Therefore, verily I say unto you, that your anointings, and your washings, and your baptisms for the dead, and your solemn assemblies, and your memorials for your sacrifices by the sons of Levi, and for your oracles in your most holy places wherein you receive conversations, and your statutes and judgments, for the beginning of the revelations and foundation of Zion, and for the glory, honor, and endowment of all her municipals, are ordained by the ordinance of my holy house, which my people are always commanded to build unto my holy name.

And verily I say unto you, let this house be built unto my name, that I may reveal mine ordinances therein unto my people; for I deign to reveal unto my church things which have been kept hid from before the foundation of the world, things that pertain to the dispensation of the fulness of times. And I will show unto my servant Joseph all things pertaining to this house, and the priesthood thereof, and the place whereon it shall be built. And ye shall build it on the place where you have contemplated building it, for that is the spot which I have chosen for you to build it. If ye labor with all your might, I will consecrate that spot that it shall be made holy.

And if my people will hearken unto my voice, and unto the voice of my servants whom I have appointed to lead my people, behold, verily I say unto you, they shall not be moved out of their place. But if they will not hearken to my voice, nor unto the voice of these men whom I have appointed, they shall not be blest, because they pollute mine holy grounds, and mine holy ordinances, and charters, and my holy words which I give unto them.

And it shall come to pass that if you build a house unto my name, and do not do the things that I say, I will not perform the oath which I make unto you, neither fulfil the promises which ye expect at my hands, saith the Lord.   For instead of blessings, ye, by your own works, bring cursings, wrath, indignation, and judgments upon your own heads, by your follies, and by all your abominations, which you practise before me, saith the Lord.

Verily, verily, I say unto you, that when I give a commandment to any of the sons of men to do a work unto my name, and those sons of men go with all their might and with all they have to perform that work, and cease not their diligence, and their enemies come upon them and hinder them from performing that work, behold, it behooveth me to require that work no more at the hands of those sons of men, but to accept of their offerings.   And the iniquity and transgression of my holy laws and commandments I will visit upon the heads of those who hindered my work, unto the third and fourth generation, so long as they repent not, and hate me, saith the Lord God.

Therefore, for this cause have I accepted the offerings of those whom I commanded to build up a city and a house unto my name, in Jackson county, Missouri, and were hindered by their enemies, saith the Lord your God. And I will answer judgment, wrath, and indignation, wailing, and anguish, and gnashing of teeth upon their heads, unto the third and fourth generation, so long as they repent not, and hate me, saith the Lord your God. And this I make an example unto you, for your consolation concerning all those who have been commanded to do a work and have been hindered by the hands of their enemies, and by oppression, saith the Lord your God.

* * *

AN IRREVOCABLE LAW. THE HOLY TRINITY.

SECTION 130—*Important Items given by Joseph Smith the Prophet, at Ramus, Illinois, April 2, 1843.*

* * *

WHATEVER PRINCIPLE of intelligence we attain unto in this life, it will rise with us in the resurrection. And if a person gains more knowledge and intelligence in this life through his diligence and obedience than another, he will have so much the advantage in the world to come.

There is a law, irrevocably decreed in heaven before the foundations of this world, upon which all blessings are predicated; and when we obtain any blessing from God, it is by obedience to that law upon which it is predicated.

The Father has a body of flesh and bones as

tangible as man's; the Son also; but the Holy Ghost has not a body of flesh and bones, but is a personage of Spirit. * * *

MATTER AND SPIRIT

SECTION 131—*Instructions by Joseph Smith the Prophet, given at Ramus, Illinois, May 16 and 17, 1843.*

* * *

IT IS IMPOSSIBLE for a man to be saved in ignorance.

There is no such thing as immaterial matter. All spirit is matter, but it is more fine or pure, and can only be discerned by purer eyes. We cannot see it; but when our bodies are purified we shall see that it is all matter.

IMMINENCE OF THE LORD'S COMING

SECTION 133—*Revelation given through Joseph Smith the Prophet, at Hiram, Ohio, November 3, 1831. Prefacing this revelation the Prophet wrote: "At this time there were many things which the Elders desired to know, relative to preaching the Gospel to the inhabitants of the earth, and concerning the gathering; and in order to walk by the true light, and be instructed from on high, on the 3rd of November, 1831, I inquired of the Lord and received the following important revelation, which has since been added to the book of Doctrine and Covenants and called the Appendix." —— A proclamation to the people of the Church to gather to Zion—Zion and Jerusalem both to be established—The*

voice of the Lord to issue from each of these centers—
The Lost Tribes to be remembered and be brought forth
from the north countries—Graves to be opened at the
coming of the Lord—The doom of those who reject the
Lord's message.

HEARKEN, O ye people of my church, saith the Lord your God, and hear the word of the Lord concerning you—the Lord who shall suddenly come to his temple; the Lord who shall come down upon the world with a curse to judgment; yea, upon all the nations that forget God, and upon all the ungodly among you. For he shall make bare his holy arm in the eyes of all the nations, and all the ends of the earth shall see the salvation of their God.

Wherefore, prepare ye, prepare ye, O my people; sanctify yourselves; gather ye together, O ye people of my church, upon the land of Zion, all you that have not been commanded to tarry. Go ye out from Babylon. Be ye clean that bear the vessels of the Lord. Call your solemn assemblies, and speak often one to another. And let every man call upon the name of the Lord.

Yea, verily I say unto you again, the time has come when the voice of the Lord is unto you: Go ye out of Babylon; gather ye out from among the nations, from the four winds, from one end of heaven to the other. Send forth the elders of my church unto the nations which are afar off; unto the islands of the sea; send forth unto foreign lands; call upon all nations, first upon the Gen-

tiles, and then upon the Jews.   And behold, and
lo, this shall be their cry, and the voice of the
Lord unto all people: Go ye forth unto the land
of Zion, that the borders of my people may be
enlarged, and that her stakes may be strengthened,
and that Zion may go forth unto the regions
round about.

Yea, let the cry go forth among all people:
Awake and arise and go forth to meet the Bridegroom; behold and lo, the Bridegroom cometh;
go ye out to meet him.   Prepare yourselves for the
great day of the Lord.   Watch, therefore, for ye
know neither the day nor the hour.   Let them,
therefore, who are among the Gentiles flee unto
Zion.   And let them who be of Judah flee unto
Jerusalem, unto the mountains of the Lord's house.
Go ye out from among the nations, even from
Babylon, from the midst of wickedness, which
is spiritual Babylon.   But verily, thus saith the
Lord, let not your flight be in haste, but let all
things be prepared before you; and he that goeth,
let him not look back lest sudden destruction
shall come upon him.

Hearken and hear, O ye inhabitants of the
earth.   Listen, ye elders of my church together,
and hear the voice of the Lord; for he calleth upon
all men, and he commandeth all men everywhere
to repent.   For behold, the Lord God hath sent
forth the angel crying through the midst of heav-
en, saying: Prepare ye the way of the Lord, and
make his paths straight; for the hour of his com-

ing is nigh, when the Lamb shall stand upon Mount Zion, and with him a hundred and forty-four thousand, having his Father's name written on their foreheads.

Wherefore, prepare ye for the coming of the Bridegroom; go ye, go ye out to meet him. For behold, he shall stand upon the mount of Olivet, and upon the mighty ocean even the great deep, and upon the islands of the sea, and upon the land of Zion. And he shall utter his voice out of Zion, and he shall speak from Jerusalem, and his voice shall be heard among all people. And it shall be a voice as the voice of many waters, and as the voice of a great thunder, which shall break down the mountains, and the valleys shall not be found. He shall command the great deep, and it shall be driven back into the north countries, and the islands shall become one land. And the land of Jerusalem and the land of Zion shall be turned back into their own place, and the earth shall be like as it was in the days before it was divided. And the Lord, even the Savior, shall stand in the midst of his people, and shall reign over all flesh.

And they who are in the north countries shall come in remembrance before the Lord; and their prophets shall hear his voice, and shall no longer stay themselves; and they shall smite the rocks, and the ice shall flow down at their presence. And an highway shall be cast up in the midst of the great deep. Their enemies shall become a prey unto them, and in the barren deserts there shall come forth pools of living water; and the parched ground shall no longer be a thirsty land.   And they shall bring forth their rich treasures unto the children of Ephraim, my servants. And the boundaries of the everlasting hills shall tremble at their presence.   And there shall they fall down and be crowned with glory, even in Zion, by the hands of the servants of the Lord, even the children of Ephraim.   And they shall be filled with songs of everlasting joy.

Behold, this is the blessing of the everlasting God upon the tribes of Israel, and the richer blessing upon the head of Ephraim and his fellows. And they also of the tribe of Judah, after their pain shall be sanctified in holiness before the Lord, to dwell in his presence day and night, forever and ever.

And now, verily saith the Lord, that these things might be known among you, O inhabitants of the earth, I have sent forth mine angel flying through the midst of heaven, having the everlasting gospel, who hath appeared unto some and hath committed it unto man, who shall appear unto many that dwell on the earth.   And this gospel shall be preached unto every nation, and kindred, and tongue, and people.   And the servants of God shall go forth, saying with a loud voice: Fear God and give glory to him, for the hour of his judgment is come; and worship him that made heaven, and earth, and the sea, and the

11

fountains of waters—calling upon the name of the Lord day and night, saying: O that thou wouldst rend the heavens, that thou wouldst come down, that the mountains might flow down at thy presence. And it shall be answered upon their heads; for the presence of the Lord shall be as the melting fire that burneth, and as the fire which causeth the waters to boil.

O Lord, thou shalt come down to make thy name known to thine adversaries, and all nations shall tremble at thy presence—when thou doest terrible things, things they look not for. Yea, when thou comest down, and the mountains flow down at thy presence, thou shalt meet him who rejoiceth and worketh righteousness, who remembereth thee in thy ways. For since the beginning of the world have not men heard nor perceived by the ear, neither hath any eye seen, O God, besides thee, how great things thou hast prepared for him that waiteth for thee.

And it shall be said: Who is this that cometh down from God in heaven with dyed garments; yea, from the regions which are not known, clothed in his glorious apparel, traveling in the greatness of his strength? And he shall say: I am he who spake in righteousness, mighty to save. And the Lord shall be red in his apparel, and his garments like him that treadeth in the wine-vat. And so great shall be the glory of his presence that the sun shall hide his face in shame, and the moon shall withhold its light, and the stars shall be hurled from their places.   And his voice shall be heard: I have trodden the wine-press alone, and have brought judgment upon all people; and none were with me.   And I have trampled them in my fury, and I did tread upon them in mine anger, and their blood have I sprinkled upon my garments, and stained all my raiment; for this was the day of vengeance which was in my heart.

And now the year of my redeemed is come; and they shall mention the loving kindness of their Lord, and all that he has bestowed upon them according to his goodness, and according to his loving kindness, forever and ever.   In all their afflictions he was afflicted.   And the angel of his presence saved them; and in his love, and in his pity, he redeemed them, and bore them, and carried them all the days of old.   Yea, and Enoch also, and they who were with him; the prophets who were before him; and Noah also, and they who were before him; and Moses also, and they who were before him; and from Moses to Elijah, and from Elijah to John, who were with Christ in his resurrection, and the holy apostles, with Abraham, Isaac, and Jacob, shall be in the presence of the Lamb.

And the graves of the saints shall be opened; and they shall come forth and stand on the right hand of the Lamb, when he shall stand upon Mount Zion, and upon the holy city, the New Jerusalem; and they shall sing the song of the Lamb, day and night forever and ever.   And for this cause, that men might be made partakers of the glories which were to be revealed, the Lord sent forth the fulness of his gospel, his everlasting covenant, reasoning in plainness and simplicity— to prepare the weak for those things which are coming on the earth, and for the Lord's errand in the day when the weak shall confound the wise, and the little one become a strong nation, and two shall put their tens of thousands to flight. And by the weak things of the earth the Lord shall thrash the nations by the power of his Spirit.

And for this cause these commandments were given; they were commanded to be kept from the world in the day that they were given, but now are to go forth unto all flesh—and this according to the mind and will of the Lord, who ruleth over all flesh. And unto him that repenteth and sanctifieth himself before the Lord shall be given eternal life. And upon them that hearken not to the voice of the Lord shall be fulfilled that which was written by the prophet Moses, that they should be cut off from among the people. And also that which was written by the prophet Malachi: For, behold, the day cometh that shall burn as an oven, and all the proud, yea, and all that do wickedly, shall be stubble; and the day that cometh shall burn them up, saith the Lord of hosts, that it shall leave them neither root nor branch.

Wherefore, this shall be the answer of the Lord unto them: In that day when I came unto mine own, no man among you received me, and you were driven out. When I called again there was none of you to answer; yet my arm was not shortened at all that I could not redeem, neither my power to deliver. Behold, at my rebuke I dry up the sea. I make the rivers a wilderness; their fish stink, and die for thirst. I clothe the heavens with blackness, and make sackcloth their covering. And this shall ye have of my hand—ye shall lie down in sorrow. Behold, and lo, there are none to deliver you; for ye obeyed not my voice when I called to you out of the heavens; ye believed not my servants, and when they were sent unto you ye received them not.

Wherefore, they sealed up the testimony and bound up the law, and ye were delivered over unto darkness. These shall go away into outer darkness, where there is weeping, and wailing, and gnashing of teeth. Behold the Lord your God hath spoken it. Amen.

CHURCH AND STATE

Section 134—*A Declaration of Belief regarding Governments and Laws in general, adopted by unanimous vote at a general assembly of the Church of Jesus Christ of Latter-day Saints, held at Kirtland, Ohio, August 17, 1835, with the following preamble: "That our belief with regard to earthly governments and laws in general may not be misinterpreted nor misunderstood, we have thought proper to present at the close of this volume our opinion concerning the same." This was inserted near the end of the "Book of Commandments," as compiled at that time.*

1. WE BELIEVE that governments were instituted of God for the benefit of man; and that he holds men accountable for their acts in relation to them, both in making laws and administering them, for the good and safety of society.

2. We believe that no government can exist in peace, except such laws are framed and held inviolate as will secure to each individual the free exercise of conscience, the right and control of property, and the protection of life.

3. We believe that all governments necessarily require civil officers and magistrates to enforce the laws of the same; and that such as will administer the law in equity and justice should be sought for and upheld by the voice of the people if a republic, or the will of the sovereign.

4. We believe that religion is instituted of God; and that men are amenable to him, and to him only, for the exercise of it, unless their religious opinions prompt them to infringe upon the rights and liberties of others; but we do not believe that human law has a right to interfere in prescribing rules of worship to bind the consciences of men, nor dictate forms for public or private devotion; that the civil magistrate should restrain crime, but never control conscience; should punish guilt, but never suppress the freedom of the soul.

5. We believe that all men are bound to sustain

and uphold the respective governments in which they reside, while protected in their inherent and inalienable rights by the laws of such governments; and that sedition and rebellion are unbecoming every citizen thus protected, and should be punished accordingly; and that all governments have a right to enact such laws as in their own judgments are best calculated to secure the public interest; at the same time, however, holding sacred the freedom of conscience.

6. We believe that every man should be honored in his station, rulers and magistrates as such, being placed for the protection of the innocent and the punishment of the guilty; and that to the laws all men owe respect and deference, as without them peace and harmony would be supplanted by anarchy and terror; human laws being instituted for the express purpose of regulating our interests as individuals and nations, between man and man; and divine laws given of heaven, prescribing rules on spiritual concerns, for faith and worship, both to be answered by man to his Maker.

7. We believe that rulers, states, and governments have a right, and are bound to enact laws for the protection of all citizens in the free exercise of their religious belief; but we do not believe that they have a right in justice to deprive citizens of this privilege, or proscribe them in their opinions, so long as a regard and reverence are shown to the laws and such religious opinions do not justify sedition nor conspiracy.

8. We believe that the commission of crime should be punished according to the nature of the offense; that murder, treason, robbery, theft, and the breach of the general peace, in all respects, should be punished according to their criminality and their tendency to evil among men, by the laws of that government in which the offense is committed; and for the public peace and tranquility all men should step forward and use their ability in bringing offenders against good laws to punishment.

9. We do not believe it just to mingle religious influence with civil government, whereby one religious society is fostered and another proscribed in its spiritual privileges, and the individual rights of its members, as citizens, denied.

10. We believe that all religious societies have a right to deal with their members for disorderly conduct, according to the rules and regulations of such societies; provided that such dealings be for fellowship and good standing; but we do not believe that any religious society has authority to try men on the right of property or life, to take from them this world's goods, or to put them in jeopardy of either life or limb, or to inflict any physical punishment upon them. They can only excommunicate them from their society, and withdraw from them their fellowship.

11. We believe that men should appeal to the civil law for redress of all wrongs and grievances, where personal abuse is inflicted or the right of

property or character infringed, where such laws exist as will protect the same; but we believe that all men are justified in defending themselves, their friends, and property, and the government, from the unlawful assaults and encroachments of all persons in times of exigency, where immediate appeal cannot be made to the laws, and relief afforded.

12. We believe it just to preach the gospel to the nations of the earth, and warn the righteous to save themselves from the corruption of the world; but we do not believe it right to interfere with bond-servants, neither preach the gospel to, nor baptize them contrary to the will and wish of their masters, nor to meddle with or influence them in the least to cause them to be dissatisfied with their situations in this life, thereby jeopardizing the lives of men; such interference we believe to be unlawful and unjust, and dangerous to the peace of every government allowing human beings to be held in servitude.

INDEX

Numerals Refer to Pages